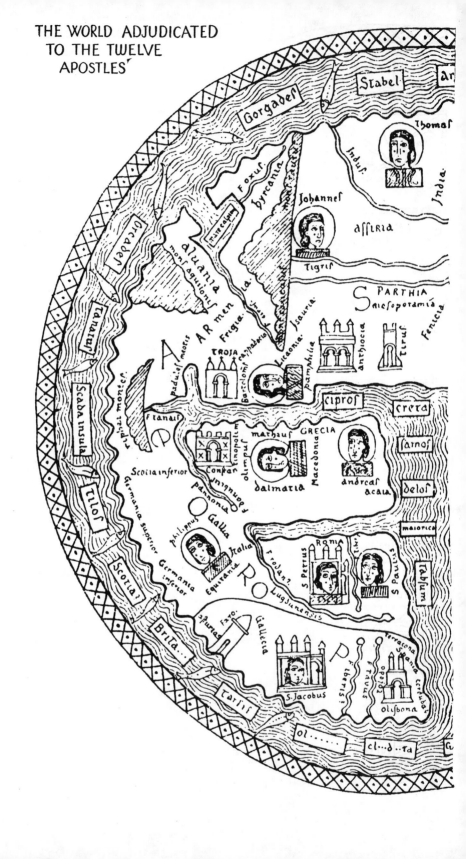

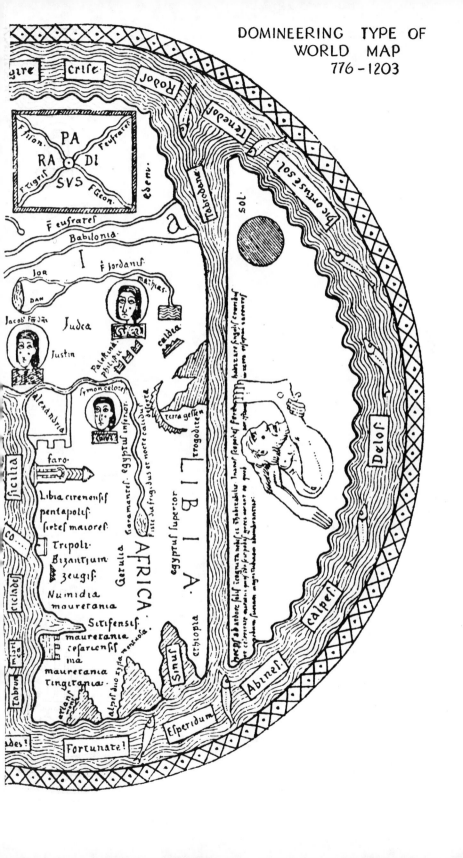

OUT OF REVOLUTION

Out of
Revolution

AUTOBIOGRAPHY OF WESTERN MAN

De Te Fabula Narratur

Eugen Rosenstock-Huessy

BERG

Providence / Oxford

Wipf and Stock Publishers
199 W 8th Ave, Suite 3
Eugene, OR 97401

Out of Revolution   I 02906, U.S.A.
Autobiography of Western Man   JK
By Rosenstock-Huessy, Eugen
Copyright©1969 The Eugen   ⁷
Rosenstock-Huessy Fund   ᵧck-Huessy
ISBN 13: 978-1-62564-019-2   y Argo Books, 1969
Publication date 3/20/2013
Previously published by Berg
Publishers, 1969   ᵉproduced
                                     ᵗ the permission
Distributed and managed by
Wipf and Stock Publishers.
For all orders and inquiries   ᵪ is available from the British Library.
please contact us at:
                                     ᵢblication Data applied for.
http://www.wipfandstock.com
info@wipfandstock.com
orders@wipfandstock.com

Printed in the United States by Edwards Brothers, Ann Arbor, MI.

TO

THE FAMILY OF

HENRY COPLEY and ROSALIND HUIDEKOPER GREENE

in their homes at

Cambridge, Mass.   Dublin, N. H.

Durham, N. C.   Mount Carmel, Conn.

In meines Vaters Garten soll die Erde
Dich umgetriebnen vielgeplagten Mann
zum freundlichsten empfangen . . .

Goethe, Nausikaa-Fragment.

ACKNOWLEDGMENTS

THE AUTHOR OWES TWO KINDS OF THANKS. ONE GOES TO A GROUP OF friendly supporters who have helped him in parts of the preparation of the manuscript; the other to friends who have made the whole enterprise their own to an unusual degree.

In the first group, I am happy to list the following names: Professor Dietrich Gerhard, of St. Louis, for going over the whole manuscript and making suggestions from the historian's point of view; my colleague at Dartmouth College, Professor W. K. Wright, and Mrs. Wright, for reading proof; Professor Adolf Zeller, of Breslau, for the use of a photograph in his work on Carolingian architecture; the Verein für Kunstwissenschaft, Berlin, for the photograph taken from Hanns Swarzenski's *Die Deutschen Buchmalerein des XIII. Jahrhunderts,* Berlin, 1936; the Baker Memorial Library, of Dartmouth College, for the use of a reproduction of Orozco's panel of Christ; Mr. Rollo Walter Brown for the passage from his *How the French Boy Learns to Write,* Harvard University Press; Messrs. A. P. Watt and Son, London, Doubleday, Doran & Co., New York, and the heirs of Rudyard Kipling for the quotation from *Her Majesty's Servants* from the *Jungle Book;* Brandt and Brandt in New York for the insertion from *John Brown's Body* (Farrar & Rinehart, Inc.), by Stephen Vincent Benét; Arthur D. Little for the quotation from *The Handwriting on the Wall,* Little, Brown & Co., Boston; Robert McElroy for permission to quote from *The Social and Political Ideas of the Revolutionary Era,* London; Professor Arthur Meier Schlesinger for the quotation from *New Viewpoints in American History,* Macmillan. Mr. Harvey J. Swann was most gracious in allowing a passage from his *French Terminologies in the Making* to be incorporated in the French chapter. Eugen Diederichs in Jena, Germany, who published my earlier book, mentioned in the "Post-War Preface," generously gave up his idea of an English translation when I explained to him that a completely new book must result from my life in the New World.

The staffs of the libraries at Harvard University, at the Fogg

Museum, and at the Germanic Museum in Cambridge, and especially at Dartmouth College, have been very patient with an author
who so frequently required most abstruse materials.

And yet, all this gratifying sympathy, such as every author would
cherish, was not enough to launch this work when it had to face the
dutiful opposition of many defenders of pre-War scholarship. My
friend C. J. Friedrich, Professor of Government at Harvard University, recognized the difficulties of my enterprise even before I
came to these shores, and as early as 1932, he mobilized Mr. Paul
Herzog and Dr. Gerald Else for a first attempt. Although his first
plan came to nought, it gave me the courage for further initiative,
and he was helpful in every possible way in each of the later stages.

My friend Thomas H. Thomas in Cambridge contributed several
historical maps which show his experience as a cartographer of history and his abiding interest in my work. And then came Professor
Richard Cabot, who, with that generosity and faith which are so
singular with him, saved the situation when it seemed impossible
to bring this work before the public.

As to Henry Copley Greene and Rosalind Huidekoper Greene—
they have become a part of the book. Obstacles in the outside world
or in the author's style meant nothing to them. I do not think there
is a page which has not definitely gained from their suggestions.
Mr. Greene has put two years of unflinching, patient labour into
the manuscript. The preparation for printing has had the same
degree of attention from Mrs. Greene. The experience itself of such
a co-operative fellowship is unique. It testifies to the thesis of this
book that inspiration, genius, talents, or simply thought, language,
writing, are not merely means for starring lonely individuals; they
are uniting people in a common life.

E. R.-H.

Four Wells
Norwich, Vt.
June 24, 1938.

CONTENTS

ILLUSTRATIONS

INTRODUCTION

By Harold J. Berman

THAT THIS BOOK – written six decades ago – is without any question an
extraordinary book, a remarkable book, a fascinating book, has not
saved it from relative obscurity. It is directed against conventional historiography, and for the most part the conventional historians have
either ignored it or denounced it. When it first appeared, a leading
historian – who had written his own book on "the anatomy" of revolution – published scathing reviews of it in four different journals.
One is inevitably reminded of other unrecognized geniuses such as
the eighteenth-century Italian philosopher of history Gambattista
Vico, who was totally disregarded in his lifetime and for some time
thereafter, but who later was seen as a great pioneer, to whose works
special courses are now devoted in the history departments of our
universities. I have no doubt that one day – perhaps soon – the academic historians will discover that Rosenstock-Huessy was also one of
the great pioneers in a new and significant interpretation of the history of mankind.

Out of Revolution is history in the best sense of the word. Although
it embodies original scholarship of the highest professional quality, it
is written primarily for the amateur, the person of general education,
who wants to know where we came from and whither we are headed.
But it is also a *theory* of history: how history should be understood,
how historians should write about it. In this Introduction I shall discuss first Rosenstock-Huessy's theory of history, his historiography,
and then the ways in which that theory is reflected in the "autobiography of Western Man" which he recounts.

xiii

I.

Rosenstock-Huessy views history as periodic in its course, as patterned, and as moving in long time-spans, with recurrent motifs. He believes that the periodization of history is not arbitrary and that the historian's first task is to establish the right periodization. He finds the right periodization in the great upheavals that have been the "birth throes" of new epochs. These great upheavals are commemorated in our holidays and in new words that they have created as well as in new political and religious institutions and ideas. The periodic eruptions of collective passions, he writes, "make epochs in history" (p. 4).

The historian should therefore count not only days and years but also, and above all, generations and centuries, if he is to "avoid the Scylla of disordered detail and the Charybdis of meaningless generalities." The "scientific" or "objective" historiography of the nineteenth and twentieth centuries, which placed the historian outside of history, has led to the continual breaking down of the past into smaller parts and the eventual loss of any sense of direction.

Rosenstock-Huessy's history is *his* history, the history of *his* generation, which came to maturity in the suicidal European War of 1914. His own experience as a German soldier at Verdun, and the experience of the entire generation of European soldiers in the first World War, created "a new basis for understanding history." It produced a new vision of European history, and eventually of world history, as our own heritage – "our own autobiography" (p. 7). Rosenstock-Huessy's book overcomes the unconscious national – and often nationalistic – bias of so-called "realist" history by telling the story of the European context in which each of the great national revolutions was rooted.

Rosenstock-Huessy's "autobiographical" historiography exposes the fallacy of applying the Cartesian premises of mathematics and the natural sciences to the social sciences and humanities. His distrust of academic pretensions to total objectivity is shared today by the best scholars, as are his basic insights into the power of language, or speech, to draw people together into a common future. Nevertheless, the practice of the social sciences and humanities – including the "science" (or "humanity") of history – remains to a large extent

Cartesian. Leading writers about history are increasingly Rosenstock-ian in their awareness of the deficiencies of Cartesian historiography in which the historian purports to weigh, measure, and count histor-ical phenomena in an effort to overcome the rational doubts which, according to Descartes, should be the starting-point of all inquiry; and in their corresponding awareness of the importance both of pas-sions and of traditions in shaping the larger patterns of historical change and continuity. But the run-of-the-mill writers *of* history, that is, of Ph.D. dissertations and of textbooks and of authoritative mono-graphs, remain Cartesian in their emphasis on skeptical analysis of historical data and in their mechanical explanations of historical development.

Rosenstock-Huessy's intensely personal style – what his great admirer, the eminent American historian Page Smith, has called his "fiercely anti-academic language" – is, as Smith has said, "essential to the statement of his vision."

For Rosenstock-Huessy, history is purposive, and its purposes become apparent in its unfolding. In that sense, he might have said that history is revelation; it is a revelation of our destiny. For Western Man, the purposes of history are revealed especially in its periodicity, its patterns of development, and its recurrent motifs. But we must not pretend that, as historians, we have the right to impose upon the read-er a finished system of thought, with its own definitions and its own methodology. The science of history is not physics or chemistry. Rosen-stock-Huessy *engages* the reader with his story of our heritage, and he asks for a creative response. The last lines in the text of this great work are at the heart of his historiography: "In the community that common sense rebuilds, after the earthquake, upon the ashes of the slope of Vesuvius, the red wine of life tastes better than anywhere else. And a man writes a book, even as he stretches out his hand, so that he may find that he is not alone in the survival of humankind" (p. 758).

II.

Out of Revolution interprets modern Western history as a single 900-year period, initiated by a total revolution – the revolution of the Roman Catholic Church, under the papacy, against imperial, royal, and feudal domination – and punctuated thereafter by a series of total revolutions which broke out successively in the different European nations. These successive national revolutions – the revolution of the Italian city-states, the German Reformation, the Puritan Revolution in England, the French and American Revolutions, the Russian Revolution – were initially prepared by European-wide movements and eventually had European-wide repercussions. The dialectic of revolution and evolution, and eventually the failure to realize the apocalyptic visions of the great revolutions, culminated in the collapse of Europe in 1914 and in the Russian Revolution of 1917.

This vision of the history of Western Man looked to the regeneration of Europe after World War I by an integration of national histories into a common European destiny, one which would be integral in the entire history of mankind. It was a vision which only now, two generations later, is beginning to be realized.

Rosenstock-Huessy starts his story – after appropriate introductions – with the Russian Revolution and works his way backward, chronologically, through the eighteenth-, seventeenth-, and sixteenth-century national revolutions, before showing their common roots in the Papal Revolution of 1075-1122. This has the advantage of placing more remote events in the perspective of more familiar ones. It has the consequence, however, that the reader must wait for several hundred pages before coming to a full discussion of the larger "European" – as contrasted with merely "national" –explanations.

Karl Marx wrote that "revolutions are the locomotives of history." In fact, it was only in the West that such historical "locomotives" originally appeared. Marx counted what he called the "bourgeois" or "capitalist" German, English, and French Revolutions, and he forecast a subsequent "proletarian" or "socialist" revolution. He never found a specific pre-sixteenth-century revolution for "feudalism." Unfortunately, the Marxian periodization of history as a movement from medieval feudalism to modern capitalism to post-modern socialism eventually penetrated conventional historiography not only in Soviet Russia but almost everywhere. Among its fallacies are its total neglect of the violent upheaval of the late eleventh and early twelfth centuries that was called at the time "the Gregorian Reformation" (after its leader, Pope Gregory VII) and is today generally recognized by specialists as a revolutionary break between the "low" and the "high" "Middle Ages." Rosenstock-Huessy was perhaps the first – in his 1932 German book that paved the way for *Out of Revolution* – to call the Gregorian Reformation "the Papal Revolution." His interpretation of the revolutionary character of the transformation of the Roman Catholic Church, and of its impact on subsequent secular revolutions (all of which were directed in part *against* the Roman Catholic Church) exposes and corrects the Marxian fallacy of economic determinism. Rosenstockian historiography emphasizes the total character – political, economic, social, legal, religious, and more – of these upheavals, to at least one of which every nation of the West traces its origin.

In the middle of the book, in Chapter VIII, entitled "Polybius or the Reproduction of Mankind," the reader is given an interpretation of what is common to the great national revolutions and of ways in which the respective national characters that they shaped have interacted to form a common European culture. The ancient Polybian cyclical theory of government taught that monarchy becomes corrupted by tyranny and is succeeded by aristocracy, that aristocracy is corrupted by oligarchy and is succeeded by democracy, and that democracy is corrupted by ochlocracy – mob rule – and is succeeded, once again, by monarchy or tyranny. Rosenstock-Huessy shows that in Europe – taken as a single culture – monarchy, aristocracy, and democracy came to co-exist, as did feudal, capitalist, and socialist institutions. The author returns to Polybius in Chapter XII, drawing parallels not only among the national revolutions but also between them and the Papal Revolution. Each revolution extends over several generations. Each goes through a period of exaltation followed by a period of humiliation, and each has a later "golden age." Rosenstock-Huessy illustrates these cycles by use not only of political, economic, and legal but also of linguistic, artistic, and other kinds of examples.

There are obscurities and ambiguities and mistakes in this great work. But there are also extraordinary insights and many original historical discoveries. The chapter on the American Revolution is of special interest, since it shows how in 1776 Americans were divided (and, it may be added, are still divided) between the aristocratic, communitarian, and traditionalist ("Puritan") heritage of the seventeenth-century English Revolution and the democratic, individualist, and rationalist ideology which triumphed a little later in the eighteenth-century French Revolution.

Each of the great revolutions started with a radical movement in a single apocalyptic direction, but each eventually reconciled itself with the past against which it had revolted. Writing in 1938, Rosenstock-Huessy saw the beginning of the settling down of the Russian Revolution in 1934, with Stalin's restoration of respect for Russian history and for traditional Russian language and with his abandonment of revolutionary internationalism. We can now see that it took fifty more years for this Restoration to be accomplished.

As one contemplates *Out of Revolution* almost sixty years after it was written, one must acknowledge that the "new science of history," which the author states he has here "put on trial," has to this day hardly influenced the professional writing of history. The professional historians have become narrower and narrower in their perspective. They strive more and more to distance themselves from the object of their study. Only a few – usually in the late stages of their careers – call, vainly, for more breadth, more depth, more insight into the significance of the past for the present and future. In fact, the time-spans of professional historiography become shorter and shorter. Calendars of great events that have left their impress on the future, and examples of inspired language created to express the passions that have motivated our forebears – these are discounted in favor of "forces" and "conditions."

Rosenstock-Huessy was a prophet who, like many great prophets, failed in his own time, but whose time may now be coming. In spite of – and because of – its unconventional character, *Out of Revolution* has much to teach us about how history should be understood, and even more important, how the history of the second millennium of the Christian era can serve as a prophesy of the future of the human race.

BIOGRAPHY OF EUGEN ROSENSTOCK-HUESSY

EUGEN ROSENSTOCK WAS BORN IN BERLIN, GERMANY, on July 6, 1888. He received his doctorate in law and philosophy from the University of Heidelberg. At the age of 24, he taught law at the University of Leipzig and continued there until the outbreak of World War I in 1914. Just before the war, he married Margrit Huessy. Rosenstock-Huessy spent the four years of the war as a German army officer at the western front.

During those years, Rosenstock-Huessy corresponded with a Jewish friend, Franz Rosenzweig, who was also a member of the German army. This correspondence became a classic exchange and confrontation between Christian and Jew. The collection of letters was first published in 1935.

After the war, Rosenstock-Huessy joined the Daimler Benz automobile company, and edited the first German factory newspaper there. In 1919, he co-founded a publishing company, the Patmos Verlag. Between 1921 and 1922, Rosenstock-Huessy also helped found and then headed the Academy of Labor in Frankfurt/Main, which was a pioneering effort in adult education.

He returned to teaching law in 1923 at the University of Breslau, where he remained until 1933. He kept active in adult education outside the university, and wrote important works on speech, the social sciences, the Church, and history. Between 1928 and 1932, Rosenstock-Huessy organized voluntary work-service camps. These camps included students, young farmers, and workers who lived communally and did manual labor together for several weeks at a time. The camps' purpose was to combine manual labor with a dedication to solving pressing problems in society.

Because Adolf Hitler had come to power, Rosenstock-Huessy immediately left Germany in 1933 for the United States. He taught for two years at Harvard University and then moved to Dartmouth College, where he taught social philosophy until his retirement in 1957. He continued to write and lecture throughout the United States and Europe after his retirement.

In 1938, he published his first book in the United States, *Out of Revolution: Autobiography of Western Man*, which you have in your hands. It was followed by *The Christian Future, or the Modern Mind Outrun* (1946) and *The Multiformity of Man* (1948). A more detailed bibliography is on page xxi.

In the United States, Rosenstock-Huessy built what is essentially a new foundation for combining work service and adult education. In 1940, President Franklin Roosevelt invited him to organize an experimental leadership training program for the Civilian Conservation Corps. Rosenstock-Huessy established it in Vermont, and called it Camp William James, commemorating James' call for a moral equivalent of war. Its task was not just the training of leaders for an expanded Civilian Conservation Corps, but also the development of a system of work service that would accept volunteers from all walks of life. The initial participants were young unemployed men, as well as students from Harvard and Dartmouth. World War II brought this effort to a halt.

Eugen Rosenstock-Huessy's home was in Norwich, Vermont, where he died on February 24, 1973.

WORKS OF EUGEN ROSENSTOCK-HUESSY

Books Currently in Print

In English

The Christian Future or the Modern Mind Outrun, Harper Torchbooks, 1966, 248pp.
Fruit of Lips (Edited by Marion D. Battles), The Pickwick Press, 1978, 144pp.
I Am an Impure Thinker, Argo Books Inc., 1970, 206pp.
Judaism Despite Christianity (with Franz Rosenzweig), Schocken Books, 1971, 181pp.
Life Lines: Quotations from Eugen Rosenstock-Huessy's Work (Edited by Clinton C. Gardner), Argo Books Inc., 1988, 83pp.
Magna Carta Latina (with Fred Lewis Battles), The Pickwick Press, 1975, 296pp.
The Multiformity of Man, Argo Books Inc., 1973, 78pp.
The Origin of Speech, Argo Books Inc., 1981, 1410pp.
Planetary Service: A Way into the Third Millenium, Argo Books Inc., 1978, 126pp.
Practical Knowledge of the Soul, Argo Books Inc., 1988, 66pp.
Speech and Reality, Argo Books Inc., 1970, 201pp.

The above books are available from Argo Books, RR2 Box 366 A, Jericho, VT 05465.

Out of Revolution: Autobiography of Western Man, Berg Publishers, 1993, 795pp.

xxi

In German

Der Atem des Geistesi, Amandus/Brendow, 1991, 294pp.
Des Christen Zukunft oder Wir Überholen die Moderne, Brendow, 1985, 288pp.
Die Europäischen Revolution: Volkscharaktere und Staatenbildung, Brendow, 1987, 590pp.
Friedensbedingungen einer Weltwirtschaft (Herausgegeben von Rudolf Hermeier), Haag und Herchen, 1988, 329pp.
Heilkraft und Wahrheit, Amadus/Brendow, 1991, 215pp.
Herzogsgewalt und Friedensschutz, 1910, Scientia Verlag, 1969, 205pp.
Die Sprache des Menschengeschlechts, Lambert Schneider, 1963 and 1964, Vol. 1: 810pp., Vol. 2: 904pp.
Die Tocher / Das Buch Rut (Herausgegeben von Bas Leenman), Talheimer, 1988, 46pp.

PROLOGUE

THE STAKES OF WORLD WAR
AND WORLD REVOLUTION

CHAPTER ONE

A Post-War Preface

OUR PASSIONS GIVE LIFE TO THE WORLD. OUR COLLECTIVE PASSIONS constitute the history of mankind. No political entity can be formed into the steel and concrete of government, frontiers, army and navy, schools and roads, laws and regulations, if people are not swayed out of their rugged individualism into common enterprises, such as war, revolutions, adventure, co-operation, by collective passions. Any political effort must single out the peculiar human passion which, at that moment in history, will create unanimity and coherence among men.

Different governments, different civilizations, will exploit and cultivate, or correspondingly defy and eliminate, different passions of our soul. Some societies, as the Puritan, will bury sex so deeply that the visible life of the people turns towards the sexless virtues and vices of the meeting-house. Another, as the Russian, may pay little or no attention to the bonfire of sex emotions, but will outlaw and persecute grimly the gambling and speculative instincts as revealed at the stock exchange or the races.

A different type of man and woman is produced by stimulating or repressing different potential passions; and any special society is based on a peculiar selection in admitting or negating the innumerable desires of our hearts.

This selective process could be overlooked in the Age of Reason because in that Age man tried to persuade himself that the increase of Reason was the summary of human history. In fact, the craving for more Reason and more Enlightenment and more Science, highly respectable and productive as it is, is a passion nevertheless.

Now, this work intends to disclose an intelligible sequence in the course of human passions, follies, and beliefs. The history of our era which, at first sight and in our times, may seem a crude encyclopedia of all possible methods of government and public morals, is at closer inspection one ineluctable order of alternating passions of the human heart. As in individual life, every one of these passions calls for the next. The deeper and truer it is, the more urgently does it call. For such is the noble nature of man, that his heart will never wholly lose itself in one single passion or idol, or, as people call it apologetically, one idea. On it goes from one devotion to the next, not because it is ashamed of its first love, but because it must be on fire perpetually. To fall for Reason, as our grandfathers did, is but one Fall of Man among his many passionate attempts to find the apples of knowledge and eternal life, both in one.

When a nation, or individual, declines the experiences that present themselves to passionate hearts only, they are automatically turned out from the realm of history. The heart of man either falls in love with somebody or something, or it falls ill. It can never go unoccupied. And the great question for mankind is what is to be loved or hated next, whenever an old love or fear has lost its hold.

But how do the eruptions of passion make epochs in history? How do they leave any traces behind?

When and where we love or fear, we are willing to pay. We are willing to spend money, or in more serious turmoil to sacrifice some parts of our own nature, and to consecrate others. We are ready to forget certain temptations, and to give free rein to others.

Thus, our energies flow into new channels each time that our hearts leap. And each leap of our hearts remakes our bodies, our habits, and our institutions. Since any heart that has the privilege of loving is willing to suffer for its love, our social customs are the fruit of these sufferings which reshape our ways of life. The Body Politic as well as the cellular body is the reward of the sacrifices which our heart has paid for its privilege to love.

The creation of humankind, then, is the topic of this book. A history of the inspirations of mankind as a sequel to its biological prehistory is being attempted today from many sides. Its plan was first conceived by Friedrich Schlegel, who founded in 1803 the first periodical to bear the name *Europe*. He knew what most of the moderns try to forget: that the crucial test for any such bridge from biology to sociology is not Egypt or Babel, but the history of Europe in the last thousand years. If this period is not explained and illuminated by our world-wide surveys, nothing is explained and illuminated if we ourselves would not be included really. Thus, our own concrete past is the test-case for all our otherwise too vague discoveries about humanity.

The idea of this book originated in an experience we went through in the trenches: that war was one thing to the soldiers of all nations and another thing to the people at home. The attempt to found a new future for the united soldiers of Europe, that is, for its manhood, on the common experience of the World War can only be successful if this generation that was killed, wounded, weakened, decimated, by the War can bequeath a lasting memory of its experience to its children. Scholars cannot demobilize until the World War has reformed their method and their purpose in writing history.

I, at least, shall not demobilize until I have made my contribution to that common enterprise of humanity.

The plan of writing the book in this particular way was conceived in 1917, on the Battlefield of Verdun.

Since then mankind has tried a thousand times to forget its experience. Sensations of all kinds have drowned our senses and our thought. Historians have tried to bury the World War under the standards of pre-War history. Many have measured it with the yardstick of the Napoleonic wars, or have simply added a new chapter to their endless chronicle.

But a great new event is more than an additional paragraph to be inserted in the next edition of a book. It rewrites history, it simplifies history, it changes the past because it initiates a new future. Anyone who looks back on his own life knows how completely a new love, a new home, a new conviction, changes the aspect of his past. How, then, can history remain a piecemeal confusion of national developments after a conflagration of the dimensions of the World War? A race that was not impressed by such an experience, that could not rewrite its history after such an earthquake, would not deserve any history. Men who did not long for a new history of mankind after the World War showed thereby that they were withered leaves on the tree of humanity. Their souls had been killed in the World War.

The present work claims one merit: it not only rewrites the history of Europe in the light of the experience of the Great War, but it confesses this dependence frankly. And thereby it enables the reader to test it. For he knows now that the book had a real day of birth. If a man refuses to accept the importance of this new date in our history which is called World War, World Revolution, Suicide of Europe, or Crusade of America,—whether he be a writer or a scholar, a teacher or a reader,—he must fight the method of this book. But he cannot refute it, because he does not share the time and period to which it belongs.

Often among the men who seem to be contemporaries, little contemporaneity exists. And a contemplative mind that is shocked by the origin of this book in the hellfire of war and revolution may be sure that he and I are no contemporaries.

But I have my contemporaries. They will understand why I insist upon standing guard on the spot where the earthquake happened: people forget so quickly and have such wonderful devices for disguising or escaping their own cruel experience of truth.

May we not suppose that all new discoveries in science were made by the stubborn patience of men who insisted on looking at everyday things with astonishment in spite of the general indifference? To the many apples which fell before Newton we may compare the many falls of man before this World War. "The War to end War" was a peculiar war indeed, a war that revealed something about the laws of the life of nations long since divined, but now really discoverable for the first time.

A pupil of the World War sees a new future and a new past. He discovers a new political biology of the human race, filling the gap between Planckism in physics, Darwinism in zoology, Marxism in economy, and liberalism in theology and political history.

Man belongs to the three realms of Earth, Heaven, and Society. He has always—from age to age—re-established these three realms and fixed their frontiers. It is the sovereign faculty of man to do so. But he must not forfeit his sovereignty by allowing disorder, disunion, disintegration, to creep in. The incoherence of modern knowledge in history and nature, physics and theology became so frightening even before the World War that nothing but a breakdown of civilization could be expected from a kingdom so terribly divided against itself. The World War seemed more a test than a surprise to those who had suffered from the atmosphere of an occidental university and the absurdities of its specialists.

This book owes to the World War its daring to be simple and general. It owes to events that far transcend our individual judgment its rediscovery of what is important and what is trifling in the life of mankind. This book owes to the sufferings of millions and tens of millions its ability to treat the history of the world as an autobiography.

I am unable to stare at history like a spectacle to be contemplated from a box. The rise of empires in the West or the downfall of civilizations in the East, the laws of systole and diastole or of Classicism and Romanticism, and all these niceties of a spectacular world history have lost their meaning since the solidarity of twenty million men has nailed all the surviving soldiers to the same cross of reality. The world's history is our own history. If it were but a world's history, its facts would be endless, the selection of its millions of dates would be undertaken in vain; it would be nothing but a hopeless library of dust.

What if it were the autobiography of our race? Perhaps the tree of life in the Garden of Eden and the tree of knowledge are not far distant from each other.

If a man or a generation confess that they have lived and

sinned perhaps they can arrive at knowledge. History is perhaps dark and confused only if we stare at it from the outside, without solidarity, without having first lived and sympathized.

Let us try to read world history as our own autobiography. Then our interest will centre equally on the future, the present and the past.

Even so, it may seem doubtful whether the tools for such an undertaking were available. Mankind certainly could not have an autobiography if it had always been like modern society: completely sensational, totally forgetful, and wonderfully devoid of memory. But mankind has always, with the utmost tenacity, cultivated its calendar. One of the innovations of this book in point of method consists in taking the political and ecclesiastical calendar seriously. A day introduced into the calendar or a day stricken out of the calendar, means a real change in the education and tradition of a nation. Mankind writes its own history long before the historians visit its battlefields; days, festivals, holidays, the order of meals, rest and vacations, together with religiously observed ritual and symbols, are sources of political history, though rarely used by the average political or economic historian.

A holiday is always a political creation and a political instrument. It is true, the importance of a calendar and a change in the calendar are not visible in the history of some ten or thirty years. Neither does creative history begin until at least three or four generations have collaborated toward the same goal. No individual can go very far. Real achievements must be based on the continuity of many generations.

We shall try to mention only those events or facts which have left their mark, or are apt to leave their mark, upon a time of more than one generation. The unicellular individual and the history of isolated events are too microscopic to interest us here, where we are concerned with the vital process of mankind's revolutions. But this does not mean that we wish to escape into the generality of abstract ideas or statistics.

The drama of a playwright, the blessing of a beggar, the prayer of a monk, the fury of a mob, can all become essential features in the survival of the race. Guy Fawkes' Day, the

Wedding of Figaro, a holiday like All Souls', and the sun-song of St. Francis are better illustrations of history than our reasoning. I have tried as much as I could to let them speak for themselves. Every human being is endowed with the wonderful gift of speech. He can express his own secret better than anybody else. We rarely reveal our true selves in the market place of life. Words often seem to be made to hide our thoughts. But the more we try to avoid emphasis, or even truth, in our speech, the more the few moments stand out in which language has the full weight of self-expression. A bride speaking her decisive "Yes" or "No" before the altar uses speech in its old sense of revelation, because her answer establishes a new identity between two separate offsprings of the race and may found a new race, a new nation. We are so dull that we rarely realize how much history lies hidden in marriage, and how the one word spoken by the bride makes all the difference between cattle-raising and a nation's good breeding.

Mankind and the groups of humankind express their secret, their choice, and their destiny as clearly as a bride on her wedding day. It is not necessary to record the everyday life of a nation for a thousand years in order to know its aim and inspiration. The great creations of history do not reveal their deepest sense nor their soul every day. But each has its wedding day; and the words and songs, the promises and laws of this period of a nation's life express its character viva voce and settle its destiny once and forever.

Unfortunately the records of the past cannot be assembled mechanically. They have to be selected. Any selection means personal responsibility; and such personal decisions and choices make the reader dependent on my judgment. But how can he rely on it unless he has a chance of checking me? I have tried to offer him that chance.

I do not start my narrative at a point or date in the past for fear of preventing the reader from testing my prejudices and superstitions. I begin with the present day because there he is in every respect my peer and will very soon find whether I am betraying his confidence or not. For he knows most of the facts as well as I do.

The narrative of the book begins with the Russian Revolution and goes back to the great French, English and German Revolutions.

All four are secular revolutions made by the temporal power. A comparison of all four shows them to be interdependent and to have created a system based on their permanent interplay. At the end of this part it will have become evident that the World War dealt with religious aspects not represented by these four revolutions. Empires, Crusades and Churches, Citizenship and Authority, were values in the World War and are values today, though of older origin than 1789 or 1688.

For that reason a second part will establish a peculiar parallel to the four great national revolutions, a parallel which has become visible through and since the World War. America, especially with its unsolved polarity between complete secularism and a powerful Catholic church, Anglo-Saxons and immigrants, cannot act reasonably in the present World Revolution without being equipped to look at it as a short phase in a millennial revolution. The American Revolution itself is treated in a special chapter, because America contributes something peculiar to the doctrine of Revolutions. It belongs to at least three different types of revolutionary events.

No nation's history remains orthodox after a war or after a revolution. That is why we divide our biography into periods defined by the great upheavals of all mankind, or at least, of all Christendom. Events which did not evoke a universal interest do not enter our plan. The World War demands a world biography, not a mosaic of national histories.

However, since the book covers a period of 900 years and claims to convey in every chapter genuine and primary new discoveries and unfamiliar facts, the specialist would expect a series of monographs and after fifty years a ten-volume book. Reader of this Preface, I longed to do that. I like monographs and have written some scores of them on subjects relating to this book. Yet the result is depressing. From many experiences I was forced to draw the conclusion: An attempt to resuscitate the memory and faith of Europe would be doomed if it appealed to the expert alone. Though it is quite impossible to write such a book without a series of minor mistakes, I have no reason to fear the expert. He himself knows better than anyone else that these minor mistakes do not diminish in the course of monographical research. They change their aspect but they remain. Clio, the Muse of history, seems to have a certain sense of humour. She stirs our passion for accuracy to the utmost, but the goal, like the wheel of fortune, always recedes.

My real sorrow is that I cannot publish more volumes on so glorious a subject. Much of the evidence could easily have been doubled; on the German rite of *Konfirmation*, the English change from Sunday to Sabbath, the historical rôle of men like Shakespeare or Tolstoi or Matthias Gruenewald, more could have been said. What a chapter "Sex in the literature of the nineteenth century" might have made! I advise the student to look up the volume of the Italian, Mario Praz, on *The Flesh, Death and the Devil in Nineteenth Century Romanticism,* a work of real importance. But my duty was to condense things so that our new science may get a fair trial before the general public.

In the meantime my German work, published at Jena in 1931, *Die Europaeischen Revolutionen, Volkscharaktere und Staatenbildung,* though treating the same problem with the old method of the romantic historical school, and from a narrower point of view, supplies a vast and different mass of material. The scholar, therefore, is asked to use the two books as a combined effort to put the source material before him.

Furthermore, I might have added a list of documents which could serve for textbook study and could form the basis for a dictionary of Europe's cultural and political language. It would be the first of its kind to transcend the limits of French, English, German, Russian, and make clear the dialectical and interdependent structure of humankind's speech. This is of immediate practical importance in the days of radio. I simply quote a broadcast of the German Chancellor Bruening to the nations of the world in 1931. Bruening, talking German, called the effort that was needed an effort of the "soul." The French newspapers rendered this by "morally"; the English by "loyally." "Soul," "moral," "loyal": all three powerful notions. Apparently they have the same ring in the ear of millions; they produce the same amount of blood-pressure in Germany, France, and England respectively. And although the fact is not mentioned in any existing dictionary, these words may take each other's place in the viva voce dialogue of real people.

We are recording the viva voce autobiography of Europe during the last thousand years with regard to its connection backwards; we are convinced, however, that any history of the evolution of mankind will prove a failure if it tries to deprive us of the greatest contribution of the last twenty years. I mean any history of mankind which fails to start frankly and modestly from the experiences and sufferings of our own generation.

The autobiography of Europe is, after all, a very short story. It covers the space of not more than twenty-seven generations. It is really all present and our own. Though it is brief and full of failures and disasters and fears and maladies and disappointments, it is the only age of mankind which is fully accessible to us; it is our present, even where it seems to be the past.

In this book we shall treat the last 900 years as one present day, the heritage of which we must all receive before it is allowed to go down and be buried.

The autobiography of a world such as Europe was and is, is no one man's enterprise. Any individual's sympathies are limited. His feeling of solidarity cannot be all-comprehensive, as it ought to be. Man's heart has and must have its predilections. But my own short-comings can be overcome by the collaboration of my readers. Most of them not only know their own country better than I but will find thousands of small traits—vocabulary, sports, customs and manners—to add to the chapter on one or the other member of the European family of nations.

This natural and spontaneous collaboration by the reader of this book would be the best guarantee of its truth. In adding from his own memory whatever he knows of French, English, Russian, or Italian history, he cannot but enlarge and round out our draft.

Without such a collaboration, how could I venture to press the wealth of a millennium between the covers of one small volume? The more our readers will begin to mobilize their own thoughts, with the help of our suggestions, the sooner will the past of revolutions become a living part of the future of society.

Any real book conveys one idea and one idea only. Its author is a man who is so slow of understanding that he has to write a whole book where common sense is perfectly satisfied with one phrase or slogan. In my case it is even worse: I am so slow at grasping the simplest rules of the game of human society that I have had to turn the subject over and over again. At last, when I was thrown into the turmoil of the Great War, revolution seemed to offer the best clues to the labyrinth; and for twenty years I have been following that clue. This tenacity may seem very cumbersome. Is not society moving with tremendous speed, progressing indefinitely? Like a Proteus, it has changed so quickly during the last twenty years that all we can do is to keep track of the latest developments. I am still pointing at the World War, and shall always do so. Surely, then, my book must lag far behind. I am conscious of this crime. I am delaying the consummation of things. But some sinners are bold enough to boast of their sins.

My predecessors in the field of political thought poured the strong wine of progress into the water of human traditions, lest their generation miss its opportunities. I wish to pour the water of patience into the strong wine of revolutionary excitement, so that my contemporaries may not waste their time in feverish and fruitless efforts.

"Too early" is the bane of most political efforts that have been made during the last fifteen years. When we act too early we are not ourselves; our intellect, our will, our efforts, are in advance of our true being, and they may easily forfeit—by their restlessness—our own secret destiny.

Obstinate retardation is, therefore, my voluntary choice. By quiet procrastination we can hope to add a few inches to the mantle of time, which modern man wishes to outgrow too suddenly and too violently.

The end of time is close upon us, in the technical sense of the word. When one man can address the whole earth at once, when a World War technically is over after four years, time has lost its retarding power. Our technical gain in respect to time is so enormous that we should be entering on a period of "plenty of time." Of all the kinds of abundance promised us by the "economists of plenty," abundance of time seems the most general and most certain. Unfortunately, the abundance of time is not quite the same thing as the fulness of time. Most people who have plenty of time never fill it to the full. They throw it away. To gain time, and to learn how to regain time, is the content of mankind's story of earth. It is the easiest thing in the world to work all the time, compared to the incredible difficulty of spending one hour or one day of rest in a proper way.

Humanity has always conquered the flux of natural time by means of a rhythm between active and passive time-spans. To reconquer his holidays, to establish a new and better time-schedule for life, has been the great endeavour of man ever since the days of Noah.

The revolutions of mankind create new time-spans for our life on earth. They give man's soul a new relation between present, past, and future; and by doing so they give us time to start our life on earth all over again, with a new rhythm and a new faith. For ordering the three dimensions of time, we need what St. Ambrose called the times of times, temporum tempora, standards for making the right distribution between past, future, and present. These standards are more easily shattered than a thermometer for measuring fever. Modern men talk so much about the three dimensions of space that they are ignorant of the fact itself that space has nothing of the tremendous triplicity of dimension which time contains.

The new science of revolutions reveals the secret of the "too early" and the "too late"—and, on the other hand, of timeliness. To you, most learned readers of this preface, I have divulged this secret too early, since you unfortunately have no time to read the book. The book itself narrates how mankind has conquered new time and overcome the waste of time, and thereby reconquered itself, whenever too lazy hearts or too nervous brains had squandered the fulness of time which is mankind's share in eternity.

CHAPTER TWO

Arcana Revolutionis: To the Revolutionaries

ALL OVER THE GLOBE TODAY CONSERVATIVES ARE APPROACHING
more or less timidly the "Arcana Revolutionis," the secrets
and mysteries of revolution. Highly respectable people are
beginning to think of themselves as possible revolutionaries
and are studying revolutionary technique.

After the French Revolution conservatives all over the world
insisted upon a Restoration, and waged wars of deliverance
against the Jacobins. In 1815 even an American statesman,
Gouverneur Morris, breathed his semicomical sigh of relief:
"Rejoice, America, the Bourbons are restored." Today the
nationalists in many countries are preparing a revolution, the
right kind of revolution, against the Hydra of Marxism. Nobody
seems afraid of starting a revolution. It is always astonishing
to find bankers, scholars, parsons, enthusiastically awaiting a
new revolution without divining the satanic character of all
revolutions, whether it come from the left or from the right.

God certainly does not grant to a revolution what he gives
to thirty or fifty years of loyal collaboration in peace and law.
Awareness of this fact seems to have vanished. A man is terribly
old-fashioned if he mentions this little difference. Conservatives now insist on being as revolutionary as anybody and defy
those who might call their undertaking reactionary. The principle of revolution no longer distinguishes the radical half of
mankind alone. It animates the ranks of conservatism as well.
Law, Legitimacy, Loyalty, have lost their flavour. Employers,
lawyers, gentlemen, generals, admirals, begin to think in terms
of Revolution.

War, external war, used to be the measles of national life, which even respectable people accepted as inevitable. The new situation created by the World War excludes war for one half of the nations. War has virtually ceased to be a weapon in the life of the European nations. They know more or less that it has become impossible. Any war in Europe would mean not only the Twilight of the Gods, but quite literally the "finis" of Europe in every respect. In a time of global economic units, any territory smaller than a sixth or seventh of the earth cannot have a separate existence, either economic or military. An individual European State is beneath the level of a belligerent power. It was below the level even in 1914. But it remained for the World War to make clear once for all that war could never be waged again by a single nation on the continent of Europe. The time of national wars in Europe is past. When frontiers are as thin as tissue-paper, and when aeroplanes fly 300 miles an hour, there is no room for a duel between two nations whose territories are less than a thousand miles in diameter.

I know how many dreams are still being dreamt to the contrary in Europe. But in spite of these dreams, the actual practice of her statesmen follows two lines of policy:

First of all, insofar as they think of war, they think of it only in terms of coalitions, alliances, and vast combinations including at least one whole continent or more. This in itself means the end of national war, in the proper sense of the word—that is, a single nation waging war to achieve a national purpose or end. The time for such private adventures, in Europe at least, is gone.

You may reply: But it can return!

The second character of all practical policy in Europe since the War is such as to make even the prospect of a later swinging back of the pendulum remote. This second line of policy is a still stronger check on the possibility of war. European statesmen are shifting their use of military, belligerent language and procedure from real war to civil war.

For the first time in history civil war has become popular, and all the glamour of war heroism, of courage and virility, surrounds the Black Shirts or Consomols or Storm Troopers who, in Italy or Russia or Germany, march against the enemy inside the nation!

In the days of Æschylus the Greeks used for civil war the name of "cock-fight," because the cock was then a new and exotic bird from Persia, and the old Greek tribes were as much bewildered by a civil war as they were by that strange Persian bird.

Civil wars have been looked upon ever since as one of the greatest evils of mankind, much more distressing than war because of the total lack of chivalry, *code d'honneur,* limitation, which a civil war involves. A war between relatives, friends, comrades, seemed atrocious. Compared to a civil war a war against Indians, Blacks, Huns, unbelievers, was easy to understand. Distance made a foreign people strange people. Today this difference between war and civil war has broken down, and we witness the funeral of the old predilection for foreign wars.

Jefferson showed the way to a new age when he asked for a nice little revolution every twenty years. Since the time of Jefferson the Earth itself overshadows all its parts; the flag of humanity overshadows all the national flags. Mere distance no longer makes us act as foes and belligerents.

When Mr. Schoen, the German Ambassador in Paris in 1914, added to the formal declaration of war the remark: *"C'est le suicide de l'Europe,"* and when Lyautey, the French Marshal in Morocco, greeted the news of the outbreak of the war with the classical statement: "War in Europe? A war between Europeans cannot but be a civil war!" War and Civil War had become as like as twins.

The World War turned the scales definitely in favour of civil war. The pacifist movement today is only an overtone of the movement of hard and unshakable facts, which forbids war and plunges humanity, with its thirst for fight, into civil wars instead. Pacifists are needed in America, because America is physically able to fight. In Europe warriors, with all their lust for battle, cannot go to war—and they know it. Therefore.

they plunge into revolutions. This explains the failure of the pre-War type of socialists all over the world, like Briand or MacDonald or Otto Bauer. It originates in their instinctive shunning of both external war and civil war.

The average Western socialist was certainly no adherent of war. He was aware that Revolution was something inevitable and natural. But by instinct, though he detested war, he also disliked civil war.

Ebert, the Socialist President of Germany, exclaimed that he "hated social revolution like the plague." The fighting instinct of the socialists was nowhere strong enough to make them feel at home in civil war. And so not the socialist worker, but only the national soldier returning from the World War, was cold-blooded enough to embark on civil war.

He could do it because he had been a soldier. In the trenches he had discovered for himself that war was obsolete. The trenches on the other side were filled with his brothers, victims of their respective "staffs," as he was. The motto, "Soldiers of all countries, turn about, unite," was a real moral experience in the trenches between 1914 and 1918.

It was more serious, more real, than the Marxian slogan of international solidarity of the workers, because it was discovered casually, so to speak, by men who had no intention of experiencing anything of the kind. It was a real discovery and conversion against expectation or purpose. It was the more convincing for this lack of premeditation.

As a matter of fact, the soldiers discovered in the trenches exactly what Marx had tried to explain to his followers in terms of class-consciousness. The German National Socialists emphasize the soldier's experience without realizing that the soldier is the proletarian in a new aggregate form. The peasants, workers, craftsmen, of one nation or the other are described by the National Socialists as a "thoroughly brotherly lot." Wicked people, especially Jews, made for war; the nations themselves are peaceful.

That is good Marxian propaganda. Princes and capitalists were Marx's bugbear; Jews and journalists seem to be the bugbear of Nazism. Both try to explain the same event: the impos-

sibility of war in the future. Both use poisoned weapons to
demonstrate the wickedness of a puzzling past where wars could
happen. They hate each other. But war is abolished in both
ideologies. To Lenin, war is nonsense, and he cedes the western
territories of Russia. To Hitler, every drop of German blood
is precious, and he would certainly prefer to shed Jewish blood
instead. "Wars destroy the élite of the nations. That is why war
is out of the question," he told a French interviewer.

However, both Lenin and Hitler agree in one thing. First
of all, they realize that farmer and worker are not interested
in war, but beyond that, both are too much the pagan and
the soldier not to use the fighting force and the discipline of
a uniformed army. They abolish war by constantly using war
machinery for internal purposes. In this respect, Mussolini is
like them. The Pontine marshes, the Lira, like the coal mines
of Donez, grain, money, raw materials, houses, homesteads, are
attacked, conquered, and victoriously annexed by this new civil
war strategy. The telegrams all read like reports from the front,
whether it be Mussolini or Stalin who receives them. Powers
usually given to the executive only in time of war are bestowed
upon it in this present emergency because the emergency is
the new warfare. Lincoln's martial law measure of Emancipation and Roosevelt's New Deal powers are closely connected.
Emergency is like war, and this holds good in many countries
today. It is a great moment in the history of humankind when
the energies of the race shift from martial laws to civil emergency laws. The armies enlisted against territorial enemies are
superseded or outstripped by armies enlisting against nature.
The change is so colossal, coming as it does after six thousand
years of warfare, that it can neither be achieved completely
in a few decades, nor its scope be understood by the passionate
masses. Still, it is true, revolution has taken the place of war.

To a mankind that recognizes the equality of man everywhere, every war becomes a civil war. Now every revolution
creates two people, two groups as foreign to each other as two
nations. This is a stage of human growth in which common
language and traditional values lose their grip on the individual. We see him falter. People proud of their ancestors, their

education, their wealth, come to be guided by the course of the stock market or by the headlines of their favourite newspaper. It is overwhelming to discover suddenly the thorough forgetfulness of modern man. People forget and betray their faith, traditions, and breeding twice a week.

The sudden shift from security and civil peace to civil war and emergency throws long-bearded colonels and "gilded youth" alike into plain madness. Suddenly discovering that the sanctified division between War and Peace is gone, they acclaim the necessary evil, class-war, as a splendid chance for excitement. Even many of the literati today shift from one extreme to the other.

The process of "Revolution" has been discovered and is being manipulated today like Mr. Nobel's dynamite, as a thing in itself. The future of mankind depends very much on the skill and courage with which "the elements of Revolution" shall be faced and considered. The empirical facts are so abundant, experiences are so eloquent, that a science of revolutions is possible. The future depends largely on the speed needed for the conscious retraining of the instincts awakened in us by the pre-scientific era which has irrevocably passed away.

A writer on revolution who, like a Cassandra, should only deplore this future would not be fit for his task, which is to face the greatest catastrophes of mankind without anxiety. But he who has himself lived through the World War and two revolutions can even less take the side of the layman who finds history simply splendid, thrilling, fascinating, and looks forward to being thrilled by the excitement of one more revolution.

Life asks of us that we bury our dearest loves, and go on. It makes allowance for tears and for joy, for despair and for hope. A blind partisan of revolution may be satisfied with mere triumph, finding everything bigger and better, believing in progress. A sense of fairness will tell the reader that neither satisfaction nor mere abhorrence can be the answer of any man who was a man and used his human privilege of love and hate in the days before the War. A peaceful civilian simply shudders when people are shot in the streets. No autobiography can kill old loves in favour of new. Going on from a funeral to a baptism, from a shipwreck to an inauguration, man must weep with the mourners and be merry with the merry. I think we have shown that the necessity of a change is felt everywhere these days. The real point is that we must *change with honour* from one faith, one hope, one love, to the next, neither insulting the dead we have had to bury nor idolizing the new house which we are just building.

To *change with honour* seems terribly difficult. Most people are like weathercocks, turning with every change of wind. They rush from one creed to the next as if a change of faith were nothing, and in the end become nothing themselves.

In a time of revolution, our own volition contributes very little to our change. Volition and intention can do very little in a world which makes a principle of changing every day. Perhaps the real danger in such a period comes from our own inertia, which makes us accept all these changes stoically but without conviction or personal decision. We cannot really change without a period of waiting and relearning.

To *change with honour* seems to be the paradoxical effort that is asked of us today. It means keeping away from both extremes, that of a rigid honour which kills the force of progress, and that of a mechanical change which leaves the potentialities of the soul untouched.

A book on Revolutions has to deal with the great forward leaps in the history of man. *Natura facit saltus,* nature proceeds by leaps and bounds in the life of the human race. But man survives death and nations survive their sudden leaps, thanks to the finest forces of the soul. The marching soldier, the fighting revolutionary, the struggling business man, have less personality than the bride who leaves her father's and mother's house for her own and that of her children. She changes with honour. She regenerates the race. She abandons and restores. She loses and wins.

Humanity will never stop acting and believing in action as long as men are men and hope to be like God. The era of revolution and the future of revolution depend on man's actions, ambitions, crimes, and aggressive theories.

The new phase of revolution which is beginning today must put the destructive forces of mankind to use. The thunderstorms of revolution have ceased to be irregular forces of nature; in the future they can be understood and manipulated like water or fire.

The future of revolution and the future of mankind depend on the readiness of the human soul to galvanize political action with a spark of that queer power which regenerates mankind.

Today the significance of revolution is not that of a disgraceful interruption between two periods of quiet and peace. The present time is—for reasons to be explained in this book—bound to attempt an organization of future society by which the dynamite of revolution may be manipulated as persistently and consciously as contractors use real dynamite in building tunnels or roads.

To use lawlessness itself as a vital force in the reconstruction of mankind was Jefferson's dream. It is the sober reality of the future.

The manipulation of "Revolution" as a vital force for change can be based only on the recognition of a permanent relation between lawlessness and law. In nature, water and fire hate and destroy each other. But man began to master nature when he was courageous enough to force water and fire to collaborate in his service. A loyalist revolutionary seems a contradiction in terms; but the mutual permeation of men's souls has reached a point where this contradiction in terms will cease to be a contradiction in life. When a potential revolutionism and a potential conservatism exist in every man, it is useless to pretend that revolutionaries and conservatives are divided like black and white, angels and devils. We are all eighty per centers or fifty-one per centers now. The old "nil humani a me alienum puto" may stand for the new truth that the forces of revolution and passive obedience are only two sides of the same thing, man's heart and soul. Since War and Peace are both in our souls, civil war and civil peace, revolution and legality, must play the rôles in the future which war and peace played in former days.

A man who fought for his country has always been honoured,

and the more so the more peaceful he was by nature. Now
that war is becoming impracticable, revealing itself in fact as
civil war, the warrior cannot simply be replaced by the civilian
of the old type. The warrior must give way to the "revolutionary loyalist," a man who is ready for both order and revolution,
law and overthrow of law.

This is neither a simple task nor an agreeable outlook. But
even in times of revolution there should be a place for truth
and for an investigation of truth such as we have tried to make
here.

To us, entering a phase of world-wide mutual permeation
where everybody knows and hears of everybody else, where the
earth is so small that words fly like lightning and men fly like
words, revolution comes upon the scene with a new significance.

By its abolishing war, or changing it into civil war, the future
revolution already presupposes the solidarity of mankind. As
long as war was waged against unbelievers, pagans or Huns,
civilized men could think of their foes as less than human.
This is impossible now. Henceforth men are equals, and all
wars are civil wars within one society. This in itself, even compared to the last war and its propaganda, is a revolutionary
kind of spiritualization.

This mutual permeation and world-wide solidarity has been
a long time in the making. The old Messianic faith of mankind
told generation after generation that man was a citizen of one
great commonwealth. The national warrior who has been converted into a conservative revolutionary or a revolutionary
conservative will find in this book the rules which governed
the husbandry of the corresponding human forces in the past.
He will see that the national warrior was always a fighter for
universal values as well. This paradox is an old paradox. It has
always been creative. It has revolutionized and regenerated the
race again and again, though the names of the forces have
changed.

And it is important to know that the things created by
genuine revolutions are all immortal. The era of revolutions
described in the following chapters has produced a sequence

of forms of characters, of types of men and of human homes, which a future revolution cannot simply destroy.

Forms created by revolution, by the most terrible sacrifices, are revolution-proof themselves. Tomorrow will fail if it does not understand why these creations of today and yesterday are immortal.

CHAPTER THREE

The Stakes: Liberties and Loyalties

JUST WHAT ARE THE EUROPEAN TRADITIONS WHICH MAY BE CON-
sidered the stakes of the present convulsions? A short list of
very simple, everyday facts introduces us best into the centre
of revolutions.

After the World War, when normalcy seemed to be around
the corner, decent progressives wished to get back to work in
their old lines: creative art, business enterprise, scholarly research, missionary work, technical inventions and so on. These
people were convinced, both in Europe and in America, that
they could rely again on the institution of the "peace of the
land." The peace of the land had been an institution from time
immemorial. Though it had been disturbed under special conditions, as, for example, during the gold rush to California, it
had always been easily restored by a vigilant community. For
nobody doubted that it was a precious thing that ought to be
restored at all costs.

But what actually happened, and is happening day after day
and year after year all over the world, is not quite in line with
this reverent tradition. Shooting, riots, strikes, kidnapping,
pogroms, not only happen on a colossal scale, but for the first
time in history they are extolled as an expression of reconquered vitality or sound class feeling or in whatever formula
the general new gospel of "Violence for the sake of Violence"
is masking itself. Thinkers like Sorel the French, and Pareto
the Italian, engineers of the new art, minds of the engineering
type which are accustomed to smelting iron, mixing concretes,
vivisecting guinea pigs, turn towards human politics with the

same faith in "thermodynamic laws" and overlook the practical consequences of any political theory of the vivisecting character. Shirts of all colours indicate the return of private armies, taking the name of free associations in order to build up semigovernmental authority. Feuds and vendetta are cultivated again under the new name of strong racial sentiment. The World War, as we can see, has rehabilitated ways of thinking and forms of action abolished a long, long time ago. Once we are conscious of this new glorification of violence, we shall glance with renewed interest over the period which felt strong enough to eradicate vendetta and violence of clan and family by creating the famous "Truce of God." In the beginning, this truce was a modest attempt to pacify as many days in the week as were dedicated in Easter week by the passion and resurrection of the Lord. Its vestiges date back to the eleventh century; it took centuries to advance from these four holy days to a complete, lasting peace of the land forever. It is, therefore, nothing but the sober truth that we progressives of today are still drawing on a political institution created some nine hundred years ago.

A similar development can be sketched for our present problems of labour and employment. The free choice of a profession has been the pride of Western man ever since the Reformation. That a farmer's son might become a physician, a butler's progeny a lord, a butcher's son a banker, is an established faith in every civilized country. Luther actually put this rule into practice when he and thousands of monks and nuns returned into the world and took up trades. These people could not turn to their fathers' trades, as had been universal tradition before. They came from their monasteries as individuals, stripped of their clannishness and their family-loyalties as no human being ever had been before. As the Truce of God had needed a superhuman effort, so it needed this superhuman emergency of some hundred thousand individuals to establish the right of every living generation to rearrange society. Thus the social revolution of the sixteenth century has given to the Western world the liberty of cleaving to the calling of our choice.

After the Great War, this liberty begins to be curtailed by a "Numerus clausus," a limitation of the total number of students in universities and in the trades as well in many countries. A hereditary peasantry is one of the goals of the present rulers of Germany and of many leaders in other countries. Workers are sent out by the hundreds of thousands in a more

HANS BURGKMAIER
The new freedom in choosing a profession.
Sixteenth Century.

or less compulsory way on public works, whole districts are evacuated or resettled, and emigration and immigration are checked to such an extent that for all practical purposes they have ceased to exist. Certain professions have been closed for a series of years while on the other hand pupils are assigned to professions which the government wishes to expand. It almost approaches the methods of cattle-raising when such and such a number of aviators, teachers, watch-makers, is called into existence each year according to plan. However, a whole public-school system was erected on the basic principle that a man was free to choose his profession. Now the liberal arts college, the universities and the public schools talk of progress on this line, while the principle and the particular institution which has enabled them to go forward in that direction for the last four hundred years is crumbling.

More recent achievements are equally imperilled. The world owes it to the British Commonwealth that during the last centuries, donations, endowments, voluntary gifts, have been the mainspring of progress in many fields. Were it not for the right of man to do what he liked with his property little would exist in religion, art, science, social and medical work today. No king's arbitrary power was allowed to interfere with a man's last will as expressed in his testament. On the independence of 10,000 fortunes a civilization was based that allowed for a rich variety of special activities introduced by imaginative donors and founders. The ways of life explored under the protection of an independent judiciary form a social galaxy. Our modern dictators, however, are cutting deeply into this tradition. This is achieved through progressive taxation of inheritance or limitation of a man's right over his property, by subsidizing institutions, like Oxford, which were independent formerly. A still bolder attempt to annihilate the freedom of wills was carried out successfully in Nazi Germany. This is all the more interesting, as Germany claims to take an anti-communistic stand, and to respect private property. The confiscation was performed without any legislation. The social principle of *"Gleichschaltung"* sufficed. Stipends, Rotary clubs, hospitals, libraries, schools, associations of artists, consumers' clubs, football unions, lodges, were forced to dismiss their boards of directors or trustees or whatever representatives ruled the foundations and new groups of Nazis took over the corporations. This was done even with corporations in business, factories, department stores. But the greatest inroad was made in the field of the institutions which had come into existence through the generosity of founders; still, this part of the national revolution was rarely noticed abroad. The famous Dartmouth case which Daniel Webster won against the State (a striking example of the progressive significance of the Whiggish principle) was tried only a century ago; yet the conditions which made it possible for Webster to win are rapidly vanishing, at least in Europe.

Turning to the American and French Revolutions, we find that they too introduced a new stimulus to progress. To the list of liberties they added the freedom of the mind. Not only were freedom of belief and creative art and science guaranteed as never before; for the first time in the history of the world it became possible for a man, thanks to patents and copyrights, to capitalize on his talents and genius. In fact, we have become so dependent on the unresting efforts of the inventive mind that we deliberately encourage genius by legislation and other means. Spinoza had to toil at the grinding of lenses. In our times, a writer, a composer, an inventor, are able to make a living by using the occasional sparks of inspiration. Once more, progress has been speeded up. Turning from hereditary trades to a life-time job has meant a new era. Now, any hour may bring a happy chance.

But again, the institutions which thus protect genius are losing their former energy. Great trusts are taking over the movies, the arts, and the process of invention. A chain-gang of hundreds and thousands of collaborating brains—in chemistry, electricity, and the whole realm of technique and medicine— asks for legislative protection.

The Truce of God, the free choice of a profession, the liberty to make a will, the copyright of ideas—these institutions are like letters in the alphabet which we call Western civilization. To be sure, they are not all the letters. The Truce of God, for example, great as it was and slowly as it was established, was not the only preoccupation of the clerical period of Europe. The institutions of higher learning, the universities, are a second element which we cannot omit from our own alphabet of everyday life. And they too antedate Humanism and Reformation. The idea of a plurality of opinions to be represented at the same time in the same place on important questions came as an illumination to the age of the great theologians and lawyers of the Middle Ages. They established an intercollegiate science unknown to Greeks and Arabs.

Our second omission is really a gap not in our list on page

32 but in the world outside. It is a gap which we ourselves
must fill by action. Our contemporaries are asking for institutions to protect the child, the labourer, the mill hand, against
exploitation. The character of the legislation and of the institutions are now under discussion, and as always the problem
is how to go forward and take the next step without losing the
gains secured by previous institutions.

As a matter of fact, each set of these institutions, when it first
was advocated, seemed completely irreconcilable with existing
ways of life. The people who invoked the new covenant cursed
the old one and vice versa. This is exactly what is going on
among us today. Labour sees nothing but labour problems;
the older classes see nothing but losses.

It seems, then, not inappropriate to look into the matter
more deeply and bring into the open what all these institutions
have in common.

They have emancipated the various elements of our social
existence from previous bondage. Each time one of these institutions came into being, it had a stiffening effect on one type
of human activity. Each time it enabled man to direct his
energies towards ends that hitherto transcended his potentialities. Less and less did he remain bound by the unchangeable
traditions of his environment. A police force means nothing
less than the emancipation of the civilian within myself; for
without it, I should be forced to cultivate the rugged virtues
of a vigilant man. To free the courts from the whims of a
changing government exalts my will and testament to a kind
of immortality: something will endure when I have passed
away. And so each of these institutions was hailed as a deliverance. Not one of them came into existence without the shed-
ding of streams of blood. Each of these institutions was accorded the greatest sacrifices.

The paradoxical truth about progress, then, is that it wholly
depends on the survival of massive institutions which prevent
a relapse from a stage which has once been reached. In general,
this is the last thing a progressive is concerned about. He must
make a real *volte-face* and learn to revere our millennium of
progress and invention as a whole. On the other hand, the

list is an important lesson for the conservative as well. All the
different sides of human nature developed and protected in
the course of time are but sides of our whole being. Whenever
people tried to dwell exclusively on one feature, on one liberty,
and were enamoured of one specialty, life began to wither, and
the inspiration left the institution that protected this special
human activity. For the sake of preserving the previous liberties, the conservative must graft a new branch on the old tree
in time.

I invite the progressive to look about and to recognize the
fact that his insatiable thirst for newness may suck the blood
out of the institutions on which he wholly depends for his
progress. I invite the conservative to recognize the fact that his
old institutions will decay if the sap of the tree is not given a
new outlet into the timely institutions of today.

The ladder of potentialities for progress and emancipation
is shown in the following list:

CENTURY	LIBERTIES	PROTECTING PRINCIPLE	CORRESPONDING INSTITUTION
20th	Freedom for growth, health	Public character of labour	(?Perhaps: adult education, decentralization of industry?)
19th	Freedom for talent, thought, genius, speech, creativeness to compete	Public character of private ideas	Copyright, patents, a written constitution
17th	Freedom of endowment	Public character of wills	An independent judiciary
16th	Free choice of profession, no vows for children	Public character of education	Public schools
13th	Freedom of competition between teachers	Public character of the sciences	Universities
11th	Freedom of movement for the men in the professions	Public character of civil life (truce of God)	Judges of the peace, public prosecution of crime

These, then, are the stakes of our present struggles.

PART ONE

FROM LENIN TO LUTHER

The Secular Revolutions

CHAPTER FOUR

Russia: The Eurasian Factory for Cereals

A Journey to Bulgaria—Little Mother Russia—The Russia of the Soviets—The Intelligentsia—Lenin's Private Life—The Failure of the Social Revolutionaries—The Bolsheviks—The Speech of the Russian Revolution—Totality and Reproduction (Karl Marx)—The Limitations of a Market-Seeking Economy—The Reproduction of Man—The True Victim of Capitalism—Dostoevski and Tolstoi—Between the First and Second Revolution—Military Defeat: A Revolutionary Victory—World War and World Revolution—The Depression—Judas Iscariot—The Interdependence of Revolutions—The First of May and the Abolition of History—The Soviet Calendar—Racial History

A JOURNEY TO BULGARIA.

WHEN I TRAVELLED IN THE BALKANS IN 1927 TO INVESTIGATE THE compulsory Labour Service of Bulgaria, huge orthodox monasteries in the midst of forests and hotels in the cities offered me hospitality. I moved through both, monasteries and hotels, as in a dream of unreality.

When I entered one of the monasteries high up in the mountains, a family of beggars was being entertained by the monks. A father and his boys, clothed in rags for which any film producer would have paid a fantastic sum, had been going to this monastery twice a week for many years. Begging was an institution. This family would find its soup ready next week and next year and forever. Charity was the most noble obligation of Christians and particularly of monks; begging was a condition for alms-giving. Procure beggars; otherwise you cannot be charitable.

In another abbey—the wealthiest of the country, and visited by thousands of pilgrims, who camp on the porches and verandas as well as in the hundreds of rooms—the abbot assured

35

us that the Creator loved bugs, lice, fleas, and mosquitoes as much as man, so that it would be sinful to lessen the excitements of a night under the beams, black with insects. For fifteen hundred years monks have given alms to the poor, and pilgrims have scratched themselves. And the gold of Eternity was around them, as it is on the pictures of Christ in a Byzantine Church.[1]

On the other hand, when I came to the pseudo-Western hotels, I met people who were not at home in their own country. I remember one heavy man who took his degree in Berlin under the best German specialist in a historical detail of the seventh century, and who was now trying to act as city councillor in modern Sofia—and another who, from his studies in Paris, had carried with him his plan for a wonderful book. His desk was full of manuscript which will never see the light of day; for the Bulgarian book-market cannot digest scientific literature. I found scores of lawyers, too, like cobblers or tailors in Southern Europe, seated in the windows of their "shops" at Trnovo, offering their skill in reading and writing to the illiterate peasants so that these might fight off taxation. As for the lawyers themselves, they were an intellectual proletariat, three times as numerous as the country could possibly feed, and foreign-born in spirit. A dead church and a foreign-minded intellectual class are the curse of the countries east of the Roman and Protestant denominations. Heaven only knows what any one of us might be guided to do, under conditions where both sources of inspiration—religion and education—are equally damaging.

LITTLE MOTHER RUSSIA.

After 1917, the Russian leaders wished to be considered as purely post-War and Bolshevik. In its totalitarian claim, the proletarian society abandoned the whole Czarist past as annihilated and deserving annihilation.

---

[1] Compare the latest report: Ralph Brewster, *The Six Thousand Beards of Athos*, Hogarth Press, London, 1935. See also Michael Choukas, *Black Angels of Athos*, Brattleboro, Vt., 1934.

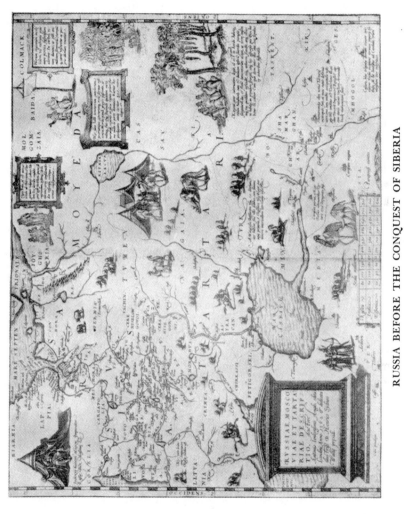

RUSSIA BEFORE THE CONQUEST OF SIBERIA

And, in fact, Czarist Russia, compared with present-day Soviet Russia, was a different country.

In 1900 "little Mother Russia" consisted of the central block of orthodox Russians, with 66 per cent of the whole population, and the western countries, Finland, Poland, and the Baltic provinces, Protestant or Roman Catholic in religion, and with an old European tradition.

The Eastern wing, Siberia and Central Asia, more than three times as large as the European wing, contained only 13,500,000 inhabitants, as against 114,000,000 in Europe. One sixth of the Earth is Russian. The territory is forty times as big as France. The Randstaaten—that is, the disannexed area yielded up by the treaty of Brest-Litovsk, and guaranteed at first by Germany and Austria and later by the Allies—is one and a half times as big as Germany.

Russia, in 1914, contained almost as many peasants' households (25,000,000) as France had inhabitants at the time of her Revolution of 1789 (24,000,000).

It was the Volga that held European Russia together in pre-railroad days. Without the Volga Russia would not be one country. The dividing range near the height of Valdai is no check, since it is transversed by a combined canal-system of 859 kilometres in length. In the old days boats were carried by men from one network of river-lines to the other. The name of the town of Volotschok, "place where the boats are carried," recalls this organization of old Russia.

The Volga is navigable for 1,900 miles. More than 2,000,000 square miles belong to the region of the Volga, and the system of canals running to the Baltic Sea greatly extends this region. The line of the Volga forms the last natural articulation of traffic on the European continent. About 160 different tribes, nationalities and cultural groups lived in this Russian territory; with the increase of Western influences, these groups showed a frightening increase in their birthrate.

The population was not only subdivided into countless nationalities, but it contained, in some of its parts, artificially compressed and suppressed, five and one half millions of that race which carries wherever it goes all the riddles of religious warfare and religious peace: the Jews. In France, where the Jews were first emancipated, there were 87,000 Jews in 1900 out of 39,000,000 inhabitants; in Russia 5,250,000 Jews out of 128,000,000 inhabitants. The proportions were: in France, 0.22%; in Russia, 4.2%. When we hear of pogroms and the outlawing and restriction of Jews as daily events in the old Russia, we must not forget this proportion, and the fact that in France it took more than twelve years to settle the simple affair of an innocent man like Dreyfus, and that almost at the cost of civil war.

The western territories were divided from Russia proper not only by religion and history, but by other economic and social conditions as well. In Finland, for example, no illiteracy existed in 1900; in Russia, 891 out of every 1,000 could not read or write. Russian Poland, though the most agricultural section in all Poland, had at least 500 cities among her 43,000 communities in 1892; Russia counted 486,000 villages and 650 cities. The proportion is almost one to a hundred in Poland and one to a thousand in Russia. In 1890 Russia had 13,000 kilometres of railroad, and England 200,000! A striking parallel in periodicals: Only 800 newspapers and magazines appeared in Russia, 342 of them in Petersburg and Moscow, and 460 throughout the rest of the country.

The greatest peculiarity, however, was the distribution of private property, 84.6% of the farming land belonging to the community, and only 15.4% being private property. "Common land" was land given as security for the taxes laid upon the land. The "Mir," the union among the peasants, was a duty, not a privilege of the community. The apportionment of taxes, therefore, was called "rolling off" or "rolling up" of souls. The measure for taxation was the labour-force of husband and wife (*tjaglo*) or of men, or of eaters, or of good will, sometimes only of souls.

In 1861, simultaneously with the emancipation of the negroes in the United States of America, liberalism forced upon Russia the deliverance of the peasants. It is interesting to know that Lincoln's first peaceful scheme of emancipation would have been carried out in 1900, whereas in Russia the last of the steps provided in 1861 for redistributing the land would have been taken in 1932.

In 1861, 22,000,000 "souls of revision" were emancipated and 15½ acres of land were given them pro rata capitis, or about three hundred and forty millions of acres of land in all. In 1917 the peasants took another 250,000,000 acres; but even of these about one third had been on lease before. This may explain why we are told today that the whole agricultural area is but 530,000,000 acres.

Eighty-five per cent of the whole population lived as peasants. But the word "peasant" should not be mistaken for the same as "farming population." Nearly a third of the peasants were homeworkers on textiles, candles, timber, furs and metals. This helps partly to explain why, out of sixty governments, only twenty-nine had grain to export. Another reason was the rather poor soil. The fertile district in Central and Southern Russia covers but 950,000 square kilometres, twice the size of Texas. Temperatures of 40° F., and 55 or even 75 are frequent even for long periods of quiet, bright and dry weather.

Only eight governments or sections were at all thickly populated (more than seventy people to a square mile). In Russia we find a marvellous example of the truism that homogeneity is no help in organizing a country. Russia was then in a permanent state of fermentation from below and artificial reorganization from above. The fermentation from below is illustrated by the wanderings of the Russian peasant in the last five centuries. He was no stable freeholder of the Western type, but much more a nomad, a pedlar, a craftsman, and a soldier. His capacity for expansion was tremendous.

In the fifteenth century Russia covered 560,000 square kilometres,

SQUARE KILOMETRES

in the sixteenth century it covered.......... 8,720,000
in the seventeenth century it covered........ 14,392,000
in the eighteenth century it covered........ 17,080,000
in the nineteenth century (1885) it covered... 22,311,992

In 1581 Asiatic Russia was opened. Russian expansion, extending even in the eighteenth century as far as to the Russian River in Northern California, was by no means Czaristic only. The "Moujik," the Russian peasant, because he is not a "Bauer" or "farmer," or a "labourer," but a "Moujik," wanders and stays, ready to migrate again eventually year after year.

Paul von Sokolovski, a well-known Russian scholar and administrator, calls our attention to the fact that the formation of sand dunes goes on continuously in Southern Russia and has wrought this unceasing change of the soil deep into the character of the inhabitants. The spring tide of peasants was the permanent riddle of Russia. A gigantic land movement—how can it be organized? Peter the Great was the first to answer this question "from outside." He founded St. Petersburg as Russia's window toward Europe. The Czarist State was a state without a people, chiefly interested not in Russia, but in Europe, in politics, in the prestige or territory which it could find abroad. The Russian lumber and hemp market was Russia's first connection with the world, and the Czarist régime was occupied from the first in organizing foreign trade. A forest was always on hand to be liquidated by a prince or a nobleman when he was short of means. In the eighteenth century the English Navy was built, to a great extent, of Russian wood. Only in foreign trade could one find the financial support to govern a country, to pay an army, a navy, a civil administration, when one got no real taxes from the Moujiks and had no cities to rely on. The timber trade, and later the export of wheat, gave revenues to princes and nobility. As late as 1904 the grand princes of the imperial family, speculating on the woods of the Yalu in Manchuria, precipitated the outbreak of the Russo-Japanese War. The Colossus with feet of clay had to go in quest of additional sources of revenue, the more he tried to organize the central power.

An example of Russian government from the outside was the forced exportation of wheat with famine raging in the neighbourhood of the exporting sections. The Bolsheviks have had to imitate this distortion rather often in the last ten years.

The annexation of big masses of land in the west seemed the first remedy against this evil, because all the western regions were more articulated, more civilized, and therefore better equipped for traffic. Russia can be compared to the United States of America in more than the question of slaves and negroes and their emancipation. Both are continents which have had to be organized during the last one hundred and fifty years. But in Russia the problem was somehow first solved from the "frontier" toward the Baltic coast. It was as if Texas or Utah and Nevada had tried to annex the thirteen colonies.

In conquering Finland, in dividing Poland, in vanquishing the free people of the Caucasus, in getting the Baltic provinces from Sweden, the Russians inherited an old investment in political and social tradition. They found a surplus for taxation more easily in the Teutonic order, the German harbours and universities, the Polish craftsmen and peasants, and the Jewish traders. For Russia, the conquest of new western districts spared organizing the purely Russian regions! This could be postponed, and was postponed. And who can blame the leaders? One quarter of Russia is composed of mire and heath; 200,000 square kilometres become sand dunes every year. Nature in this country draws towards decay. As a matter of fact, Nature, left to herself, is everywhere in decay, though this may sound like a strange paradox to Europeans who are intoxicated by Rousseau and by his childish belief in nature. But Rousseau, in the vineyards of Neuchâtel, is easily excused. The decadence of nature is felt more sharply in the middle of vast continents like America or Russia. The French revolutionaries in *la douce France,* the owners of rich plantations in Virginia, or even the crews of clipper ships from Boston, could believe in fortunes to be made with the support of a charitable and helpful nature, prodigal of her treasures and wealth.

But in Russia nature is devastating and depressing. Nowhere is nature so unimproved, or, better still, less closely married to the soul of man. The Russian peasant sold his manure to the "Nemez," the German colonist next door. The busy German had a use for manure because he was really settled. But the German freeholder and yeoman had been protected and trained by centuries of education in the Western church. The reward of such an education is a new relationship to nature and our duties toward nature. In Russia the Church had never conquered its liberty from the Empire. It had been petrified for a thousand years. Nothing had moved within the Church since the famous monasteries of Mount Athos were founded during the tenth century. Beginning with 922, the old church of the saints had concentrated in these monasteries all their forms of praise, thanksgiving, adoration and worship.

These traditions were well-preserved in Russia. The Russian church, it is true, kept all the joy and delightful cheerfulness of ancient Christianity, and since there was less struggle with popes or reformers or puritans, it upheld the old tradition much better than Western Christendom. The childlike joy and glee which the members of the Russian and Greek Church feel and express at Easter are strange for a Roman Catholic, to say nothing of a Protestant. The last genuine representative of this pre-War Christianity in Russia, and, for that reason, the last link between the dynasty and the people; Rasputin, wrote home from his pilgrimage to Palestine: "I saw the Easter of the Roman Catholics in Jerusalem, but the holiday was not to be compared with that of the Orthodox Church. The Catholics did not look cheerful, whereas with us all the world is merry on that day, even the animals. The faces of the Catholics are sad, even at Easter. I think, therefore, that their souls are not truly glad. I do not wish to compare the two denominations, and to condemn the Catholics, but I feel how with us all the world is happy when the bells of the church ring and how then the holy spring blossoms for all of us."

Without knowing something about this unchanged life of the Orthodox Church, it is useless to become excited over the Bolshevik attitude toward religion. This Church never tried to change the world, to teach, to translate, to reform. It is the old church of adoration, attacking nobody, leaving the world alone. The arrow of religion always pointed away from the world and never back into it. To the Russian Moujik the church gave one special instrument of communication with the majestic world of God and his Saints, an instrument well adapted to a far-off village in the country. In the lowlands of the Volga, earth is expanding and the individual is quite lost. Man is, in Russia, but a blade of grass. To this powerless man the church presented the Ikons, the painted images of the Saints. Art helps man to look at the world with the eyes of God because in art he is lifted up above his natural environment of village and hut. The Saints visited the poor as witnesses of a united Christianity far away, and as sponsors of a stream of power and strength going on from time eternal.

Says John Sergiev, famous "Father John" of Cronstadt, in *My Life in Christ:* "Ikons replace for me the persons themselves whose names they bear. The images of the saints upon our Ikons represent to us the nearness in the spirit of God's saints who are always near to us. For what can be far away from the spirit of God who is everywhere present? We have Ikons in our houses in order to show that the eyes of God and of all the heavenly dwellers are constantly fixed on us."

Today the Bolsheviks use the Ikons in their statistics; to them anybody who wears Ikons, or worships them, is a Christian, so much does the Ikon seem identical with the Christian faith. As a matter of fact, this is not true even for the Orthodox clergy in Russia. Pobedonostsev, the famous head of the church under the last Czar, Nicholas II, had no Ikons in his office and was proud of that puritanism. Art is never more than an image. However, one has to admit that the Ikons reflect very clearly the situation of a church evangelizing scattered units, isolated villages, whilst it was itself ecumenic and universal. A polarity existed between an economy that covered the smallest possible circle and a church that filled the largest possible circumference. Today we see just the opposite, a world-wide economy and parish-wide sects or creeds. In a world-wide economy the connection with far-distant events becomes natural. In a period of electrification, the church need not emphasize this side of its mission, particularly to the believers. Unity now belongs to the realm of knowledge instead of the realm of belief. The world of knowledge is an economic world, and the world of faith is ruled by the church or whatever takes its place. The

Ikons proved that the Russian church was not a civilizing institution of reform and progress, but a place of pure adoration
and glorification; in Russia in 1914, and in Russia only, the
Christian Church was still what it had been everywhere in 900:
a place of worship and devotion without any ambition to transform the world or wrest it from the devil.

The Western churches had not been afraid to redeem some
part of human life, and to build up different new stages of
civilization. In the West, universities, free cities, shipping,
banking, are closely connected with stages of ecclesiastical activity; in Russia, modern technique and modern capitalism en-
countered a form of Christianity which had never committed
itself to a reform of the world, like the Roman or the Lutheran
or the Puritan Christians.

For that reason, the Ikons symbolized a pre-War Russia in
which the church stood for unity and world-wide standards,
and the economic unit of the village for isolation and weakness. The Bolsheviks hate the pictures and hate the religion
represented by the pictures, because it seems to perpetuate a
division of labour between faith and knowledge which they
know they can outstrip.

The Soviets must be against the Ikons because these reflect
village economy. Their mistake is not to be found so much in
the warfare against the Ikons; that fight is connected with the
industrialization of Russia. The atheism of the Bolshevik becomes tragic only because of his confusion of Ikons with Christianity.

THE RUSSIA OF THE SOVIETS.

To the endless plain of Little Mother Russia, the cradle of
a hundred million unconscious Moujiks, post-War Russia forms
a complete antithesis.

The Institute for the Economy and Organization of Socialistic Agriculture has published a plan for the exploitation of
the soil. In this plan the regions of the U.S.S.R. (Union of
Soviet Socialist Republics) are divided into five sections. The
first section is adapted to crops for industrial use and intensive
cattle-raising.

ICONOSTASES

The essential of the Iconostasis is its being employed to shut away completely from the congregation the view of what is going on in the Sanctuary.

Hemp
Sugar
Turnips
Indian corn
Soya beans   }   Southwestern Ukraine, Black Earth
Tobacco   Basin, Northern Kuban, Far East (par-
Cotton   tially)
Girasole
Hogs

The second zone produces:

Flax
Dairy farm prod-
   ucts   }   The grazing country from the Baltic
Vegetables   via Moscow to the Ural
Hogs

The third zone produces sub-tropical plants:

Silk
Tea   }   Southern Crimea
Grapes   Caucasus
Oranges   Asia
etc.   Central

The fourth zone produces:

Cattle   }   Buriat–Mongolian Republic
Sheep   Southeastern Steppes east of the Volga

The fifth zone is marked as:

Reservatión for
  Agriculture   }   From Archangel to the Pacific
Forestation Zone

This classification of Russia destroys the distinction between Russia and Siberia. It no longer looks at Russia from the West, from St. Petersburg, nor even from Moscow. The plan is a new concept of all Russia as one sixth of the globe; it shakes off the old yoke of European discriminations between European

and Asiatic soil and carries out the resolution of the Tenth
Communist Convention in 1921: "The destruction of the actual inequality among the nations is connected with the destruction of the historically conditioned inequality in their
economy. The economic iniquity was expressed in the fact that
the territories on the edge of Russia were treated like colonies,
or half-colonies, and were held by force to their function of
delivering all kinds of raw material for the manufacturers in
the 'Central.' "

The "Central" is treated like a criminal in this statement.
Now, the "Central" is nothing else but Little Mother Russia
herself. The sentimental cradle of the Moujik is degraded to
the same status in which the territories of the edge were before.
It is like a sinner's repentance. "Central" and colonies move
towards each other. They are brought to the same level. They
become sections of the area upon which one big industrial
trust, called the U.S.S.R., builds the branches of its industrial
system. What an estrangement from all sentiment and feeling!
What a Genghis Khan-like attitude! Montesquieu said in writing his *L'Esprit des Lois* that he wished to look at Europe as
though it were Madagascar. Lenin, as a Bolshevik, taught the
Russians to manipulate their homesteads as if they were colonial soil. The ruins of Mother Russia are just a foundation on
which the real factory for cereals can be built, covering 20,000,-
000 square kilometres. This is the gigantic achievement of the
Revolution. By a process of abstraction the earth, the natural
environment, is estranged from the man who lives on it to such
an extent that anybody with roots in the soil must be extirpated.

Now the type of peasant or farmer whom we know best is
the independent owner of, let us say, one hundred acres. The
pre-War reforms of Stolypin had taken this type as the normal
man for agriculture. Stolypin had imported, so to speak, the
wealthy farmer, in the form of the famous Kulak. The Kulak
became the target against which the most violent cannonade
of the Bolsheviks was directed. The expropriation and expatri-
ation of the Kulak is parallelled by the construction of factories for cereals. Thirty million acres were given to the grain

trust. The territory was divided into Sovcoses, big estates. From the beginning, bad harvests were taken into account; the vastness of the area compensated for them. The biggest Sovcose is as big as Rhode Island or a German principality of former days, 22,000 square kilometres. In Belgium, or in Saxony, or in Massachusetts, a million people live in such an area. The nearest part of Germany to the east and to Russia, Silesia, is very thinly populated, especially along its borders. Yet in this border district 200,000 people live on the same extent of territory. On the Sovcose "Gigant" there are seventeen thousand people. Such an emptiness of the fields was well-known to the soldiers of the World War. We called it "the emptiness of the battlefield." Our war-time experience is being exploited for the first time by the Russian economy. The war against nature, against the wind of the steppes, against the drought, is carried on by an army of young warriors. Ninety-five per cent of the workers among the Sovcoses are under thirty years of age. But their force, vigorous as they may be, is only a fraction of the tremendous force moved in this warfare. It is the warfare of machines. Ninety per cent of the personnel are technicians; not more than ten per cent are agricultural labourers. Cultivation is standardized at 100 per cent. These national farms were scheduled to deliver the same amount of grain in 1930 which the Kulaks had delivered in 1927: 100,000,000 Pud.[2]

Here we find a government actually carrying on a ferocious competition against its inhabitants for political reasons. For any pre-War order of things, these proceedings are incomprehensible. In the pre-War countries government had to deal with economy as it was. It had to protect, perhaps to develop, but in any case to acknowledge the existing economic interests; silver, farming, oil, building, could not be abolished by governmental action. The Soviets have reversed the relationship between the nation and business. They have abolished the Kulaks. And they have sacrificed some billions in this civil war.

In 1927 the situation of the grain market had made the Soviets depend upon the Kulaks. Nobody except the Kulaks

[2] A Pud is about thirty-six pounds.

could offer a surplus of products for exportation. And we know already that Russia depends upon exports for balancing her budget. In another country the effect of this dependency would have been a strong support of Kulak interests by the government. Their influence would easily have doubled. But in Soviet Russia this very fact of dependency led to the opposite result. Communism boasts of its "jump out of the realm of necessity into the realm of freedom," which was forecast by Karl Marx's twin, Friedrich Engels. The individual liberty of the Kulaks is a threat, it is corrupt and corrupting, it leads to the slavery of others. The organization of production must be torn out of the hands of owners or proprietors: "Nobody but the party can regulate consciously the producing forces of society." (Lukasz.) The destruction of old economic values or forms is no argument by which you can frighten a Bolshevik, for England may rule the waves, France may rule the ideas of the civilized world, but the Bolshevik rules the means of production. Economy and property are no given facts for this government. They are interesting, not because they exist, but because they can be planned. All members of society are interchangeable; and they must be interchanged. If any one of them claims political privileges for economic reasons, he must be annihilated. To the Bolshevik, the Kulaks are but the Russian example of the destruction which threatens all the so-called capitalistic powers. Capitalistic powers are nations which have to take into consideration the vested interests of groups of the population, nations which feel incapable of extirpating classes from their social order.

In the Russian five-year plan (piatiletka), the key which designates the relationship between the output of consumers' goods (production) and of capital investment (reproduction), represents a kind of last judgment over whole classes and groups of society. The key means that a series of starvations has to be undergone for the next five, ten or fifteen years, that a million people have to be turned bodily into civil engineers, that this and that group of artists, or *spez*, has to disappear. The Bolsheviks mean business when they speak of "has-beens."

Poets, or ladies, or bourgeois, are "has-beens." They still exist, but in bare physical nakedness. Since no social use can be made of them, they are "extra commercium," as the Romans said. Under favourable conditions they might get their maintenance, out of compassion. But they "have been," they are not citizens of the Soviet and their existence has lost all meaning, because they are not labour forces. With the key of the "Piatiletka," a power of binding and loosing is given to the officials which surpasses by far all the powers of government in the nineteenth century. That is why we focus our attention on that power more than on any annual statistics of output, etc. Because, after all, the figures in the statistics of Russian production will change in her plans for reproduction. The figures, therefore, are not interesting in themselves. The political and human interest in the Soviet experiment centres in their contribution to the social organization of men and nations.

Let us look at this key of distribution once more:

a. Branches of Economy

	Industry	Power	Transport	Agriculture	Housing	Others
1927/28	14%	1.4%	16.6%	41%	17.2%	9.8%
1932/33	22.8%	4.1%	17.2%	30.4%	12%	13.5%

b. Types of Economy

	Socialistic Sector	Co-operative Sector	Private Business Sector
Oct. 1, 1928	51%	1.7%	47.3%
Oct. 1, 1933	63.6%	5.3%	31.1%

c. Products for

	Consumption	Circulation	Means of Production
Oct. 1, 1928	42.7%	18%	39.3%
Oct. 1, 1933	35%	20.5%	44.5%

Thus it becomes clear:

The Plan is in Russia what the constitution is in a democratic country. Through the Plan not only does the soil become an area for temporary factories, and the factories moveable pins on the map of the general staff, but the kinds of men are produced like goods, too. In the accounts of society, everybody is reckoned as a force. The gospel preached to everybody is that he be changed into a force, an element in the electric stream that organizes production. "From Body to Force," the

Russian Revolution could well be christened. From this point of view the offences of Bolshevism against our individual liberties vanish. Bolshevism is not interested in individuals. It scarcely knows of such a thing. At the end of the World War it found the bleeding, mutilated, starved body politic in complete disillusionment and paralysis. The resuscitation of this body was the first endeavour of the proletarian revolution. To say "Rise up and walk" to the corpse of broken-down Russia depended upon everybody's courage in this incantation. A man was welcome if he could conduct electric current, new energies. If not, nobody was interested in him. In compensation, anybody useful in the electrification of the corpse was freed from all Sin. Man has no personal sins. Personal sin is abolished in the U.S.S.R. This impresses a European mind, especially in questions of love; the tremendous well of personal life, love, is watered down into sex. Krupskaya, the wife of Lenin, wrote a book on the life of the working bees, doing away with all the confusion of sex, love, passion. Modern youth in Russia has no special interest in sex. There are no privileges, there are no secrets, there are no inhibitions. Sex has ceased, therefore, to be an obsession.

The exaggeration of its importance is closely connected with the exaggeration of the individual in the bourgeois civilization of the nineteenth century. But let us be careful! In abolishing, or not acknowledging, personal sin, the Bolsheviks did not abolish sin. They came back to an older, pre-subjective meaning of sin: there can be public sin in society, without any personal fault, merely by the corruption of institutions. This sin prevents the regeneration of life.

All civilization is simply order, but order repeating itself. The cultural level can only be maintained where there is room for renovation, reform, repair and reconstruction. Self-perpetuating forms of life must breed, nurse, and educate men. How are men reproduced? is the real question of history, and the true question of our book.

Other periods of history tried to reproduce the citizen, the gentleman and the Christian; in the Russian Revolution the institutions for reproducing types of men are shaped according to their usefulness in the process of production. And this is one side of our nature, too. We have in ourselves non-human forces of nature as steam, electricity or water, forces which can be used like any other raw material in an industrialized world.

After the terrible losses of the War—in which 15,000,000 inhabitants of Russia are said to have passed away—the Soviet Union found no reliable supply of skilled labour, technical staffs, economists or explorers left from the pre-War organization of society. So decisions were forced upon them for the reproduction of different kinds of men: teachers, technicians, skilled workers, farmers—nowhere else but in the piatiletka can the ground be found on which they can base their *raison d'être*. If they are not put on the map, they will become extinct, not physically and personally, but typically and as a class. In Dante's Purgatory the crown of a man's life, his personal immortality, is called to judgment; has he a soul, a redeemable soul, or is he condemned? In the piatiletka, the original sin of society is judged. Not the crown but the roots of the tree of life are tested. We are punished for the original sin of inheritance, for the form of character and outlook into which we were introduced in the historical course of social events. The last judgment is based on older orders of society, older divisions of labour, older class conditions and social functions.

This is an impersonal and earthly judgment, put into effect not against our soul or person, but against us as children of earth, against the material subconscious labour force which is judged, reorganized, redistributed. To understand the indifference of the Soviets to all questions of personal morality we must take care to limit the despotic power of the piatiletka to its real scope. Man as a creature among other creatures, man as a labour force, is the object of the piatiletka. In its system, the Moujik in the cradle of Little Mother Russia, always a minor, is a minor again. He is not an individual; as he was treated before as a helpless child of God, now he is treated as an atom of the raw materials and labour forces of the globe.

The Soviets dropped the name of Rossiya (Russia). They wish to be the nucleus of a universal, pan-global order. They started a world-revolution. So much stress is laid upon that non-

Russian side of their enterprise that the aim of the piatiletka reads as follows: "By means of the energetic industrialization of the U.S.S.R. and the gradual strengthening of socialistic elements to attain and then surpass in our time the level of the most advanced countries, in order to secure the victory of the socialist system in its historical struggle against the capitalistic system." [3]

The non-Russian duty of the Russian proletarian is to fight capitalism. The Bolshevik, G. Grinke, writes about the pig-iron front: "The reports in the Soviet Press from this constructive front recall the reports of actions at the most important sectors of the fighting front during the War." The Russian experiment was started as a non-Russian affair. This fact makes it the more astounding. Is it really the world revolution? Is every event in the newspapers, in Spain, America, Germany, France, only a step toward universal Bolshevism? In other words: Is the international component in the Russian Revolution growing or declining?

We contrasted old pre-War Russia with the piatiletka. We shall now speak of the groups of men and the set of ideas which transformed one into the other. We are going to narrate the rise of the governing class in Russia and the standards of European Marxism. Lenin united in his synthesis the Russian Intelligentsia as a social group and the doctrines of Western Marxism. He destroyed, as we shall see, both the Russian intellectuals and the Western Marxists, who were not capable of forgetting their respective beginnings. Only a few passed through the eye of the needle; those are the men who govern Russia today.

THE INTELLIGENTSIA.

Which is the governing class of Russia? We are told the proletariat. But there exists a queer test for admission to the Bolshevik Party; people are taken not because they are proletarians, but because they have a tested revolutionary disposition. Besides the social setting of the piatiletka, a personal and individual disposition must mark the man who wishes to

[3] Malevsky-Malevitch, *Russia/U.S.S.R.*, p. 529, Payson, New York, 1933.

belong to the select men of the Party. A stratum of fewer millions of men than the old governing class in pre-War Russia governs Russia today as the Bolshevik Party, and it is kept together by the tested revolutionary and proletarian disposition of individuals.

One could recognize a Bolshevik during the first fifteen years by the fact that he was not allowed to earn more than 225 rubles a month. He was not allowed to dance or to show that he liked dissipated life. Even today, kissing your sweetheart's hand in public may get you into difficulties. But in pre-War days the test was much simpler. The disposition and conviction were tested by suffering. Had he been in prison? Had he been to Siberia? Had he lived disguised, without a passport, under a false name, among the people? Then he had the real disposition. On the whole, the women or men who suffered in this or similar ways before the War were of good family. Lenin was the son of a gentleman, Mr. Ulianov; Trotsky of a big land owner; Tolstoi and his friends, like Paul Birkov, were nobles, officers in the guard. The Intelligentsia of Russia was not at all a greedy group of suppressed proletarians. As early as 1825 the man who had defended Moscow against Napoleon, Count Rostoptschin, exclaimed: "I can understand the French citizen with his revolution for the acquisition of rights, but what idea can a Russian gentleman have in starting a revolution in order to lose his privileges?"

What happened to these people that they went against their personal interests for more than a century? Their crusade was described as follows in 1886: These people denied their past completely. They no longer had private property. If anybody hesitated to give away everything he excited pity and contempt. Like the first Christians, they said, "I disavow Satan and all that comes from him and all his pride. I spit on him." [4]

The history of Russian literature is of more importance for the evolution of Russia than the history of any other literature is for its own nation. This has been valid at least since the days of Peter the Great. In the other countries of Europe, civiliza-

[4] See Tikhomirov, *La Russie*, Paris, 1886, for a contemporary description.

tion is, so to speak, the result of all the social and political
struggles of corporations and estates. In Russia the reverse was
true. There, political life began by detour via culture. In Europe the parties are founded by corporative and social interests.
These groups elect and found their organs. In Russia it was
the press and the organs of literature which called new parties
into life and enabled them to exist. Whilst in Europe every
efficient individual represented a profession or a corporation,
and was supported by his group or the privileges of the group,
in Russia the individual could succeed only as an individual,
never as a representative of his kind.

Through the importing of Western erudition, the individual
found ways of social activity. The exchange of literary reflections might make him influential. It was for that reason that
poets and literati exercised such a great influence in Czarist
Russia. Only a few of the leading spirits could end their days
without being troubled by exile or administrative discipline.
The rulers themselves propagated their reforms by literary
productions. Peter the Great introduced plays which were
meant to make people laugh at the foes of his reform. Catherine II founded satirical journals, and herself wrote plays and
essays. The sense of political satire is so fierce that even today
the normal Soviet newspaper has its *daily* page of caricatures.

In Russia literature brought men into groups and excited
them to political activity. You could mingle with a circle for
years without divining whether or not this or that member
were a nobleman. The only question was which line of literature he preferred. There was an astounding number of reviews. There were monthlies, often two or three hundred pages
thick, and around the magazines political parties were formed.
Belles-lettres were the battlefield of politics; esthetic appreciation was impossible.

The existence of censorship had led to a real art of reading
and writing between the lines. Sometimes books passed the
censorship but the authors were disciplined for the secret sense
of the writing.

The violence of Peter's reforms, and the formation of a staff
by sending young men to foreign countries, or by having them

educated by foreigners, had this odd result that the literature of Russia began with satires, with the criticism of existing society. It had an eye that was detached, like a foreigner's, and a pen that took a negative and didactic line.

The very first poet, Prince Cantemir (1708-1744), was educated in Paris, and his Parisian education made him think how queer society was at home. He became a satirist. Later, Karamzin began an epoch (1765-1826). He was sent to the West for his instruction and published immediately afterwards (1791-1792) his famous *Letters of a Russian Traveller*. Up to that time Europe and her great men in art and science had been known from translations only. Now Karamzin introduced the nature and society of Europe by faithful and lively descriptions. His readers seemed to meet the leaders of European literature and scholarship personally. Karamzin founded the review, *The European Courier (Vestnik Evropy)*. St. Petersburg's aim to be the window towards Europe is well illustrated by this title of the leading national review.

The Napoleonic Wars had a great effect on the national conscience. The army, which marched as far as Paris, contained a mass of educated Russians. On April 15, 1814, the Te Deum of the Allies on the Place de la Concorde was celebrated by six Orthodox priests. Everyone could now verify for himself the reports of Karamzin. Young men came home with Western ideas, and again they went into Literature. No field for practice seemed open to them. The neologists fought despite censorship, exile and jail. In 1825, the martyrdom of this specific intelligence, conjured up by Czarism, began. This year marks the final estrangement between the government and the youth of the leading classes, because the government tried to make undone its own work. The Czars owed all their success after 1697 to the introduction of Western techniques. And they knew it. Catherine II (1763-1796) corresponded with Voltaire and Diderot; she anxiously awaited what Professor Schloezer of Goettingen had to say in his magazine about her policy. Now, in 1825, this cornerstone of Czarist expansion broke. Freedom of thought, the very instrument that had founded St. Petersburg, the bureaucracy and the army, was thrown away. 1825 was the point of departure for the Russian drama.

The facts are very simple. Alexander I, "the monarch who, in his own kingdom, had worked so much into the hands of the Revolutionists, succumbed mentally and bodily in the fight. Seeing himself deceived in all his calculations, under the necessity of himself striking at a class of his own subjects who had been led astray and instigated by men and principles whom he himself had long supported, his heart broke." [5]

A conspiracy broke out against the succession of Alexander.[6] The soldiers understood little of the French ideas of the young officers. They cried: "Hail, Grand Duke Constantine, and hail his wife, the Constitution!" There was no nation behind the innovators. But these idealists themselves paid a terrible price. The leader of his generation, the poet Ryleev, was hanged in 1826. Bestuzhev, the Prince Odoevski, Polejaieff, ended their lives in exile in the mines of Siberia, or were degraded into private soldiers in the Caucasus. Alexander Pushkin escaped banishment to Siberia only by a miracle, and had to live on his estate under the supervision of the police.

The women of these Dekabrists accompanied their husbands as volunteers. They shared the sufferings of the men and were ennobled by this rare companionship in permanent misfortune. Russian women were emancipated and exalted by their rare quality of being fellow-sufferers. This makes for an equality with man which surpasses all the legal or moral equality in Western society.

Pushkin was the first to speak poetically, in the character of Tatiana in *Eugen Onegin*, of this new type of Russian woman. The state of mind after 1825 is well shown in the comedy, *The Misfortunes of Being Clever (Gore ot uma)*. Anybody who did not bow before bureaucracy and the army was taken to be a politically dangerous man, and was finally declared mad. The malformation of Russian society, its hunched back, so to speak, was permanent after 1825.

[5] Clemens Metternich, *Memoirs*, Vol. I, p. 332, New York, Scribner, 1880.

[6] Compare also Anatole G. Mazour, *The First Russian Revolution, 1825: The Decembrist Movement, Its Origins, Development, and Significance*, Berkeley, Univ. of Calif., 1937.

The Intellectuals were all preoccupied with Western problems, even though they divided themselves into Westerners (*Zapadniki*) and Slavophils. It was a period of heavy oppression. In the textbooks the history of the French Revolution was cancelled. A period of despondent literature opened. Lermontov's *Hero of Our Times* torments himself and others with fruitless grief and seems to be destroying himself because he can be of no use in Russia. Nicholas Gogol opened the procession of novelists who wished to unveil social wrongs. Alexander Herzen drew the consequences of the situation. He published, in 1843, his *Who Is Responsible?* The hero of this book, who aims in vain at greater activity in Russia, leaves the country and wallows in distinguished slothfulness.

The defeat in the Crimean War and the death of Nicholas I opened the sluices. For the first time the fruits of suffering seemed to ripen. Alexander Herzen rang *The Bell,* his London journal. Though an exile, he gave audiences like a future Regent. The highest dignitaries visited "the criminal" with great reverence. The revaluation of values affected all the "pillars" of Church and State in Russia; nowhere could jail and banishment so little degrade a man as in the best circles of St. Petersburg.

The new era was announced in Turgenev's *Eve,* and the hero of his novel *Fathers and Sons* (1861) chooses for himself the name of Nihilist. The innovators had found their shibboleth. *Nihil,* i.e., nothing, of the old loyalties was to be kept. A complete break was the only condition for a new future.

But this future was still far off. Turgenev, in 1867, full of despair, wrote *Smoke.* Nothing had come of the emancipation of the serfs, and he declared the absolute bankruptcy of "Fathers and Sons," parties and groups of the better classes of society. He was right. The *"Gebildete Gesellschaft,"* the upper classes, were rotten. Intellectually and mentally, everything had been thought through and fought through.

No wonder that all educated people threw themselves into socialism. Socialism made literature into propaganda. The socialists pretended to conform to the class-consciousness of the proletariat. But in Russia no proletariat existed. Here the brunt of class-war was not borne by the proletarian worker whom Marx and Engels had seen starved in the cotton mills of Lancashire. Though the Russians were the first nation to translate the *Capital* of Marx, its attack on capitalism was devoured by non-capitalists and non-proletarians. Members of the feudal class devoted themselves to the study of Marx with the same eagerness which had led Tolstoi twenty years before to study the school system in Goethe's Weimar, or which produced incredible enthusiasm for European music and musicians throughout Czarist Russia.

Now Marxism meant the importation of a European Utopia which was still being persecuted in the rest of Europe. From the Russian point of view it had, therefore, one great advantage compared to all other European goods: it could still be made a genuine Russian product, if Russia amalgamated it first.[7] For the first time, the critical attitude of centuries could be replaced by a faith in the pioneering rôle of the Russian intellectuals. They could scorn the obsolete mentality of the average Western man. The last invention of the West, the dynamite with which to blow up all traditional order of Western civilization, was now in the hands of these restless Nihilists.

Tshernychevsky had already summoned youth to gather round Socialism in his *What to Do?*, written in 1863—the novel for which he was rewarded with twenty years of Siberian exile. Turgenev describes this new Marxism in 1876 in his book *New-Land*. It is a socialism without a capitalistic society, a Marxism without a proletariat. It is the great opportunity for the Intelligentsia *to go among the people*.

From 1825 to 1880, two generations of intellectuals had suffered for thinking, reading and writing. By 1880 the conflict with the government had become irreconcilable. The Russian Revolution was inevitable, for that reason, as early as 1890. Our statistical figures for pre-War Russia were purposely chosen from these older times, since conditions of the eighties and nineties became fixed in the minds of the revolutionary gen-

[7] A personal reminiscence: When the German jurist, R. von Ihering, was writing a—later famous—book, Prince Leon Galitzin bought for a high price the privilege of publishing it in Russian one day ahead of the German edition.

erations of later days. No progress in agriculture, no school reform, no constitution offered by the government in later years, could influence the future essentially, because it could not reach, and even less change, the picture of Russia which the revolutionaries had in mind.

Like a stream divided into branches, the life of Russian society split. One branch flowed on the surface, the other delved into a new bed deep underneath. From 1880 onward a class existed in Russian society which had cut itself off from all loyalties toward the existing order. The Nihilists went on a subterranean crusade. Everywhere abroad groups of them studied. At Bern alone, in Switzerland, six hundred Russian students registered, all utterly devoid of means, but all more or less the type created by this emigration; a type which may be described as student, intellectual, conspirator and politician rolled into one, but first of all a man who says "no" to the existing order. These men did not wish to miss their calling in the history of the world. They forgot their individual conditions, wealth, family, creed, and identified themselves with the people. Very often they acted as hangman and executioner to their own material interests. Their own families, their own futures, their own intellectual treasures and needs, counted for nothing. Before murdering the Czar or the Grand Duke, they committed moral suicide and became emancipated from all earthly interests. The code radiating from people like Lenin or Savinkov was the code of those who died to themselves ten times over because they clung to their mission. More fanatical than the Spanish Inquisition, they were not interested in their own salvation. They wished—and it seems to have been their only genuine desire—to be ahead of the West. Once, at least, this damned West would not be the pioneer; Russians would be the leaders of future society! While Europe counted confidently on a permanence of the century of progress, they knew, once for all, the secret of her total revolution. That is why the loss of civilization was no longer a bugaboo to them. Civilization was bourgeois. Liberty was bourgeois, because civilization and liberty already existed. Conscience, Honour, Faith? *Nihil!*

They had all been in prison, using the language of knocking through the walls and floors. This was a point of honour. The revolutionaries were the pariahs of the existing Russian world. Their way led from the seditious students' union at high school via study abroad to propaganda in Russia, into prison, back into the party, abroad again, back, to Siberia and into jail again, and so on. That is the rotation of their lives; every stage in exile or in separation. Separation from the domestic circle, separation from liberty, banishment from home, separation from their own social position and the necessities of life.

That all this came not as the result of external causes, but as a free choice, made the new order more solemn still. An order of revolutionary intention drew youth out of their classes and out of their senses as well. All over Russia the contrast existed between the obedient and pious son, becoming a despised Chinovnik, or office holder, and the revolutionary. The life of the latter is a life of separation. Now, a life of separation is like a life of vows. To leave your parents, faithful and loyal subjects of the Emperor, to leave your profession, to desist from having children, to lose your fortune, and to give up your civil honour, all for revolutionary conviction, makes for a league of more practical proof than any religious order. What more could the Jesuits ask, or the Trappists, where you had at least benevolent Superiors? How trifling the test of the Free Mason seems compared with Siberia, with exile, with the danger of being executed! These are risks that they took voluntarily with the deepest serenity for the sake of a materialistic theory of events, because the clock of history was soon to strike.

Comparing the dangers undergone by the French before the Revolution in 1789, we can say that neither Beaumarchais nor Voltaire nor Diderot had to suffer like thousands, nay, tens of thousands, of Russians between 1870 and 1914. No wonder, then, that the new league must have more weight than the lofty genius of 1789. He who suffers wins in politics. The martyr does not obtain the victory personally, but his group, his successors, win in the long run.

In the materialistic philosophy of Bolshevism there seems to be little room for what they would call theological babble.

But the Russian Intelligentsia offers a startling example of vicarious suffering. The tears of the Dekabrists, the hardships of the exiles, the courage of the terrorists, the abnegation of the Nihilists, were not wasted.

The great lesson of Russian intellectual history for our day is the truth that *in Russia it was not the proletarian who suffered.* The intellectual made himself an intentional martyr, a specialist in deliberate renouncement.

That is the reason why, instead of the proletarian governing Russia, the old order and league of revolutionaries, tested in disposition and action, exerts the dictatorship over the proletarians. As early as the eighties Lavrov, Kareev, Vorontsov, raised the question who ought to govern Russia, and they saw clearly that something like a monastic order was needed. All this was forgotten later, because the Marxians scouted the whole problem. They were not only too much interested in the goal, but they wished too much to be like the Western proletarian and therefore detested all plans which smelt of aristocracy or oligarchy.

But their hatred and chiding cannot veil the fact that the proletarian does not govern Russia, because he did not suffer for Russia like the Bolshevik. That is why even today you cannot become a member of the Bolshevik Party by being of proletarian descent, but only by being of revolutionary disposition. The pre-War revolutionary disposition is the highest recommendation for any candidate.

LENIN'S PRIVATE LIFE.

The sacrifices of pre-War days were not in vain. The modest story of one of these lives, that of Lenin himself, may round off our picture of the Intelligentsia. We quote from the memoirs of Madame Lenin, Nadeshda Krupskaya:

"For the Revolutionaries, any big apartment house with a thoroughfare from front to back, was a fulcrum against the secret police. Lenin was famous for knowing all houses with such ways through. Then Lenin knew enough chemistry to jot down invisible notes in books." He made the acquaintance of his wife when she listened to the reading of his revolutionary article on *The Friends of the People* in 1894.

In 1896 Lenin was jailed and his so-called "fiancée," too. After the imprisonment Lenin was exiled to Minusinsk, and Krupskaya to Ufa. Under the condition of being married by a priest, Krupskaya was allowed to share the exile of Lenin.

The complete revaluation of values by the revolutionaries can be seen in the effects of this alliance on the new Madame Lenin's mother. Old Madame Krupskaya, of a good bourgeois family, declared that she would share the exile of her daughter and her son-in-law. "She became a true comrade, helping in the revolutionary work. In the periods of domiciliary visits by the police, she would conceal illegal books, bring precious tools to the comrades in prison, deliver messages. She lived with us in Siberia and abroad, kept house for us, entertained the many comrades walking in and out, sewed letters in coats or belts, prepared chemical inscriptions." In Siberia she taught her daughter how to fight the Russian stove, provided a Russian book on cooking when they were abroad, gave Lenin, who had no fur coat himself when he was sent from Minusinsk to Pskov, her muff which had at least a fur lining.

Before 1905, the Lenins lived in Munich, London and Geneva. In 1905 he secretly returned to Russia. In 1907 he left again for Switzerland. Then he moved to Paris. But finally he settled in Poronin, Galicia, where he could more easily smuggle illegal pamphlets across the Russian frontier and keep in contact with his party in the Duma. In 1914 the Austrian police thought the stranger might be a Czarist spy, and, in order to be on the safe side, they expelled the unknown man into Switzerland. He was without money. Now his mother-in-law had a sister who had been head of a girls' school in Novo Sergiyevsk for thirty years. She had willed to her sister all her savings, some silver spoons, some Ikons, dresses, and 4,000 rubles, more than 2,000 gold dollars. The money was deposited in a bank at Cracow. A Viennese broker succeeded in quashing its sequestration. Ironically enough, the old schoolmistress in Novo Sergiyevsk had pinched herself in food so that the revolutionary who hated everything she loved might carry on anti-war propaganda from abroad.

As to Madame Krupskaya, she thought herself still a good Christian, and homesickness destroyed her health. But she shared Lenin's life to the last. Her body underwent the sad, and certainly not Orthodox, ritual of cremation. The Lenins waited two hours in the cemetery, "till a supervisor brought the urn with the warm ashes, and pointed to the spot where they should put the urn in the soil."

Her self-denial had been the prop of an impossible life, which was rewarded in 1917 by an equally incredible success.

THE FAILURE OF THE SOCIAL REVOLUTIONARIES.

Not all the revolutionaries were successful. Like all the Russian generations between 1825 and 1905, the last precursors had to undergo their disillusionment, too. The bewildering cruelty of the Russian Revolution against its old revolutionary allies is one of the striking features. But I am afraid we must say that without this cruelty it would not have had any importance for the rest of the world. Only by a new separation into two groups inside the revolutionary party could the Russians reach a point where their experiment coincided with the real problems of a simultaneous world-economy.

The first group which went among the people in 1881 called itself "Soil and Freedom," a name well known in America from the "Free-Soilers" movement. But in Russia, as an open preaching of the gospel was out of the question, every soldier stood alone in hidden, subterranean trenches. No wonder that the close contact with primitive rural conditions turned most of the social workers into friends of the peasant, the Moujik. These Socialists, as they were by virtue of their European education, began to revolutionize the Moujik instead of the non-existent industrial worker. The slavery of the peasants was felt, after the emancipation of 1861, as an unsolved problem. Their hunger for more land became a natural platform for the intellectual who lived among them. The intellectuals derived their program more or less from the horizon of the Moujik himself. He was the germ of the party of "Social Revolutionaries." They wished to reform the single village in Russia. They gave in as far as possible to the instincts of their fellow-countrymen at home. This party was very numerous and very popular until 1918; and it is difficult for any superficial observer to understand why it did not take the lead, and why the Russia of today is not governed by this party, which was completely devoted to eighty-five per cent of the population and represented their interests in the way these interests appeared to the eighty-five per cent themselves!

To answer this question means to understand the iron laws of history. Not before the end of this book will the reader be provided with all the material which will enable him to see the failure of the Social Revolutionary as the obvious and natural event which it is.

At this point in our story it may be enough to point out that the Social Revolutionaries shared one prejudice with the Moujik which blinded them against the historical order of the day.

The Social Revolutionaries and the Moujik wished to reform the village, and by doing so they hoped to reform Russia. But this was not a proper aim for any revolutionary scheme, because it meant a cult of the village as an individual thing. It is one of the common slips of the romanticist to transfer his love for the unique from the human soul to any other social unity, family, village, country, and to try to make this area or group the treasure-house of everything he likes or values. Now the human soul is unique; and a man whose profession is the care of souls must be more interested in one soul than in the whole world. Unfortunately this realm of the soul cannot be transferred into politics. It is useless to treat the Russian village as an invaluable soul for political purposes, when the difficulties of Russia rise from its gigantic, unorganized, continental impenetrability.

In Russia, the lumber trade, the wheat export, the wars of expansion, had to pay the budget of the central power. The Social Revolutionaries, in starting from the particular needs of the suffering Russian individual, and wishing to distribute land, took a very human attitude, but did not even notice the disease which they were venturing to cure. The fate of the village under the impetus of capitalism cannot be solved if it is taken as outside the history of mankind. The wish to help Russia in all her parts was sterile as long as it did not give some constitution to this unruly continent forty times as big as France.

The superficial and colony-like organization of Russia had to be reconstructed. This had nothing to do with sentimentalism.

THE BOLSHEVIKS.

The lack of intellectual sentimentalism, of prejudices originating from the "beauty" of an idea, was the outstanding feature of the second group in the revolution. It tried to deal with the totality of mankind's economy as disclosed in or applicable to Russia. Not to be found missing in the historical hour of progress for the economy of the world as a whole, was the obsession of this austere group. In their opinion, the economy of the Moujik was too archaic to offer any future. Political action and economic thinking that intended to be of consequence had to turn in the direction toward which the latest revolutionary outbursts in Western Europe pointed. In these outbursts the abuses and short-comings of the domineering economic trends were attacked. The Commune in 1871 in Paris offered a sketch of what had to be done to get rid of both precapitalistic Russia and capitalistic Europe by one and the same decision. The Commune presented the alleged representative of the historical hour: the proletarian. The worker in the suburbs of Paris was the product of modern factory life, a cog in the machine, a townsman uprooted from the soil, and a free-thinker in religion.

This later group, the real Marxians, had the courage to confess that the bourgeois society which they wanted to destroy did not exist in Russia. Capitalism first had to be introduced before they could form it into socialism! This is a grandiose conception though completely unreal. "We are enemies of the capitalistic order. In Russia the capitalistic order is only in its beginnings. Let us hasten its coming because we hate it so much that we cannot bear to live without our foe. We must kill him, and to be killed he must first live."

Unless we keep in mind this situation of a starved Intelligentsia, the attitude of Russian youth is completely inconceivable. It was not Russian, and not proletarian, but European thought, that was suffering in Russia. In their quality as European thinkers and readers and students, the Russian Intelligentsia were welded together into a fearless battalion. They were nothing more nor less than disappointed Europeans. And they were disappointed Europeans because the older chapters of European history were not their history as orthodox Russians. They had had no partnership in the history of European civilization since the schism between Rome and Byzantium in 1054. They came to know Europe again only later, i.e., in the form of the eighteenth-century enlightenment, which ended in the French Revolution and brought Napoleon's expedition as far as Moscow. They knew the industrial expansion of the Western states, and their capitalistic invasion of Russia, building the Russian railroads and factories and destroying the rural home-industries of the country.

Beside enlightenment and colonial exploitation, capitalism represented itself to their eyes in the form of fervent nationalism; so nationalism, too, seemed closely connected with the reign of the bourgeois class. As much as capitalism, nationalism, coming as it did from outside, showed only its reverse side in Russia.

The nationalism of the nineteenth century was the natural thing in France, where the national language, the spoken language, had been exalted for centuries into the bright instrument of literature and where the good taste of Paris was a barometer for the spiritual and intellectual climate of the whole nation.

The "window into Europe," St. Petersburg, could not possibly play the nationalistic part of Paris because it was only a port for foreign goods. Furthermore, all the western territories of the Empire, Poland, the Baltic provinces, were more national than Russia herself. How could a Russian schoolmaster convince the Poles in Lodz, the Lithuanians in Vilna, the

Germans in Riga, that they had to undergo "Russification"?
The idea was perfectly meaningless because the democratic
nationalism of the nineteenth century had the strong presupposition of a real economic togetherness and a real historical
community.

Nevertheless, about 1880, at the same time that the invisible
stream of the Revolution delved into its subterranean bed,
Czarism ventured to begin the "Russification" of its western
possessions. It even thought of conquering large parts of
Austria and the Balkans. From 1878 to 1917 Czarism hoped
for new western territories for "Russification." This was the
"war-guilt" of Czarism in the World War.

In consequence of the complete failure and the cruelty of
this task, the instinct of the revolutionaries turned against this
kind of nationalism. We must neither forget their disappointment over prevailing European trends, nor their pride in being
pioneers of *European* thought, if we wish to understand the
Russian Revolution.

As Europeans, the Bolsheviks did not capitulate to the villagers, but kept their own independent non-Russian standards.
As disappointed Europeans, they chose a new standard which
had been tried nowhere in Europe but in the revolt of the
Commune in 1871. Because the Russians were souls expatriated
from Europe, seeking the true solution of Europe's society, the
French Commune became their great model. Lenin always had
the chronology of the Commune at hand. In 1917 he oriented
his own course by the course of events in 1871. And when they
had held out in Moscow as many days as the people of Paris,
he cried: "This was the last thing we had to accomplish. Now
our honour is saved!"

Childish as this dependence may appear, it is natural to
brains that try to think about the political future in terms of
the dialectical continuity of European thought. They had to
be European Marxists first and Russians second, because only
so could Russia obtain its leading place in Europe.

It is certainly true that super-consciousness in a political
actor sterilizes his endeavour. In the greatest epic of the nineteenth century, *War and Peace*, Leo Tolstoi ridicules the hero-

worship of the time and all its affectation. And then he goes on as if wishing to warn his compatriots: "In historical events more clearly than anywhere else the command runs: Don't eat from the Tree of Knowledge of good and evil. Nothing but unconscious action bears fruit. An actor in an historical event never understands its significance. When he tries to see through it he condemns himself to sterilization."

But the Marxist thinks he must know exactly what historical hour has struck, because that is the only dowry he brings home from Europe to his virgin country.

The consciousness of the historical hour is the core of Marxian theory. It is clear, therefore, that we must pay attention to the theory of Marx before we can investigate what the Russians have done and what they actually represent, in spite of their own theory.

This is all the more important as Marxism offers a scientific theory on revolutions.

Historical materialism, as Marxism is also labelled, considers all history as a series of class-wars and revolutions. The world-revolution, which was started by the Russians, breaks down as meaningless if its place in a proper succession of revolutions is not the place assigned to it by the general staff. The general staff knows the algebra, calculus and interpolations of Revolution. The Russian Revolution is but a sub-species, or a practical application, of the general laws of revolution. Revolutions mark the epochs in history. To know the theory of Marx makes men masters of history.

The old maxim of Horace, *"Nec scire fas est omnia,"* i.e., we are not permitted to know everything, seems to have given way to the application of the Baconian "Knowledge is Power" to human, social and political affairs.

It is one purpose of this book to show that the Baconian formula, "Knowledge is Power," has misled the Socialists all over the world. The truth of "Knowledge is Power" may be valid in all the connections between man and nature. It does not work in human affairs. When a man knows how steam reacts in a boiler, he can force the steam to work for him. The same holds good with electricity, oil, coal, and so on. But when a man knows that his neighbor is a rascal, this truth does not make him secure. The knowledge of an individual man among ignorant people makes him more helpless than he was as an innocent member of his group. The man who invents a machine may be perfectly powerless in society in spite of all his knowledge. "Knowledge of what?" we must ask. Only the knowledge of organized and united mankind gives power over nature.

Marxism tries to give to the knowing individual the power *within* society which united mankind has over external nature. That campaign is of world-wide significance. If it should be victorious, it would change the aspect of things. No country in the world could fail to adopt the government of the knowing. The philosopher of nature, the cosmologist, ruling society, is the ultimate vision of Marxism. Society no longer a blind piece of nature, but mastered, like the chaotic world of matter, by human knowledge. At this point the order of men who have renounced every normal desire in social life takes on a particular significance. Men who wish to govern the bundle of passions and interests which we call society cannot belong to it themselves. "He who aims at the guidance of others must be able to forego a great many things." (Goethe.)

The voluntary Nihilism of the Russian Intelligentsia cuts off the roots which make men members of social groups like family, tribe, nation, class. Society must become nature; men must become scientists, beyond the good and evil of their private passions.

THE SPEECH OF THE RUSSIAN REVOLUTION.

Surveying the vocabulary of the new order we find arrayed on the side of society all the terminology of the natural sciences. A Bolshevik dictionary might contain:

Quantity: The masses. Quality: The Bolshevik Party. Society: The forms of co-operation. Human interests are explained by class situation. Class situation is explained in figures and statistics. Changes in human history become visible in statistical changes, as in the key of distribution.

This is provoking language. Any revolution must speak a provoking language, because it must move men in a new direction. The common slang, the traditional worn-out expressions of cultivated language or of daily talk, lack power to make us turn about. Old speech goes in one ear and out the other. Revolutionary speech has to be new speech because new speech rings effectively in the ear.

The old Biblical phrase, "He that hath ears to hear let him hear," is for the individual soul, which can be struck by eternal truth even though clothed in old words.

A political party cannot wait for the individual. It must thunder in order to be heard and understood by the masses. The speech of Socialism is the reverse of the language of the Bible. It does not try to speak to us in our mother-tongue or in our tradition, as the speech of prayer always does. It is strikingly opposed to familiar and usual conceptions. It uproots man by uprooting his speech. In the social movement of the last fifty or a hundred years, the revolution is present wherever this new uprooting language is spoken. Very often the language is spoken by individuals who mistake themselves for tories or conservatives. But wherever the new language has its grip on a man, we can be sure that he is promoting the revolutionary identification of Society with Nature.

The fascination of figures, diagrams, curves, is generally felt in the modern world. We are all taken in by this method of argumentation. Towns and States and Empires are ruled by statistics, though God punished David for having numbered and counted the Jews.

Instead of the high-brow quoting of a classical poem, it is much more impressive to begin a speech or a book with dates and figures. The reader is grateful if he can hold the eel of science by the tail at least. The vocabulary of modern political success is the mystic speech of figures. Each age has its specific political melody: ours in the music of numbers. The masses, which you cannot feed on high sentiments or questions of personal conscience, willingly listen to numbers. Wages and taxes, battleships and armaments, unemployed and students, are shifted about with amazing frivolity if the statesman can put figures before us which seem to show a necessity for it. No moral sermon can melt the indifference and reluctance of modern masses. Figures do.

And they have another merit. Figures do not blush. In speech it is a little indecent to talk about prostitution, crime, slums, famine. Our heart, our taste, our eye and ear are hurt by any mention of the "reverse of the medal." In society, we are expected not to swear and not to quote hell and the devil and the vices by their real names. The part of the body which contains the seats of our passions was taboo. In English society not long ago, man had no thigh, no genitals, no bladder. In the famous International Thesaurus of English words and phrases which appeared at this zenith of the Victorian régime, in 1852, Mr. Roget includes in his classifications time and space, inorganic matter, organic matter, the five senses, the intellect, the volition and the affections of man. But the poor human body is scattered everywhere. His feces are put under the esthetic headline of cleanness, his genitals under the abstract term of production. The stomach is veiled under the generality of "receptacle."

The figures of the materialist do not blush. They are icy and indifferent. Whores can be counted, feces evaluated as fertilizing the soil. The hinterland of humanity can be decently described by numbers and figures. In the language of the Russian Revolution neither the pleasant nor the beautiful, neither the true nor the good, is at the top of the scale of values. The side of life which escapes light, which ordinarily remains in the dark, is brought up first. The heart and its desires are eliminated. Marxians reckon in their arguments, on stony hearts and dead souls. Their logic is illuminating: "First let us have food, then I will be good." If they succeed in convincing those parts of us which represent the element of indifference, of unbelief, of greed within our nature, the rest will be conquered even more easily. An appeal to the best qualities of our nature would overlook the inertia of its other elements; but figures can interest even the beastly part of us. The "proletarian" who has nothing is always suspicious. He always thinks he is being cheated or exploited when he hears a fine speech. The proletarian has no ideas. Very well, let us talk business. Things speak

their own language. Please count. The yearly production of
steel or coal can be the first figure; further steps show imports,
wages, exports, increase of production, accumulation of capital,
amortization; the maze grows larger and larger, and at the end,
world economy, world war, world revolution, and world order
are but natural results of the first few figures.

The universe is encircled in a dialogue between brain and
belly. The Soviets compare the index of living in pre-War days
with the index of today. The proletarian character of the Revolution is demonstrated by the fact that the industrial worker
gets more than he did in 1914. It does not matter that there
were but 8,000,000 industrial workers and 80,000,000 peasants.
More figures might be disturbing: for example more people
were killed during the Russian Revolution than during the
War. Or it might be said that the governing class in Russia
numbers not half so many people today as its counterpart in
pre-War Russia. However, these figures can simply be omitted.
To an observer, it is true, the language of numbers seems no
better guarantee that one has chosen the right road than any
other language.

But despite this limitation, it remains remarkable how successfully this particular tune is played today on the keyboard
of political languages. It is successful in every country. Marxism gives it a monopoly over all others. The outstanding feature of this revolution is less the mere use of numbers than
their exclusive use. The equation between nature and society
is true as long as we express everything in size and measures.
Modern architecture, with its square and cubic forms, its hatred
of curves and illogical details, is a striking illustration of the
monopoly claimed by the abacists and trigonometricians of this
revolution.

When Stalin declared in 1934 that the new architecture had
failed, that the people should get baroque and irrational forms
of houses, pictures and dresses, the spell of the algebra of
revolution was broken for the first time. "Russia Goes Main
Street" was the judicious headline for this event. The monopoly
of the proletarian language was abolished and other emotional
forms of speech were re-admitted. In 1934, Maxim Gorky pre-

sided over a congress for the restoration of the language of Russian classics. This shows that Russia is entering on its period of Restoration. The execution or suicide or exile of all former co-mates of Stalin tells the same story. Communism has restored Czarism minus its alliance with Western capitalism. And Peter the Great, reappearing in Russian movies, shows that the revolutionary period, as symbolized by Trotsky, is over.

TOTALITY AND REPRODUCTION.
(Karl Marx)

A grandiose caricature of Western civilization had entered Russia in the forms of cynical satire, colonial exploitation and hypocritical nationalism. This caricature accounts for the violent Russian repercussion. However, at the core of this Western civilization, an energetic protest had been filed also in the form of Marxism. The liberty of Western Man never was lulled into sleep by any existing order of things merely for the reason of its being in power. Karl Marx represents the last protest against the existing order of things. And he formulated it because he grew up in its actual centre, between the rivers Seine and Weser which, to an industrial sociologist like Le Play, are the lines of demarcation for highest industrialization.

Marx was born in 1819 in a German district ruled by codes of Napoleonic origin, of a Jewish family that owed its emancipation to the new ideas of the French Revolution. He lived in a sphere (Rhineland, Berlin, Brussels, Paris, London, Westphalia) of big cities and industrial progress. He studied in Berlin, it is true, but had no intention of making a contribution to German philosophy. He laughed at the sterile works of the idealistic Sisyphi in Germany who were satisfied to reason about the existing order. On the battlefields of the Napoleonic Wars he felt that the Revolution of 1789 cried for a continuation. Since the ideas of French liberalism went around the world, the continuation could not do less.

The first Marxian principle is this: For any real change in humanity the category of "World-Wide" is essential. The revolution is a total revolution, or it is none at all. To fall behind the diameter of the area revolutionized by the ideas of 1789, deprives any subsequent event of its claim to importance in the history of the world. That the category of totality dominates, is the criterion for the revolutionary principle in any science.

This category of totality reappears distorted in the modern talk of the totalitarian state. The Fascists denied the category of totality as it applied to the spatial side of history. They wished to keep their national territory out of touch with the rest of the earth. But feeling that totality is a powerful god, they build a totalitarian order within the boundaries of a single state.

No European, no human being, can preserve his full humanity and his true human countenance as a member of his nation alone. Mankind must be reflected across the border lines of nations. Man as mere Italian, mere Russian, mere German, would not be man. Our thoughts are rooted in and our feelings are moved by forces which scorn geographical limitations.

This Marxian principle of totality is immensely fruitful. It prohibits the historian, for example, from going on with national history, as he did throughout the nineteenth century. In the history of the American Civil War, the simultaneous emancipation of the serfs in Russia did not seem worthy of mention. The Czarism of the tragic era was not to be compared with the corresponding periods during which capitalism was installed in other countries. The exhibition in the Crystal Palace in London was not understood as a decisive victory of the French and bourgeois idea of the "spirit of the times" over English ideas, because totality was not a working hypothesis for the national historian.

Hegel had realized that it is not a historical fact, nothing of permanent significance, when a king is killed or a battle lost. Too many accidents of that kind occur all over the world. They are important as personal reminiscences. They have the same inestimable educational value which the stories have that a child gets from the lips of its grandparents. They are the necessary enlargement of man's horizon, that which makes him feel his own limbs, his roots and branches, his racial identity and ancestry. But the memory of humankind has to do something better. In its book of history nothing should be put down but what has been settled once for all.

Once in a long while it happens that a great question is brought up and discussed and fought through once for all. The equal right of every human being is a fruit of the French Revolution which was conquered once for all for Moujiks and Jews, blacks and yellows, men and women. The French Revolution may prove a failure. The equal rights of men may be abolished. Undoubtedly this is possible. But if it happened it would diminish the significance of the French Revolution, because an event which has not settled something once for all is of no importance to living men and women. We must know so many things that it is enough to know what must be known once for all. The rest of history is the history of failures, experiments, abuses. This rest can perhaps be made interesting too, but not without the yardstick of the true history of humanity. A preposterous attempt, a precursor, a stormy petrel, becomes valuable when we bring it into relation with the successful "once for all" achievement. The "once for all" principle works like a great sieve, sifting out quantities of superfluous traditions. And Marxism was able to single out the important events of history by virtue of its inheriting from the history of philosophy this principle of totality.

The second principle of Marxism is what Nietzsche called in his last vision "the permanent recurrence of the same." In the economic language of the Marxians this takes the shape of reproduction. They insist on a distinction. "We produce goods, or we draw an income from a certain capital; this belongs to the sphere of production. Reproduction is something more. Our gold mine may cease to produce gold; and then we must know how to replace it." Marx and Engels went further. They enlarged the concept of "Reproduction" beyond the economical sphere. Quite often this is ignored by "Reds." The larger concept is by far more human as the vulgar Marxian knows. Accumulation of capital is a sub-species of reproduction. Governments too must be reproduced. I go far beyond Marx in this line of thought. It is not enough to have a sequence of good presidents or virtuous kings; the constitution itself must be remade one day. For instance, in a monarchy, if there is too much intermarriage among kings, decay is the inevitable result; and it may take a revolution to get a new dynasty. The two-party system may prove too lukewarm; and it may take a revolution to get, not a new president, but a new type of president. A real man, unlike a politician, cannot be secured by mere volition. Manhood is a quality which is imperilled by certain forms of environment and favoured by others. Most of the time men are glad that they have a new president or another king. They forget, even, that the type of president and the kind of dynasty is much more vital, and that the several individuals will be formed if the nursery, the place for their breeding, is prepared in time. The blindness of men toward the re-production of kinds is healed by revolution. Revolutions bring forward the question of the type of society which ought to exist. This question is even more vital than a war. A war, according to whether it is won or lost, expands or contracts the political order of a country. But revolution creates this same political order. Wars carry out, export into new regions, what revolutions create. Revolutions are the creative movements of history because they reproduce the standards of society. To be sure, the word "revolution" does not apply to the events like the hundred and twenty revolutions in Mexico. It belongs to the few events of totalitarian character which have settled a question of re-production for the human kind once for all.

The third and last principle of Bolshevism is less general, less revolutionary and less convincing. It claims for Marxism the merit of understanding the sufferings of the proletarian better than anybody else, and of knowing more about his emancipation than anybody else.

In this field of social policy, Marxism has always had many rivals. Marx's first working hypothesis was that capitalism permitted a special kind of exploitation by the capitalist. Values created by the labour of the worker were not paid for as they ought to be, but a surplus was kept in the pocket of the exploiting business man. That is to say, Marx construed a kind of immorality as the lasting relation between entrepreneur and wage earners. Marx pretended that the capitalist made unjustifiable profits, withholding a legitimate share from his fellow-workers.

It is worthwhile to follow Marx for a moment into the thicket of his calculations. He seems almost like a deer-stalker in his eagerness to penetrate the dark secrets of bookkeeping and business calculations. The fascination of figures which we observed in Bolshevism and in all modern social science led in his case to a remarkable result.

What happened in a modern factory during the last hundred years was an attempt to calculate wages and prices by the piece. An order comes in for a thousand pairs of silk stockings. The problem now is how much money the firm must get for this order. In Marx's day the cost-accounting office would begin a queer vicious circle. It would fix its attention on the hours of manual labour needed for the production of one pair of stockings. The units of production and of labour—one pair of stockings and, let us say, half an hour of work—once arrived at, the wages which had to be paid to the manual workers for this piece of work would be called the productive wage. None of the staff work in the factory, that of the director, agents, charwomen, porters, or calculators, could be referred in this way to a single piece of the order. The expense of keeping the staff, paying interest on mortgage, meeting overhead expenses, were estimated roughly at 100, 200 or 300 per cent of the "productive wage."

Thus, in the calculations of modern business, the share of the manual worker is brought into the limelight. His activity seems to be the only primary force; the activities of the "white-collar" men rank as secondary. The men whose earnings account for the overhead expense appear like drones and the manual workers like the only productive bees. All higher social functions are apt to be taken as a superstructure on this foundation of manual labour.

CALCULATION: ORDER:
Unproductive wages: 1,000 pair of
                                     silk stockings.

Salaries ⎫
Interest ⎪   250 per cent
Taxes   ⎬ = of the pro- =   0.50
Light, etc.⎭   ductive wage

MATERIAL 0.40
_____
Productive wages for one piece.
Hours: ½   @   .40   =   0.20
        TOTAL: $1.10 *per pair*

To cut down the overhead expense means moral and economic progress. The upper class seems more remote from the forces of production than the manual worker, the only man who can get productive wages.

Now the capitalist is not always expecting orders. Sometimes he produces first and finds his market later, after his calculation has been made. He now tries to get more than $1.10 on the market. Perhaps he can get $1.50. But then he seems to have cheated his workers; for he could have paid more if he had anticipated the final price. The fictitious price on the day he started his production induced him to offer his workers a fictitious productive wage. And his claim that he is paying the utmost which he could reasonably calculate is refuted if he repeatedly gets higher prices on the market.

The fictions and play-rules of business calculations are misleading. The spies on the other side of the counter, the Communists, observing the bare processes of wage-fixing, are perfectly right in denouncing them. The only mistake they make is that they take the abstract scheme of wage-fixing too seriously. Practically, a modern industry which sells, let us say, five kinds of products, will get the "normal" expected prices for only one kind, two kinds will be sold higher, and two will have to be given away without profit, or even at a loss.

Department 1 gets a 100 per cent higher price
Department 2 gets a 10 per cent higher price
Department 3 gets the expected price
Department 4 lowers its price 10 per cent
Department 5 lowers its price 25 per cent

In four out of five cases the whole process of calculation of wages and prices was only preliminary and provisional. The workers of Departments 1 and 2 have gotten too little, those of 4 and 5 have gotten too much, if the principle of the "productive wage" is pursued to its last consequences.

Marx did pursue it to its last consequences, because he had to find an ex post facto justification for his instinct that the economy of his time was destructive. But it is not true that it is the permanent trick of capitalism to pay low wages. Computation by the piece leads quite as often to a wage that is too high as to one that is too low. Profit-sharing by the workers is no solution of the social question, because profits are not the exploiting factor of industry.

Neither Russian practice nor the later writings of Rosa Luxemburg, the only real successor to Marx, bear out this theory of exploitation. The Class-War between Capital and Labour is as true and as untrue as the sex-war between man and wife, the age-war between old and young, the border-war between neighbouring groups. But the whole process is as complicated as the other conflicts mentioned above. In the struggle between the sexes the man can exploit the woman, and the woman can exploit the man; but there can also exist, after all, a happy marriage. In the Class-War, Capital can exploit Labour, but Labour can also exploit Capital, or there can be real peace as there was in England between 1850 and 1882, to the great disappointment of Marx. English workers exploited the world in peaceful co-operation with English capitalists from 1846 to 1914. German workers exploited the capital-owning class, together with the employers, during the inflation of 1918-1923. During these years the workers improved or at least kept up their standards. The people of means lowered theirs to little more than zero, because the inflation did not abolish wages, but capital.

In Russia industrial labour exploits both peasantry and capital, because the few millions of "productive" workers are constantly overpaid. Only since 1933 has the Russian bureaucracy tried to correct this. In Russia the wrong application of the wage-fixing principle has starved the rest of the population, the standard of the peasant being 70 and that of the industrial worker 135 compared to the norm of 1914.

A mere technicality of transitional and provisional character, the incompetent work of calculators, has been used to rationalize fantastic emotions among the modern masses, and is leading them into a blind alley. The real human question put by the waste of a market-seeking society is the interest in reproduction, and not the wages paid by the producer for productive work. The Russian Revolution, in running a race with a world which was already industrialized, may teach Trade Unionists, Marxists, and capitalists alike where the real problems of the future are to be found: not in the production of goods, because this is settled better than ever, but in the reproduction of real and all-round men, which was never less assured than today.

THE LIMITATIONS OF A MARKET-SEEKING ECONOMY.

What is the permanent and actual interest in the field cultivated first by Marxian theory can be cut down to two main statements. These, our statements, are themselves not Marxian, and are not acknowledged as Marxian. They are an attempt to explain not only the problem that baffled Marx, but also and at the same time the causes and motives of the peculiar Marxian answer. Our own answer is given without a Marxian bias and therefore claims to be post-Marxian, because it is true that the liberal did not see the dilemma, as it is true that the Marxian was not able to solve it.

Our first statement starts from the great achievements of the nineteenth century in the field of production. Millions of goods unknown to our grandparents are thrown upon the markets of the world at an incredibly low price. This miracle is achieved by an economy which can be described most briefly as a market-seeking economy. If a factory produces cars, it can hope to sell more cars next year on condition of seeking new markets. By doubling its production it can, perhaps, reduce its overhead expenses and so both earn more and sell cheaper.

The seeking of new markets is the world economy during the last hundred and fifty years. Market-seeking salesmanship is the reality behind the attacks on capitalism. Quoting at random from a textbook, I cite this lamentation: "A century and a half of monetary chaos lies behind us. This century and a half of chaotic history of prices which meant prosperity or ruined the lifetime opportunities of innumerable individuals, was not due to acts of Providence. It was due to lack of knowledge of economic principles or failure to apply the little knowledge that there was. The common assumption at any given date has always been that the conditions were world-wide and inevitable, either as a punishment for present sins or because of some benign force working for the good. Prices are as chaotic as was medical practice before bacteria were known." How can they be otherwise in a world of perpetual expansion and contraction of markets? And this principle involves another. The markets, their expansion and their shrinkage, prosperity and crisis, remained changeable under one condition only: the employer could not be obliged to deal in his calculation with the fate of his employees. Starting on a race for bigger markets, he had to be freed from all responsibility for the political, moral and educational order of his country. When a city was founded in 1250, the founders were responsible for the craftsmen of the place. As in marriage, they belonged to each other for better or for worse. We call feudal and patriarchal that stage of society where man and man belong to each other by social discipline without being relatives.

The pre-capitalistic employer owed security to his employees, they belonged to each other like landlord and tenant. The capitalistic employer owes wages to a mercenary. The wages under the capitalistic system are much higher than in pre-capitalistic days. It is futile to find fault with the market-seeking system for paying low wages. The exploitation is not in the payment. The wages are as high as in any mercenary army of the seventeenth century. The measure of the stipend always depended on the booty and the luck of arms.

The relationship in the modern factory is not a relationship of exploitation. Nobody is deprived of the fruits of labour. Only the relationship is cut down to a certain number of hours in the day. And some fruits of human labour do not grow under such conditions. No harvest has been stolen, but the species Labour is limited to one certain kind of it, the kind which can be paid by hour, day or week.

The tremendous novelty of the market-seeking system was the principle of payment by the hour. In all pre-capitalistic times labour was related to the physical nature of man, and the shortest unit of work was, for that reason, a day. A man's work was paid by days, meaning that a day of twenty-four hours, with sunshine and moonlight, food and sleep, family life and resting time, stand as a natural vision before the mind of the employer. To hire a charwoman meant to take one day of her life, such as her life was.

A modern worker at Zeiss-Jena, a wonder of precision though his work may be, is himself less to the factory that employs him than the charwoman was to her mistress. It is not his biographical day of day and night, of sunrise and sunset, that is bought by the firm. He may be in the factory for twenty-four years; but the twenty-four years are only the sum-total of eight hours a day, forty-eight hours a week, ninety-six hours a double-week, 2,400 hours a year and $24 \times 2,400$ hours in twenty-four years.

The hour in the life of the modern wage-earning class is something completely different from the day in the life of the old labourer or charwoman. The hour for which I am paid wages is not my hour. This hour and this sum-total of hours are an element in the employer's schedule. The employer in his struggle with nature to produce goods has a time-plan, but his time-plan should not include the same words which signify elements of human life, because here they mean something in the external world organized by science. The employer's working hours are abstract units of a plan; they may run into millions. They always are related to the interest he has to pay for his invested capital. In some countries the capitalistic and scientific abstraction is carried so far that in February, with its twenty-eight days, interest is paid for the abstract length of thirty days. The old-timers, objecting to daylight-saving time, have a good name for their pre-capitalistic dial: they call it "God's time." Capitalistic time is manufactured time, indeed.

In the card-index of a factory men appear like any other

force of nature. Water is used for three hours a day, electricity for six hours, men for eight or ten hours. It is the economic day, the day of society, the day of finance, which is subdivided into hours when such forces are used. The only justifiable name for the workers in the factory is "labour-forces." All other expressions betray the truth. The worker, the employee who enters a factory, becomes a proletarian because he is divorced from his own time rhythm. He changes his status. Instead of a person with his own time of life, consisting of year, lustrum, and score of years, he becomes a labour-force.

This is the point of exploitation by the market-seeking economy which Marx scented without being able to define it.

The principles of the mining industry dominate our industrial organization. We all work in shifts. We are all interchangeable. We have all lost our anchorage in the rhythm of a community. Who will regenerate the forms of social life which function like harvest home, and funerals, and sunsets, as the framework of our life?

It is incredible how quickly a man degenerates without this background. The same chemist who as the assistant of a great explorer worked all his nights through for the sake of an experiment, will begin, as an employee of the dye trust two years later, to clean up his work-table at half-past three, because at four work ends for the day.

"The proletariat signifies destroying the old order of the world," says Marx, "because it is, in itself, its destruction." The phrase is true, because to the proletarian even his holiday is but a prolongation of the work-a-day world. His individual "leisure time" has nothing to do with a general Sunday or sabbath. He is thrown out of the rhythm of the earth and of his life-time work. He is one atom in a mass of atoms. The organization of masses can, perhaps, get hold of him. But their rhythm is artificial, too. The masses of men can celebrate mass meetings, they can observe the world holiday of the first of May: but the man of the masses no longer knows what is arbitrary and what is necessary. Shall he go hiking, to the movies, to a lecture course, or shall he march in procession? He crumbles. What the proletarian needs is a cure against atomization.

"In a man's life things that do not endure more than a year are worthless," says Goethe. When man lives on this side of good and evil, as an atomized labour-force, the cure must be to strengthen the longer periods of his life, and to emphasize the epoch-making turns of three-, or five-, or seven-year periods, by which this whole life can be restored and revalued. But Marx could offer no remedy, because he tried to describe the "exploitation" in terms of money and prices. The loss of status, not the lower wages, makes the proletariat suffer.

THE REPRODUCTION OF MAN.

Marx and Engels were the first to study the problem of Revolution and Reproduction seriously. They made it plain to what an extent business is behind all history, how much the Duke of Wellington, as his monument in front of the London Stock Exchange shows, was bound up with the market of the world on the banks of the Thames.

But they did not complete their analysis.

We sum up our statements thus: It is not valid to pretend that the workers are exploited by the capitalists because they get low wages. The real outcry of man's offended nature should be that he is degraded because his boss does not care for his past or his future, and because he, the worker, is deprived of the power to weave past or future into his own day of work.

The boss, by virtue of the privileges conferred upon him by liberalism, hires a man's force and skill and presence and brains as a ready-made product. All the traditions that were needed to concoct this man's talents, and all the props that are needed to keep up his character, are degraded into his own private affair. Modern society and the fellowship of our modern society use present-day forces, disregarding their past and their future. What you are paid for is not a slow growth or an organic evolution, but something that can be ground out immediately by the mill of social life. Modern society exchanges goods, and man is used as a ready-made product. His own mystic process of reproduction, his long way of birth, education, apprenticeship, discipleship, hope and faith in the intrinsic powers of his nature—all this is of no interest to the business man who hires him for an hour or a year or ten years. Schools, parents, friends, foundations, can take care of his personality. For his boss he is not a growing child of God, but a standardized labour-force, number such and such, output such and such, reliability such and such. A modern factory requires above all regular and repetitive work of the same kind; a man is taken as a machine of regularized, standardized capacity, doing his 7,325 "ergs" or "ergons" per X Y Z calories an hour. But that is only another expression for a thing which has no past and no future. Electricity, coal, linen, have no past and no future. A labour-force has no past and no future. In the world of physical experiment we base our behaviour on the expectance of recurrence. A labour-force may last a long time, or may be wasted very quickly. But fifty years or five days of repetitive labour in the factory are equally devoid of any meaning for the past or future of its owner.

This world of bodies is a world of mechanical time, repeating its sixty minutes every hour. The other world must be sought through an other gate than the "business entrance." We live in a plurality of worlds. In one world, Mr. Smith, the employer, is at home. He sits at the breakfast table, perhaps as an autocrat, but nevertheless as a man, a father, a husband, who has a past when he was unmarried and belonged to his father's family, and a future when all his children will have founded their own homes and ceased to listen to his orders. He is an autocrat, yes, but if he is not a fool he feels happy at being limited in time by his own experience and by his own purpose and intentions. He feels how his present day stretches out between two other ages of equal worth. His present is no better than his past or his future; at its very best it can only rival them. Such a house is a world where death almighty mitigates the arrogance of mere life. Here life is a conscious adventure of man between youth and old age. In this world both past and future exist in a positive sense, because they assist in keeping the family alive and in setting its real standards.

In the business cycle and the circle of business we are in a world of bodies: neither past nor future is represented. They may be preserved in schools and museums, as history, as education; but business itself cannot use them. It has a different concept of time, as a mechanical recurrence. But this kind of time occurs only in the dead world of physical nature.

Thus we are right in saying that we treat ourselves and our neighbours as though we had to obey the laws of two different worlds at once. In one world we deal with a man's individuality, in the other we deal with ourselves and others as bodies. Body and soul are not objective parts of the outside world. They are the two constituent elements of two different worlds which we ourselves are constantly building by our own actions and reactions. The world of bodies embodies our way of *working,* and the world of souls our way of *living.* We shall soon see that there is a third world, of another type, which we are building all the time by our way of *thinking.* Our mind is a creator, too, and constructs a third world. But for the explanation of the Communistic reaction the discovery of the two worlds may suffice.

The important conclusion is that all raw material can be transferred from one world to the other, since our own attitudes create both worlds and since we can tell which occurrences in our lives we ought to treat as elements of real life and which we should treat as business. Lumber, electricity, a man's talents, can be commercialized; or they can acquire a past and a future, enter the real life of the soul, as soon as we become or feel responsible for their reproduction.

Suppose all the kinds of raw material we use in our business begin to grow scarce: rubber, wood-pulp, children, poets; forest-fires begin to destroy our timber, and drought our fields. . . . At that moment the employer becomes deeply interested in the process of "Reproduction"; a new world opens before his eyes: a world of change. The circular process of raising rubber, replanting forests, educating foresters, resettling the country, begins to present itself to the minds of business men who up to that time had thought of nothing but the logs they bought from the farmer who needed cash.

Or again: artists, civil engineers, composers, publicity men, are hired by an employer who assumes he can get them by a simple advertisement in the *Times* or *Herald.* But one day he discovers that this recruiting in the labour market does not work. Hundreds and thousands of men wish to be employed; and not one of them is up to the standard of the men he could buy on the market a year before. The irresponsibility of the employer for the *reproduction* of the forces he hires, uses, and eventually destroys or wastes, is the curse of capitalism.

No system ever worked so well in producing goods. This side of capitalism cannot be improved by any nationalization. The immediate production of goods was never achieved with such marvellous success, and socialism is completely hopeless if it aims to abolish the very best side of capitalism, its insuperable capacity for producing all kinds of ready-made goods.

All life is production and reproduction at once. While the donkey turns the mill, the next donkey must be bred. While the coal is being burned, new coal mines or substitutes for coal must be found. While men are painting, teaching, buying, inventing, building and planning, new men must be recruited to dream of future building, planning, buying, and painting. The bad conscience of the employer about "reproduction" often induces him to spend incredible sums for educational institutions. But in the modern world, these educational institutions have little chance to co-ordinate their activities so as to reproduce the kind of men who are the real need of the future.

Be this as it may, we have discovered the real injustice of an acquisitive society. Since its great aim is to produce goods cheaply, it has no direct interest in reproducing men. And any answer to capitalism must let alone Mr. Ford's production of cars, because that is working satisfactorily; what it *must* find is a means of preventing Mr. Ford's waste of men in skimming the cream of the labour supply, regardless of their Past and Future.

This injustice of the acquisitive society is misrepresented in Marx's theory. This distortion in Marxism is based on an acute observation of facts and is, therefore, not easily discovered. But it misleads socialists into seeking the failures of the economic system in the wrong place, and fancying that socialism is a question of higher wages. We hope to have shown that this is not true. Employer and employee are natural allies in their common enterprise of exploiting older forms of society, in which employers must bear the responsibility for the lives and the reproduction of their labour-forces, forms such as old farming communities, feudal societies, groups of primitive tribes, or any society without marked variations in the size of its market. Capitalism must conquer new markets or it ceases to be capitalism. Wherever a market becomes stable, the reproduction of the social forces becomes a burning problem for society, because in such a limited community the background of *permanent* relations outshines the short-lived relations between wage earners and employers.

THE TRUE VICTIM OF CAPITALISM.

The unrest of the labour-forces all over the world has its background in the breakdown of the moral "cadres" which support men's social rhythm. But the factory schedule has a result which is nearer to the heart of the Russian. The home industries of Russia were ruined by the cheap import of industrial goods from outside. Russia is the best example for the colonial expansion of the market-seeking economy. Liberalism puts to death the old orders of society which cannot compete with its low prices. But the paradox is that its prices are low only so long as capitalism can find pre-capitalistic markets. In these pre-capitalistic regions the social order of reproduction, the whole framework of society, church, and art, and holiday, is still included in the price of goods. The naked production of the acquisitive society can sell cheaper because it is without this responsibility for the rest of the natural day.

The lord of the manor feeds his workers all the year round because year and day are felt to be unshakable elements in the life of both lord and workers. The farmer next door who pays by the hour can easily ruin the manor. But the school and the church and the hospital are ruined, too, when the manor ceases to pay. Now the farmer innocently supposes that school and church and hospital will continue to exist as they existed before he began to produce. The modern employer comes into a settled community like a bull into a china shop. He lives by murdering the pre-capitalistic orders. But he and his own labour-forces still receive all the moral order they have, from the values of this same pre-capitalistic world which capitalism underbids.

Marx did not see that the financial exploitation of employer and employee, of capital and labour, is directed against the pre-capitalistic world. In times of inflation, employer and employee together exploited the older classes of society. We cannot decipher the riddles of economic unrest by staring at the factories in the industrial countries. France or England are not the field of an industrial exploitation. "Capitalism," as a market-seeking society, is impossible in the world in which there is but capital and labour. There would be no profit! Capitalism can make profits only so long as it can escape the cost of reproducing the political and social order. That is why it is imperialistic. Unlike the feudal lord, the owner of a factory is allowed to pay hands by the hour, instead of men by the year. The government is responsible for the police, the relief of the poor, and all social policies. Naturally, the capitalist prefers to sell in markets for whose political order he bears no responsibility. As long as he sells in foreign markets he need not pay for the destruction of the old "cadres." Capitalists earn a dividend as long as there are markets for which foreign political organizations are responsible. Capital and labour are never alone. There is a third man in the game. The exploited are the natives of every pre-capitalistic group, class, country. "Capitalism is the first form of economy with the power of propaganda, a form with the tendency to expand over the earth and to eliminate all other forms of production. At the same time, it is the first economy which cannot exist without using the other forms of economy as its alimentary soil and milieu." (Rosa Luxemburg.) Colonial expansion is the nutriment of any market-seeking society. This discovery explains why in the Great War the proletarians of all the Western countries did not behave as the Marxian theory had expected they might.

The working classes of all the industrialized countries collaborated in the warfare of 1914. The Socialist parties had to follow willy-nilly the belligerent instinct of the proletarian masses. Even the great Russian Marxian, Plekhanov fired up at the outbreak of the War. This astonishing fact was often belittled as the result of superstition, atavism, patriotic hypnotism, surprise and similar causes, because it was a terrible shock to Marxian theory and discipline. Nowhere had the masses been better "Marxians" than in France and Germany. And nowhere did they fight more courageously for their country. A Marxian wrote: "The failure of all working-class parties in the Great War must be taken as a fact of universal importance, as the result of the former history of the class movement." (Lukasz.) But it is much simpler to say that labour is not exploited by capitalism, and that the English worker had been repaid by the sacrifice made for his sake in 1846 when the rural interests of England were finally abandoned to secure cheap bread for the cotton workers in Lancashire.

The only country which went against the Great War was Russia. Russia mutinied not because her proletariat had nothing to lose, but because she was much more of a pre-capitalistic world exploited by capitalism than any other European country.

Our conclusion is: The most backward country started the Revolution to abolish capitalism. The vulgar theory of progress says that evolution makes the most progressive country more progressive still. In the case of a revolution this theory fails. Russia starts the Revolution because it is the most backward country in the world of liberalism. "We will march under full steam toward industrialization, toward Socialism, and leave behind us the centuries-old Russian 'belatedness.' We will become a country of metals, of tractorization, of electrification, and when the U.S.S.R. climbs into the automobile and the Moujik upon the tractor, then let the honourable capitalist, who boasts of his civilization, try to keep up with us. Then we shall see which countries are backward and which are progressive." (Stalin.) Keep in mind the lesson that the most belated country started the Revolution against the market-seeking economy of Western nationalism, and turn once more to the soil where this eruption had been prepared.

DOSTOEVSKI AND TOLSTOI.

In the sixties, after the emancipation of the peasants, when the split between official Czarism and the Intelligentsia had become final, when the revolutionary youth vanished from the surface and sank into the people, the soul of old Little Russia began to expire. But some poets caught the sigh. Through their voice and through the atmosphere created in their writings Russia could still breathe between 1870 and 1914. This literature, by being highly representative in a revolutionized world, became the contribution of Russia to the rest of the world. Without Dostoevski and Tolstoi, Western Europe would not know what man really is. These Russian writers, using the Western forms of the novel, gave back to the West a knowledge of the human soul which makes all French, English and German literature wither in comparison. Step by step Russian literature works its way closer and closer to the work-a-day world of the Russian peasant, pedlar, soldier, prisoner.

The title pages of Dostoevski's novels tell the story: *The Idiot, The Humiliated and Offended, Reminiscences of the Dead-house* (which means Siberian forced labour), *The Demons.*

Dostoevski extricates the types of men who will become the standard bearers of the Revolution. To read Dostoevski is to read the psychic history of the Russian Revolution. All the facts, of course, are different; he ignores any quantitative questions of society. On the other hand, state and government must disappear, as in the Marxian theory of society. Since the artist and seer is unwilling to see life in terms of quantities, the only future he can think of is a church-like order. In *The Brothers Karamasov,* his greatest book, the venerable Staretz, an orthodox abbot and somewhat a saint, exclaims prophetically: "Not the Church becoming State, but the State becoming Church, mark that well!" Government by military or police force no longer has any meaning for Dostoevski. The men he describes have nothing to do with the hilarious and creative geniuses of Western civilization. They are as dirty, as weak and as horrible as humanity itself, but they are as highly explosive, too. The *homeless soul* is the hero of Dostoevski, the nomadic soul.

In this inner vision of Dostoevski, the prodigal son is the central figure, the prodigal son, yes, but paralyzed midway, impenitent, obdurate, hardened, refractory. Incendiary, blasphemous, criminal, he sometimes is, but only because he cannot find the way home to his father's house. In a miraculous way, the situation of the man who leaves home at fourteen to go into a factory and never goes home again because he never starts on an independent career, the proletarian form of life, is anticipated in Dostoevski. To a certain extent, the disillusion with our first home and its reconstruction after a time of homelessness has to be experienced by every man during the years between fourteen and thirty. If he escape this crisis it is true he would never become a man. But in *The Adolescent* (another of Dostoevski's novels) all life seems to be concentrated in this unique phenomenon of the wandering between the old home and the new. This type of man is "in becoming." He is open to every temptation, he is agnostic, he is immature. All the hell of humanity lives in the visitations and manias of the eternal revolutionary.

Society has always had to deal with this side of our nature. But man preferred to appear strong, rich, human, intelligent, and the rules of the social game were based on the pretence that the human being is rich, good, and beautiful. Dostoevski lays the corner-stone for a new building of humanity. In the new house, the prodigal son becomes the basic element. Hell is opened. Mankind, always frightened by hell before, now resolves to bear its presence consciously. The class consciousness of the proletariat, a favourite topic of Marxism, finds its explanation in the fact that the uprooted outlawed stranger, the idiot, the proletarian, have nothing but their consciousness. He who lives in peace and has roots in the earth, has little need of consciousness. The Russian intellectuals need consciousness.

Something eternally human gains form and shape in these Russian figures. These novels, therefore, belong to the Russian Revolution and to the history of the world. The deepest stratum of our being, the one most alienated from light, is lifted up into the clear day of history. The reverse of all our creative power, namely, our capacity for destruction, our demons, our self-contempt, hatred and laziness, envy and indifference, greediness and jealousy, are faced without the fury of the moralist, or the indifference of the anatomist, but with a glowing passion of solidarity in our short-comings. The revolutionary pure and simple is bodied forth in these novels as an eternal form of mankind.

The Russian Revolution, in proclaiming its permanence, eternalizes the revolutionary, too. The Russians try to use this side of our potentialities for solving the universal economic problem. The destroying features of life impersonated in the "revolutionary" shall form the basis for a new society which will avoid the casual destructions that came from concealing or ignoring altogether this element of our nature.

A permanent revolution will invest the fierce element of destruction in time into the process of regenerating our sources of income, and this perpetual investment will ward off the sudden economic catastrophes from which we have suffered. The revolutionary element will become a daily neighbour of our life, just as dynamite, the explosive invention of Nobel, became a blessing to contractors and the mining industry. The courage to incorporate a part of hell-fire itself into society and the readiness to use dynamite as the only way to a relative security, is the answer given by Communism to Dostoevski's disclosure of hell within our own bodies.

Tolstoi—not exiled to Siberia like Dostoevski, but living as a voluntary hermit in the social prison of his environment, Tolstoi, the wizard of Yasnaya Polyana—became the centre of enlightenment and encouragement for the Eastern nations. His letters, published by Paul Biriukov, are full of political counsel for the emancipation of Asia. The importance of the Russian Revolution for Asia is well illustrated by Tolstoi's influence.

He too offers no solution of the social question. Less orthodox than Dostoevski, he even taunts the church which he detests. The Sermon on the Mount, the sermon to the masses, is all he keeps of the Christian tradition, dropping as he does all that Jesus taught in the inner circle of the disciples. Tolstoi, who is a saint in Russia even today, prepared the way for the Revolution by his song of the majesty of the people. Dostoevski revealed the individual. Tolstoi's theme is the majesty of the people, not the nation in the Western sense of the word. The people's face is like that of the simple Moujik. As long as it is not corrupted by consciousness, as long as it does not ask for a constitution, the people in its pre-Adamitic stage that lies before all political volition opens like a door so that the higher power may enter and take possession of the soul.

To be sure, Tolstoi has no solutions to offer. But by his assertion he destroys everything superimposed upon his genuine layer of "the people." Tolstoi and Dostoevski together composed a new creed. One gave to it his doctrine of the weak and trembling individual, the other enriched it by his faith in the majesty of the people, which reacts like the ocean, the cornfield, the forest, because it is patient, passive, obedient.

The Revolution itself practically abolished literature. The statistician superseded the novelist. The poet was a man "in the air," as the term is. One of the few better novels of postwar Russia is called *Concrete*. Concrete took the place of the air, economy the place of poetry.

The period of realization began: realization of Marxism, realization of Russian leadership.

BETWEEN THE FIRST AND SECOND REVOLUTION.

Lenin, originally a gentleman named Ulianov, was Europe's plenipotentiary to Russia to stop its exploitation by a Western market-seeking economy.

In 1904-05 the loss of the Japanese War enabled the bourgeoisie to ask for parliamentary reform. Lenin soon saw that in the absence of a Russian proletariat the revolution could not serve socialistic purposes, and so took no part in it. Instead of the expected "Socialist Revolution" the battleship *Potemkin* started a revolution; the marine and the soldier, overlooked by Marxism, were the dangerous proletarians of the revolution of 1905. After 1905, a stormy period of reform brought factories, Kulaks and workers into the country. But the revolutionary fever died down for a time. Youth was corrupted by "Nashinism," for the novel *Nashin* laid bare the despondency and dissipation of society after the disappointments of 1905.

For nine years Russian youth was less revolutionary, more inclined to corruption and dissipation, than it had been before 1905. To a retrospective observer these nine years seem like a period of subterfuge all over Europe, a last attempt to overlook, to eschew, the catastrophe. In Western Europe the nations tried to ignore war. In Russia youth tried to ignore the Revolution. In this period of temptation the loose leaves of the tree were shaken. Anyone who resisted the corruption (Nashinism) was proved the incorruptible soldier of the Revolution.

Lenin was such a soldier. His teacher, Plekhanov, the leading Marxian authority of Russia, was not. When the War broke out, Plekhanov was blinded by it and forgot his loyalties to the World Revolution. And most of the other revolutionaries did the same.

But some did not. "Why, you won't help us to crush the Czar!" cried a young Russian revolutionary, trying to rouse some Bavarian soldiers who were reluctant to go to their barracks in Munich on the first of August, 1914.

The exclamation is important, because it already takes the Great War as the first phase of the Russian Revolution. For the War was the most important part of the Russian Revolution. The one hundred and fifty million inhabitants of the "exploited colony of capitalism" could not be reached in peacetime. Mobilization of the army and concentration at the front was the only way of getting them under control. An organic evolution of a liberal economic system, with private property and high wages, would have threatened the plans of the Socialists; the War ruined this potential evolution of the reformers. In 1917 two per cent of Russian industry was working for the needs of the population, the rest was working for the army. In other words, 98 per cent of Russian industrial production was nationalized in its market, two per cent, that is, nothing, escaped. The home market was a perfect blank. No trains, no roads. Bolshevism found a *tabula rasa*. But the War also brought another condition for success: it emancipated the non-

Orthodox territories of the West. The victories of the Central
Powers freed all the sections of Russia with old European
traditions of private property, farming, craftsmanship and
education.

When the unsuspecting Kerenski started his milk-and-water
revolution, he overlooked the fact that the classes on which to
build a national democracy no longer existed in the Czaristic
empire.

Therefore Kerenski was bound to fight for the re-conquest of
the Western Provinces. His tragic mistake of going on fighting
was perfectly consistent with his political program. He unchained the real revolution by deposing the Czar, and thought
that the country could be aroused to "national defence" like
the French in 1792, merely because democracy had been proclaimed. But the moral values of national pride and "fight to
the last" were too much a corollary to the rule of the bourgeois-
class and to the *beginning* of a war to fit into the Russian situation after three years of bloodshed. Nationalism, as practised
in Russia since the laws of Russification, only showed the
strong hold of Western influence upon the upper classes in
Russia. The Moujik could be loyal to the Little Father Czar,
but the Petersburg ideology of a corrupt society had no roots
in the vast mass of the peasants. Their sentiments were much
better represented by the monk and ranter Rasputin. Dissipated as he seems to have been, he was certainly a better barometer of Russian instincts than Prince Yusupov who boasts of
having murdered him. Yusupov invited, poisoned, shot and
knocked down Rasputin because he, like all Westerners, was
afraid the influence of Rasputin on Emperor and Empress
might bring about a separate peace between Russia and the
Central Powers. For Rasputin, being neither a nationalist nor
a democrat, was unmoved by the code of honour of the die-
hards. He, like his better predecessor, Father John of Cronstadt,
expressed to Emperor and rabble the primitive Christian traditions. As to any pre-capitalistic and naïve type of man, war was
to him simply and plainly an evil. It had to be avoided, and
eventually to be stopped, at all costs. The loss of a war was no
reason to blush. The townspeople of the big cities, fed by

literati and newspaper headlines, are easily intoxicated into frenzies of patriotism. The real stupidity of the average citizen betrays itself precisely in his readiness to become over-excited in times of emergency, and in his incapacity to balance the pros and cons soberly when he is told that the national prestige is at stake. Of this superstition, at least, Rasputin was free, though the superstitious super-patriots found him very superstitious indeed.

They sacrificed him to their idol, patriotism. But in killing him they cut off the last, however corrupt, vein that, weak as it was, still ran through Little Mother Russia even in 1917, and which had connected the Little Father Czar with the common man. After Rasputin's stupid assassination, the Czar was just a constitutional monarch like any in the West. The fact that Western capitalism had Russia in its grip, and that the governing class, though they might call themselves princes, barons and counts, were really an excrescence of the money-making class of Europe, had begun to leak out when the Czar went to Paris for foreign loans, and especially when, in 1889, in exchange for this financial help, he allowed the *Marseillaise* to be played before him. All the efforts of Czarism after that were aimed at keeping a balance between the fact that Russia had become dependent on Western economic methods and the traditional feelings of the Moujik. The enlightened upper classes were only disgusted at the fanatical orthodoxy shown by the German-born Empress. We are usually blinded by this cheap enlightenment of the free-thinker which ignores the irrational loyalties of group life. A ruler and his followers move in a common faith as in a fluid which enables them to turn the Ship of State wherever it must be turned, even if it be to the harbour of a hard peace. Rational relations in government do not survive, because the ship must be steered across the rocks of political misfortunes. Wars and foreign policy are apt to be most fatal in democracies; for there they are fought out to the bitter end.

This truth can well be learned from Russian history itself. The Russo-Japanese War in 1904-05, and the first Russian

Revolution have to be considered as a prelude [8] to the greater
events of a decade later.

In 1904 the world crash began to appear on the horizon.
Irredentism became more violent. The most sensitive writer
on the *Fin de Siècle* decay, Joyce, dates his witches' sabbath
of civilization in *Ulysses* back to June, 1904, with an astounding instinct for the epoch made by that year in the soul of
the European. The catastrophe to which Europe had long
since been driven as if "in a torture of tension," according to
Nietzsche's phrase, first became visible in this year.

The first rapids of the cataract through which mankind has
been passing ever since appeared when the Esthonians set fire
to their landlords' estates on the Baltic coast, and when a yellow
power defeated the white man for the first time.

The first Russian Revolution pleased all the Democrats,
Liberals and Humanists. But Lenin refused to take part in it.
And as the pre-liberal, pre-democratic *ancien régime* had the
courage to make peace in time, it survived. These two facts
are the outstanding features of 1905. The fighting fronts
grouped themselves for the first time, and the uselessness of
the bourgeois ideology of the liberal and national revolutionaries was already visible.

MILITARY DEFEAT: A REVOLUTIONARY VICTORY.

In a country as badly organized as Russia a military defeat
was always possible. Now the ruler of a country is the pivot
between war and peace, and peace and war. He is not on one
side of the door, like his ministers or the generals of the army;
he has to choose every day between the use of peaceful means
and adopting brute force. He is the pivot between peace and
war because he decides with whom his people shall be on
speaking terms and with whom not. The reader will understand
that "peace" and "war" are not merely the extreme cases of
complete disarmament or open warfare, but imply a daily decision, because a country has to move every day at least one inch
toward solidarity or towards isolation in its policies. A ruler

---

[8] Stated with great clarity in 1905 by Joseph Conrad in his "Autocracy and
War," *Fortnightly Review,* reprinted in *Life and Letters,* p. 111 *ff.,* 1921.

is worthless as a ruler (king, president, Czar, congress, parliament or dictator) if he no longer has the authority to swing the door freely between peace and war. As soon as a government has finally closed the door on one of the two possibilities, it has lost its proper value.

The Nationalists in Russia were worthless because they could not make peace in 1917. The statesman who could was the ruler of Russia. All measures, laws and programmes of government are minor questions compared to this main issue which concerns the very existence of a nation as an independent group.

In 1917 a German pullman car carried Lenin from Zurich through Germany. Lenin was sent home by the German army staff. Well knowing his main duty in the future, he protected himself from the very beginning against the easy impeachment of collusion with the Germans. When he stepped on the train he had in his pocket a document signed by a French, a German and a Swiss Marxist, saying that they did not object to his bargain with Prussian militarism. Later, in Petrograd, he became the great man, not for his radicalism or his economics (he had to give in to the greed of the peasants, and painfully disappointed Rosa Luxemburg by accepting at first the seizure of the land by the individual villages and peasants), but because he concluded the treaty of Brest-Litovsk. He alone turned the Great War into a World Revolution; for he was the only man, even in the Russia of 1917, who had the courage to do it. No intellectual Russian who had lived through the last three years in Russia had escaped the infection of current nationalistic ideas. Rasputin, as a pure-blooded Moujik, and Lenin, as a Nihilist and refugee, were not blinded by patriotic fury. Lenin came into the country in order to conquer it for Socialism. It was the field for his task, and raw material on which to work, an object in the full sense of this word in natural science. To him the amputation of all the Western territories from the trunk of Russia was justifiable because it was the way to peace. No mere Russian mind imbued with nationalism could sacrifice the Balkans and Bessarabia and Warsaw and Finland and Riga and Lithuania. Lenin was isolated when he first pronounced his "peace at all costs." Coldly, with the relentlessness of a masseur, he began to repeat his formula. The intoxicated patriots could not understand him. He was in a hopeless minority for a relatively long time. But he uttered his monstrous formula like a curative treatment day after day. The subconscious part of men, "their visceral sensation," their diaphragm, was kneaded and rubbed, and became aware of their true situation: "It does not matter how much of our territory we lose, provided we can build up Socialism in the rest."

With this formula he dedicated the rest of Russian territory to a world-wide mission. The surrender of the western border became the honourable price of a new organic function of the Russians within the world. They screwed their courage to the sticking point: they accepted the amputation as necessary to Russia's task.

It was a fight between reason on one side and faith and instinct on the other. All the phraseology of passion, of emotional slogans, had been used up for war. The new language of Socialism could not but be cool, harsh, grey, like a doctor's prescription or a chemist's formula. Finally, Lenin won, and the treaty was signed. Thus the new language of Bolshevism was created in the autumn of 1917: cynical, icy, cooling instead of warming.

All the procedures of the Bolshevik keep and must keep this standard set forth by Lenin. The subconscious mind of man, his fears for life and bare material existence, his suspicion of his own idealistic intoxication, is used to build up a materialistic organization for every*body* instead of for every *mind* or *soul*. The new language does not cease to rely on sacrifice, self-denial, self-discipline and the forming of ideals for millions of individuals. This materialism is strictly opposed to sensualism. It is an asceticism of the individual soul for the sake of material solidarity in the body politic. The material needs of the body politic, wheat and iron and cotton and electric power, are the ideals expressed, as we have seen, by the piatiletka. Yet they appeal to the indivdiual in the form of scientific prescriptions, because otherwise they might be mistaken for the airy and dreamy lies of bourgeois ideologists.

The only man who had the detachment to use this new "language of the diaphragm" against the intoxication of the brain by war propaganda, became the demigod who founded the U.S.S.R., and when he died he was embalmed and enshrined like the founders of cities in ancient Hellas. The creation of a new political scale of values always seems the achievement of a demigod. Ordinarily, the pilgrimage to Lenin's grave is compared to the pilgrimage to the relics of a Christian saint. But the dust and bones of the saint's corpse bear witness to an invisible world. Lenin's corpse is kept carefully embalmed because he provides food and clothing for the masses, like an Egyptian Pharaoh.

By sacrificing the favourite topic of the nationalized intellectuals in time of war, that is, military victory, Lenin brought intellectuality home to the reasoning of the man in the street. He forced Reason to look down, instead of staring up or around the universe. He humiliated the free, idealistic outlook of the period of liberty and patriotic citizenship. This famous phrase, "liberty is a bourgeois prejudice," must be understood in the light of the peace of Brest-Litovsk.

WORLD WAR AND WORLD REVOLUTION.

The Russian Revolution remains indebted to the World War. The War, as we have seen, gathered the organized manhood of the country for centralized military service, delivered it into the hands of the Bolsheviks, and later handed over to Lenin what the Czar had lost: the power of concluding peace.

This has been the paradox of the Russian situation ever since. It was closely connected with Europe, not by economic strings, but by the War. The mobilization of the army and the war against Central Europe created the new unity of the U.S.S.R. It changed both the territory and the population. It made it a power of "Eurasian" character, as the new geography in Russia styles it. A hundred years ago the famous traveller-prince, Pückler-Muskau, wrote: "My book will treat in its first part Europe, in its second Africa, in its third Asia, and the fourth will deal with Russia, because it can be considered, with good reason, a continent of its own."

The result of the Russian Revolution fits well into this definition. A new continent was established economically, not a new world. The World War saw the greatest geographical expansion of direct Russian influence. The high-water mark of Communism was the year of 1919. Since then Communism has been more and more limited to the government of Russia, as one government among others, and the close connection with the West has been replaced by a growing isolation from all Western contacts or exchanges. Russia is more Russia today than she had ever been since Peter the Great. She is an isolated continent of her own. This significance of the World War is well-expressed by the terms of the treaties. Being dovetailed into Europe by the system of western territories, Russia had been a part of the Western market-seeking economy. When the dovetailing was destroyed she moved away from the rest of the world. The cold philosophy of the Bolsheviks failed to grasp this point. Being primarily Europeans, they went so far as to drop "Rossiya" from the official name of their government. When Mr. Troyanovsky, the first Bolshevik minister to Washington, presented his credentials to Mr. Roosevelt, the name of Russia, curiously enough, was not used on either side. U.S.S.R. was the expression of the Russian hope for worldwide revolution. Starting from the world as a whole, they were reluctant to see that they were creating an isolated system.

Instead they went on carefully studying the French Revolution, the tactics of Robespierre and Hébert, and the importance of sparing the heads of the left- and right-wing opposition because in France "the Revolution had devoured its own children." Thus they missed the main point of a comparative study, namely, that between 1789 and 1815 there had been three and a half years of revolution at home and twenty-three years of war abroad, whilst Russia saw three and a half years of war and then a permanent revolution.

After the exhaustion caused by the external wars, a second revolution, in 1830, had to be started to win back France and Europe to the maxims of its bourgeois revolution. This second revolution set up a bourgeois king who gave the first real expression to the material interests of the governing class. 1789 and 1830 are like the drama and the explanatory epilogue.

In Russia a prologue clears the scene. The events of 1904 and 1905 are called, with perfect right, "the first Russian Revolution," because they really prepared the main drama of the second. The general staff of the second revolution was ready forty years before the existence of a real proletariat in Russia, and waited impatiently for the economic evolution of the country to catch up with it. The French Revolution was a perfect model for the Marxian theory that a class interest builds up a class ideology and that the philosophers of the movement therefore depend upon the material interests of their group. But with all their knowledge of this relationship, the Bolsheviks themselves could not help existing before the proletarian in Russia. The ideologist awaited, seized, educated and won over the proletarians in Russia! The emancipation of a class "must be the work of the class itself," is a famous phrase in Marx, condemning the right of the intellectual to be more than the executive of a social will. But in Russia the emancipation of the proletariat is the work of the intelligentsia. The intelligentsia suffered for a century, and its vicarious suffering gave Lenin the right to enforce his "Laws." Socialism was a theory devised by a bourgeois, with all the corollaries of bourgeois thought, since atheism, free-thinking, and the belief in natural science are merely the accompaniment of bourgeois thought in the middle of the nineteenth century.

Finally, the Russians, being hypnotized by the example of the French Revolution, misunderstood their own relation to the World War. If the Napoleonic Wars had infected the rest of Europe with the germ of the ideas of 1789, the Great War, on the contrary, preceded the so-called revolution and pervaded Europe for three years as a catastrophical force quite apart from any formulated programme. The war was the great revolution for all European civilization. Compared with its terrible bloodshed, destruction, and despair, Communist propaganda was simply a drop in the ocean.

As the distance from the Great War increased, the influ-

ence of Russian policy on the rest of Europe could not but
decline.

We shall see later what happened to the rest of the world
as a result of the Great War. At this point we are dealing with
the effect of all these self-deceptions on the Russians themselves. It took them ten years to realize their real tendency
toward complete isolation. Once they discovered their destiny,
they lost interest in Communist theories of 1918 or 1920 and
resumed, instead, their connection with the economic problems
of 1917. Then the country made a desperate effort to organize
itself. Lenin himself had fervently admired the efficiency of
German organization for all the purposes of war economy, an
efficiency which was certainly far distant from Communism.
The "Piatiletka" is the Hindenburg line of the Bolsheviks, the
problem of war economy renewed on a gigantic scale. For
them it means drawing the conclusion from their isolation
and limiting their planning to an autarchy of the U.S.S.R.

The years 1929-1934, read in the light of the disillusions
and mistakes of the Russians in both theory and practice, are
a sober acceptance of the real results of the Great War. The
War took the intelligentsia by surprise. Their revolution actually did not begin as a class-war! Instead, a civil war which
cut across class lines broke out between the European nations.
The differentiation of the European nations according to their
economic and geographical conditions was made clear by the
War, which brought into sharp relief Germany's efficiency in
holding the fortress of Central Europe, England's dependence
upon the rest of the world, and Russia's backwardness in her
internal organization.

The materialistic outlook of the Marxists was much truer
than they imagined. According to their own theory, changes
in economic conditions create new thoughts in men; but in
spite of this fact, most of the Russians believed in 1917 that
the dream of a world revolution could be realized after a
World War. They habitually overlooked the fact that the War
itself had created new economic conditions unknown to Marx.
The soldiers of the Great War, in their humble and unconscious rôle of soldiers, made the real revolution. Like Hamlet,

they could say to any Marxian dogmatist, "Our withers are unwrung."

When the French bourgeoisie began to take the first steps toward revolt, about 1750, its leaders had in mind specific economic conditions and abuses which were recurrent for the next forty years. The Great War, on the other hand, made a complete change in the economic conditions of the world. Not until the depression of 1929 was the change taken seriously. Prophets, Cassandras, demagogues, had foretold it; but the overwhelming majority of governments and parties had tried to return to the conditions of 1914. These conditions were progress, bigger and better conditions of living, an upward trend for everything, a cheering up from year to year. In so far, the Communists in the Kremlin shared the illusions of the people who held the World Fair of a Century of Progress in Chicago as late as 1933. For had not Socialism and Marxism been born under pre-War conditions? According to the Marxian creed itself, how could a theory be workable after a change in its material environment? It was a triumph of Marxism over the Marxists when the Great War, a real and substantial material fact, proved to be of more importance than any volition on the part of parties or individuals. The World War was a World Revolution: it ended Marxism as it ended liberalism.

The Marxists clung to their pre-War notions as long as they could. The same was true of the rest of the world. In all the nations the years 1924 to 1929 mark a period of stubborn refusal to recognize the new facts. Every country exaggerated its pre-War economy. The problems which America has had to face since 1929 were exactly the problems foreseen by Theodore Roosevelt in 1912. The thoughts of men are slow. It is true our brains can register news and information day by day; thought seems, on the surface, to be quick and dashing. But this quality belongs to the particular statement only. The framework of our thoughts is the most conservative part of our bodies. The grey cells of our brains are the only cells of the body which are never rejuvenated during our lives. They survive ten or more complete restorations of all the other cells. The processes of our judgment often go on for centuries in a changed environment. Less easily does a scholar change his methods than nations their religion. American lawyers follow the method of English common law Anno Domini 1934 as they did in 1634. . . .

Valuing everything in terms of expansion, "bigger and better," boom and prosperity, growth and progress and evolution, thinking, in other words, in terms of a market-seeking economy and society, was the common mistake of both Marxists and liberals after the War. The Marxists longed for the success of a pre-War social theory, the liberals for the success of a pre-War economic practice. Both failed because the facts of the War were catalogued under the old headings that dominated pre-War brains, instead of forming new headings themselves. A curve could show the ups and downs in our willingness to see the War as a break in our habits of thinking. The willingness varies. We avoid realizing that our new situation is connected with the World War. In the United States the depression is blamed for what was really done by the War and the Treaty of Versailles. In Russia the "Piatiletka" which bids farewell to the Marxist World Revolution and means the organization of Russia as an independent and invulnerable state even in time of war, is hailed as the triumph of Marxism.

THE DEPRESSION.

The economists call the crisis an economic crisis, which it certainly is. But the pattern of the business cycle is not applicable to a case like ours. Our intentional suppression of what has happened makes all the difference between 1912 and 1929. A crisis in 1912 was a crisis only; the crisis of 1929 is of double force, because people have tried to forget and to make others forget that the open-market period since the War is gone. The destruction of Austria, for example, by the treaty of St. Germain, was simply a step backward from a bigger market into many smaller ones. We cannot carry out what our own language of progress calls a "regress," and then believe that the regress will affect us like a progress. But that was exactly what all the nations did. In the vocabulary of the market-seeking economy and the Century of Progress, the victors of the Great War had to create the greatest possible market. One provision would have settled all the economic difficulties of later years: "The earth is one and united for all business purposes." All the other paragraphs of the treaties could have been omitted, and a World Peace would have followed the World War. But in 1919 this one proposition could not have been made without imperilling the life of the man who uttered it. Even today it is merely a logical *tour de force,* and has nothing to do with any of the acts, speeches, and plans in the diplomatic chancelleries.

From the facts of our World War experience we must draw the inevitable conclusion: property, or in other words, the endless production of goods, is certainly an endeavour which can unite mankind in its struggle for life all over the world. This production of goods is all very well, but the nations thought first of reproducing their exhausted man-power. They wished to restore the nation's vitality, to reproduce man himself. Now, the reproduction of man is not a formula which can unite all men, because man is reproduced in different ways. From the attitude of the nations during and after the Great War, the Russians themselves came to learn that even in capitalistic countries production is a less sovereign motive than others. The rest of the world sacrificed its cash interests to other interests or values. Capitalistic interests were outweighed everywhere by obligations toward the reproduction of national character.

JUDAS ISCARIOT.

The tenets of Marxism were too narrow. In opposing Capitalism to Communism, an existing order to a mere unhistorical theory, it missed the real situation. And it was able to go on with this illusion as long as the self-deception of the other pre-War governments lasted. Its merit was to label things as revolutionary before this word was popular in Western countries. Today "revolutions" are as plentiful as blackberries; but their meaning is watered down to the cheap notion of quick changes in the technique of moving pictures or textiles, or the making of codes for industry. The discovery made by the Marxist theory that mankind goes from revolution to revolution needs a broader framework than the Marxists were equipped to give.

The anti-economic result of the World War gives testimony to the truth of what has often been said: Marx understood some things in economics better than anybody among his contemporaries, but of men he knew less than the simple housewives in a village. The souls of men can be trained to amazing purposes. In Russia they are drilled to deprive their own bodies of all pleasure, for the pleasure of acting as a force in an organized "body economic." In Russia the governing class proudly call themselves the "proletariat," though actually they form a religious order, revolutionary in intention and disposition, which owes its authority to the procession of vicarious suffering, century-long martyrdom, among the Russian nobility and intelligentsia.

The souls of men seem to hide their actions under a strange veneer of ideology. Men are much more reserved than rationalists suspect. Marxism unveils our ideologies; it strips off the moral pretexts that cover our naked interest. But it cannot change human nature. By the nature of our souls, even Marxists are doomed to wear clothes. Man is not naked and never will be. There is a province in man's realm, it is true, that belongs to tense body, gnashing teeth, clenched fist, stamping foot, where the "brother donkey" of St. Francis of Assisi seems to be all of us that is left. The stretch and strain of labour brings the labour-force inside us so close to the surface that the drone and hum and whetting and pawing and swearing and screaming silence the other parts of our being. Labour even acquires a universal language. The labour forces "waft a sigh from Indus to the Pole." The curses of the individual labourer carry no weight; but once united the labour-forces can break their chains. We can organize labour as part of the universe. Labour is the curse by which God has blessed mankind. Labour is a curse for the lonely worker, but it can be made the happiness of a co-operative fellowship.

This grandiose effort of the Bolsheviks is a permanent and unforgettable contribution to human reality. But it is meaningless if it is left alone. How meaningless is made apparent by a symbol used by the Bolsheviks themselves. In Perm there stands a monument to Judas Iscariot. We are living in a period when treason, high treason, is revealed as an essential feature of human frailty. German National Socialism is beset by the problem of the traitor. Now the category of treason reveals the very nature of man as a social force. Instead of a personality, man is a frail bundle of nerves: he follows his leader as far as his nerves will carry him, and then treason is the next step.[9] In psychoanalysis, treason is well-known as the revenge of the weak against the strong. Nietzsche's apostasy from Richard Wagner is a modern parallel to the case of Judas, and is celebrated by Nietzsche himself as a victory. Judas appears in many modern books as the twin of Jesus, with the better instinct for this world. Judas wished power and success; and in a century when D. H. Lawrence wrote *Blessed the Powerful,* when the thirst for power becomes the basic creed of great nations, poor Judas appears as a martyr to the true creed of mankind. Judas would have saved the Kingdom of Judea! He would have driven out the Romans. He would not have deserted to Christendom! The Bolsheviks challenged the old rule that in a misfortune a man does not argue against his country. They deserted old Russia. The desertion made them discover Judas.

The martyr Judas is extolled in both psychoanalytical and Communist literature. One might expect the successful ruler of Jesus' day, Cæsar Augustus, to be hailed as the model; but Augustus is not mentioned. The pagan emperor has no connection with the history of our soul; Judas has. The revolutionaries prefer to set up Judas, the permanent natural and pre-Adamitic force within ourselves, in opposition to the perfect man who healed Adam's wound.

In human history, in so far as it dates from Adam and Jesus, the pre-Adamite is represented by the traitor. "No manual worker can be virtuous," said Aristotle.

Modern society has to recognize that man, in so far as he is a cog in the machine, must be looked upon as frail, unrelia-

[9] In Western literature, Edmond Rostand, in the nineties, created the rôle of a treacherous youth in *La Princesse Lointaine.* His traitor, Bertrand, however, though corresponding to the Russian type, is, in the French setting, vanquished by the hero.

ble, traitorous—and all this not from bad intentions, but through his lasting weakness, helplessness, fear, and disappointment. But this recognition does not mean that exalted heroism or the virtues of strength and faith and reliability are abolished or denied. Only, the mass man in his tribal fears and nightmares cannot reach them. He is haunted like any Australian bushman. "We are afraid," is the great outcry of the proletariat. But let us not overlook the peculiar relation between this outcry and the old virtues of the liberal, the self-possessed individual. The proletarian soul is visited by weaknesses which are the logical antithesis of the old scale of values. The proletariat negates and ridicules these values because of its inferiority complex; *but it has no other values of its own.* It lives without values, without ideals, without any trimmings or embellishments. It is the eternal incendiary of this so-called and so-despised higher civilization.

It is the universal and perpetual mission of the proletariat to maintain this negative attitude, says Trotsky; for the revolution is permanent and must be permanent. The very concept of the Russian Revolution perverts the old order of connection between means and ends. Revolution had been a means to the end of better government; for the Bolshevik, revolution is perpetual because there is no "better government." Over and over he repeats: "The State must be destroyed once more!" The polarity between the capitalistic world and Marxism is to be eternal. On the day of the Last Judgment the Revolution can die down, not before. Like Hébert in the French Revolution, the Bolshevik has a clear conception of the mass man's own incapacity for government. Like the waves of the ocean drawn between two tides, the masses tear down in eternal recurrence whatever takes the shape of exploitation and government. Hence a peculiar eschatology: the process of attack, lawlessness, destruction, must be perpetual, because the solution cannot be found until the Last Day of Creation. The final vision is a peaceful earth; but the whole period between today and the end is bloodshed, force, treason, struggle and fight. History means war, class-war. Not until history is ended can there be peace.

A peculiar eschatology because it enables the law-giver, the leader of a government, the reformer of society, to clothe himself as a ferocious revolutionary. The governing class in Russia, these simple administrators of an economic order, rather than be revealed as heirs of the old Chinovnik, the Czarist bureaucrat, prefer to wear the blood-red mantle of the revolutionary. Being a very pedantic kind of social worker, they wear a mask of nakedness. But it is a mask. The Bolshevist fashion is to appear naked, without ideals; but this naked skin is painted, like the dancing costume of the medicine man in an Indian tribe, and the idealistic fanatics who govern because they have suffered, govern in the name of the devil of materialism.

THE INTERDEPENDENCE OF REVOLUTIONS.

Why do the Bolsheviks choose the blood-red flag? Why do they scorn idealism? The tricolour and the ideals of the bourgeois nations are their enemies. They are the symbols of the West which, as we have seen, the Intelligentsia in Russia was resolved to overtake. As the antithesis to the polished civilization of Europe they chose their language of complete denudation. The language of the Bourgeois Revolution had to be outdone.

One is struck at the outset by the fact that to a Bolshevik mind revolution is an end, not a means. The term is given a queer sense of permanence. This concept of a continuous, never-ending state of affairs to be called "perpetual revolution" certainly is cumbersome for any liberal mind. However, all the post-War revolutionaries agree in the new terminology. Hitler and Mussolini, as much as Stalin, are attempting today to bring about a complete change in our political vision. They are proclaiming "revolution" to be the only decent political status for human beings. Intervals of mere legal and peaceful order are branded as treason against the true concept of life. Darwin's "struggle for existence" is transformed by these political dogmatists into the new term, "continuous revolution." Order, stability, peace, security, are dethroned. They are inexcusable symbols of darkness and cowardice. To such minds the darkness of capitalism is the more inexcusable because capitalism itself is of revolutionary origin. How can the sons and daughters of a revolution forbear living on the interest from the revolutionary investment of their forefathers?

Bolshevism is less concerned with showing its true faith than it is with tearing off the mask of the French Revolution worn by the governing class. Its perpetual revolution goes against a temporary revolution. With the French it is anti-bourgeois, anti-liberal, anti-democratic, anti-national. It is the dissolution of the existing order, the only paradox being that it is its *perpetual dissolution.* A perpetual dissolution is a contradiction in terms. But this contradiction is at the root of Bolshevism. Bolshevism learns, buys, borrows from capitalism, relies on its organization, taps its very source and vigour; it must have capitalism to live. Because the proletarian is the negation of the bourgeois his creed begins with *nihil,* and the dissolution of Family, State, Law, Art, and Religion is its revolutionary desire.

The way to understand the Russian Revolution is, in fact, to study the French Revolution. The Russians studied the French as a pattern for their own behaviour. They curtailed their study by divorcing the Napoleonic Wars from the Revolution; but they took the French Revolution as their own dialectical antagonist. We shall consider the French Revolution in its polarity to the World War of 1914, and in doing so we shall discover the process by which the French Revolution became a necessary step in the life of all mankind, not of France alone. We shall discover in it that same interplay between real events and the veneer of speech and ideology which helped us to understand the Bolshevik régime. The French régime is based on an assumption no less universal than the Marxian "labour-force." Man is free, equal, and the brother of every man because he has reason, says the Frenchman. The revolutionary dynamite of the proletarian is no higher an explosive than this "reason" of the citizen who created *La France une et indivisible* during the Great Revolution.

In the eyes of the resentful Stalin, Russia was an exploited colony of European capitalism. It was on the circumference of the circle that surrounded the Mecca of civilization, the capital of France, during the nineteenth century. Napoleon I, the warrior of the French Revolution, barely touched Russia by the burning of Moscow. During the régime of Napoleon III the ideas of 1789 wrested from Russia the emancipation of the peasants (1861). In both cases French ideas brought a pressure to bear upon Russia without solving the problem, without carrying through what they intended to achieve.

What a strange period, when ideas led a personal existence, and the march of ideas into Russia in 1861 proved more irresistible than the march of the Grand Army in 1812.

With so much power at the circumference of the circle, these ideas must have produced a hundredfold greater phosphorescence at the centre.

The reflected glow of the French Revolution permeated the world of European civilization. Citizenship and civilization, in Argentina and in Rumania, in Sweden and in Egypt, proclaimed their indebtedness to the French enlightenment of 1789. Even today this brightness still shines above the horizon for most of us.

It may be difficult for an author to be impartial toward the Russian Revolution, because he must fight its claim to absoluteness. It is an even more delicate matter to deal with the French Revolution, because very few of my readers will be inclined to confess how completely their whole scale of sentiments and values is pitched in its key.

To prepare our ears for the "soft language of liberty in France" we here sum up the creed and dogma of the proletarian revolution in Russia.

THE FIRST OF MAY AND THE ABOLITION OF HISTORY.

The Russian Revolution acts like a brick-layer. Men are tiles piled upon a wall that grows higher and higher. One of the few good pieces of revolutionary literature is *Concrete* by Gladkov, in which he describes the disappearance of everything atmospheric. The Revolution transforms men into concrete. Everything is to be as tangible as concrete, and everybody, too. The thinker, the writer, the poet, is called a "man in the air." He is impossible and is disappearing. Living souls, with individual faces, smiling and sobbing like personal beings, lose their form and vanish as soon as the stamp is pressed upon them. Like a trip-hammer, the daily process of industrialization mechanizes childish, naïve faces into nationalized labour-forces. The Russians, trying to bridge the gulf of a thousand years, are paving the road towards industrialization with religious devotion. If it were not a kind of worship, they probably could not be so reckless. When we see them acting like the watchmen upon Mount Zion we must remember that their Zion is a work-a-day world in which every man is just every-*body* and nothing else. Since our nature presents this colourless, physiological, physical, mechanical aspect as well as others, it is a side of us which is real indeed, but in the same way as any mechanism—that is, it is monotonous. The monotony of the ore-crusher, the trip-hammer, the steam-roller, is antihistorical because its principle is mere repetition.

The worship of mechanization recalls the prayer-mills of Tibet—the same prayer repeated 50,000 times or 100,000 times is the spiritual counterpart of the same manipulation repeated a million times: at best there is the same sleight of hand. A famous Bolshevik moving picture boasted that the Russian Revolution had shaken the world in ten days. Instinctively we feel that it shook the "world" less than it shook the ground under our feet. Fascism and Nazism, which will have to be analyzed later in connection with the Italian and German revolutions, are struggling hard to revolt against this dry and monotonous clatter of the mill. They revolt against the use of chemical formulas like hexamethylene, tetramine, or zoological terms like dysmeromorph or antherozoid to describe human moods and tempers, against chromosomes being made to explain the results of love or lack of love. But the Russians worship nature in the garb of chemical formulas. Medicine is the religion of the Soviets. Good and evil are abolished, healthy and ill are the only qualities of the labour-forces. Hundreds of physicians are drilled in Moscow and then sent out to lonely regions in the North and East as the new evangelists of the medical gospel. Every physician and every physicist is thought of as a standard bearer of the new pre-Adamite gospel of man as a bundle of energies.

The first of May marks this return of men into the womb of society. The social masses are redeemed when they can move like the forces of nature in spring: untried, rejuvenated, juvenile, endless, impersonal.

All natural religion tries to double the cape of human responsibility or freedom by persuading us that sun and moon and rain and climate rule over us. Sunwheels and rainbows, meteors and trees, are venerated wherever man feels himself too weak to be man. The Communist revolution must deal with the weakness of man. It does so by offering him the sensations of recurrent nature. (Nazism has not only adopted the first of May, but added similar nature festivals.) But it was neither the "Nature" of lyric poetry nor the dangerous nature of prehistory which was to form the wings of the political scene. It was a mechanized nature, with chanting choruses of thousands, with loud-speakers all over the place, with men themselves changed into drops in the ocean or into leaves of grass by the most refined technique of mass-hypnotism. Men, afraid, inarticulate, are galvanized by the new technique of handling thousands. I myself have heard a thousand children in a stadium repeating monotonously a chorus on the suppression of the worker in the Saar:

> For - cing - Ger - man - wor - ker's - hand
> with - beast - ly - rank - ha - tred
> in - to - serf - dom.

The members of such a chorus are not actors. Taken separately, they are simply nothing. Not one of those children could use the phrase quoted above personally. It is the impersonal character of the chorus which makes it possible for the words to be used. The text sung by modern choruses in mass-meetings may be irresponsible and detestable. But it would be unfair to treat its content as seriously as we were taught in school to treat poetry. We learned to worship poetry as a flower. In the modern cult of the proletariat the chorus is filled with steam, and off it goes. The civil engineers of the mass turn their steam on and off. The flowers of poetry are superseded by gas—call it poison gas or intoxicating gas—but in any case something that moves a host of mass energies toward unanimous action.

The symbolism of the holiday of labour, the first of May, is based on the abolition of responsibility. The sweating labour-force gets its proper reward. Georges Clemenceau wrote a great page on this march of the underman against the individualistic civilization which he himself loved so passionately. Forecasting the approach of the modern masses, he wrote: "In this heart-rending hour, who will not pity the ennobled pangs of hope, lost in the shadow of the past? Yes, our sons will see a day when the horrible massacres of historical times, and even primitive barbarism, will seem to them to represent human happiness in the face of the terrifying catastrophe which with irresistible step will gain ground upon them. It would be a monstrous climax of pain, even into the last phases of decay, if the notion of the necessary end were not already present and did not awaken in us the superior philosophy which permits us to brave any destiny without growing pale.

"The horrible prostration will be accomplished imperceptibly before our eyes. Senility will gradually deaden consciousness, already diminishing in sensibility to the blows; and step by step, along the road of death he has already travelled into life, man, coming from the earth and returning to the earth, will find his grave in his cradle, drowned in forgetfulness at the very source of pain. Pitiless, the slow regression will perform its work. The last human being then alive will be extinguished in the same mystery from which the first man arose. Thus will be ended, in supreme wretchedness, the struggle for life which was begun at the happy hour of birth in the enchanted world. The life of man had exercised a fatal domination over all inferior life. New conditions of life now create new conditions of struggle. The hour has come for the *great revenge* of lower against higher nature. The inferior organism, less pretentious than its greater competitors, is satisfied with second-rate conditions of life. In proportion as the conditions of life are narrowed, man, beast, tree, are impoverished, become anemic and are eclipsed. Incapable of repressing any longer the obscure growth of primitive forms, they now recoil; and the inferior life invades the immense domain where the superior life had formerly kept it in check. It will be the last battle, the great rout of life in defeat, yielding its ground step by step, under the indifferent eyes of centuries, to some humble moss which in an undiscovered retreat has been biding its time until now.

"I see our cities crumbling, among shapeless remnants of humanity, the last ruins collapsing upon expiring life, all thought, all the arts . . ."

Clemenceau describes the sentiments of a civilized man faced by the marching battalions of the proletariat. Do not be misled by the natural metaphor in which he speaks of mosses and inferior life. Such a vision always goes too far. The French thinker, writing in pre-War days, recorded like a seismograph the approaching catastrophe of his civilization, where thought and science and art prevailed. His mosses are the modern masses. From their point of view, nothing is lost, everything is to be gained. "The proletariat has nothing to lose but its chains."

Recurrent nature is the great dream of the manual worker. He is the forgotten man, the unknown soldier on the battle-field of mankind. Why should he worry about a superior life that is unknown to him? Why care for the dishes on a table when he has only the doubtful honour of washing them? In a proletarian song of the German workers, they are called "people of the night." It is an excellent expression to describe the absence of clearness and brightness, of all the glories of French "clarté," in this lower life of the primitive worker in the coal-mines and factories. There is something subterranean about the long slavery of manual work. It is no accident that subter-ranean gnomes and dwarfs fill the old fairy tales, the literature of a race that was better acquainted with fire and earth than with the easily moved air and water. The darkness within us, suppressed by the diaphragm, ruled by the clear eyes, the lucid thought, the loving heart, remains darkness nevertheless. Mod-ern machinery digs it out of its deep dens and caves, and for the first time the internal forces of fire and earth hear a word of hope. The sighing and groaning of the creatures become audible, as it is promised in the gospel, a sighing and groaning not palliated, to be sure, by the poet's flowery phrases or the reflections of the philosopher. The people in the dark of night and the watchmen upon the Mount Zion of this work-a-day world, abolishing civilization as they certainly are, do not live without an historical vision. Since its beginning, scientific socialism has turned towards anthropology and ethnology. Prehistory is the great projection of the proletarian vision into the past. In 1921 the radical Marxist wing of the German Socialists, the independents, instructed their leader, Ledebur, to work into the programme of the party the "newest results of scientific research in the field of anthropology and prehistory." Books like James Henry Breasted, *Dawn of Conscience*, with its ardour for an age preceding the despicable age of revelation, or like Frazer's *Golden Bough*, pave the road for an age where Jerusalem, Athens, and Rome can be eradicated from our children's textbooks, and where the life of Indians, negroes, Egyptians, Sumerians, Teutons, and Celts will seem much more attractive than the so-called classics of Greece and Rome.

The primitives know no history. That is why the modern masses adore primitivism. They are told that the worker has always paid the price of history: he fought the battles of kings and oil-kings, of prophets and popes. He will no longer be fodder for cannon. Perhaps prehistory offers a way out of this ridiculous thirst for world history which intoxicates the ruling classes all over the world. An American statesman, defying Europe and European imperialism, exclaimed: "Happy the country that has no history. America has not much of it, and should try to have even less." He was a man who had come from Europe and with ardent love had adopted the new world as his country. He is seconded by a modern sophisticate of infinite timeliness, the hero of Joyce's *Ulysses*, who exclaims: "History is the nightmare from which I will awake." These words may help us to decipher the prehistoric Messianism of the modern masses. They don't bother about Church and State. The monotony of their life is not to be interrupted by crusades of the soul or reforms of the mind. They long for the ritual of a primitive clan.

According to orthodox Bolshevism, therefore, the first of May is the first day of a permanent revolution which tends to eradicate history and dive into the recurrent waves of pre-history. The last day of the permanent revolution will be the last day of the dictatorship of the proletariat. The provisional arrangement of this dictatorship is necessary for security against any capitalistic aggression or reaction. But it is provisional. All governments are provisional, legislators are provisional, the State is provisional. They are all too much like historical pow-ers. The salvation of mankind is the abolition of all historical powers, and especially of the power of history over the brain and heart of men.

The classless society, the goal of Bolshevism, is beyond his-tory; it is prehistory regained. In the meantime, Lenin or Stalin and the order of the Intelligentsia must govern the Union of Socialist Soviet Republics, U.S.S.R., as the nucleus of the class-less society. Their rulership stretches out, so to speak, between the first of May and the last day in the calendar of history. It is curious to see that any attempt by an outsider to dis-cover symptoms of a classless society in Russia always meets with a stern reprimand from the Marxists. Their rule being temporary and provisional, it is of no use to look for any symptoms of a situation beyond it! Reproduction can never become natural as long as the party must plan it every year. Like the Pope in Strindberg's legend, who triumphantly lis-tened to the clock going on after the hour of the fixed Dooms-day of the world, the *"last syllable of recorded time,"* had passed away, the watchmen upon the tower of Bolshevism state tri-umphantly every day that the revolution continues, that no symptoms of a classless society are available yet, and that the historical function of the proletariat has to be performed day after day.

The Messianism of the Bolshevik Revolution divides the life of humanity into three stages. First Period: history before the World Revolution, the history of class-wars, symbolized by dates of battles, dynasties, heroes, etc. Second Period: Permanent Revolution of the masses against this history of class-wars, started by Lenin and symbolized by the celebration of the first of May. The first of May anticipates the anti-historical Third Period: the classless society, when man has become a part of recurrent and reproduced nature and can live like the people of prehistory.

Are we here breaking into a new era? The worship of the first of May is not a question of Russia alone. It echoes the non-historical side of every man's nature; it reminds us that man is permanent, recurrent, natural, physical, and that many of his actions and activities are quite unhistorical. In a century when history studies a poet's indigestion or a prince's unhappy marriage under the microscope, it is refreshing to learn that after all there is something among men which is not historical at all.

Birth and death and food and clothing and joy and pain are as permanent as they are recurrent. The monotony in the recurrence of generations on this earth is not interrupted by the petty sensations of theatrical politicians.

We have cleared the way for the few events that are really worthwhile when we have learned to differentiate between the historical and the unhistorical or prehistoric elements in ourselves. Christianity had always preached a complete indifference toward history, and Eastern Christians can still find today, in the monasteries on Mount Athos near Thessalonica (Salonika), the quintessence of this complete remoteness from the world. The Greek Orthodox Church, more than any other branch of Christianity, has preserved the energies of the human soul which defend her from the temptation of time. The history of this world is a bad dream to the monk on Mount Athos. The glory of God is visible whenever man can resist the temptations of time. Today orthodox Christianity is fighting history again. The materialistic form of Bolshevism seems to preclude any parallel with the doctrines of Christianity. It seems a mere revolutionary intoxication. But against a world which mistook "The history of the world for the Last Judgment" (Schiller), which believed that we could experience history as in a theatre, the monotony of Russian anti-historianism is like an antitoxin. The theatre is not all. The comedy on the stage of history is not the whole truth of the tragedy of mankind.

THE SOVIET CALENDAR.

Tampering with the calendar began as far back as 1918. Russia had remained true to the Julian calendar, but the Revolution adopted the Gregorian instead, thus coming into line with Western countries. This was decidedly more convenient for international intercourse, but local authorities began to emulate the French Revolution by altering the names of the months and days, substituting the names of old peasant leaders for Easter and Christmas, for example. But when the central government obtained real control of the country, all these local innovations were cancelled. The government made its first determined assault on the seven-day week in September, 1929, with a decree ordering the general introduction of a five-day week. The avowed purpose of this reform was to combat religion by abolishing the common rest day. Factories were to be kept working incessantly day and night. The operatives were divided into five colours, or "labour calendars." On any given day or night four "colours" would be working, and the fifth colour enjoying a day of rest. A man and a wife would never have the same day off unless they were in the same "labour calendar." In a family of more working individuals it became still more difficult to synchronize the leisure time. Consequently, family ties were broken up as much as religion.

The colour system was given up in 1932; the labour week was lengthened to six days. A common rest was reintroduced for all. As in the French decadic calendar of the Revolution, the ultimate goal was not reached permanently. After a long period of conferences, the system formulated in 1936 seems to stabilize a calendar, which, though less radical, shows certain unique features still.

Whereas the year of 365 days remains divided into twelve months, two parallel weeks have been introduced, one of seven, and the other of six days. Labour, industry and rest are to be regulated by the shorter, government and international inter-

course by the longer. The rest days of the labour week fall
on the sixth, twelfth, eighteenth, twenty-fourth and thirtieth
day of each month, with March 1 taking the place of the fifth
rest day of February.

The number of extra holidays has now been fixed at five
of the first order and ten or twelve of secondary rank. They
were much more numerous before the revolution and during
the first ten years of the new régime. The first of five great
holidays is on January 22, and is known as Lenin's Day. Formerly there were two holidays, January 22, the anniversary
of the Father Gapon demonstration in 1905, when the police
fired on an unarmed crowd in front of the Emperor's palace;
January 21, the death of Lenin. Now, the two festivals have
been run into one. Curiously enough, Lenin's birthday on
April 22 is not observed as a full holiday. The next general
holiday is May Day, celebrated on May 1 and 2. November
7 and 8 are similarly put aside to celebrate the Bolshevist
Revolution in 1917. The character of the minor holidays is
mainly concomitant to the idea of May Day: Youth, Women,
Sports, Anti-War Days are typical of a movement that emphasizes the recurrence of human energies. A new polytheism of
group ideals is established. Great powers and principalities:
Labour, Youth, Womanhood, Peace sway this world in endless recurrence. They did not begin at any moment in time;
they are the essentials of the social order; one might expect
them to go on forever.

How far is the Russian Labour Calendar the practice of
Western Man already? How far is it not? With the Russians
work is made into a public function of the people united,
leisure is a private business. Formally, this calendar contradicts
our tradition in which each individual is toiling, bent on his
work, during the week, and comes into the common fellowship on Sundays only. However, the Russian shift in family
and religious tradition, its making work into a public function,
and rest into a private one, crystallized a movement that was
in progress throughout the industrial world. For even in Anglo-
Saxon countries, the common day of rest was slowly losing
its importance for more and more millions of people. Maids,

waiters, clerks in drugstores, people working in the pleasure industries, taxi drivers, telephone operators, are required to take off, not Sunday, but some other day picked at random, to allow production to continue more or less undiminished. And in this change in calendar, this abolition of "Sunday" for parts of the population, is implicit an emphasis upon the community of labour. The difference between the practice (not the theory) of Western Man and of the Russian Labour Calendar is one of degree. Leisure is becoming more and more a private affair, production is coming to the front as a common destiny. In America, some great manufacturing plants have rejected the twelve-month calendar and apply a thirteen-month calendar, each month containing twenty-eight days. This thirteen-month calendar enables a plant to check more conveniently the amount of production per month. It glorifies production and the goods that are produced; it no longer cares for the holidays of the whole community. It stands halfway, then, between a calendar which united people for worship only, and a calendar which unites the pepole who are working in shifts together.

RACIAL HISTORY.

History is dissolved into economics by the Russians, and the calendar pushes events into the background and presses the viewpoint of perpetual reproduction. A system of repetitive character challenges the human soul to its depth. For if all these dominations and powers rule our lives incessantly, liberty is gone. The only loophole for man's freedom under such a firmament of social constellations is to shift emphasis from some of these powers to others.

And in fact, the counter-revolutions against Sovietism were not capable of shaking off the framework of recurrent social forces. Instead, all the so-called national revolutions in Europe, opposed as they were to the Russian dictatorship of the proletarians, gave precedence to other abstract gods in their calendar, yet abstract dominations these gods were, too. The native elements of man, equally unhistorical as "labour" or "woman," are trimmed. Nordic profiles, motherhood, fatherhood, race, nation are celebrated. The fight against the class-war reaches its clearest expression in the invention of Racial War. Against a purely economic history, racial history is the appropriate antitoxin. Economics and race are both the least historical elements of our existence: they are the material into which the Promethean spark of history must fall in order to produce changes.

Racial history and a racial calendar flourish everywhere because they are the simplest way of reacting against economic Communism. They, too, camouflage the abolition of history by an allegedly historical cloak (like the birthday of the Roman nation in 753 B.C.), although the real issue is to present the peoples with something unchangeable and perpetual. The two facts, that man is born and that he is hungry, are the same everywhere and always; whereas history tells us what happened only once.

The economic and the racial historians are no longer historians in the old sense of the word; they are scientists of a new millennium of recurrence. On May Day, 1936, it was officially stated that the German people would follow the Egyptian example of the Pharaohs and their peasant-slaves and organize themselves into a body politic for the next four thousand years.

For a horizon of four thousand years, facts and events of fifteen or thirty years appear pretty meaningless. Pragmatic research is easily replaced by mythology; forgeries are welcomed which do away with petty particularities. The eyes of eternity scorn accurate detail and date.

Similar ideas advance today all over the world; with irresistible pressure they invade the textbooks of Turkey, Russia, Germany, Italy, etc.

Nations and individuals will always get what they sincerely crave. They may, therefore, be drowned in the economic and racial cycles into which the masses put their faith, precisely as the business men get their business cycle since they fail to revolt against it. However, there is a plurality of cyclical beliefs, a plurality of recurrent powers, and a plurality of calendars.

History-writing, in any responsible sense, cannot compromise with any group's one-sided myth or tales or holidays. Economic and racial history are a challenge to thought: we must transcend each fragmentary myth, each partial calendar. Each partial choice of man for one or the other eternal value is a decision made by inspired people in an hour of danger and despair. As an inspired decision the introduction of a new myth, a new calendar, a new social order, represents a part of the total order of things. No opposition can destroy the values represented by Labour, Nation, Constitution, Youth, etc. And we do not oppose, with analytical scepticism, the irresistible march of the group mind.

Instead, in our crucible, the calendars and values of the antagonistic groups are fused. Reality is bigger than any one of them. The races of faith are manifold. Economic recurrence itself has a birthday and origin in dramatic struggle. Our book goes beyond economic or racial history, because these are both only the last style imposed on history in our time. The style of history changes. We have had so much personal, dramatic, constitutional history that a correction is most appropriate.

However, the totalitarian history of mankind deals with the interplay of revolutionary styles and antagonistic inspirations. It understands each new type of history or calendar as a new branch on the same tree. The modern interest in recurrent life reacts against the interest taken during more than a century in individual life; for the myth of the French Revolution was neither racial nor economic. It dramatized the powers of genius and individuality. In taking stock of the permanent achievements of the French Revolution, we shall turn from economic history to history dramatized.

CHAPTER FIVE

France: The European Genius of the Île de France

Dramatized History—The Womb of Time—The Fight for "Europe"—The Cradle of Europe: Greece—Frankish Europe—Paris and the Rhine—Versailles— Huguenots and Jesuits—Privileges—The Nation: How the Bourgeois Was Made a Citizen—Voltaire's and Rousseau's Ideas—Freemasonry—The Constitution—The Tyranny of the Decimal System—Madame Curie—The "Nature" of France—The French Calendar—Capitalism Around France—The Emancipation of the Jews— Digression Alpha and Omega: Gentiles and Jews—The New Messianism—The "Affaire"—The Three Qualities of Higher Life—The Great Electorate: Who Can Govern a Nation?—Adam and Eve—The Pitfall of Reason—The Peasant of Paris —Checks on Individualism

DRAMATIZED HISTORY.

THE FRENCH REVOLUTION IS HIGHLY THEATRICAL: IT IS FULL OF dramatic events. *"Nous ne cédons qu'à la force des baïonnettes!"* exclaimed Mirabeau on June 23, 1789, being sure that no bayonets were at hand. The abolition of the privileges of clergy and nobility was voted in August with such enthusiasm that the members of the National Assembly sobbed and laughed. The gathering on the field of Mars to take the constitutional oath, the festival (or holiday) of Reason, the execution of King and Queen and so many thousands of aristocrats, were highly spectacular, aye, even histrionic.

In the Russian technique there is no place for a *bon mot* like Danton's remark to the executioner when Robespierre sent him to the scaffold: "Take care of my head—*Il vaut la peine*" (it is worth the trouble).

The terrible transportation of the royal family from Versailles to Paris, the wonderful eloquence of the convention— all this is performed with more charm and spirit than in the greatest tragedy. A monument in the Pantheon tries to express the fascination of the French Revolution by showing the lawyers arguing fervently, while out of their passionate words a gigantic drummer and an army of young men grow up and march eastward against the despots of the rest of Europe. Another sculptor gave to the Revolution the features of the tragic muse.

Early enough, the uniqueness of the French Revolution was felt by its contemporaries. Klopstock acclaimed the "bold Diet of Gaul" as the sunrise of a new day of mankind. Goethe proclaimed that the rather harmless manœuvre of the cannonade of Valmy, in 1792, began a new era in the history of the world.

The key of the Bastille was sent to Mount Vernon, and by its enshrinement in George Washington's home the taking of the Bastille on July 14, 1789, was baptized in the spirit of the American Declaration of Independence.

It had never happened before and will never happen again that events and minds, external decisions and internal reflections, should be on all fours as they were then. People knew what they did, and did what they knew. While history, up to that time, had been a foggy and misty process of accidents, catastrophes, causes and influences, mere turns of the wheel of fortune, crises and intrigues, now it suddenly ceased to be incomprehensible.

At once, everything became perfectly clear. There seemed to be, for good or ill, a harmony between the brains of men and the nature of events, a harmony which made Hegel remark: "It was a unique moment in the history of mankind. The world literally stood balanced on the human head. History had become conscious of itself. Heaven and earth seemed reconciled, because for the first time external fate and internal thought met in the same hour." The old order of things in France passed away irresistibly, as if by an earthquake, and men were mature enough to rise to the situation.

Most people have forgotten today that the French Revolution seemed a miracle because of this coincidence of free will and inevitable crisis. The Russian Revolution, with its century-long preparation in cold blood, has weakened our sense of

wonder at such a coincidence. We assume that revolutions happen because they are planned. But this supposition is without
foundation in reality. Announced revolutions do not happen.
Killing, murdering, destroying, breaking down, cannot be
planned. The revolution in Austria in 1934 failed because it
was planned. A revolution must overwhelm us as other passions
do. Jealousy can lead to murder. All the passions, we know
from the stage, can lead to personal revolution and rebellion.
The French, with the sure instinct of dramatists of life, knew
that Reason could not make a revolution: Reason could only
master it when it had happened. For the French Revolution
any notion of a previous plan, conspiracy or premeditation
would be worthless. The miracle of it is the marriage of an
unreasonable world with the reason of man. Hence the French
use of the word *"Révolution"* is different from its use in Russian or English, or German or Italian terminology. This is what
I wish to demonstrate first.

Liberal historians of the nineteenth century identified the
outbreak of the French Revolution with the first acts of the
Three Estates, as they were summoned from their grave and
met at Versailles in May, 1789. Mirabeau's remark to the King's
Lord Chamberlain about the force of bayonets is one of the
occasions which, to the peaceful writer of moderate imagination, symbolize the outbreak of the Revolution. But nobody
thought this way in 1789. In re-reading Mirabeau, Camille
Desmoulins, or the foreign diplomats, one nowhere finds the
word "revolution" applied to the events either of June or of
the first eight days of July. The courtiers and diplomats, very
pessimistic as they were, spoke of rebellion, insurrection, civil
war; the reformers desired "reforms," restoration of old rights,
and regeneration of France. "Regeneration" especially was the
favourite expression of Mirabeau, and was obviously the slogan
of the day. These two lists do not meet. The liberals saw the
blessings of a new order which they desired in the future; the
old statesmen felt the illegitimacy of the means.

The term "Revolution" became the plank which bridged
the gulf between backward- and forward-looking thought.

On the fourteenth of July the Parisian mob defeated the garrison of the Bastille, the state prison corresponding to the Tower in London. The demagogue, Camille Desmoulins, the King's Lord Chamberlain, Count Liancourt, the American diplomat Gouverneur Morris, and a detached French scholar all agreed immediately, on the fifteenth of July, that this was the Revolution. Here it was. An explosion had occurred which belonged to the realm of fact. This change in the world of Fact could be matched and had to be matched by an intelligent judgment in the field of Reason. This dualism became the attitude of the French throughout the next twenty-six years. They were either revolutionaries, loyal to what had happened, or else counter-revolutionaries, trying to *undo* what had happened! A long essay by one of the standard-bearers of the first revolutionary years, the popular philosopher Condorcet, reveals the startling fact that the word "revolutionary," as a noun or an adjective, did not exist before 1789. The English used the word "revolutionist" for the adherents of the Whigs after 1688. The Americans had no adjective throughout the whole Revolutionary War. As late as 1791 Patrick Henry had to speak of the "Revolution War" in his speeches, because "revolutionary" did not exist! It would have meant "insurgent"; and the Americans did not want to be insurgents. They stood for civil law and order against the British troops.

But the French invented the word [1] to designate the men who stood *with their reason on the side of the revolution!* The whole modern vocabulary of "revolutionize," "ultra-revolutionary," "counter-revolutionary" is French. It is an old objective and descriptive word which is now embraced as the expression of subjective passion:

". . . and, too, the word *Révolution*. This word also had always existed. There had been revolutions in Rome, in England. There had been one recently in America. This word was known, was used on occasion, like such a word, say, as phalanx or centurion, but

---

[1] The only older quotation I can find is in the early papers of Gouverneur Morris. He there allegedly uses "revolutionary" in the general meaning of unstable, revolving. But the phrasing of the whole passage is probably an invention of the editor Sparks, who is well known to have been careless about his sources.

the occasions were rare. And then all of a sudden one day a king is told: *'Une révolte? C'est une révolution!'* And the word commences its whirlwind career. *'Une révolution? C'est la révolution!'* Its article is changed from the indefinite to the definite. It acquires a capital R, if not capitals throughout. It becomes a proper noun. From being the mere general name of a political movement, a word on a par with 'battle' or 'war' or 'invasion,' the mere synonym, more or less extant, of *révolte, sédition, insurrection, rébellion,* it now becomes one of the most individual of words, one of the most powerful. He who could say now: *'La révolution, c'est moi,'* would wield a greater, a more violent power, than had he who said, *'L'État, c'est moi.'* *La Révolution,* in the minds of many, now replaces *l'état, le gouvernement, l'église, le roi,* even *Dieu.* It has swept all these from their seats of authority. The most potent word to conjure with is now not these, but *La Révolution.* It now does for the people what these words once did for kings.

"The power of the word may be seen by the vigour of the growth it put forth. Before 1789, the family consisted, as given in Féraud, of the solitary word *Révolution.* Now we find *révolutionner, révolutionnaire* (noun and adjective) . . . fourteen words as compared with a single word before." [2]

From France the word was imported into the other countries. Slowly "revolutionary" came to replace "revolutionist" in England. As in cases like "Lord Treasurer" or "Whig," it took the English a century to adopt the French terminology. If the English today speak of the Prime Minister, instead of the First Lord of the Treasury, or of a Liberal instead of a Whig, of revolutionaries instead of revolutionists, they are using words of French origin.

After the fourteenth of July, the whole French nation reacted to the destruction of the Bastille in the same way as Liancourt in his famous reply to Louis XVI. The King had stammered: "But this is a rebellion." "No, sire," the courtier replied, "this is the Revolution." For the rest of that summer the country was visited by the inexplicable *"grande peur."* [3] In the depths of their souls the people felt that the world was

[2] H. J. Swann, *French Terminologies in the Making,* p. 163 f., New York, Columbia Univ. Press, 1918.

[3] Georges Lefèbvre, *La Grande Peur,* Paris, Armand Colin, 1932.

out of joint. It was like Goethe's intuition in *The Natural Daughter:* "These great elements will no longer embrace each other with the force of love unceasingly renewed. Now each evades the other and withdraws coldly into itself." *"La grande peur"* is the majestic reaction of the popular instinct to a decisive break in tradition. Mad rumours spread over the country. None of them proved true. But their content was not the significant event: it was this complete paralysis of will and reason, the deep insight that one was no longer safe on land. A sea of passion had opened, and the French nation was destined for long to be on this high sea of Revolution. Thus the allegedly inexplicable *Grande Peur* of the summer of 1789 is the most explicable event of the whole Revolution. Shall dogs and horses scent a thunderstorm, and man not sense the breakdown of a social order that has lasted a thousand years? It shows the hopeless aridity of bourgeois historiography that the *Grande Peur* is always treated as something special and provincial, whereas without such an evidence we should despair of finding any deeper instinct in our race.

All the actions of men between 1789 and 1794 are attempts to find a rational formula for the Revolution. First the good and superficial men thought they could find the open sesame in English principles. Self-government was their slogan: every part of France was to get autonomy. This would have meant turning the wheel of history backward beyond the reign of Henry IV; and it very soon proved impracticable. Condorcet exclaimed, on July 23, 1791, "A nation of 24,000,000, or an area of 27,000 square miles—can it become a republic?" Robespierre and Napoleon were both monarchists in 1791. Two days after the assault on the Bastille a leader said: "A Mediterranean kingdom like France, lying between two terribly great powers, needs an executive which is completely in the hands of the King." Federalism was a still-born child. But Republicanism seemed impossible, too. The republics of the time were aristocracies: Venice, Switzerland, Geneva, the United States (in pre-Jefferson days), were clearly oligarchic. We shall see later why an aristocracy was much more offensive to the French than a monarchy. Here we discover again the complete candour of the French revolutionaries. They tried to find out what the principle of the Revolution was: a revolution raging in the streets had to be interpreted by the orators in the assemblies! Reason, the interpreter, expounds the meaning of the pictures that move swiftly across the streets and squares of Paris. Now that the Bastille was destroyed, *a strong executive without a Bastille* was the problem before the French nation—a true paradox. Each successive government set to work to interpret the true nature of the Revolution. First, in 1791, a "law paramount" to supplant royal caprice. In 1792 the Convention mobilized the nation against the despots of Europe. *"L'Étendard sanglant est levé."* In 1794 Robespierre defends the Revolution against both the ultra-revolutionaries and the infra-revolutionaries (left and right wings). The adherents of an English system and the precursors of the Bolshevik solution (Hébert, with his idea of permanent, recurrent waves of mob-revolution) are both crushed. From 1795 to 1798 the *"Directoire"* tries to compromise between a powerful executive for war and a moderate government at home. When it fails, in 1798, the whole nation embarks on the European campaigns of Napoleon, postponing the internal solution for which neither men nor measures exist. Napoleon fills the gap between the Revolutionary events and ideas and a stabilized order of things. Napoleon was the son of the Revolution. His letters to Josephine from the Italian campaign affect us like the poetry of a lover who touches off the whole outside world like a display of fireworks in honour of his mistress. In the days of the Terror "the Revolution had devoured its own children." But this saying was even truer of Napoleon's own destiny. He was the giant of the third estate, summing up in himself the talents and qualities, the desires and passions, of the man of the street. He was no hero in the high sense of the word. He did not make himself. He was made by time, by the Revolution; and he was undone when he was no longer able to interpret the Revolution. His mother, Letitia, had felt this dependence when, hearing of his success, she said, "That's very pretty—'*Pourvu que cela dure!*' (Providing it lasts)." It could not last when Napoleon ceased to be a child of the Revolution. His second marriage, his idea of quoting Louis XVI as his uncle, made him impossible. As a legitimate and hereditary ruler, he was finished. When the regicides of 1792, Talleyrand and Fouché, kissed the hands of His Majesty Louis XVIII, because he seemed the lesser evil, Napoleon was superfluous.

Louis XVIII, to be sure, was no interpreter of the French Revolution. But his remark on his return (1815)—"Everything is unchanged, only one more good Frenchman is in France"— shows the compromise that had been reached at that time. The government is no longer the interpreter of the great volcanic eruption; the Revolution is ended. But on the other hand, the government remains passive toward the actual results of the Revolution; these results—the distribution of the wealth of clergy and aristocracy among the buyers at the Revolutionary sales—were recognized. And a "charter" guaranteed the old Law Paramount of 1791. The Constitution made its entrance into Paris in the train of Louis XVIII himself.

Before returning to the "interpretation of the Revolution" by its reasonable adherents, we may briefly survey its later steps. The upheaval of 1789 was levelled out in 1815, and the Bourbon restoration lasted from 1815 to 1830. But the stupidity, or the sincerity, of Charles X threatened the ownership of the revolutionized lands, and the rights of Revolutionary minds. The Revolution of July, 1830, was mentioned in our first chapter, though as an epilogue instead of a prologue, as a parallel to the first Russian Revolution of 1905. Being an epilogue, the July Revolution was like an explosion in the air, compared to the earthquake and fires of the great Revolution. When old Lafayette mounted his horse, as if it were 1789 again, he made a poor show. Flesh and blood were gone; only an anæmic ghost was left upon the scene. But it was again a theatrical and conscious scene. As in 1789, when National Assembly and populace rivalled each other, so in 1830 the two props of the Revolution acted separately. The doers and fighters met at the City Hall, and the interpreters, Guizot, Thiers, and Talleyrand, at the Palais Bourbon. As in 1789, the "real meaning of the Revolution" was not discovered by the military forces of the Revolution, but by the unarmed intellectuals on the other bank of the Seine. On their advice, the Bourgeois King, Louis Philippe, dressed in a general's uniform as "lieutenant-general" of the kingdom, and wearing the tricolour, rode across the river from the Palais Bourbon to the Hôtel de Ville. Crowds of people watched this famous ride, for the point of it was to see what the republican fighters would do. It was Lafayette who ended the crisis by appearing on the balcony of the Hôtel de Ville and embracing Louis Philippe before all the people. The doers had recognized the interpretation of the thinkers.

After 1830, the dramatic course of the French Revolution leads to the third act: a time of extreme presumption and vanity on the part of the ruling class. Though they owed their close victory to the helplessness of the armed republicans around Lafayette, they plunged into orgies of capitalism. France was then the paradise of "gigmanity," as Carlyle called the middle classes, the *"juste-milieu."* Between 1830 and 1848 corruption penetrated to the very marrow of the bourgeois society. In carrying the umbrella, despised by the English gentleman of those days as a poor middle-class invention, the King, with all his great talents and merits, had capitulated to the wealth of this class. Even today the umbrella has political value in France. In the strike of 1908 the Préfet de Police of Paris, Lépine, won his popularity by being visible everywhere with his great umbrella. The head of the police, unarmed, but with an umbrella!—Louis Philippe, himself a gentleman, encouraged the middle class with his famous phrase: *"Enrichissez-vous."* Lamartine pronounced this tragic verdict on the period: "France was *annoyed* by the untheatrical régime of Louis Philippe and his *juste-milieu.* His reasonable policy broke down because it could not make up for the unsatisfied lust for glory and expansion."

This period of arrogance was relieved by a fourth act, the period of humiliation. When, in 1848, the republican workers again mounted the barricades, and tried to avoid the mistakes of 1830, they fell into the trap of a much worse reaction still. The tender dream of 1830 had resulted in the careful policy of a *juste-milieu* King. The real atrocities of 1848 conjured up a real Cæsarism. Napoleon III was not definitely replaced by the Law Paramount until 1875, when the republican form of government was carried by one vote.

The reign of Napoleon III was a period of shame and disillusion. *"Passivement subi, le second empire a marqué, d'une façon décisive chez nous, une diminution de foi dans l'idéologie combattive de la révolution française aussi bien que dans la supériorité des armées libératrices."* (Clemenceau.) Ideas and events, revolutionary interpretations and revolutionary wars, were devaluated during this painful fourth act, which ended in the loss of the Franco-Prussian War, the quartering of the Prussians at Versailles, and the shooting and deportation of 50,000 Communists in Paris.

The fifth act established the republic. The solution, a *"république des camarades,"* was what it had to be after 1789: it meant a strong executive without a Bastille. The Chamber, meeting at Versailles from 1871 to 1879 on account of the unrest in Paris, felt that it had to reconcile the monarchical traditions of Versailles and the liberal aspirations of Paris. It proclaimed that the Fourteenth of July, 1789, should be celebrated as the great Birthday of Liberty. It enacted that the election of the president of the republic should take place in Versailles by the vote of the Senate and the deputies of the Chamber. Who knows whether, in the raging tempest of 1919, if the election had been held in Paris, the electorate would not have voted as it had promised, for Clemenceau, father of victory? But in the tranquillity of Versailles the quiet citizen, Paul Deschanel, though a paralytic, was elected.

The five acts of the French Revolution bear sharp marks of beginning and ending. There is no doubt when a period begins or ends. It is a great play acted in the sunlight of consciousness, with all the *clarté* of the French *esprit:*

1789   July 14—Bastille demolished

1789   Rest of the summer—*Grande Peur*

$$\text{I}\ \begin{cases} 1789\text{-}1792\ (95) & \text{Internal Revolution} \\ 1792(95)\text{-}1815 & \text{External Revolutionary Wars} \end{cases} \begin{cases} \text{Period of} \\ \text{volcanic} \\ \text{eruption} \end{cases}$$

The different forms of government "interpret" the Revolution.

II   1815-1830 The results of the Revolution upheld; the government pre-revolutionary. Period of incubation.

III   1830-1848 July Revolution.
        The bourgeois monarchy.
        Period of pride.

IV   1848-1875 February Revolution.
        Napoleon III—*La Commune*.
        Period of humiliation.

V   1875   The Third Republic.

THE WOMB OF TIME.

The dramatic course of events enables us, in looking backward, to perceive a curve. Legal tradition once washed away in 1789, floods inundate the country like a mighty unleashing of subterranean forces.

As long as the floods increase, people try to hold them back (period of internal constitutional experiments, until 1792). But the revolutionary tides prevent any partial salvation. The inundation is complete, the only possibility is to swim on top of the flood. Wars become the natural outlet in face of the impossibility of finding solid ground at home. They create the environment in which the new France can live. In 1815 the inundation ceases. The flood, after all its changes and devastations, seems to have gone down.

In 1830 it is realized that the waters are streaming still, and a permanent curb for the well of revolutionary ideas is built for the first time. The curb is frail. The waters seep out beyond control.

From 1848 to 1875 they are suppressed again; the symbols of the previous period of revolutionary wars act as a soporific (Napoleon III).

Neither the suppression nor the soporific is effective. Napoleon III cannot conquer, as his uncle had done, because there is no flood of real revolution to support him. He himself must hurry to announce, *"L'Empire, c'est la paix,"* in sharp contrast to the frequent wars he undertakes.

The fifth act, the "government by inspired individuals," we will analyze later. Here we are contemplating the curve as a whole; and it points to the important fact that human affairs seem to follow in a reasonable order.

One break in legality leads to such a period as the First Republic, of which Victor Cousin remarked: "The First Republic was not a form of state, but a crisis." The name must

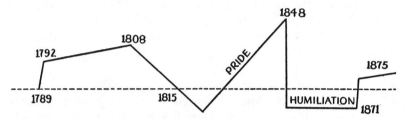

not mislead us. The babble of dictators or revolutionary leaders crying for legality is not legality.

The constitution of France is based on a period of twenty-six years during which it lived without real legal foundations. "Revolution is the larva of civilization." (Victor Hugo.)

But it is impossible to pass from the stage of revolution to the stage of evolution by a mere lapse of time. The mechanical evaluation of time might lead us to suppose that the French Revolution should have developed farther in 1855 than in 1840. This is a fallacy which makes history the slave of natural science. The curve 1789–1815 Inundation, 1815–1830 Incubation, 1830–1848 Pride, 1848–1875 Humiliation, shows that the history of man is very unmathematical. It goes by leaps and bounds.

The scheme given above does not at all claim to be perfect, but is inserted as a protest against the flat notion that time is a straight line reaching from 1789 to 1934, with years marked off upon it like inches or centimetres on a yardstick. Man's time, unlike space, has no yardstick!

The curve will have to be studied more carefully later, when we know more about the other total revolutions of mankind.

The Russian curve, of course, is still unknown, but we can keep its contrast to the French curve in mind from now on.

The curves of history are not like the recurrent formulas of physics; but they exist and remind us that "nothing disappears which the hours of men have conceived in their womb." The days of the sun, the years of the stars, are not the same as the hours of men. The hours of history are created in a special field of force where distant events call to each other from century to century.

In Russia the two streams of action split as early as 1825 and 1861. The Revolution was inevitable once a reconciliation between them had become impossible. This "nihilism" began in the sixties, two generations before the open and visible outburst. The body politic was afflicted by the bursting of old sores; by themselves, they were long forgotten, but they had a decisive effect on the course of events even a century later. The date 1685 in our diagram hints at a similar problem in France. Superficially, the Huguenots, the Protestants, had as little to do with 1789 as the Russian nobles of 1825 with the proletarians of 1917. But without their grievances the French Revolution might have been nothing more than a national event. The sore spot of the body politic in France was of European, world-wide, origin. The Huguenots represented a Christian and a human injustice. It was not a French, it was a human, reaction which found expression in the French Revolution. We all, in so far as we are human, are present and represented on the stage of the French Revolution. To it, the category of totality applies. National, even nationalistic, as it worked out in the end, it began as a great crusade to discover the nature of the individual man in Europe. The expulsion of the Huguenots could not be expiated by the simple restoration of Protestantism in France. Interwoven as it was with the fate of *the* oldest University in Christendom, that is, Paris, it could only be avenged by a more general restoration of nature, by a total revolution in the relations between individual will and natural law.

THE FIGHT FOR "EUROPE."

France, one fortieth the size of Russia, is "the centre of Europe." This alone is a revolutionary statement. And it is perfectly fitting to say that *"L'Europe"* is the creation of the French Revolution. For us, who live in the same world with "Eurasia," that is, of a Russia which has become a global force and a special continent, the idea of such a sudden creation may have lost its oddity. But the average dweller in a European town during the nineteenth century believed dogmatically that *"L'Europe"* was an eternal reality and Paris, its established and undoubted centre, "the Mecca of civilization," as Victor Hugo had christened it.

When, after the War, M. E. Ravage wrote his *Malady of Europe,* and G. Lowes Dickinson his *The European Anarchy,* they honestly believed that Europe was one civilization which could and should be rebuilt and reorganized.

But it is not without its danger that America's schoolboys are taught to believe in the real existence of a thing called "Europe." "England," for example, seems rather European to the man from Nebraska. But in 1927 there was published at Oxford *A History of Europe and the Modern World* by R. B. Mowat, which expressed a different opinion. The book covers a space of 400 years (1500-1918); but Elizabeth, Cromwell, Pitt are not mentioned. And this is not a slip of an inattentive pen, for the author wishes "to increase the understanding of the unity of European civilization!" A man cannot be more in earnest. Here, an Englishman divides the apple which the American schoolboy calls Europe into two parts, and lumps the whole continent outside England as one separate civilization!

The Russians, again, have destroyed the unity of Europe from their Eurasian viewpoint. As early as 1853 a book of Danilevski's became the bible of the Panslavists because it denied that the term "Europe" could be of any geographical value. Danilevski could rely upon the fact that before 1730 Russia was not reckoned as European. Before that year the maps showed Europe bounded, not by the Ural Mountains as

today, but by the river Don, leaving two thirds of what we
call European Russia to Asia! Europe had a moving frontier
toward the East! No wonder that an influential writer, Mr.
Spengler, waged war on the largest scale against the use of the
word "Europe." It has no meaning whatever to him, and he
himself prefers the expressions West, Occident. But this, too, is
obviously ambiguous. One quotation from the geographer
Ritter, in 1817, might have warned Spengler. Ritter exclaimed:
"When America was discovered, the European Occident became an Orient"—a change which is very inconvenient for the
"Occident."

The few instances given here seem to justify the sullen remark of Disraeli in *Lothair*, one of his novels on early Victorian
policy: "The change of name from Christendom to Europe has
proved a failure, and a disastrous one. And what wonder?
Europe is not even a quarter of the globe!"

But failure or no failure, it has been done. You cannot kill
a word like "Europe" simply by ignoring it; it must be buried.
And the words of Disraeli open the door at least wide enough
so that we can see from which room our patient must be taken
to the cemetery. Europe, as Disraeli says, is not even a quarter
of the globe. At the same time, it is a change from Christendom.

> Christendom is pre-French
> Europe   is French
> Globe   is Russian

This little list protects us from the misapprehension that in
"European civilization" "Europe" was thought of as one continent among others. The words "Christendom" and "Globe"
clearly stand for a totality. Now wherever the word "Europe" is
used with emphasis it rests on the same ambition: it shall be
valid for all mankind. Combinations like European civilization,
culture, science, arts, cathedrals, make sense because they embrace Spain and Sweden, Ireland and Dalmatia in a tacit unity.
The multi-coloured political map of the small Western peninsula of Asia is illuminated as soon as we use the word "Europe"
for it. Then its geographical variety is dignified. Europe means
diversity in unity. The wealth of European civilization, its

marvellous paradoxes and achievements, are all dependent on the complete freedom of its nations. Europe is a kaleidoscope of independent parts; that is a condition of her cultural superiority.

"Europe" is not a geographical but a moral value. It may be criticized by German, Russian and other writers; but the name expresses a desire for the *independence of many nations in one universal civilization,* and as such it has served its purpose well. It cannot be dismissed until its origin and aim have been more clearly stated than they can be by attacks from the outside.

THE CRADLE OF EUROPE: GREECE.

Europeans, *"gute Europäer,"* good Europeans, in Friedrich Nietzsche's term, must tell us what they wished to express by this appellation. What, indeed, did Europe stand for? It was intended as a response, and a loving response, from the West to the old myth of the East. Everybody knows of a similar response: I mean the response made by the Western tribes to the East during the Middle Ages, when the Frankish Knights vanquished the troops of the Sultan and conquered Jerusalem. They gave back to the Holy Place in the East the physical liberty it had lost. For this Christian gentry owed its intellectual deliverance from the fetters of fear, human sacrifice and demoniac superstitions to the gospel which hailed from Jerusalem.

The Crusaders quoted the verse of the Bible: "I will bring thy seed from the East and gather thee from the West," and they said what the Europeans might have said later: "God has already brought our seed from the East. But he will also gather it from the West, provided he repairs the wrongs of Jerusalem through those who have to be the first witnesses to the ultimate faith, that is, through the people of the West."

These words of the French chronicler Guibert of Nogent apply equally well to the spirited response which is given by the French, and especially by French revolutionary ideas, to the eastern parts of Europe. The French Revolution enamoured Western man of the classic traditions of Hellas, of Greece.

Replace Jerusalem by Greece, and the stream of inspiration

which freed the Eastern cradle of humanity, Greece and Crete, from the yoke of the Turks during the nineteenth century takes its legitimate place in the history of the ideas of 1789. All Europe rallied to the resurrection of Greece. Lord Byron, the very genius of modern Europe, went there. As late as 1897, during the Turko-Greek War, we are told that Benjamin Wheeler, President of the University of California, roused his students to a frenzy of enthusiasm for the modern Hellenes. The terrible mistake of the Greek in expanding in Asia Minor after the Great War was the furthest step in this Greek Renaissance, which was carried on under the protectorate of Western civilization throughout the nineteenth century. When Kemal Pasha smashed Greece, drove 10,000 Greeks into the sea, and created a new Turkey, the climax of Greek regeneration had passed. Here, too, the Great War brought about a moral revolution. Today Greece is one nation among others. In the nineteenth century it was much more: it was a hostage, a pawn that had to be ransomed. The *"esprit" de l'Europe,* the modern mind, reflected itself in Greece. Any French scholar or politician, even in a special monograph, will end by burning a few grains of incense in honour of Athens. In the France of the nineteenth century such different men as Clemenceau, Renan and Taine offer this same eulogy. The Count de Gobineau, in writing a poem on his mediæval hero Amadis, cannot help a complete outburst when he mentions the classics:

"Et toi, Athènes, Athènes, Athènes, Athènes."

"Hellas ewig unsere Liebe" (To Hellas our eternal love), sings the most influential German poet of the last generation. The nineteenth century might be called *the Grecianizing century.*

The Olympiad again united all the nations of the civilized world into one Olympia bent on winning the prize in fair and loyal sports and games.

A loving arm stretched back from the West to the East, a grateful echo of the former hegemony of Greece—this is the attitude of the Occident when it calls itself "Europe."

And the matter has an even wider bearing on all our cultural values. I ask permission to narrate more in detail the resurrection of "Europe" as an ultimate ideal.

FRANKISH EUROPE.

A thousand years ago Charlemagne tranformed the Gaulish tradition of his Frankish kingdom into a larger conception. On his expeditions through the Continent he went as far as Hungary. His empire was no longer the Gaul of St. Martin of Tours, but neither did he, since he hated the New Romans in Byzantium, wish to be the head of a Roman Empire. So his enlargement of Gaul into a whole continent was first labelled the Kingdom of Europe. This Europe centred in "Francia," and stretched from it toward the other parts of the continent: Spain, Italy, the Balkans, Germany, Denmark, and so on. Here already was a complete break with the ancient notion of a Europe which began in Crete, had its sharply defined boundary at the Dardanelles, and extended westward to the Pillars of Hercules. Two points show the difference. The latitude of Charlemagne's Europe is about ten degrees more northerly than that of the classical, and its centre of gravity is exactly on the opposite side of the continent.

The Carolingian conception is still true today. Wherever Europe expanded, as in the "European Messenger" of St. Petersburg, it expanded eastward from the old Frankish centre.

But another feature had to be added later. The Europe of Charlemagne was one Empire; and this united rule by an emperor soon came to be labelled again with the traditional word "Roman." Europe disappeared for a long time, to be restored by the Humanists of the Renaissance. In 1450 Pope Pius II, Æneas Silvius, wrote a book on Europe in which he praised the humanistic and classical associations of the name. His contemporary, Lorenzo Valla, who detected the great forgeries of documents in the Western church, recommended the use of Europe as a fresh, unspoiled word to replace Occident. A century later the geographer Wechel dedicated a map to the emperor Charles V, which showed Europe as "The Queen Virgin." His successor, Postel of Augsburg, explained it thus in 1561: "Europe is portrayed, as a woman, beginning on the side of Spain. Spain is the head, France the left shoulder, Germany the breast, Italy the right arm, and Turkey and Poland the lower parts of the body." And Postel adds: "This picture of Europe can be associated with the unity of Christendom and the true hegemony of Japhet."

Here again "Europe" was used like "Christendom" as a value for *hegemony* and of *unity,* in spite of its many different political divisions. The term "Europe" keeps neutrality between Pope and Emperor, kings and princes, nations and countries. Europe is the expression of a faith which believes in unity *without visible political unity.*

In this sense of an invisible moral unity behind the separate political bodies, Europe served as the title of the great review of the seventeenth century, the *Theatrum Europæum.* Yet it is often equated with the word "Christendom," as any selection of tracts of the time will show. For example, in 1690 the English, in debating their future policy, waver somewhat between the three expressions "Christendom," "Europe" and "World," exactly as Disraeli did in *Lothair.* The famous rule of the balance of power was explained in this way in 1690: "Our predecessors ever held this to be a fundamental Maxim of their Conduct, to hold the balance equal between these two great Monarchies in Europe. By which means they made themselves the arbitrators of Christendom. By remaining neutral we cannot eschew being exposed friendless to the reproaches of all the rest of *Christendom,* whereby the name of Englishmen will remain so much in the oblivion of *Europe* that nobody will scarce remember there is such a nation in the *World.*"

As late as 1800 a German poet wrote a proclamation entitled *Europe or Christianity,* with the intention of putting both on all fours again. But it was too late. In one country at least, Europe and Christianity had ceased to be interchangeable. This definite break was due to the French Revolution. The same French who dared to ally themselves with the Infidel Turks as early as 1524, the French whose King Louis XIV locked himself up in his room in a great rage when all Christendom was in glee over the defeat of the Turks before Vienna in 1683, the

French who were the first nation in Europe to enjoy the foreign customs of the *Lettres Persanes* and the *Arabian Nights,* now abolished all audible and visible connection between the Christian past and their European civilization.

In the mouth of the Frenchman *"Europe"* means a field of action for the philosopher, the artist, the thinker, the democrat, the Republican, the soldier and last, not least, a market for the fashions of Paris.

Shortly before the Revolution a Minister of Louis XVI wrote to his king: *"France is situated in the middle of Europe."* France is—in every respect—the centre of the field of force which we call Europe in terms like: "Trip to Europe," "European standards," "European literature," "European civilization."

None of the other European countries is in the centre of Europe in this deeper sense. The Central Powers were called "Boches" "Huns," "barbarians," and *"Autres chiens"* during the War, but certainly not Europeans. This seemed perfectly consistent with the ideal use of "Europe," because Central Europe is only a geographical section of a continent, whereas the centre of Europe is something very French, lying in the French sphere of influence. Europe is the totality for which France sets the pattern. In other words, Europe is Christendom restored to the classical values. These values are threefold:

> Democracy
> Liberalism, and
> Nationalism;

and the essence of all three values is contained in the French word *civilisation.*

The ideas of the French Revolution repeated in national and natural language the claims of France within mediæval Christendom. In the great days of the University of Paris, Ægidius of Corbeil (1224) could sing of

> *"Francia, cuius ad exemplum reliquus formabitur orbis . . .*
> *Inque brevi spatio*
> *Totus ab Ecclesia fidei purgabitur error."*

"France, to the pattern of which the rest of the world will be shaped, and in a short time all error of faith will be purged from the Church." This could have been written in 1789, with the slight difference that the new conformity to the pattern of France is based on a natural orthodoxy instead of on the faith of the Church.

This natural orthodoxy is embodied by the nation. But a nation, in the European sense of the word, is its literature! And the sources of this new French pattern for the organization of Europe are literary sources. This sovereign literature is studied or written in France, acclaimed by the clerics (as the *"écrivains de France"* can still be called today in a famous book, *La Trahison des Clercs*), made known in Paris, made into law in France, and carried by Napoleon's soldiers across Europe.

Even the antagonists of the French Revolution soon bowed before the idea of "Europe." The leaders of German romanticism, in 1810, founded a review called *Europe*. The King of Prussia published a summons to arms against the French in 1813 with the argument, "My cause is the cause of all the men of good will in Europe." In 1814, when the Allies against the French began to organize the Continent, they built up the European Concert, without the pope, as a purely secular community of nations. (In 1856 the Islamic Sultan of Turkey joined the European Concert.) The leaders of the emancipation of the Jews called Christian baptism the ticket of admission to European civilization! Another example: in the thirties of the nineteenth century all the non-democratized governments of the old world faced revolutionary movements of young Poles, young Germans, young Italians, etc. All these groups recognized their affinity by calling the whole movement "Young Europe."

In the time of Napoleon III the Germans and the Italians, even without or against the French, waged wars that were clearly French in ideology. The ideas of the French Revolution, democracy, liberalism and nationalism, brought about the union of Italy and Germany, brought about the Civil War in America and the emancipation of the peasants in Russia; it brought about the universal franchise, even without taxation, in England and Germany in 1867.

Europe was a great and powerful reality during the nineteenth century. This reality of course exercised no absolute domination. Romanticists like Disraeli complained of its failure, Russian prophets slated it for death. Yet it was the war cry of a real crusade; and whoever, in any part of Europe, carried on this crusade for liberty, fraternity, equality, was the partisan of the French Revolution. Any liberal (manufacturer, banker, artist, physician, Jew, writer, journalist, tradesman) tried to be a good European because this meant nothing more nor less than being a citizen of the liberal civilization introduced by the French Revolution.

Through this survey we have reached the conclusion that Europe, with its peculiar culture centring in France and radiating eastward and all over the world, though it had a long previous history, became a definite power and tendency only through the force of the Revolution. The contribution of the French Revolution to European civilization very often seems to be exaggerated in French tradition. But the French are perfectly sincere, because European civilization is the result of the French Revolution, and conversely the Revolution had just one world-wide purpose and programme: to civilize Europe!

The American reader will perhaps object: "How is it possible to limit the effect of the French Revolution to 'Europe'?" One answer is that America had started her revolution so early that she was safe and did not need help like the unfortunate countries in Europe which had kings or emperors. But this answer would not be quite to the point, because Bolivar did in fact depend on French ideas for the deliverance of South America.

But to France the value of "Europe" was immense and irreplaceable, because it suggested the old Greek and Classical world. The French Revolution, in going back to ancient Rome and Greece, intentionally kept within the limits of "Europe," because the very word guaranteed the new boundaries of France.

Francia, the territories of the Kings of France, became *"la France une et indivisible"* of today, thanks to the support which the French found in antiquity. Without the vocabulary of the Classics, neither Nice nor Savoy nor Alsace-Lorraine could be French today! It was the classical passion of the French that made them call the historical map of antiquity the "true Nature" to which Europe had to be restored. France became the Gaul of Cæsar's day, with the Rhine, the Mediterranean Sea, the Alps and the Lake of Geneva (Lacus Lemannus) for its frontiers, as described by Cæsar in his book on his wars in Gaul. The Netherlands, which the French tried to annex during their first revolution, had at least, as an outcome of the second French Revolution in 1830, to be divided into Belgium and the Netherlands; and the very name Belgium, a schoolmaster's invention, is a good example of the incredible dominance of classicism over the Europe of the French Revolution. Unable to replace the old name of France by "Gaul," the French succeeded at least in communicating their main idea to their Northern neighbours by transforming them into a third of Gaul, into the "Belgæ" of antiquity. It is ironical enough that the most Germanic and Frankish part of Europe, Flanders, should be called by the pre-Germanic name of Belgium. It reminds one of the story about King Albert. When he was hailed at Paris as the great representative of French and European civilization, the official speaker was asked what he personally thought of the Belgian ruler. He is said to have answered, *"Il n'y a pas de plus Boche."*

PARIS AND THE RHINE.

Napoleon III was the last Frenchman who tried openly to annex the "third third" of Cæsar's Gaul—Belgium. But the history of the "natural frontier" of France keeps its fascination even for the present day. The rest of Europe had to pay the bill for this natural frontier, because all her border-lines were changed to agree with it. Wilson's Fourteen Points and the frontiers of the Peace Treaties are the high-water mark of "natural frontiers." In America the natural frontier seems easy to find: the continent is encircled by two oceans. But even there, Canada and Mexico, Puerto Rico and Bermuda, Alaska and Hawaii, are as many demonstrations of the absence of natural frontiers.

The history of France can be read as a highly realistic lesson in the frontier problem. A millennium before 1789, Gallia and Germania, that is, a bundle of old Roman provinces, had been conquered by the Franks. Later, the Frankish Kingdom was divided. One third of Gaul remained under the old dynasty, one third, Burgundy and the South, was given up, and the last third of the old Gaulish territory remained united to the eastern territories. Trèves, the German "Trier," "Augusta Treverorum" of the Roman emperors, was always called the capital of Gaul during the Middle Ages; at the same time, it was the See of the chief prelate of the German emperors, and remained so until 1806. Aachen, Aix-la-Chapelle, was the regular scene of the Teuton kings' coronation. Strassburg, Basel, Worms and Speyer, all on the left bank of the Rhine, in Cæsar's Gallia, were the residences and the financial backbone of the Holy Roman emperors during the Middle Ages.

The Western Franks were concentrated around the Île de France, the region formed by the River Seine, which contains Paris and Versailles, and which gave its name to the proud liner of the French merchant marine which carried its Prime Minister to the United States.

"L'Île de France" is the country of the *"Francs des Francs."* The name immortalizes the best stock of the immigrants and settlers who perpetuated the work of the conquering Franks. The domain of the French Kings centred around that region: but its frontiers had no traditional significance. The older unity of Roman times was upheld by the Church alone. The *Gallican church* was larger than the realm of Western France during the Middle Ages. And it was truly Gallican, not French. Many Gallican bishops did not obey the kings of France. On the other hand, the kings of France had one jewel in their crown, the rays of which shone far beyond the Gallican church and filled all Christendom. On its splendour, their glory was based. The empire, it is true, was governed by the Eastern Franks, the Teutons; and the papacy (the authority of the Church) was centred in Rome. But the Île de France became the centre of Christian thought during the Middle Ages. People would say: "Allemannia has the empire, Italy holds the sacerdoce, but France possesses the 'studium,' the learning." This learning was brought to Paris, to Mount Geneviève on the left bank of the Seine, by the powerful Descartes of the Middle Ages, Abailard.

Abailard (Abélard) was the first complete Frenchman. The history of his "calamities" is well-known. His love for Héloïse offended her family: a gang caught and castrated him. With tremendous energy, he compensated for his physical ignominy by a glorious adventure of mind. He was the first man in Europe who dared to build a church in honour of the Holy Ghost. Never before had it been permissible to isolate the Holy Ghost, the life of thought, from the Body and Soul of the Church. Abailard, in his bodily frustration, threw himself body and soul into the arms of the Spirit, and called his home the house of Paracletus. All his passions he threw into the intellectual fight. He became the founder of Scholasticism by his famous Treatise on *"Sic et Non"* (Yes and No).

French style, with its brilliance, clearness and lucidity, can well be traced back to his method. And since this method still dominates much of our thought, it deserves an explanation. For a thousand years before Abailard the old Church had had its doctors, fathers and writers. They had had all the possible experiences of personal and ecclesiastical life, and their authority seemed to hover over the life of Abailard's day as every established authority does, lingering and threatening life with petrifaction.

Abailard acknowledged fully the authority of the first millennium of Christianity. He avoided the cheap solution of a Bohemian mind, which throws off the heavy yoke of tradition for its own personal convenience. But he urged upon men's thought the conception of totality, completeness. He refused to listen to any single authority, any arbitrary voice of the past. He asked for their togetherness, their simultaneous representation. When the authorities were gathered, their voices were by no means unanimous; they contradicted each other. And this simultaneous representation of contradictions was the dawn of science. The narrow way into a new science was opened by this completeness, which laid bare the contradictions between the sacred traditions. The *"Summa,"* the complete collection of Church traditions by the scholastics, allowed them to criticize and use their own judgment freely. This wiser road of "Freedom through totality" was inaugurated by Abailard. The reader will perhaps remember the great part played by "totality" in any revolutionary conception of the world. Abailard and his followers started a revolution in independent thought by introducing into it the conception of totality, of summing up.

The Bishop of Paris, upset by the amazing success of this dangerous man, established or enlarged his own cathedral school also. And this competition has been the secret of Paris ever since. Schools exist in many places, and there seems nothing extraordinary in their existence. But in Paris two great schools existed in the same place; this made room for a real university. The difference between a School of mere learning and the Higher School of fundamental thinking has been an element in European life since Abailard. Acknowledged competition between two schools of thought in the same place is what gives the Higher School its value. Wherever the disaccord of various and contradictory principles is born, the higher life of the mind begins to reveal its power. The forms of human life are indivisible and individual (you are a physician or a boy or a grandmother), whilst the forms of the life of thought are exactly the reverse. Thought is created and promoted in a *dialectical* process, by polarities and paradoxes, in a dialogue between pro and con. The existence of at least two complete sets of doctors at Paris gave the proper form of existence to thought and thinking for the first time in history.

The Marxians love the dialectical method in history. But the method applies, as far as we see, first of all to philosophy, to teaching and thinking. The dialogue is a condition of our intellectual existence.

Our theory of revolutions leaves the narrow landmarks set by Marxism as soon as we trace back the institutions of dialectical progress, of systematic competition in thought, to their proper place.

The rivalry of the dialectical schools established at Paris explains why a dialectical element became inherent in European history, and why universities ever since have played a leading part in the history of the European revolutions.

Before the different nations of the old world could march out in different social and political directions, the mediæval university whetted the sword of thinking by the formidable training of students who gathered in Paris.

Paris was the brain of the Occident, the School of all Christendom, and had neither Gallican nor French limitations. Paris was, therefore, reluctant to play any leading part in the political organization of a united France during the Middle Ages. It was a free port of learning much more than it was a monarch's stronghold. It reflected like a mirror all the speculations of Christian thought. The words "reflection," "mirror," "speculum," "speculation" were all very popular in mediæval writing, but revealed by their novelty the prismatic and fragmentary aspect of scholastic truth. We are shareholders in the truth whenever we think. But thought is and must be, by its very essence, dialectical. Being a shareholder, the individual mind never owns the whole capital of truth. We are thrown on others; our thought provokes other and contrary thought! On the bare physical plane one individual or one group can easily cope with the life of many other groups and individuals: indifference and a peaceful equilibrium are possible at that level. But thought changes the peace of the world. Thought is always provoking its own contradiction. This eternal dialogue of thoughts and principles organizes humanity into schools of thought. The parties of policy, the armies of war, and the classes of interest, are embodiments of this power of the mind to act like a sword, to distinguish and to polarize, to live by paradox and conflict, by dialectical revolutions.

The organization of the independent University of Paris apart from empire and papacy is one of the reasons for the revolutionary character of the history of Europe. This was its universal effect on all the European nations. What was its gift to France? The French Revolution, as we know already, did not share the Christian tradition of the Sorbonne of the Middle Ages. It was the eclipse of mediæval Paris which was responsible for the French Revolution. Paris was by far the biggest city in Europe at the end of the Middle Ages. During the democratic movement of the great Councils of the Church the doctors of Paris triumphed over pope and cardinals. This presumption was violently resented. The popes returned from Avignon and re-established their absolute power at the Curia without any regard for the doctrines of Paris (1450-1517). After 1517 the progress of the Reformation destroyed for good and all the scholastic authority of Paris over more than one half of Europe; Wittenberg and Heidelberg and Marburg gained the authority lost by Paris.

About 1530 the great Spanish thinker, J. L. Vives, writes against the "pseudo-dialecticos," criticizing the higher school of Paris: "Don't you think that the University of Paris in the 800th year of its age is raving with decrepitudes?" Then for the first time Paris was confined within the narrow circle of Gaul and France. Paris had never been a French or Gaulish institution like the Kingdom. Its lofty speculations were supported by the universal interest of all Christendom. The repercussion of its imprisonment in France could not but be tremendous.

The universal rôle of Paris being in decline, its 500,000 inhabitants had to come to terms with the Kingdom of the Valois and the Gallican Church.

In this state of affairs the seed of modern France was sown.

Before the Reformation the French kings had fought the English in the North and the emperors in Italy, whereas the eastern frontier towards the Empire was always the River Maas (Meuse). The Reformation turned the face of the Kings of France from Italy and Brittany toward the east. In the October of 1551 a Crown Council was held, at which the traditional plans for a campaign in Italy were discussed. News came that Charles V intended to station troops near the French border at Metz, Toul and Verdun. The Marshal Vieilleville advocated that France should steal a march on Charles. And so the century-old fight for Italy, an unreal, abstract obsession of French policy, was given up for the first time. The Kings of France began to look eastward.

Five years later, in August, 1557, Charles V saw his son a victor before St. Quentin. "Why is my son not in Paris?" he

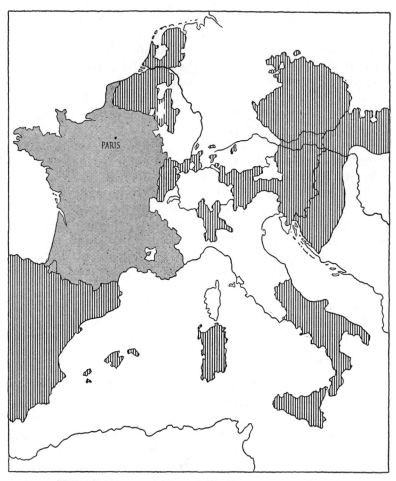

THE HAPSBURG DANGER TO FRANCE—CIRCA 1535

The French territory (shaded) and the lands of the Spanish and Austrian Hapsburgs (lines).

asked impatiently. The threat that Paris might be invaded was felt for the last time in the Great War; it became effective for the first time in 1557. The new policy of France meant a new military situation for Paris. That great centre had now realized the colossal danger of its unprotectedness against the East. And it resented it. The eastern frontier increasingly attracted attention, and the more it did so, the more the King of France and Paris fell into the same line of interest.

But now, for the first time, Paris underwent a long period of starvation and humiliation. Russia, before 1917, suffered from its exploiting capital, St. Petersburg, while Paris, before 1789, suffered ignominiously from France. The old university of Christendom tried to cope with the threat of Protestantism in France in a way deserving of the great times of Paris, when Thomas Aquinas (1276) and Gerson (1410) had taught all Europe. Originally, Paris had believed that her Catholicism was a presupposition of her own rôle in the world. And later, after Luther's heresy, she abhorred any peaceful compromise in matters of religion between the different estates of the realm. The University did not understand the new *"raison d'état"* which was opposed to the reasoning of theologians. *"Que Dieu nous protège de la messe du chancelier"* was a Paris saying against the royal chancellor Michel de l'Hôpital, who tried to avoid the massacres between Catholics and Reformers. Paris scented heresy everywhere. Immediately after the death of the chancellor, the fury of the parties led to the famous massacre of Saint Bartholomew. On the night of the twenty-fourth of August, 1572, at the wedding of the King's daughter with the young Henri Bourbon of Navarre, the Protestants were murdered by thousands.

The despotism of the most Catholic University of Paris made it impossible for the French Government to come to terms with the Protestants. The reasoning of scholasticism seemed to be of unassailable logic: "The Île de France can never be governed by a Protestant king, because the King's orthodox faith is the only basic element on which the Lord of the Royal Domain can found his rights over and in the Gallican Church. A Protestant king, ruling a smaller territory than was ruled by the traditional body of the Catholic clergy, would have withdrawn from this Gallican circle of influence." Paris stood for the future when it impressed upon the King this respect for the larger field of Gallican responsibility.

Henry IV was not blind to the partial authority of Paris. In 1589, the first year of his government, he called it *"l'abrégé et le miroir"* (summary and mirror) of the country; his followers celebrated it in verse as *"l'asme et le cœur de la France."* But the theological reasoning of the professors was not reconciled by the praises of a reforming Huguenot. In 1590, on the fourteenth of May, 1,300 clergymen went in procession through the streets of Paris, the Rector of the Sorbonne at their head, to protest because *"Henri de Bourbon, étant hérétique, relaps et nommément excommunié, ne pouvait être reconnu pour roi, même s'il obtenait son absolution du Saint Siège, vu que la perfidie et la dissimulation étaient à craindre de sa part."* As a heretic, renegade and therefore anathematized, he could not be acknowledged as King, even if the Pope should absolve him. In the last hour of her theological sovereignty, Paris was more papal than the Pope. In her arrogant assertion of her importance in the realm of ideas, she encroached on the rights of the territorial realm.

Suddenly the theoretical croaking of her teachers was silenced when Henry went to Mass and took the City of Paris by an unexpected stratagem. The Sorbonne was crushed and a party of "politicians" emerged who repudiated the use of theological principles for political purposes. The *"raison d'état,"* a political reason for purposes of peace, wealth and welfare, pervaded the nation for the first time in spite of the international glory of Paris.

After this, the decline of Paris went on throughout the next centuries. René Descartes (1596-1650), the Abélard of modern times, who was hailed by the poet La Fontaine as *"Ce mortel dont on eût fait un Dieu dans les siècles passés, et qui tient le milieu entre l'homme et l'esprit,"* left Paris and went north to one of the free universities of Holland, Franeker. In his *Discours de la Méthode,* Descartes establishes a philosophy which keeps away from any servitude to theology. Here, for the first

PARIS IN 1610

time in more than a thousand years, philosophy claims to be self-supporting. Descartes regenerates the pagan independence of the individual mind.

From that dates the strange conception of "spirit" which reigns in French and European civilization. Wherever *"l'esprit"* has superseded the Holy Ghost, you may be sure you are on territory that belongs to French or "European" civilization. The voluntary exile of Descartes from Paris announces an anti-theological, humanistic meaning of *"l'esprit."* The future reconciliation between *"l'esprit"* and Paris becomes the problem of the next centuries. As soon as Paris would incorporate and politically organize this spirit of the modern world, its international and European rôle could be resumed. The French Revolution was to be this fusion.

Between 1594 and 1789 Paris was impoverished, deprived of her old privileges, and always feverishly awaiting the true heir to her former glories. But she lay in the dust for a long while. In 1645 a sculptor was ordered to erect a monument in the City Hall of Paris, showing Louis XIV contemptuously treading a rebellious Parisian under his royal feet.

The monument was graciously removed in 1687, it is true. But then the humiliation of Paris had already become permanent. The King had left Paris for Versailles. Between 1675 and 1805 no new building was done on the royal palace, the Louvre, in Paris. After the second of May, 1682, Versailles was the permanent residence of the King. In it lodged 2,200 horses and 1,500 officers and clerics. 100,000 candles burned at its feasts. 100,000 people lived in Versailles, while today, in spite of the growth of most cities during the nineteenth century, its population is only 30,000. What is more, Versailles was made the centre of the fine arts. In 1680 a critic observed that Italy had yielded the palm in architecture, sculpture, painting, gardening, and water-works, to France. "Versailles seul suffit *pour assurer à jamais à la France la Gloire qu'elle a à présent de surpasser tous les autres royaumes."*

Another expression of the same author is more instructive still: *"C'est une ville, c'est un monde, que ce palais."*

The Kings, suspicious of Paris, finding its population, as Voltaire says in his description of the *Siècle de Louis XIV,* more "bourgeois" than "citizen-like" (*"plus bourgeois que citoyen"*), decided to *"épater les bourgeois."* In their ante-chamber, the *"œil de Bœuf," "se tiennent chaque jour, attendant le lever du roi, ceux qui par leur naissance, leur charge, ou la volonté du roi, ont droit aux diverses entrées, sans parler de la foule des gens de qualité, cardinaux, archevêques, ambassadeurs, ducs et pairs, maréchaux de France, gouverneurs de province, lieutenants généraux, présidents de parlement qui se donnent rendez-vous à Versailles."* Versailles became *"tout frémissant de toutes les gloires de la France."*

The *"esprit,"* the inspiration of this realm, worked passionately to overcome all natural obstacles. The fountains of Versailles were wrested from a dry and waterless soil! The Duke of Saint-Simon, chronicler of Versailles, speaks of the glorious pleasure of enslaving nature. And nature was enslaved. The physical and the social traditions of France were overshadowed by the Kings' domination over nature. And what was the ultimate goal of this new power established in an arbitrary centre? The new standard was expressed by Richelieu in his Testament: *"Le but de mon ministère a été de rendre à la Gaule les frontières que lui a destinées* la nature, *de rendre aux Gaulois un roi Gaulois, de* confondre la Gaule avec la France, *et partout* où fut l'ancienne Gaule d'y rétablir la nouvelle."

This was already the regeneration of a pre-Christian order of things. The successor to St. Louis was slated to become the absolute conqueror of ancient Gaul. The absolutism of the dynasty destroyed the estates, which assembled in 1614 for the last time. It began its wars of conquest, robbery, and reunion against the east and northeast. The scar of St. Quentin, in 1557, was never forgotten. The "siege-trenches of the Île de France" were carried forward toward the east year after year. Louis XIV, entering Strassburg, the old imperial and German city, in 1681, distributed a medal with the legend: *"Gallia Germanis Clausa."* Gaul had won over France.

The tendency of this policy pointed from the traditional rights of an anointed King over clergy, nobility and cities of a Christian realm to the absolute power of a Cæsar over Gaul. But on the way to this goal the government was caught in a trap. The very allies it needed to help it go back beyond the real traditions of France to this abstract notion of Gaul, led the King astray. All went well so long as he had no allies. In fact he tried desperately to represent the new character of a secular France all by himself, by making his life in Versailles more public than any monarch had ever done. Every Sunday the gates of the Palace were opened, and people could see the royal family and the King as close at hand as they liked. Lenin was exposed to the public gaze after his death, Louis XIV during his lifetime. The King's handkerchief, his foot-stool, his shirt, his cough or smile, were observed with sympathy and interest.

But this sun of France was a mortal after all. The *Roi-soleil* had his sunset, too. It was all very well to found Versailles for the sake of a triumph over Paris. But who ran the realm when the King was asleep, or lazy, or a minor? Three groups encroached on the new god-like power of the King: priests, royal family, and nobles. Under Louis XIV (1680-1715) the priests prevailed, under the Regency (1715-1722) the liberties taken by the royal family were those most violently felt, and under Louis XV it was the insolence of the nobles which overshadowed all the merits of Versailles.

By being in the company of these three groups, which wished to share the royal privileges, royalty exposed itself to the attacks of the Parisians. The Constitution of modern France is largely a condensation of the attacks of the Parisians against these three exploiting groups, and not against the organization created by the Kings at Versailles. It is therefore worthwhile to define these abuses more carefully than is commonly done in textbooks. Because abuses in themselves do not lead to revolutions. Graft and irregularities are the unavoidable companions of power and government. Only adolescents can dream of revolution as an appropriate means to the end of clean government. Force calls for force, lawlessness for lawlessness.

That is why any established order is better than a complete break. When Henry IV was accepted as King, the vanity of Paris was sacrificed to the common sense of the French for continuity. The traditional assumption of an innate frivolity in the French or the Parisians is not true at all. Voltaire wrote of them: "They come to everything late, but at last they come to it."

Lest we underrate the angelic patience and real conservatism of the French nation, we ought to discover their grievances. These had little to do with the private pleasures of the Kings. Their mistresses were expensive, but no more expensive than the usual patronage in an aristocracy or the inevitable graft in a democracy. Money is wasted in different ways, but wasted it is everywhere. The grievances of the French had a deeper meaning, which no virtuous king like Louis XVI could outweigh. They endured the government of their dissipated rulers, because then it might still be doubtful whether it was a question of personal vice or of basic rottenness. But when Louis XVI turned out to be perfectly honest, decent and brave, they started the Revolution.

The same may be said of Nicholas II of Russia, or of Charles I of England, or of President Buchanan in America. Because they were innocent in their personal attitude, their governments ended in revolution. Their good personal character made it perfectly clear that something was rotten in the State which had nothing to do with sentiments or personalities.

Moral talk about despots and revolutions imposes on our credulity, inasmuch as it ignores the deep instinct of a nation for its permanent organization. The downfall of the virtuous Louis XVI happened not because he was King, monarch or despot, but because he could not be awake all the time. There was no remedy which could save the King from the corruption of the three pillars of his throne: priesthood, family and nobility. The French Revolution installed a sovereign who was independent of priesthood, family ties, and privilege. The French Revolution was not directed against the successor of Louis XIV. The fact that no reasonable leader in France wished to weaken the central government kept Louis XVI in power until 1792. France was not and is not anti-royal, but anti-clerical, anti-aristocratic, and anti-dynastic. Napoleon I, for example, emperor though he was, did less to violate the principles of the French Revolution than the federalists of 1790, who tried to go back to the estates of 1614 and to decentralize France. They were the first to be crushed by the fury of the real successors of the King of Versailles, the courtiers of the new Queen of France, Paris.

In order that the courtiers of Versailles might cease to influence the King, the rôle of kingship was invested in the Queen of Cities, Paris; and her courtiers were allowed to rule alternately!

HUGUENOTS AND JESUITS.

The priests made the French Cæsar a bigot. In 1685, when Louis XIV drove out the Huguenots, the friends of his great-grandfather, Henry IV, he expelled the progressive part of his nation, whose courage alone had made it possible for him to govern the country by *"raison d'état,"* against the "reason of theology." The reason of State was overruled when Madame de Maintenon and the Jesuits secured the repeal of the Edict of Nantes by which the Huguenots had been allowed to stay in France. Most of them left France, carrying her best blood into the world abroad; but many of them left—for Paris. Strangely enough, the cruel execution of the *Édit de Versailles* by the "Dragonnades," that is, by military quartering, seemed impossible in the King's *"grande ville de Paris."* Some 10,000 Huguenots remained in the place, outlawed, it is true, but for that very reason so much more an element of permanent unrest. In this persecution, the provincial priesthood of the country acted without the Sorbonne. Paris, however, though proud of its Catholic university, did not mean to bow before the lower clergy of the King's provinces. The parochial and provincial character of the Gallican Church deprived it of all the essential loyalties owed to the great Faculty of Theology. The edict of Versailles was a triumph for the provincial and royal clergy, and though the Jesuits only joined in the triumph, it unchained the fury of Paris against them as well. As a Spanish order, seated in Rome, to fight English, Dutch and German

Protestantism, the Jesuits overruled, so to speak, the Île de France, the old centre of speculation. Having an international reputation as schoolmasters, they were apt candidates to take over the rôle of the old Catholic Paris for the rest of Europe, but certainly not in Paris itself. Nowhere else was the fight against the Jesuits so much a nationalistic crusade against invaders from outside. From 1590 to 1761 the Jesuits were anathema to Paris. Richelieu had sensed this when he founded the Academy of Paris, to replace the dying Sorbonne, and when he included Huguenots in its ranks from the very beginning. Later the great soul of Blaise Pascal represents the French genius in its struggle for a new orthodoxy. By turning to Pascal we can learn about the French Revolution. Pascal attacked the Jesuits because they were parochial and no longer had the magnanimity of Thomas of Aquinas or Bonaventura. He was fighting against a church which had become too visible and used reason only for apologetics. Pascal turned the scales of French thought in favour of the new principles by depriving Jesuitism of all dignity, and by unveiling its moral cowardice in his *Lettres Provinciales,* the first great piece of modern French prose. We should give up the superstition, of literary histories, that great men are read and admired for their literary merits alone; as if literature were a water-tight compartment where pens and tongues are used for the sake of book-writing. Pascal could perhaps have written a better book than the *Lettres Provinciales.* I found an American friend "disappointed" with it because he disliked its sarcasm! The poor man had taken a course in literature and expected something to suit his literary palate. The French read Pascal because Pascal was a free-lance in a desperate enterprise, more desperate than the enterprise of the Minute Men at Lexington and Concord in 1775.

Yet, bold though he was, Pascal himself was no desperado. His fight, the natural exhalation of a virile spirit, was dignified by his own humility and restraint. Though he collaborated with the discoverers of the world of space, he knew that space was hell for an isolated man. "Most crimes are committed because man cannot remain calmly and quietly one hour alone in an empty room," he wrote. This is perhaps the deepest utterance of this brilliant thinker, fighter and Christian. The fear of empty space was not to be vanquished by the isolated soul. Pascal tried to think in connection with a living community. He wrote his *Pensées* in connection with Port Royal, the austere praying centre of Jansenism. He could not think unless supported by love.

Pascal, then, is a great figure in the French Revolution. In his three-fold activity of preparing the defeat of the Jesuits, supporting the victory of Cartesian science, and also of saving the social and communal character of our psychic and creative life, he condensed into his short life (1623-1662), the permanent features of the French character: the cosmological vision of a sensualist and rationalist, the personal courage and faith of a crusader, and the heart of a troubadour.

Pascal and Port Royal are pillars in the middle of the broad stream which had to be bridged before the French nation could escape the intellectual impasse created by the Reformation and Counter-Reformation.

But the gulf was bridged. In 1761, under the pressure of public opinion, the Jesuits were exiled from France. By this capitulation the Kings lost their only intellectual allies of international standing in their fight against Paris. Diderot, the great sensualist and rationalist, could write (1761): "With the suppression of the Jesuits, absolute monarchy in France is ended."

PRIVILEGES.

Now the old French constitution, which had to be carried over the abyss between the Middle Ages and modern times, had three elements:

(1) Paris: intellectual centre of Christendom.
(2) Isle de France: a King ruling over a score of provinces.
(3) Gallican Church, throughout ancient Gaul.

These three elements had to remain in the same equilibrium, and yet they all had to be modernized. Now the chasm between the Middle Ages and modern times proved to be much broader for France than for, let us say, England or Germany. The Germans began their New Times as early as 1517, with Luther; the English too, as we shall see, had started a new era, finally dating it from the Glorious Revolution of 1688. The French nation, having lost its international Christian reputation at Luther's hands, had to wait until 1789 to end its Middle Ages, or what the French called *"ancien régime."*

Situated in the middle of Europe, they had two neighbours who had long since radically modernized their institutions: Germany and England. This backwardness made the French restless; their revolutionary energy was bottled up for 250 years. They could not borrow their solution from abroad; but on the other hand it was not enough to decline the remedies offered by the Lutheran Reformation of the Church and by the Jesuit Counter-Reformation. The English model was another attractive possibility; and so the remedies of the English Revolution were tried out. Then, when it became evident that they did not fit into the French triangular problem, the counter-revolutionary forces of absolutism, which went against the English system, were given their turn. But they, too, left France without the international function to which it had a right.

It was only then, after having flirted with the solutions offered by her neighbours, that Marianne definitely discovered her own revolutionary way into modernity, into Gaul and Europe.

Between France and Gaul stood one permanent obstacle: the traditional rights of the Frankish Regions, embodied in the nobility, dukes, counts and barons. These owed allegiance to the King, but their estates divided France into a crazy-quilt of thousands of little scraps of soil. "In Lorraine," wrote Voltaire, "you change the law as often as the horses of your mail coach." And this was true of Picardy, Artois, Poitou, Brittany, Aquitaine, Normandy, and all the other provinces. These countries each had a common law of its own in which Burgundian, Gothic, and Frankish law had been fused with Roman and Canon Law and blended with charters and privileges granted by kings or popes or bishops. The living voices of the law were the Lords of the Manor, the Fief-holders whose rights reflected at the same time the public law of the district. Local government, the pride of every Anglo-Saxon country, was invested in the "*Coutumes,*" the customs of the estates in all the "*pays de France.*" "*Pays*" is "fatherland," patria; and *Patrie* meant "Béarn" or "Languedoc" to a Frenchman in 1700. Here he had his rights, his natural roots, his home. The Huguenots, who founded New Rochelle in New York State after the repeal of the Edict of Nantes, kept the name of their "*pays,*" because the fortress of Rochelle had served for thirty years as the anchoring place of their rights as citizens. A man could not be French without first having a "*pays.*" The Huguenots, being outside the regular organization of the bishoprics and parishes of France, could not exist except by being assigned to certain Huguenot districts. Law and legal standing without a "*pays*" would not have seemed feasible.

The French fatherlands were kept together and united by the fact that the living voices of their customs, the 270,000 nobles and clergy, were vassals of the Frankish King. The King governed each fatherland according to its laws, just as the President of the United States of America has to reckon with forty-eight State constitutions.

No sooner had the living voices of the regions of England made themselves unmistakably heard during the great Civil War, than the gentry of France took a deep breath and plunged into the troubles of the Fronde (1645). The King of France victoriously stopped this English infection and began to kill the soul of the "*pays*" by taking away their leaders. He moved them to Versailles. The countryside was practically deserted, and royal intendants took over the work of administration. The nobles were turned into absentees. In the course of fifty years, the third Duke of La Rochefoucauld spent twenty nights outside Versailles. The castles became summer resorts or hunting seats. And Versailles had to be filled artificially. Of its 100,000 inhabitants in 1750, the greater part was made up of all the gentlemen of France. This was the price that the King had to pay for competing with Paris. He used the gentry of the country as a battering ram against Paris. We must keep this in mind when we read Molière: his *Bourgeois Gentilhomme* was written in the years of the gentlemen's revolution in England. But in England the governing class would never have dared to deal so cruelly with the merchants, because its very revolution against the King made it feel responsible for the other classes too. The French King allowed his gentry, in their concentration camp at Versailles, to be filled with cynical contempt for the *"crapule,"* the bourgeois; for the gentry no longer had any responsibility, and yet had to be kept in good temper. The irresponsibility of the nobles of France was the plague of the régime of Versailles! As long as the "grandeur," the greatness of the Court, overshadowed the pettiness of the courtiers, as long as the King was "great," the century *"le grand siècle,"* the Duchess of Orléans "the great Mademoiselle," Condé "the great Condé," all went well. But things ceased to be great at Versailles when Louis XIV passed away. The drones at court, with their empty hauteur, became incompatible with the humming bee-hive of Paris.

The result was: *at Versailles a privileged class without functions; in Paris a functioning society without privileges.* The concentration of leaders of the *"pays"* in Versailles had uprooted the foundations of French society. And the concentration of the privileged class resulted in its being pitilessly exposed as a privileged class. Now its privileges had made sense as long as they stayed within the framework of local government. In the past, a count who was distinguished by the King had added honour to his *"pays."* Thus, through the privileges of its leaders, the countryside had succeeded in maintaining its equality with the intellectual centres of commerce and teaching, like Paris.

Now this balance between the *"pays"* and Paris had broken down. The provinces stood naked, governed as they were by royal officials; the nobles, wrapped up in titles, ceremonies, privileges, no longer moved in a real world of social obligations. The cities sparkled with activity. Their busy life seemed to avoid the extremes of both Versailles and the provinces. They set before the eyes of the nation the *"juste-milieu,"* the golden-mean form of society. The cities, and especially Paris, seemed more than senseless agglomerations of egoistic individuals or masses. Our modern impression of a place like Pittsburgh or Liverpool or Charleroi in Belgium cannot be applied to the ideas of the French Revolution about citizenship and civilization. Its civil order aimed at the mean between the empty privileged class and the denuded peasantry. This mean already existed in 1700 or 1750 in a city like Paris (which had 600,000 inhabitants in 1789). This *juste-milieu* needed no economic revolution, no industrial revolution, no change in the forms of trade or business. France is the only country in the world where the word "industry" has never lost its meaning of skilled craftsmanship. "Industry" was not big machinery, not Ford or General Motors. When the French consuls inaugurated the exhibition of industries in Paris in 1800, the public saw furniture, jewellry and Gobelin tapestries.

The French Revolution wished to expand the organization of the cities of France, as the true bee-hives of life and production. It wished to avenge the bourgeois who had been scoffed at for imitating the gentleman.

Make the bourgeois a citizen, and no other class can compete with him. The dignity of the word *"civilisation"* depends on this moral background, where Paris stands over against Versailles, and Versailles over against the provinces. The privileged class in Versailles could not offer any common denominator for the nation; the people in the country could not do so either. As soon as the bourgeois took the risk of being more than a bourgeois, he could be turned into a citizen.

THE NATION: HOW THE BOURGEOIS WAS MADE A CITIZEN.

This process deserves a closer investigation, because during the nineteenth century the other countries of the world tried with varying success to imitate the methods of the French Revolution. The Revolution marched all over the world, as had been forecast by Napoleon. But nowhere else could the process of civilization work as it did in France, where the bourgeoisie of Paris held the centre between a privileged class of aristocrats and a denuded class of peasants. Without this polarity, no *juste-milieu* of citizenship and civilization!

As the word "industry" shows, the French vocabulary is

unique even today. The French *civilisation* has the same peculiarity, centring as it does in a special concept of the nation.
"Nation" is something which needs no king and no nobility
to feel itself a nation. France is a democracy; but it is by no
means the government of the people. The word *"peuple"* is
no less abhorrent to the French than the word *"aristocrate."*
The French Revolution built up its European civilization of
national democracies by avoiding both extremes, "aristocrats"
and "people." The nation is not the same thing as that labelled
by the word *"peuple."* People of Paris, people of Flanders,
signify the man in the street or the man in the fields, with his
native instincts, his inborn superstitions. "Nation" is the people
restored to a truer and greater nature; it is "people" minus
superstitions or instincts, plus reason and speech.

"Nation" is the glory of a natural humanity which also bears
the torch of enlightenment, gleaming like Lucifer, the morning
star, stealing light and fire like Prometheus, and defying the
gods of tradition by the majesty of human genius.

In English we can speak of "the people of this nation," which
makes it perfectly clear that people and nation are not the
same. Neither is the national government of France identical
with the *"peuple français."* Most of the mischief done to the
map of the world has happened because well-meaning people
overlook the rigid standard implied in the French conception
of "nation."

It is of practical use to lay bare the foundations of the term,
for we are all taken in today by the promiscuous use of "nation" for all kinds of purposes. The domination of French
ideas has lamed our sense of self-orientation in the social world.
We have French words for everything. The oldest parliamentary country, England, bows to France and calls the First Lord
of the Treasury by a French title, "Prime Minister"; the British
parties are called "Liberals" and "Conservatives," which are
purely French names.

"Nation" is used even by careless Americans who forget that
the continent of America is a new world embracing all kinds
of nations and open to all kinds of nations, and that Anglo-
Saxons should believe in the Commonwealth, not in National-

ism. A true American patriot should avoid the word "nation" like the plague.

The origin of the French conception of "Nation" is a fascinating story of the self-defence of a social group and the appointment of revolutionary leaders by an inarticulate society. The French bourgeois saw the emptiness of the privileged classes and the bareness of the rural area as early as 1750. Everybody expected a change, a break, even in those days. But though the field was ripe for mowing, no labourers were ready to harvest it. The creation of a group of intellectual leaders was the *conditio sine qua non* of the Revolution. In Russia, factories had to be built to help the intelligentsia; in France an intellectual class had to be trained up to help the industrial classes. Hence the desire of the French to become intellectual, their devotion to all the idealistic superstructure of society. The *tiers état,* the industrial classes, feel that they will become France just as soon as the moral atmosphere can be made to agree with the economic facts.

This new order of things was anticipated on the stage. The theatre became the hothouse for the ideas of 1789. For the actor, formerly despised and outlawed by society, can show a solution on the stage which does not exist in reality. The theatre becomes an institution for the political education of the nation.

When Molière wrote the *Bourgeois Gentilhomme,* he had acquiesced in the existing order. A hundred years later the word was passed along: "The son of Molière is found." The phrase was coined about Caron de Beaumarchais. But this "son" was not one to acquiesce. Beaumarchais was a banker who had financed, at the King's order, the deliveries of war material to the American Colonies during their Revolution; and he had won a great success with his play, *The Barber of Seville.* In 1778 he wrote *The Wedding of Figaro.* The history of this play turned out to be the prologue in miniature of the French Revolution. It took four long years to write it, and in following the proceedings of censor, King and Queen, press and public, we get nearer and nearer to the catastrophe of 1789.

The comedy of Figaro, so full of wit, brings a count and countess down to the level of their servant and maid. This poet represents the new society. He aims at the same time at the defence of his legal rights, the conquest of public fame, and the making of money; that is, at the three things which form the queer alloy of the emerging society. Beaumarchais' rights are less clear, his fame less noble, and his money less pure than the legal rights, the moral fame, and the honest money of a good citizen. But he is the prophet of the new earthly paradise, and acts as its precursor on the stage. His character, his money-making devices, and his legal proceedings contained fewer grains of gold than those of the average honest merchant; but he showed better brains, he showed genius.

In Russia the intelligentsia had to show greater character than the average Russian. In France the moral virtues are seated in the normal citizen. The *littérateur's* task is to show *génie, vrai génie;* he must have *esprit,* he must be a master of expression. Then society will be indulgent toward his dissipations. Society, laden as it is with politcial electricity, hails the electrician. The Russian Maxim Gorky tells in his diary of a practical case of Leninism. Lenin had always repeated: "Electricity plus soviets equals socialism." Whereupon an electrician went into a Russian village, gathered the peasants about, and made the following speech: "You have a pope, an Orthodox priest in your village, haven't you? You feed him well and he maintains the eternal lamp in his church. Now you appoint me as your mayor, pay me such and such a salary, and I will produce electric light for everybody in the village." His offer was accepted. The electric light and the electrician took the place of the lamp of eternity and its engineer, the priest. In France the electrician is the man of *"esprit."* He is extolled because he is able to master the political clouds, and to elicit from the atmosphere the sparks which lead to change and reconstruction.

"Esprit" cannot be translated into English, but it must be understood by anyone who wishes to understand French politics. It is the translation of the Holy Ghost into its most personal and single-minded form, that of the *inspired individual.*

The thunderbolt, the flash, may burst out through any person. Government by inspired individuals becomes the endeavour of the national society.

Figaro sings in the final chorus of the play:

"Par le sort de la naissance
L'un est roi, l'autre est berger;
Le hasard fit leur distance;
L'esprit seul peut tout changer.
De vingt rois que l'on encense
Le trépas brise l'autel
Et Voltaire est immortel."

"By the chance of birth
One is King, the other shepherd;
Their difference is haphazard,
Inspiration alone can change everything.
Incense for twenty Kings
Vanishes with their death,
But Voltaire is immortal."

Figaro sings this creed of a world changed by inspiration after having taken his witty revenge on his lord, the Count Almaviva. The great of this earth, viewed from below, cease to be great: "My lord Count, because you are a great lord you take yourself to be a genius? You have taken the pains to be born, nothing else. For the rest you are a very ordinary man."

The accident of birth, the privilege of birth or birthright, are scorned with all possible energy. Beaumarchais promised to devote some of the profits of the play to a home for unwed mothers! But now let us tell the whole story of the play.

When people heard of its length, that it would last three full hours, they predicted a failure. The manuscript was circulated among Beaumarchais' friends; and the poet could not resist the temptation of reading it in certain salons. Parties were formed "pro" and "con." In 1779 people offered to bet 200 louis d'or ($1,000) that it could not be acted in public.

The great Royal Theatre, the Comédie Française, enjoyed the privilege of making its own decision on the acceptance of a play, when the censor had no objections. Accordingly, Beau-

marchais, approaching the Comédie Française in 1781 and se-
curing a favourable censor, thought he was safe. But general
rumour made the play so famous that the commissioner of
police thought it wise to ask the King himself. The King and
Queen heard it read. In the fifth act, during the monologue
of Figaro which we quoted just now, the King, with astounding
instinct, scented the revolutionary dynamite. He jumped to his
feet, shouting, "That is abominable! That shall never be acted!
The Bastille would have to be destroyed, to make the performance of this play anything but an act of the most dangerous inconsistency." [4]

Eight years before the taking of the Bastille, Louis XVI
anticipated it in idea through the inspiration of a playwright.
The prophetic use of the stage for political changes can be
seen particularly well in this case.

Naturally, the public demand was aroused by the royal
criticism. What a play it must be that had an effect equal to
the destruction of the Bastille! For his many lectures on the
play in the salons, Beaumarchais wrote a special preface "to the
Ladies." The Russian Empress, Catherine II, true to the Czarist interest in social satire, thought of acting the play at St.
Petersburg. All this led to the intervention of the keeper of
the Great Seal. He interested the President of the Académie
Française, M. Suard, who condemned the play. All seemed to
have come to an end.

Then the royal family showed its dissipation and dissolution.
The play was going to be acted for the brother of Louis XVI,
the Count of Artois (later Charles X, 1824-1830, the reactionary
of reactionaries), at a private festival in Paris on the thirteenth
of June, 1783, and to this performance all the great dignitaries,
the princes, ministers, ladies, in short, the aristocracy, were
invited. The streets approaching the theatre were obstructed
by the throng of arriving carriages. At that moment came a
royal order forbidding the professional actors who had parts
in the play from participating in the performance. The throng
was so disappointed that it burst into shrieks: "Tyranny! Suppression!" But after all, the play was not acted.

[4] Mme. Campan, *Memoirs of the Court*, London, 1843, I, pp. 272-3.

Three months later, however, on September 23, in a country place, it was performed, and again in honour of the King's brother! The pretext was that the poet had agreed to certain cuts which would have to be tried out in performance. As a trial performance it was permitted. To be sure, the new censor now approved of the play. But the royal order was still in force. The King asked for further cuts. Two other censors must give their approval. Only one of them vetoed it; the other's vote was favourable, and was backed by a superior authority.

Finally (the frightened bureaucrats shrank from all responsibility), Beaumarchais himself summoned a real council: the chief of police, the keeper of the Great Seal, a Minister of the Cabinet, one of the censors, and two connoisseurs of literature. This council met at the beginning of 1784. Thanks to the plea of the "father" himself, who explained every detail with brilliancy, the play, this child of natural genius, was legitimized by a unanimous vote. The King was told that all the scandalous passages had been expunged. Someone added that the play would be hissed off the stage anyway. On the other hand, the actors of the theatre petitioned to the effect that they needed a play that paid. In March, 1784, the King withdrew the prohibition.

Was not everything smoothed out now? Not at all. The political tragi-comedy of this play was just beginning. The author himself and his friends were afraid that people of good taste might find fault with its unmeasured insolences. But the King's brother set their minds at rest. "The play will be a success," he said. "People will think they have won a battle against the government!"

Democracy in Europe has always wished to win battles "against the government." April 27, 1784, the play was received with such applause that enmity and envy began to stir. The play dominated the stage, it is true; on October 2 the fiftieth performance took place. But Beaumarchais was overwhelmed with invective. His old censor, Suard, attacked him in the Académie. The Archbishop of Paris denounced him in a pastoral letter. Finally Suard used the newspaper he owned, the *Journal de Paris,* to attack him violently.

March 2, 1785, Beaumarchais answered in a public letter.
He exclaimed: "Well, I had to vanquish lions and tigers so
that the play might be allowed to go on the stage, and now,
after all its successes, you think of condemning me to kill
bugs?"

The bug, Suard, immediately declared that Beaumarchais,
in referring to lions and tigers, was hinting at the King and
Queen. On the ninth of March, in the fifty-third year of his
age, Beaumarchais was taken to St. Lazare, a jail for youthful
offenders. We are told that the King wrote the writ of arrest at
a game of cards, on an ace of spades.

Public opinion was divided. The tremendous impudence
of the speculator had aroused much enmity. But his imprisonment was not to be maintained. Eight days later he was free.
At first he refused to leave prison. He protested against the
injury inflicted upon him; he condemned himself to a voluntary confinement indoors, and sold his coaches to demonstrate
that he was serious about the matter. His petitions became
such a nuisance that in time the King sent orders to reach a
compromise with him. He was offered the order of St. Michael,
the effect of which was to ennoble the receiver. Beaumarchais
insisted that he was already a noble, and asked for a pension
from the Civil List.

And what happened? By order of the King, Calonne, Minister of the Cabinet, had to write a flattering letter to Beaumarchais; and the poet received his pension from the King's
privy purse. *Figaro's Wedding* was acted in the presence of the
whole Cabinet of the King, after six months of delay, on
August 17. At Figaro's observation: "Since they cannot humiliate *l'esprit,* the genius, they take their revenge by torturing
him"—the whole audience burst out in a frenzy of applause.

The climax was reached when, on August 19, 1785, the
author was invited to the little palace of Trianon, built in the
style of Rousseauism by the Queen, Marie Antoinette. There,
in the disguise of shepherds and shepherdesses, the royal family had taken up the fashion of natural life and abolition of
privilege. In this environment, Louis XVI, King of France,
and Caron de Beaumarchais, banker, citizen, and poet, sat

down together and saw the other play written by this *enfant terrible:* his *Barber of Seville.* The main part in that play, Rosine, was acted with great charm by the Queen herself, Marie Antoinette. That evening the Bastille was destroyed.

In 1789, on July 14, the people of Paris tore down the Bastille—the event which Louis XVI had instinctively foreseen at *The Mad Day, or Figaro.* When the Lord Chamberlain announced the event to the King at Paris, Louis XVI said: "This is a rebellion." "No," the courtier replied, "this is a revolution." The moral conquest of Paris by Henry IV in 1594 was turned into its opposite. Paris ceased to be a royal city.

The theatres of Paris had prepared a new audience, the nation. The most passionate German poet, Schiller, spellbound by the sounds that came from France, wrote on *The Theatre as a Moral Institution.* And not only did the actors try to play "the mad day," but the madness of the Revolution was embodied in an actress who had to play the Goddess of Reason on the Field of Mars in 1794. It was an actor who first wore the costume of a sans-culotte. An actor and an actress infused into the French Revolution a bit of histrionic gesture, ardour of declamation, inspiration and *verve.* The French Revolution introduced the clapping of hands from the theatre into public life, where it had been unknown before. One wave had to flow from the ocean of theatrical passion into the newly organized nation to foment its new covenant; and it did.

The true heir to all the political passions of 1789 was Georges Clemenceau. This man was French of the French and revolutionary of the revolutionaries. When Clemenceau made his will, a hundred and fifty years after *Figaro* was written, he ordered that nothing should be put into his grave but an old edition of *Figaro,* an heirloom of his family.

The theatre changed the audience; it communicated the sentiments of Daphnis and Chloë to the King and Queen of France and the passions of the Great to the *roturier,* the business man. The stage was a training camp for the new equality of citizenship, and the educators of the movement had to be behind the scenes. The men of *esprit,* the inspired individuals who could "change all that," to use Figaro's phrase, were the writers of French. To the *écrivain*, the literary wielder of language, went the incense of the "twenty kings" whose lives were overshadowed by the immortality of Voltaire.

The revolutionaries of 1789, finding a great church built and dedicated to St. Geneviève, changed its destination. Recalling Abailard's teaching on St. Geneviève, and all the intellectual glories of the place, they turned this church into the "Panthéon"—the place sacred to all gods and geniuses. In this hall we find a monument dedicated to the *"écrivains de France"* killed during the World War. The *écrivains* are constitutional elements of a civilized nation. They give expression and they give standards to the national existence.

The French language has had a *culte* in France, ever since. An American teacher once made a scrupulous study of this question: "How the French boy learns to write." One might expect this to be something rather special and dry; and in fact our author set out with the idea that it was only a special question of how to co-ordinate algebra, geography, Latin, English, German, and history into one school curriculum. That, indeed, is all it seems to an English or German pedagogue, except that he might emphasize Latin or history or biology. But in France Mr. Rollo Brown found it very different indeed.

The French physicist would say: "If Latin helps us to write French better, we must keep Latin!" The Latinist would say: "Latin makes you write a more elegant French." No one would take his arguments from his own field; instead, the arguments in the case would be built up around the problem of how to get a perfect French style. "The French have chosen to be influential through their speech and writing. As Brunetière pointed out somewhere, the literary classes of France long ago recognized the possibilities of influence through speech and writing, and they set themselves, accordingly, to the task of making their native language a powerful force in the world. The schools served as the necessary means; and during the nineteenth century, when educational systems were developing most rapidly, this care for language came to be the ideal of the nation at large. The so-called disintegrating tendencies in language exist in France as in other countries of the world just now, but they meet with a stronger, more perfectly organized resistance. The French schools stand as a deeply established safeguard for the better use of the mother tongue. They have held to the conviction that whatever else the school should stand for, it should be the exponent of good French. The organization of the system and the character of the instruction given in the schools have, together, borne this conviction to every corner of the country and to every social class. It may be seen that the tradition of good language does not merely exist as tradition in spite of some vague 'spirit of the times,' but instead is organized, made not only defensive but positive, through the national system of education." [5]

Language is the idol of any democracy. Yet what is a virtue in France becomes a vice in Russia and a crime in Czechoslovakia or in Hungary, where there is neither a Paris to epitomize the speculations and reflections of a continent nor one single nationality with an exclusive territory. As the only symbol of togetherness and nationality, it is misleading in Serbia and Croatia, or Austria and Germany. But at the source of our century of progress and our national civilization, in France, language has a very complicated significance. Before the War the German historian, Lamprecht, and a French colleague were travelling in Northern France, where so many Flemish places remind us of the fight for the natural defences of Paris. Lamprecht was trying to defend the *raison d'état* in relation to different nationalities and the masterpiece of the Austrian Empire, then containing fourteen nations, against the French conception of an identity between linguistic and political units. Pointing to one of the Flemish villages they passed through in their car, Lamprecht asked: "What about the language of these people? Don't they speak their German idiom? Why isn't there a single Flemish school to teach them to read and write?"

"*Oh,*" replied his friend, "*ce n'est pas une langue, c'est un patois.*" (It's not a language, it's a dialect.) This answer betrays the French idea of language. They think that a national lan-

[5] Rollo Walter Brown, *How the French Boy Learns to Write*, p. 208 ff., Cambridge, Harvard Univ. Press, 1927.

guage needs a permanent centre of unification: *Literature.* Thus the written word, sublime, exalted, is the upper level on which a nation must live to be in permanent contact with inspiration. This is illustrated by the fact that a *fin de siècle* author—Anatole France—could venture to take the name of the whole nation as his own device. A nation is not a geographical or racial fragment. Nations are divided from barbarian tribes by the one reality of Inspiration. Where a nation organizes its inspiration into an endless stream of literary production it becomes civilized, it counts, it belongs to humanity in the sense of the humanism of the French Revolution.

We shall see that the key to the French Constitution cannot be found until we know of this endeavour to keep true inspiration alive, to keep pouring into the body of the nation the living breath of divine genius. It was this idea which made Hilaire Belloc explain the French Revolution to his suspicious English readers as a truly Catholic enterprise, because the belief in universal inspiration, in a permanent guidance of the Saints and the Holy Ghost, is the outstanding difference between the historical adventure of Christianity and the natural religions. Inspiration, forming a real stream, a continuous current of electric power, is perpetually transforming humanity. There are no established privileges, no water-tight compartments in the world. *"L'esprit seul peut tout changer."* Inspiration is at work all the time changing the surface of the earth and the essence of things and men.

VOLTAIRE'S AND ROUSSEAU'S IDEAS.

The cult of an inspired literature is a real creed, and involves a theory of revolution; like Russian Marxism, French Jacobinism created a dogmatic creed. Therefore, an understanding of Voltaire and Rousseau, the two dogmatists of "national inspiration," will make transparent most of the changes in the map of Europe during the nineteenth century. Rather than sacrifice two hundred pages more to the ups and downs of the national democracies all over the world, we shall do better to investigate the revolutionary system at its literary centre.

The first two bodies to be transferred to the Panthéon on Mount St. Geneviève were those of Voltaire and Rousseau. Voltaire had always feared that he would have no definite resting place. The "immortal spirit" who was acclaimed as the successor of Louis XIV was caught in a most inconvenient dilemma, between *ancien régime* and revolution. On the border of Switzerland and France, he lived in a sort of foxhole with two exits, so as to protect himself against both Huguenot Geneva and Catholic France. He wished to conciliate the clergy, which he had relentlessly pursued, because the abiding nightmare of his old age was that his bones would find no peace after his death. This divination came true in an astounding way. He managed by a bold trick to get a Catholic funeral in 1778, before the government knew that he had died. Later he was brought to the Panthéon; and this exaltation brought the swing back. In 1814 the hotspurs of royalist reaction dug up Voltaire's bones and scattered them, to their own satisfaction, to the four winds.

Like Dostoevski and Tolstoi, Rousseau and Voltaire unconsciously divided their labour, one aiming at the individual, the other at the institutions. By the depth of their teaching they forestalled a petty romanticism. Their situation reminds one of the victory of Tolstoi and Dostoevski over the sentimental point of view of the social revolutionaries, who fought for the poor Moujik against St. Petersburg, but who mistook the reform of the village for a satisfactory synthesis between the Christian soul of the Moujik and the social regeneration of all Russia. The danger in Russia was that romanticists identified the deliverance of the individual soul, and the liberty of the village, with the end of Czarism. People who had seen the salvation of the individual and the village in a mechanical destruction of Czarism were forced out of their dreams by Dostoevski; for he told his readers that a new concept of man, a new type of mankind, was in the background of all their desires. Tolstoi, too, prevented any mechanical solution by creating an endless longing for a new heaven and a new earth, not to be satisfied by local, Russian solutions, but only by one valid for all Europe and Asia.

Rousseau and Voltaire are to be credited with the same merit, though it is difficult for us to recapture their achievement. Their vocabulary appears rather trite today after six generations of constant use. We should forget all we know about Jefferson, Bentham, Spencer, and Wilson for a minute. These men, like the other liberals, are deeply indebted to Rousseau and Voltaire; yet they flattened out the real depth of their thought.

The French situation in 1759 was still very much the three-fold problem of Pascal, as it was explained above. Pascal had distinguished:

1. Sublime Science, on the highest level (his mathematics).
2. Provincialism, to be fought against as the murder of the intellectual life by mere inertia (his *Lettres Provinciales*).
3. Port Royal, the free harbour of the soul, which is not created to be alone (his *Pensées*).

As long as mystical homes like Port Royal were a possible escape for the individual, the bourgeois of the cities of France could desert his sensual, earthy, political environment for those asylums. But when, in 1750, the country cried out for stays and uprights to build a new political roof for the house of France, point three in Pascal's scheme had to be replaced. And it was.

Pascal had taught: *"Le moi est haïssable"* (The I is odious). Jean Jacques Rousseau began his confessions: "I wish to reveal to my fellow beings a man in all the truth of nature, and this man will be myself! . . . myself alone!" The two sentences illustrate the revolutionary change.

The Christian who escaped into a Sabbath purity of church or sect or mysticism was replaced by the "man of nature." Rousseau had the courage to exhibit himself as the first individual of the new society, the citizen of the future earthly paradise. But his personal nervous fits and ugly acts—he went so far as to treat his legitimate children as natural children and to banish them to a foundling asylum—needed certain auxiliary constructions. Jean-Jacques restored Adam, and Adam was to replace Jesus. Jesus, the first citizen of the city on Mount Zion, was supplanted by the natural man and wife. As pure water—Adam's ale—had existed before the refinements of wine or beer, so Adam himself was the natural man who existed before the original sin of division into classes; when Adam delved and Eve span, who was then the gentleman? The Creator had bestowed on the natural man the gift of freedom. "The God who gave us life gave us liberty at the same time," said Jefferson. The words "at the same time" are the essence and the Achilles' heel of this natural philosophy, for they mean that a man is to be considered *a priori* as a free being. An Easterner going into the Mississippi or Ohio Valley in 1800 was a free man. A man skilful in his profession, a jeweller or painter, was free. The government of Ohio or the Chamber of Commerce in Paris could be organized by these free men who "knew," who were "competent," who were responsible for soil and work.

The obvious weakness of the new-born child, of the old man, of the dependent servant, of the ill or weak-minded man, the bondage of irrational loyalties, even the slow growth of man into independence, contradict Jefferson's idea that life and liberty were "simultaneously" given to man. And the Russian Revolution exploited this fallacy of Rousseauism by establishing its cult of the proletariat. But the bourgeois civilization deals with one actual skein which does run through the pattern of our life. Man's liberty to change at different stages in his life was the point that interested the restless Rousseau. He saw that the adult, the man of forty or fifty years of age, the pioneer in a new country, or the pioneer in thought or art or discovery, is the most striking proof that life and liberty are identical. Our physical life is certainly not free. It depends every minute, from the day of our birth, upon the care, benevolence, interest and sacrifices of others. But our creative power of changing our environment, of changing the world, depends on liberty. Adam the digger, the chopper, but especially Adam the pioneer, is like the Creator, free and divine. Goethe expressed the new gospel when he wrote: "Allah need create no longer. We instead create his world."

In fact, the word "creation" itself changed its meaning com-

pletely during the nineteenth century, at least in French, and
to a certain extent in other languages too. The *"dernière
création"* of a fashion, an industry, can be advertised in this
new world because man himself becomes the Promethean
creator of a new earth organized by free human will. The
"demiurge," the magic hero of antiquity, is turned into the
"creative mind" of genius.

Mr. Groethuysen, in an excellent book,[6] has studied the
sermons preached to the French middle classes before the
Revolution. Everywhere the pride of "doing it oneself," of
craftsmanship, was emphasized. To the power of skill, knowledge, and talent went most of the praise in these sermons. Adam
was glorified, not merely as a piece or a child of nature, but
(and it is important to keep in mind this side of the simile)
as a man who masters nature. Man is by no means simply the
natural man, but a man on his soil, a man with his tools, a
man free in the choice of his activities.

Now we do not act in empty space or time. Action presupposes a fair chance. Adam is, inevitably, a capitalist, perhaps
a small one, like a free-soiler on fifty acres of land, or a poet
who owns nothing but his leisure time—but ownership is the
presupposition of Adam's creative liberty. Rousseau's gospel fits
the owner of land, the owner of property, the owner of capital,
the owner of talent, because it sees man in action according
to his own free choice. No choice without opportunity. Therefore the "fair chance" is our real social property and fortune;
the simplest expression of liberalism is that everyone shall have
an opportunity. Opportunity is the electron in the field of
force created by Rousseauism. The agglomeration of opportunities in a few hands may lead to wealth; but the only essential feature is that everybody shall get at least one opportunity.
That is enough to justify Jefferson's equation of life and liberty.

When Rousseau made the "I" presentable and exhibited
his "ego," he revolutionized the average conception of Adam.
Adam suddenly became more interesting before the fall than
after. His passions became as innocent and natural as the fire

6 B. Groethuysen, *Die Enstehung der bürgerlichen Welt*, p. 30, Halle, 1927.

of a volcano or the water of a great cataract. French sensualism has never been understood either in England or in Germany: in both countries philosophy remained a subject for brown study. All German philosophers are disguised theologians. In France the word "philosophy" is a much more general term. A girl of the street will shriek when a passer-by does not listen to her offer: *"Quel philosophe!"* For to philosophize means to reflect on your own passions and to be sincere enough to apply their force to your creative life.

All the other countries of Europe suffered during the hegemony of the French Revolution from suppressions and inferiority complexes. Psychoanalysis was discovered by and for all nations except the French. When the psychoanalysts organized their clientele in Europe and America, an Austrian tried to find out why the French were not interested. When he came back from Paris, he exclaimed: "Of course they don't need it. They have dances in their hospitals."

The French escaped the reign of complexes because French philosophy was too natural, too sensual, too aware of man's passions. They succeeded in looking at themselves in the mirror of life without fainting. The "speculations" of the mediæval Abailard were, as we have seen, uses of the mirror; for "speculum" was used quite literally in the sense of mirror, looking-glass. The new word for this natural mirror is "reflection." To reflect is to look at one's own passions. It was only one of the derivations of this principle when Taine uttered the famous dictum: "A work of art is a bit of nature seen through a temperament." The meaning of Spirit, Holy Ghost, turned more and more into that of "clear idea." To a Christian this may seem to degrade the dignity of the original Holy Ghost; but for a believer in liberty a clear idea is not as poor as it looks. After all, men are free, creative, powerful, they are proprietors or capitalists. The degradation of the Holy Spirit into a mere subjective view is counterbalanced by the power of the individual man to carry out his own views and ideas. Provided a free man has ideas, the difficulties of carrying them out do not matter. If man can only express his clear ideas, his inspiration will move the world. Rousseau's endeavour had to be, therefore, to equip every man with the power of expressing his views. When the spirit was nothing else but the creative liberty of every individual, it was sufficient to set this liberty a-going and a human paradise would inevitably result.

The auxiliaries for this new political enterprise were, of course, found not only in the biblical Adam but in the natural wilderness of new continents besides. Jean Jacques himself and his Émile and his creative Adam were rounded off by all the pictures of life in non-European countries! The French, preparing themselves to regenerate Europe, were perfectly willing to place Christianity below the noble savage. For the purpose of turning the scales from Pascal's Christian humility to the creativeness of the man of nature, the noble savage was a wonderful foil. Robinson Crusoe was an even better example, because he recovered from a rotten society by setting all the miraculous energies of his brain to work on an isolated island. And since Robinson Crusoe became the model of classical economics, his relation to Rousseau's Adam must be stressed. The whole prehistory of Robinson Crusoe, his upbringing, experience, equipment, standards, count for nothing: all our interest centres in this man who represents society in a nutshell, before the division of labour, that is to say, before the fall of man.

Today it has become a commonplace to lament the lack of a reasonable distribution in our economy. But any economic system which starts from Robinson Crusoe *must* overlook distribution. Production and consumption are Crusoe's only gods, because he is society without the problem of distribution. Distribution takes a back seat; it is introduced too late to get a fair hearing in the economist's reasoning.

Liberalism owes its very existence to these godfathers: Adam and Robinson Crusoe. Wherever economists begin with human consumption and production, they are doomed to end where liberalism did end: in the World War for a world market. Whoever starts with the individual must end with the universe. Once the standard unit of power is conceived as one man, enterprising, free, well-equipped, no barrier can be found to his activities. His field is the world. The naturalistic viewpoint of an Adam is valid for all mankind without any difference of creed, faith, church, denomination.

The wonderful *equality* of man is as close at hand as liberty itself wherever Adam sets our standards. Politically, the world seems a rather uniform place from Rousseau's point of view. And it is difficult to understand how France or Europe could emerge out of such a universal ocean of equality. When space, political space, is identified with space in nature, all the properties of physical space descend upon the political territory. Descartes, in applying the notions of God to Nature, assumed that space was endless and unlimited. The new Copernican view of the solar system made man a particle of dust on a minor planet. His roots in eternity were cut off. These roots had been secured by the doctrine of the Fourth Gospel that the Logos —"inspiration"—was with God before the creation of Space, that man therefore, by the process of his growth and salvation in time, is above space, and that space is nothing but the three shabby dimensions into which, for our mortal eyes, time is dissolved.

The Cartesian world put time into space, made time at its best a fourth dimension of space, and pretended that a man's lifetime was nothing but a portion of the astronomical periods. Modern men believe implicitly in the natural calendar of 365 days—as if man's lifetime could really be measured by clocks. In reality it is so far from uniform that one day can count for a hundred, and a thousand years be like one day—and this because we are able to rest, to keep the Sabbath, and to choose on every Lord's Day whether we are to repeat the existing order or are called forth to create a new. Nature has no rest and has therefore no choice; man has. Human love condenses an eternity into a drop in time's ocean. Human law can keep life unchanged for centuries. But Cartesian philosophy could not master this paradox. It bowed before the scientific vision of space. We have already mentioned that French sensualism did not need the recent discoveries of psychoanalysis. We can add now that the domination of space has been avenged in France in our time. Bergson's discovery of time as the Creator was like the flourish of the trumpet against the walls of Jericho.

Bergson was not a native of France, but he wrote his book in Paris for the French. And wherever it affected men as something new, you can be sure that Cartesianism and Rousseauism had reigned there and dried out the human soul.

In the French system, the Holy Ghost of old, *l'esprit*, does not mean much more than the views and opinions of such and such an individual. His soul, passions, hopes, became raw material for the "ideas," reflections and speculations begotten by man's genius. Man became a bundle of nerves. Both God and the soul were passed over by the *"esprit"* of the free man and by the world of nature as seen by this free man. Man acts as the womb in which nature begets. The offspring of this procreation are man's creations: art, science and industry. To sum up: philosophy of the French type can be recognized by two fallacies. In the first place, all the books written on space and time put time after space, make time secondary to space, and only later modify their observations on space by confessing that time comes in too. This helpless attitude toward time is mostly unconscious. In a great American library where I investigated the philosophy shelves, not one of the textbooks on time and space mentioned the methodological possibility of beginning with time. The Cartesian migration from theology into philosophy is a migration from eternity into space, and into space alone.

The second fallacy of the minds which were dominated by the ideas of 1789 is the artificial and arbitrary way in which they identify mind with soul. Scores of books have been written on "body and soul" and "body and mind," without asking the simple question whether dualism is the only solution of the problem. Now the Christian church, for example, has always maintained that soul and body belong to the individual, but that mind and spirit are not individual qualities. Intelligence gives the individual soul a share in the universal inspiration: that is all. Modern clergymen themselves have forgotten this fundamental truth. By giving way to the famous *God of Nature*, by abandoning the sharp distinction beween mind and soul, they condemned the soul to be nothing but a mind— God's information bureau. Now it is not our minds but our souls to which God is a secret and a revelation. The mind of the philosopher can know nothing of God. But Cartesianism makes the mind boast that it has through its own power a notion of the Supreme Being, a God of Nature. It was not Rousseau but Voltaire who established this deistic enlightenment. The usual teaching of economics in a modern university depends on the fallacies of Rousseau; the ordinary teaching of philosophy and psychology or political science is based on Voltairism.

Thus both systems became our common fallacy, and the political and social life of the modern world was based upon them. Hence, to most men today they seem truisms, but I am afraid they are really nothing more than a middle-class programme for economic expansion. We must try to understand them better.

Rousseau had revealed the odious "I" which Pascal had hated. It was not pleasant in Rousseau either; but this artifice made Adam and the noble savage the cornerstones of man's second creation.

Voltaire did something similar with the world of Descartes. In 1644, in the gloomiest year in the history of Paris, Descartes, from his self-chosen exile in Holland, began his *Principles of Philosophy* with the astounding postulates: 1. That in order to seek truth it is necessary at least once in the course of our life to doubt, as far as possible, all things; 2. that we ought to consider false everything that is doubtful.

The dynamite of these two principles can blow up any social order. It is true, Descartes had cautiously added, "that we ought not, meanwhile, to make use of doubt in the conduct of life." But even before, in the *Discourse on Method,* he had introduced the following argument: "It is not enough, before commencing to rebuild the house in which we live, that it be pulled down, and materials and builders provided . . . but it is likewise necessary that we be furnished with some other house in which we may live commodiously during the operations."

Thus there were three "houses" for mankind: 1. the new house of perfect knowledge, of science; 2. the traditional house of prejudices, of old age; and 3., between these two, a sort of apartment to give temporary shelter to the searching mind.

Voltaire, the man who changed the letters of his name "Arouet" into "Voltaire," who lived literally in an apartment with two exits, one on French and one on Swiss territory, who throughout his life published revolutionary books of which he was forced to deny the authorship, who never earned a penny from his books, but lived like an aristocrat, Voltaire took Descartes' idea of the three houses more to heart than Cartesius himself. To be sure, Descartes had pretended to be a fervent Catholic, but he had lived in Protestant countries during the last twenty years of his life and thus accepted the existence of Protestantism. Descartes had further asserted that the house number three in which to "live commodiously during the operations" had to be built according to the laws and customs of the particular "country"—which is quite simple if you succeed in living outside your own country as he did. In this way he had avoided giving a special character to the "temporary shelter." Voltaire realized much more clearly than Descartes that the mind of a man who doubts everything, who is independent and enlightened, has already sacrificed his real "old" house; that to get to the new house it was not enough to borrow a social order in the meantime by simply obeying the laws and customs of a Protestant country. There had to be a certain peculiar formation between old and new, distinctly hostile to the old and unquestioningly devoted to the new. Voltaire, in fighting Catholic and Protestant bigotry from his "fox-hole," lived the future life of the age of reason by kindling "the revolution of minds," or, as he said in French: *"la révolution des esprits."* Voltaire converted "revolution," up to his time the physical rotation of the stars, into an *intellectual* process. He was not an isolated mind like Descartes, but made himself the grand master of enlightenment, the idol of the European reading world. It was the *readers* of Europe who had to fill the breach between the old house of tradition and the new house of natural science.

Voltaire levied upon Europe an army of readers who should hold themselves ready until the actual material revolution came. And come it must. We give some quotations from him: "Twenty volumes in folio will never cause a revolution. The cheap little pamphlets you buy to carry in your pocket are the ones to be feared." "Everything around me is scattering the seed of a revolution which will inevitably occur, though I shall not have the pleasure of witnessing it." "The French come to everything late, but at last they come to it. The fog has become thicker and thicker, until at the first opportunity there will be an outburst. And then the noise will be tremendous."

And the goal of this revolution? A reasonable world must take the place of the world of miracles, revelations, and saints. For "the machinery of the world can be explained philosophically in two ways: Either (1) God once created it and nature has obeyed ever since, or (2) God unceasingly gives existence and changes of existence to everything. A third point of view would be inexplicable."

Now we all know, and Voltaire knew, that one half of the world is regular and recurrent, a lawful nature, and the other half is love, change, grace, surprise. We could not take a railroad train to go and propose to our sweetheart without this dualism. The train obeys the schedule, and we rely on it because it is the mechanized part of our existence. But we tremble until we have surprised our sweetheart and changed her mind by the sudden breaking in of a new vision of a life in common. The world is old and new at once. Progress means nothing if it is not in permanent contact and contrast with the starting-point from which it proceeds. On a road, the man who does not keep his starting-point in mind will make no progress, but only move in a vicious circle.

Law and love, nature and creation, are in perpetual opposition and struggle with each other. The third viewpoint, which was inexplicable to Voltaire, is the viewpoint practised by everybody every day.

But to the grand master of enlightenment, whose army is to enlist against prejudice, ignorance, tyranny and despotism, the process can never be a polar antagonism. The old can never be bright, the new can never be dark, because the old means the impossible constitution of France and the new means the possible solution of all the riddles of life.

Voltairism, like Rousseauism, sacrificed the Christian dualism of law and love, repetition and surprise, custom and revelation, to the *fighting monism of an army of enlightenment.* Monism was the bent of the whole nineteenth century, always willing to pervert the State into the Church, love into law, penology into education, charity into politics, war into peace, men into women, and women into men.

Monism dominated the whole world between 1789 and 1914 (or 1934), in the form of an attempt to identify future with progress and past with darkness. This monism was perfectly true and admirable in the field of science. Space and the forces of space became known better and better from the times of Copernicus and Galileo to those of Planck and Bohr. The "enlighteners," the authors and prophets of mechanism, can boast that under the guidance of this principle modern science has made its greatest progress. The services it has rendered to modern science can hardly be overestimated. Monism created an alliance between all men to observe, to march as one legion against nature, to explore, to compute and to organize the powers and forces of the universe. Man is monistic in so far as he is a scientist, because in his fight against nature he is united like one man, aye, one body, and the observations of astronomers in Australia and in Nova Scotia can be of the same immediate value for the scientific result. Nature makes mankind one observer, one mind. The monism of the scientific enlightenment lets men take the place which God took in monotheism. We, as a body, are treated like one person, one Adam, one Robinson Crusoe. We all agree in observing the same facts, in carrying out the same chemical experiments, in comparing mathematical calculations or dates of exploration.

Monism is the solidarity of mankind as it marches forth from bodily, political divisions to the intellectual union of minds. This monism can be found everywhere in the modern world as a principle of wonderful driving power. Most people are not aware that this monistic principle prevails even in their social and humanitarian activities. They think it only natural that another man can be united with them if his thoughts about the outside world are on all fours with their thoughts.

The revolutionary process itself refutes the Voltairian "either-or." The dialectical antithesis between innovation and repetition is always before our eyes. The creation of the world is not at all complete. "Creation's Lord, we give thee thanks that we are in the making still." Mother Earth does not develop purely according to the original laws of nature, seeing that millions of years ago she was only original mud. At every moment original life and developed life exist side by side, one "in becoming," the other stabilized. The revolutionary and sacrificial life, devoted to change, coexists with the hard and fast recurrence of old forms. Only after rigid testing is new life embodied into the world; but once received, it runs in its fixed groove as long as it is faithful to its origin.

Mechanism and freedom exist together in man's world. This is the "third constitution" which Voltaire thought impossible. He was perfectly sure that man's logic faced only two alternatives: either the world was a mechanical clock-work or it was a tissue of miracles; and he chose the clock-work. It is a wonderful piece of logic, and a very French logic too. The *Sic et Non,* the "yes and no" which Abailard had used to cut a path through the jungle of quotations from church-fathers, was used by Voltaire to clear up nature. Now dialectical quotations from human writings can always be answered by a verdict of true or false, yes and no, because man's judgment is always capable of revision. But Creation cannot be revised: it speaks a final language. God does not speak to us in words, he speaks in forms and creatures. For the discussion of the values of a plant, an animal, or a civilization, our logical yes and no are of little use.

The fallacy of all enlightenment is the extension of dialectical logic to questions wholly removed from a logical approach. What is called the romanticism of the nineteenth century was the constant fight against the abuse of Abailard's method by Voltaire. Friedrich Schlegel formulated it well when he said, "Let us distinguish the permanent qualities of mankind and the changes in its quality which add some new quality

in the course of history." Schlegel was writing during the
French Revolution. In the days of the Russian Revolution,
an ornithologist, speaking of his beloved birds, wrote bitterly
of Voltaire's solution: "It cannot but be a pagan religion
which manages to assign to its God the rôle of a retired civil
officer or that of the captured Samson blindly turning the mill
in the service of the Philistines."

What Hegel and Marx called the dialectical process of history, was exactly this same discovery of the illogical possibilities
of reality, as against the simplifications of the human brain.
The famous dialectic of the Russian Revolution means that
in the world of facts logic does not prevail, that yes and no
can both exist. Very often, however, the adherents of Bolshevism have been too good Voltairians and Rousseauists, and
have forgotten this protest of life against logic, which was represented by Marxism. They cannot understand how Communist
Russia, the negation of liberalism, can live in the same world
with France or the United States of America. Voltaire could
not have understood it either. We can.

The Russian Revolution, called forth by the onesidedness
of the French, is a new creation, a new reality; far from being
a thing of the philosopher's study, it is lived by real men and
women, millions of men and millions of women. These new
men and women came into being and live by continuing the
process of creation, but without destroying its former results!
We, therefore, can recognize the results of the Russian Revolution without believing that it excludes all other principles.

Thus the preceding discussion is highly practical, because
without it the reader might feel that we ourselves must be
either Voltairians or Marxians, and that after all, writing on
revolutions, we should be either a Jacobin or a Bolshevik.
This black-and-white logic is futile. But the thing is much
more serious than that. It is not the platform of a political
party but humanity itself which is at stake. Is man to be re-born
and regenerated? Is Creation all around us, or far away, tens of
thousands of years ago? Are the history of nature and the history of man one thing or two? Finally, how can the soul, which
refuses to take a partial view, be justified and redeemed?

Our book is an attempt to solve this paradox, an attempt by which history and science, law and theology, are joined into an indissoluble unit.

FREEMASONRY.

During the eighteenth century, in the days of Voltaire, the army of enlightenment formed the lodges of Freemasonry. Freemasonry came into existence as the political organization of the European reading public. It was the expression of the desire of contractors, artists, scientists, to build a new world. God, the omnipresent Creator, was banished to the first days of creation; He himself was only the Master Builder. It is an interesting fact that Voltaire and the Freemasons did not fight God as the atheists are doing in Russia. The full-blooded revolutionary, the Bolshevik, must destroy God because, as a matter of principle, since the revolution is declared to be perpetual, he must vindicate his right to destroy everything.

The French *révolution des esprits* is but the temporary shelter before the house of reason is ready. There is real building, real constructive work, a real second creation, which is expected to develop after the revolution. The revolution is a stage between house number one and house number two. None of the furniture of the old house is abandoned. Every piece is kept; but it is enlightened, improved, refined, analyzed, modernized. All the novelties of French liberalism are given out as the old ideas of humanity purified from the dross of superstition.

God, too, is such a purified idea, which it would be a pity to lose. "If God did not exist, we should have to invent him," is a famous utterance of Voltaire. But cleansed the idea must be. The same Voltaire could say: *"Écrasez l'infâme"* (Crush the infamous one), that is, the Church, the vessel in which the idea of God had been preserved. "We, as grown-up men and Freemasons, will keep the idea of God. Children may believe in the Lord's outer vestments; we know better. The idea of government, too, is a good idea. We do not abolish government like the Marxians, who in their perpetual revolution cannot leave any more room for the State than for God. But

the shell of this idea, kingship and old régime, is crumbling.
Our idea of government is constructive, architectural. *Ancien
régime* is *vieux jeu:* old government, bad government. The
very idea of government implies the reform of government.
Laws—we like laws because we are going to make laws.
Grown-up men are law-makers." The Bolsheviks despise laws
as ideology; the reader of Voltaire, the enlightened Freemason,
marches back into his nation to become a citizen through the
right conception of law. Common law, customs, the living
voices of the fathers?—all bad law. Let us make new laws, many
new laws, which will reflect the clarified idea of legislation.

God, liberty, immortality, were the three ideas to which
Robespierre clung like a real creed, as if they were the foun-
tainhead of the national constitution. And Jefferson and
Franklin shared his views. The belief in ideas assured the standards of the new régime. Without "ideas," the loss of values
would have been terrifying. Ideas are the clothes of the new
man's, the parvenu's mind. The man of nature or the man of
passion must get his "ideas," his values, his foundation somewhere. And he finds them in the house of Reason. "Ideas" are
the arsenal with which to equip the new legislators of France.
The bourgeoisie who devoured Voltaire's writings devoured
them to become the governing class of France! Their creative
mind, their constructive ability, their virile will, must be furnished with a set of positive values; and so a compromise is
reached between the philosopher and the free man of private
property. The old wine must be put into new bottles; the
eternal "ideas" must be kept, but freed from the old institutions which had corrupted them: Church, kings, and customs.
Both the philosopher and the citizen agree. The guardian of
the new civilization is he who upholds the values corrupted by
kings, priests and aristocrats.

Both the merit and the inconsequence of Freemasonry lie
in this idea of purification. All its ceremonies tend to emphasize this purpose. Since most of the members of the lodge
prefer to believe that it came down from the old stone-masons
who built the cathedrals of the Gothic period or from the

Knights Templar, it is worth mentioning that this is a typical case of mystification.

Freemasonry, this temporary guild which Descartes saw to be essential to the revolution of minds, which tried to keep the kernel without the shell, God without Church, government without authority, and law without prescription, had its origin in England between 1710 and 1730. It was the characteristic reaction of the left wing of Whiggism against the petrifaction of the Anglican Church. It made for the real union of English and Scotch, despite their religious differences, following the remark of Hobbes in his *Leviathan:* "It is strange to me that England and Scotland, being as they are but one island, and their language almost the same, and governed by one King, should be thought of as foreigners to one another. And, therefore, for my part I think they were mistaken, both the English and Scots, in calling one another 'foreigners.'" Freemasonry in England abolished the term "foreigner" between these two nations living on the same island and using the same language. It was a new common society for the United Kingdom. The union of the English and Scottish parliaments was delayed until long after the reign of the Stuarts and the fusion under Cromwell; and the lodge followed the political union which was consummated in 1708. Freemasonry in Great Britain was, therefore, no revolutionary enterprise. But in spreading over the Continent it did become revolutionary. Its secret ritual (Mozart's *Magic Flute* is an apotheosis of Freemasonry) made it the provisional home between the *ancien régime* and the age of reason. Masonry became the seed-ground of national democracy; for the lodge was always national in its aims, though international in its original creed. Today it is hated and attacked by Fascism, not for its alleged internationalism in foreign affairs, but for its other side, its unshakable anchorage in the rights of the individual against the government.

THE CONSTITUTION.

The "ideas," the weapons of the new and reasonable rulers of France, must accompany regenerated humanity into practice. How can they descend from the bright heights of leisure and philosophy into the dust of men's interests and struggle for life? Man, in his effort to remain a creator even in the daily heat of passion, is sustained by ideas in the form of the "Constitution." The idea of a "Law Paramount" had first been discussed in 1647 by the Levellers, the precursors of democratic ideas during Cromwell's Puritan revolution. The "Law Paramount" had been thought of then as a Christian and Biblical law, a covenant of the chosen people; but even so it had been the "idea" of a formulated and written constitution. This was something fundamentally opposed to the Common Law of England, the very paradise of aristocracy, with its privileges, precedents, and customs. The Levellers had been trampled under foot, but the ideas of natural philosophy, the reason of man, still cried for a visible home or shrine. The Constitution of Virginia had begun to carry out the idea of a law paramount.

The French Revolution did the same, in spite of the almost geological pressure of the many strata of ancient privilege. The place of the Past was now taken by Reason, and the laws of the land were replaced by the law of Reason. But it was the past whose place Reason was to occupy. Neither the present nor the present ruler was to be set on the throne which the tradition of the estates had preserved ever since Charlemagne. The Reason of the Law Paramount, the Constitution of the Year III, the Ideas of Voltaire or Robespierre, transcend the day-to-day opinions of politicians. As majestic, as far away, as high and venerable as tradition, the Constitution dwells on an Olympian level above the passions of politics. The Constitution must be removed from the struggles of faction or party.

The idea of a written constitution attests to the unlimited belief of Freemasonry in the power of the mind. Surely the minds of men would instinctively obey the summons of Reason. Man would always prefer the fundamentals of the Law Paramount to the changing temptations of the day; for the Constitution would move his best and deepest emotions, it would apostrophize the part of man through which he was man. The Constitution would be safe because it would flatter every free man's genius, every citizen's pride. Does it not remind him of his inalienable rights? Does it not grant him life, liberty, health, honour and property? How can a man ever prefer the despotism of a confiscatory, arbitrary, communistic, bureaucratic, tyrannic or aristocratic government to a Constitution which prohibits confiscation, arbitrary arrest, communistic neglect of privacy, bureaucratic crippling of enterprise, tyrannical suppression of speech and aristocratic contempt of genius?

As long as the middle classes, holding the mean between aristocrats and peasants in their form of life, marched forward under the flag of the Law Paramount, the choice was indeed mostly in favour of the rights of man. The "tricolour" is the flag of this creed. Wherever you find a tricolour, you are in a country whose foundations were laid after 1789 and are based on the distinction between Constitution and everyday legislation. After the deepest humiliation of the French genius, after the downfall of Napoleon III, the defeat in the war against Prussia, the loss of a part of "natural Gaul"—Alsace-Lorraine— the atrocities of the "Commune" and the equally atrocious counter-revolution, when the French citizen seemed to be ready to pay any price for stability, peace, order and security, the party of the *juste-milieu* (MacMahon, the Orléanists, and Thiers) went so far as to offer the crown to the Bourbon Count de Chambord. The Count declared that, once King, he would hoist the white flag with the lilies of Bourbon. This announcement brought the decision instantly. In refusing to give up the white flag, the Count de Chambord was really refusing to recognize the validity of the fundamental principles of the Revolution—the principles of popular sovereignty and equality of rights. The Orléanists were wise enough to know that the French people, although not at all loath to accept a king, would not and could not deny the glorious strugge of Ideas and Constitutions against aristocracy and privileges. "If we proclaim the white flag, the muskets will go off of their own accord," said Marshal MacMahon. That was as much as to say that the Ideas, even at freezing point on the revolutionary thermometer, still contained enough dynamite to blow up mere Tradition. After this cold and sober test of its inevitability, the Republic was installed, being carried by one vote. Final decisions are not made triumphantly and unanimously; on the contrary, like Lenin's Peace of Brest-Litovsk, they are carried by a bare majority. In this way France retained the tricolour.

The whole character of the French Revolution can now be better understood. It was not an anti-royal revolution. It was, and remained to the end, an anti-aristocratic restoration of Adam's equality.

The King remained King three years after the complete abolition of the privileges of the nobles in 1789. He was beheaded as a Prince of the Blood, as a supporter of aristocracy, not as a misruler, like Charles I. Napoleon I, the sword of the Revolution, Louis XVIII, faithful to the Charter, Louis Philippe, the Bourgeois King, in short, any later Constitution held that Reason, instead of tradition, had to be consulted as the divine oracle for settling conflicts of interest.

But, alas, man is not always proud of his genius, and nations cannot always be supporting the rights guaranteed by the Law Paramount against the temptations of the hour.

Where national democracy had come into existence, politics easily degenerated into lobbying. For this national democracy was soon besieged by the blind forces of the fearing, expropriated, illiterate, and uninspired masses. The lodge of the philosophers declined into a lobby of the lawyers and the governing class of the new nation. Yet they still claimed to be the people bound together by nature in defence of the Constitution.

We say "by nature"; but we already know that the nature which transforms "people" into "nation" includes *literature*. A nation is comprised of people *who are enlightened, led, and inspired by the same literature.* The important rôle of the *écrivain* in France, the political organization of the reading class all over Europe in Freemasonary, the marvellous fight of the French schoolteacher for his language, all have the same tendency. The modern "idea" of the nation, like the other "ideas" we have surveyed, is the result of a purifying process. The old concept of nation had been that of a geographical subdivision within the Church. A nation was a group of scholars, doctors, and princes at one of the Christian Councils.

At the great councils of the fifteenth century the French nation was led by the University of Paris.

Now, in the eighteenth century, the nation had to be organized outside the Church, outside Christianity, in the natural world: the doctors of theology were replaced by the writers and expounders of philosophy, and the estates of France—King, clergy, and nobility—by the Freemasons of reason. These elements formed the "nation." Wherever modern nationalism in Europe succeeded in founding a national state within natural borders, literature and the lodge were at its back. The modern nation is therefore not a product of nature but of literature, not a body of mere inhabitants but of listeners and readers of modern philosophy and science.

Like the nations in the mediæval Church, the nations of the civilized world are shareholders in a common spirit and a common thought. Literature and science, art and newspapers, are the universal framework of this civilization. It is even easier to grasp the cosmopolitan idea of the new civilization than to see any natural subdivisions within it. And, it is true, the nations of enlightenment, the national democracies of Europe and America, were built on the presumption that their common heritage was safer and clearer than their special demarcation. Science, information, common thought and common ideas seemed capable of linking men as closely as the Church, the international hospitality of monks, and the unity of faith and learning, had linked the Occident before. *To know* became the mark of man. In the schools of France the masterpieces of ancient and modern foreign literatures were introduced because, as Sainte-Beuve said, "No one is a man who does not know them."

European civilization once more secured its unity through the study of a common literature. The study of Greek was made compulsory during the nineteenth century as it had never been before. Plato and the Greek tragedies were made the common denominator of civilization. The enthusiasm for the Greeks has already been mentioned in connection with "Europe." But, for France, this Renaissance of Nature and the Classics had a much deeper meaning than for any other country. The difficulty of determining the political subdivisions of the cosmopolitanism which we have tried to describe, that is, of defining one "natural nation," existed in less degree for France than for any other power in Europe. Here literature had from time immemorial been more or less centralized in Paris. And Paris gained when literature was brought to the front. The classical *Gallia* of Cæsar could easily be confused with the natural defences of Paris. "The left bank of the Rhine!" became the natural outcry of the Revolutionary Wars. Practically, the classical quotations and the natural science of the revolutionaries have not made for the happiness of Paris: she has suffered more since she took up this theory of natural boundaries than before. She was threatened or conquered by foreign troops in 1792, 1814, 1815, 1870-1871, and 1914-1918 —all this after the Revolution. But in the field of cultural influence these sacrifices were outweighed a hundredfold, because France became the model of national democracy. For example, the language of science had to be national as it was in France. Thus the Magyars, immediately after the settlement of 1867, introduced the Magyar language into the proceedings of the Royal Academy of Budapest. What to a French Academician was a means of communication with the whole world showed its reverse here by excluding the Hungarian writer from any important audience. The Czechs, when they established their republic, had no organized readers or listeners; so they paid a lady in Prague to run a "salon." Even the wish of Austria and Germany to unite after the World War seemed more or less the natural result of the French belief that a common language and a contiguous territory make for one national democracy. Now the classical conception of *Gallia* being favourable to French literature, the classical notion of Germania has always struck the French as being terribly dangerous. Their own norm and yardstick proved fatal as soon as it favoured the union of Germany. But how to fight against it on the French basis of national rights and national literature? Obviously, the argument against the *Anschluss* had to be found in the same pharmacopœia of 1789, where the remedies were labelled "liberalism," "national democracy," "rights of nations," etc. But even this was achieved. On March 26, 1931, Herriot, the leader of the French radical party, wrote in *L'Ère Nouvelle:* "Austria cannot be allowed to join Germany, because a nation must be a circle (vide France) with one centre (vide Paris). But Germany would become an ellipse, with two focuses: and this is of course impossible!" The deduction seems perfectly absurd. New York and Washington, St. Petersburg and Moscow, tell the story of how impossible it is to make a state a circle around one centre. Mathematics means nothing in social life. But I am sure M. Herriot's readers were satisfied. The fact that geometry does not apply to society is easily understood. But Herriot is not speaking of society, he is dealing with nations; and it was the misfortune of the nineteenth century that it incessantly and intentionally confused nations with nature. Now in nature mathematics is applicable. It is not as ridiculous as it may seem at first to arrange nations in the form of circles. After all, the French Revolution stamped out the confusion in standards of measurement.

THE TYRANNY OF THE DECIMAL SYSTEM.

We can see this French use of mathematics very clearly in a question of world-wide interest: the decimal system. The fog of avoirdupois and troy weight was dispersed. Water, Adam's ale, was made the cornerstone of the new natural system of weighing and measuring bodies and distances. A thousand grams of water are one litre, and a litre is a cubic decimetre or 1000 cubic centimetres of water. The metre, again, is in connection with all nature, being the ten-millionth part of a quadrant (a quarter) of a meridian, from the Equator to the Pole. Its standard is a piece of platinum kept at Paris. The grand conception of "nature" could not be better expressed than by this new constitution for nature. The old measures, foot, yard, acre, rule, grain, pint, etc., were all taken from the near environment of man: his own body, his fruit, his soil, served as sources of his language. The French Revolution speaks in the name of nature. It starts from the Equator and brings home one forty-millionth of its circumference for practical use. The idea is universal, the adaptation is made by subdivisions. Man truly becomes a grain of dust on the globe in the same measure that he believes in the metre as one ten-millionth of the quadrant of his planet.

Decimal numeration and decimal systems are not "natural" in the way of common sense. Dozen, score, and hundred-weight contradict the hypothesis that ten and five are more natural than 4, 12, 20, and 112 or 120. They are not. Not even the natural logarithm can be based on ten-ten in the abstract. The decimal system ought rather to be called an abstract or reasonable system.

Furthermore, the decimal system reveals the real meaning of "nature" in the French language. "Nature" is not the noble savage, but the reasonable Robinson Crusoe, not the blushing Adam, but the reflecting Voltaire; it should not be called "nature" but "reason," and should be written in capitals: R E A S O N. In 1821, John Quincy Adams, later President of the United States, wrote about the revolutionary scope of the decimal system:

"The substitution of an entire new system of weights and measures, instead of one long established and in general use, is one of the most arduous exercises of legislative authority. Weights and measures may be ranked among the necessities of life to every human individual and society. They enter into the economical arrangements and daily concerns of every family. They are necessary to every occupation of human industry; to the distribution and security of every species of property; to every transaction of trade or commerce; to the labours of the husbandman; to the ingenuity of the artificer; to the studies of the philosopher; to the researches of the antiquarian; to the navigation of the mariner, and the marches of the soldier; to all the exchanges of peace and all the operations of war. The knowledge of them, as in established use, is among the first elements of education, and is often learned by those who learn nothing else. This knowledge is etched into the memory by the habitual application of it in the employments of men throughout life.

"To change all this at once, is to affect the well-being of every man, woman and child, in the community. It enters every house, it cripples every hand. Tables of equation must be circulated in such a manner as to find their way into every house; and a revolution must be effected in the use of books for elementary education, and in all the schools where the first principles of arithmetic may be taught.

"All this has been done in France. The system of modern France originated with the Revolution. It is one of those attempts to improve the condition of human kind, which, should it even be destined to fail ultimately, would, in its failure, deserve little less admiration than in its success. It is founded upon the following principles:

"1. That all weights and measures should be reduced to one *uniform* standard of linear measure.

"2. That this standard should be an aliquot part of the circumference of the globe.

"3. That the unity of linear measure, applied to matter, in its three modes of extension, length, breadth and thickness, should be the standard of all measures of length, surface and solidarity.

"4. That the cubic contents of the linear measure, in distilled water, at the temperature of its greatest contraction, should furnish at once the standard weight and measure of capacity.

"5. That for everything susceptible of being measured or weighed, there should be only one measure of length, one weight, one measure of contents, with their multiples and subdivisions exclusively in decimal proportions.

"6. That the principle of decimal division, and a proportion of the linear standard, should be annexed to the coins of gold, silver, and copper, to the moneys of account, to the division of *time,* to the barometer and the thermometer, to the plummet and the log lines of the sea, to the geography of the earth, and the astronomy of the skies; and, finally, to everything in human existence susceptible of comparative estimation by weight or measure.

"7. That the whole system should be equally suitable to the use of all mankind.

"8. That every weight and every measure should be designated by an appropriate, significant, characteristic name, applied exclusively to itself.

"In Paragraphs 6 and 8, the system reveals its world-wide ambition. 'It forms an era,' not only in the history of weights and measures, but in that of human science. Every step of its progress is interesting. It approaches to the ideal perfection of 'uniformity' applied to weights and measures, and whether destined to succeed, or doomed to fail, will shed unfading glory upon the age in which it is conceived, and upon the nation by which its execution is attempted, and has been in part achieved. In the progress of its establishment and use, it has often been brought into conflict with the laws of physical and of moral nature, with the impenetrability of matter, and with the habits, passions, prejudices and necessities of man. It has undergone various important modifications. It must undoubtedly still submit to others before it can look for universal adoption. But if man upon earth be an improveable being, if that universal peace, which was the object of a Saviour's mission, which is the desire of the philosopher, the longing of the philanthropist, the trembling hope of the Christian, is a blessing to which the futurity of mortal man has a claim of more than mortal promise; if the Spirit of Evil is, before the final consummation of things, to be cast down from his dominion over men, and bound in the chains of a thousand years, the foretaste here of man's eternal felicity, then this system of common instruments to accomplish all the changes of social and friendly commerce, will furnish the links of sympathy between the inhabitants of the most distant regions; the meter will surround the globe in use, as well as in multiplied extension, and one language of weights and measures will be spoken from the equator to the poles."

When this eloquent praise was printed, in 1821, the chances for the success of the system were rather poor. In spite of an invitation sent to Great Britain, in spite of the collaboration of Spanish, Italian, Dutch, Danish and Swiss scholars in the proceedings of the French Academy of Sciences, in spite of precious discoveries on the occasion of the geographical field survey, France herself had turned the clock back. At first, for twelve years (1792-1804), the mensuration of time, the calendar itself, had been included in the decimal system: the Christian Era was to disappear. The equinoctial, or Republican, calendar, based on the new metrology, divided the solar day into ten hours, each of 100 minutes, and each minute into 100 seconds. This part of the reform was abolished on the ninth of September, 1805. The navigators and astronomers continued to divide the sphere into 360 degrees. Continental France proved unable to rule the waves. The lapidaries and dealers in precious stones throughout Europe also continued to have a weight peculiar to themselves, under the denomination of the carat.

In 1812 a Napoleonic decree established a compromise between philosophical theory and inveterate popular habits. Retaining the principle of decimal multiplication and division for the legal system, it abandoned them entirely in the weights and measures which it allowed the people to use. It gave them back a *toise* of six feet, an inch, a foot, and a gross. But the old names now covered new things, because they were reintroduced as fractions of the new system.

John Quincy Adams himself confesses:

"The French system, admirable as it is, looked in its composition to weights and measures as more exclusively matters of account than as tests of quantity; in its eagerness for extreme accuracy in the relations between things it lost sight a little of the relations of weights and measures with the physical organization, the wants, comforts and occupations of man; it forgot the inflexible independence and the innumerable varieties of the forms of nature, and that she would not submit to be trammelled for the convenience of the Counting House. The experience of the French nation has proved that neither the square nor the cube, nor the circle, nor the sphere, nor the revolutions of the earth, nor the harmonies of the heavens will, to gratify the pleasure, or to indulge the indolence of man, be restricted to computation by decimal numbers alone."

The whole process is highly instructive for the methods of real transformation. A change in human affairs is never a simple process. It is usually two steps forward, then one and a half backward; and all possible wisdom is needed to avoid the vicious proportion of two steps forward and three steps backward!

The final victory of the decimal system in France itself was won in 1840. Not until then did the villages really accept it. America allowed its adoption after the Civil War. At the climax of their liberalism Italy and Germany introduced the system, having already imitated France in their national union. John Bull, the hero of common sense, resisted this new, all too reasonable nature most successfully. The new national democracies in the rest of Europe all introduced it, giving the ideas of 1789 an overwhelming success.

Réaumur had previously divided the thermometer into eighty degrees between freezing and boiling point, whereas Celsius had used the "normal" division of a hundred degrees. But though Réaumur was French, the use of his scale was exiled to Germany and Russia, and the French introduced the European system of Celsius, who was not a native of their country. The naturalization of a true citizen of Europe, a man of ideas, was always natural to the French. The papers of citizenship were quite naturally given to Americans or Germans or Poles who joined the rank and file of the Revolution. Nature redeemed, Nature regenerated, did not halt at the toll-gates of national or regional divisions. "The system involves nothing that savours of the peculiarities of any country; in so much as the Commissioners observe, that if all the history were forgotten and the results of the operations only preserved, it would be impossible to tell in what nation this system had originated." [7]

MADAME CURIE.

One of the most moving examples of the victory of this spirit is the biography of Madame Curie. Since we gave some details on the revolutionary life of Lenin and his family in our Russian chapter, it is only fair to illustrate the majesty of the French Revolution by the biography of a typical pioneer in the field of the exploration of nature.

The case is the more fascinating as Marie Curie was a convert. She had been exposed to the temptation of the Lenin type. She was a Pole. "Grown up in a patriarchal atmosphere, nourished by the oppression to which Poland was exposed, I intended like the other young people of my country to give all my forces to uphold the national spirit of Poland. Scientific devotion meant that I was to abandon the social and patriotic dream, to part from family and home in Poland. At the time when this question was raised, I had lived for three years in

[7] John Playfair, *Works,* IV, 257, Edinburgh, 1822.

Paris, studying physics at the Sorbonne. I lived on the seventh floor of a house in the *Quartier des Écoles,* in a miserable room, because I was short of means. But I was very happy. In the spring of 1894 I met Pierre Curie. He respected my simple life of study. He imbued me with the dream of his life, scientific work; he asked me to share his life. He wrote to me: 'Let us lead a common life, immersed in our dreams, the patriotic dream, the humanitarian dream, the scientific dream. Of them all, the scientific, I think, is the only justifiable one.' We married in July, 1895. I had to keep house without any help. For eleven years my husband and I shared our whole life, theoretical inquiries, experiments in the laboratory, preparation for courses and examinations." But after Pierre Curie became teacher at the School of Industrial Physics and Chemistry of the city of Paris, Madame Curie worked independently for three years. During these three years she discovered the radio-activity of the atoms of uranium and thorium. Then she classified all kinds of minerals, rocks and metalloids, some of them more radio-active than uranium itself. Pitchblende and chalcolite have a radio-activity so strong that Madame Curie was led to the idea of a matter much more radio-active than uranium. The outcome of her search was, therefore, the task of isolating the new substance by means of chemical analysis. In this promising situation Pierre Curie decided to join his wife's work; he gave up his own work for hers. The Austrian government presented them with one metric ton of pitchblende produced in the mines of Joachimsthal in Bohemia.

How was the thing to be done? They started in a glass-windowed room that served as a shop and a storage-place for machines. Later, they moved to a deserted shed. "In this shed, with its bituminous floor and its glass roof which did not really protect us from the rain, suffocating us in summer with the heat and rather poorly heated in winter by a cast-iron stove, we passed our best and our happiest years, devoting the whole day to our work. Without any of the amenities which facilitate the labours of a chemist, we had much trouble in running through a great number of experiments on raw material that was always increasing in quantity. When the experiment could not be done outdoors, the windows were opened to give a passage to the obnoxious vapours. Our furniture consisted of a number of old pinewood tables. On these tables I arranged my precious particles of concentrated radium. As we had no chest in which to put the radiant products of our work, we placed them on the tables or on planks. It was hard work to move the vessels, to pour the fluids from one into the other, and to stir them for hours with an iron rod, the fluid seething in a platter on the ground, and I defenceless against the coal and iron dust. But I can remember the delight it gave us when we happened to enter our laboratory at night and saw in every corner the outlines of the products of our labour, feebly radiant through the dark."

Twelve years later, in 1910, Madame Curie presided over the first conference of physical and medical radiology. The greatest physicists, led by Lord Rutherford, paid homage to her achievements. The conference established a new physical unit, the unit of emanation, and called it the "Curie." The Curies had succeeded in analyzing a ton of pitchblende; and some centigrams of pure radium were the result of their effort. Twenty milligrams of radium chloride, sealed in a glass tube, are kept in the *Pavillon de Breteuil,* the laboratory of the Faculty of Sciences in Paris, like the metre-rod, the standard of the metrical system, to serve as a norm for the secondary quantities kept in the chief civilized countries.

To Madame Curie, after the death of her husband, his chair was entrusted. But she also became a member of the French Academy of Medicine. Except for Clemenceau, she was the only person who did not present her candidacy herself. It was her colleague, the Professor A. Henry Becquerel, who moved her reception in the famous phrase coined for Molière: *"Rien ne manque à sa gloire; elle manque à la nôtre."*

It is a wonderful fairy-tale of progress in science and progress by science, producing at the same time a complete and successful naturalization of the explorer into the nature of the civilized nation where his work is done. It is a great lesson for the mad nationalism which constantly mistakes being for becoming. Nations—like all life—are only possible as long as they are in the becoming, in the making, as long as pioneers, geniuses, great—and small—individuals are making their contribution, not with any national aim, but with one far beyond earthly ambition. Without this inexplicable and irrational service for something beyond, any social group is plunged into Egyptian darkness, into the hell of self-adoration.

THE "NATURE" OF FRANCE.

During the Revolution, all France was thrown into the melting pot and stirred around with an iron rod. Her own scientific nature was discovered and established, and she was recreated *"une et indivisible."*

Since the unenlightened classes, clergy and nobles had governed the inhabitants of the different *pays* according to their different customs and laws, the words *"une et indivisible"* became the new chemical formula, which was used with emphasis by all the patriots of 1792. In speeches, on coins and monuments, in laws and bulletins, *une et indivisible* was proclaimed aloud as the original formula for the body politic. In opposition to the federalism or self-government of English origin favoured by the moderates, the "patriots" discovered the real nature of a civilized nation. In ten years they created the new French form of *patrie,* the outline of a centralized republic of twenty-five millions of citizens without any federal counterweights.

So completely was the tradition of federalism destroyed by the new conception of *une et indivisible* that the present slight unrest among Alsatians or Basques, tending to counterbalance the evils of centralization, is called by the poor and unimaginative word *"regionalism."* This anæmic and purely logical term "regionalism" illustrates the decay of the living voices of the land in the scores of *pays de France. "Patrie"* supplanted *"pays";* the names "Picardie," "Artois," "Provence," "Limousin," ceased to be heard. All the departments were baptized with the "natural" names of rivers. Even the Île de France lost its eminence as the stronghold of the Franks, and was named Département of the Seine. It is highly pathetic to read the inscription on the Dôme des Invalides which explains why the ashes of

Napoleon I were brought there from St. Helena in 1840. In it the passion of genius and the equality of *La France une et indivisible* are well balanced. The two aspects of the French Revolution are fused into one in these words on the mighty sarcophagus of the Imperator of the Revolution, upon which you look down from a gallery: "Napoleon I asked that his body might rest near the banks of the Seine, among the people he loved so well."

Not only did the rivers of France, covering 600,000 square kilometres, give rise to the new system of names for the regions, but Napoleon organized them into a central system. It had been an old dream to connect the ocean and the Mediterranean Sea with the centre of the realm and its capital, as Bilistein wrote in 1764. In 1783 Grivel proposed that a postern gate be found, common to all the provinces, like the canal which connects all the provinces of China with the centre. This central system of canalization so hypnotized the nation that the natural rivers which it was meant to connect were left to be choked up by sand. The system of the highroads of France reflected the same desire for centralization. When the Revolution began, there were twenty-eight highways running from Paris to the different borders. Even today you find before the Cathedral of Notre-Dame in Paris a stone in the pavement marking the spot whence all these roads depart. It is true that ninety-seven other highroads existed in 1789, connecting the frontiers without touching Paris. But while these ninety-seven highways measured 17,000 kilometres, the twenty-eight roads from the centre were 15,000 kilometres long. These 32,000 kilometres of roads for public use, taken together, ought to be compared with all the rest of the roads in France, measuring not more than 20,000 kilometres. As a token of the force of centralization under the *ancien régime,* that great novelty of the nineteenth century, the railroad system, still followed the routes of the old highroads and canals. Of the new spirit of central order, Paris itself offers a good example in the Place de l'Étoile, with the Arc de Triomphe and the fire at the grave of the unknown soldier.

That this spirit of logical order, of *clarté,* of the decimal system, should be embodied in a great civilization is an achievement to be welcomed even by those who prefer to muddle through. For their muddling through would prove disastrous if at least one great nation were not willing to go the whole way. Even the English use the decimal system in some fields. This use does not go very far, but so far as it goes they are indebted for it to the French army of civilization, fighting for *clarté* and a natural, reasonable order.

THE FRENCH CALENDAR.

The French tried, during the Revolution, to deal with time as they did with *"la patrie."* The calendar was changed, too. The new era of liberty began with the fourteenth of July, 1789, and was made up of units of ten days, *"décades,"* instead of the Jewish week of seven days. But the real calendar of the French spirit is not to be found in these attempts to overthrow the Christian calendar, interesting as they are. Every great revolution creates a new era, as we shall see still better at the end of the book. French calendar-making, from first to last, betrays its real conception of time. Its favourite days are days of great passions, great loves, great geniuses. In 1788, 1789, and 1790 many private attempts were made to draw up a citizen's calendar. The last attempt I can find was made in 1893, in a *"Calendrier de l'Ère Révolutionnaire."* Héloïse, the mistress of Abailard, the Aspasia of Periclean Athens, and other geniuses of love are always included in these lists of dates.

For the true French calendar is not one of eternal recurrence, like the Russian calendar with its First of May. The true idea of the French Revolution is expressed by time taken as a means of novelty and surprise. In nature as restored by the French, time is the power which produces novelties and *sensations.* The nineteenth century became the century of news and newspapers. Hunting for news was legalized as the spirit of the times by the French Revolution. The finest expression of this spirit is the sequence of exhibitions. In the Fine Arts it is the annual exhibitions of the "salon" which collect the sensations of the day. The comrades marched forth in groups linked by time, by contemporaneity, into the arena. Taste and

Fashion became the expressions of contemporaneity. French painting won the leadership of European painting because it became a perpetual campaign carried on by groups of contemporaries. The passion of the French for contemporaneity in painting was well-exposed by Voltaire when he confessed that the French were no musicians, and declared that music was bound to be national and sectional. "But the painters," he went on, "must represent a nature *which is the same in all countries* and *which is seen by the same eyes.*" The same nature and the same eyes—but seen at different times! That made for the tremendous rapidity with which one fashion followed another throughout the century of impressionism. The poets too marched in groups: Naturalists, Parnassians, Symbolists, Impressionists, succeed each other in the leadership of the times.

This passion for exhibitions was more or less clumsily imitated by other nations. America, the country which stands next to France in its revolutionary origin, also stands next in its passion for exhibitions. But the great series of exhibitions in Paris, 1856, 1867, 1878, 1889 and 1900, only dot the I's and cross the T's of the superstition of the French *esprit* concerning time. Nature in space has to be "clear," organized, centralized. It is well to observe that organization, in its French origin, means "to create a natural organism by reason." "Organize" lies halfway between the two extremes of mechanical and organic. It means to create something organic—a process which to a romanticist of the German type is just as horrible and unthinkable as any mechanism. But the French mind excels in the organization of space and of sensations in time. Paris is the queen of cities as long as it dominates women's fashions. Even after losing her importance in the series of "world" expositions every eleventh year and the annual exhibitions of painting, Paris still continues to dominate the tastes of the seasons. Where the rule of contemporaneity does not work, French taste is at a loss: French museums and collections are colourless. The spirit of a museum is to have no spirit of the times. In Paris the Louvre receives the old masters, tested by time, and the Luxembourg the pictures of living artists, still fighting the battles of genius as contemporaries. But the Louvre has none of the atmosphere of the Hesperides. The past is lacking in spirit, in genius; it is unsensational. The Louvre is depressing to anyone who loves life and antiquity for their own sake. Where novelty cannot give the stretch and strain of ingenious surprise (in the ordinary run of public buildings, for example) the French imagination is completely eclipsed. Either time is a chain of surprises or it breaks down into a helpless conservatism.

CAPITALISM AROUND FRANCE.

The French citizen, teeming with new ideas, crazy for new and fertile efforts of productive genius, is himself more conservative in all business and family traditions than people who live in Asia or Africa.

It is true that French liberalism has allowed the importation of all kinds of foreign goods. M. Avenel, the historian of French capitalism, explains the new world-wide organization of commerce very well when he says: "Look at the simplest family of French peasants in its village. You will find that many of the things they use come from far away, and that many goods would become too costly if produced by themselves and thus hurt the producers themselves if they could not be multiplied by foreign imports. In its daily consumption the average French family uses coffee from Brazil, sugar from the departments of Aisne or Pas-de-Calais, stock-fish from Newfoundland, petrol from the Indian Ocean or the Black Sea; its candles are made out of foreign hides, and out of garbage chemically treated; its tractors come from America, its ploughshares and the steel for axles from Lorraine. The ribbon around their caps is made of fibre from Manila or of Riga hemp; planks and beams for their roofs come from Sweden or Norway, ready-made, and the same countries furnish the paper for French newspapers; shirts and towels are derived from Texas, and the cloth of their coats from the Cape or Australia."

But all this importing is carefully grouped around the industry in France. Nine tenths of the French were still rural in

1914. The French Socialists have always voted for the tariffs which protected the farmers. Family enterprise and personal credit remain through all the orgies of capitalism as the skeleton of French production. The world is well received in France; but you must not ask the French to leave their country or to introduce foreign forms. The French language was the only one which called the devastating form of capitalistic enterprise by its true name: *"société anonyme"*—the society without a name. Whereas in Germany or America the corporations were given all the privileges of free and individual men, because they were treated as persons (it was the tragic story of the Fourteenth Amendment that a privilege meant for the negro was turned into a privilege for industry by the corporation lawyers), the French sense for the *juste-milieu*, kept alive the notion of the artificiality of the thing in the word *"anonyme,"* thus warning the citizens that this individual was less trustworthy than a true individual with a proper name.

A French carpenter or cobbler may, with perfect peace of mind, close his workshop during the summer and put up a sign, *"À la campagne"* (in the country). The French have opened the sluices of capitalism, but they have not allowed themselves to be submerged. It seems to me that this is the reason why the reaction against capitalism was so much briefer in France than in other countries. The French worker is the most personal craftsman in the world. M. Paléologue, who was the French Minister to Petersburg during the Great War, shocked the Russians by remarking that one *poilu* or one French intellectual was a greater loss to civilization than a thousand Moujiks. He might have included the craftsmen, the artisans of France. The reaction of this type against the monotony of modern industry was syndicalistic, anarchical. It was the result of a real individual nature. In Russia the Bolsheviks can play a higher trump than the private capitalists by using the mass-man; but in France man revolted against the threat that capitalism might degrade him into a proletarian. This was the tragedy of the Commune in 1871; it was a revolt of the non-proletarian individual nature of man against proletarian conditions. Thus it could not overthrow a constitution which in spite of all its sore spots was based on the nature of man. No country is as safe against Communism as France today. The Russian Communists themselves published a statistical report for the year 1924 which demonstrates this truth in actual figures. In considering the configuration of classes in the countries of the world they gave France the smallest concentration of proletarians. They give the figures in thousands:

COUNTRY	TOTAL PRODUCTIVE CLASS	PROLETARIANS	SEMI-PROLETARIANS	RULING CLASS AND ITS HENCHMEN
Great Britain (without Ireland)	18,400	16,010	560	1,830
Germany	33,900	26,000	3,500	4,400
Italy	20,000	14,000	2,500	3,500
Denmark	1,350	850	100	350
Bulgaria	2,500	1,600	260	640
United States of America	42,000	27,500	6,500	8,000

In each of these countries the proletarians form two thirds or more of the productive class. But the figures for France are given as follows:

20,900	10,700	3,900	6,300

France was able to raise 50% of her productive population to complete or semi-complete independence, while Great Britain had not more than 15% on the side of independence.

These statistics, interesting as they are, are not the whole truth. England's Commonwealth cannot be understood by looking at the 15% at home who feel themselves independent. The French figures, too, are much more the result than the explanation of the French constitution. The French *citoyen* has fought for a *juste-milieu,* and he has gotten it. And that is the most effective refutation of the Marxian theory, because at the very centre of liberal ideas the horrors of capitalism ought to be at their worst. Instead, as we found, the system worked perfectly in France, where it was carried out to the extreme. It did not work well in countries into which it was imported without a corresponding emotional and revolutionary effort by the nation. The French nation established the moral equality of citizenship, without which the burdens of the factory system

would be intolerable indeed. Without perfect and firmly established equality, the lot of the employé is hell itself. It was
natural that in America the employé should look freely into
the eyes of his employer, because the ties of industrialism are
not overburdened by older, pre-industrial forms of dependence;
for in the United States the old relations had scarcely existed.
But in France, where old loyalties to church and *pays* had
dominated the relations and the characters of men from time
immemorial, it was only the political enfeeblement of the
French clergy and nobility through their de-localization in
Versailles which enabled Paris to destroy these old codes of
society and to create a real equality based on ideas.

THE EMANCIPATION OF THE JEWS.

Like any great process, the French Revolution introduced
new elements into the old mixture of forces. The Jewish question is not solved and will not be solved in a day, because its
very meaning is that it must be solved every day. The Jew is a
stranger among the Gentiles, a reminder to them that their
Christianity is always threatened by a backsliding into mere
paganism. Against this, baptism is no guarantee, church-going
is no guarantee. There is no absolute guarantee against the
hardening of our hearts. No institution, no pope, no priest or
theologian can prevent the relapse of man into his natural
indolence. The Jews are a scandal. They do not believe in the
Christianity of the Christians. As far as I know, the Jews in
1789 did not discriminate in their language between pagans
and Christians. They did not believe in the genuineness of the
Christian faith. The nearness of God the Father to the Chosen
People makes the "Our Father" of the Lord's Prayer such a
minimum of faith for a Jew that he only feels how much paganism must be left over in Christianity. All the follies of philosophy, of abstract ideas and scientific notions were characterized
to me by a great Jewish scholar as "moral insanity," as crude
as pagan superstition. And it is true that many pagans use
Christianity as a veneer. Baptism was the cheap price at which
many tribes originally hoped to buy and store up Roman
civilization. Christianity came to the nations as something old

and distinguished, as an indispensable equipment for their march on the high road of history. Many converts cursed a faith so exacting that no pagan impulses were safe from its challenge. When this challenge of Christianity slackens, paganism immediately creeps in. The nations of Europe were on the way to complete repaganization in the eighteenth century; the churches themselves were open to this attack. All this was changed completely by the emancipation of the Jews.

The non-Christian side of French Jacobinism is really its most Christian side. It offers to the Jew a common meeting-ground on the basis of humanity, of humanism. "Adam," in 1789, was more than a figure of speech. He was the great symbol of a unity that preceded the division of Jews and Gentiles. Adam became a great messianic figure standing for the end of time when all men should meet again. The nation was changed from an origin into a final destiny.

This national messianism of the French had to outbid the messianism embodied by the Jews themselves. The French could not bear that any nation should be more messianic than their own. That is why it was not the respectable, kind, well-educated, enlightened Jew who was emancipated by the ideas of 1789. Any notion of a selective process for certain particularly welcome and agreeable individuals must be rejected before we can understand the principles of the emancipation of the Jews. The deeper cause of emancipation was the new equality. The last Polish or Russian Jew had the same right to it, from the viewpoint of 1789, as the "philosopher," because citizenship was due not only to the actual philosopher but to any man who was capable of using his reason in the cause of humanity. The philosopher was to form the leading class of this new race; but potentially everyone had his own mind to offer as a pledge of his humanity and of his fitness for citizenship.

In emancipating the Jews, the European ideals of 1789 reached their farthest limits. It was fifteen years before it became evident that European citizenship could not stop at baptism. Not until 1804 did the emancipation which had been urged before, actually take place. When Napoleon was anointed by the Pope, when the son of the Revolution began his dizzy-

ing process of legitimation by the Church, the danger was great
that the Revolution had already failed and that France would
relapse into a pre-Revolutionary stage. The emancipation of
the Jews was begun during the birth-throes of the empire, in
1803. The 100,000 Jews living in France were just enough to
help Napoleon keep his revolutionary character.

The process of the *assimilation* of the Jews followed upon
their *emancipation:* it was their grateful answer to the emancipation. Karl Marx's father could become a lawyer in Trier
without abjuring his faith. No wonder that his son wrote the
greatest libel against the Jews ever published in any language
by any anti-Semite; for he was trying to disclaim his Jewishness.
He knew only the economic question of the Jew as an individual, and forgot, thanks to his philosophical education, that
Judah had another reason for existence besides retail selling
and usury.

The emancipation of the Jews was a stroke of the pen on the
part of the respective legislators; the assimilation of the Jews
was their attempt to answer this opening of the doors of Europe.
Most of them simply entered the doors of modern Europe, not
bothering about the older strata of European life. In a way,
the emancipated Jew could not possibly forget who and what
ideas had emancipated him and his people. When the great
conservative leader of Prussia, Julius Stahl, fiercely supported
the right of the Christian King and exclaimed, as a good royalist: "Authority, not majority," Bismarck said: "He is a liberal
nevertheless." He wished to say, without irony, that Stahl himself could not, though now a pious Christian, betray the principles which had made his own emancipation possible thirty
years before. Stahl depended on the idea of equality. Thus the
Jews became the natural bodyguard of liberalism all over Europe, not from any preconceived general ideas on God and
Nature or Man, but because liberalism stood for emancipation.
Any discussion between the Jews and the nation made sense
only if emancipation was agreed upon. Since many forces,
throughout the century, still denied the very essence of emancipation and equality of rights, the Jewish population remained

a devotee of liberalism as long as the slightest danger of oppression remained.

An argument which is often heard is that the higher bourgeoisie and the Jews were connected by business interests, both being bankers and financiers. This argument is a good example of shallowness and superficiality. Competition and business rivalry has stood in the way of the Jews for centuries. For two hundred years the Lutheran patricians in Frankfurt had prevented even their Calvinist competitors from living in the city. Not until 1780, nine years before the conquest of the Bastille, did the Calvinist merchants get permission to build their church in Frankfurt itself instead of in a neighbouring village. The danger of competition should have led the capitalist class in France, as the new rulers, to suppress the Jews even more. The economic argument does not explain anything, because it can be used both ways. Anti-Semitism is always backed by the greed, envy and jealousy of the middle classes. It is largely a question of desperate competition for jobs. As a matter of fact the Jews had no monopoly on financiering or trade; they had always had Christian competitors.

DIGRESSION
ALPHA AND OMEGA; GENTILES AND JEWS.

The French conception of the Jewish destiny within the national boundaries was restricted to emancipation. But the destiny of the Chosen People is unsettled despite 1789. France did not and could not conceive of the function that the Chosen People had performed and that must be performed in one way or another to the end of time. Thus, the French accomplished no absolute solution: this digression seeks to evaluate the objective problem that will remain when all individual Jews are emancipated.

It is incorrect to explain the mode of life of the Jews in the well-known way, by pretending that they were by nature a nation of usurers, pedlars and traders. They certainly were not. In both the Old and the New Testaments they are farmers and craftsmen and scholars. Cause and effect, perhaps, run in the opposite direction. When they were scattered over the earth

after the loss of Jerusalem in 70 A.D., they had no other function than to bear witness to the "economy of revelation," to the
growing Kingdom of God. Without their existence, the gospel
of Jesus might have come to the Gentiles like a myth or a
legend. Christianity becomes an historical fact only through
the existence of the Jews. The natural inclination of men and
nations to take flight into dreams of ancestral pride or the
cobwebs of abstract philosophy always leads to excesses of ag-
nosticism and mythology. The Jews, simply by their existence,
bar the nations from a relapse into that comfortable self-
adoration which makes Jesus himself into a blond Germanic
hero instead of a despised Jew. To accomplish such a thing
over thousands of years may seem a trifle to the average philosopher, who overlooks the simple sociological conditions of
everyday life and does not perceive that a very important result
can be achieved by the simple fact of doing a small thing every
day. This is precisely what the Jews are constantly doing. They
exist, and by their existence remind the Gentiles of their own
deficiency, their unfinished wayfaring. The Gentiles would like
to treat Jesus as a myth. Modern literature is full of such
idiocies. The Jews are the living refutation of these fictions.
When Frederick the Great said to a pastor: "After all, there
is not the slightest evidence for all your Christianity," the
pastor was quick to reply: "Certainly, the Jews."

But in order to exist, the Jews must do something, and the
business which is the least prejudicial to their mission is trade.
The Jews are therefore traders and not farmers, because thus
they are removed from the soil which leads Gentiles to idolize
tools of human government, earth, agriculture, countries and
cities and machines, and set them up as Gods. The formlessness
of the Jewish existence emphasizes its clerical, priest-like character. The Jews, as one of them wrote in the first book which
tried to explain our Christian faith in Jewish terms, "the
Hebrews are like the coals in the heart of the fire, powerless
in the hands of God," unable to form an earthly political order,
a national organization, a worldly culture. But unlike the
Christians, they are not even able to evangelize these pagan
strongholds of empires, industries, civilization. The true Chris-

tians can preach the Gospel among the Gentiles. They are the rays sent out from the central fire, which actually transform the world. As coals in the heart of the fire, the Jews are prisoners of God. The Gentiles themselves represent the third rôle: climate, earth, trees, deer, cattle, metals, lions, sheep—in short, the gifts of nature. Natural humanity is the mouthpiece of all the treasures of creation. To be a physician, a gardener, a chemist, a carpenter, a bridge-builder, a cattle-breeder, means to be the mouthpiece and the culmination of some form which was pre-destined by the pre-human part of creation and only waited for accomplishment through the love, faith, and hope of man. In all his professions of the natural, the earthly, and the secular type, man is the chosen administrator of a part of creation. As such, he advances like nature itself from the birth of life to its death. He takes the side of natural growth. Messianism, on the other hand, draws back the curtain from the end of time: it is eschatological. It begins with the end, the consummation of things. One of the questions put to the Jew after his death is: "Hast thou believed in the Messiah, in the end of Time?" If we had to ask the natural man for his faith, he would probably answer: "I have conquered, I have been a faithful administrator of those gifts which were entrusted to me." But to a people of priests, the sacrifice of inborn talents is more natural than their use. The most general expression of the natural man is his thirst for power, his love of domination. But the Jews had little of that representative power which makes presidents and dictators. They could be patriarchs and kings, perhaps, but they never succeed as self-sufficing rulers, as sheer dominators. It is not their business.[8]

Thus far we have deduced the character of the Jews theoretically. Without any metaphysics, an experienced administrator, the Russian Paul von Sokolowski, has stated [9] that though all the properties of man occur in Jews, though they vary as

[8] A good expression of this fact, though in Chapman's erratic form, may be found in *John Jay Chapman and His Letters* (p. 274) by M. A. De Wolfe Howe, Boston, Houghton Mifflin, 1937: "It is foolish to rule the world, and the Jew knows it."

[9] *Die Versandung Europas*, Berlin, 1929.

much and are as different among themselves as other peoples, although they have many talents and gifts that are rare among others, yet they lack the instinct for government. "Some of them try it, and some achieve great things; but it is not their nature to rule."

This is an important fact. The ruler who gives his name to an hour of history must be absorbed completely in that hour. He must dive into its waves and be lost in it more than any other man. For it is the ruler's business to mark the epoch, to appear on the stamps or coins of his country. Rulership, because it personifies an epoch, always finds itself in a polarity to the workings of Eternity. It is in order not to discredit the Jews, but to honour their priestly qualities, that we mention their predicament in relation to political leadership. An intelligent being like Nebuchadnezzar sympathized with his prime minister, Daniel, because the man did not bow the knee before him. But the people cried out that Daniel was a national traitor because he did not, and Daniel was deposed so that the races of the empire could exercise their hero-worship for a man of flesh and blood. In Germany, the failure of Heinrich Bruening was largely due to his aversion for mass idols. Bruening behaved like a monk; he abhorred the cult of the masses. Hitler, on the contrary, lives on this need of the masses for hero-worship.

The pagan leader is the servant of time. The Jew can never "believe" in time; he believes in Eternity. Since every Jewish leader or prophet thinks of Eternity or of innumerable generations, the star of Judah always shines most brilliantly in times when there are no pagan heroes. When a nation is despoiled of its governing class, when a national failure has brought a darkness without comfort or illumination, the nation is struck by the fact that the Jews are less shaken by this darkness than the Gentiles. The Jews are not leaderless in the absence of a king or emperor. Anti-Semitism always becomes especially violent in times of a lost war. The Jews must be guilty: this is the word that is quickly passed round. For are they not as ready to shoulder hard times without a complaint as they were to profit in the good? The star of Judah shines bright, and po-

groms break out, whenever the Gentiles have just buried their
Nebuchadnezzar or their Tiberius and are faced with disintegration.

Naturally, the Jews had to make their living in collaboration
and co-operation with the Gentiles. But for the degree of this
co-operation they depended upon the Gentiles. This dependence upon foreign mercy for mere subsistence often makes the
Jews eager and restless. Like any clergy or profession or group,
they are not all believers. The fears of the individual Jew often
make him lose his trust in God; and such a Jew is a prey to
all kinds of demoniac forces, because he has lost his faith in
his priesthood and yet suffers from all the anxieties and external dangers of his extraordinary vocation. This Jew of little
faith is the excrescence of Judah. In the years before 1789 he
became the usurer, the Shylock of pagan tradition. But the
pious banker is as frequent among the Jews as the ruthless
usurer. It is not a question of the profession, but of individual
moral balance. The greed of the farmer who loses his faith is
diverted into acquiring more and more land; the Jew who
loses his faith becomes greedy for money.

The average Jew is no more and no less unpleasant than any
other individual. But by his restlessness he frightens his neighbours, whereas lazy or vicious Gentiles do the same harm in a
less aggressive way. Nations, as units and on the average, are
always horrible, as Count Keyserling courageously said. The
Jewish character includes all the human qualities; for all men
are equal. But because of his exceptional, imperilled condition
the Jew exaggerates. "Jewishness" is not a material quality, but
a certain "too much." Too much charity, too much smartness,
too much understanding, too much devotion, too much self-
denial, too much egotism, are the Jewish eccentricities and
dangers.

Gambetta, Marx, Rathenau exaggerated. Take, for example,
Rathenau. In 1918, when Hindenburg and Ludendorff had
lost their nerve, and the Gentiles in Germany from top to
bottom, emperor and farmer, professor and worker, knew that
not another drop of blood could be spent for war because the
body of the nation had already nearly bled to death, Walther

Rathenau blew the trumpet of national resistance. Some years later he was murdered as a national traitor, and simply because his model behaviour exasperated the whole military class which had failed to show the same energy.

The individual Jew, believer or unbeliever, having the same human weaknesses as any Greek or pagan, gives no cause for hatred of the Jews. The conflict is much wider. The terrible antagonism between the nucleus of God's devouring fire and the circumference of God's creation is the fatal antagonism of death and life. The nations all wish to live, to grow, to expand, to be immortal. The Jew lives beyond the end, the doomsday of all the empires of the world. He had to outlive the Pharaoh of Egypt, Nebuchadnezzar, Alexander and Cæsar, popes and emperors and kings and presidents, so that no golden calf and no man-god might overshadow the glory of the living God. This attitude is a threat to all the national pride of man. The opposing tension between Judah and Greece is tolerable only so long as Christian evangelization pervades the countries of the Gentiles, the "Greeks," and so long as the serenity of the peace of God pervades the hearts of the Jews.

The average historian can neither admit nor explain the existence of a Jewish question; it is the man in the street and the layman who knows, by instinct alone, but by a sure instinct, that such a question exists. Our history of revolutions would be as tame as Macaulay's or as poisoned as Trotsky's if we too should leave the Jewish question to the man on the street-corner. Let us take account of his instinct, and ask our question of both Jews and heathen. Without seeing that mankind is divided into the component elements of paganism, Christianism, and Judaism, we can see and understand nothing of the world around us. Like the three tenses of grammar, past, present, and future, or like beginning, middle, and end, Paganism, Christianism, and Judaism together make up the world, though in a different proportion and interrelation in each period of history. A special proportion between Paganism, Judaism, and Christianity is the sign manual of every epoch; for the proportions between the three are in constant change. Without this yardstick, world history becomes meaningless. Yet the French idea that with the abolition of the three divisions, with the union between Adam (Nature) and the revelations of Church and Synagogue a new era would begin, is natural enough. For history, chronology, time (that is, the great system of periods on which our idea of humanity is formed) has been treated in a different way by the Gentiles and by the Jews. We today, beguiled by the long-established use of the Christian Era, forget that it is only a creative way out of the indissoluble dilemma between Jewish hope and pagan faith. Yet this dilemma is not a thing of the past. Both calendars still threaten the Christian Era, the pagan counting from the beginning of the race or the foundation of Rome, and the Jewish looking forward from day to day and year to year to the end, the Messiah, salvation, and burying all past time in the greater glory of the God who will be what He will be.

The anti-Semitic hatred of the Jew, in all its simplicity and straightforwardness, has always and necessarily been the hatred of the Beginning of things for the End. The outlook from the beginning is impossible once you have looked at the same thing from the end; yet that was the permanent conflict or tension forced upon paganism by the existence of the Hebrews.

In the Bible God is called the Alpha and Omega. But we are seldom conscious of the fact that he has created the natural nations of men in His power as Alpha and the Jews in his power as Omega. The Jews represent the end of human history before its actual end: without them pagan history would not only have had no goal, but would have gotten nowhere. The pagans represent the eternal new beginnings of history, and without them history would never have acquired any shape or form or beauty or fulfilment or attainment.

God's Alpha was lived by the Gentiles, and God's Omega is embodied in the Jews. This antithesis brought Pagans and Jews into a conflict of principle. The Jewish community, as a community, was created by God to be his witness against the blindnesses of the Alpha-nations. This is the viewpoint of Revelation. But from the viewpoint of the natural nations, Aztecs and Egyptians, Moab and Assur, their own faith was created as a bulwark against the precipitous end symbolized

by the "Omegas." In this antagonism the Jews can exaggerate
and the heathen can exaggerate, because God has left them
both the freedom to sin. And both are perpetually exaggerating, the one by loving the idols of the past and the other by
cherishing its endless hope for the future.

Now the periodical persecutions of the Jews were the metaphysical warfare by which the Gentiles combated the pressure
of a hostile calendar. Through the pogrom they tried to throw
off the yoke which joins Alpha and Omega. Wherever an old
form is reluctant to go to its doom, like the Church in the
fifteenth century, or like Czarism before 1914, it defends its
own obsolete and dying institutions by persecuting the Jew,
the eternal symbol of a life beyond any existing form of government. Wherever a young generation tries to relive the first
day of creation, it attacks the Jew because he smiles at this
passionate belief in fugitive forms. In Germany during the
orgies of Hitlerism a certain Jewish journalist was asked to
correct the book of a Nazi authoress; and in return for the
favour she agreed to take him to see Goebbels and Goering.
After tea with them he came back as though enlightened and
told his friends: "They cannot help persecuting us; they are
playing Red Indians, and they know that we cannot take their
game seriously."

The persecutions of the Jews are, to the relation between
Alpha and Omega in time, precisely what wars are between
neighbours in space. Wars require territories, governments,
armies. To avoid a misunderstanding, let me add this on the
question of war: A Jew can, of course, serve in the armies of
his country with passion and devotion. But the Jewish community, as a community, has nothing to do with war between
geographical units. It was created above and beyond all human
divisions. It reminds men of the hope beyond their daily hopes,
of a more important step to come. By their persecution the
Gentiles defy this challenge from the side of Eternity and finality. They always accuse the Jew of provocation, because although he is quite capable of playing Red Indian out of love
for his neighbours, he is incapable of any of their idolatries,
and though he can shed his blood for his country, he will always

feel that no skyscraper, no man-of-war, no Venus of Cnidos, and no glory of arms is more important than the tears of the widow or the sigh of the orphan. And this is provoking as long as countries must arouse enthusiasm for great patriotic sacrifices.

I give an example, the remark of a young German lieutenant who had been hearing of Walther Rathenau's services to Germany during the World War. He was told that Rathenau, a Jew, had been the first and the only man to foresee that Germany was going to be short of war-materials, that he had created the war-economy which was introduced successfully then and is being imitated and repeated by the anti-Semites in Germany today. He was told that in 1918, when Ludendorff ignominiously broke down, Rathenau tried to become the Gambetta of the nation and venture upon a last national resistance. The lieutenant answered: "It is not true: and if it is true, it is a shame." This is the quintessence of the pagan hatred against the Jew. First of all, the Jew has no merits in our national life. Secondly, if he has, he ought not. "It is a shame," because it shows *that the Omegas must play the part of the Alphas!* Creation feels itself humiliated when Revelation must send troops to fight its battles. Creation, paganism—what is mildly called "secularism" today—resents its own failures.

The fifteenth century offers a good example of Jewish persecutions at a time when Christianity was frightened by the approaching downfall of its visible unity. The fear of Reformation and dissolution spread all over Europe between 1450 and 1517, and led to violent pogroms. The pogroms were the lightning-rod that protected Papacy; they averted Luther's Reformation for fifty years. The same could perhaps be said of Czarist Russia. There, too, the Jews were one of the lightning-conductors of the régime. These atrocities of a senescent institution fighting for a longer span of life are always peculiarly insulting and outrageous. But as mankind's propensity to war is not explained by condemning iniquitous wars, neither are persecutions explained by condemning iniquitous persecutions. Generally the nations take advantage of the liberty of choice which is granted them to remain in a blind alley as long as they can escape conversion. Pogroms seem to indicate a situation during which a painful fact, like the loss of the World War, cannot yet be swallowed by the nation. It will swallow it later; but first the Jews—so the pagan exclaims—must suffer. For the Jews knew of the blind alley too soon, they saw through it from the very beginning. "Now, if we must bury these dreams, at least we will not be ashamed of them. We are determined to remain proud of them. We wish to remain sons of the earth, builders of its stone walls and states, artists and architects of this world. Therefore let us distinguish ourselves from the Jew who knew of our defeat beforehand."

There is permanent hostility between the wisdom of the serpent and the naïveté of Adam. There is permanent hostility between worshippers of the birth of forms and the beauty of things and worshippers of the living God, with his fire burning high above the shapelessness of man's soul. The genius of Greece or of any pagan nation always tries to blossom and bear fruit so divinely that people will forget everything except itself. It is intoxicating to live the life of natural growth. The artist, the statesman, the hero, fascinate us by their personalities; their humanity concentrates all our love, all our interest, all our attention on them. But lest the reader think that genius or hero-worship alone was meant by the "Alpha" side of life, I must perhaps add that any beauty of form, any organization of society, any sweetness of friendship or self-realization can intoxicate our hearts.

Both Jewish and pagan life try to honour God, the pagan by being as much the Creator as possible, the Jew by being as much the creature as is permitted to a son of Adam. Their twofold endeavour stretches the rope between earth and heaven. But originally the Gentiles did not see the other end of the rope. That was revealed only to the Jews. They could see both sides: to the tragic conflict between the naïve sons of men and the guardians of wisdom, the word "and" could be added only by Israel itself. Thus pagans and Jews lived as members of one community, but without the pagan having any understanding for the Jew. He saw only commerce, usury, shabbiness, greed, fear, clannishness, because the rest did not interest him. Within the narrow limits of his national creed he laughed at the idea that he should depend on the Jew. This miserable pedlar could not have any message for him. Later the pagans and the Jews were connected by Christianity, and the innumerable histories of tribes and cities on one side and the sufferings of Israel on the other were changed into one world history. During the march of the Holy Ghost through the nations, the distance between beginning and end becomes shorter and shorter. Yet it remains a difference in principle, because at any given moment of history man can represent one or the other aspect of his evolution. Nevertheless, the emancipation of the Jews brings a real change.

Here for the first time the rôle of the Messiah was played by the nations rather than by the Jews. The end of time, announced in Paul's Letter to the Romans, began in 1789, when a great nation felt itself to be the true and chief vessel of Messianism.

THE NEW MESSIANISM.

Up to 1789 Christianity had undertaken to bring together the heavenly Creator and his chosen people on the one side, and his creatures and their earthly work on the other. The Church balanced creation against revelation; the values of the Last Judgment and of evolution were interwoven in the slow march of the Cross over the earth.

But in France in 1789 the situation was peculiar, because there the normal instrument for this task, the Christian Church, was no longer usable. France, by the degradation of Paris, by the expulsion of the Huguenots, and by the abasement of its gentry, had been deprived of the regenerative forces of three different periods of religion. Scholasticism (Paris), Reformation (Huguenots), and Puritanism (gentry) were all kept outside the political field and their life-giving power dried up. Yet these had been the vital forces of Christianity for the rest of Europe from 1200 down to 1750. The exclusion of these vigorous forms of Christian life was not compensated for by the troops of Jesuits, those negative defenders of the faith. They smelled of the narrowness inherent in any "counter"-movement. Any counter-revolution is sterile. When the Jesuits were expelled from France in 1761, it was because the nation felt

them to be only a make-shift for the true religion. To understand the French free-thinker, we must keep in mind the completely abnormal situation of the Gallican Church about 1750,
with a great university derided in Voltaire's pamphlet, *Tom-
beau de la Sorbonne,* with the Huguenots active in Paris or in
exile, and with an irresponsible, ungodly, and unrighteous
gentry; then we shall understand why France went "messianic,"
and with its natural messianism tried to outstrip the Christian
church and the Jewish synagogue. The church seemed too
defiled to serve as an instrument of the future, and the Jews
seemed worn and shabby under their ancient curse of the
Wandering Jew. After all, church and synagogue had been
established as means to an end: they had been founded to
spread the Gospel and to preach the Lord. Yet the fortress of
Popery built up by the Jesuits impressed people as a very
earthly and defective thing, with no ultimate end beyond
itself; and the usurer, too, was a perversion of the Jewish
mission. Usurers and Jesuits seemed to demonstrate the defeat
of messianism by its own instruments.

Logically enough, the French attacked the two old spiritual
homes of mankind with the war-cry: Humanity. Humanity
itself was the only possible aim which could inspire the new
messianism of the French Revolution, with its hatred of the
Christian church and its abolition of the ghetto. Humanism is a
sincere purging away of revelation; and through this means it
has emancipated the church and the synagogue. Of course this
humanity, like the others, needed a home with walls. For a
thousand years the unity of the Christian world had been an
actuality embodied in certain institutions, like the emperor
who summoned the Councils, the monasteries which gave hospitality and instruction, the papacy which guaranteed the purity of dogma, the University of Paris which reproduced and
reflected theology, and so on. The Jesuits, the fighting army of
the Church, having failed, there was no doctrine, no institution, no soldiers, teachers, language, school, or office, which still
stood for the unity of mankind. A new unity had to be built
up. It was planned on a field covered with the debris of church
and synagogue.

The natural inertia of the people was inflamed by a real enthusiasm for this new world of Europe. Science, newspapers, railroads, academies, congresses, Leagues of Nations, the decimal system, all testify to the success of this reorganization. As long as the task was sincerely religious, the Jews could enter the rank and file of the new secular messianism with perfect honesty. For messianism it was. But what was to be the content of the new religion? The nineteenth century professed a creed no less sincere than that of any other great period; and its priest was the man of genius.

Many Frenchmen have professed this faith. I quote at least one example: In a lecture delivered at the Collège de France in 1870, when the German armies were at the gates of Paris, and the French patriots were belittling German science, the great philologist Gaston Paris said: *"Je professe absolument et sans réserve cette doctrine, que la science n'a d'autre objet que la vérité, et la vérité pour elle-même, sans aucun souci des conséquences, bonnes ou mauvaises, regrettables ou heureuses, que cette vérité pourrait avoir dans la pratique. Celui qui par un motif patriotique, religieux ou même moral, se permet dans les faits qu'il étudie, dans les conclusions qu'il tire, la plus petite dissimulation, l'altération la plus légère, n'est pas digne d'avoir sa place dans le grand laboratoire, où la probité est un titre d'admission plus indispensable que l'habileté. Ainsi comprises, les études communes, poursuivies avec le même esprit dans tous les pays civilisés, forment audessus des nationalités restreintes, diverses et souvent hostiles, une grande patrie, qu'aucune guerre ne souille, qu'aucun conquérant ne menace, et où les âmes trouvent le refuge et l'unité que la cité de Dieu leur a donnés en d'autres temps."* Scientific research, undertaken in the same spirit in all the civilized countries, forms a great fatherland above our nationalities, limited, diverse, and often hostile as they are; and in this high fatherland, not stained by any war, not threatened by any conqueror, men's souls find the refuge and the unity which the City of God gave to them in former days!

The equation is complete. The revelation of Zion is supplanted. And the grandeur of this faith cannot be belittled.
Theodor Mommsen answered Gaston Paris' confession with a
similar one from the German side in his famous "Preface" to
the third volume of the *Corpus Inscriptionum Latinarum,*
dated December 28, 1872: "I had endeavoured to confess in
public my sense of gratitude towards every one of the men who
promoted this work.[10] Alas, even this cannot be done today in
the way I intended; the world and the nations within it being
torn to pieces, most of the men whose munificence and friendship helped to build up this volume were changed from friends
into enemies and from enemies into personal foes. And now,
I am not sure which among these men wish to go back on the
benefits that they previously have conferred on a foreigner
before these things happened, neither can I venture to publish
the names of those of whom I know that they will not go back
on their benefits, because I am ignorant where to draw the line
and how far to compromise with the ungenerous mob and the
whims of its blind wrath. And yet, the classical studies have
this eminent and rather divine quality, that they call forth
every scholar out of his narrow birthplace into one common
field, and that they, by reminding us of the common origin of
humanity, associate the very best men from various nations.
I was congratulating myself for having obtained not the last
place in this society, and I nourished hopes of seeing this
volume becoming a testimony of this community and cement-
ing it. And now, it is true, it testifies only of a community that
belongs to the past, whereas disunited peoples receive what was
achieved through united strength.

"However, the book will last, and studies will last; and
whenever, after our part is over, the *republic of science (respub-
lica litterarum)* comes to life again, they will continue our
beginnings as though they were not broken off, but only interrupted."

THE "AFFAIRE."

But the revolutionary faith was sincere only so long as
humanity took first place in the minds of the French. In 1870

[10] Among them Napoleon III.

this humanity, or "Europe," as Thiers phrased it, was nowhere discoverable when the French asked for help against the Prussians; and as a result their faith in the reality of any internationalism abated. When Clemenceau said in 1919, " 'Humanity' is a beautiful word, but 'France' is more beautiful," the dream was over. The repercussion of this disappointment can be recognized by various symptoms. We limit ourselves, however, to mentioning its effect upon the Jewish question. The wandering Jew, as a permanent note of interrogation or mark of suspension between the nations of this earth, could no longer remain the naïve soldier for national democracy which he had been during the period when "humanity" was the sincere equivalent to an ideal revelation without priests or Jews. Even then a Jew could only serve as an individual in the fight for a better European civilization. Israel, as Israel, has a longer breath and a more difficult task than the ideas of 1789.

It was not by accident, I am sure, that a Catholic Frenchman, Paillière, after the World War, discovered the eternal religious burden of the Jew. Where the Revolution had sought to emancipate sons of "Adam," Pallière discovered "the unknown temple of God" (he published a book under that title). Ernest Hello, another great French Catholic, whose *Paroles de Dieu* is the most French and the most Christian book I know, and Léon Bloy, the Catholic Nietzsche of France, tried to justify the rising anti-Semitism in France in the nineties by the repulsiveness of the average Jewish usurer and second-hand dealer in the ghettos he visited. But one day Bloy saw an anti-Jewish placard in Paris, showing St. George's spear piercing the body of Moses; and then he knew that creation was once more threatened with the extinguishing of the light of revelation. St. George piercing Moses meant perverting St. George into a pagan and destroying Christianity. Bloy sat down to write his book, *Le Salut par les Juifs*. Reconvincing himself that there was still something to be expected from the Jews in days to come, he opened the door to a new phase in the relation between the Jews and the nations, one not covered by the conception of the French Revolution. Léon Bloy, in the country of emancipation, restored religious depth to the Jewish question, much as Franz Rosenzweig did in Germany later on.

In the meantime the Dreyfus affair was raging in France. In connection with many other atrocities of the failing "Boulangism," the unsuccessful Hitlerite movement in vanquished France after 1887, a captain of the French general staff, who was an Alsatian and a Jew, was made the scapegoat for an irregularity in the *service d'espionnage*. His condemnation and degradation was accompanied by a tremendous outburst of hatred against "the filthy Jew"—so tremendous that a Jewish correspondent for an Austrian newspaper, a fervent "assimilant" up to that date, lost his faith in "Europe," left Paris after the insulting scene at Christmas, 1894, and went to Vienna, convinced that assimilation had failed. He was Theodor Herzl, the man who wrote *The Jewish State* and who became the father of Zionism and of the resettlement of Palestine.

This same affair, which by creating Zionism ended "assimilation," brought French emancipation to its decisive test. We have stressed the fact that emancipation was granted before assimilation existed, that emancipation must be viewed with the eyes of the Jacobins and not with the eyes of the Jews. Emancipation of the Jews—like emancipation of the slaves to the Northerner—was an article of French faith and French humanitarianism. Jews like Herzl might abandon assimilation; but to the French Republic excluding a Jew from the Rights of Man would have been equivalent to hoisting the white flag of the Bourbons.

Thus the Dreyfus affair became the decisive trial of the French Republic. Through all its turns and twistings it became clearer and clearer that the essential problem was not Dreyfus but the Rights of Man.

In the course of the struggle the forces of pre-Revolutionary France, church and army, proved nearly as strong as all the forces of the three or four generations since the great Revolution. A century is a short period in which to spread a new gospel. France was not capable of settling the affair until 1906. Meanwhile all the *écrivains* were called upon to support the cause of humanity. *Humanité* was the name of the newspaper which published the famous *J'accuse* of Zola, the novelist, against the government. And Anatole France was another who fought with the League for the Rights of Man. He who had usurped the name of his country wished to restore to France the true ideal of equality.

THE THREE QUALITIES OF HIGHER LIFE.

Emancipation has not ended the Jewish question, because the Jews are not like the Armenians in Turkey or the Japanese in California or the Irish in New England. The Jews were created as a counterfoil to the Gentiles; and whenever the third element, the Christians, grow weak in their faith, hope, and love, then the glowing nucleus of revelation and the inanimate forms of creation diverge and threaten to destroy human history, which is a process of the salvation of the world and the conversion of the pagans by the Word.

But emancipation *has* permanently changed the aspect of the Jewish question. Emancipation cannot be abolished. All nationalism will be hoisted by its own petard if it breaks off the emancipation of the Jews. Government is not everything in the life of man: this is the creed of the French Revolution. Bourgeois France showed that it meant business when it proclaimed the equality of Jew and Greek, the vessel of God and the vessel of genius. Furthermore, when the instruments of revelation and of creation both became citizens in the post-Christian body politic of Europe, all lifelong priesthood was dissolved. Henceforth the priest, and the Jew as well, was first and foremost a natural man. *This is irrevocable.* The scope of the event is reflected by the humanism which accompanies the political events of the French Revolution. The movement which restored Hellas and Rome, Philosophy and Law, made the history of Jews and pagans one tradition. The mutual impenetrability of Rome and Greece, and of Jerusalem and Athens, was melted down. The new Europe blended and mixed the powers which had ruined the ancient world by their isolation.

When Louis XVIII accepted the emancipation of the Jews as a fact in 1815, he accepted the great idea of humanity as conceived by the French Revolution. This humanism, or, better still, humanitarianism, in which Rousseau and Briand, Diderot and Barthou, Jefferson and Wilson, Mary Wollstone-craft and Ramsay MacDonald, were baptized, had discovered man behind men, nature behind nations, Adam behind Shem, Ham and Japhet, and the great identity of all men behind creed, faith, colour and race. It baptized Gentiledom by giving a mission to every nation! Nationalism makes every nation a chosen people in competition with all the others. Messianism, originally limited to the Jews, later communicated to the heathen by the Church, is transferred by the European nationalism born in 1789 to the nations in general, which now enter upon a common race of *messianic nationalism*.

What would have been pure and ridiculous arrogance for the different nations if it were only a vaunting of their own nature, became reasonable through the emancipation of the Jews. For by the addition of the element of Omega, the chosen people of God, the "Alphaic" nations have acquired one touch of finality and predestination. A modern nation, since 1789, differs completely from the old natural, pagan groups called nations, because it is a task, not a fact, a movement, not an established house, a future and not a past. The admixture of the Jews, who can never be treated as pagans, secures the nation from backsliding and mistaking mere existence for growth, inheritance for heritage, Alpha for Omega. Henceforth the secular literature of a nation could be treated as of equal religious and educational power with the Bible. True inspiration was recognized in national poetry; secular art was sanctified as an instrument of divine inspiration. The unleashing of a competitive race in national inspiration filled the gap created by the disappearance of the "Omegaic" nation. The cult of art and literature and science betrays the religious character of "inspired nationalism" during the nineteenth century.

But the scrupulous accuracy with which one messianism (that of the Jews) was supplanted by another, more general one (that of the nations), the exactness of the correspondence between national government by inspiration and the disclaiming of any reliance on priests or prophets, shows how deeply the history of Christianity delves its channels even where neither church nor dogma, neither pope nor parsons, still play any part in the drama. Pagans, Christians, and Jews carry out the commands of revelation long after these commands have ceased to be represented by a clergy.

The crisis of modern history came when nationalism threw itself into a fiery messianic crusade for a common future. The "promise of America," for example, is such an attempt to put the real life into the future. It is the great courage of those who think that the full life is going to be lived not now, but later. With such a hope, all the failures of the past and the scars of national pride and memory are easily forgotten. Then the nations can march forward toward a common goal. Then the Jews can be dismissed, because the nations are now inoculated with the Jewish promise.

On the Jews themselves, this inoculation has reacted in the form of Zionism. Zionism has inoculated Judah with a drop of worldly realism, of European nationalism.

In spite of Hitlerism, we are living in a new era, because henceforth the functions of Gentiles, Christians, and Jews are no longer invested in a visible race, a visible clergy, and a visible Israel. In the future the character and function of a man can no longer be judged by the outward signs of race, creed, or country. He has to choose for himself. He may not even know whether he is going to act as a representative of Beginning, Middle, or End. Anybody can act, at any given moment, as the representative of body, soul or spirit, that is, of paganism, Judaism or Christianism. The yoke of embodiment in a clergy has ceased to be universal. The three properties of any higher life are now accessible at various times to various men.

THE GREAT ELECTORATE: WHO CAN GOVERN A NATION?

In 1912 Raymond Poincaré published a popular book on *How France Is Governed*. The whole book dealt with "equality": equality of votes, equality of departments, equality of students, equality of cities and villages. Neither Paris nor the colonies were mentioned. Yet in the same year, according to d'Avenel, one fourth of all the mobile capital of the country was concentrated in the Île de France. The written constitution of France is backed by an unwritten constitution which guarantees that mixture, that osmosis and concentration of all energies, which are needed to represent messianic humanity in France. Catholics, Jews, and free-thinkers must meet. Provincials and Parisians must meet. Poles, Italians, Germans and French must meet. Old fighters and new geniuses must meet. "Paris will remain what it has always been, the great point of concentration of French thought." [11] There is no other intellectual centre in France and never will be.

The capital of France is a real sovereign. It is still a higher school in the meaning of the law, where the word "high" means sovereign. The less its rôle is mentioned in the Constitution the more important it is to understand its sovereignty. What makes Paris the queen of cities? For two hundred years she has held this sovereignty through her salons.

Stendhal (Henri Beyle) partly described the function of the salons in his *Life of Henri Brunard:* "Dear Cousin, if you wish to make a figure in the world, twenty people must have an interest in speaking well of you. Therefore, choose a salon, go there regularly every day that they receive, take the pains to be amiable, or at least very polite, to everybody. Then you will be playing a part in the world, and you can hope to please an amiable woman as soon as two or three salons intercede in your favour.

"After ten years of perseverance, these salons, chosen from among our circles of society, can promote you to anything and everything. The main point is perseverance and regular appearance."

This advice has been sound in Paris ever since Voltaire's success in the salons at the beginning of the eighteenth century. The Dreyfusards had their salons, those of the *"précieuses radicales."* The last man of great note in the dynasty of writers on the passions of society, Marcel Proust, frequented, so we are told by Leon Pierre Quint, the salons of:

11 *"Paris est resté ce qu'il a toujours eté, ce qu'il sera toujours; le grand point de concentration de la pensée française."*—Georges Clemenceau.

1. Princess Edmond de Polignac
2. Madeleine Lemaire, a painter
3. Madame Aubernon and her niece Madame de Vierville
4. Madame de Loynes
5. Count d'Haussonville
6. Princess Mathilde Napoléon
7. Madame Strauss-Bizet

It was in the last salon *"où il se forma véritablement"* (where he was really shaped). The salons of the great ladies of society select the candidates for Mount Parnassus and the Areopagus. "A salon is never complete; all the time, it must be supplemented and embellished. You may be plain or vicious, no matter, as long as you have connections. Each time that you swing open the door of a salon, your value increases. You are nobody by yourself. You begin to exist when you are admitted to the evenings in some salons. And you are the perfect man when not one of them is closed to you at any time of the day." (Marcel Proust.)

French democracy votes on an equal footing. However, there must be a certain machinery to put candidates before the voters. In America the candidates are named by bosses and conventions, men and groups of men; in France, by the salon. The salon fills the necessary function of an aristocratic process of selection which enables the machinery of democracy to work.

The word "aristocracy" is outlawed in the political life of France; it had to be supplanted by the notion of an *"Élite de cœur et de génie,"* or *"les privilégiés de l'esprit."* As a democratic voter, the Frenchman can say "Yes" or "No." But to put up a new man, to launch a new talent, is the privilege of the French women. They need no vote in the rank and file of men. No country has been less interested in votes for women than France; for it is their salons which select the candidates. This is the unwritten part of the French constitution, the part which makes it possible for the French to change the government as often as they do, to live in a perpetual cabinet crisis, with a prodigality of ministries that baffles the foreigner. The single individual gets a chance to play his part in a Morrisdance of inspired individuals. But the sequence of inspired individuals, not the putting up of any single leader, is the essence of government. The queen of cities, Paris, has replaced Versailles because her salons have replaced a dynasty of kings by a dynasty of inspired individuals whose candidacies the ladies of the salons have previously approved. Thus the keystone of the French constitution is not a rational thing. The society of Paris is the illogical premise to all the logical constructions on paper.

There is no boss, no party whip, to hold together the members of Parliament in France. No party leader can force candidates upon the constituency. The whole apparatus of politics is split into many small groups. Every candidate is an individual, making his career by changing his allegiances from day to day. Society and its "intrigues" elude all efforts toward strict party discipline or leadership. Political treason has lost the bad savour it has in England. *"Trahison"* is a natural weapon in the maze of intrigues in Paris. The ambiguity of our social connections in a republic of equals, exaggerated by men like Talleyrand and Fouché, those masters of vice and crime by indirection, remains the eternal secret by which the government can be revolutionized, so to speak, every day. The comrades must overthrow the government today in order to take it back tomorrow. In no other country can a political leader lose and win so often and in so short a time. The "inspired individual" acts his part for weeks, even months; then the next one strikes the key-note of the day more successfully, and gets his turn. But *the opportunity for change* is at the root of the system. That is what makes society, not the master, but more accurately the mistress of government. Where else in the world could Congress be compared to a salon? In *Le Télégramme du Pas-de-Calais,* a provincial paper, I find this phrase: *"Les couloirs de la Chambre ne sont pas le dernier salon où l'on cause."*

It would be a mistake to think of the French *Chambre des Députés* as a parliament in the English sense of the word. The thing which corresponds to it in the English constitution is Election Day in the different constituencies. For in England the place where passion reigns is not Parliament but the constituencies. Here people really act according to the emotions of the moment. Here enthusiasm, applause and inspiration collaborate in the final issue. In France, this is true of the *Chambre* itself. The *Galérie* was a weighty factor in French politics from the very beginning. When a motion was made to exclude the public from the meetings of the National Assembly, a deputy exclaimed: "How dare they propose to exclude from this place our constituents, our masters?" [12]

That is why the dissolution of Parliament would be a real break of the constitution in France, whereas it is perfectly normal in England. In England it is a device for recapturing popular support; in Paris, it means that the very honour of the Chamber is at stake for not having reflected faithfully, in the nation's greatest constituency, the passions of the day. The Chamber itself is the *"foire sur la place,"* Vanity Fair. One dissolution would be a blow to its required function from which it could never recover. The passage from England to France is like a passage from *Pickwick Papers* to Victor Hugo. The passions of the electorate are taken humorously in England, and they work at random. In France this weed-like growth is dignified: the crop is ennobled by the new domination of the *esprit* over the passions. Whereas the English Parliament is the Grand Jury of England, the *Chambre* of the Palais Bourbon does not debate, but pleads, and could well be called the great electorate of the nation.

In 1835 a Russian princess interviewed the deputy Berryer, a distinguished French politician; and in this interview the indirect "intrigue" and the incessant "change" are both well indicated.

"What do you think, M. Berryer, of the new laws proposed by the French government?"

"I approve of them in principle, and that is why I intend to absent myself from the Chamber, where my position would oblige me to oppose them."

"Do you think the government will last?"

"No."

[12] John Simpson Penman, *The Irresistible Movement of Democracy*, New York, Macmillan, 1923.

"Do you think there will be a republic?"
"No."
"Do you think Henri V will come in?"
"No."
"What, then, do you think?"
"Nothing; for in France it is impossible to establish anything." [13]

In August and September, 1914, French public opinion held: "The State (*l'État*) has failed, Society has saved us!" For by a spontaneous, unorganized effort the deepest reserves of French faith and courage had improvised a form of resistance behind the front of defeat and retreat organized by a pedantic and legalist government. In 1911 Francis Delaisi, who had foreseen the disintegration of society, had invoked the decision of 1914 in his startling book *La Guerre qui Vient: "Faites la guerre ou faites un roi."* (Make war or make a king!) The War took the place of royal restoration, and confirmed the responsibility of "society" as organized by the higher bourgeoisie and its 100,000 families. Wars are the final test of a constitution.

The French nation will be able to live in the framework of its democratic constitution as long as the queen of the Île de France bears the torch of genius and can bestow her laurels on the inspired individual of the day. In this, the queen of cities is the true heir of the monarchs of Versailles. The best statement that can be made of this system of French government was made by Louis XIV in his memoirs:

"Wisdom requires that under certain conditions one leave much to chance. Reason itself recommends further that we follow all kinds of blind stirrings of instinct, which escape our reason and seem to come from Heaven. No one can tell when to ward off and when to yield. Neither books nor rules nor experience teach us this. A certain acuteness and a certain boldness of *esprit* will always make us find the right thing."

Paris has distributed this royal wisdom through society. This new monarch, by her "élite of the spirit" turns the wheel of fortune and genius in an organized way, nevertheless leaves much to chance, to instincts which seem to come from Heaven,

[13] *Diary of the Duchesse de Dino,* September 17, 1835, p. 264 f., London, 1909.

to acuteness and boldness. The Cartesian and Voltairian perfect order of the universe is kept alive by this irrational trust in the lightning-flashes of surprise.

The French have made a special effort to organize the *"milieu,"* the environment, in which government can be prepared. They specialize, not in good government, but in preparing the conditions for good government. Now this is a universal problem. All governments need a social playground for the governing class. A revolutionary government needs a pre-revolutionary meeting-place to prepare the minds of the people and to prepare its own organization. The austere character of Bolshevism is derived from the exile-character of the meeting-places of the revolutionary group. They met in exile and in prison, in Switzerland and in Germany, in France and in Siberia. They conquered Russia from outside.

France was fortunate in beginning her revolution from the inside, from Paris. The salons prepared the way for the revolution and have kept it going ever since. And the society of Paris has urbanized the manors of the nobility of France; the beautiful castles along the Loire and the Seine were turned into summer resorts for the wealthy bourgeoisie. The *"patrie"* invaded the *"pays,"* and grafted its social customs onto the trunk and core of the nation.

One of the roots of regionalism had been the aristocracy of bishops throughout France. Now, even the Church has been centralized. A description of the technique of this centralization will round off our survey of the sovereign society of Paris.

Napoleon I, in his concordat with Rome, imposed upon the Church the organic articles which empowered the government to censor any utterance of the Holy See. Before any communication can be made by the shepherd of Rome to his sheep in France (so say the first three organic articles of 1802) Paris must give its permission. Through Paris the Pope can affect France, never without it. Even ecumenical councils are not allowed to raise their voices in France without the permission of the French government.

The Third Republic, during the Dreyfus affair, tried to destroy the Church by opposing it. Convents were dissolved, parishes dispossessed of their churches. But during the War the Catholic priest earned a new halo by his heroic efforts on the battlefield, and the Freemasons like Briand began to be frightened by the increasing vigour of neo-Catholicism. Therefore they preferred not to attack it—martyrs are the best propaganda for a creed—but to control it. Against the mild protests of the real Catholics in France, the Pope's representative was made to supplant almost the whole French hierarchy. The nuncio, the Pope's minister to the French government, became the mouthpiece of the latter so as to assure its influence over all appointments in the Church. Practically speaking, no bishop can be appointed who has not been recommended by the government. No meeting of the French bishops can deal with any important matter on its own initiative. The simplest way back into an independent life for the dioceses or regions of France is successfully barred by this surprising nationalization of the Roman Catholic Church. When the government wished to see the *Action Française* outlawed by the Pope, pressure was brought to bear upon the French episcopate to such an extent that the bishops themselves petitioned officially for its banishment. But their signatures were really furnished by the nuncio, so that the bishops had to submit or else accuse him of having forged the signatures. The plan succeeded. One bishop protested against the use of his name, the rest bowed. The *Action Française* was suppressed. (See the accurate account in the *Mercure de France*, May, 1932.)

Obviously, this system, though the ideal of any nationalistic government, cannot but be unique. In no other country can the Catholic Church be governed by Freemasons. The unwritten French constitution is not an article of export.

ADAM AND EVE.

That scene of the impudent speculator, Beaumarchais, watching Marie Antoinette act in his play in her Rousseau-like house of Trianon anticipated the concentration of the living voices of French life in the capital and the capitulation of the gentry to the bourgeoisie.

All the other countries of Europe experienced the shock of

this Jacobinism. When people like Byron and Shelley invaded English society, Satan seemed to have entered the quiet houses of old England. Lucifer, Milton's fallen angel, the ultimate threat to the Commonwealth of a Christian world, set foot on the British Isles when these geniuses introduced the rights of free love and suicide, free-thinking and libertinism, into the settled social order of England.

The eccentricities of the *"esprit libre,"* the orgies of free genius, were the background of life in French literature and society; passion was the *conditio sine qua non* for the rule of equality in France. The legitimate wife and the mistress coexist in a Frenchman's life. Without the eruptions of passionate feeling, passionate love, passionate creation, the republic would lose its anchorage in the nature of man. The *Human Comedy,* as it was described by the great Napoleon of French literature, Honoré de Balzac, is the tragedy of love and greed, ambition and jealousy. Balzac reads the runes of this society; he draws back the veil which covers the skeleton of its organization. The grandeur and wretchedness of the human heart (compare Clemenceau's *Grandeurs et Misères d'une Victoire*) drive the machinery of life. Balzac described the devastations of passion in the life of the individual, the price which was paid by thousands of Frenchmen for the fireworks of liberalism and progress. The literary men themselves were the victims of this law of the smelting-furnace. Sainte-Beuve described it when he said: "Whereas the classical writers wrote only with the higher and purely intellectual part of their being, today the conditions of the time force the writer to wrest from his nature all and everything that it can sell." "I must express my century," said Balzac.

This means condemning a man to swim with the stream of change to the limit of exhaustion, to struggle against death and weakness in the agony of his heart. And the strain is the more terrible because, in the age of genius, heart and spirit are no longer distinguishable. The heart no longer has an objective order of the spirit to fall back on, as it has in civilizations where the spirit is public and the heart individual. The French monism of heart and brain, spirit of the community and spirit of genius, leads the individual into endless effusions and catastrophes. This monism is the great French contribution to the nineteenth century. Of Pierre Loti his biographer, L. Coquelin, could say: "Among the remedies for escaping the flight of time he found, however, one noble way, the way of literature. Loti thought that 'the necessity of fighting against death is the only reason a man can have for working.' He therefore composed novels in order to prolong the memory of himself beyond this short life, and, what was even more important to him, to prolong this life by living the past over again." The morbidity of a soul which believes in its obligation to become immortal through intellectual means was compensated only by the brilliance of the sparks struck from such a troubled soul in its search for immortality.

Balzac, Zola, Proust are artistic lenses focussed on reality. Their "immortality" is not their fault. Lenses and prisms of society as they are, they only reflect its functioning. It is true that they mark the rapid decline of love from an exalted idea to a passion (Balzac), to a vice (Zola), and to a crime (Proust). Human love, the love of Adam and Eve, is mortal and sinful unto death. The magnificence of the pictures drawn by the novelist does not alter the fatal down-hill course which individual passion took between 1789 and 1918, once it had been let loose. The God of the French Revolution is the God of passion. Even Ernest Hello, the devout Catholic, in whose work the tears, the misery and the faith of man are transmuted into pure sounds that can be understood in every quarter of the globe and in every clime, cannot help ending this book with a typically French expression. Theoretically, the sentence could just as well have been written by anyone else, an Englishman or a Russian; but it would not stand as the last word of a book of edification: "For what is God's supreme quality? *Dieu qui est feu brûlant, Amen, Amen.*" (God is burning fire, Amen, Amen.)

Passion burns us to dross; passion dies. It is true that the words of the genius were brought up from the well of life, the poem was written, the picture painted, the discovery made; and in the Panthéon of immortality not only are the poet and the chemist and the *écrivain,* Victor Hugo, Berthelot and Zola, present, but Madame Berthelot rests at the side of her husband whom she loved so passionately that they died together.

Passion excuses crime in France, and Madame Caillaux was absolved by the jury for having shot Calmette, the detractor of Joseph Caillaux who had infuriated the capitalists by sponsoring the sacrileges of sacrileges, the income tax.

Balzac wrote after Napoleon I. After Napoleon III, Émile Zola, facing the social struggles between classes, supplemented Balzac's *Comédie Humaine* with his tragedy of the race. In the twenty volumes of his *Rougon-Macquart* he draws back the curtain from the destruction of the race by the passions of sex and greed. Syphilis and loveless marriage ruin body and soul of the tree of life.

The third generation, represented by Marcel Proust, went further still in its bold investigation of the forces of life behind the scenes of society. The inversion of the instincts of life scar society as Proust describes it in his great fifteen-volume work: *À la Recherche du Temps Perdu.* Man loving man and woman loving woman sterilize the natural flowering of youth, sterilize the hope of natural regeneration. *"J'appelle ici 'amour' une torture réciproque"* was Proust's terrible definition of love.

Like Balzac and like Zola, Proust was denounced as an Herostratus, a destroyer of decency. But intellectual courage was an established god in French literature; and so Proust explained proudly and calmly to his friend Louis de Robert why he had to write on Sodom and Gomorrah and their unnatural vices: "I am serving a general truth which prohibits me from thinking any more of my agreeable friends than of the disagreeable. To have won the favour of the Sadists will have its reaction on me as a man once my book has been published; it could not modify the conditions under which *I experience truth,* and which I did not choose from any personal caprice."

THE PITFALL OF REASON.

Reason, *l'esprit,* the intellect of the writing and reasoning nation, is constantly fighting against the darkness of "illiteracy." You must know how to read and write to be a real member

of a civilized nation. The illiterate is a poor devil in this enlightened world. He clings to symbols, he is dependent on
superstitions. He is not a pure "individual"; he wears all kinds
of blinkers. He marches, perhaps, in procession on Corpus
Christi day; as a husband he wears and respects (perhaps!) a
gold ring; as a gentleman, he takes off his hat when a lady
passes, though this is an old feudal abuse. In brief, the irrational part of man's nature is a slave to forms and symbols, and
looks upon life through a glass darkly. Reason sees straight
through all the symbols. It is free of superstition. It needs no
emblems, no flags. It is not subject to the fury characteristic
of the illiterate, who are roused by bugaboos. It is not deceived
by the cheap intoxication of lies and fairy-tales.

This is the creed of the modern mind, or was its creed twenty
years ago. It is one of these self-betrayals which any revolutionary party unconsciously produces as long as it is storming the
walls of Jericho. A revolution on its way, a movement in its
first century, is perfectly honest in thinking that the twilight
of the gods exist only on the other side.

In clearing up the underbrush of privilege and prejudice,
liberalism or rationalism was convinced that it held in its
hand the naked truth, undisguised, unstained by dogma or
tradition. Reason discovering nature can test everything by
experiment. There is no room for traditional habits: fashion
takes the place of habit. But it is precisely fashion which en-
slaves Reason. The philosophizing mind has its prison of sensu-
ality and drudgery exactly like a pupil of the Jesuits or a child
in a backwoods village. Its fairy-tale and its prejudice are
not dependent upon miracles or dogmas or incense or witch-
craft, but the apparatus of Reason is subject to the same laws
of sensuous disguise as any other part of the human soul. Superstition sends us to the medicine man, physical pain to the
physician. We have a native sense that urges us on toward Reason and Philosophy: this sense is curiosity. Without a sense for
novelty, no thinker can succeed or affect the life of the community. The self-indulgence of Reason is its predilection for
the new. The newspaper is the true expression of this quality
of philosophical perception, the sensuous form which enables

man to recollect truth in its disguise as news. New facts and new ideas inflame our imagination. Without this flame the best idea, the wisest thought, remains useless. Any influence upon our senses is useless so long as our senses do not react. Indifference is a state of perfect equilibrium. When we feel neither cold nor warm, our internal thermometer is not registering anything. As long as we feel neither joy nor pride, our emotional system is quiescent. Philosophy has recognized the external dependence of all our senses. It is aware that they are all based on impressions, and react to influences from outside.

Now Reason is exactly the same kind of servant. It serves us well whenever its proper centre is stimulated. It is created and given to us for the purpose of distinguishing between new and old. It begins to move and to be stimulated by sensations which are new, unheard of. Reason is tickled by novelty. The nineteenth century changed the oldest truths into sensational news. We are willing to believe that the wind bloweth where it listeth, or that to him who hath shall be given, if we read it on the front page of our newspaper as the latest cable from Seattle. As the latest news in the newspaper, the oldest truth is welcome to Reason. The Age of Reason reveals truth by proceeding from news to news. It believes that the age of Revelation is gone; it believes in Enlightenment. But it itself is wholly based on Revelation. Reason cannot understand eternity or old age. It scorns tradition, *ancien régime,* customs, irrational weights or measures. It is clear, precise; but it also destroys everything which cannot be made either bad or happy news. Anything that is not willing to break out or happen or change is hidden to Reason. The nineteenth century forgot all eternal truth which was not ready to step down into the arena of Latest News, telegrams and publicity. A man had to become a sensation lest he be a failure.

To secure the electric current from which permanent sensation could be drawn, Reason had to conclude an alliance with the almighty power through which mankind enters the realm of sensation. Venus had to be propitious to the adventure of Reason. Without Venus, Reason is dry and sterile. All ancient languages express knowledge and knowledge of a woman by the same word. And it is true that the world comes to us through our most worldly quality: sex. That explains the erotic obsession of the Age of Reason. This erotic sensitiveness reproduced a great mythology nourished by the ebullition of our flesh and blood. The art of the nineteenth century is quite different from the art of other periods, of the Italian Renaissance, for example. The use of the same word for both is highly misleading. In the liberal art of the "French" century in Europe, Reason invested all its faith. The fate and destiny of Reason were trusted to the process of sensuous revelation. A manifest logic seemed to govern the sensations experienced by one genius after the other. One blood, it was supposed, runs through the veins of all the artists who are members of the cult. The pleasures, the excitements, the fashions, the curiosities of genius, are no longer considered to be casual impressions of private individuals. They follow each other—from Chénier to Anatole France, from Beethoven to Strauss, from Byron to Wilde, from Leopardi to d'Annunzio—with the trans-personal logic of evolution. This evolution is necessary and inevitable even if it is fatal.

The experiments in the art of this last period are based on a mythological faith in the lawfulness of our sensuous reactions; to the labyrinth of our passions and true nature, only pleasure itself can serve as a clue. In its manifold phases and changes, its restless transformations, pleasure seems to have little dignity and less reliability. But the artist's pleasure is ennobled, for it is believed to be part of a universal process. The sequence of sensations and intellectual emotions through which four or five generations of writers and painters and composers passed in majestic procession, this *"érotomanie cérébrale"* which tapped every possible source of pleasure and excitement, was sanctified as the true self-revelation of the deity of Life. With Life as its sovereign, art is freed from any code or creed which is not based on pleasure. Barbey d'Aurevilly, a most Catholic French writer, in a letter, in 1877, explained the rules of the game to a baffled ultra-Catholic youth, Léon Bloy, by this startling paradox: "In questions of morals we must do what we don't like. . . . But in the life of art and literature the opposite is true. There the only safe rule is to do what gives you pleasure." It is no mean pleasure; for it is not individual. Our scattered, particular pleasures are made human because they are integrated into a human body of common experience. The humanism of the last century must not be mistaken either for the licentiousness of libertines and *déracinés* or for a pedantic revival of classical humanity. The artists serve on a humanistic expedition which utilizes every shock, every nervous fit, every emotion or sensation of its members as another successful way of reconnoitring man's terra incognita: himself.

In the nineteenth century art is no longer the expression of undoubted values through the medium of our senses. Art itself is doubt, and every artist is ready for death, disease, paralysis, destruction whenever passion forces him to meet life on dangerous ground. *"Ils ne mouraient pas tous, mais tous étaient frappés."* Baudelaire would say: *"J'ai cultivé ma hystérie avec jouissance et terreur."* For this service he was rewarded by Victor Hugo's praise: *"Vous créez un frisson nouveau,"* you are giving us a new sensation. Through the creations of art the lives of the poets are integrated into the great uniting force: Life, in the singular, comprehending us all. *"La Vie"* is the common denominator of a century of individualism. It is its deity because it is the unity among all the innumerable *"frissons nouveaux."* Life, it was presupposed, was unitarian, monistic, running through all the brains of creative individuals, as one evolutionary stream. Without this one mythical unity of "life," Reason, in its fury of analysis, would have destroyed the very conception of unity.

These, then, are the *"grandeurs et misères"* of the victory of Reason. Reason, abstract and unreal, without roots in the soil, without rhythm in its movements, cannot govern its world without submitting to the directing power of sensation.

Today we are somewhat tired of this self-indulgence of Reason. The titillation of our sense of novelty is expensive and ruinous, because world, facts, truth and values lose their roots in the timeless when they are made to depend upon being rediscovered from time to time. Under the dictatorship of Reason, man begins to live like a solitary and one-celled animal.

This unicellular life can get nowhere except by eating and swallowing. Multicellular life can depend upon older achievements without eating and digesting them. The modern society of the nineteenth century kills everything which cannot be swallowed in the form of news and sensations. It is unicellular. Now civilization does not form visible cells; its cells consist of generations, ages, periods. The repressive and outstanding feature of the age of Reason is its "single-aged," one-generation character. Such an age may go on for two hundred years; but it will always remain a one-generation affair as long as its values depend on reproduction in the form of novelty. We meet reality through various senses. Any sense which states a difference is able to inform us. A consideration of our modern life will reveal how much of its information is based on a mere sense of curiosity. Curiosity arranges the things of the universe according to their quality of being *new;* and this produces an order of things of remarkable futility. The movie star comes to the foreground, wisdom is ridiculed, forests are sacrificed without a qualm because they grow so slowly, and skyscrapers are adored because they go up so fast. It is a very limited outlook on the universe which we gain through our instruments for news. There are other instruments, like hunger, reverence, patience, faith, which work in a different way and discover very different parts of the world.

The sense of novelty has been organized in the last hundred and fifty years as our main highroad of information. We say: it has been *organized.* The nineteenth century did not make discoveries or inventions in the same way as any other period of history. It invented the technique of invention; it formulated the methods of discovery. The secret of the French Revolution is the organization of discovery. We no longer stumble from one invention to the next; we have learned to plan our inventions and discoveries.

The sensation of novelty is sanctified by the campaigns carried on in our laboratories into the unknown. But like any sacrament, this one is stained by terrible superstitions. No one wishes to minimize the miracles performed in the laboratory; but we must overcome this appalling destruction of family, discipline, faith, by curiosity and by the growing paralysis of the rest of our senses. Because everybody has been trained in curiosity, most people have neglected their other senses; our deeper, wiser, better and more important links with reality have degenerated under our system of newspapers, radios, phonographs, movies, with their organization of novelty. They are the bane of modern life. The prohibition of news would restore the peace of many families. Truth will die if the masses see it based on nothing but novelty. Truth is not new, it is all around us. It was before we were. The original thinker knows that true originality consists in being as old as creation.

At the installation of a minister, at which I was present, neither the examiner nor the minister being examined cared in the least for the old dogma of the pre-existence of Christ. They were faithful believers in the ideas of liberty, Class of 1789, and did not suspect that truth must be as old as the world in order to be truth at all. "Pre-existence of Christ" is but an old expression for a law completely forgotten by the century of progress, which says that truth has been and will be when all our sensational news has withered and faded away like the morning dew. Dew is refreshing; dew is morning-like; the dew of novelty is an image of the morning star, called "Lucifer" by the ancients. But Lucifer and all his projects for our earthly happiness are very apt to presume too far. The happiness of the individual is limited by his mortality. The species must survive one individual's shortcomings. Lucifer's pride brought his downfall. The heresy of the nineteenth century is its utter disregard of the eternal recurrence of life. Unable to hear or to understand through any medium which is not telegraph, telephone or radio—that is, which is not sensational or new—our period is doomed because it has not taken thought for reproduction and regeneration.

The Russian Revolution, in trying to end history, was striking against this nightmare of liberty and reason. The trap-door underlying Reason bears an illuminated sign "Latest News," "Sensational Report." In the laboratory, where progress can be organized, this trap-door leads into a real and important room, the storehouse of raw material and provisions. In the world of society, the trap-door with this inscription leads into the gaping pit of much ado about nothing. Sensation cannot distinguish between the permanent and the sham, between Vanity Fair and the Holy of Holies, between short-lived Noise and long-lived Silence.

The French Revolution sharpened our senses for change; it blunted them to the deeper sensations that precede the coming earthquake of world-war and world-revolution. No civilization was ever taken so completely by surprise, as was Europe by the World War. The Age of Reason fell into the abyss of time without any understanding of how to make a war or how to conclude a peace. The period of the French Revolution, because it was a period of "Reason first," was ensnared by the absolutism of the latest news, and in spite of all intellectual warnings, no wisdom, no religion, and no reverence were left to prepare the nations for an honest war or a reasonable peace. Reason was overruled by blind passions, because Reason had degraded the peers: Hunger and Love, Old Age and Tradition.

The shortcomings of the Age of Reason are usually treated as economic shortcomings. Marxians content themselves with exposing "capitalism" behind the mask of liberalism. They can see only matter where the liberals saw ideas. The red intellectuals are very harsh against the material interest, but they are less eager to criticize their own failure as intellectuals. A clever Frenchman unmasked the bad conscience of the red intellectuals in a book that he called La Trahison des Clercs, the treason of the clergy of our modern civilization, of the literati themselves. Therefore, instead of relaxing in the rocking chair of economic statistics, we discussed the rôle of reason in any age, be it Bolshevik, liberal or feudal, and thereby circumscribed the relative place of the French Revolution.

THE PEASANT OF PARIS.

Today Paris, the *"ville de la lumière,"* is threatened with darkness. In 1931 Aragon wrote a great novel on *The Peasant of Paris (Le Paysan de Paris)*, in which he treated Paris as one of the many *"pays de France."* The most radical thing in this book is the turning away to a France without the *tour d'Eiffel* of Paris and the ocean of light spreading from the City to the villages. Aragon thinks that personal life will have to disappear from the surface of our earth. *"Les personnes ont fini leur temps sur la terre."* Worker and agricultural labourer, the inferior organisms of Clemenceau, are advancing. The number of artists and foreigners is dwindling down. The lights of the *tour d'Eiffel* and the lightning flashes of genius are, after all, artificial lights. Any strike in the electrical power-plant, this city of light, Paris, must result in the disintegration of France. The lack of regeneration in the governing class of France since Clemenceau and Poincaré is tremendous. Of course, as in England or Germany, the best men have died during the War. And the *"pays,"* the old countries, the regions, are being spoken of again. The Basques, stimulated from the Spanish side, begin to rub their eyes. Brittany was always something apart; Alsace-Lorraine is influenced by her nearness to Switzerland and her German experience.

But it seems improbable that regionalism can make real progress in France. It is too early. The outcome of the French Revolution, the concentration of the élite in Paris, is not to be undone after only a century of trial. Some colonial adventurer from Tunis or Morocco might perhaps give reality to the rather theoretical revival of the regions in France. But France's universal function, the part she must play against Bolshevism, will hold her for the time being to her moral and political constitution. Today, as always, the French are approaching a rather slight change with great violence.

CHECKS ON INDIVIDUALISM.

The world could not exist without severe checks on the French system of government, and we look around for the forces which were vigorous enough to balance French individualism during the nineteenth century. We have already mentioned the deep shock which characters like Byron's produced on the British Isles. When the naked statue of Shelley was erected in University College, Oxford, something "French" took possession of England which was as revolutionary as the words "Prime Minister" or "Liberal," imported during the nineteenth century.

But behind these influences the old organization of England persisted. No Paris swallowed up the English countryside, no bourgeoisie hung the tricolour over the fireplaces of the old manors of England's green and pleasant land. The English Constitution remains unwritten, unreasonable, and old. To be like one's ancestors, to have privileges, to exist by precedent, to be a gentleman, offensive as these things are in France, are recommendations in England and Anglo-Saxon countries even today.

Revelation of genius, inundation by passion, are not the key to a career in England. Another creed, a different faith, created the British Commonwealth. The French system of an age of Reason and Nature following upon the *ancien régime,* with its prejudices and unreasonableness, would not have functioned for an hour without its active counterpart, an age of precedent, prescriptive right and experience of the world.

In turning from the French Revolution to the British Commonwealth we shall find the key to the situation of America today, standing as she does midway between the English and the French. But we shall find more. In opposing precedent and novelty, customs and written law, experience and reason, "world" and "nature," we shall look deep into the variousness of man. A revolution produces a national character as one combination of the vast possibilities of the human soul. The nations of Europe are not pebbles, not bodies which developed like atoms in the universe. They came into existence to save the life of the soul from deviation and one-sidedness.

The eternally valid discoveries of the proletarian and the bourgeois revolution would make no sense if they were not related to the preceding attempts to express our desires through the framework of political forms. The French Revolution was not a continuation of the English Revolution; it came as its logical antagonist. Without this permanent opposition it loses its meaning. And all Europeans are called upon to nourish themselves, not upon one or the other revolution, but upon the totality of institutions created by the great revolutions of the human soul.

CHAPTER SIX

England: A Commonwealth Within the Western World

Detective History—The Realm—Common Law—The Restoration of the Common Law—Economics and Budget—Particulars and Precedents—The Pedigree of Oliver Cromwell—The New Environment: The Western World—The Theft of a Word—The King in Parliament—A Parliamentary Church—Public Spirit—The End of Convocation—The Language of a Gentleman—The Fifth of November—The European Significance of "Glorious Revolution"—The Three Restorations—The Loss of the First Commonwealth—The Adaptation to the Bourgeois Revolution: Sportsmanship and Liberalism

DETECTIVE HISTORY.

WHY SHOULD A FOREIGNER MEDDLE WITH THE ENGLISH REVOLUtion? The English, in any case, will not care what he says about England. While the French always claimed a European scope for their undertaking, the British tried to make theirs a family affair, for people of good breeding; and it need scarcely be said that you must be an Englishman in order to be well-bred. It was English gentlemen who told the story of the British Revolution to the new middle classes of the Victorian era: Thomas Babington Macaulay immortalized the virtues of William and the Whigs in the Glorious Revolution, and Samuel R. Gardiner published all the documents concerning the atrocities of Cromwell and the Civil War, from 1640 to 1660; while other writers concentrated on the obscenities of the Restoration (between 1660 and 1685) at court, on the stage, and in Pepys' diaries.

Unfortunately, the British Revolution is in sore need of being retold by a foreigner—not for the sake of any reader in the British Isles, only for the less happy peoples of the world.

For they are being compelled to readjust themselves, and they cannot do so without fitting England into the European pattern. The British Revolution has been splendidly isolated from any possible explanation, by a tacit conspiracy among English historians and lawyers, which stands in the way of any reasonable treatment of politics in our textbooks on history, political theory, economics, and law. Hence, a German World History, in dealing with Europe in the seventeenth century, had only two sentences on England; and this was outdone by an Oxford *History of Europe* that did not mention the author's own country at all. So well have the English contrived to make the world believe that the Anglican Church, the English Parliament, and the British Empire are institutions not on earth but in heaven! The catholic, European, universal character of their experience, the correct and precise place of its faith and vocabulary in the European concert, had no place in their institutions and their outlook. They used every spark of wit and genius to conceal what they did from the unworthy gaze of the princes and peoples on the Continent. They were exclusive and insular for a great purpose. And the result is that school-children everywhere suffer; for without the part of the road that led mankind through the green lawns of England, history and law resemble a maze. The English Revolution ought to be saved from its English detractors, because in spite of their insularity it was a human, a Christian, a universal event.

First of all, the English split their literary traditions of the decisive hours of their past into three sections, one idealistic, one materialistic, and one realistic. The pride of the nation centres about the Glorious Revolution; the depravity of the Stuart Restoration allows English men of letters an insight into the otherwise hidden sides of man's nature and body; and the documents and pamphlets of the Civil War can be published and registered in a completely matter-of-fact way, without ever coming to an end. The Continental reproach of English hypocrisy and perfidy dates from the unwillingness of English writers to conceive of the years from 1640 to 1691 as one distinct and continuous period.

It is true that recent authors have written valuable books on the seventeenth century which repair this splitting up of the political tradition. But these writers go to the other extreme. When the whole of the seventeenth century is surveyed at once, or the sixteenth and seventeenth together, the peculiarities of our fifty years are levelled over. Instead of two separate peaks (Civil War, 1640 to 1660, and Glorious Revolution, 1688), as they appeared in the old, fictitious tale, the moderns make the stream of history run through a monotonous plain. Either way, the fifty years of gigantic struggle, which tower up like a real mountain—the "highest time in history," as Hobbes rightly christened it—are flattened out.

The very use of three different names enabled the English to disguise what is really one drama in the form of three different plays. "Great Rebellion" is the official label for the years 1640 to 1660; the years 1660 to 1668 are styled "Restoration"; and the "Glorious Revolution," 1688 and 1689, is appended like a stroke of Providence with almost no extension in time. Now these three names:

> Great Rebellion
> Restoration
> Glorious Revolution

are in themselves great accomplishments of the British Revolution. They are marvellously well-chosen by its contemporaries in order to confuse the issue and befog the reader as to the principles involved.

Constitutional history, in the field of Anglo-Saxon public law, is like a detective story. We shall try to detect the motives of this intentional camouflaging, and to recover the lost names of the three parts. Under an English pen this disclosure probably would read like a detective story. For a real theft, or, if you prefer, the embezzlement of a name was perpetrated in the midst of the Revolution. I would not go so far as to suggest that the revolutionary crime corresponds to the peculiar English worship of detective stories. However, why may not a nation with a theft in the very centre of her political existence become detective-minded?

Since we are analyzing the theft in the capacity of outside observers, we cannot successfully compete with Blackstone or Conan Doyle. And therefore we are not going to imitate their strong point: we shall give away the whole plot before the story begins. The Drama of the English Revolution may be called "The King in Parliament." It is a drama, though it lacks the unity of place and time which is so fascinating in the dramatized history of France. In fact, it begins like a morality play, becomes a pageant in its middle part, and ends as a miracle play. In other words, it contains three parts:

The Puritan Restoration	1640 to 1659
The King's Restoration	1660 to 1685
The Anglican Restoration	1685 to 1691

In retracing the English adventures of the words "revolution" and "restoration" we shall relocate this drama in the spiritual pedigree of Christendom as a whole. Nevertheless, let it be said from the beginning that the British used the word "revolution" in a sense opposite to the French and in contrast to our present-day use. In our eyes revolution is connected with the schemes and intentions of revolutionaries, and points to the day of the first violent outbreak. The British coined the term "Glorious Revolution" for precisely the reverse idea; it was meant as a full stop at the end of a sentence. Not the first, but the last, day of that stormy period was labelled Glorious Revolution, and with the intention of ending all revolutionary efforts forever.

Once the unity of the drama of the King in Parliament is restored, the English Revolution is no longer insular. As the French period from 1848 to 1875 tested the ideas of 1789 to the uttermost, so the King-in-Parliament of Great Britain was rigidly put to the test in a period of humiliation which lasted forty years, from 1774 to 1815. The periods previous to the humiliation resemble each other in both countries also. A majestic rhythm becomes visible, comparable to the Continental movements of the political symphony.

The third and last statement in this survey will give a clue to the sequence of our tale. It is concerned with the point of departure for the specifically British evolution. In the preceding chapters we found that the point of conflict came long before the open outbreak. In Russia the intelligentsia, this artificial creation of Czarism, definitely broke with the government as early as 1825. In France something irreparable happened with the revocation of the *Édit de Nantes* for the Huguenots in 1685. The British, too, had their skeleton in the closet, for more than a century. Their fate was determined in 1535 by the execution of the Chancellor of the Realm, Thomas More. Thus the periods of the English Revolution are circumscribed:

POINT OF CONFLICT	UPHEAVAL	PRIDE	HUMILIATION
1535	1640-91	1745-74	1774-1815

This is the part of the story that is purely British. However, the particular charm of this evolution is its interplay with later European revolutions. After 1815 the nation had to adapt itself to the results of a later, equally universal conflagration, the French Revolution. From this process conclusions may be drawn for the present, in that we, too, have to adapt ourselves to an event which presses upon us from the outside. Adaptation is a process, not in the bottom of our hearts, but on the surface. During the nineteenth century Great Britain managed so well to disguise her proper constitution that today Americans or Frenchmen can speak of her as a democracy. This gives us reason to hope that some day France and America will be called Bolshevist by the Russians, without having gone any further in the direction of dictatorial Communism than the British have in the direction of egalitarian democracy.

Alas, in making this remark, I realize how, for a large class of readers, this chapter on Great Britain is under a more serious handicap still.

Though Americans do not share the English creed, they hold that the English creed should be stated in the terms of the English themselves. The unity of language, though it does not at all imply unity of ideas, yet reserves to the English the privilege of being known directly, without any foreign interpreter. The common-law lawyer and the person of literary tastes in

America, in natural response to their heritage, grant the English what they do not grant any other European tradition: that it be left untranslated and not reduced to a common, all-human denominator.

My studies of Roman, Canon, and Germanic law, for instance, have not protected me from the violent outcries of jurists who knew nothing but the common law and their Blackstone, Maitland, and Holdsworth. And what was so terrible? That I spoke, like Burke, with perfect ingenuousness, of the common law of all Europe. Common Law had to be Anglo-Saxon, not universal. This lack of humour of the English-American, with regard to any Continental intervention between himself and his direct knowledge of England, is in itself a virtue. You do not want to protect the English, but you do want to protect your own decency about the English. Thus, when I must get on your nerves, don't forget that this may be, not so much the result of irreverence or ignorance, as the dire need to recognize the English contribution for our common life.

THE REALM.

The frequent failure of parliamentarism on the Continent of Europe is explained by the fact that few parliaments have understood the wisdom of the English solution. English national liberty depends on the existence of a Norman Realm. In sketching the British Commonwealth we must first explain the permanent features of this Realm.

The Norman Realm, Royaume, Kingdom, is a Christian and Continental power established over England by the right of the sword and the blessings of the Church. When the ushers announce the sitting of court in England they cry, "Oyez, oyez!" (*audite!*), the old French-Norman word. When the Prime Minister of England appoints a bishop, he asks the King to write a letter to the chapter of the cathedral containing the name of the candidate, and summoning Dean and Chapter to exercise their "*droit d'élire*," their fictitious right to choose this candidate.[1] When the King accepts the grievances and bills

[1] For a recent example, see Viscount Alverstone, *Recollections of Bar and Bench*, p. 256-8, London, 1915.

passed upon these grievances by his faithful militia in the Lower
House of Parliament, he uses the Norman formula: *Le roi
remercie ses bons sujets, accepte leur benevolence et ainsi
le veut.*

In 1628 the lawyers of the House refused to receive a gracious message in plain English from King Charles I. A verbal
message from the King is no full royal declaration. The customs
of the realm prohibit any answer outside the framework of
Chancery. Coke, the leading lawyer, formulated the Petition
of Rights. Again the King tried to answer it by a long speech
in English. But the House continued to mutter until the King
gave in, and used the Norman formula: *"Soit droit comme il
est désiré."* These lawyers preferred Norman stones to English
bread. The strong roof of the Realm seemed to them a better
shelter than an English popular government.

The English had little luck with their dynasties. With the
exception of the Tudors (Henry VII, Henry VIII, Edward,
Mary and Elizabeth), no English dynasty has been English since
1066, and even the Tudors descended from the "butler of a
Welsh Bishop," Owen op Mergent, and the French princess,
Katherine of Valois! No ruler of purely English blood has
been on the English throne from 1066 up to 1935. The throne
is foreign. But the Throne is surrounded by other royal insti-
tutions of Church and State. The Church was Norman, too.
The first Lords Spiritual, Lanfranc, Anselm, Thomas, were
French clergymen. The Lords Temporal were Normans: Simon
Montfort of Leicester, though called *Protector gentis Angliæ*
in the popular songs, was a Norman who took sides with the
English people against the Realm.

The King's Council and the King's Court were Norman.
Parliament is a French word, too, a translation of the old
German-Frankish *"sprakka," colloquium,* into the Normanized
Frankish term "parliament." The Realm consisted of the

King and Queen
The King's Council
The King's Court
The King's Parliament, Earls, Dukes, Marquisses, Bishops and
  Abbots.

The Norman Lords, Bishops and Abbots were summoned to Parliament individually, by their proper names; the Knights of the Shires, "gentry," and the burgesses of the towns, by their generic names.

Thus within the Realm the only members distinctively English were not recognized as personal dignitaries. The yeomanry of the shires, however, looked up to the squires as their nearest native leaders, after they were deprived of all native higher nobility and royalty.

$$
\text{Realm}
\begin{cases}
\text{King} \\
\text{Bishops} \\
\text{Lords Temporal} \\
\text{Gentry}
\end{cases}
$$

$$
\text{Gens Angliæ}
\begin{cases}
\text{Gentry} \\
\text{Yeomanry} \\
\text{Serfs}
\end{cases}
\quad
\begin{array}{l}
\text{(The gentry is to be} \\
\text{found on both sides;} \\
\text{realm and nation)}
\end{array}
$$

War Lords and Church Lords were foreigners. The strange aversion of Englishmen to the German title of the Emperor, "War Lord," seems utterly unfounded to a Continental, because he knows that War Lord is a limitation, and denies unlimited power to the War Lord in peace times. But in England it sounds as if a foreigner were presuming to command good English blood. The *"Angestammten,"* the native princes of Germany, being unknown in England, English blood became the slogan of every English political movement. A gentry of truly English descent was in itself a guarantee of the English birthright. The gentry were looked up to by the simple yeomanry because they gave a voice to the English blood within the Realm.

During the whole period of the Middle Ages, the Realm also governed the counties of England. It looked down upon the gentry as it did upon the Commons of England. The pride of the gentry in belonging to the people, or at least in representing them, is derived from the haughty viewpoint that prevails in the Realm. The gentry of the shires are Commoners when viewed from the Throne. They are Squires, Leaders and Chief when looked at in their local situation and environment. The Commoners boast of being the Commons because their access to the People outside the Realm is certified by the expression Commoner. This access gave them an advantage in comparison with all the other powers in the Realm. The very names of the other members, Lords and Counsellors of the King, nullified their capacity for representing anyone but themselves! Individualism barred the great members of the Realm. He who wishes to be the head of a living unity must not have a name of his own, he must owe his name and leadership to the body whose head he is to become. The Commons had the good luck to be nameless in the Realm of Great Britain and Normandy.

In the old days of the Realm, during the Middle Ages, the Norman King—like all the other Christian Kings—had summoned a parliament that would pledge his subjects to the taxes which his chancellor proposed to lay upon the people, rich and poor, of the Realm. To go to Parliament was a burden for any member of it, and a merciful King spared his subjects this heavy service so far as he could; for they knew perfectly well how difficult it was to withhold their consent, and how much pressure could be brought upon them when they appeared in the King's presence. In times of little traffic and inadequate transportation, any government was weak as long as its subjects were far away. A Russian proverb said: "Russia is big, and the Czar is far away." This is the secret of the Middle Ages, too. Organization was difficult because distances always meant loss of authority. The King's servants had no better ways of communication than any recalcitrant subject.

Today airplanes, cars, trains and ships, telephone and radio can be seized by the government with relative quickness; in cases of emergency this monopoly of information and transportation gives it an overwhelming power with which no private man can compete. The French Revolution, by abolishing the privileges of any single region and by making men equals, has so weakened the individual power that it cannot be compared with the central powers. We have been spoiled by the

French Revolution to the point of thinking any government, even the weakest, infinitely more powerful than its individual citizens. But we can see even in our day how the equality of men is abused by the corporation lawyers, when they establish persons, companies, trusts, corporations, which cripple the government because they can manage information, propaganda, votes, influence, lobbies, to such an extent that they become states within the State. We must multiply the power of the princes of modern business considerably in our imagination if we wish to get a proportionate picture of mediæval England.

It took so much time for any central power to get information and to act upon it, that, practically, the local lord was the real master of his tenants, and royalty no more than an overlord. Only his feudal allegiance to the sovereign diminished the local power and kept down the local arrogance of such a powerful lord. In Parliament the great became small and the proud humble. The local governors came under the control of a higher ruler, with better standards of administration and justice, because they had to face his eye and listen to his words. The Christian and anointed King, owing a part of his rights to the support of the Church, would fight against the arrogance and intemperance of the great. He would humiliate Powers into citizens, and he would exalt the humble servant of such a Lord into a free man by taking him into the service of the Church or the King. The disgusting utterance of James I, that a prince could cry his subjects up and down, resounded in the ears of an English peasant as his only hope of justice in this world. Peasants and kings, serfs and princes, stood united in a time of rare and difficult communication, against the local powers of land-owners and chiefs of clans.

Parliament was a means of breaking the resistance of the local governors and of co-ordinating them. No wonder that the members of Parliament pleaded for as few parliamentary sessions as possible. Kings were praised for not summoning Parliaments! It was dangerous, expensive and burdensome to go to Parliament; taxes had to be granted. The only relief for so much hardship was the opportunity to denounce the King's servants, to tell the chancellor and the King about the complaints against a judge or a bishop, or any other employé of the Realm. The chance to utter grievances was the compensation for the burden of Parliament's duty of granting taxes. The King, in his pleasure at getting his money, was willing to listen, and would instruct his chancellor to go into the matter and abolish whatever abuses there might be. Perhaps it would take a certain time, between the opening and the closing of the session of Parliament, to formulate their wrongs. The Commons would debate for a long time in their special meeting-place before their speaker was ready to join the Lords of the Upper House, kneeling down at the bar of the House of Lords and there giving voice to their grievances. Even today Parliament includes all its bills in the final grant of the budget! The budget is still the chief act of Parliament, and all the bills for the redress of abuses are enacted together with the budget. This practice was universal all over mediæval Europe, and in many countries the grievances included petitions of the estates that such and such a counsellor be deposed, or such and such a trustee of the powers gathered in Parliament be appointed as chancellor of the kingdom.

The practice of the Norman Realm was that the chancellor should be: first, not a local Lord, and second, if possible, a man who knew the laws of the land. Both circumstances give point to our description of the ideal which was really cherished in olden times. The chancellor must not belong to the powerful in a local district, representing as he did the central and governmental sense of justice. And though a bishop, he must know the English language, customs and traditions. The English chancellor of a King who had other interests outside the country, in France or Ireland for example, was the guarantee that English customs would be respected by the Realm. *He was the Keeper of the King's Conscience* in English affairs. This great name, derived from his duty of hearing the King's confession, was more than a name. Ordinarily, the chancellor kept the Great Seal of the Kingdom. Nothing could be enacted, therefore, without his co-operation. The will of the King became visible only under the Great Seal of the English Kingdom, administered by the chancellor.

At the beginning of the Puritan Restoration the chancellor still was called "Mouth, ear and eye, the very heart of the prince," and his Court was "the King's High Court of Conscience, bound by no custom." Coke, the leader of the move for a petition of Rights in 1628, called the Great Seal *"the Key of the Kingdom."* As Chancellor Haldane said on the fourth of November, 1924: "The Great Seal under the Constitution of this country was an extraordinary instrument. Whoever had it in his possession was Lord Chancellor, with all the powers of the Lord Chancellor. Constitutionally, he could exercise them. It might require a statute to undo things which he could do at that moment, if evilly minded." [2]

No wonder, then, that in the Glorious Revolution of 1688, the Great Seal played a rôle, too. James II flung it into the River Thames, and thought that by doing so he had effectually defeated the enterprise of the Prince of Orange, and Parliament would not have legal authority. The Seal was worth 212 pounds sterling, the enormous amount of money spent for it in 1686. But James II was mistaken. His deed turned against himself. A King who left the country "without so much as leaving a guardian or Great Seal behind him" (State Tracts I, 234; 22. I. 1689) seemed to have divested himself of all authority. The taboo of the Great Seal would not work in 1689. The Lord Chancellor had ceased to be the most important link between the King and his English subjects. The Prince of Orange signed the checks for the Treasury with his own hand, "let this be paid." His name was now as good as the Great Seal.

Let us glance, for a moment, at later times. The power of the Great Seal survived in the imagination of the people. In 1784, while the government was desirous of dissolving Parliament, the metropolis was thrown into consternation by the news that the Great Seal was stolen, the Great Seal, enclosed in the two bags (one of leather, the other of silk), was stolen from the Lord Chancellor. And many imagined that, for want of it, all the functions of the executive government must be suspended. This power of the Great Seal, moreover, was ex-

[2] Haldane's speech is given in the Report of the English County Library Conference of 1924.

ploited as late as 1788. Then the King was mentally ill, and, instead of a regency, the use of the Great Seal seemed to satisfy the need for continuity in government. And officially, the Lord Chancellor still seems to hold the same power today as in the days of Sir Thomas More, taking the Woolsack in the Upper House and presiding at its sessions. Actually, the Lord Chancellor belongs to the obsolete House of Lords, which was justly called by Disraeli as unreal as the Abode of the Blessed, a lifeless Elysium; and he is charmingly caricatured as the "susceptible Chancellor" in Gilbert and Sullivan's *Iolanthe, or The Peer and the Peri.*" The Lord Chancellor has shared with all the Upper Powers of the Realm the destiny of being overruled by the Lower House.

But, to return to the Revolution, in no sense was the fundamental idea of the mediæval chancellor then alive. Nevertheless, the keeper of the King's conscience played a great part in the Puritan Revolution. Certainly he was no revolutionary, no Puritan; he was not even a living man. The ghost of the chancellor, the spectre of the last true keeper of the King's conscience, wrongfully beheaded, the shadow of the greatest chancellor of Englnad, loomed over the horizon of the Puritan Revolution as the shadows of the Huguenots loomed over the French Revolution.

COMMON LAW.

Why did the very breath of English liberty depend on the functioning of Chancery?

Through Chancery the conquering Realm and the conquered nation both hearkened to the civilizing influences of the Church. Thanks to Chancery, England was not a merely military and barbarian country, but a part of Christendom. For the chancellor embodied an order of things in which new ideas of righteousness incessantly made their way from the sanctuaries of the Church into the nation. Chancery created the pride of Anglo-Saxon public life, the bulwark of England and America, the famous and mysterious Common Law.

Since the Common Law is regarded today as of national and native origin, we must devote a few pages to making the reader acquainted with certain elementary facts about it. And this is by no means an antiquarian discussion. Without an understanding of the values embodied in the Common Law, public opinion regarding the education of lawyers can scarcely be developed to a satisfactory degree.

Before Henry VIII (1535) Common Law was not a fact or a collection of rules, but a process. It was a product of the mutual permeation of the Canon Law of the Church, the Roman Law of the Franco-Roman Empire and the Norman law, as well as of the different laws of the land.

There was no Common Law, but anything could become and be made "common law" by the intermediation of Chancery. The lawyers of today think of Common Law as opposed to Roman Law or Canon Law. To the pride of modern Anglo-Saxon jurisprudence, Common Law seems a popular and native kind of law, in short, Anglo-Saxon Law. But Common Law was the product of a union between universal Christian laws and local customs; and the union was legalized by the office of the chancellor.

Henry VIII abolished this fruitful osmosis and interpenetration of two equally important streams of life. Local customs and universal justice were both suppressed by the King's justice and law. Instead of a vivifying process of give and take, a stable order was erected.

The Reformation raised the question, on the Continent as well as in England: The Roman Church having lost authority, what are the sources of the syncretistic law applied by the general courts, the "placita communia" of the land? Hence, the hitherto merely technical term "Common Law," had to be clarified.

It is refreshing to see that the lawyers of the seventeenth century did not share the superstitions of their grandsons in the nineteenth century. They knew pretty well that Common Law was Christian law. A programmatic pamphlet of 1653 explains the true meaning of Common Law. This *Reply to a Draft of an Act or System proposed, as it is reported, by the Committee on Regulations concerning the state* supplies ample material for reflection even today. Printed for the use of the

Commonwealth, as it says, it recommends its plan with this exhortation: "Will not such Counsels, Clerks and Attorneys thereby grow and proceed to be expert in the Law, as formerly, and be a means of preservation of the ancient law of this Nation, being grounded at the first upon *the Old and the New Testament?* According to the direction of Papa Eleutherius, Bishop of Rome to the noble King Lucius of this Nation of Britain and first Christian King in the world, in his Christian epistle (in answer to the message sent by King Lucius to him for the Roman Laws to govern the people of this nation), by putting him in mind that when he was in Rome (where he was raised up in the Christian religion during his youth, among the Christians of the primitive church, in the Second Century after the passion of our Saviour), with his Christian brethren there he received the Old and New Testaments; advising him that out of the same he and his people would take a law to govern by; intimating to him that thereby he should govern well and that so long as he should govern well, he was King, otherwise cease to be King."

The authors, it is true, misdate the origin of Common Law by a thousand years. It originated, not under King Lucius I in 150, but at the time of Pope Lucius II, about 1150, at the time when in Bologna, Magister Gratianus first published his *Concordia Discordantium Canonum* and Thomas à Becket forced a reluctant king to recognize the validity of Canon Law. However, our quotations show how little the nationalistic pride of being English prevailed as late as in Cromwell's day. Common Law was the good law which could not be depreciated by the King's arbitrary power. It did not claim a national origin, but was the dowry of Christian baptism. It was not the nature of the English people but its public inspiration at its conversion that gave rise to the Common Law, which could therefore contain, as it really does contain, elements of Hebrew, Roman and Ecclesiastical Law. Common Law is European law. Hence Burke could write:

"Europe is virtually one great State having the same basis of general law, with some diversity of provincial customs and local establishments. The whole of the polity and economy of every country in Europe has been derived from the same sources."

We found that in France a hundred and four years elapsed between the crime against the Huguenots and the full revenge of 1789. In England, in 1640, a hundred and five years had elapsed since the Chancellor Thomas More was sent from the Tower to his death by the King and Parliament of England. That had been in the days of Henry VIII, who had won from the papacy, in its terror of Luther, the title of "Defender of the Faith," but who later pronounced himself head of the Anglican Church. He had cut off the connection with Rome by means of the absurd fiction that the Anglican Church was the true old Church, without any break, and that it was Rome which had gone heretical. The King married six wives, and beheaded or divorced four of them: one died. He confiscated the wealth of the monasteries, and made himself master of the Canon Law. This reversed the relation between King and Church. Equity, Christianity, progress, had always worked through the keeper of the King's conscience, the chancellor. The quality of mercy was not strained so long as the chancellor could constantly promote change; his reforms and mitigations of the strict law were based on equity, Canon Law, and all the ecclesiastical recommendations for a better social order, divine justice against the Lords, and Christian freedom for the underlings. This constant stream of equity and mercy flowed toward the King. When the King became the head of the Church, the sound circulation of equity from the Christian Universe into the British Isles was stopped. The coin we reproduce here with the King's Hebrew, Greek and Latin titles, contracts effectively with the Hebrew, Greek and Roman elements of Christian law. It illustrates the new claim of the English King to be in himself the source of universal law.

Henry VIII mistook the makeshift of a right to reform, which Luther and the doctors of theology on the Continent had granted to the princes only in case of emergency, for an apostolic office. He thus cut off the prince's dependence upon the "magisterial" teaching of a universal priesthood, and denied independent and universal preaching its legitimate influence. Yet he himself had originally recognized that he was bound in conscience to listen to the universal Church when he sent his embassy to Wittenberg for the divorce from Anne Boleyn. When Luther and Melanchthon gave him as little comfort in his Protestant marriage as the Pope had given him in his Catholic, Henry VIII gave up the universal Church for a second time [3] and withdrew into the fortress of Anglicanism. This was clearly a perversion of Luther's teaching. In England, the King's counsellors had no line of retreat into a universal body of doctrine if they disagreed with their overlord. The prince's conscience was a public institution only so long as his counsellors had to deduce their proposals from the principles of a Church which lived and thought and taught in a sphere not exceeded by the radius of the King's power.

In England the King's conscience was now reduced to the level of a private affair. When James VI of Scotland ascended the English throne in 1603, he tried to teach his subjects the Continental theory of government. But he overlooked the fact that any Continental prince was limited by his membership in a body of reform called a "Party of Religion." Moreover, all the Protestant princes on the Continent ruled such small territories that they were constantly obliged to hire counsellors from abroad and thus tacitly recognized a sovereign learning on which they depended and by which they themselves were informed and reformed. James I, on the contrary, ruled over England and Scotland and Ireland, three countries with three different churches. He was the only prince in Europe whose government far exceeded the extent of the respective denominations. On an island the royal counsellors were terribly dependent upon the whims of the sovereign. The ecclesiastical claims implied by the "Head of the Church" were the ruin. of the liberties of England. And Thomas More, in defending the supremacy of the Church over the King's lusts, was defending the true liberties of England. It was Parliament that deserted these liberties when it co-operated with Henry VIII. No

[3] H. E. Jacobs, *The Lutheran Movement in England*, p. 75, Philadelphia, United Lutheran Pub., 1908.

king ever honoured Parliament more highly than Henry VIII. He used it freely to carry his measures against the Church, and neither the Lords nor the Commons have formally abolished the King's supremacy over the Anglican Church. Today, in 1938, the King of England is its supreme and undisputed head. The Commons preferred inheriting the King's rights over the Church to abolishing them. When the power of the King in the Church proved too much like popery, it was taken over by the Commons, who thenceforth furnished him his college of cardinals. Today, the Prime Ministers govern the Church of England.

Like the Huguenots in France, the Chancellor of England was finally defeated. Parliament was greedy. Parliament escaped taxation by plundering the property of the Church. Parliament was the prop of the King in his effort to pay the expenses of his government by confiscation. All the great Whig families of 1688 derived their property from donations of Henry VIII. The British Commonwealth is largely the wealth of the Commons under Henry VIII, earned under his rule and the rule of the "hammer of the monks," Thomas Cromwell. The charity, generosity and hospitality of the English gentry is a well-justified mortgage on their country-seats. Hallam, telling us that these great families, Lords or non-Lords, owed their ascent to the period of the Tudors and the confiscation of ecclesiastical property, adds characteristically: "This class which was presented with the land of the convents, always excelled—and especially in the first century after 1540—in charity and liberality."

No wonder; for this class took over the important rôle and function of the mediæval Church. And therefore, it could never go back to the period before the Reformation. It had to remain reformed. It was an accomplice in Henry VIII's tyranny over the Church. It had to swallow all the pretensions of the thirty-nine Articles and the Act of Supremacy, because its own fortune was at stake. After 1535 Parliament consistently supported the King in his destruction of the checks which the existence of a free Church had exercised upon the monarchy.

But the shadow of More's scaffold, the ghost of a Catholic

Lord Chancellor who had guaranteed the influx of equity and the checks upon the King's arbitrary power, loomed on the horizon of the five reigns which followed. For Thomas More was the conscious victim of this change. He had been the most popular of the Chancellors. People sang of him, with a pun on his name:

> "When More one year had Chancellor been
> No case did more remain;
> The same will never more be seen
> Till Morus comes again."

His wit was proverbial. Shakespeare borrowed from More his art of dialogue. When the innocent blood of the last Catholic Chancellor of England had been shed (July 6, 1535), the biography written by his son-in-law, Roper, gave the nation its first picture of a gentleman's wit and behaviour. Thomas More would tell his stories with complete detachment, not a line in his face betraying the irony. When the Chancellor's office was reduced in importance, the private manners and habits of the last true chancellor became the future model for British lawyers. The lives of the Chancellors became a favourite in legal literature. But no later chancellor could equal More. With his death the office began to lose its political importance.

The fictions of the modern lawyers carefully veil this break in the tradition. A talk with a leading American authority on the Common Law taught me a valuable lesson in how far this suppression goes. He quoted certain precedents from the fourteenth century, in which the English courts had denied that the King could become a parson and take the income of a parish without the consent of the Supreme Head of the Church, that is, at that time the Pope! He took these precedents as valid, even today; they showed how the courts could overrule the Executive. My natural question was where these same courts had been in 1535, when the monasteries were dissolved and their property confiscated, and the King himself became head of the Church. His reply was simply: "Well, no case was brought into court!" This answer is a good example of the legal and parliamentary art of dressing up facts. The lawyer did not ask *why* no case that attacked the King's religious authority could be brought into court. But Sir Thomas More asked that very question. He saw that the coincidence of King and Supreme Head of the Church deprived the courts of any chance of acting as they had acted before. He died for his conviction, one of the greatest and wisest characters in history, worthy if any of the name of Saint. More, with his clear and sober intelligence, recognized that Common Law had been, not an established reality, but a campaign of action by the King's conscience, against the interests of the King and the other powers. He refused to sanction with the Great Seal of England the stopping of this wonderful process. But the lawyers intentionally overlook the fact that after 1535 the Common Law completely changed its character. The orgies of fictionalism begin; the so-called legal "facts" pass over the real facts of common sense. A historian of the Glorious Revolution, Traill, has described this attitude with masterful precision:

"All our great constitutional precedents are the parents of principle, rather than its offspring; we deduce our theories from accomplished facts of our own creation; the creation of such accomplished facts being itself determined by no theoretical considerations, but by certain practical exigencies of the moment." [4]

After 1535 the King of England had no organized conscience. Whereas on the Continent the conscience of any Protestant prince was kept active by the astringent force of his membership in a large religious party which controlled, stimulated, and co-ordinated all his particular reforms, the King of England was alone among his servants, who had no background outside the mercy and favour of the King himself. The Protestant counsellor on the Continent represented to his prince the considered advice of the new world-wide learning. The counsellor could draw upon a conviction and a teaching common to all the Protestant faculties and theologians: he was their mouthpiece at the king's court. And therefore he was not a courtier. The prince could dismiss a single counsellor, but he could not silence the voice of the Christian conscience, proclaimed by

[4] H. D. Traill, *William III*, p. 57, London, 1888.

Luther when he used the doors of his prince's church to propagate the evangelical, universal truth of the new learning.

THE RESTORATION OF THE COMMON LAW.

Finally the gentry avenged More. But just as the French philosophers could never think of going back beyond Versailles, even though Versailles had killed the Huguenots, so the lawyers of the English gentry could not think of destroying the supremacy of the King, even though his supremacy had killed Thomas More. The vengeance took quite a different shape. Instead of restoring the liberties of the Church against the King, the gentry put its claim for a control over the King in the form of a secular restoration. The liberties of England had to be *restored;* the wrong side of the British Reformation had to be repaired.

The Commons never called their actions anything but a restoration. Neither Great Rebellion nor Civil War, nor, of course, Revolution, was the native name of their enterprise. With all their hearts they were convinced · that they were beginning the real great and glorious *Restoration of the liberties of England.* It is true, as we shall soon find out, that radical changes were made in the Church, which enthroned the united Commons as a religious sovereign, as the Anglican Christian people, in church assembled. But these changes were not allowed to give their name to the Puritan struggle. The name of the struggle was selected, not by the zealots who tried to abolish the Episcopal constitution and the Book of Common Prayer, but by the parliamentary lawyers who looked at the matter from the secular point of view. Taxation was the principle which was put in the foreground by the lawyers. Finance, budget, grievances of his majesty's loyal subjects were at stake. The King, as a secular prince, needed an army and he needed a revenue. And the lawyers argued with him over these two questions under the caption "Restoration."

Now a name may seem a trifle to the reader and he may think that we are wasting too much effort on recovering the proper name of the Puritan Restoration. But a name is much more powerful than a mere noun. Names are never without serious consequences. For centuries the English historians have overlooked the frank profession of the Puritans that they were *restoring* England but, as good heirs of the Puritans, they contended that from Magna Charta down there was no break of continuity in the English Constitution. But this legend is precisely the revolutionary invention of 1641. It was then that the English became traditionalist on purpose. They dug out old forms and gave to Magna Charta and many an old statute a significance which they had never had before. The Common Law was restored *because it had been interrupted*. England, since the Puritan restoration, has been making herself old by artificial means. The features of English life which fascinate the observer as reflecting an unbroken tradition of nine hundred years are in fact the outcome of a restoration which restored a broken tradition by revolutionary means.

It is, therefore, impossible to understand the English passion for old precedents, if we take it to be a native passion of the English from the days of Alfred or William the Conquerer. It is an acquired quality of the national character, acquired in the great Puritan clash of the seventeenth century. The national character was not a permanent, native or inborn quality of the race. It was produced in an historical struggle, where to be *"old"* became a weapon in the hands of a *new* class.

At the outbreak of the Puritan resistance, when Cromwell was inclined to leave the country and go to America, insecurity haunted the gentry. Members of their class had been condemned to bodily punishment for resisting taxation. Arbitrary taxation without consent of the Commons was the centre of parliamentary complaints. The Commons wished, therefore, to restore Magna Charta. And so the knights of the shires clothed their resistance in phrases such as "from time immemorial," and "prescriptive rights."

But "Restoration"—that is, restoration of the old laws of England—evaded the question whether these laws were of national or ecclesiastical origin. The technique of the Puritan Restoration was to restore the Common Law. To that end it was cut off from its connection with the Papacy, with the clergy and even, to a certain extent, with Chancery. It was put into the hands of English judges and lawyers and juries. The class which was fitted to act in the courts of the country as jurors and justices claimed the right to interpret this Common Law.

The "Restoration of the Common Law" is the great fiction of the first half of the English Revolution. On the Great Seal of 1648 we read: "In the first year of freedom by God's blessing *restored.*"

The Restoration of the Common Law had to create safeguards against any codification by the King's counsellors or any professor *regius* from Oxford or Cambridge. For the King's judges and scholars had served the King's purpose *too often and too willingly.* They had upheld the fiction that even the Protestant King, under the Great Seal of his Kingdom, could do what he liked. In the famous question of taxation, in 1637, the King's judges had decided:

"When the good and safety of the kingdom in general is concerned, and the kingdom in danger, your Majesty may, by writ under the Great Seal of England, command all your subjects of this, your Kingdom . . . and we are also of the opinion that in such case your Majesty is the sole judge both of the danger and when and how the same is to be prevented and avoided."

Therefore the Common Law had to be rescued from the King's Great Seal and from the King's legislation. The English have no written constitution and no systematic codification, because centralizing and codifying are the artifices of kings. The Common Law relies on precedents. Precedents cannot be overruled by royal prerogative. Precedents are a safeguard against despotism. A king and his counsellors rationalize, they systematize, they bring order out of the chaos of precedents. The answer of the Puritan Restoration is: "Let us intrench ourselves behind this chaos of precedents." Socially, the power of the judiciary became intimately enmeshed with the interests and ways of life of the aristocracy. The Inns of courts became self-perpetuating bodies with the right of co-operation. The famous separation between parliamentary legislation and royal executive never existed in England, but it was emphasized because Parliament was the Highest Court of all and its independence lent glory to all other courts. The crown lost the power of interfering with the judiciary.

Materially the judiciary worked even faster. Whereas the real safeguards against the crown came into existence under William III and Anne, the law of contracts was changed in favour of the wealthy classes in the middle of the seventeenth century. Clever safeguards against any confiscation of property by the crown were established. An accusation for High Treason would find the peer without a penny; his son owning the family property already. For these and similar purposes, freedom of donations during lifetime and freedom of testation were essential. On the other hand, the rigid enforcement of all contracts against debtors was extended beyond all equity. To their candid surprise, Continental lawyers stated the paradox of a law protecting individual liberty to the utmost against the government but extraditing it completely to the private creditors: In 1835 a French writer exclaimed: *"C'est dans le pays où l'on professe le plus de respect pour la liberté individuelle, qu'elle est le plus facilement sacrifiée aux intérêts pécuniaires. Il suffit de quelques actes simulés pour mettre un citoyen hors la loi."* This writer, Bayle-Mouillard, after showing that some statutes of the Tudors had already made all reasonable concessions to the creditor's interest, goes on, "Still, as if any restriction imposed by the law should be an insupportable bridle for the English lawyers, they were unable to comply with the principles of these statutes, and by the means of fictions they finally established the rule that a personal debtor could be arrested without any preliminary proof." "Habeas Corpus" was good against the Crown; it did not protect the mighty's poor debtor. The producer mercilessly fell into the hands of the wealthy in this aristocratic revolution, called Restoration of the Common Law.

ECONOMICS AND BUDGET.

In fact, the financial transactions of the new aristocracy became as much an expression of religious faith and Christian morals as the equity of Chancery had been before. The poetry of figures, the popularity of economics, the love of expressing great national achievements by the sums that have been spent upon them, are impossible and inexplicable on the Continent. Englishmen seem cynical when they begin a book on the enemies of England, as did G. Peel, with the statement: "To insure against European enemies, a grand total of £32,000,000 is spent. The charge, capitalized at the proper rate, amounts to the sum of £1,280,000." Only in England can a parliamentary paper on finances include a careful investigation of the dates of the beginnings and endings of wars since 1688. Only in England can the commonwealth become poetical about money. In 1665 the Speaker told his Majesty that the Commons had prepared a security for all such persons as should bring their money into the public bank of the Exchequer. "As the rivers do naturally empty themselves into the sea, so we hope the veins of gold and silver in this nation will plentifully run into this ocean."

In 1816 the abolition of the income tax was hailed by the largest applause ever heard in Parliament. But more striking was the simultaneous decision to burn all books and accounts which might be reminders of the existence of this tax. Taxation was not merely taxation. Ever since the Puritan Reformation the control of taxation had stood for Equity and Religion and Progress and Morals and Prosperity, in short, for everything important. Where else could a parliament address the populace in the way Parliament did in the Great Remonstrace of 1641? This document which was to call the rabble to arms spoke in the language of dry figures. Adam Smith's *Wealth of Nations* was written as a part of his moral philosophy, his intellectual faith.

The poetical quality of numbers is demonstrated everywhere in English life. A man's inheritance is published to the last farthing. Every bequest is printed. The wealth of the rich is an item in the budget of the nation. A gentleman uses his wealth as the King uses his civil list. The administration of this wealth is the backbone of English self-government. Hospitals, museums, public schools, are maintained by founders and donators because the great wealth of the country is the

prop of the country's expenditures. They are all inserted in
the Golden Book of the Commonwealth as *stationes fisci,* self-
governing departments. In nations where the central government is responsible for schools, hospitals, police and roads, the
badly paid officials are envious. Envy is the vice of a nation
in which civil service is preponderant. England is spared the
vice of envy. The budget has educated the nation to understand figures and to appreciate their significance without
jealousy.

The rôle held in Germany by philosophy, in France by science, is held in England by economics. It is the popular science
of the British. When Disraeli wished to turn the laugh against
the people who believed in the eternal necessity of wars, it
needed no more than the simile: "They are like men who think
of 5% as a natural rate of interest." Frantic applause and
laughter greeted the statement. On the Continent neither the
comparison nor its emotional success is easy to understand.
In other countries you cannot produce a general effect of religious dignity and prophecy by the use of figures.

For this new economic and financial order of the kingdom,
the old Chancellor, with his interest in the law, was not the
natural representative. And so, he was pushed aside, despite
all protestations of restoring the former constitution.

That no full restoration of the Common Laws was planned
is shown by the development of the chancellorship. It was not
restored to its full power. In the search for a check on the
King's Conscience, the Puritans abolished the royal courts,
like the Starchamber, and the whole jurisdiction over morals
which these courts had inherited from the ecclesiastical courts.
During the Puritan Restoration "keepers of the liberties of
England" were appointed for a short time, obviously as a parallel to the old controlling keeper of the King's Conscience.
During the Restoration the most shocking moral misbehaviour
could not be punished because no courts existed for such
offences.[5]

---

[5] The American Puritans of the "Scarlet Letter" type acted as good Englishmen, in the same emergency into which their home country was thrown by the
disappearance of ecclesiastical courts. There is nothing "American" in the at-

By the end of the seventeenth century it became evident that both Puritan and Stuart restoration had bestowed on Parliament the power in spiritual matters by which the Chancellor had restrained the King's arbitrary power. The Lord Chancellor ceased to be the link between the King and his English subjects. The first successor of More, the reckless Chancellor Thomas Cromwell, was called the "Hammer of the Monks." He was a self-made man, or better still, "a man made and cried up" by the King. There was true logic in the fact that his great-grand-nephew, Oliver, who got his name from Thomas Cromwell by adoption, avenged Thomas More, that great Christian soul and last true keeper of the King's conscience. He atoned for Thomas Cromwell's destruction of the old constitution. But the political heir-at-law of the Chancellor became the political agent who manipulated the secrets of the country's wealth. The prophet of finance and figures became the new political leader in the Commonwealth, replacing the prophet of equity. Tacitly this new leader took over the rôle of the Lord Chancellor and his Great Seal. Officially intact even today, the Chancellor was in fact removed to an upper sphere, where he presides over the House of Lords. For serious business he was replaced by somebody with quite different duties in the King's council: the First Lord of the Treasury. Formally this Lord of the Treasury took the place of the Comptroller, who had become the heart of the government. Today the Prime Minister of England is called a Prime Minister only by a twentieth-century innovation. In truth, he is still the First Lord of the Treasury. The Committee on legislation which gives its advice to the Cabinet and the Prime Minister in all technical and legal questions is called Parliamentary Counsel of the Treasury. The interests of the Treasury are what connect Crown and country. The Restoration meant business in making finance and religion the two cardinal points in the relations between King and Commons. The rule prevailed that on

tempt of New Haven or Massachusetts to use the precedents from Holy Scripture for jurisdiction against moral misbehaviour. This was an *English* problem at that time. The case of Charles Sedley led to a new solution.

questions of finance and religion the House must always sit as a committee of the whole.

The First Lord of the Treasury annually had to fight for his budget (the name has been on record since 1733), that is, the little pocket which contained his accounts. He opened this pocket on budget-day. In no other country in the world has budget-day become a popular holiday. In England, the minister who opens the budget has the name of Chancellor of the Exchequer. On budget-day he walks from his office to Parliament, even though very often he must force his way through a thronging crowd. The career of a statesman is counted by the budgets which he brings before Parliament. Pitt, Asquith, Lloyd George, Snowden, became popular through their budgets. Pitt made his fame by comprehending all revenue under one common denominator. But it would be entirely inappropriate to suppose that dry greed or avarice are behind this English liking for the budget. The same Pitt was bold enough to add 650 million pounds to the public debt because the British Commonwealth had to fight the French Revolution which imperilled all privileges and all precedents.

PARTICULARS AND PRECEDENTS.

The Common Law was restored by as many reaffirmations as possible. Coke exclaimed, on March 26, 1628: "All laws of the King which contradict Magna Charta are void." Magna Charta *was* reaffirmed thirty times; thirty times England's kings approved it.

Burke's famous dictum on man as a link in the chain of generations illustrates the concept of the English constitution.

"Because a nation is not an idea only of local extent, and individual momentary aggregation; but it is an idea of continuity, which extends in time as well as in numbers and in space. And this is a choice not of one day or one set of people, not a tumultuary and giddy choice; it is a deliberate election of the ages and of generations; it is a constitution made by what is ten thousand times better than choice; it is made by the peculiar circumstances, occasions, tempers, dispositions, and morals, civil and social habitudes of the people, which disclose themselves only in a long space of time. It is a vestment which accommodates itself to the body. "The individual is foolish, the multitude, for the moment, is foolish, when they act without deliberation; but the species is wise, and when time is given to it, as a species it always acts right." [6]

Anyone who wishes to deal with this English mind must attack it by precedent. A Continental Christian thinks of the conflict between Catholics and Protestants as a problem of truth. At Westminster he learns that it is a matter of precedent. The Anglicans point, not to the truth, but to the age of their branch of the Church. The fact that the indifferent word "Anglican" occurs in documents as early as the fifteenth century seems to them important. And the Catholics of modern England have realized that they must meet this challenge. On a pillar in their stronghold, the Catholic Cathedral of Westminster in London, they have carved a list of bishops of England who were in communion with Rome from the year 600. Precedents make law.

When the nineteenth century, with its liberal indoctrination, invaded England, Disraeli had a happy way of defending English precedent against the principles of logic. "A precedent embalms a principle" was his formula, which embalmed, in a century of abstract principles, the English principle of precedent.

Nevertheless, this ideology was as much a fiction as the idea of a natural Gaul was a fiction with the French. For the purpose of the English revolutionaries was not really to restore the Middle Ages, but to wrest from the King the ecclesiastical power which Parliament itself had bestowed on him.

The City of London paid 62⅔ pounds of horseshoes annually for its franchise. Why? When some pert fellow moved, in 1862, to commute the obligation, his motion was lost. The custom had always been so. It was too dangerous to change it, because something might result which would imperil the liberty of the City of London. "Never ask why," is the English golden rule. "Why?" is a question worthy of royal courtiers and think-

---

[6] Burke, *Works*, VI, p. 146, London, 1856.

ers who plan and systematize. Principles are an inheritance from the party of religion, the Protestant princes. Princes establish principles; gentlemen prefer particulars.

The word "particulars," like public spirit, is untranslatable. Anybody who asks an English lawyer's opinion gets this answer: "Let me know the particulars." In 1933 a questionnaire was sent out by an international institute to the bars and courts of seventy nations, asking for information about the legal procedure of the respective countries. The English barrister was the only one whose answer began thus: "It is impossible to answer all your questions seriatim, because every case will have to be approached from its own particular set of facts, and more particularly still, from the actual terms of each contract of sale." The word "particular" occurs twice.

"Particular" and "particularism" are poor words in French or in German, signifying something irrational, shapeless, partial or fragmentary, or a bad tendency towards egotistic provincialism. In England, precedent and particulars reach into the depths of the earth. Like the Greek titan Antæus, who drew new vigour for his struggle every time he touched his Mother Earth, so in England every particular adds vigour to a case and roots it more deeply in the Common Law, where a King's arm cannot reach. Give everyone his particular charter, his particular privilege, and the world is safe against arbitrary power.

Thanks to the Puritan Revolution, Englishmen have stamped out all feeling for system and economy of thought. They prefer to deal with a sea of particulars, because through particulars they feel protected against the King's officials. Particulars—they are the significant feature in the explanations of the man who acts as your guide through the Tower of London, of the English novelist or historian, of the reformer or speaker on the budget—particulars are rooted in the past. They can only be held by memory. In a country of particular charters and privileges *for everybody,* the word "old" became a charm of the first order. " '*Ancien régime*' or 'old France' is objectionable in France; 'Old England' is a eulogy." (Boutmy.) In France the aristocrats of the *ancien régime* are hated; the gentry of England embarked on their revolution with the war-cry "Old!"

And the gentry was adored by the lower classes for this odd choice of "Old" as its device. The Man in the Street, the shopkeeper, the tenant, who could not boast of being gentlemen, felt themselves protected and relieved by the existence of an old gentry. Thanks to this pedigree of age proper to the gentry, the whole people was ennobled and made "ancient." And an increase in age meant an increase in strength against the innovations of foreign-born kings and tyrants. "Innovation" was an insult. In France, as in any bourgeois society, novelty and sensation are a merit in themselves. "News"papers are the weapons of democracy. Records are the guarantee of aristocracy. In 1794 so simple a thing as a matter of order was solemnly broached by a member of Parliament with a very incantation of antiquity:

"He wished the House to adhere to the principles, the practice, and the forms of proceeding adopted by our ancestors, and handed down to the present age by them, in the manner in which he hoped they would be able to hand them down to their successors, and that they might uninterruptedly descend to posterity." [7]

Coke had said the same thing on May 8, 1628.

I do not know whether in any other language one can speak of "the wise old world" as a generalization of our experience and custom. To have a "high *old* time" is as reasonable in English as it is atrocious in French to be "*vieux jeu.*" The older a fashion the better. Since the Puritan Restoration, forms and customs of social life have become an end in themselves. The wigs of the English judges are no trifle. They exactly express the aversion of the English law toward any sign of novelty.

This worship of the "old" is a comprehensive and, as we shall see, religious view of the world which dates back no earlier than the seventeenth century. The European and American democrats, in turning against the *ancien régime* and the old prejudices of the past, in fighting against superstitions and iniquity, privilege and abuse, became to a certain extent the dupes of this English passion for the old; for they did not and could not, perhaps, distinguish between the real and innocent

[7] Woodfall II, 422, May 25, 1794.

meaning of "ancient" and the revolutionary and emotional power of it for the establishment of aristocratic government. In 1789, and later on, the innovators fought against all the prejudices of popes, princes, clergy and nobles, because they saw in every former institution something that boasted of being "old." Such an exaggeration is comparable to the bad habit which leads a Communist nowadays to call any fact he dislikes "capitalistic." To him the past is all painted in one color, the color of class war and capitalism. "Capitalism is whatever I hate," a young boy once said to me; and in that spirit he will minimize all the differences that existed in the pre-Communistic world. Similarly, the liberals overlooked the differences between all previous forms of society. But some of these forms had actually been rather recent. They were preceding stages of society, which had disguised its hierarchic rule by priding itself on being "old." The Jacobin's attack on feudalism was not directed against the real feudalism of the Middle Ages, because that did not exist in any country in 1789. Feudalism is a term of invective coined by people who suffered from a young gentry which had made feudalism and traditionalism a shibboleth for revolutionary purposes. Practically, the Whigs in England were young families dating from the sixteenth century. They had nothing to do with feudal times and feudal society. But they used feudal forms because these gave them a "patina" of old age and prescriptive right. For the English "old" served the purpose of a legal theory and a legitimist tendency; it was not an established fact. As a tendency, it was spread all over the world by the aristocracy. It was officially exported to the Continent in 1815, when "legitimism" was invented to "restore" the *ancien régime*. But though it had an immense circulation, nowhere did it fit the situation so well as in England.

THE PEDIGREE OF OLIVER CROMWELL.

In England the gentry, perhaps five thousand families, stood for the rest of the country as a bulwark against the danger of a royal caliphate. They had no doctrine, no intellectual theory.

University faculties seemed to them royal or ecclesiastical; so the gentry based its claims on precedent and pedigree.

Cromwell himself, for example, was shown to have a pedigree as excellent as the Stuarts. His Highness Oliver Cromwell who made the "glorious revolution of our monarchy" and delivered the Commonwealth from slavery and arbitrary power was praised for having one of the finest of English pedigrees. Cromwell, as people believed in his day, was of English, Scotch and Welsh blood. The alleged Scotch relation had already been invented by the ancestor who had profited by the Reformation of Henry VIII. He claimed to be a "Stuart" also. The royal Stuarts had a dark spot in their pedigree because of the fact that Owen op Mergent was the son of a butler. The Cromwellian pedigree, poor on the English side and equal on the Scotch, could compete most successfully in the Welsh field. A descent from some good Welsh lords could easily be feigned. Thus the hero of the Puritan Restoration appeared by no means a self-made man, but a true native of the three nations of Great Britain.

The pedigree of the Russells, Salisburys, Churchills, is an important part of the English Constitution. The history of human thought would be incomplete if it overlooked the extraordinary prop which the new order of English society found in the dignity of the "old." This insured the success of the fictions which were brought forward against the "innovations" of the Protestant kings. In the Puritan ideology, the precedents for action corresponded to the pedigree of men.

Cromwell himself did not care very much about his nobility. He said, "I was by birth a gentleman, living neither in any considerable height nor yet in obscurity." (September 9, 1654, in Parliament.) His genius was enmeshed in difficulties not to be solved by genealogy. Cromwell's pedigree might or might not be equal to the Stuarts. However, Sir Oliver neither could nor would point to any precedent for his actions. In a restoration of precedents he was condemned to stand out as a singularity, as an individual who had to do all kinds of things for the first time in the history of the world. This was shocking. His actions could be liked only when they were repeated later without the newness of the first moment, his vision was admitted only when it became trite. He himself never won over his frightened fellow-creatures with his outbursts of immediate inspiration and his fresh faith in the new things before him.

The "New Model" of the Army betrayed in its very name his contribution to the Revolution. He carried the New Model over to the Navy. He built a navy of ships wholly independent of merchant auxiliaries. "But Cromwell gave still more. He gave the sentiment for using the instrument. For he bequeathed to the restored monarchy a definite naval policy in the Mediterranean and an *indestructible ambition* for what we now call imperial policies." [8] In this quotation the author himself is aware of the impropriety of "imperial" for the days of Cromwell. Cromwell's own vocabulary will disclose his point of view.

Many scholars hold that Cromwell acted by instinct, unconsciously. They can list in their favour the fact that his vision was not expressed in a war-cry as simple as Restoration, or, later, Glorious Revolution. It is indeed not a new word but the new shading of a word which expressed his table of values. Still, this re-colouring of an old world embraced a fresh concept of England's place in the world.

The novelty of the situation was widely felt. However, when Milton tried to describe it, he had no new sound for his "trumpet from Zion." He simply called for a "reforming [of the] Reformation." His formula was correct. The English Revolution had to reform the results of a perverted Reformation of the Anglican Church. But the conceit of a "reform of the Reformation" was no slogan for the masses. After all, there was no longer a Roman Church to be reformed. The cry was taken up in a slightly different form by another contemporary. Winstanley, in his *Platform of the Law of Freedom,* asserted of the atmosphere of his day: "The spirit of the whole creation was about the reformation of the world." In this passage he changed one little word; instead of Reformation of the *"Church,"* he said: of the *"world."* But this is the most essential change of the world. It was the layman's world, the world

[8] Sir Julian Corbett, *England in the Mediterranean*, II, 298, New York, Longmans, 1917.

of action, not the Church of prayer which had to be reformed. Reformation of the World was the decisive step from Anglican to universal concepts. Cromwell used it when he replied to the Little Englanders of his day: "God has not brought us hither where we are but to consider the work that we may do in the world as well as at home."

That part of the world which the British organized in the ways of their "home" country was the redeemed part of the world. A new term was introduced that labelled these redeemed parts of the world. On May 19, 1649, England, with all its dependencies and dominions, was made a *Commonwealth*.

The word "Common," which appears in the phrases Common Prayer, House of Commons, common sense, reached its climax in the enthronement of "Commonwealth." The word communicates the thrill of pride over the fact that Church and State were now united into a Commonwealth, whilst formerly the Chancellor had to alternate, so to speak, between the two. Baxter, the leading Puritan moralist, well expressed the new patriotism when he exclaimed: "Every man as a member of Church or *Commonwealth* must use his powers utterly for the good of Church or Commonwealth." Commonwealth is a religious unity as much as Church.

THE NEW ENVIRONMENT: THE WESTERN WORLD.

Each inspired form of society must reshape its environment before it can begin to influence the world. Russia, in order to become a "global" state, related to the whole of the earth instead of being the eastern promontory of Europe, had to be cut off from Europe by the World War. When it was forced to abandon the countries, from Finland to Bessarabia, that belonged to the Roman and Protestant faith, its own faith had to be re-stated in revolutionary language; and immediately, by the change of environment, Russia began to live a full life of her own. France under Napoleon smashed the relics of feudalism from Portugal to Memel. In the old feudal and Roman environment the germ of the ideas of 1789 would have withered. "Europe" became France's war-cry because she had to find a new world commensurate with her new ideas.

The same rule applies to England. Because of the constitutional character of the English detective story, the change of environment is not discussed on principle and largely, though it is mentioned in particular again and again. Yet the British Commonwealth also broke through a wall of enmity and hostility and surrounded itself with a new world sympathetic to its principles. It called into being the Western World. Like all creations of political geography, the Western World was manmade. The globe does not contain it. It has unnatural measurements and proportions all of its own. One might say that the Western World was created around England on the basis of equations like these: the distance from Liverpool to Boston shall equal the distance from Liverpool to the Canary Islands. Or, the distance from Newcastle-on-Tyne to Oslo shall equal the distance from Newcastle-on-Tyne to St. Petersburg (Leningrad). Or, the journey from Plymouth to Malaga is the same as the journey from Plymouth to Alexandria. These equations, of course, do not alter the actual difference in mileage between the various places; but that difference shall not matter any longer for commercial, political, and social purposes or relations. So, by a great inspiration, the oceans of the five continents were turned into one united Western World. Selden, the author of the *Mare Clausum,* expressed the new law of the oceans well when he rhymed: "The Seas now made appropriate and yield to all the Laws of State." He asserted that since Britannia was called "the Island of the Ocean" in antiquity it was permissible to turn about and to call the Seas "The Ocean of the Island." "Without question it is true that the very shores or Ports of the neighbouring princes beyond seas are bounds of the sea territory of the British Empire, but that in the open and vast Ocean of the North and the West, they are to be placed at the utmost extent of those most spacious seas which are possessed by the English, Scotch and Irish." [9]

We know of the smashing blow dealt to the millennial order of things when Napoleon I erased the Roman Empire from the surface of the globe, and, brushing away the litter of two

[9] Selden, *Mare Clausum,* p. 416, 1662.

thousand years, called the area so cleansed "Europe." The British under Cromwell did an equally bold piece of political map-drawing. England, still for Shakespeare "that utmost cor-

VISION OF THE WORLD, FOURTEENTH CENTURY
Britannia on lower rim.

ner of the west," is relegated, on mediæval maps, to the margin. Now, she is in the centre of the map and is hailed as acting "In the Light of the Sun, in the World's Amphitheatre, all Europe looking on and wondering." [10] They conceived of a world in which the waves of all seas and oceans were considered, for the first time in the history of mankind, as one single

[10] *Purchas, his Pilgrim,* p. 73, London, 1625.

water. "The Sea makes all the world an island." [11] All this one
world of waterways was destined to carry goods and men under
the English flag in free trade all over the world. The French
panorama of "Europe" is parallelled by the "marinorama," the
oceanic view of the English for the Western World. For the
first time in history the waters were put before the continents
and treated as giving laws to the continents. Oceans and Continents: in this order the two halves of the world were organized. The new conception was boldly announced by the Navigation Act of Oliver Cromwell. (This document, by the way,
is known to the modern lawyer mostly in its later redactions
where it has been watered down and has lost some of its greatness.) Among his other visions, Cromwell had a design on
Gibraltar; he planned to take it and transform it into an
island.

In the old days the English had not been sailors; they had
been conquered again and again by Continentals. England's
outposts south of the Channel made it clear that the Realm
had been established from the side of the Continent. The
permanent tendency of England had been to face south, and
to defend her communications on the south. Like the French
kings who looked toward Italy until the Council of the Crown
in 1551, the English kings had sought their glory in France
and Belgium, inside the old Church and Empire of Rome.
Within the frame of these two old political forms, it was
enough that neither pope nor emperor should be overbearing.
After their decline in importance, the various nations tried to
find a working system for coexistence. Henry VIII had formulated the balance of power by saying, *"Cui adhæreo, præest"*
(Whom I join prevails).

But this slogan of the Tudors is a rather negative one; though
it is already on the road to the system of a balance of power,
it does not tell us anything positive about the goal of English
policy. The English Revolution is bold enough to supplement
the *negative*, Machiavellian wisdom of the princes with a new,
positive message from the country. Church and Empire become

[11] *Purchas, his Pilgrim*, p. 58, London, 1625.

the arena of Continental powers. Here it is always sufficient to keep down the mightiest, be it Spain, France, Germany or Russia. But outside this rotten, torn old world there is something better: the Western World.

When an Englishman says "world" he means God's free world redeemed from worldliness. Where a Lutheran prays for God's Kingdom from eternity to eternity, Anglicans pray: "World without end." This has no connection with the genuine Latin text, *"et in secula seculorum";* but it is perfectly correct in an atmosphere where public spirit has stimulated each local unit to join in an inspired movement for a country-wide understanding. The country became the model and the nucleus of a world governed by public spirit.

As early as Shakespeare's day, Lord Essex had given a play in honour of the Virgin Queen which anticipated this turn. Here you feel England trembling before the new task of ruling an immense world, without settled government, without tradition, without the clear governing will of a King. As early as 1098, the Archbishop of Canterbury had been addressed as pope and patriarch of a second orbit of the earth. An old Saxon king had played with the notion of being *"alterius orbis imperator."* Now, in Essex's pageant, the character of England's burden between two worlds is stressed. "Atlas himself," says he, "did not bear such a burden." And it is true. The new English task is *Trans-Atlantic.*

To understand Essex's poetic license we must remember that in the sixteenth century "Atlas" was limited to Morocco and the Mediterranean. What we call the Atlantic Ocean today was called the Occidental Ocean in the sixteenth and seventeenth centuries. This made it easy for the English Revolution to establish a new term, the "Western World." "Western World" replaces Western Church and Roman Empire, but it keeps the supernatural, religious background and atmosphere which surrounds these two millennial words. Western World was a programme of hegemony, as "Europe" was for France. The word "Western" had an appeal. It announced a beginning and a

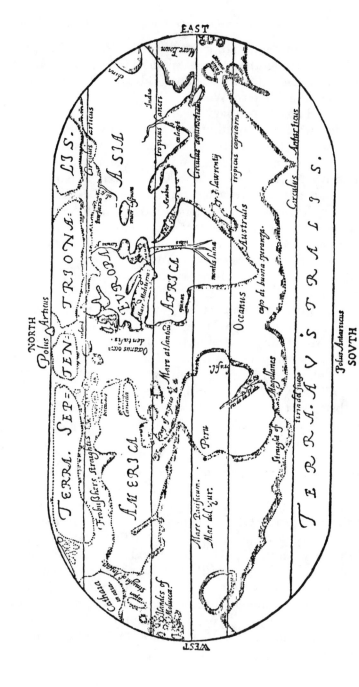

ENGLAND BETWEEN THE OLD AND THE NEW WORLD, 1578

prerogative of Western man. Today the French word *"civilisation,"* valid for Europe and the civilized nations, is mixed up
almost indiscriminately with the British vision of a new Western World governed from within by the public spirit of the
Christian people of England. This French influence makes it
difficult today to isolate "Western World" and treat it again
as it was treated in 1688 or 1658. But it is worth while trying
this revival. The important change of *"mundus,"* a religious
term used for the secular worldliness in the Middle Ages, from
a chaotic sequence of time *(seculum)* into a lawful realm in
space, took place during the seventeenth century. We already
know how much Descartes did to secure this new understanding of "world." But the English "world" is never Nature in the
sense of French philosophy. World is not nationalized, discovered, known, by the force of human brains.

Milton, the poet *par excellence* of the English Revolution,
wrote a line which dissipates all doubts as to the character of
this world: "The world was all before them where to choose
Their place of rest, and Providence their guide," are the last
words of *Paradise Lost.* The world was all before them. The
English countrymen, facing a new world ascending out of the
salt waves of the seas, were frightened. *"Illi robur et æs triplex
circa pectus erat,"* the verse of Horace inveighing against the
dangers of sea-faring, must have been in their hearts and minds.
It required no normal courage, but a revolutionary effort, to
leave the island regularly and permanently, and found the
British Commonwealth. Without a religious belief in God's
guidance through this world, it could not have been done.

Up to the Tudors, the Kings alone had cared for the world
outside England, and foreign policy was a secret of State. Since
Cromwell's Revolution, foreign policy has been in the very
bones of every Englishman who goes abroad. The English Commonwealth would never have been made by Kings and Kings'
ministers alone. Abroad, any Englishman, and particularly any
English ship, learned how to be England's ambassadors to the
world. The islands and coaling stations, the coasts of five continents that belong to England, were not conquered by a King
or a planned foreign policy, but by lightning strokes of public

spirit, flashing through groups, committees, ships. The sale of the majority of the bonds of the Suez Canal in 1881 to the English government was not the result of a diplomatic manœuvre, but of a commercial chance suddenly noticed by private people and supported by private people in its financial realization.

England's foreign policy can be so flexible, can muddle through, because ten thousand amateurs in foreign policy scattered all over the world are its eyes and ears. Perhaps they sometimes seem a nuisance, and bureaucracy in Downing Street sighs. But Downing Street is dead the moment it is possible for a lawyer to govern foreign policy without the support of Englishmen abroad. As this stage seems nearly to have been reached in the days of Sir John Simon and Sir Samuel Hoare, it is well to think of the stream of emigrants who left England year after year, *yet remained English*. Other nations migrate; but the Anglo-Saxon inhabitants of the British Empire are the only emigrants who take with them a ready-made constitution covering the whole field of government, that is to say, Christian spirit, democratic consent, authoritative government, royal independence of the courts, and respect for public opinion.

This ready-made constitution is the export article of the mother-country to the Western World. "The world was all before them." The Englishman, leaving his country, felt himself to be taking possession of a world promised to him by Providence. Predestination was no abstract principle, but a deep faith in an established harmony between the country at home and the world ahead. The world abroad expected you. The world needed the new inspiration. But you, too, were not to be imprisoned in the little island. As your passage was promised to a world that thirsted for public spirit as the hart panteth after the water-brooks, it was no less clear that the world was yours. An Englishman going out into the world *comes into his own*. The world and he meet because he brings to it a message which is as wide as the world.

We shall see how a special form of prayer "to be used at sea" was invented in 1647. It is the only "left-over" of Puritan origin in the Book of Common Prayer today. Two more powerful symbols of this new world (to repeat, not Europe, but the Western World) were erected in the time of the Civil War.

When the new world was divined by Essex as emerging from the waves, it still had to be clothed in the symbols of the Church. Under Elizabeth man still sought his salvation behind the protecting shield of Church and State. The nation, too, was personified as an ecclesiastical power. When the Armada was destroyed, the medal in memory of its defeat showed England as a kind of Rock of St. Peter in the middle of the sea, playing the part of the Church. In another version it is an arch, or a laurel tree, and the Spanish Navy is shown outside, helpless and incapable of harming the English soil. The sea in these pictures was still inimical.

In the Civil War, a new vision makes its way into the official symbols of the nation. The later idea of a Britannia who rules the waves is expressed in a way which unfolds the thought behind these words more clearly than the proud anthem itself. The quintessence of the new doctrine was that the seashore was no longer to be considered the borderline of England. Soil and waves, land and sea, previously kept carefully apart, were brought together into a new unit.

Up to 1640, the Great Seal of the Realm had always shown the King in his sacred vestments, with crown and sceptre on the throne or on horseback. In 1642 Parliament began to think of a new seal that might better express the new influence of the House of Commons. Parliament itself was portrayed upon it. And finally the ultimate purpose of the Revolution was made visible by the able artist who designed the seal of 1651. The reverse shows Parliament with the table of the House, the Speaker, the mace, etc.; on the obverse the map of England and Ireland is given with wonderful precision. And the seas with ships filling them are given, too.

Looking back to the seal of 1640 and before, we feel the totality of this Revolution; the old world of the anointed, sovereign King, dealing with secrets of State in religious majesty; and a new world, an inspired community, ruling at once over a country and over the waves of the British and Irish Seas. The beautiful design of two fleets at sea makes it perfectly clear that the new Commonwealth has usurped something never conquered before—the sea itself—as belonging to the nature of the Realm committed to the hands of the Commons. Royal power is eclipsed by this greater vision, by this overwhelming discovery of the physical world as an object of faith. The Commons had faith in the predestination of the physical world, land and sea, to become the footstool of the nation's policy and power.

The Great Seal of 1651 already has the full depth and scope of the Glorious Revolution, because the physical and corporeal world is seen with new eyes. Whereas, before man had believed in the *sacraments* and symbols of a Church, the world itself was now sacred and symbolical; whereas the home of men had been ecclesiastical and eternal, "from eternity to eternity," it now became worldly and permanent, "world without end"!

Our interpretation is supported by the Navigation Act, of the same year as the new Seal. It equals in words the grandeur of these designs:

Resolved by Parliament and Law by its authority:
[Acts and Ordinances of the Interregnum 1642-1660, II, 559 (1911).]
For the increase of shipping and the encouragement of the Navigation of this Nation, 9, Oct. 1651.
For the increase of the shipping and the encouragement of the navigation of this nation, which under the good Providence and Protection of God, is so great a means of the Welfare and Safety of this Commonwealth; be it enacted that . . . no goods or commodities whatsoever, of the growth, production of manufacture of Asia, Africa or America, or of any part thereof, of any island belonging to them, or any of them or which are described or laid down in the usual Maps or Cards of those places, as well as of the English Plantations as others, shall be imported or brought into this Commonwealth of England or into Ireland, or any other lands, islands, plantations or territories to this Commonwealth, belonging, in any other ship or ships, Vessel or Vessels whatsoever, but only in such as do truly and without fraud belong to the people of this Commonwealth.

MARINORAMA

THE GREAT SEAL, 1651

THE KING'S SOVEREIGNTY ON THE SEAS, 1662

No sort of salty Fish, usually fished for and caught *by the people of this Nation,* shall from henceforth be imported (in foreign vessels) . . .

By the way, the untranslatable term "people of this nation" has remained a property of Anglo-Saxon language. The Roads of the Sea belong to the chosen people who are "the people of this Commonwealth." "The sea is not a foe, not an enemy of men. It is subdued and transformed into a field of man's activity." In the English "counties" of old, manor or house and garden formed the centre, and around them fields and meadows and pastures and woods and forests and marshes were the objects of man's struggle for life. They were cleared, cultivated and exploited from the established centre of a country-seat.

Now the whole country becomes the home, whose inhabitants plough new fields on the seas and oceans abroad. The table in the House of Commons replaces the table in the manor, around which the husbandry of the community had centred. The new vision had been revealed on which all later English accomplishments were based. Disraeli creating an Empire of India, the Imperial Conference of 1932 formulating a system of impartial agreements, are but the latest descendants of the Acts and Drafts of 1651.

To my mind, the Seal of 1651 has never been surpassed for eloquence in painting a new country and a new world. Wherever such a new vision occurs, the world has really changed. A complete revolution has taken place, replacing all the old concepts by new tables and new commands and values. We are right in calling such a process a total revolution, in the same sense in which we had to call the French or Russian Revolution a total and complete change in language, thought and character.

THE THEFT OF A WORD.

The period of the Civil War and of Cromwell, between 1641 and 1660, is the real revolution, because the Restoration of Freedom led to a wholly new concept of a commonwealth within the Western World. The leaders of such a spiritual

movement cannot be called rebels. The use of the word for
people who cared so much for the law that they carried the
ghost of a King in Parliament with them in battle against the
physical person of Charles I, is an insult. It may be the only
adequate description of them from a Cavalier's point of view;
but if you call Cromwell or Pym rebels you are a Jacobite, a
Stuart. No Whig, and no impartial writer, can speak of the
time between 1640 and 1660 as Civil War or Great Rebellion.
Horace Walpole was perfectly outspoken about that. Seas
"made appropriate to all the Laws of State" as much as the soil,
were a precious heritage to the returning Charles II; he was
shown, in 1662, on a Seal, riding on the waves of the ocean, a
trident in his hand, drawn by sea horses. The inscription
pointed straight to the conclusion. It did not say "Britannia
rules the waves"; it used the beloved name of "world": "Britons
over the whole world are kings" (et penitus toto regnantes orbe
Britannos). General Monk handed over to the monarch the
Portuguese alliance which meant the Atlantic coast of the
Spanish peninsula, and the port of Tangier. Tangier, between
1661 and 1684, played the part later performed by Gibraltar.
Jealously the Stuart king clung to it, faithful to Cromwell's
vision. Here, as in all questions of European scope, the Commons failed Cromwell. Parliament refused the subsidies for
Tangier if the Catholic succession was not abandoned. It was
the last act of a parliament under Charles II. The Restoration
preserved the legacy of the Commonwealth as far as the King
was concerned.

Why, then, was there a break between the Protectorate and
the Restoration? And why was the Restoration of the Stuarts
so short-lived?

The death-warrant of Charles Stuart in 1649 hung on the
wall of Walpole's bed-chamber, and he called the precious
document, comparing it with the Magna Charta of 1215, the
"Charta Major," the Greater Charter! But Walpole is a rare
exception. Many a kindly Englishman would censure Walpole
very severely for his bad taste. They would praise the cowards
and traitors who invited in William III. But they tried for a
long time to get rid of any connection with the Roundheads

of the Civil War. Historians tried to prove that Cromwell, Pym, Hampden, Lenthall, Hutchinson, Undlow, had not been real gentlemen. A Frenchman, Boutmy, had to silence this attempt. He showed that the gentry presided over the political clubs in all the counties during the Civil War. All the leading families of the gentry were appointed or recognized by the revolutionary government, and Oliver Cromwell himself was the most remarkable type of a country gentleman, using exactly the terminology already ascribed to the Lower House when he stated that he was born "neither too high nor too low." He was even too modest in that respect. His friends, as we have seen before, did not find much difference between the pedigree of the Cromwells and the blood of the Stuarts.

May it be sufficient to say here that a Whig and any friend of English parliamentarism must acknowledge that he depends much more on the Rebels of 1641 than on the Whigs of 1688. The peculiar reserve and shyness of the gentry springs less from the bad behaviour of their Puritan ancestors than from the Freudian repression of later days. For it is true that something terrible did happen, not in acts but in speech, not in deeds but in words. The proper name of the insurgents of 1640 had been stolen between 1660 and 1688. The honest title of their enterprise had been perverted into shame. Because in normal times no one can condone a civil war or a rebellion, people disassociated themselves from their fathers and masters.

The Royalists, under the clever leadership of Clarendon, committed the theft in cold blood. They covered the memory of the twenty years before Charles II came back, as King of the practically united kingdom; they profiteered on Cromwell's unification of the three kingdoms, in a way similar to the technique of modern conservatives who call their counter-revolutionary methods "revolution." The ways of modern reaction against Bolshevism help to explain the Stuart "Restoration." Today "national revolution" is being planned or brought forward in many countries to stop world revolution. Thus the word "revolution" becomes ambiguous, and is used by both armies in the civil strife. The embarking of the conservative elements on a "revolution," though with exactly the opposite aim, is a recognition of necessary change, and prevents a mere reaction. But its main importance is to spread confusion and to weaken the position of the groups which thought they had the privilege of being the only original revolutionaries.

That is what happened in England, too. The "restorers" were over-reached by a royal restoration. This theft of the real name and fair title of the Puritan Revolution could not fully be understood by the historians of the nineteenth century because the term "Restoration" was used by the Bourbons in France after 1815, as a protest against a preceding "Revolution." Thus the word "Restoration" emphasized the end of the French Revolution.

But in England there was no "Revolution" to be overcome when the Stuart Monarchy was "restored" in 1660. Here the term "Restoration" did not follow, but preceded, the term "Glorious Revolution." It had, therefore, quite a different meaning in 1660 from that which it had in 1815. In 1815, Restoration was opposed to Revolution, and served to disconnect the new era from the preceding revolutionary period. In 1660, Restoration was chosen intentionally to *connect* the Puritan Revolution as closely as possible with the new mission of the King. Restoration made for identity between the Puritan endeavour and the aims of the dynasty. Restoration was the word of reconciliation. It stressed the fact that the new King recognized one half of the Puritan Restoration. It was selected to calm the anxieties of the nation. In telling them that the King would restore, the King's ministers cunningly took up the very war-cry of the Puritans themselves. They showed that they did not shrink from the dangerous and seditious word "Restoration," and that the King also wished to restore. Charles, too, like the Puritans, was going to restore the Constitution of King and Country.

The Royalist leader, Hyde (Lord Clarendon), had the intelligence to draw up the first proclamation of Charles II, the so-called "Declaration of Breda," in 1660, in these terms; "To the end that fear of punishment may not engage any . . . to a perseverance in guilt for the future, by opposing the Quiet and Happiness of their country in the Restoration, both of King,

Peers and people to their just, ancient and fundamental Rights . . ."

The document shows clearly that he tried to go as far as possible in his adaptation to the vocabulary of the gentry. He acknowledged the victory of parliamentary speech. And when Charles II disbanded his army, the King also appealed, in words written by Clarendon, to the good will of his countrymen "in *restoring* the whole nation to its primitive temper and integrity."

As soon as the Royalists had transferred the label "Restoration" from the Roundheads to themselves, they erased the memory of any popular restoration from the textbooks. In the Book of Common Prayer, after 1660, we read under the date of May 29 the name "Great Rebellion" for the years 1649-1660. Here, for the first time in the history of the world, a political period of twenty years came under official liturgical diagnosis and treatment. Never before had the calendar of any church mentioned political events. But the theft of the word "Restoration" was sealed with the greatest solemnity the Church could offer. Politics abused the most sacred of instruments to brand the restorers of 1640 forever as rebels.

By thus inserting the rubric "Great Rebellion" in her timeless missals, the Church created an impasse. The Roundheads could no longer move modestly on the plane of human affairs. If they wished to make a breach in the wall erected by the sacred curse of the Anglican Church, their authority had to become divine also. The Roundheads came back as Whigs. And we shall see how they managed to replace the decrees of the King in Parliament by the decrees of divine Providence. It was not their fault that Heaven itself had to be adjured. It was the victors over the Great Rebellion who, by adding the blessings of the Church to their political manœuvres, prepared the way for the new theology of the Glorious Revolution of 1688.

THE KING IN PARLIAMENT.

Every Anglo-Saxon schoolboy is taught that facts are at the core of human understanding. But British facts are not what an innocent Continental mind would call facts at all. English facts are all *parliamentary* facts: they are a preserved variety, which is changed into matter-of-fact on the table of the House. The alleged interest of the English mind in facts languishes as soon as the facts can no longer be construed as matters on the table of the House.

Now the table in the House of Commons is a curious piece of furniture. It is a communistic institution. One table serves for all the members of the House; even today they have no private desks, no tables. All other parliaments equip their senators or deputies as comfortably as possible. The Mother of Parliaments is proud of offering as little comfort as possible. The one table really means that the Right Honourables are members of a family assembled round one table, one instrument. The members may have no tables and no rooms for *themselves,* but *they* can put their feet on the table of the House in order to show that they are at home there and that this house is their house. The transactions in the House are all carried on under pressure of a most intimate character. The debates are really a preliminary talk and exchange of views. They are a precondition of legal procedure, but not legal in themselves. "Politics," in English, means literally an aggregate status before legislation and law begin. The debaters *are not the legislators.* Their attitude reflects, not the formality of law, but the informality of an exchange of opinions. The members inform the Speaker, the only member of the House who can raise his voice in the Realm, the Council of the State. The Speaker is the Voice of the House, the only voice that is audible outside. The speeches inside, considered from the legal point of view, are nothing but a whisper and a murmur. No one can or shall know who speaks in the House of Commons. In the debates the names of members are not mentioned. The speakers whom these different gentlemen try to inform call upon them as "member for Ipswich," "for Bath," "for Liverpool," because they are present as representing the shires of the Realm. The country is represented by delegates from the different counties, fifty-two in England, thirty-three in Scotland. The Knights of the Shires, and the Citizens of the Boroughs of the Realm meet in the House of Commons, like the Grand Jury of the nation, to give their verdict on the grievances of the King's subjects and the demands of the King's budget. They are without personal character, anonymous like a good jury, where twelve ordinary men are the embodiment of public conscience. The jury has one voice, and the judge has one. Thus, in respect to personality, the twelve men who make up one voice count for one twelfth each. Similarly, the members of the House of Commons are not units, to be counted from 1 to 658—though they can be subdivided into, for example, 219 representatives of counties and 307 of cities and boroughs in England and Scotland. No, the individual member is really $\frac{1}{658}$ of the unit, the will of which is voiced by the Speaker.

The anonymous character of the single member is at the root of the institution. This becomes clear when an M.P. behaves badly and thereby forfeits the recognition of his membership. The censure imposed on such a member by the Speaker is the use of his personal name. When other members are annoyed by an unparliamentary remark from a debating member, they cry: "Name him, name him!" For as soon as the Speaker names him, the member ceases to be a member. He stands naked, cut off from the tree, a fallen leaf. That is all that happens. The discipline of the House cannot go farther. Naming the member means refusing to recognize his membership. It is excommunication.

Surely this is paradoxical enough: a man is excommunicated by being given back his real name. But the atmospheric intensity of the meetings of the House of Commons cannot be better tested than by stating the fact that men are in a different aggregate status as long as they serve in Parliament. Like any group of men who are led by a chief, for instance, like soldiers in a company (eating bread together), under a "captain" (caput—head), like students in a college under one head, like jurors on a panel led by a foreman, the absence of names changes their character. The French citizen carries his name everywhere. Like most of the results of the French Revolution, this quality of having one's own name is thought today to be the essence of political physics. A man is considered to be permanently one and the same atom: Mr. Smith, the voter, full name, with his taxes paid, and a fine record.

We have already observed, in the Russian Revolution, how different man as a *labour-force* is from man as a citizen. As a *labour-force*, he is No. 7,966 in a power-plant which uses hands in the same way as amperes and H.P. A French individual is a personality. An English squire serving on a jury or in the House of Commons has the aggregate status of a member.

Charles I tried to arrest five members of the House for High Treason, and asked the Speaker where they were. "Upon that the Speaker fell on his knees, and desired his excuse, for he was a servant to the House, and had neither eyes nor tongue, to see or say anything but what they commanded him." [12] Even the Speaker, as long as he is in the House, is not an individual kinsman of the King's Majesty, but a part of a body from which no single member can be torn without violating the body.

The body politic of the Lower House owes its privileges and its constitutional rights to the specific aggregate status of anonymous membership. In the Upper House, of the Lords Spiritual and Temporal, each person has his own name. Every Lord is called, as a dignitary, by his full name. Any peer can have his dissent entered in the journals of the House of Lords, together with his reasons for such dissent. Such a protest is valid. But a Commoner cannot do the same. When, in 1641, certain members protested against the Great Remonstrance by which the Lower House, for the first time in history, appealed "downwards" to the people instead of upward to the King, they were sent to the Tower. No single member in the House of Commons can move anything alone. He must be seconded, and he can speak only once in defence of his motion, because he is not an individual.

The House knows no split into parties. In questions of debate and the order of the House, the English Parliament never moved along party lines. Every member helps jealously to protect the privileges of the minority, because the privileges of

[12] *Verney Papers,* Camden Society, p. 139.

the minority are never the rights of another party, but those of the whole membership.

The immunity of an M.P. does not depend on his individual merit or exemption. The fact that he cannot be prosecuted for anything done, said or thought in common with his fellow members is derived from the central fact that the House of Commons is the body politic, which cannot be deprived of any of its members during its session, and which cannot allow any individual to bear responsibility for the course of procedure followed by the House.

Most of these principles are overlooked or misinterpreted on the Continent. The Mother of Parliaments has usually been imitated without being understood. For example, "opposition," the astronomical expression of the movement of the stars, is misunderstood on the Continent as a fixed and final situation. It is hated and crushed. But in England this sterile situation was called division, not opposition, and divisions of the House were irregular. Robert Walpole managed to conduct one session with no more than three divisions of the House.

"Opposition" was borrowed from astrology, because it was an expression of *temporary* localization. Opposition is a particular constellation among others. Stars which are moving steadily are in opposition and will soon be seen in conjunction again. Conjunction and opposition are stages in a permanent system of movement across the sky of events. The leader of the opposition can even be paid, as he is in Canada, by the government, because the political solar system necessarily produces curves and situations which include opposition and conjunction. The perfect harmony of the revolving stars being the model on which political life should be shaped, opposition is *essential* to the life of the body politic. The Corporation of the Commons, embracing members without name, the Grand Jury *of the Realm,* is itself not treated as a human being, but as an astronomical character, a celestial power. And its ways are taken to be as sovereign, as much a matter of experience, as the sovereign course of the stars in the sky.

The world of Parliament is a real world of its own. "To be out of Parliament is to be out of the world," wrote Admiral

Rodney in 1780. And this world is not the world of reasoning science, of abstract measurements, of a decimal system, but the empirical system of earth and sea, stars and sun, day and night, ebb and flow.

A PARLIAMENTARY CHURCH.

The latest historian of England in the seventeenth century called the Church "the key of the whole constitutional building." But we might better have called the Church the building for which a key of extraordinary subtlety was needed, sought, and finally devised. The Christianity of England being older than its Whiggism, the Whigs, with their passion for the old, *had to take possession of the Anglican Church*. That is the creative act. The combined impact of the words Restoration and Revolution, though apparently tending in opposite directions, delivered the Church of England into the hands of the Commons, and did what neither the Puritan Restoration nor the Whig Revolution could have attained without the conquest of the Church: it gave to the knights and officers of militia of Merrie Old England, who were "Junkers" as much as any Junker in Prussia or Poland or Hungary, the treasures of a liturgy, a religious supremacy, and a godly sovereignty to which no gentry and no lower house on the Continent of Europe, except the Hungarian gentry, could pretend.

The British Junkers described their goal as the restoration of Magna Charta. Magna Charta dates back to 1215. Now in this very year 1215, the greatest universal council of Western Christendom was held in the Lateran at Rome, with more than four hundred bishops present. Obviously, in 1215, the Church of England was not a "church" of its own at all. It had been established as a province of the Church by the Popes of the seventh century. Lanfranc and Anselm of Canterbury had sought the commands of the Pope for their second world, their *"orbis secundus,"* as it was called in 1090. Thomas à Becket had shed his blood for the liberty of the Church, against the King and for the Pope. Christendom had strongly admired his Catholic courage, and had canonized him as a saint two years after his death. From 1172 to 1535 Thomas was the saint of the thirtieth of December, who during Christmas week itself represented the fact that no priest could be appointed or judged by a secular power. Throughout the Middle Ages the pilgrimage to his tomb was the symbol of Christian liberty against kings and lords, and when it was abolished by Henry VIII he was reminded by the Pilgrimage of Grace (1536), for a last tragic moment, of the rights of the populace. Henry VIII did not invade the liberties of Parliament; he led a Parliamentary invasion of the liberties of the Church. "The Church of England lost the liberties granted by Magna Charta. These were liberties denied by Parliament and not to Parliament." [13]

The paradox of an Anglican Church ruled by the Commons because these laymen wished to restore the Common Law of mediæval England is, I hope, now clear. The Commons wished to restore one half of the mediæval constitution and to destroy completely its other half, the independence of the Christian spirit from kings and parliaments. For both purposes, restoration and destruction, they used legal fictions; but these fictions were opposite in character. To destroy the universal and clerical character of the Church it was important that the King be one of themselves, a gentleman of the same religion they held, and willing to grant them complete influence over the stipends and appoints within this Church. The clergy was to consist of a "Christian gentleman" in every village. The theologians of the universities were to be without any influence on the evolution of the creed; for they represented either royal interests or the un-English, universal influence of scholarship.

In this mighty task the gentry could rely on an important precedent. The King, in introducing his supremacy over the Church, had deferred to his subjects by calling the reformed missal the Book of Common Prayer. This beautiful book has now lived over four hundred years; and its title has contributed more than anything else to the religious colouring of the word "Common" in the English language. From the Book of Common Prayer and from the "Commons" in Parliament originated the two mighty streams of feeling, thought and imagination

[13] Albert F. Pollard, *The Evolution of Parliament*, 2nd edition, p. 215, New York, Longmans, 1926.

which finally led to the vision of the British Commonwealth of Nations.

This book, then, by its very title, made every reasonable concession to the presumptions of the common man when it was published by the King's bishops in 1549. It avoided the hierarchical claim by replacing the words "divine service" with the words "common prayer." [14] The introduction runs as follows: "There was never anything by the wit of man so well devised or so sure established which in continuance of time hath not been corrupted: As among other things, it may plainly appear by the common prayers in the church, commonly called divine service." This was an astounding concession on the part of the Anglican Church to the spirit of the Commons. Here "common prayer" is suggested, or supposed, to be the original expression; and the hierarchical phrase "divine service" is reduced to a later, surreptitious alteration of this original meaning. By a stroke of the pen the proper order of things (sacraments that radiate from a holy centre to the circumference of the community) is replaced by the unhistorical fiction of a self-sufficing community, created not by apostolic succession but by a granted equality of all the members, old and new.

There was a further concession in the Book, in that the praying community was made the subject of the service. In the Lutheran churches—as in the Greek or Roman Catholic— the priest made the confession of sins in the singular: "I, poor sinner." It had been Luther's pride that he bestowed on every Christian soul as much of a personal right to say "I" in church as had the priest who prepared himself individually to sing the Mass. But the Book of Common Prayer abolished the "I." All Anglican ritual uses "we." When, in the eighties of the last century, the Lutheran churches of America established a common ritual, the one concession they made to the tradition of Anglo-Saxon congregational life was to replace "I" by "we" in the confession of sins made by the Lutheran pastor. So strongly did they feel the pressure of their Anglo-American environment. This tradition goes back to the year 1549, the

[14] For the first appearance of the phrase, see Th. Lathbury, *A History of the Book of Common Prayer*, p. 9, Oxford, 1859.

oldest year of the Book of Common Prayer. Here the central prayer of the Mass, the Canon, was changed into a form that shaped the character of the Christian people of England for all future times. Instead of praying for "all here standing around" (circumstantium),[15] the priest now prayed for "this thy congregation which is here assembled in thy name." The Anglican congregation was thus filled with the inspiration promised to every gathering in his name; and never, after 1549, could it be at rest until its inspiration was recognized as the public spirit of England. The conquest of the service by the congregation found a first conspicuous outlet in the Responsory of the Psalms. Unknown in the Lutheran Church, the Responsory not only gave the congregation a share in the service, but endowed the English people with a real language. It made them into a "Christian people" by bestowing upon them the language of Canaan! Like the Commons in the Realm, "Congregation" became a living body politic in the Church. The old Church had always known a distinction between clergy and people. The order of voting in ecclesiastical elections had always been "clerus et populus," clergy and laymen. The form of the Book of Common Prayer exalted the "populus Christianus" into a leading partner in the Service. Congregation, "grex," became the leading element in religious life.

The popular concessions were summed up when the "parson" was turned into a "minister." Whereas Luther had been a magister, and taught all the preachers of the "new learning" at Wittenberg to wear the gown of a university magister (the Lutheran frock is the doctor's gown), the English "magisters" became "ministers." Now "magister" is derived from "magis," "minister" from "minus." We find Thomas Hobbes already contrasting the Lutheran and Anglican conception. He says: "We look at the pulpit not as magistral, but as ministerial." Francis Bacon had already attacked "magisterial method" and recommended "initiative method."

This ought to be connected with the love of low, "Lower," and "Common" in English, as against the aura of unreality

---

[15] See prayer Suscipe in Offertorium of the Mass, in the Roman Missal.

which surrounds everything that is called High or Upper; then the change from magisterial into ministerial clergy will be appreciated.

All these concessions to the special English political situation were made by the Book of Common Prayer. But of course it could not renounce the very idea of the unity of the Anglican Church. It had to keep a calendar. The English Church could not give up the great festivals of Christmas, Easter and Whit-sunday—all imperilled and attacked by the Puritans—without cutting itself off from some of the very deepest symbols of mutual recognition between the Christians of England and the Christians of the world. The same is true of the ritual. Without the core of the Lord's Prayer, the Nicene Creed, the Agnus Dei, and certain other cardinal prayers and sacraments of the Church, such as baptism, Christianity evaporates into something like Masonry or philosophy.

But the Non-Conformists, descendants of the ranters as they were, smelled papacy and superstition everywhere. They wished to abolish godfathers and godmothers and put their whole trust in the inspiration of the congregation, the gatherings in church. There the living spirit of the Christian people should fill the mouths of prophets and ministers. And serving as mouthpieces of the people, ministers should be fed by the Holy Spirit of their congregations and synods.

In the first period of the British Revolution, the very meaning of what was being done had to be discovered step by step. The men who fought for the Rights of Parliament, quite capable of understanding the legal fictions of the Realm, were incapable of using the same fictions for the Kingdom of God. As gentry, they were ready to accept a visible head of the Kingdom. But as Puritans, their Kingdom of Heaven was not likely to tolerate a visible head of the Church of England. The Commons were too deeply inspired by the Scotch to bear the religious yoke of a "King in Church" church. John Knox, in the sixteenth century, had taught that the Lower Estates were responsible for the Christian faith in any case of emergency; i.e., at any time when the supreme head delayed the reform called for by divine law. Calvinism favoured everywhere a local church system, with a local government of elders. This would have meant the splitting up of a great national institution into pieces; and the fragments of this presbyterian church would have fallen into the hands of the squires, except for the institution of synods which were lacking in authority.

The Presbyterians tried this experiment; they abolished the hierarchy. The local group was made omnipotent. But in so doing they went against their own parliamentary principles. For, as we have seen, it was not that "such and such an esquire" at Stokeford Grantham had rights in the Realm, but that the assembled Commons exercised power in the United Kingdom. Without this rigid discipline of a single body, the Realm would have been dissolved into petty local governments. England would have become like chaotic Poland where every gentleman exercised a personal veto in the Imperial Diet and could block all procedure. The membership in the House of Commons, by excluding names, prevented chaos. It barred any return to the feuds of a lawless aristocracy. The very word "Commons" guaranteed that the peace of the land, the praiseworthy unifying gift of royal power, was to be inherited by the new King in Parliament.

Now it was completely inconsistent with this policy of the Commons to dissolve the other half of the Realm. The Church, schools, hospitals, universities, prayer-books, calendars, in short, Christian civilization was in danger of being watered down, and losing all its standards, if parochial and provincial presbyterians were to govern these institutions. Like any utterance of the higher life of man, the spirit must be able to move where it listeth. Parochial fetters suffocate the life of the spirit. As a matter of fact, animosity against the universities and the cathedral schools ran high in the Long Parliament. The Presbyterians hated Oxford and Cambridge as they hated the bishoprics. They were seats of the whore of Babylon, of a royal and central power in a much too visible church. Parliament began by abandoning the liturgy of a united Anglican Church to the local ardours of Puritanism. In 1646 the Book of Common Prayer was abolished. But in 1647 the peculiar situation of the British Isles was suddenly rediscovered by Parliament. One thing at least made the sacrifice of a united and hierarchical church as impossible as the sacrifice of the royal peace. England did not live on land alone; one half of English life was enacted on the sea. The waves of the British sea were crossed day after day by hundreds of ships. Few men-of-war and practically no ship of trade carried a minister on board. But Christians they were, and pray they must. In abolishing the Book of Common Prayer, the Presbyterians had ignored the weakness of any institution which is merely local and self-governed; its incapacity to provide, all the time and everywhere, good, responsible, highly trained leaders. Intellectual leadership, religious leadership, is scarce. Talent is not as plentiful as blackberries. Democracy believes that it is, but the belief is false. Without a Central Power, which could be nothing but the authority of the Anglican Church more or less disguised, the seamen would have been lost to the religious cause of the Presbyterians. They would have clung inevitably to the royal Book of Common Prayer, because in order to face shipwreck and death they needed some form of spiritual comfort.

The Presbyterians, therefore, in 1648, issued a decree that a Directory should supersede the Book of Common Prayer. The Directory took its position at the heart of the constitution of the Realm. The union of Scotland, England and Ireland, which was after all merely a royal union by dynastic inheritance, was vindicated. A prayer was framed for these sacred covenants, and for the churches of England, Scotland and Ireland, and the King in Parliament was read a moral lesson by the cursing of his evil counsellors: "Whereas there are thousands of ships which have no ministers with them to guide them in prayer, and therefore either use the old form of Common Prayer or no prayer at all; the former whereof for many weighty reasons hath been abolished, and the latter is likely to make them heathens rather than Christians; therefore, to avoid these inconveniences, it hath been thought fit to frame some prayers, for example, this: 'We pray thee send thy blessing upon all the Reformed Churches, especially upon the churches and kingdoms [sic, the churches precede!] of England, Scotland and Ireland, now more strictly and religiously united in the solemn league and convenant. We pray thee for all in authority, especially the King's majesty, that God would make him rich in blessings, both in his person and government, establish his throne in religion, save him from evil counsel, and make him a blessed and glorious instrument for the conservation and propagation of the Gospel.' "

This time the Presbyterians were as "Anglican" and "Episcopalian" as they well could be. In publishing the Directory they completely abandoned the Presbyterian principle of local church government. The Directory is the "sin against the Holy Ghost" of the Puritan Revolution. Such a great document is not even mentioned by Gardiner in his books on the Great Rebellion and the civil wars of England. It would, in fact, be too much to ask of a Liberal of the nineteenth century that he should divine the real dangers of the Puritan days. But the whole imperial development, the Commonwealth of England, was at stake when the Church of England was given over to petty local pedants or congregationalists. In forbidding the use of the Book of Common Prayer, Parliament abdicated its religious dignity as a member of a Realm mighty in the things of the spirit, such things as universities, schools and the calendar. The introduction of the Directory was the first event which stopped the threatened suicide of the Mother of Parliaments.

One year later Parliament had broken the resistance of Charles I. The King agreed to all the secular demands of his enemies. But in their blindness they could not see what they had already done in publishing the Directory; it seemed merely an exception to the rule they had established. On land, the inspired congregationalists did not shrink at the backward step into chaos; they mistook the isolated local congregation of each parish for the united members of the Commonwealth. Charles I did not lose his life because of his temporal power. He had agreed to all the demands of Parliament in matters of finance and war. But he was clear-headed enough to understand his father's famous "No bishop, no Kings" in the sense in which it was meant; namely, that a government over the counties of England and Scotland was impossible if all that we call today the civil departments of government were to be excluded from its co-ordinating power. All civil departments today are of ecclesiastical origin, derived from common law, the monastic orders, theology, or university traditions.

Charles I died, not as a fanatic for a personal faith, but as a clear-headed fighter for the rights of the King's rôle in the Anglican Church. When he was beheaded one half of his fight was won. His secular rights, by his own consent, were gone. But the return to the catholicity of the Anglican Church was made possible by his tenacity. Had he once given up his claim it would probably have been impossible to restore it at any later time. Religion would have fallen into the hands of a special body. The British Commons would not have acquired the religious sovereignty of their House. The words on the Great Seal of the Commons in 1642, *Pro Religione, grege et Rege,* turned the scales between Rex and Grex, King and Parliament. But it was the mistake of the Presbyterians not to stop there, but to mistake *grex* as meaning ecclesiastical congregation. The Great Seal of the Civil War would be valid only if *grex* preceded *rex* and religion preceded both, embracing the whole Kingdom at once. Then *grex* could not be "congregation," but had to mean the *Christian people of all England.* Not the isolated minister and congregation, but the united ministers and the united congregation of all England, represented by Parliament, had to be the bearers of the inspiration.

Actually, Charles I became the martyr of this united Christianity and the protector of Parliament against local government of the Church. "The King in Parliament," by climbing the scaffold, helped Parliament against its own blindness, along the road to parliamentary glory and sovereignty. Charles I saved, not a royal Church as against a democratic Church, but an Anglican and a parliamentary Church as against a Derbyshire, a Norfolk, a Kent, a Warwickshire and a ministerial Church! By doing so, he acted as the true trustee of Parliament itself against Parliament, appealing from this misinformed Parliament to its wiser successors!

Charles I is the only saint of the Anglican Church. No other martyr or saint was ever inserted in its calendar. Charles I adorns it with good reason. For it was not the "arbitrary power" of a monarch, but the *Realm* of Great Britain which spoke through him in favour of a Church of the Realm, regardless of the conflict between King and Commons.

PUBLIC SPIRIT.

Thus the King stood out for a sovereign Public Spirit pervading all England. Inspiration, in France the contribution of the national genius, was exposed in England to the terrible danger of becoming the attribute of Hyde Park corner prophets and ranters, levellers, sectarians of all kinds of cheap spiritual excitement. The Commons of England, by shouldering the religious task, gave support to what is called with untranslatable force, in Anglo-Saxon terms, "public spirit." These words cannot be translated literally into any other language. *"L'opinion publique"* is a poor echo from the nineteenth century, which distinguished between individual *esprit* and public opinion. But in England you can only be public-*spirited*—you could not be public-opinioned!—and you have no *esprit* of your own.

Public spirit is the inspiration of the *populus christianus* in revolt against the fossilized Realm in State and Church. Public spirit is the power to which the Commons appealed when they turned from the King to the people in 1641 and explained their Great Remonstrance to the man in the street. "To thy tents, Israel," was the war-cry of the man in the street when Charles I returned from his attempt to arrest five members of Parliament. This command voiced the public spirit. By phrasing it in biblical terms, the people emphasized the religious character of this spirit, its equality with true Christian inspiration.

After 1641, England could never be governed against the public spirit of the nation. Public opinion, the shallow, critical, muttering, and uncomprehending intellect, can never prevent the government of a great nation from acting grimly and sternly. But public spirit is serious. It is positive. It knows where the country has to go, not for cheap profits, but for the sake of the soul. Public spirit makes the whole man move, not merely his intellect. Public spirit surrounds parliamentary life in England as waves bear a boat. Without public spirit, Parliament is utterly lost.

All reforms in England have been carried out, not along party lines, but by the evolution of public spirit. Wilberforce's successful fight against slavery, continuing as it did for twenty-five years, is a great example. He was a Tory, and it seemed to be the worst thing in the world that the emancipation should come from that side of the House. But he succeeded. When the last bill accomplishing emancipation was voted, the whole House of Commons rose in a body and honoured the man who had won his battle against all odds.

Public spirit is conjured up by Harrington in his *Oceana*, written under Cromwell, and is the idea under whose ægis Anglo-Saxons will always keep peace and understand each other. It is the first great attempt to secularize the gifts of the Holy Ghost. Once imprisoned in the strong walls of synods and councils, the decrees of popes, and the books of universities, it now invaded this "precious stone set in the silver sea" with the force of union and enthusiasm. No wonder that at first it swept the Presbyterians away past the limits of the real situation. The Kingdom of God had invaded the kingdom of this world.

It was the idea of the Scottish Kirk which conquered England in the years of the Civil War. Here John Knox had taught men to distinguish the two kingdoms, and to be mindful that the King of Scotland held no higher rank in the Kingdom of God than any other man. This ecclesiastical law of the Scotch swamped the Puritans. It was like being drowned with inspiration. When the waters receded, Public Spirit remained as the permanent result.

By its reception, not an isolated word was added to the English vocabulary. The Great Seal, by reversing the old Continental

(1)   (2)   (3)

Mit Gott für König und Vaterland

and making it

(1)   (3)   (2)

Pro religione et grege et rege

broke the old tablets and established a new value, the inspiration of the *grex*, of the united congregation of England. Everything had a new colour, a new sense. Faith in Public Spirit made the British believe in frequent elections.

For every topic in which the Church had been concerned, this lay conception of spirit suggested new words. I mean "country" and "commonwealth." These new words are the last link we have to fill in the chain of language that united the Christian people of England; for they were re-created by the Puritan Revolution.

Public spirit, permeating the Island of Great Britain, catching up great and small alike, obliterated the boundaries of Convocations, countries and shires. The word "country" was of ambiguous character. Usually it signified a county; sometimes it was used for the larger unity of the whole kingdom. Now, under the inspiration of the general and common spirit, country and county were differentiated. When we look into the books of the time, we find the same author using the word "country" sometimes in the old, particular, and sometimes in the new, general, sense of one country, represented by the gentry of the counties meeting in London. (In Württemberg the country in this sense was called the *Landschaft*.) The united estates of the land, when assembled, represented its unity. The country now became the new fatherland, the *patrie*. For "country" has all the flavour of the French *"patrie"* or the German *"Vaterland."* It is the first native, domestic representation of England within the Realm, no longer suffering passively as in the Middle Ages, no longer the widow who had been lamented in 1540, during the Reformation, in the famous first English tragedy *Gorboduc*, but a vigorous motherland of vigorous men, of fighting Christians, and godly English squires. The movement, which replaced the narrow Calvinist conception of a local congregation in a particular town by the great idea of a public spirit embracing 100,000 square miles, brought the countries together until the abstract unity of their representation in Parliament was reflected in the notion of the "country." "My country, right or wrong"; the famous phrase expresses the revolutionary fact that Realm and local congregation have met half-way, in the conception of a country represented by the Commons of the Realm and moved by a public spirit reigning throughout the counties of the Commonwealth.

THE END OF CONVOCATION.

But there was still a gap in the constitution for which not even this grandiose idea of a united country led by public spirit could compensate. Oliver Cromwell had to fill this gap single-handed: he had to make himself Lord Protector. Under Cromwell the English constitution was in effect this: the Lord Protector (himself a gentleman) represented the Realm, i.e., King and Lords, while the gentry of the Lower House represented the Commonwealth. The gap was in the constitution of the Church. For the Realm without an ecclesiastical hierarchy was not the real Norman Realm; it was a purely military organization of the King's feudal army, taken over by Cromwell's "Ironsides." Cromwell and the army made desperate efforts to overcome this obstacle and make themselves into a church-like institution, to fill the cultural and moral portions of the old Realm with religious life. But their ranting and praying and fanaticism could not make up for the old royal, high Church of Norman tradition. The tragedy of Cromwell's "Ironsides" lies in this: there was an evident, unbridgeable gap between Church and piety, palpable institutions and palpitating faith. The Christian people of England could not be put on all fours with the Anglican Church of the Realm by simple enthusiasm and godliness. Cromwell, restoring the liberties of the Commonwealth of England, was incapable of destroying the need for a Church of England.

It was Charles II who carried through the parliamentarization of the English Church. In the cavalcade of "restorers" and revolutionaries, it was the part of the monarch of the Restoration to subjugate the Church to the "King in Parliament," and do away with its loyalties to the "King in Council." All this was attained more or less indirectly. For example, Convocation, the ecclesiastical parliament, was dangerous because York and Canterbury each had its own Convocation, which could be used by a fighting King to get money from the Church without Parliament. But as early as 1662, Waller could sing:

"Convocation no longer continues to sit,
Because nobody sees any use for it."

It was no revolutionary, but Clarendon himself, the minister of Charles II, who managed to get this settled without Parliament. The lawyers—amongst them a famous Speaker of the House of Commons—have always held that his abolishing the financial independence of the Church through the tacit assumption that the lower clergy could be represented by the gentlemen of the Lower House, was one of the boldest and most revolutionary acts in English constitutional history. It was only possible because henceforth the Church was not governed visibly, by Presbyterian zealots, but invisibly, by the courteous mediation of his Majesty's Minister.

We can say that this was really the great revolution: the control, not of a mere sect, but of a real branch of the Christian Church, the Church of England, by the gentry of the shires. The transfer of the King's rights in the Church from the King as spiritual overlord to the "King in Parliament" was the subtle key which finally opened the doors of the cathedral. This process lasted from 1660 to 1685; and the Stuart Restoration, far from preventing it, was a part of it. It was under Charles II that Parliament embarked on Church legislation, the surveillance of morals, and all kinds of crucial religious questions. The authority of Parliament in matters of religion was questioned for the last time in 1689, when the Non-Jurors, a little group of Royalists in the Anglican Church, refused to take the oath of allegiance to William and Mary at the command of Parliament, and went to Scotland. In 1927 Parliament was still able to reject the reform of the Book of Common Prayer, though it was proposed by archbishops, bishops, and the regalvanized Convocations of York and Canterbury.

THE LANGUAGE OF A GENTLEMAN.

The Commons use the figures of the budget as an expression of their political influence and power. They pay the King, the princes, the judges; and the more they pay the more they enjoy their own wealth. But when it became necessary to speak of the duties of the country and the nation, instead of its privileges, the gentleman had no natural language at his disposal. Yet Burke, the hero of English eloquence, called all of Europe "virtually one State." The duties of England within this larger Commonwealth had to be elucidated by rules and notions of authority. Plain English was not enough to inspire these hunting, drinking, gambling, hard-riding country squires. The old Merry England of Falstaff and Shakespeare could not have bridled the natural pride and arrogance of the gentry. A code had to be found which should be valid for every gentleman. This code had to avoid all theological or philosophical *raffinement*. It had to find *old* words for the wise *old world* in which Englishmen were determined to live; but it need not be a religion. This faith knows no tabernacle. The secular Catholicism of modern English society has replaced the ritual of the Mass by the ritualism of daily life. From tub to dinner, everything is done in a deacon's way. I need not dwell on the rigours of an English Sunday; they are world-famous. But the week, too, has a special routine. The so-called "hours" of monastic life in 1400, prime, matins, nones, vespers, and so on, have been replaced—without blasphemy be it said—by breakfast, luncheon, tea, and dinner.

Whistler, the American painter, with his provoking wit, neatly hit off the islanders' ritual when he fell into the midst of them on a P. & O. steamer during the Boer War: "Nobody but English on board—and after months of not seeing them, really they are amazing. There they all were at dinner—you know—the women in low gowns, the men in dinner jackets— they might look a trifle green, they might suddenly run when the ship rolled—but what matter—there they were—men in dinner jackets, stewards behind their chairs in dinner jackets —and so all's right with the country! And do you know, it made the whole business clear to me down there in South Africa. At home every Englishman does his duty—appears in his dinner jacket at the dinner hour—and so what difference what the Boers are doing? All is well with England." [16]

The ships are England herself; that is the result of the Revolution. There is no reason to believe that the English have, by birth, "hearts cased in triple steel," which Horace thought necessary for those who crossed the sea. The gentry overcame the awe which seafaring inspires by a moral conquest. Profligate and lustful the Stuart Restoration was, but its most frivolous poet, Wycherley, went to sea himself and exclaimed in *The Gentleman Dancing-Master*—with a phrase impossible in Shakespeare's time—"All gentlemen must pack to sea."

The language of the Christian gentleman was formed on the vocabulary of the Old Testament. Until very recently, every educated Englishman learned the Psalter by heart and learned to master the language of the Psalms by paraphrasing them in writing. A young gentleman of the earliest days in the United States, Gouverneur Morris, wrote a description of the Gentleman, using only words of the Fifteenth Psalm; and Thomas Jefferson liked it so much that he copied it with his own hand:

> " 'Tis he whose every *thought and deed*
>   By *rule of virtue moves,*
> Whose *generous tongue disdains to speak*
>   The *thing his heart disproves.*
> Who *never* did *a slander forge,*
>   His *neighbour's fame to wound;*
> Nor *hearken to a false report*
>   By *malice* whispered round.

> "Who *vice,* in all its *pomp* and *power*
>   *Can treat with just neglect;*
> And *piety,* though cloth'd in *rags,*
>   Religiously *respect.*

[16] Joseph and Elizabeth Pennell, *Life of James McNeill Whistler*, II, 267, Philadelphia, Lippincott, 1908.

> Who, *to his plighted words and trust*
> Has ever *firmly stood;*
> And though *he promised to his loss,*
> *He makes* his promise *good.*

> "Whose soul *in usury disdains*
> *His treasures to employ,*
> Whom no *record* can ever *bribe*
> *The guiltless to destroy.*" [17]

That this ideal was painted during the war against England is remarkable. It is important for our political theory that the ideal contains no features proper to a man who needs help or support or money or advancement or office. Gouverneur Morris was a man whose grandfather had been Governor of the State of New York. Robert Peel once said: "It takes three generations to make a gentleman." There is not one trait that alludes to a condition where a man depends on others or rules others. The Gentleman is the embodiment of independence; it is in his power to destroy the guiltless, or to act as a usurer. These possibilities presuppose wealth. He is a good loser, too:

> "And though he promised to his loss
> He makes his promise good."

The gentleman, the rich and independent man who "makes his promise good," even if it be "to his loss," is kept in moral discipline by his abandonment of any high-brow arrogance of intellect. He shrinks from self-introspection, the very food of the French mind. He wishes to find his way by visceral sensations, by instinct, not by a logical chain of deductions. The highest praise accorded Lord Asquith by Stanley Baldwin was that he was able to sense instinctively the temper and opinion of the House, and was willing to let these impressions react on his own judgment.

The cardinal virtue of an Englishman is presence of mind. Whereas the German, in his speech, offers a result of past thought, and the Russian presents plans for an abstract future,

---

[17] *The Historical Magazine*, 13, 1868, 178 B.

the Englishman would think it impolite to intrude on the present any suggestion of his own past thinking or his future purposes. His language excels in understatement, in the tropes of "meiosis" and mild irony. Self-control, self-mastery, self-suppression, self-effacement, self-command, self-conquest, etc., this inexhaustible list of words indicates one of the Englishman's great achievements. "He had the regular English tendency to hide away any taste or talent that might conceivably seem to imply a claim to superiority," Sir Gilbert Murray says of a young friend.[18]

The French take into consideration the sudden turns in the wheel of fortune; the English take the full risk and are good losers. It is no accident that a gentleman's agreement became the safest contract in international relations. Property, wealth, ownership, belong to the English Commons; even today the franchise is given, not to everybody, but to a householder, a head of a household. It is only by legal fictions that almost everyone is treated as a householder. But Common Law wishes to deal with men who have something to lose, who belong to a well-to-do family. In America, for a certain period in the eighteenth century, the names of the graduates of Harvard College were arranged in an order of precedence according to the estimated rank of their families. Thus we are told, for example, that in a class of twenty-four, John Adams, later President, held fourteenth place. So the fireside of an English country-seat became a place used not merely for voting purposes but for all social existence, a symbol of England which has resisted all changes, including central heating. The fireplace, the hearth, the rug, accompany Englishmen all over the world; it is part of the ritual of establishing an English home, an outpost of the beloved country which their ancestors restored to its old liberties and which a Glorious Revolution made happy forever.

When the Commons wished to please Sir Robert Walpole, who was their leader for many years, and who liked to call himself a simple country gentleman, they introduced the week-end so that he might hunt the fox and shoot the deer at home in

[18] Æneas on Siegecraft, ed. L. W. Hunter and S. A. Handford, Oxford 1927, p. 11.

the country. English civilization does not aim at the transformation of *"paysans"* and "nobles" into citizens, it tries to "countrify" the cities and boroughs. It is true that the words "countrification" and "to countrify" are now archaic. But anything in England may be called "countrified," even today. So far as the gentry's Restoration is concerned, all England should be called "countrified," and "countrification" would be the clearest description of the goal which English public spirit has pursued for the last three hundred years.

Sentimental affection for the low roof, the old brick, the fireplace, sometimes rose to the level of true poetry, as in Thomas Gray's (1716-1771) *Elegy Written in a Country Churchyard.* The success of the poem was due to the simple things which it opposed to grandeur, pride, "the boast of heraldry, and pomp of power." Gray praised:

> "Some village Hampden that with dauntless breast
> The little tyrant of his fields withstood;
> Some mute, inglorious Milton here may rest,
> Some Cromwell guiltless of his country's blood."

And the secret is out when he sings:

> "Along the cool, sequestered vale of life
> They kept the noiseless tenor of their way."

"Noiseless" is the way of a gentleman. Wordless deeds are best. This passage from *Tom Brown's Schooldays at Rugby* should not be omitted in a chapter on the English Gentleman:

"All the way up to London he [the father] had pondered what he should say to Tom by way of parting advice, something that the boy could keep in his head ready for use. . . .

"To condense the Squire's meditation, it was somewhat as follows: 'I won't tell him to read his Bible, and love and serve God; if he don't do that for his mother's sake and teaching, he won't do it for mine. Shall I go into the sort of temptations he'll meet with? No, I can't do that. Never do for an old fellow like me to go into such things with a boy. He won't understand me. Do him more harm than good, ten to one. Shall I tell him to mind his work, and say he's sent to school to make himself a good scholar? Well, but he isn't sent to school for that—at any rate, not for that mainly. I don't care a straw for Greek particles or the digamma, no more does his mother. What is he sent to school for? Well, partly because he wanted so to go. If he'll only turn out a brave, helpful, truth-telling Englishman, and a gentleman and a Christian, that's all we want,' thought the Squire. And upon this view of the case, framed his last words of advice to Tom, which were well enough suited to his purpose.''

The love of understating facts is a well-known trait of English humour. An Englishman is happy if he can describe a big event with a small word. This English tendency to minimize has often been contrasted with the American habit of exaggerating little things. The love of understatement runs through all the institutions of England. The oldest and greatest insurance company in the world is Lloyd's, which insures against all risks of shipping. This firm was a coffee house, and for a century the directors were called the waiters of Lloyd's Coffee House. It was not until the Foreign Office declined to continue correspondence with the waiters that they clothed themselves with the title of secretaries. In America the "waiters" would have been "presidents," and in Germany "general directors," before the firm was started.

A tragic example of such a life and such a language was presented by Sir Edward Grey, Foreign Minister of England in 1914. His real language and thought is the more significant as most people on the Continent thought of him as a Machiavelli, a cunning and intriguing politician who deliberately brought about the World War. But when we meet Grey himself, we find that he corresponds perfectly to Gladstone's remark: "Edward Grey—there you have the Parliamentary manner." He had the oratory that is also conversation. It is so simple, this speech—and it seems to put everybody else so utterly in the wrong. Yet when this gentleman, by a single hour of eloquence, had moved Parliament to declare war, he had gone so far that his only retreat was country life. This champion of tennis, this lover of stream and forest, this famous angler in country waters and in the troubled waters of world politics, had passed the bounds of the parliamentary manner. The matters on the table of the House could no longer be dealt with by parliamentary conversation or debate. Grey began to brood over his responsibility, and he could scarcely eat. His eyesight failed, and in later years, as death drew on, he sat under the trees, the squirrels worrying him for their nuts, and the birds, whose language he had learned as his own, fighting with one another for a place near his friendly hand. And this was Grey, the man of the third of August, 1914.

The "countrification" of the Commonwealth would have been rustic, tiresome, and insupportable without the language of Canaan, without speechifying. The anti-intellectual attitude of the country had to be leavened by some higher inspiration than peasants or Roundheads seemed to offer in the eyes of courtiers and Cavaliers. The responsory of the Psalter in the divine service, later changed to the "common prayer" of a congregation, the paraphrasing of the Psalms in Sunday-school, this unique *public service* performed by the householder on Sundays, the use of the language of the Psalms at the fireside on week-day evenings by pious and witty laymen—all enabled the country to counterbalance the culture and refinement of the court, where Shakespeare's plays were acted and Bacon was read. The Commons did not fully succeed, however, until the nickname "Roundhead" was superseded by another nickname —"Whig." "Whig" was the designation of the Scotch Covenanters. It was a play on the religious language of the Revolution, as "Roundhead" had been on the hair-cut of the gentry. It was in turning from Roundhead to Whig that the English discovered the full meaning of the new ideal: *an England countrified by the Psalms.* Behind this island of Great Britain lay the Promised Land and the chosen people. The Common Law, as we have already seen, was old because it was Jewish and Christian. So the country was old because it was Canaan, and the English were the chosen people.

William Blake's wonderful verses on England and Jerusalem presuppose the kinship of England and Canaan:

"And did those feet in ancient time
Walk upon England's mountain green. . . .
And was Jerusalem builded here
Among these dark Satanic mills?"

Cromwell beat his drum through the whole of the Old Testament and summoned up every name from Abigail to Zedekiah. The lunatic fringe of the English Revolution went Anglo-Israelitic. The search for the ten lost tribes of Israel became such a habit that 150 years later, in 1794, an Englishman who had thrown his faith and enthusiasm in the scales with his brothers, the patriots in America, in a laudatory speech written for the foundation of Washington as the capital, discovered the ten tribes to be the red Indians of his day! Even in the year 1934 one suddenly finds a full-page advertisement in a leading English newspaper explaining why the English are the ten lost tribes of Israel.

We have seen that the isolation of the Jews was ended by the French Revolution, dissolved in the common descent of mankind from Adam. In the English Revolution we are at a half-way stage between Christ and Adam, and our model is Canaan, the God-governed commonwealth of Joshua and Gideon. The *Judges of Israel* are the great figures of the past, the true prototypes of the British statesman. I know very well that Macaulay preferred to call himself a British proconsul, and that Lord Curzon loved to be Viceroy of an Empire. But in the British Empire the imperialists only belie the feelings and good conscience of the common man. They estrange labour and they produce "Little-Englanders," by a natural reaction against their crass and worldly imperialism. The imperialists are the enemies of the empire. For the imperialists simply mean customs or immigration laws, or subsidies, or other limited issues. They are essentially non-religious.

Now the political value or force of religion is its endlessness. Politics, being a process of realization, must be driven by the force of some unlimited faith. Only the infinite can move the finite. There lies the fatal superiority of faith over reason. The faith of the British sounds less clearly in the challenging outcry of "Britannia Rules the Waves" than in the refrain of the English missionary hymn:

"God is working his purpose out
As year succeeds to year;
God is working his purpose out,
And the time is drawing near.
The time that shall surely be,
When earth shall be filled
With the Glory of God
As waters cover the sea.

* * *

"That the light of the glorious gospel of truth
May shine throughout the world;
Fight we the fight with sorrow and sin,
To set their captives free,
That the earth may be filled with the Glory of God
As the waters cover the sea."

What audacity! The continents risen out of the waves can do no better than to follow this example and praise the Lord as unanimously as the waters that cover the sea. The religious faith of the English Parliament, that it is entitled to rule Catholic Ireland and Buddhist India and the Anglican Church and the Colonies and all the shores of the promised world, rests on this vision of the infinite sea. The infinite has conquered the finite.

Perhaps the upper classes of England, with their empire, their secularism, and their loss of religious faith, are going to destroy the unanimity of this English faith in a Commonwealth guided by the decrees of Providence and the law of God, as Israel had been guided by the Lord in the times of the Judges, when God alone was King.

THE FIFTH OF NOVEMBER.

In purloining the word "Restoration" in 1660, the King left the genuine political idea of the British Commonwealth in shadow. Eager to deny the charge of "royal innovations," he borrowed the vocabulary of the Commons, so that they were no longer able to set forth their purposes in plain legal language. The secular and terrestrial vocabulary being thus destroyed, the last phase of the great transformation was filled by the growth of a new vocabulary. New names and titles had to be coined to express the spirit of the new society and the "marinorama" of its new world.

It was a slow growth: It took twenty-nine years, from 1660 to 1689. During these twenty-nine years the nation suffered as much morally as it had suffered physically during the Civil War. Bunyan's book, *Pilgrim's Progress*, written in prison, is one of the great documents of moral suffering. It was not the return of the King that caused the moral nausea; it was the intolerable ambiguity of the nation's vocabulary for praise and blame, virtue and vice. On the one hand, Charles II seemed willing to respect the liberties of England; on the other, it was ominous that the restorers of these liberties were and remained ostracized as regicides. While the "King in Parliament" respected the outcome of the great upheaval, the heroes of the revolution and the Protector of the Commonwealth were both expunged from the book of the national life, as rebels.

It is true that on one day a year at least the relative rights of Parliament were mentioned. Guy Fawkes' Day, the fifth of November,[19] was celebrated in the calendar of the same Anglican Church that scourged the rebels on May 29. Guy Fawkes' Day, as everyone knows, is a popular holiday all over England; bonfires are lit, and the boys sing, "I remember, I remember the Fifth of November . . ." The basement of the Parliament Buildings is searched annually by its guards for a possible *cache* of gunpowder. It is less well-known that as late as 1859 the Book of Common Prayer contained a form of thanksgiving for the happy deliverance from the Gunpowder Plot. The Commons of Charles II might look upon the forms set aside for this

[19] Compare for its introduction the German chapter, section nine. I. H. Benton, on page XL of his book on the "Anglican Agenda" (1910) says that the Fifth of November did not become a holiday until after 1662. This would strengthen our case considerably; but it seems not to be true. See also Vernon Staley, *Liturgical Studies*, p. 66, London, 1907.

day with relative satisfaction. The defeat of a plot against King and Parliament was, it is true, only a negative event. However, since the lawyers so loved their "old" prescriptive rights, a day inserted in the calendar to celebrate the salvation of an old constitution from a band of conspirators was an acceptable political demonstration in favour of the "old." To be sure, a more positive statement, defending the country not only against Popery but against King and courtiers as well, would have been a far better counterpoise to the ominous twenty-ninth of May, on which Charles II entered his city of London and ended the Great Rebellion. So long as this latter date was the most recent symbol of the state of affairs in the kingdom, the King had not clearly committed himself to the limitation of his power. Royal tyranny might flame up again at any time.

With the succession of the Catholic Duke of York in 1685, the lack of any compelling symbol for the religious rôle of Parliament made itself felt with new violence. Already, between 1678 and 1680, the Commons had done everything in their power to exclude him from the throne. When James became King the rebellion began; and when a son was born to him the possibility of a compromise for the period of his lifetime was superseded by the threat of a continuous Catholic succession. Now on the Continent this problem did not stir up bad feeling. In Saxony, the very motherland of Protestantism, the prince became a Catholic so that he might ascend the throne of Poland, while the country was governed by Protestant ministers. But in England a great new form of life had come into being: Parliament had been made superior to Convocation. And now the revenues of the Whig families from the confiscated monasteries were at stake. This threat precipitated events. The great Whigs asked William of Orange to help them in the fight. The birthright of the new-born Prince of Wales was attacked in absurd manifestoes in which the daughters of the King by a former marriage denied that the Queen of England had been pregnant at all. Civil war raged. William entered London on December 19, 1688; and in the same month James sailed for France. Parliament convened without a royal summons, and decided after endless debates that the King had forfeited his crown by quitting the country without so much as leaving the Great Seal behind him. In other words, James II had committed a felony by being driven out of his realm! But William forced the lawyers to go further; he sent a message that the only acceptable solution was to make him King. In 1689 a settlement between King and Commons was reached; in 1690 and 1691 Ireland was subjugated to the new order of things. If we look at the facts without bias, it appears that in a struggle which lasted over a period of years the Commons succeeded in making the childless William Protector for his lifetime—with the title of King, it is true, but without the right of interfering in his own succession. The bill of rights, guaranteeing the financial and religious sovereignty of Parliament, was signed by William as pretender to the throne, *before* he was declared Sovereign. The sequence of the two declarations tells the true story.

In this whole course of events the usual revolutionary methods were used: high treason was committed, civil war let loose, international support secured, law and order violated. The similarities between Puritans and Whigs, between Cromwell and William, are striking. As a matter of course, there is the same difference between them as between 1789 and 1830 in Paris, that is, between original and copy. The business-like tone of 1689 differs from the moral preachments of 1640 because everybody was tired of solemnity or excitement and concentrated solely on the essentials. But why was the grandeur and the originality of the first magnanimous effort forgotten, and only the pusillanimity of the Whigs recorded in the Book of Fame? It was because the nation needed records, not events. In order to get a clean record, unspoiled by any association with struggle or dissent, the similarities between 1649 and 1689 were suppressed and the contrast stressed to the utmost.

Not only was this done in the first moment, but it was repeated for two more centuries. Macaulay is the most naïve witness to this artificial suppression. A Whig disliked the notion of owing the glories of his Empire to the Puritans. The divorce of the Civil War between 1688 and 1691, from the Civil War in 1642, is carried so far that most school-children never think of bloodshed in connection with 1688, nor of peaceful evolution during the Great Rebellion. William's moderation is always exaggerated, and on the other hand the dire necessity of Cromwell's domestic policy is not appreciated. William came to England, as he literally expressed himself, for the sake of the safety of Europe: he was obliged to gain the military support of England for his wars on the Continent. He forcibly suppressed the Loyalists in Ireland and established English tyranny over it for another two hundred years. William left only one seventh of Irish soil to the sons of Erin; the rest fell into English hands. Well and good; this perhaps was inevitable. But then do not tell us that there was no bloodshed, no war, no violence! On the other hand, Cromwell was put into power by Parliament; he did not ask for a crown, like William; he tried to act for the world at large; he united the three kingdoms for the first time. And still, in the eyes of the later Whigs Cromwell remained a dangerous rebel and William a legitimate king.

Blackstone, the leading lawyer of the eighteenth century, describes William as an "hereditary monarch" and Cromwell as a "usurper"; though he has to admit, with a priceless expression, that "the title to the crown is at present, *though not quite so absolutely hereditary as formerly"!* Thus it was not admitted that the Revolution of 1688 had been a civil war, which it had been nevertheless. And the Civil War, according to Blackstone, was nothing but downright confusion, instability, and madness. The Civil War and the Glorious Revolution were kept as far apart as possible. We should miss the secret of English parliamentary cant if we overlooked this violent attempt to separate what belongs together. William III, the new Lord Protector, and those who followed him, those life-long First Gentlemen of England who are called Kings, must have nothing whatsoever to do with that blood-shedding, tyrannical gentleman, Oliver Cromwell.

Being thus averse to any possible comparison of Cromwell and William III, the English were given to the point of view which we have called detective history. In a detective story endless particulars are revealed one after the other, and the solution must not come until the last page. The British treated forty-nine years of their history as a detective story, obliterating all parallels and all continuity, listing hundreds of disconnected executions, coronations, and so on and so forth, suppressing the universal character of the struggle, and finally concentrating all the limelight on one short moment near the end. In American or French tradition it is the first days, the Fourth or Fourteenth of July, which get all the publicity; the first days of the revolutionary era are the epoch-making ones. The beginnings are heroic, divine, dramatic. The end is more or less disappointing; it drags. No Frenchmen can possibly understand the English on this point. How can he be expected to celebrate the ghosts of the revolution of June, 1830, and forget the heroes of 1792, or Napoleon? Yet this is exactly what the British did when they celebrated the last decision of the Supreme Court of history and dropped all interest in the previous long trial.

The limelight of consciousness was concentrated on the final act because consciousness of the foregoing stages was neither wished nor accepted. English memory is *scarred* by the preceding acts, the Parliamentary War, the Cromwellian Commonwealth, and the Restoration of the Stuarts. Any such scar in a nation's life obstructs truth. Scars produce myths and legends. Every myth is the self-defence of a body politic which cannot bear to see its wounds re-opened and bleeding once more. By fixing unswervingly on 1688, the English avoided touching their scar.

But the contrast between Whigs and Roundheads, William and Cromwell, Glorious Revolution and Great Rebellion, usurper and hereditary king, legality and madness, is carried to its extreme when it comes to the chronology of the two periods. For instead of contrasting nine years for the first Civil War, with a period of three or five years for the second, English writers speak of twenty years on one side (1640 to 1660) and a single day on the other. Rebellion against James II? Not at all; the transformation took place on a single day of the year 1688, a day which happened to be the Fifth of November! Pamphlets had been spread among the Stuarts' army and navy: "Remember the year '88"—alluding to the Spanish Armada and its defeat one hundred years before. Thus the landing of William III at

Torbay was compared to the defeat of the Catholic aggressor. And whereas in 1660 it was the entrance of the King into London which had been epoch-making, the accent, in 1688, was placed on the miracle of the landing at Torbay. All the later events were simply omitted. The illegal convening of Parliament without a royal writ, the fruitless debates of the Commons, William's usurpation—everything was turned into an automatic and legal consequence of the decrees of Providence as manifested on the old holiday, the Fifth of November.

The popularity of Guy Fawkes' Day in modern England does not really go back to 1605. So old-fashioned and restorative were the methods of the English revolutionaries that they even managed to "restore" a holiday and disguise their triumph over a modern event as the celebration of an old one. But the liturgy of the Church betrays the secret when it adds to the prayers of thanksgiving for the failure of the Gunpowder Plot the concise lines: ". . . and also for the happy arrival of his Majesty, King William III, on this day for the deliverance of our church and nation . . . for giving King William a safe arrival here, and for making all opposition fall before him." Here we have the cant of the English Revolution at its climax. Church and Parliament speak differently about the same event. Parliament declares that William's title to the throne dates from a felony, and that James II has committed that felony by leaving England in December; the Church extols William as a lawful monarch on the anniversary of his coming in November.

Legally, the Fifth of November, 1688, the landing at Torbay, did not create the Whig government of England even in the eyes of Parliament, for James did not leave England until later. But morally and religiously the Fifth of November is the glorious revolution of God. In fact, it seems to have impressed William III himself as such. Landing, on his second attempt, by the help of a favourable wind, one hundred years after the Spanish Armada had been scattered in the same attempt, he took the Anglican bishop, Burnet, by the hand and asked him as a good Calvinist: "Do you believe in predestination now?" Not man's volition, but the decrees of Providence, had brought on the Revolution. The Colony of Connecticut clearly expressed this distinction when it congratulated William and Mary in the unctuous phrase: "Great was the day when the Lord who sitteth upon the floods, did divide his and your adversaries like the waters of Jordan, and did begin to magnify you like Joshua [who after all, was not a king!] by the deliverance of the English dominions from Popery and slavery."

The epilogue of the British Revolution, embracing at least three months' time, was not put into the calendar because the Glorious Revolution had to be a final, superhuman intervention from heaven.

He who underrates the liturgy of the Church as evidence may look at the attitude of the *Revolution Club* of the eighteenth century. Year after year, down to 1789, on the Sunday following the Fifth of November, it celebrated the miracle of that day. The members of this Club were doing homage to a fact, an event. Revolution had no adjective in the English language up to 1789. A revolutionist was merely a devotee of the miracle of 1688, a supporter of the Protestant succession and the right of Parliament to exclude non-Protestant branches of the dynasty from succession to the Throne. The word "revolutionist" had nothing of the meaning of the word "revolutionary" today. The revolutionary fact was the landing at Torbay, an objective event not brought about by any Englishman. There is a wonderful lightening of conscience compressed into this word "Revolution." Heaven has spoken. Englishmen, this time at least, are innocent and humble. The Lower House of the Realm is delivered from unnatural pressure by intervention from above. No dictator, no usurper, no protector, no pretender can share the loftiness of God's Providence. Once and forever men had to distinguish between the level of their actions on earth and the level on which God acted, beyond the sky.

The lasting abhorrence and detestation of any super-elevation of the individual, a striking feature of the English national character, has deprived the English language of even a correct word for the vice of eminence, *"Überhebung,"* self-aggrandizement and pride.

The political tracts of the years after 1688 all agreed in this distinction between human action and superhuman interference. The State tracts from the year 1689 were published in 1692 as an account of "our late *happy* revolution." The religious word "glorious" of the Psalms is parallelled here by the secular expression "happy." As early as the end of 1688, the writers of the Proposals to the Convention expressed with emphasis this idea of *revolution:* "In a word, if the Hand of God is to be seen in human affairs, and His voice to be heard upon Earth, we cannot anywhere find a clearer and more remarkable instance than is to be observed in the present Revolution. . . . If one considers how *happily and wonderfully* both persons and things are changed in a little time, and without bloodshed. It looks like so many marks of God's favour, by which He thinks fit, to point him out to us in this extraordinary conjuncture." The editors of the first edition of Clarendon's *History of the Rebellion* (of 1640-1660) point again to the events of 1688 as a period "where a revolution became necessary, during which the *fundamentals* of Earth left their regular course to carry through a Reformation."

The analogy of an earthquake or a celestial catastrophe is used to explain the difference between a rebellion from underneath or below, and the final stroke of 1688. This did not come from below, from the valley of earthly volition! It is important to understand why, on the one hand, all the men involved in the revolution claimed to be *restorers,* while on the other, the totality of the event could not be called a restoration. This is a paradox indeed. William III, in his Proclamation, claimed to be restoring the laws of England. And so claimed the lawyers who by their subtle precedents cleared his way to the Throne. Maynard, born in 1602, was in his eighty-seventh year when he quoted the precedents of the thirteenth and fourteenth centuries to exclude the succession of the Catholic Prince of Wales, and, in order to cool his Protestant fever in the bloody persecution of the papists in Ireland, based his hatred and passion on the duties of a mediæval king. He, like all the lawyers of the revolutionary century, was restoring Magna Charta, restoring the Common Law, the privileges and liberty of the Commons of this Kingdom.

Why, then, "Revolution" and not "Restoration"? For the

sake of the honour of the revolutionaries, their Restoration of Freedom had to be ennobled by the word "Revolution." When the Commons acted, Heaven acted along parallel lines. There was a miraculous correlation between the actions of Englishmen and laws of a supra-English scope and importance.

The universal significance of the British Revolution which saved Portugal, the Netherlands, Belgium, Denmark, and many other small nations in Europe from annihilation, which raised scores of political movements all over the world, from Transylvania to Pennsylvania, which saved the dwindling ranks of Protestantism on the Continent and set up the English Parliament as the Mother of Parliaments, is the important side of the British seventeenth century for any philosophy and sociology of revolutions. We found that the Bolsheviks, who habitually spoke of the World Revolution and even dropped the word Russia, had to be seized off their guard and observed in their process of "going Russian." The English, on the contrary, have such a fear of being anything but English that their revolution has to be caught by detective methods in the very act of becoming universal and exercising universal effects. Elizabeth, in the times of the Armada, had compared England to an arch; that is, she had limited herself to a biblical parallel. The breadth of heaven and earth had remained within the narrow horizon of Church and Empire. The English Revolution looked up to the majesty of the infinite heaven of natural science, and by doing so gained the courage to comprehend a far bigger world. The earth in which the new Commonwealth was placed soon extended over five oceans, into continents unknown to the Roman world. In this actualizing of a new astronomical and geographical vision the English Revolution was a forward step for all mankind toward a new form of existence.

Revolution and Restoration are like head and tail of one coin, minted jointly by Cromwell and William III. It was the division of the English tradition into two separate chapters, one for Cromwell and one for William, one for the Puritans and one for the Whigs, which created the protective colouring of English politics, so often called hypocrisy by people on the Continent. In reality, the phrases of English parliamentarism are a plainsong in an act of religious worship. Taken literally, the meaning of this plainsong is lost; it can easily be unmasked as cant in its worst sense, that of pious lying. J. W. Croker, writing in a period of parliamentary decay, masterfully described the latent dangers of the institution:

"There is something in the very atmosphere of the House unfavourable to bold and uncompromising conduct. It is, de facto, *a sort of overgrown club*. This is the most important part of the whole business. Things are every day admitted in private among the members, which are studiously denied or concealed in the speeches reported from the gallery. Whoever, therefore, should endeavour to rend asunder that veil, which by all parties in the House is held up before the public, would lose his character and caste." [20]

THE EUROPEAN SIGNIFICANCE OF "GLORIOUS REVOLUTION."

Humanity as a whole underwent a revolutionary change during the seventeenth century, and expressed this change through an English vocabulary. We have already remarked on the word "glorious" in "Glorious Revolution"; but the word "revolution" deserves some further notice. The new terminology sanctified revolution as a lawful event—naturally lawful though politically illegal. Something bigger than legality had made its entrance into the Western World.

As early as a generation before 1688, individual writers had begun to use the word "revolution" in a sense which implied a parallel between the rotations of government and the great motions of the stars. In the Middle Ages politics were thought of as depending wholly on the "revolving" wheel of fortune. By the seventeenth century the new astronomy of Copernicus and Kepler and Galileo had impressed the public deeply enough to make it apply the notion of astronomical revolutions to earthly events. Mathematics and the physics of space stimulated the imagination. Hobbes wrote, in physical terms: "If in time as in place there were degrees of high and low, I verily believe that the highest of time would be that which passed between the years of 1640 and 1660." In another chapter he expresses himself in this way:

[20] *Quarterly Review,* Vol. 42, January, 1830, pp. 271-272.

"I have seen *in this revolution* a circular motion of the sovereign power through two usurpers, father and son, from the late King to his son. For it moved from King Charles I to the Long Parliament; from thence to the Rump; from the Rump to Oliver Cromwell; and thence back again from Richard Cromwell to the Rump; thence to the Long Parliament and thence to King Charles II, where long may it remain."

Clarendon himself, in his later years, when he was no longer a responsible minister of the King, called the royal restoration of 1660 "the revolution."

Through this new usage the laws of nature made their entrance into the world of politics. "Depression," "opposition," "influence," "conjunction," are words of the same stamp. The notorious phrase "the business cycle" is also descended from this stock. All of them deserve our interest. Take, for instance, "influence": "Certain occult streams of power believed to emanate from the heavenly bodies." [21] Revolution brought about an astronomical order of things in which the body politic is no longer moved by the High of this earth—in which a new "influence," God's glorious will from above, has opened unforeseen channels of power to the lower estates of the realm. This belief in an "influence" more powerful than the written or formal law is related to the belief in the Revolution. The vocabulary of politics always has to deal with the intangibles which move the heart and mind of a ruler, without even being mentioned by the law of the land. The lawyers of pre-revolutionary England had set up the law against those secret influences of the court which made the King's power arbitrary. They tried to exclude influence and act by law alone. But influence is a fluid, as law is a solid body. Ice and water are no more closely related than politics and law. Influence cannot be excluded by law, but only by another influence. Otherwise the origin of new law is made impossible. Thus legitimate and illegitimate influence are the real opposing elements in the English revolution. As the Great Remonstrance of 1642 put it, the King should entrust the business of the State to no other persons than those who had the confidence of the Commons.

[21] Trench, *Study of Words*, Oxford, 1894.

The word "conjuncture" points in the same direction; it is an astronomical term. When Charles II returned in 1660, he said that "a happy conjuncture had removed a malignant star." "Opposition," the common expression for a political antagonism, is also an astronomical word. It was the insight into the inevitability of opposition in heaven which overcame the reluctance of human brains to tolerate opposition on earth. When we find the Leader of the Opposition legally established in the Canadian constitution we should not forget that the discoveries of the astronomer had to give man a glimpse of the revolutions of the stars before he was bold enough to legalize human opposition.

We should add, however, that this cosmic point of view did not mean that the individual politician was governed by the motions of the stars. Cheap astrology, the drawing of horoscopes, and so on, methods freely used by princes and military leaders all through the seventeenth century, were a kind of black magic which a great nation could not tolerate. No, the application of natural law was, not to the politician, but to the whole of politics. These new words were acceptable only because they were applied, not to the individual Englishman and his freedom, or to the King, but to the balance of power in the body politic as a whole. Astronomical metaphors were welcomed because no Christian soul, no named individual, was caught in the net. The new vocabulary emphasized the anonymous order of things described above, in which gentlemen had no names of their own, the Speaker of the House no eyes or ears of his own, and Members of Parliament no desks of their own. This was the sense in which, by a happy conjuncture, the Lower House had secured its co-ordination with the upper spheres.

We shall understand the meaning of "Glorious Revolution" still better if we ask ourselves what bodies were involved in it. Was it everybody, every citizen, who got his share of power in this revolution? Or was it the great individuals, dignitaries of rank and influence, lords and aristocrats, who became the governing class? Either assumption would miss the point of the British Constitution. The Whigs of 1688 wished their word "revolution" to be taken literally. Individual men moved on this earth; but the model of the body politic was the celestial bodies on which Copernicus had written his famous treatise *De revolutionibus corporum cœlestium* (1543). Arbitrary power was banned. There was no Popery left to dim the light of moon and stars by the alleged glories of its Roman court; there was only the majesty of the galaxy above a benighted world—supra-individual, supra-personal. And the mighty of this world were revealed as nothing and of no account compared with this celestial system of moving bodies.

THE THREE RESTORATIONS.

Perhaps it seems strange to a modern mind that the people of England should have looked up from below to an upper Realm of superhuman powers, and that they should have celebrated a sudden co-ordination with this upper realm of Church and State as an act of deliverance. But this is the secret of the English Revolution, that by a penetration and undermining of the upper powers of the Realm from below, high became low, mountains valleys, and humble gentlemen of England the proud masters of Church and State; and that, although Upper remained Upper, High remained High, and Sovereign remained Sovereign, they all had to give way henceforth to the opinions, grievances and wishes of the Commons of England.

The power of the House of Commons would vanish the moment either Realm, Anglican Church or House of Lords ceased to function. All proposals to abolish the House of the Lords Spiritual and Temporal were and are doomed, because they are all infected by the Continental, democratic point of view. These proposals are founded on the assumption of a nation which governs itself. But the English people do not govern themselves. They are governed by consent, which is something very different. Undoubtedly, to secure this consent they have bored through the foundations of the Realm, which governs England even today, and have transformed King and Queen, Lords and Archbishops, Chancellors and Judges of the English nation, for all their pompous wigs and scarlet vestments, crowns and processions, ritual and privileges, into willing servants of the English people. But the superstructure cannot be abandoned. Cromwell, describing himself as neither very high nor very low, was the model of the Commoner of England.

The limelight of French tradition plays on the first years of the French Revolution. The fourteenth of July, 1789, is the christening day for a period of twenty-six years. Awaited with impatience for forty years, the Revolution was realized in its universal importance from the very beginning. Reality and the consciousness of reality reached a harmony unheard-of in the annals of our race; in the very dawn of events consciousness was fully awake.

"Glorious Revolution" emphasizes a different kind of parallelism. The French were intoxicated by the perfect harmony between mind and body. The English expression does homage to the perfect harmony in God's creation of heaven and earth, and to his power to act without man's help in His government of the world. And this vision came to the British nation as a farewell to forty-eight years of civil unrest. It was the final ceremony of a long struggle; the name was uttered like a deep sigh ending the fifty years of strain and precluding any return to civil war, insurrection, or illegal procedure in the future. A great solemnity prevails. It is the finality of the event that strikes us most. As an illustration, I have saved one line from the divine service for the Fifth of November. In it the note, sounded in the first hour of the struggle, resounds admirably in the last. I hope that the reader will share the reverence I felt when I discovered, under the surface of the "Glorious Revolution," the old word "restoration." So says the Book of Common Prayer on the Fifth of November: "The glory of God made William III the instrument of His will in *restoring* the rights and liberties of England."

We have re-established the unity of the Puritan and royal restorations, and we have pointed out that 1688 was a third restoration, trimmed and embellished to suit the limelight of consciousness, and guaranteeing the Anglican character of the English Church. Now we can rename the phases of the English Revolution:

The Puritan Restoration of Freedom 1641-1660
The Royal Restoration   1660-1685
The Anglican Restoration   1685-1689 (1692)

It is the secret of the English Revolution that the real revolution was deprived of its birthright, and that a later event carried off the glories of victory. The Glorious Revolution is an aftermath, like the July Revolution of 1830. Now we have already had occasion to compare the epilogue of 1830 to the prologue of 1905 in Russia; and we asserted that 1830 played a similar rôle, in relation to the end of the French Revolution in 1815, to that played by the prologue of 1905 in relation to the outbreak of the World Revolution in 1917. In each case the truth had to be proclaimed over again; the effort had to be made twice before it could be final. Without 1905, the World Revolution of 1917 could not have been aware of its own finality. Until 1830 the French Revolution was without self-consciousness.

The English crisis obeys the same law of a two-fold beginning. Without 1688, the great change of 1651 could not be brought fully into consciousness. Though it had long been in effect, it needed the dramatic events of 1688 to become legitimate and be made a formula of recurrent order. But since the English Revolution preceded the French and Russian, the English were not able to see 1688 as the sequel of 1649, as the French could when Lafayette rode through the streets of Paris in 1830 as he had ridden in 1789. It is true that many members of the Convention of 1689 had seen the Civil War. It is by no means a mere accident that Maynard could be so active in 1688, when he was eighty-seven years old. But the point is that in 1689 everyone did the opposite of what the French did in 1830. Instead of comparing the old days with present events, the British in 1689 were haunted by a firm resolution not to see any similarities and not to permit any comparison.

THE LOSS OF THE FIRST COMMONWEALTH.

Though all comparison with the times of Cromwell was suppressed, the British gentry honoured the European obligations incurred through William III for another fifty years. Only after the death of Robert Walpole was the balance of rights and duties in this aristocratic government definitely destroyed. A period of insolence followed, for which we may draw a parallel with the corresponding French period, 1830 to 1848. Bribery and dissipation reigned among the gentry. The Duke of Newcastle cynically pulled the wires of patronage. On one occasion, when the opposition was saying that everybody whom the Duke had brought in was to be turned out, without any exception, somebody replied, "Save the King!" In the country, the absence of a central royal police led to the orgies of highway robbery described in *The Beggar's Opera* of 1727. The Prime Minister boasted openly of this lack of any central government. He stated in 1749 that it was his duty to inform the nation: "We are not in a position to fight our enemies."

The moral shamelessness of Lords and Ladies in their dealings with the other classes surpassed belief. Gentlemen like Lord Holland deliberately trained their sons to be irresponsible. "For him [i.e., Lord Holland's son] there were no rules, only prerogatives. He was taught to gamble, he was taught to drink himself drunk, he was taught to be gay. His debts were soon incredible and had to be handled by funding operations. His habits—but I forbear. They were the *reductio ad absurdum* of education." In these sentences Mr. P. W. Wilson [22] is speaking of a leading English statesman, Charles James Fox. Edmund Burke was referring to this state of affairs when he said in 1780: "We have had so much power and luck that even the most modest among us is degenerated into the vices and stupidities of kings." And Horace Walpole wrote in 1763: "You could not recognize your own country. You left it a private little island, living upon its means; you would find it the capital of the world. . . . The city of London is so elated that I think it very lucky some alderman did not insist on matching his daughter with the king."

The English in 1763 had enough arrogance to tread the Colonies, France, Ireland, and the plantations all under foot

22 *New York Times Book Review*, August 16, 1936.

at once. The climax reached in this year reminds us of Boniface VIII, who published his bull on the omnipotence of the Roman Church in 1302 and immediately afterward was made a prisoner by the King of France. So 1763, like 1302, was the climax of a long period which preceded it. No wonder that the anticlimax came as the result of an outburst of hatred on all sides. The French minister, Vergennes, put it in these words: "If England looks outside to the other countries of the world—from Buenos Aires to New Orleans, from Dunkirk to the Antilles (except Portugal, whose defence is only one more burden)—she sees only enemies."

The First Commonwealth underwent a terrible crisis, both internally and externally, during the American Revolution and the Napoleonic Wars. This crisis is too often spoken of slightingly, and so the totality and completeness of its threat to the first British Commonwealth is overlooked. The truth is that the whole outside world and all the isolated interests inside turned against the arrogance of the British Parliament in the years between 1774 and 1815.

The Colonies lost faith in the Commonwealth; each one assumed the name separately. "God save the Commonwealth of Massachusetts!" replaced the old "God save the King!". John Adams wrote in 1774: "If the American resistance to the act for destroying your charter [i.e., the charter of the city of Boston] . . . is treason, the Lords and Commons, and the whole nation, were traitors at the Revolution."

Our picture of conditions within the British Isles can be taken from John Wesley. The father of Methodism, who travelled from four to five thousand miles annually, likened the times in 1774 and 1775 in every detail to 1640. In his letters to Lords North and Dartmouth he says:

"I aver that in every part of England where I have been (and I have been east, west, north, and south within these two years) trade in general is exceedingly decayed, and thousands of people are quite unemployed. I aver that the people in general all over the nation are far more deeply dissatisfied than they appear to have been even a year or two before the Great Rebellion, and far more dangerously dissatisfied. The bulk of the people in every city, town, and village where I have been do not so much aim at the ministry, as they usually did in the last century [sic], but at the King himself. He is the object of their anger, contempt, and malice. They heartily despise his Majesty; and hate him with a perfect hatred. *They wish to imbrue their hands in his blood;* they are full of the spirit of murder and rebellion, and I am persuaded, should any occasion offer, thousands would be ready to act what they now speak." [23]

Of the emotions of present-day Englishmen towards royalty we cannot find a trace in Wesley's report. In another letter he wrote:

"We have thousands of enemies . . . they fill our cities, our towns, our villages. I know the general disposition of the people, English, Scots, and Irish, and I know an huge majority of them are exasperated almost to madness. Exactly so they were throughout England and Scotland *about the year 1640;* and in great measure by the same means—by inflammatory papers, which were spread, as they are now, with the utmost diligence in every corner of the land. Hereby the bulk of the people were effectually cured of all love and reverence for the King. So that first despising, then hating him, they were just ripe for open rebellion. And I assure your lordships, so they are now: they want nothing but a leader."

We see that the comparison between 1640 and the present day was on all lips. But this time the "King in Parliament" was attacked by all the Nonconformists with exactly the same violence with which the absolute Stuart king had been attacked by the gentry. Soon Ireland was in rebellion. Freedom of the press was abolished. For many years the Parliamentary reports were not offered for public sale. Habeas corpus was suspended. In 1810, 1811, and 1812, as the figures of the Annual Register show, England almost collapsed. When Burke said, "Our most salutary and most beautiful institutions yield nothing but dust and smut. The harvest of our law is no more than stubble," he indicated that this series of humiliations cannot be understood as a series of accidents; that it was a single long attack lasting

[23] John Wesley, *Journal,* Standard Ed., VIII, pp. 334 *ff.,* London, 1916.

from 1776 to 1815. The English have habitually refused to see the whole period as one time-span; but it is the only way to understand how fundamentally the English Commonwealth was tested during these years.

Here it is useful to look at the rôle played by the French. In 1778, the French declaration of war called on the world to put an end to *"the tyrannical empire* usurped by England, and which England pretends to exercise over the oceans."* From outside, the Commonwealth seemed to be nothing but a tyrannical empire. The French, first by the munitions delivered through the firm of our old acquaintance, the poet and banker, Caron de Beaumarchais, and later by their fleet, armed all the internal enemies of England. In 1781, the French victory off Cape Henry finally saved the thirteen colonies of America. And now France's appeal to the other nations was answered. "Every nation wished to see England humiliated," said Franklin. In 1780, France, Spain, the Netherlands, were engaged in open warfare against England. War raged in India. Ireland was in full rebellion. Nay, more: Russia, Sweden, Denmark, England's old ally Prussia, Austria and Portugal were all united in an "armed neutrality" against the pirate.

"The American War of Independence was a European event. It was the great powers of Europe that brought about the heaviest calamity in English history, the 'breach with America.' This is the essence of the whole struggle which extended over eight years and was fought on all the seas of the four continents." (Emil Reich.)

An outline of three distinct periods becomes visible:

1640-1689		Total revolution
1730-1776	(1774)	Presumption
1776-1815		Humiliation

The period of humiliation, in England as in France, runs strangely parallel to the first revolutionary period. First, it covers a similar length of time.

	England	France
Point of Departure	1535	1685
Total revolution	1640-1691	1789-1815
Humiliation	1776-1815	1848-1874

Then there is an even more striking parallel in the distribution of particular phases and sections.

Parliament fights the King 1642-1649	The Colonies fight Parliament 1776-1783
A second rebellion seals English liberty 1688-1691	A second war seals American liberty 1812-1815

THE ADAPTATION TO THE BOURGEOIS REVOLUTION: SPORTSMANSHIP AND LIBERALISM.

In so far as the American Revolution and the English period of humiliation led to the independence of the United States, we shall look at them more in detail in another chapter. For us and our present-day problems the fascination of English history lies in the fact that we can find in it an example of how a nation reacts toward a new revolution. The British nation adapted itself to the ideas of 1789 in a way rather similar to that followed by the French and Americans in our day. This parallel will be further illuminated when we can cite Italy's and Germany's processes of adaptation to the British revolutionary system.

England did not give in to the French Revolution until 1830. A nation does not make concessions to a foreign spirit under pressure! It was in 1830 that J. W. Croker coined the name "Conservative Party" for the Tories—a concession which Peel called "un-English." Everyone knows that the Reform Bill of 1832 and Disraeli's Reforms of 1867 installed "Liberalism" in power, abolishing rotten boroughs and the excesses of local self-government, extending the franchise, and so on and so forth. It was even done in a rather cheerful manner, as for example when Ludgershall lost its seat: "I am the proprietor of Ludgershall. I am the member for Ludgershall. I am the constituency of Ludgershall. And in all three capacities I assent to the disfranchisement of Ludgershall."

However, the moral survival of a House of Commons ruling Church and State and colonies in a secularized world and a nation of shopkeepers and workers is not explained by electoral franchises. The first step had to be a moral step. Adam Smith showed in his moral philosophy that the "Wealth of Nations" could be restored by industry, "even without territorial expansion." The loss of the American Colonies, the fatal result of tyranny and heartlessness, could be repaired by industry and an industrial revolution. Adam Smith became a national prophet because he taught the English to take wealth as national wealth. He enabled the English language to fight the new nationalism of the French Revolution by stressing, in a way no other language had done, the industrial revolution. As Charles II had made a Royal Restoration, with the aim of outdoing the Puritan Restoration, so the English of the first half of the nineteenth century concentrated on an "Industrial Revolution." They fell in love with the phrase, and opposed it to the French idea of revolution as an outburst of human passions.

But one concession had to be made to "nature and humanity." To the model of the Christian Gentleman there had to be added a new, purely natural type, the sportsman; for even the fox-hunting and tennis-playing gentleman is more than a sportsman. It was then that sport became a religion of the masses. Tom Sawyer, the boxer, was fêted as a hero by the citizens of Liverpool in 1850; they went in procession to welcome him. The Frenchman, Boutmy, compared this excitement over the sportsman to the day when the Florentine populace walked from Florence to Borgo Allegri to honour Cimabue, who had just finished his picture of the Madonna. The feelings which the art of painting aroused in 1300 were unleashed in England in 1850 by sport. The Derby became the most popular holiday in England. A young man could look forward to his life being crowned by three achievements: becoming Prime Minister, marrying a rich heiress, and winning the Derby. Perhaps in any country a fool could dream of three such things, but in no other country would Lord Rosebery have been able to carry out his plan: to become Prime Minister, to marry a Rothschild, and to win the Derby.

Today we hear the tragic news that hunting the fox may soon become extinct in England, because it is too expensive. If this terrible loss must be borne, there is comfort in the fact that the ancient symbol of true sport can go down with honour. A wealth of other sports, drawn from every nation, have taken its place: golf from Scotland, cricket from Ireland, polo from India. The penetration of England by these sports is a part of its political revolution too. For example, golf is perhaps a symbolical expression, in the field of sport, of the tremendous Scotch influence in English politics during the nineteenth century. So many English statesmen were Scotch that it seemed as if sport and politics were a two-fold sign of the Covenanters' influence. The spirit which had ennobled the Roundheads and made them Whigs was now translated once more into plain English by golf and Carlyle, by Campbell-Bannerman and Ramsay MacDonald.

This spirit of sportmanship, then, was a second growth of the mystical union between the Commons of England and the Scotch Kirk, a second growth which no longer used the religious war-cry of the Puritans. And yet the old definition of Puritan in the Great Remonstrance still held good: "The Puritan, under which name they include all that desire to preserve the laws and liberties of the Kingdom, and to maintain religion in the power of it." Any leader of the nineteenth century might have subscribed to this definition of his aim. The odd situation of the Presbyterians agreeing in 1648 on an authoritative directory for seamen in foreign waters, was duplicated in 1933, when the Presbyterians in India permitted the union of all the Indian denominations into one Episcopal Church, because political and religious liberty at home and political and religious unity abroad are woven into one indissoluble fabric. And a second growth of the religious Commonwealth was brought about, too.

The Lambeth Conference of the Anglican Church, including the bishops of the United States of America, reminds one

of the larger moral union of all Anglo-Saxons, beyond the conflicts of political independence. This larger union triumphed
in the World War when Lloyd George laid a wreath on a
memorial to the American "Rabble in Arms," because, as he
said, they had taught the British in their crisis how to organize
a true commonwealth of peers.

After the English period of humiliation not only the constitution but also the type of the ruling classes was regenerated.
About 1780, a hundred years after the Revolution, the type
produced by the public schools began to verge on caricature.
Self-control had led to spleen, and the accentuated mildness
among men to a terrible reversal in the relation between man
and woman. By putting all the charm of human intercourse
and common life into men's clubs, colleges, debates, the gentry
deprived English women of their bridal character. *Flagellantism in England* is the name of the famous book by a Continental physician, describing the scars left by this lack of
wooing, of courtship, between the Englishman and his wife.
Perhaps it is fair to say that the phase of courtship—well-
known as a problem to every biologist—remains a thing by
itself in the life of the Englishman.

The clubs of England, the counterparts of the French salons,
excluded women from all political influence. In France, nothing was Salic (i.e., excluding females) except the throne; in
England everything is "Salic" except the throne. Queen Elizabeth and Queen Victoria could not help their sisters. Suffra-
gettism, an absurdity in France, became a necessity in England. Mrs. Pankhurst, with all her energy, had to shock the
frequenters of clubs and taverns into restoring, by the poor
means of external, political measures, what the Puritan revolution had stolen from the women of England.

England, old England herself, being the bride of Englishmen for whom they longed during their campaigns abroad,
the individual wife became more a comrade than a bride. The
sailor wishes to find everything at home just as he left it; the
English Constitution, by virtue of "precedent," grants the man
in Singapore and Sydney the privilege of finding his country
unchanged after twenty or thirty years of absence. It always

remains "old England" in its methods, though it may have changed enormously in other respects. But the daughter of man is likely to be starved in England because she is not allowed the privilege of being new and surprising. In the feminine character, Venus Anadyomene, the foam-sprung goddess of glistening novelty, always lies hidden. Women may be young, beautiful, a good sport, gentle, pretty and "nice"; but she cannot be the Beatrice of a new vision, the muse of inspiration. There is no English Jeanne d'Arc.

The terrible letter of Jonathan Swift to Jane Waring—"I will marry you on certain conditions: First, you must be educated so that you can entertain me. Next, you must put up with all my whims, and likes and dislikes. Then you must live wherever I please. On these terms I will take you, without reference to your looks or to your income. As to the first, cleanliness is all that I require; as to the second, I only ask that it be enough."—can perhaps only be excused in the light of the fact that it was she who had proposed to him; however, he would have been less censurable had he struck Varina with his fist, or kicked her. But his mental cruelty is an extreme, comparable in France only to the cruelty of women like George Sand towards Musset or Chopin. The gentleman, before the regeneration of his type under the pressure of the French Revolution, paid for all his isolation; his independence was offset by torpor and fastidiousness. Self-adulation, the germ of death as it always is, invaded the upper classes and made them snobs and prigs. Like "Whig," the nickname for the superficial, worldly man, "Dandy," is a Scotch word, first used about 1780. An essay which was written shortly afterwards, on "the look of a gentleman," reveals that the stage of self-idolatry was near.

But after a period of hard struggle the ritual of the gentry was successfully transferred to new classes. The admiration and love of the new middle class revived the integrity of the old gentry, lest it be found unworthy of Tennyson's lines:

> "And thus he bore without abuse
> The grand old name of gentleman."

On the other hand, the circle of society was sufficiently enlarged so that its features could be revitalized. England counted about ten thousand "independent fortunes" in 1850. Nine tenths of these independent fortunes were made by middle-class men, who were accepted as ranking with the born gentleman. In his charming book, *The English, Are They Human?*, Mr. Renier has described this shift which occurred in the nineteenth century, and the loss of vigour and naïveté it involved, but without seeing that it was only the downward step from the gentry to the "gigmanity" which made the ritual of eating and drinking, love and leisure, a little unnatural and inhuman.

On the whole, the amalgamation worked quite well on the two levels of gentleman and sport, Commonwealth and Empire. But the lower classes remained outside the charmed circle of ritualism. On the eve of the proletarian revolution, after 1900, Labour, Lloyd George, and the Fabians renewed their attacks on the gentleman. Figures like Lord Curzon or Haldane or Morley impressed them as the *fin de siècle* of gentility. But in the long run the odds are not in favour of Labour or the Fabians.

The attempt of the lower classes to overthrow the secret constitution of English society does not seem very promising. For the life-span of the British Commonwealth is not yet closed: It is too deeply rooted in the divine conception of a Christian world which "lies all before us where to choose," an expression secularized by Young, in the diabolical line, "The world their field, and humankind their prey."

Nature, without secrets, rediscovered and refashioned from day to day, is the idol of the French. *Earth,* without history, time returning upon itself, is the Bolshevik dream. The English adventure is a movement toward the unknown, from a home as old as Revelation. This is the English vision of a *"world without end."*

The gentleman does not repeat nor innovate. He fights, he muddles through; and he does so because he is led from on high. Oliver Cromwell, the badly mistreated Protector of the First Commonwealth, whose statue was finally permitted, in

1906, to stand on a very, very low pedestal in front of the House of Parliament, expressed this mixed state of irrational security, of blind faith in the promises of God, when he said: "Never is a man lifted higher than when he does not know where he goes." [24]

[24] The Cardinal de Retz, in his *Mémoires*, for August, 1651, quotes the Président de Bellièvre, on Cromwell, and his own response: "'Cromwell . . . me disait un jour que l'on ne monte jamais si haut que quand l'on ne sait où l'on va.'—'Vous savez,' dis-je à M. de Bellièvre, 'que j'ai horreur de Cromwell; mais, quelque grand homme que l'on nous le prône, j'y ajoute le mépris s'il est de ce sentiment: il me parait d'un fou.'"

CHAPTER SEVEN

Germany: A Nation's Forests and the Soul's Chorale

The Christian Soldier—Personal History—Martin Luther—The Civil Servant and His Religious Party—Militarism—The Professions under Civil Law—Bound in Conscience—Prophet and King—"Your Highness"—Reform of the Churches—Why Teaching Is a Public Trust—Neither Machiavelli nor Bodinus—University Leadership—Music and Government—The Green Mountain Glade—Trunk and Branches—Goethe's Faust—Protesting Policy—Hitler—Non-Resistance—The Birthday of the Modern Constitution

THE CHRISTIAN SOLDIER.

THE ENGLISH REVOLUTION GAVE BIRTH TO A WORLD OF SEAS, WITH a silver island set in their midst, a home of sailors, missionaries, and colonial officers, that was freed from the burden of a royal army and its expression on the Continent of Europe: general conscription. The symbol of this delivery from the King's military domination by a standing army is preserved in the annual ceremonial of Parliament. To prove that Royal Prerogative has been cut to a harmless minimum, a member of the House wears the uniform of the militia on the day on which the answer to the speech from the throne is first brought up for debate. It is the duty of this M.P. in uniform to move that the Mutiny Act be passed which grants the King only six months' service from his army.

When kingship was restored in 1660, the disbanding of the army was the essential feature of the event; for it marked the progress beyond the military protectorate most illuminatingly.

The freedom from military service and the prerogative of a "War Lord" has remained ever since an outstanding feature of the national temper. As a Frenchman once put it to Rudyard Kipling: "We Continentals are more separated from your world by our compulsory service than by anything else. How can you English understand our minds if you do not realize those years of service—those years of service for us all? When we come to talk to you about life, it is like talking to children about death."

This advantage for England is vanishing fast, today. "In these days the face of England is changing so rapidly that a man does not have to reach the age of Rip Van Winkle in order to suffer Rip's experiences." [1] Or, as Rolf Gardiner put it, in his *North Sea and Baltic*, "a conservative revolution is transforming the former island into a part of the mainland." Gone are the happy days when, after a severe storm, the Londoner would laugh over the telegram: "Storm raging in Channel; Continent isolated."

With armaments in the air, with gas masks for women and children, Mars returns from the British Sea to the British Home. Military service is again a vital problem on the island itself.

Of course it is only the motherland to which it returns as something new today. Abroad, England has always relied on military service as much or more than any other nation. The efficient army and the discipline of military service which are distasteful on the British Isles, are respectable when the British fight in India. Rudyard Kipling, in his *Jungle Book,* makes the English army the symbol of a European accomplishment. He relates how natives of Afghanistan attended a review of the British army in India. The impression which the manœuvres make on the Afghans has nothing to do with England or the British in particular; but it has everything to do with Europe and the totality of Western Civilization. It runs as follows:

"Then I heard an old, grizzled, long-haired Central-Asian chief who had come down with the Amir, asking questions of a native officer:

[1] R. W. Chambers, *The Place of Saint Thomas More in English Literature and History*, p. 3, London, 1937.

" 'Now,' said he, 'in what manner was this wonderful thing done?'

"And the officer answered: 'There was an order, and they obeyed.'

" 'But are the beasts as wise as the men?' said the chief.

" 'They obey as the men do. Mule, horse, elephant, or bullock, he obeys his driver, and the driver his sergeant, and the sergeant his lieutenant, and the lieutenant his captain, and the captain his major, and the major his colonel, and the colonel his brigadier, commanding three regiments, and the brigadier his general, who obeys the Viceroy, who is the servant of the empress. Thus is it done.'

" 'Would it were so in Afghanistan!' said the chief, 'for there we obey only our own wills.'

" 'And for that reason,' said the native officer, twirling his moustache, 'your Amir, whom you do not obey, must come here and take orders from our Viceroy.' "

England remained a European country, reserving the central organization of the King's service for its maritime empire. Now this is the State, this is the meaning of "Higher" and "Upper," against which the Lower House protested desperately, but the essence of which it wisely kept for the running of its colonies. Here England relies on an art and faith that were developed, not in English self-government, but on the Continent. The universal significance of such a hierarchy is not limited to military form. In India the army is less important than the English Civil Service. And for fifty years the English government at home has increasingly reformed and enlarged its Civil Service.

PERSONAL HISTORY.

Even Americans are faced today with the problem of a bureaucracy, a brain trust, a centre of *civil prerogative.*

Now, no seed can spring from a sterile tree. Red tape, bureaucracy, brain trust, central power, are all very well for purposes of academic discussion, but they cannot produce branches, because their trunk is dry and sapless.

Without an emotional uplifting of the soul, no nation can

hand over its liberties to a new or reorganized system of government. The only basis of any radical change is radical faith. The urgent questions of a radical change in the organized work of society cannot be solved until we reach the depths of every man's innermost creed and conviction. Civil service as a purely mechanical organization will never work efficiently. To understand the real inner justification for the strict discipline of a civil service, we must turn to the German revolution; for it alone gave the civil servant a religious position in his country. In the German revolution the drab, grey life of the average bureaucrat was suddenly transformed, as if by a great volcanic eruption. Graft, bribery, the spoils-system, stain the character of the civil servant in every country which has not been touched by this great revolution. In the land of its origin, on the contrary, the civil servant became a proud, leading character, the torch-bearer of a special form of European life, an organized unit. As man he took upon himself a new duty towards his mother earth.

This revolution is the German Reformation. Unfortunately, its caricature, Henry VIII's Anglican Reformation, has detracted from it in the eyes of the British. Since Milton summoned his nation, "Ev'n to the Reforming of the Reformation itself" (*Areopagitica*), Englishmen have seldom gone deeper into the details of Lutheranism. It seems all a dark century, the sixteenth.

But the same Milton, in order to express his belief in a new age, coud find no better word than—Reformation! "Why else was this nation chosen before any other, that out of her, as out of Zion, should be proclaimed and sounded forth the first tidings and trumpet of Reformation to all Europe?"

Thus, in the midst of the terrible devastation of the Thirty Years' War (1618-1648), in 1644, Milton still used the word which had been sanctioned by Luther's nailing of his Ninety-five Theses on the door of his Prince's chapel at Wittenberg.

And there is another thing which proves the universal scope of the German Reformation. Our division of the Christian era into the darkness of the Middle Ages and the light of modern times is a Protestant creation. Luther's followers were bold enough to begin a new era, as Cromwell tried to do by dating his Great Seal "In the III year of freedom restored," and the French by the new calendar of a ten-day week.

But whereas the English and French era did not last, the German dominates all our textbooks. Later we shall find out the tricks by which French historians have changed the border-dates between modern times and the Middle Ages. Perhaps it was only by a trick that they could keep the Protestant arrangement of human history. However, the trick itself shows the impression left by the German Reformation upon all Europe. The German Reformation ventured to declare that between 600 and 1500 *"densissimæ tenebræ"* had obscured the earth. The Pope had governed as the Anti-Christ, and had poisoned the real Christian gospel. A "new learning" was begun by Luther and Melanchthon to restore the pure Pauline faith. Luther himself sometimes thought of being St. Paul *redivivus.* For four hundred years St. Paul has been the symbol of a new church, fighting Petrine Rome and popery, preaching the gospel in the mother-tongue and integrating Church and State, monasteries and hospitals, universities and schools everywhere, into one great organ of culture.

Deep and vigorous motives must have been at work when the mere reading of certain books written by a professor of theology could make men discard a nine-hundred-year-old method. "Reformation" must weigh heavier in the scales of history than "World Revolution" if we compare their achievements. It was no theologians' quarrel, no mere clergymen's dispute, but a revolution in the modern sense of the word: a breaking of all moulds, a pointing toward a new order of things, something totalitarian, universal in its aim, which had been unknown till then.

Being a Reformation of the Church, it of course took every member of the human race to be a member of this Christian Church. Its gospel restored Christianity within the Church. Luther's greatest pamphlet announced "the freedom of every Christian."

But since half of the world was "church" in those days,

the destruction of the visible church was nothing less than the reconstruction of the world.

Formally, it is easy to show what the Reformation has in common with the later revolutions. As in the others, the first period is one of upheaval. The second is a time of carelessness and arrogance, which leads to deep humiliation and abasement. Furthermore, the problem of a double start, a two-fold beginning, is very clear in the German Reformation, because Luther's religious movement and the political moves of the German princes are distinct and separate. The monk, Luther, dominated the public scene from the sensational moment when he nailed up his theses against indulgences and papal securities in 1517, up to the equally sensational event of his marriage in 1525. In that same year the princes themselves became reformers during the war against the inflamed and fanatical villagers, and remained so until the peace of religion in 1555.

During the first eight years Luther spread his gospel all over the Empire, aye, the world, and every Christian man was moved and startled. The Imperial Diets tried in vain to silence him. From 1525 on, the Empire ceased to be the centre of Luther's struggles. The various nations and territories began to articulate the right of reformation more carefully; not everybody can reform the Church. Thus Luther's religious trumpet-call made clear that Reformation of the Church was inevitable, here and now; in the later period the High Magistrates settled the question of who could and should reform the Church.

With a similar dualism, the Thirty Years' War, the time of deep mourning for reformed Germany, first ended in an external peace; only six years later did the Empire find the energy to settle the economic and juridical questions raised by this religious war: at the "Last Recess" of any imperial diet (*Recessus imperii novissimus* of 1654).

1517-1525   Luther—1648-1654—Internal Insecurity.
1525-1555   The Princes—1618-1648—External War.

The German reformers used a war-cry already familiar to the reader in its revolutionary technique. Perhaps a list will best help him to visualize this parallel.

Russia: Every proletarian a capitalist.
France: Every man of talent an aristocrat.
England: Every gentleman a king.
Germany: Every Christian a priest.

We found that these slogans presupposed a clear vision of territorial unity, of God-given borders which considerably modified the rational constitution. Every proletarian a capitalist; yes, but within one economy held together by the Communist Party. Every talent an aristocrat; yes, but within an indivisible nation. Every gentleman a king; yes, but within the United Kingdom. The real progress and the tragic bloodshed of each revolution were both caused by the paradox contained in this "yes, but." The clue to the success of the English, French and Russian revolutions was that none of them bribed the respective supporters at the price of diminishing the size of the body politic; they all reached out for a political organization bigger than anything attempted before. The Commons shook off the yoke of the Congregationalists because the Congregationalists would have dissolved the united Anglican Church. The French beheaded the Girondins because Federalism would have dissolved the central power of an individual France built up in royal Versailles. The Russians killed the Social Revolutionaries because these people loved the Russian village and would not have had the hardness of heart to sacrifice it to a united economy for all Russia.

In all these cases there is some comprehensive, uniting force —kingdom, nation, economy—which is upheld in the face of the ranters and romanticists. Something pre-existing and preciously united is reformed and transformed by the revolutionaries in order that everybody may participate in the circulation of its blood.

The same is true of the German revolution. "Every Christian a priest" is restricted by the "yes, but" only in the universal religion as it is reforming one whole territory. The German revolution killed the leaders of the local reforms, the anabaptists and peasants, ruthlessly, because their dreams would have meant an individual religion of every village. Instead, a

unified economy in Russia, a unification in France, a united
kingdom in England, a universal religion are the realistic
requirements which the great revolutions cannot give up.
Minor rebellions may pick up an arbitrary course, they may
destroy units. The majestic rhythm of the Great Revolutions
of Christianity is characterized by its lack of arbitrary additions or omissions. They never go behind what has been
achieved before. No previous accomplishment is revoked by
the Revolutions of the Faith.

MARTIN LUTHER.

The person who changed a clerical world into an era of
universal priesthood had to be a priest and a Christian himself. On the other hand, his new equation, "every Christian
a priest," had to be fought through and secured, not for a
single farm-house or a single village or town, but for the
largest units of Christendom then in existence. In those days,
this largest unit was the single State, a State the size of Rhode
Island and Providence Plantations or Saxony or Tuscany. The
priest and the Christian who brought about the German Reformation was eager to resist the "Ranters" and to establish
the State as the minimum receptacle for a universal religion.

In order to do this it was not enough for Martin Luther,
Augustinian monk and professor of theology, to marry a nun
and become a layman; unless he risked being mistaken for a
bohemian or vagabond, he had to take upon himself the yoke
of a definite allegiance. He had to become the loyal citizen of
a particular State. The way of expressing this intention and
of asking for naturalization in his days was to become the loyal
servant of a High Magistrate.

Thus, the German Reformation hinges on the personal biography of Martin Luther. In England, the theft of a word was
the clue to the ideology of its revolution. In Germany, every
realistic, material, social or political aspect of the Reformation
was veiled behind a curtain. And this curtain, rewoven year
after year by all the candidates for Chairs in Theology, was
labelled "the Life of Martin Luther." The political facts of
the high nobility's Rebellion against the Pope lie carefully

hidden under the scores of theological biographies of Luther. The new sovereignty of the secular princes, in the nation of its most glorious establishment, did not boast of its own righteousness. It borrowed its glamour from the priest who exchanged his clerical priesthood for a universal one. In other European regions, like England and France, the new political experience was soon evaluated in abstract terms like "Prerogative" and "Sovereignty." In the "Fatherland" of the Reformation, Protestantism was victorious only so long as it insisted on remaining in the shade of Luther's personal experience. Of course, this concealment of a political earthquake in the religious biography of an indivdiual had its inconveniences for the German mentality. The realistic sides of the struggle remained concealed. In Luther's life itself the social aspect was not given its proper due. Martin Luther, the civil servant, the new-born citizen of a civil State, disappeared behind the "mighty personality," the "hero," the "Great German," the "deliverer." The overstatement of his personal contribution led to an understatement with regard to his concrete social function. His will, for instance, a legal document of the highest importance, has never been analyzed. His condemnation of the peasantry's rebellion was always treated in the style of a Sunday-school argument. The great political stakes were obscured then, and in many later phases of German politics, behind personal issues, allegiances and sentimentalities.

Nevertheless, this strange subjectivism is generally recognized as the source of German strength and originality. The German Declaration of Independence is a one-man declaration; and the elements that regenerated the Church and emancipated the world were personal first and institutional later.

A chronological survey of the Reformation is divided into two halves, one giving Luther's part in it, the other showing the part played by the secular authorities, called High Magistrates.

A. LUTHER'S PART IN THE REFORMATION.

1517 Luther publishes ninety-five theses against the securities promised by the papacy to the Christian soul.

1520 He burns the Papal Bull which excommunicates him.

1521 He is outlawed by the Emperor at the Diet of Worms. His books are to be confiscated; but the princes, including the Archbishop of Mayence, Chancellor of the Empire, frightened by Luther's popularity, refuse to execute the Emperor's edict.

1524 The universities and the princes determine to meet to debate upon the Reformation. The Emperor forbids this transformation of the Imperial Diet into a council of the Church.

1525 Luther, the monk, is married to a nun. Henceforth his own legal status and that of his family remains doubtful.

1541 He makes his last will without regard to the laws of the Empire or the Church or the land, requesting the affirmation of his prince as its only guarantee.

1546 He dies before open war breaks out.

B. THE PART OF THE SECULAR AUTHORITY, CALLED "HIGH MAGISTRATES," IN THE REFORMATION.

1525 The war against the supporters of native resistance and local military traditions is successfully carried through by the secular princes.

1526 The princes "protest" the decrees of the Empire against the Reformation. Hence "Protestants."

1530 The princes present to the Emperor the creed composed by the theologians, and form a religious party on an equal footing with the Emperor.

1546-1547 The Emperor crushes the Protestant League.

1552 The princes ally themselves with France and defeat the Emperor.

1555 The estates of the realm are empowered to reform their respective territories. Peace of religion.

THE CIVIL SERVANT AND HIS RELIGIOUS PARTY.

The civil servant is the result of the mutual permeation of Luther's prophecy of the universal Reformation and the princes' carrying out of their special reformation.

The civil servant is the man who first hears the prophetic voice of universal truth, and who later enters the service of a secular authority to carry out his part in the Reform.

In a system based on civil service no brain-trust governs, no pure intellectuals meddle in the affairs of government. The scorn of Andrew Jackson and his followers for a high-brow officialdom does not obtain in Germany, the native land of efficient civil service. Its system was more subtle; and I think in a period when efficiency and planning are current slogans in America, and hard thinking and methodical reconstruction are inevitable in England, it is worthwhile to study the problem of a paternal government more carefully.

Let us state the general principle first: any German who intended to go into government service underwent two completely different influences during his life. Both influences were exercised by two sovereign jurisdictions independent of each other, and their mutual sovereignty guaranteed the relative intellectual liberty and reliability of the individual who had passed through the two jurisdictions of a teaching church and a listening government.

The second jurisdiction was, of course, the sovereignty of a High Magistrate, one of the hundreds of principalities of the German Federation. At the beginning of the German Reformation there were many High Magistrates of many different kinds in the German part of the Holy Roman Empire. For example, there were:

7 Electors (Palatinate, Saxony, Brandenburg, Bohemia, Treves, Mayence and Cologne)
50 Archbishops and Bishops
70 Abbots and Abbesses of the Empire
31 Secular princes
128 Counts of the Empire
81 Free cities of the Empire

As late as 1750, in the Germany of Schiller and Goethe, Frederick the Great and Maria Theresa, there were about three hundred and fifty princely houses.

Each of these authorities occupied a different rank in the Holy Roman Empire. As in the Norman Realm of England, the hierarchy of this empire descended the scale in subtle gradations. The ladder began at the top with the Emperor; under him were placed the Electors spiritual and temporal, like cardinals under a pope; then came

the spiritual Princes,
the secular Princes,
the Abbots and Abbesses,
the Counts,
the Cities.

The Reformation changed all these dignitaries into peers in a new order of government. The old gradations were no longer valid in matters of religion. For the first time in history, the great prince and the little count, the diocese of Cologne on the lower Rhine and the small district of the Abbots of Säckingen on the upper Rhine, became equals in their responsibility for the religious salvation of their subjects. The earthquake of the Reformation, which has long been treated by Catholic historians as a real revolution, turned the hierarchy of the Holy Empire and its Diets, with Emperor, Princes Electors, Princes Spiritual, Princes Temporal, Prelates, Counts, Barons, Knights, Cities and finally Imperial valleys and villages, into a federation of peers, all of equal rank, that is to say, into the "German Nation" embodied by its some hundreds of High Magistrates.

Of course, these High Magistrates were not equals in power, in military force or in wealth. The Emperor himself, for example, held a ring or bulwark of countries surrounding Germany proper, and these he governed as a hereditary prince. He was Count of Holland, and Marquis of Namur, Duke of the Hennegau and Brabant, Landgrave of Alsace, Count of Breisgau, Count of Hapsburg and Kiburg, and the Thurgow in Switzerland, Count in Bregenz and of the Tyrol, Prince of Brixen and Trent, Marquis of Styria, Archduke of Upper and Lower Austria, King of Bohemia and Apostolic Majesty of Hungary, Marquis of Moravia, Duke of Silesia, Grand Duke of Transylvania, Lord of the Cities of Trieste and Cattaro, King of Dalmatia, etc.

All this was contained in the Great House of Austria which for many centuries protected Germany proper on the west, south and southeast, and especially against the Turks, who twice besieged the Emperor's capital, Vienna, in 1529 and in 1683.

Compared with this Imperial crown and mantle, embracing the heart of the German countries, a Prince von Hohenlohe or an Imperial Baron von Stein did not count materially. But morally, for the sake of the highest good of mankind, these petty Lords were peers of the Emperor. In matters of religion any High Magistrate could not only raise his voice as freely as any Christian, but could act like a pope. His resolutions in matters of Reform did not depend upon the approval of Emperor and Diet. The individual High Magistrate became responsible individually, and did not need the permission or dispensation of any superior to act as he believed he was bound in conscience to act. The result of the Reformation was the German Liberty, the *"Teutsche Libertaet,"* which consisted in the fact that any High Magistrate was bound to shape his own conscience in matters of religion without depending on the authority of pope or bishop or emperor.

Every High Magistrate became a pope in his own big or little territory. For most of the territories, because of their very smallness, the Reformation was a spiritual, religious and political movement; it was not a military or belligerent enterprise at all. On the contrary, the princes of central Germany, because they felt protected against wars from outside by the Emperor's colossal ring of countries, took up the Reformation in order to consolidate the administration of their own territories. Reformation to them was a revolution for the purpose of co-ordinating all ecclesiastical institutions under the jurisdiction of one High Magistrate. The outcome was the creation of *civil* government and a civil service, to replace *ecclesiastical* government and the employment of the clergy in political office. The word *"clerc"* (clerk) can still be used in French and English. In German the word "clergy" was extirpated, because in Germany the civil servant appeared as a religious rival of the clergy. The civil power and the Civil Law became sacred weapons against ecclesiastical power and against legislation by Canon Law. The old Latin word *"civis,"* used by the middle class in France as the basis of their *civilisation,* was used in

Germany to build up a civilian order. What progress this was can only be felt when we realize how we today think of such an order of things as natural and proper. In our minds everyone is first and foremost a civilian; only exceptionally, in cases of emergency or war, will men join the militia or the army and so put themselves under martial law. Ordinarily a man looks upon it as his birthright to live under the Civil Law. Now this was completely unknown before the Reformation. In the Middle Ages a man was either a layman or a clergyman. In the first case he was governed by martial, feudal and canon law. His marriage was regulated by the canons of the Church, his inheritance by the customs of the land, his trade and his contracts by the king's justice. There was no Civil Law and no Common Law in the Middle Ages. Common Law, the pride of England, is, as we have already seen, a seventeenth-century invention which replaced the Continental Civil Law. The Reformation abolished the presupposition that a man was a warrior first, and only secondly a peaceful citizen. It created one fundamental civil law for all the inhabitants of one territory and all the subjects of one High Magistrate, a law which protected them from birth to death against all the threats of popes or papal legates or bishops, guaranteed them equity against the cruel laws of the land, and delivered them from the expensive decisions of Roman courts.

Civil Law was the pride of every High Magistrate, because it meant, for the first time in the Occident, the unification of a man's civil position. The High Magistrates took from their subjects' shoulders the burden of being primarily soldiers, and only exceptionally and occasionally civilians. By concentrating the duty of defence in their own hands, they made the inhabitants of their territories free to give most of their time to the works of peace.

MILITARISM.

The new situation was emphasized by the borrowing, from the inexhaustible resources of ancient Latinity, of new words for the warrior: the words "militia" and "military." Military forces are the forces of a civilized country, and by that very token they are no longer essential to the rights of the individual! Every subject is under the lawful protection of the government, even though he is not a feudal knight or tenant. The modern world was created by the High Magistrates, who cared for their subjects as civilians and provided a militia only as a second and secondary group, to protect the main body of civilians.

The High Magistrate, when he created a civil law and a civil service, separated his generals from his civil servants and made them generals pure and simple, without any claim to be made governors, either then or later. How strange and surprising this division of labour was and is, is shown by the lives of George Washington, the Duke of Wellington, of Jackson, Taylor and Grant who were both Generals and Presidents, of MacMahon in France and Hindenburg in Germany. So natural is it for a nation to entrust political leadership to a successful general.

But the Reformation abolished this confusion. From Luther's time down to 1890, ordinarily no German general was invested with civil power! Hindenburg was a great exception to the rule. German militarism consisted in the strict exclusion of generals from politics. This cardinal contribution of Germany to democracy and civilization was not adopted by the democratic countries.

Only one general ever tried to become a political leader in Germany, namely Wallenstein. It was at the very blackest hour of the Counter-Reformation, when all the achievements of the Lutheran Reformation might have been regarded as lost, that Wallenstein, the successful general of the Emperor, thought of making peace as he had made war. Instead of a prince governing *with* an army, he would have become the Cromwell type, who became a prince because he *commanded* the army. Wallenstein was stopped immediately. He was assassinated in 1634 by orders from Vienna, and the supremacy of the High Magistrate over the Field Marshal, of justice over power, was restored. Barely as the victory was won, it was final, because it was won at the weakest and most despondent hour of German Protestantism. The victory over Wallenstein should be compared to the one vote by which the Third Republic was carried in France in 1875. It was decisive because it happened at the zero hour of revolutionary faith. In 1634, as in 1874, the result of the previous Revolution had already become an objective, living reality that was stronger than the physique or morale of exhausted and depressed men.

THE PROFESSIONS UNDER THE CIVIL LAW.

Luther himself, the leader of the Reformers, can serve as a good illustration of the new realm created by the civil law of the High Magistrate. Martin Luther had been a miner's son in the county of Mansfeld. He, with his family, lived, therefore, according to Saxon tribal law. In 1509 he entered a monastery. Now, a monk died to the world and its jurisdiction. A monk had no property, no affinity, no relationship in the *mundus,* the world outside. He took a new name, and he was ruled, not by Saxon law, but by the religion of his order, the monastic rule laid down in the charter of the monastery and "professed" by the entering novice. This particular monk entered one of the hundred different monasteries in Thuringia and Saxony which lay in the territory of his prince, the Elector of Saxony and Landgrave of Thuringia. This prince had a domain one ninth as large as England—a normal size for a state in the sixteenth century. Parts of six different bishoprics were included in his territory. The pope in Rome, the superiors of the hundred monasteries, the archbishops controlling the six bishops, and finally five of the six bishops themselves, lived outside the prince's jurisdiction. He had to transact and negotiate with Mayence and Magdeburg, with Rome and Bamberg, to settle any religious matter at home.

The monasteries held a great deal of land, as much as one third of his territory, exempt from taxation. Each one had a "religion" of its own, granted by a pope. Religion in those days was a special form of monastic life by which a group of people had chosen to live together. Each order claimed its special religion as the one way to holiness. Hence religion was a source of rivalry, disorder and confusion.

The only way out for a prince who, like Luther's prince, Frederick the Wise, was also a devout Christian, was to found a university. If he could compel the clergy and the bailiffs, priests and parsons, all to study in his territory, then a certain co-ordination seemed possible.

In the shabby and sandy region of Wittenberg—a town of three hundred and eighty-two citizens in 1512—a university had been founded in the year 1502. Luther was a professor there, and since, as a university, it stood under the patronage of Emperor and Pope, Luther's position as a professor was regulated by Canon and Roman Law. This monk, who had been a Saxon and who had joined the "religion" of an order, was now involved in canonistic and imperial regulations. But, after all, the prince who had founded Wittenberg paid Luther's salary. This foundation was the apple of his eye, and the rights or wrongs of any member of it involved his own rights and privileges as well. The future of his administration might be determined by the prosperous or unprosperous growth of the university.

Luther did not interest the Elector as a personality. They were not friends. We are told that, in spite of the importance and vast scope of Luther's actions and the smallness of the country, the Elector never exchanged a word with Luther. The whole relation between prince and professor, High Magistrate and Reformer, was, as this lack of personal intercourse shows, completely abstract and objective.

While in this situation, the professor, Luther, lost the support of the pope because he attacked his power of dispensation. He was banished; and when he and his students went outside the walls of Wittenberg to burn the papal bull, they created a new order, a world which had not existed until that day. They had the courage to live under the curse of Rome and under the threats of all its minions.

One year later Luther was summoned to the Imperial Diet. The fetters of Canon Law had been broken so successfully that even so strict a Catholic as the young Emperor, Charles V, could not venture to act as his forefathers had done. All previous Emperors had thought of themselves as bailiffs of the Church. They had defended the Church and made war on anyone who attacked it. When Magister John Huss had as-

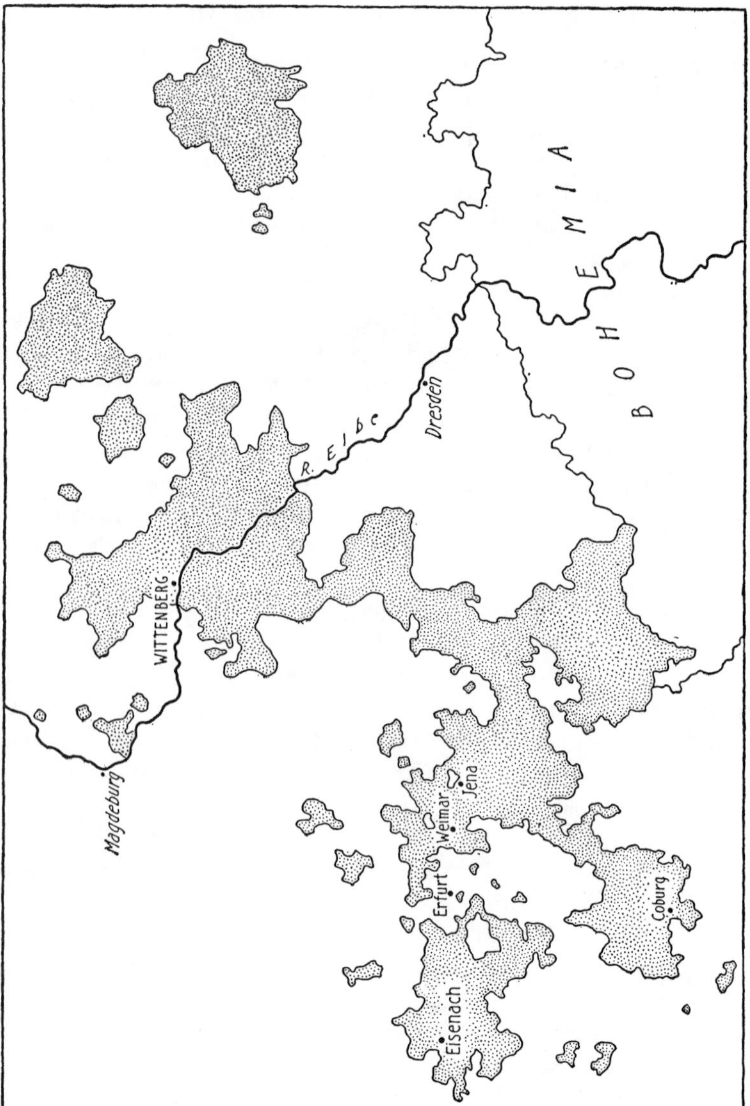
BOHEMIA
R. Elbe
Dresden
WITTENBERG
Magdeburg
Jena
Weimar
Erfurt
Eisenach
Coburg
FULDA

THE CASE FOR

These two maps cover exactly the same territory and indicate the conflict
outline) held jurisdiction of some part

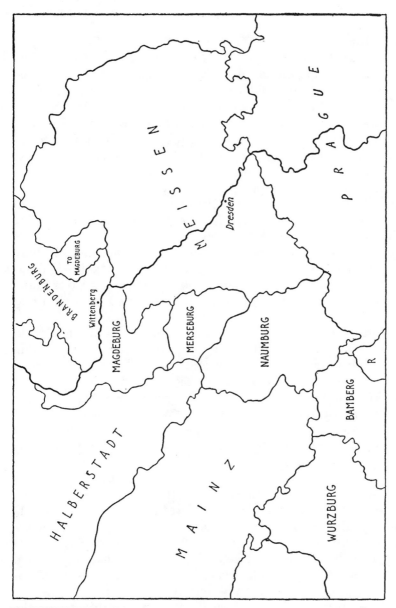

WITTENBERG

between ecclesiastical and secular authority. The ten Dioceses (shown in
of the land of the Elector of Saxony.

sailed it, and when the Œcumenical Council of Constance had condemned Huss in 1415, the Emperor Sigismund had risked his own claim to the throne of Bohemia and executed the judgment of the Council. Fifty years of terrible warfare, 1419-1471, had followed the carrying out of this anathema. The desperate Hussite wars were the fruit of the ill-omened day when John Huss looked down at the old hag piling wood about his feet and exclaimed: *"O Sancta Simplicitas"*—O Holy Simplicity!

The tragedy of Huss had been caused by Sigismund's readiness to break his Imperial promise of safe conduct, because the Council had outlawed Huss as a heretic. A convicted heretic could have no legal defence in this world. In Luther's day the martyrdom of John Huss was not forgotten. A queer prophecy went the rounds: "When one hundred years have revolved you shall answer God and me." In 1515 a neighbour of the Duke of Saxony, a count who owned certain silver mines between Saxony and Bohemia, had medals struck off with that legend.

Luther profited from this century-old scar. Charles V did not wish to commit himself as Sigismund had committed himself. Therefore the Emperor and his Diet usurped a privilege never before granted to the secular arm, but now sought by kings and princes everywhere, the privilege of passing on the decisions of the Roman Church. With the bloodshed and devastation brought about by the Hussites before their very eyes, Emperor and Diet refused to act as mere executioners for the Church. Luther was invited to explain his position at a meeting of the Diet. The secular arm showed its desire to inquire into the proceedings of the spiritual arm; a question which seemed to have been settled when Gregory VII successfully excommunicated an Emperor and Innocent IV successfully deposed the Emperor Frederick II of Sicily, came up in a new form. The new principle was that the Church could not bring troubles, warfare, civil war, upon kingdoms and empires without even asking their consent.

The question of the Reformation was really this: Could the High Magistrate refuse his consent when the Church commanded him to act? Could the High Magistrate doubt and test the constitutionality of a measure of the Church? Under the Common Law any judge can test the constitutionality of a law. That was exactly the problem of the Reformation. Could the High Magistrate examine the constitutionality of a papal bull or a Christian custom or a Canon law?

The Diet of Worms tried a halfway solution. Luther was summoned. He was in high glee: having defied Canon Law, and having lost his Saxon law, he thought Imperial Law would protect him. He asked for a legal pronouncement of the united Diet on his orthodoxy. Now this was more than he could get. These laymen, knights and feudal lords, and even the Emperor himself, had never claimed to be theologians! How could or should the Estates of the Empire, fat abbots or illiterate counts, suddenly pass judgment on the subtle writings of a monk about purgatory and hell, salvation and worship? Luther's hope that the military hierarchy of the Diet would close the gap which the burning of the papal bull had made in his legal status, proved chimerical. He was examined at Worms, it is true. But the Emperor limited the trial to the question of whether or not Luther had written all his alleged heresies.

The difficulties of Charles V are still our difficulties today. Censorship of movies or plays, controversies between fundamentalists and evolutionists, prohibition of books or news, occur daily. The function of the papacy has been taken over by nationalistic priests or Communistic fanatics or elderly society ladies. And though the authorities are multiple, the result in any particular jurisdiction, in Russia or Tennessee, Italy or Germany, is as final and suffocating as it was in 1521!

Religion, the real formation of an inner life in protest against the conventional despotism of society, is never safe; it is always a challenge. We may congratulate ourselves, therefore, that the Diet of Worms arrived at no solution. For in matters of conscience and belief the clear-cut black and white distinctions of those in authority are likely to be tyrannical. Conscience gains whenever the men in power are doubtful and reluctant to act.

When Luther exclaimed: "Yes, I wrote the offending, in-

criminating texts. Here I stand, and can do no other," the Diet,
that high pyramid of feudal lords and vassals, was at a loss.
Surely their assembly could not judge heresies. But to persecute their own subjects with fire and sword, as the Hussites
had been persecuted, seemed equally impossible.

When the Emperor tried to impose on the princes of the
Empire the execution of the pope's ban, the first of these
princes, the Archbishop of Mayence, Chancellor and Keeper
of the Great Seal, refused his Seal and signature; and later he
wrote in a letter to the Emperor that he could not carry out
the order without the joint action of all his neighbour-princes.
An archbishop of the church, in his capacity as a secular ruler,
could not set fire to his own house. Now this archbishop was
one of those who had ecclesiastical authority in the territories
of Luther's prince. The weakness of these ecclesiastical rulers
was obviously their secular power. They dared not put into
effect as High Magistrates what they had to approve as Lords
Spiritual. The neighbour of this archbishop, the Duke of Saxony, was in a much simpler position. The archbishop at least
owed special allegiance to the pope. If even he shrank from
unloosing a civil war, the Elector had still greater reason to
do so.

But there was another side to the question. Frederick the
Wise had in his university a stronghold of reformation and
control over a third of the wealth and the area of his territory. As long as this university could be denounced as heretical
by the pope whenever it so pleased him, the university had
to be closed or opened whenever Rome intervened. The only
weapon the Duke had against his one hundred and six different "religions" and religious authorities would have been
knocked out of his hands.

Since universities were not old in Germany, the question
was a new question indeed. But a prince who cherished his
university as the apple of his eye could not admit the right
of anyone else to pass judgment on its orthodoxy, since its very
raison d'être was to check other peoples' (that is to say, foreign-
clerical) influences over his territory.

Charles V perceived this obstacle. In framing his Edict of

Worms he gave the right of censorship in all matters of religion, not to the bishops, but to the theological faculty of the universities. The Emperor himself thus implied a kind of exemption and sovereign privilege for the theological faculties of the universities. They were appointed as acting censors, and nobody else could officially rebuke them. This regulation in the Emperor's Writ outweighed his approval of the pope's decision in respect to Luther's past actions. For the future, men like Luther who, after all, was a member of a faculty, were acknowledged as competent judges of orthodoxy, public morals, and Christian principles.

Luther's prince, therefore, was not protecting Luther as a personal friend; he was standing for the right of a High Magistrate to harbour a sovereign university in his territories.

All German Catholics and Protestants were completely unanimous on this point. In 1524 the Diet and the Imperial Vicar, the Roman King Ferdinand, brother of Charles V, agreed on a solution which would have enacted the sovereignty of the universities into a Law of the Empire. A special form of Diet was proposed, to which princes and universities should send their envoys. This would have been a strange mixture of a Diet and a National Council: the professors and the war-lords would have met on equal terms. This idea had, in fact, been conceived as early as 1460.

The plan failed in 1524 as it had in 1460. Charles V saw immediately what a hopeless confusion it might bring about, and shut the door on the experiment. The professors did not meet with the Diet. From that time on, every prince had to decide for himself whether he preferred to defend his university and its decisions and teachings in matters of religion, or to obey the judgments of pope and bishops.

This decision was not very difficult. He who had to deal with several bishops or orders in his territory, dignitaries whose religious foundations and jurisdictions had their centre outside his own territory, would be inclined to defend his own right of control. As a High Magistrate he would claim or usurp the right to cry his professor up as a Reformer or down as a heretic. Princes whose territories included cathedral towns were inclined to compromise with pope and bishops. The Duke of Saxony or the Elector of Hesse could not make the same concession. Wittenberg and Marburg, Jena and Helmstedt, became the centres of the new learning because, for large parts of Saxony, Thuringia, Hesse and Brunswick, the Episcopal See was a foreign See.

The Imperial Law could not protect Luther; the law of the land did not apply to him as a monk; Canon Law had put its ban upon him. No one but the High Magistrate, who wished to protect his university, could endow the members of this university with a new legal status.

In 1525 Luther married a nun. With Katherine of Bora he founded a family. Both man and wife in this marriage were not only without law, but outlawed. The High Magistrate alone could supply something like a legal standing for the thousands of nuns and monks who returned to the world and for Luther's children, who could not inherit anything from a monk's and a nun's household. It was pathetic for any ruler to see the despondency of these thousands and tens of thousands who were deprived of all law and legitimacy and longed for a new status as civilians.

BOUND IN CONSCIENCE.

The problem could be solved only if the High Magistrate could decide how much of the Canon Law should remain a part of the Civil Law, in his territory. The protection of the university led inevitably to the conclusion that certain chapters of Canon and Imperial Law could be abolished by the prince's decision, that a High Magistrate might find himself *bound in conscience* to supplement the law of the land by his own initiative. In an emergency which demands immediate action, without time for discussion, the government of a nation is obliged to initiate and act on its own responsibility.

This prerogative of any government to act in times of war, of rebellion, of famine, of earthquake is an established principle. The English, fighting the king's prerogative, stripped "prerogative" of its innocent and necessary character. We can spare "fervent democrats" the use of the word. As a matter

of fact, in the country of its origin, it never was classified
among the rights of the prince but among his duties. Since
all good Christians wished to mobilize the princes against the
abuses in the Church, they told the princes that they were
bound in conscience to do something about these scandals. In
politics, it is more fruitful to claim duties than privileges. The
High Magistrate was in duty bound to act in this religious
emergency. The pressure of circumstance weighed on his conscience. Although I think that no other expression gives a
better description of the "general welfare clause" for any government, I don't think that the terms of German Protestantism
can be resuscitated. But we cannot do without the thing itself.

If it were not for emergencies, if it were not for war and
the dangers of life, little initiative in government would be
needed. In all these cases, "government by talk" would be no
government at all. The government has to decide; and he who
decides what has to be done is the government. One, or a few,
must command in cases of emergency, and the rest must obey.
Government by the people is a good expression when you wish
to surround the executive with safeguards and controls, but
all this is torn like a thread the minute a real emergency
occurs. Then the prerogative of the ruler stands up alone
and isolated in all its glory, power and monstrosity. It is brutal,
it is cruel, it is diabolical; but without it the world would
relapse into chaos. For the emergency is here, before us, among
us, around us. The crisis shuts the banks, ridicules the pleas
of creditors in courts and the humanitarian effort to educate
people in jails. The bankers have no money, the debtors have
no cash, and the community has so many unemployed that
their need comes first, far ahead of the objectionable fellows
in jail.

In a case of war or real emergency the normal life, the very
existence of the best, most energetic stock of the population
is imperilled. The withered leaves of the tree can be cared for
in peaceful times. Government stays in the background; private
initiative spreads and helps the poor, the sick, the abnormal,
the weak, to reach the general standard. In normal times the
prerogative descends to individuals. They cultivate with par-

ticular care the fading leaves of the tree, they bring back individuals to normality.

But what about a loss of the very standards for normality? In times like the Great War or the depression one begins to doubt everything. Is life worthwhile? Is a man out of work still a man? What is it all about? Why found a family which you can no longer educate for any definite profession or denomination, because there are no definite professions or denominations left?

These are the times to try men's souls, because what we feel is not so much the external pain or attack or danger, but a worm at the root, eating our faith, killing the seed of love and conviction in our hearts.

In such times the prerogative of a leader is indispensable. Without his iron grip on the country all standards would become debatable, doubtful and dissolved. The dilution of faith caused by the emergency forces upon the leader the responsibility of uttering the cry of alarm and commanding, brutally and harshly.

We can even say that he who commands efficiently in such times is or makes himself the leader, even though legal procedure may not take account of him. Timely prerogative creates and restores actual government, legalizes conquest and force. To be sure, the legitimation of brute force is never to be found in its external success. Tyranny remains tyranny, and iniquity is never bleached into the genuine white of sacred authority. Nay, the test of domination is not "success" in an abstract sense, that of a man's being called Emperor or President or leader by intimidated slaves. It is *the success in this emergency,* and in this particular emergency only. In one special and definite emergency the new government will rise or the old government will be regenerated. Its test, then, is this particular emergency. If it succeeds in its fight against this enemy, this dilution of faith and standards, this famine, people will feel gratified and support or tolerate it in spite of all its other faults.

Now the curious thing in the history of Christianity is that the primitive emergency which gave rise to the modern state was not an economic emergency. We today are sure that economic forces pull all the wires. Washington was the richest man in the colonies, the Federalists speculated in Western land, the Whigs owned ecclesiastical estates, and the French middle class wished to exploit the farmers. This is all true, but no truer than the fact that economics is part of all our lives every day. Bread and butter is an everyday question. For that very reason it is not the permanent question of history, because history selects one or the other everyday question and makes it the centre of attention for a certain time. History is the passing from *one* question to *another,* the putting of different questions at different times.

Because of the very fact that economics is so important all the time, it cannot be *the* question for every period. History would not be history but a recurrent mechanism if it were one and the same question which raised human fury to the pitch of war or revolution in every age. We vary, the seasons vary, mankind varies in its furies, passions, aims and ends, and the emergencies against which we need government vary likewise.

The secular state of the Reformation was the result of an *emergency* in religion and law. The monk and the nun relied on someone's prerogative to give them back their rights of citizenship, of normality. He who had the power, and who used that power in order to make their situation regular, was bound to be hailed as their sword of justice, righteous governor, and true leader toward prosperity and happiness.

The Reformation discovered the marvellous comfort that a powerful prerogative can give to a world which is troubled in conscience and which is losing its accepted standards of clergy and laymen, monks and indulgences.

On the prince and the High Magistrate centred all the enthusiasm of the Reformers of the Church, because the High Magistrate alone remained as a beacon on the ocean of life. The visible church once attacked in its power of binding and loosing, the great flood of disorder inundated a world, which, only a year before Luther's theses, had seemed completely clear and well-organized. The canons of the Church had dealt with everything on this earth. The organization of the Middle Ages was complicated, it was most refined; but it was clear and safe for the individual. Good and evil were known quantities.

The Reformation overturned all values, by denying the distinction between clergy and laymen, between a security granted by the pope and any other worldly security. Luther refused to believe that any clergy could influence hell or heaven. Says Luther in his Ninety-five Theses:

THESIS 8: All paragraphs of penitence are valid for life, not for death. It must clearly have been the Holy Ghost in the Pope who told him to make allowance, in all his laws, for our last hour and cases of emergency.

THESIS 27: It smells of the ways of men when preachers pretend that the soul enters heaven as soon as the vendor of indulgences gets his money.

THESIS 32: Whoever teaches that we can buy our salvation by any letter of indulgence will go to hell with all his *sibling*.

THESIS 79: It is blasphemy when anybody mistakes the visible cross on the armour of a crusader for the Cross of Christ.

THESIS 16: Hell, Purgatory and Heaven must be like Despair, Semi-Despair and Security. No one of them can be given to anybody from outside, by a visible remedy.

Luther's final admonition was: *"Exhortandi sunt Christiani ut caput suum, Christum, per pœnas, mortes, infernosque sequi studeant ac sic magis per multas tribulationes intrare cælum quam per securitatem pacis confidant."* This exhortation to the Christians, against the love of security and in behalf of an enduring state of insecurity, reads like a Bolshevist pronunciamento against bourgeois security. With one stroke of the pen it annihilated all that pleasant structure of security which we love to piece together like a mosaic, counting over the examinations we have passed, our marriage and our children, our books, our friends, our house and our car, and figuring that after all we have done pretty well and gathered together what a man should gather during his life.

The somewhat deeper and more serious civilization of the Middle Ages had asked less what cars or books a man owned than what good works he had performed as a public-spirited man. He had gained some comfort, say, from building a hospital, from founding a school or from going to Rome or Jerusalem on a pilgrimage. In this way the terrible debt of man to his Creator seemed to be redeemable in instalments. And how much is the situation of the modern man different except that we are on the cruder level of instalments on a radio or a car?

Luther destroyed the belief in the sense of this slow, methodical progress toward salvation. "All or nothing," was his war cry. We cannot win battles against God by isolated actions. Either He has us—and then nothing belongs to us, nothing is owned by us, but He leads, governs, commands what we shall do—or we are completely lost, and no percentage of "good actions" will interest Him or save us.

PROPHET AND KING.

In March, 1522, with the Imperial Edict of Worms over his head, with the other Saxon Duke, George of Leipzig, raging against Lutheranism, with the ranters in Wittenberg running mad with iconoclastic radicalism, and he himself kept by his prince in the Wartburg near Eisenach, Luther suddenly left his hiding place. He explained his step to his frightened Prince-Elector in a letter which I insert here in extenso; for it is the most general statement that can be made of the relations between an invisible Church and the visible State.

In the abstract constitutional era of modern times, the general character of the letter, with its "I" and "Your Grace," its apparent character of a missive from one individual to another, is a hindrance to its understanding. In point of fact, the real duel is between Church and State, soul and power, man and big business. I should like to direct the reader in each case to translate the "I" of Luther into the sovereign claims of any church or inspiration of genius, and the "Grace" of the prince into the sovereignty of any government, be it in Washington, Ottawa, or London. Then, through the old pattern of style, the permanent truth and external conflict seem to me well stated, even for our modern times.

"Grace and peace of God, our Father, and our Lord Jesus Christ, and my most humble service. Serene Highborn Elector, most gracious prince: Your Grace's letter and reflections reached me Friday night as I was just about to leave the Wartburg for Wittenberg on horseback Saturday morning. That Your Grace intends the best needs neither acknowledgment nor witness in my eyes, for by all human inquiry I am assured of the same; that I too intend well, I trust I know from a higher source than human inquiry. But with that alone nothing is accomplished.

"I perceived from Your Grace's letter that my letter shocked Your Grace a little, in that I recommended to you more wisdom. But I have dismissed the thought, for I am confident that Your Grace knows my heart too well to suppose I wished to belittle Your Grace's renowned wisdom. [In fact, the Elector was surnamed the Wise.] For I hope my heart clings ever to the love and inclination which I have always sincerely and without hypocrisy discovered toward Your Grace more than toward any other Prince or Magistrate.

"What I wrote was written with the care of comforting Your Grace and not in my behalf, for of that I took no thought. I wrote only by reason of the troubles in Wittenberg, which sprung from our friends' great dishonouring of the Gospel. I feared this would cause Your Grace much pain.

"I myself was so distressed that, were I not assured the pure gospel was with us, I might have desponded of our case. All that has happened to my pain in this cause was as chaff and nothing. I would gladly have redeemed it with my life, because it was done in such a wise that we cannot justify it either before God or before the world. Yet it rests on my shoulders, and especially on the Holy Gospel. This makes me sick at heart. Therefore my letter did not purpose to treat of my own affairs; its intent was only to desire Your Grace not to look at the devil's countenance that appears in this game. Such an admonition, if it be not helpful to Your Grace, yet it was necessary for me to give it.

"As for my own business, my gracious Lord, I answer in this way. Your Grace knows, or if he does not know, let him be informed now, that I have the Gospel not from men, but from Heaven alone, through our Lord, Jesus Christ, in order that I might (and shall in the future) call myself His servant and evangelist. That I have offered myself for inquiry and trial was done, not as professing any doubt on my side, but in voluntary humility, to attract others. But since I see that my excess of humbleness has brought humiliation upon the Gospel, and that the devil pleases to take the whole when I give him so much as a hand's breadth, I am brought by the force of my conscience to do otherwise. I satisfied Your Grace by yielding this year, for the service of Your Grace. For the devil knows very well it was not through fear that I yielded. He saw my heart well when I entered Worms, and that though I had seen as many devils taking aim at me as there were tiles on the roofs, yet I would have sprung right upon them with joy.

"Now Duke George is much less than one single devil; and since the Father of bottomless compassion has made us joyful masters over all devils and over death, and has given us so great trust in Him that we dare call Him our dearly beloved Father, Your Grace can well conceive that it would be a great shame to such a Father if we should so little trust in Him as not to remain also masters of Duke George's anger. I know that if things were in Duke George's city of Leipzig as they are now in our city of Wittenberg, I would ride into it though it rained Duke Georges for a week, and though each of them were nine times more fierce than he.

"This is written to Your Grace that Your Grace may know I am coming to Wittenberg under a much higher protection than the Prince-Elector's. I have no mind to ask for Your Grace's protection; nay, I hold that I could protect Your Grace more than he could protect me. Moreover, if I knew that Your Grace could and would protect me, I would not come. In this, no sword can direct nor help; God alone must act in this matter, without all care and seeking.

"Therefore he who believes most will protect most; and because I feel that Your Grace is still weak in the faith, I cannot by any means think of Your Grace as the man who could protect or save me."

The voice of the prophet speaking to the kings of Israel, the voice of Paul speaking before the governors of Rome, was made a public institution of the German nation when Luther offered Frederick his protection. Thomas Paine offering George Washington his protection would seem ridiculous. Victor Hugo in 1870 accomplished nothing when he challenged the King of Prussia to a duel in these words: "Because, as he is a great Monarch, so I, Victor Hugo, am a great poet, and therefore his equal." But Luther, believing more strongly than the Elector who, being weak in the faith, had nothing but his secular power—Luther's voice became a national institution for twenty, forty, eighty millions of people, and a need and necessity for the rest of the world. A college professor in America, an Oxford don, is certainly no leader in his community by virtue of his position; in Germany, by the queer contrast between an immense nation and hundreds of High Magistrates, the universities became the heirs of the bishops' chair, the cathedra. The professor's chair was called *"Katheder."* These Katheders became a churchlike institution, like the Commons in England. The French historian, Ernest Lavisse, wrote long ago that universities were national battlegrounds in Germany. He was right.

In 1542 Doctor Luther wrote his last will and testament. Here again his faith is boundless. His authority in the beyond gives him authority in this world. Avoiding all formulas of human or Canon or Saxon Law, he exclaims: "Lastly, I beg of everybody, though in this deed or testimonial I make no use of legal forms and words (wherefor I have had good cause), that I may have leave to be that person which I really am, namely a *public person* known both in heaven and on earth and in hell, and having so much of respect or authority that more trust and belief may be put in me than in a notary. For seeing that God the father of all mercy hath entrusted unto me, poor damned unworthy miserable sinner, the Gospel of His dear Son, and hath made me, kept me, and found me true and faithful therein, so that many in this world have accepted the same because of me and hold me for a teacher of the truth, notwithstanding the pope's ban and the wrath of emperors, kings, princes, priests, yes, and all the devils; then I ought much more to be trusted in these smaller matters, forasmuch especially as I here give my hand, which is well enough known, in the hope it will suffice if it may be said and proved, this is Doctor Martinus Luther (who is God's notary and witness in His Gospel), his earnest and well-considered intent, as proved by his own hand and seal, passed and given on the day of Epiphany 1542."

The will corroborates our sketch of the balance of power in a Lutheran government. It was for these smaller matters that the prophet had to ask a prince's favour in the visible world. In God's Kingdom he was a public person. The prince, for whose support the prophet was concerned, could do no more than appropriate his fund of faith, power and authority to the uses of the visible world, of territory and policy.

"YOUR HIGHNESS."

Whoever knows the terrible fears of men knows that they will do anything to buy security. We are so tormented by fears, the pains of a troubled heart are so agonizing, that we will pay any tribute to the wonder-worker whose sorceries mitigate our anxiety. The standards of our spiritual advisers vary widely. The sorcerer may bear different names; he may be a black magician, an astrologist, a psychoanalyst, a clergyman or a medical man. Luther certainly attacked the purest one of all, the real and sincere Christian priest. In breaking the power of the best and purest type of priest, he broke down all the lower grades of priesthood or sorcery as well.

The struggle against the witches is a necessary feature of the Reformation. Wherever man tried to purchase safety too cheaply, to insure the issue without exposing his faith to God's intervention, he was the servant of the devil. Luther went against the sorcerers of Pharaoh who promised the life of happiness and plenty instead of preaching penitence. Men have to listen to God passively, and then to act for themselves. But between the hours of listening and of action there is a middle period to be endured where everything is uncertain.

"It is easier to enter heaven through many tribulations than through trusting in an external assurance of peace," runs Thesis 84. Suddenly darkening all the bright order of the Madonna, the Holy Family, Apostles, Saints, Popes, Bishops, Luther extinguished all the friendly lights kindled for the night of life by faithful generations before him.

·The darkness created by Luther was tremendous. The complete invisibility of good and evil was his final word to the soul. Each soul was left alone with its God. "God and the soul" became the religious party of the Reformation, fighting "God and the world"—which included the visible church—as the other, the fallen and sinful side of life. In German, "*Gott und die Welt*" is a scornful expression for the merely external. "World" is always something indifferent.

This new religious party—each soul a priest of God Almighty, but each soul alone with God and having no security during its lifetime as to God's plans or decrees, except the boundless faith and trust in His mercy—needed a support, something to lean on; for otherwise its fantastic effort to stand on the side of God must necessarily have led to utter confusion of society in all practical matters. The new beacon of souls on the ocean of life was the Christian law of the High Magistrate. He regulated the civil order, marriage, property, trade, in the world of Christian states. His very highness became a strength that comforted the soul of every Christian who lived in his territories. "Let him stand high, let him speak out clearly what the law is, let him be strong enough to protect our property and our family against emperors and popes," was the necessary and genuine prayer of a Lutheran in any of the territories of the Empire and of the omnipotent Catholic Church.

We have already discussed the predilection of Englishmen for understatement: a Lower House and a Low Church are the natural outcome of a revolution made by the Commons of the land against the Highness of the Realm.

In Lutheran countries "High" is the favourite word; the Prince, the High Magistrate, is addressed as "Your Highness." The subject honours himself when he puts the secular authority as high as possible; for in bowing low before the prince he is fighting the pope and all priesthood. Luther abolished the institution of kneeling before the priest. Dutifulness, loyalty, the lust for obedience, make the Lutheran; for all these characteristics are so many symbols of his fight against clerical domination. Your soul is perfectly free, it is not involved, in your obeisance before a secular Supreme Judge. That is simply a regulation of this world, to direct people on their social way. It is convenient to have civil conventions; but they do not wound the conscience like a devotion to relics, pictures, priests and sacraments. Nobody can understand the German's exaltation of the "State" unless he knows that it is rooted in the depreciation of a visible church. Today, four hundred years later, the Hitler régime shows the reverse of the medal: his government commands more religious devotion than was ever asked by any pope or clergy. The balance between Church and monarchy has been upset because the Church has ceased to be real. For that reason German Protestantism has become shallow. A Protestant must protest against a too visible Church, against cheating offers of security and salvation from priests or magicians, saints or sorcerers. Protest against a Church is the presupposition of service in the State. The religious background of civil service in the Lutheran countries was the revolt against the visible Church. The permanent protest against its visibility was clothed in a passionate devotion to the prince or monarch, because this monarch was no pope, no saint, no sorcerer at all. When Goethe celebrated the three hundredth anniversary of the Reformation on October 31, 1817, he spoke as a good secular disciple of Luther: he promised never to stop protesting in the arts and sciences, i.e., in his own field. The protesting servant of a law-giver: this is the Protestant type. This Protestant character—on which Hitler is leading a central attack—this Protestant character has been decaying for the last century; but in the meantime the peculiar balance of power in Lutheran hearts had created a great European type.

It is not astonishing, considering the fears and anxieties we are subjected to, that men pervert their worldly governors into idols, messiahs, tyrants. It is more surprising to find that the Protestant remedy for idolatry kept its efficacy for four hundred years, and purified all our superstition by making us subjects of a High Magistrate in this world. The independence of a lofty thinker and the dependence of a humble servant are strangely mixed in the German character. The balance between a protesting subjectivism in matters of belief and a splendid objective efficiency has baffled observers of German discipline as recently as the World War.

Let no one suppose that blind obedience or drill can be so efficient. The key to the riddle of German efficiency lay in the education of a Protestant, who was his own priest in church on Sundays and was therefore ready to become a humble civil servant on week-days.

In fighting ecclesiastical government, the German civil servant restored his own balance. No Anglo-Saxon will believe this. He will ask: "But why did the whole system not work in a country like England?"

The main reason for the long-time efficiency of the method was this: no prince, no High Magistrate, in Germany was likely to become a real pope in his territory. They were too small for such an attempt. These princes could not protest separately against emperor and pope; they had to unite. The first Lutheran Confession, which they brought before the Emperor at Augsburg in 1530, was drafted by Melanchthon; the High Magistrates of eleven German territories, led by the two Middle German princes of Saxony and Hesse, agreed on a common *"confessio augustana."* In matters of religion they formed a community. The living word of the Gospel could not be represented or embodied by one tyrannical potentate. No danger that the Church of God might be made completely invisible in brick and stone, or in the laws and ritual of a Saxon or a Hessian "church." Unquestionably, *"Landeskirchen,"* territorial churches, grew up, but they were all based on a foundation broader and larger than the territory in which they were established.

The so-called "established" church of the Continental territories was not an established church in the Anglican sense of the word, because its real sovereign was not limited by the boundaries of the territorial church. The Kings of England were the heads of the Anglican Church, Oxford and Cambridge were its faculties of theology, the bishops were Anglican bishops, etc. On the Continent, as we have seen, the Elector of Saxony acknowledged the sovereign claim of the Wittenberg faculty of theology to settle right and wrong in matters of religion by its own authority. The prince only defended the orthodoxy of this claim. Now this faculty of Wittenberg was sovereign only as a mouth-piece of the convictions of the whole German nation. The professors of Wittenberg, though officially civil servants of His Highness, the Prince, were also ministers plenipotentiary of the German nation within his little State or Dukedom.

The chairs of the universities derived all their authority from the fact that they were Christian chairs of the German nation. The Lutheran Confession was the yardstick by which the faculties measured their learning and doctrine. But this "new learning," as it was called, could be judged only by the faculties themselves and by nobody else. No prince, no High Magistrate, could tell them what to teach in matters of religion. He had no understanding in religious matters. They were as sovereign as he was. They were Higher Schools in the same sense that has made High unpopular in England and led the Puritan ministers to decry the university magisters. The universities were sovereign in preaching the Gospel; the prince was sovereign in making the law. He, like any layman, had to listen to them, be informed by them, be instructed by their learning, or he was no true Christian. The well-informed, well-educated, well-equipped Christian had his duty to perform in the external world, the prince giving laws, the cobbler patching shoes, everybody according to his calling; each man a master and king in his field of action, the husbandman a king and the king a husbandman. "Every man ought to serve God in such a way whereto he hath best fitted him by nature, education or gifts or by graces acquired." [2] But the prince had no grip on the universities, no more than the cobbler. The universities represented the life of the Holy Ghost in the German Nation, whereas the prince and his State were blind and deaf in matters of religion without the help of the preachers and teachers of the faith. State and government were not at all glorified by Luther. "Princes are God's hangmen and jailors," he said.

2 Thomas Dudley, Governor of Massachusetts.

REFORM OF THE CHURCHES.

This, then, was the result of the Reformation; all the High Magistrates became equals in matters of the external manifestation of the faith. The one Christian faith had to take its worldly form, religion, from them. In 1530 the central idea of "a party of *religion*" was clearly formulated: The Emperor himself and all the great princes, and also the smallest member of the Diet, should be equals, like parties pleading in court. The word "party," so reduced in significance today, was expressly used in the declaration of Augsburg as the legal term for the equality of religious sovereignty between Emperor and estates. In matters of religion, the Protestants held: No Pope or Emperor or Diet or council can vote us down. We, the High Magistrates of the nation, are one party to the matter; you, the Emperor and the old Catholic princes, are the other. We may compromise on the subject, but of a surety we have no earthly judge above us.

On this account all the High Magistrates needed what the pope alone had possessed before: a staff for religious questions, a consistorium. The Catholic and the Protestant princes did not differ very much in this respect. The formation of a Bavarian (Catholic) territorial church was for centuries the aim of the ecclesiastical policy of the Dukes of Bavaria. In the very period when Bavaria expelled the Protestants in Munich a clerical board was established, a sovereign ecclesiastical authority comparable to the consistories of the Lutherans. In 1563 the Dukes of Bavaria granted to their estates the use of the chalice in Holy Communion. In 1620 the Hapsburg Emperor reformed the Bohemian church with a strong hand. He did not so much as ask the pope before he inserted a new Holy Day, the day of the Immaculate Conception, into the Christian calendar: the eighth day of December is a princely Holy Day. Thus the two parties of religion vied with one another in their consistorial policy. For such a consistory the High Magistrate of a very small town (a place of three thousand inhabitants, surrounded by a few villages and a large forest which provided firewood for his subjects, and pasture for their

THE NORMAL RELATION OF STATE AND CHURCH IN LUTHERAN TERRITORY:
Sovereign Prince and Sovereign Seat of Learning.

AN ABNORMAL SITUATION:
Henry VIII proclaiming himself, in Hebrew, Greek, and Latin, Head of the Anglican Church, 1535.

hogs and sheep), this High Magistrate would try to get a magister from a good and reliable university. He knew he could not do the job himself. The High Magistrate of a hamlet like Forst (500 citizens) established an independent consistory. His neighbour of Sorau followed in 1597. Both sought their directories from the university; the title of a book which was printed in 1571 gives perhaps an idea of the strange position of the universities: *Final Report and Declaration of the Theologians of the Two Universities, Leipzig and Wittenberg, and the superintendents* [members of consistories] *of the churches of Saxony, concerning the learning which these universities have uniformly defended from the beginning of the Augustan Confession, in all its articles.* And Philipp Melanchthon, the famous Preceptor Germaniæ, stated, in 1543, his creed with stupendous ingenuity, against the glamour of the papal court, in these words: "I follow and embrace the doctrine of the Church of Wittenberg and its associates which without any doubt represents the consent of the catholic church of Christ, i.e., of all the better instructed in the Christian Church." [3] How far away we here are from the procedure of the English Henry VIII. The Church of Wittenberg stands up against the Church of Rome as the Commonwealth of Massachusetts stood up against the British Commonwealth.

WHY TEACHING IS A PUBLIC TRUST.

Luther, the man who offered comfort to his prince, was no isolated individual like Thomas Paine; he was the rightful spokesman of the City of God, the guardian of the opened and re-opened Bible, the trusted interpreter of Holy Scripture, one of the ordained seventy interpreters invested, not like Peter and the priests of the old Church, with the power of binding and loosing, but with the authority to open and close a public discussion in matters of national interest. The German professor was always careful to keep as part of his title the addition, "Public Professor," in order to make clear his

---

[3] *Opera*, ed. Brettschneider, 21, 603. The exact term is "*Consensus eruditiorum*," consensus of those who are "*gebildeter*." See p. 405.

political sovereignty. The Germans, untrained in debate or discussion and as little inclined to pay attention to matters of that sort as, let us say, to a cock-fight, could always be interested in questions propounded by the Chairs of their University. Such questions would ring in their ears like the public theses of Luther.

A public teacher, then, had uttered this "All or nothing" from his public *Katheder* (chair). No wonder that the Germans saw in him, not a ranter or mere private person, but a public and official spokesman taking thought for their salvation. They were grateful for the division of labour between two sovereign powers, and supported it faithfully to the very end. This situation, therefore, was stamped upon all relations between public affairs and public opinion. The public in Germany thought of the universities as *keepers of the nation's conscience*. Once a question was broached in public by a university man it was difficult to avoid practical consequences. Public opinion would feel that an important issue was at stake, a responsible spokesman of the nation having opened the *"Erörterung"* of the topic. Like "debate" in English, like *"discussion"* in French, the German *"Erörterung"* seems untranslatable into another language. It is derived from the word "topic," translated into German. It means to put a question in its right place. No topic is decently *"erörtert,"* settled, until it is *placed* in a larger context.

The theologians, when they had occasion to deal with the creed, would take up one topic this year and another ten years hence—indulgences, say, in 1517, and the use of the seminaries for priests in 1522—and would try to determine what systematic place must be given to this or that question before it could be answered. A systematic and hard-thinking mind was required to follow this long campaign against so many papal traditions point after point, paragraph after paragraph, brick after brick, so to speak, the whole framework of the old visible church was to be tested and rebuilt, lest the new learning lose its reason for existence. Every year brought a new question; but not one of these questions could be treated alone.

The result was a passion for systematic thinking in Germany. These heavy German minds developed an unheard-of technique of systematic training in generalities. While Englishmen, as we have seen, for good reasons of political self-defence, were wading in particulars, the Germans were drowned in systems and generalities because the individual thinker was fighting against the whole system of mediævalism, the whole united front of the visible church. The little pebble flung by the thesis of a young German scholar seems to us now nothing more than a pebble, and in Anglo-Saxon countries, with their eye for particulars, the idea of the Ph.D. thesis as a pebble still prevails. But in Germany this pebble was David's pebble hurled at Goliath. Any dissertation might dislodge the keystone from the Holy Sepulchre of the real Christian faith, as Luther's ninety-five theses had done in the year of salvation 1517.

This salvation-character of scholarship, utterly foreign to the rest of the world, is the religious key to the political building erected by the Reformation.

"The topic is *erörtert*" means that a new battle against the foe of darkness is opened: a new abuse of the pure gospel is discovered.[4] From this minute of the first declaration of doubt the war is on. It is now a public question and a public affair. To an Anglo-Saxon mind a battle of books may seem rather dull. The professor publicus, the German public teacher, bears an attribute which in English intellectual life attaches only to the "publisher." British public spirit needs better weapons than scholars' books.

In Germany the only public war that could be waged was scientific and scholarly. The *"Weltanschauung,"* the most sacred principles, would come into play. The issue would be decided, not by a lay public, not by public spirit, but by the hot contention of experts from different faculties all over the

---

[4] The anti-Catholic bias of the German method of topics is clearly stated in its first important example: the common topics, the *Loci Communes,* of Ph. Melanchthon when he writes, in the preface: "So we should recognize Christ in a way that differs from the method exhibited by the scholastics!" "Scholastics" and the new learning are the two intellectual parties.

country. The German professor, of course, cuts as comic a figure as the English country squire. John Jay Chapman called them monsters, and saw clear that Nietzsche was their last and most terrible descendant. English matter-of-fact empiricism, and German pedantry, with its eternal search for reasons, *Gründe,* are both blind in one eye. But since it has become fashionable to scorn the whole tribe, let us quote old W. H. Riehl: "Do not forget that almost all the great reforming minds of Germany, from Luther to Goethe, had much, and not the worst side, in common with this type of professor who was an authority of the first order for the nation." The professors opened the warfare against *"Misstände,"* i.e., unjust conditions. The struggle would end the moment a High Magistrate's council took the matter under consideration and extended to it the *"Staatliches Interesse"* (public interest), because then the *living voice of the interpreters of the true faith* would have successfully informed and moved the organized conscience of a prince. Thus *"Wissen"* and *"Gewissen,"* science and conscience, met in a happy constellation. The formula, *"nach bestem Wissen und Gewissen,"* is the formula of German oaths; but is also the German constitution at large; it means the audible and visible organization of a person's conscience. Without *"Wissen"* and *"Gewissen"* a man is not a person. The German cult of personality is based on a faith in the conjunction of science and conscience. The counsellors of the government, evil demons in the eyes of the Commons who impeached Laud and Strafford, were hailed as saviours in the countries of Reform. It was their task to translate the gospel of the university chair into the bread-and-butter policy of a prince. He might be too lazy, too evil, too wicked to listen to the Divine voice of truth; but the counsellor could insist. Amidst the inertia of a splendid court, of palace cabals and intrigues, he would not forget his teachers at the university. Truth would penetrate the walls of the council chamber in which the prince and his servants deliberated. Goethe and Schiller were both occupied with this problem (*Egmont, Don Carlos, Maria Stuart*).

It became the passion of every German to be, or at least to get the title of, privy counsellor to a High Magistrate. The uni-

versal spread of this title *"Rat"* was finally reduced to absurdity in Germany. Dentists insisted on becoming *Sanitätsräte,*
lawyers *Justizräte,* postmasters *Posträte,* and tax-collectors financial counsellors (like Mr. Hugenberg). In the material world,
the baker and the barber longed to be called at least Purveyors
to the court of Reuss—Schleiz—Greiz—Lobenstein.

Yet it was a good thing that any man of importance should
feel it incumbent on him, not to write a letter to the *Times* as
an Englishman would have done, but to gain the ear of his
Monarch. For after all, any ruler has only a limited amount
of force and time to spend in listening; and to fill out this
square of force and time with the best counsels is a serious
problem for a democracy in Washington or for a Dictator in
Moscow. The pride of being a counsellor of the High Magistrate was, then, very pardonable in the Germans, and it was
natural that a university professor should be made in most
cases a *consiliarius a secretis,* a counsellor in the inner secrets
of State. *Arcana imperii,* state secrets—so obnoxious to the
English mind because of their results in the form of Starchamber and ship money—were the very centre of activity for any
responsible German thinker, worker, or public servant. To
inform this intimate and secret circle where the wheels of government turned was the highest he could hope for.

This duty of every prince to inform himself at the purest
fountain of truth was well expressed by the rule of precedence
at the Saxon court, where the rector of Leipzig walked in
immediately after the princes of the royal family and before
the generals and ministers of the court. He represented the
teaching guild which opened the debate on a new law, a new
bill of reform, a new purge of old abuses. He was a sovereign
in the realm of the spirit, as the king was in his wordly realm.
It was very much like the relation between Paul and Peter in
the Catholic Church. The princes took over the functions of
the popes, the successors of Peter. They founded consistories
and passed laws governing clergymen and monks and universities and schools, as the popes had done. But in the old Church
there had been a Paul too. He had left to Peter the visible
power of the bishop, but he had remained the prophet of the

Kingdom of God everywhere. He was the carrier of the Gospel before there was any shelter to be found in an established church. He was the teacher of the established churches, to inspire them, fight their abuses, move them forward.

The Reformation bestowed the function of St. Paul on the universities. The universities would yield to the emergency authority of the High Magistrate in all questions of decision and legislation, but the inspiration was theirs. They would not "cease from mental fight"; to raise one question of reform after another was their uncensored and uncensorable, inalienable duty.

This held good for all questions of principle. Down to 1870 every German court of justice was obliged to send the records of a case to a faculty of law whenever a principle was at stake. The records were laid before the faculty with strict precautions against bribery or intrigue by either of the parties. The parties were forbidden to know which faculty had been asked for its decision, and the "Acts," as the records were called in German, were sealed in the presence of the parties, lest the attorney or the judge insert any arbitrary remark.

The faculty based its decision solely on the facts in the "Akten." "Quod non in actis non erat in mundo": What was not in the "acts" (records) did not exist. This famous sentence can only be explained by the fact that the faculties stood for the national will against the interference of any arbitrary power. The transmission of public papers to the faculty was the guarantee of national control. The matters on the table of the House in the English Parliament enjoyed the same prestige. The "Acts," Reports, in Germany were as "popular," as truly German, as the Parliamentary Papers in England. The bookishness of the Germans was based on this clear distinction between arbitrary oral procedure and reports which were tangible and referable to a distant scholar, a professor of national standing exempt from any local partisanship.

A German "Act" is like an English action, because the conscience of a learned man has taken over its content and discovered the "principle embalmed in it." Surveying four centuries of German Reform, from 1517 to 1914, we find the German universities in the van of national thoughts, hopes and fears. Four hundred years of unbroken tradition made every capable German student think of the study of theology, philosophy or law as the road of honour. It was the respectable thing, in the same sense in which the American calls business a respectable profession. To become a teacher in a university was the ultimate desire of men who in any other country would have written articles in newspapers or made speeches in clubs. In Germany nothing but the public chair was surrounded by this halo of partnership in the national spirit. To become at least a *Privatdozent,* a candidate for such a sacred company, was the ambition of every intellectual. It is remarkable how this passion has once more sowed its wild oats in the years since the World War. From 1918 to 1933 the German universities were inundated by a flood of readers and professors who had previously been ministers, generals, or the like, and as a result the quality of the teaching staff was watered down. A lowering of the level of the institution had been perceptible for years; but the sudden inflation of post-War times burst all bounds. Because of this influx the national revolutionists of 1933 found a country in which the successors of Luther and Melanchthon had become too numerous to be respected; and they could therefore abolish the achievements of the German Reformation. The German professor's *"Katheder,"* of which the Empress Catherine of Russia could say that she trembled before its criticism, has for the moment no public voice in the national affairs of Germany.

The inflation of 1918-1933 was a wild carnival of a doomed order of things. For without a plurality of High Magistrates the sovereignty of the university could not have survived. Up to 1932 a German professor would be judged by the number of his "calls" to other universities. He would take his degree in one faculty, begin his career in another, become a full professor in a third, and so on. The republic of scholars liked to supervise the local faculties, to corroborate the vote of one by the votes of as many others as possible. The professor came into a state, to serve the community, with a prestige won in the wider field of the nation. The German nation was always bigger than any particular government. Even after 1871 Austria and Prussia remained as the Protestant and the Catholic antagonists. There were twenty-six different ministers of instruction to compete for the best candidate. And this was true not only for the universities but for all officialdom.

When all is said and done, the ultimate secret of German efficiency lies in the fact that in the labour-market for civil servants competition was constantly at work reshaping the type. Long before big business, the princes were hunting for the best man. And they did it for centuries, carefully and conscientiously. Moltke, the Field Marshal of Prussia, came from abroad; Goethe went from his imperial city of Frankfurt to Weimar, into the service of an unknown young prince; Spinoza got his call to Heidelberg, Hegel went from Württemberg to Prussia, Schlegel from Berlin to Vienna, Schelling from Württemberg to Munich. But Fichte, Schelling, Hegel, also met for a short time in Jena, under the eyes of Schiller and Goethe; for the universities, as a matter of principle, exchanged their best men back and forth. Many of the leading Prussian administrators came from outside: Schmoller, who started the social insurance legislation and put German social policy fifty years ahead of the rest of the world, was called from South Germany to his chair in Berlin. Niebuhr (1776-1831), the famous Roman historian and president of the bank of the Kingdom, came from Copenhagen; Stein, the first great Reformer after the defeat by Napoleon in 1807, was an independent High Magistrate who cast in his lot with Prussia; Prince Hohenlohe, an equal of the Hapsburgs and Hohenzollerns, became president of the cabinet of the Bavarian King in 1867 and chancellor to the King of Prussia in 1894. Beust was at first Prime Minister in Saxony, and later chancellor of Austria. Hertling again, the last in this long line, was Prime Minister of Bavaria before he was called to fill and to liquidate the Prussian Chancellorship in 1917.

The free competition between many governments increased the independence and moral value of their servants. Being free to leave his present master for another who might be more inclined to listen to his ideas, the servant felt that he represented the learning of the nation as against the deaf and blind mechanism of the *"Racker Staat"; the voracious Leviathan of Hobbes, the "State," could only be enlightened by faithful servants who had been informed by learning and were learned themselves. To be learned meant to be a free man, even under the very eyes of a despot. The connection, the brotherhood and comradeship which were felt by the English in the word "Common," were felt in Germany as attaching to the word *"Gebildet."* To be *"gebildet"* (formed or educated) meant to swim in this stream of reforming thought.[5] A *"gebildeter Mensch"* participated actively or passively in the intellectual adventure of the nation as it was represented by the professors' chairs in the universities, and in the artistic movement as it was represented by the musical service in the Lutheran churches. With these two roots, he was at home in an invisible church. The more *"gebildet"* he was, the less could he be conquered by the outside material world.

While Calvinism speaks of predestination and links man's fate with the stars of his birth, with his upbringing, the German word *"Bildung"* emphasizes a conscious formation, a preceding stage which we might label "pre-information" if the reader will understand that the individual is formed during the first half of his life by being taught and informed in the visible church of German inspiration, *den "Deutschen Geist."* [6] Individual Preformation precedes political and collective reforms. The spiritual and invisible community preforms (= *bildet*) the individual; reforming one part of the visible world is the task of government. Thus, *"Bildung"* (*preformation*) and *Staat* (the organized body for *reform*) condition each other. Man passes through two different orders during his life: the order of the Church, instructing, teaching, informing him, but making no decisions whatever for him ("the Word is free"),

---

[5] See p. 397, our note on the usage of Melanchthon.
[6] The so-called *"Konfirmation"* was the austere climax of this preforming process. At the *Konfirmation,* the young Christian appropriated his fund of Christian teaching. In the Weimar of Goethe, in 1779, the great Herder asked the hereditary prince 255 questions, which the poor boy had to formulate himself, for the *Konfirmation.*

and the order of the State, using him, appointing him, listening to him, and claiming his obedience.

Free acceptance of the word of Scripture in the audible Church and loyal obedience in the service of a Christian State mutually balance each other. One would be intolerable without the other. But together they give the soul what it needs in order to be human and to breathe freely.

The civil servant acquired his dignity through his *"Bildung."* It raised him above the level of a plaything in the hands of an unjust master. And the State acquired the inspiration which was lacking in the Machiavellian prince by relying on the informed and instructed service of its whole staff; from top to bottom, prince, minister, counsellor and teacher had to be *"gebildet"* in order to win anew each day their duty or their right to govern others. This *Bildung* made Frederick the Great of Prussia "the first Servant of his State," and it distinguished the princes of the German Reformation from the *principe* of the Italian Renaissance.

NEITHER MACHIAVELLI NOR BODINUS.

Luther really saved a world which was going Fascist. About 1500 the decay of the Catholic Church had led to a blind struggle for power in Italy. When Machiavelli jotted down his acute observations on this state of affairs it was a state of affairs only, without the least tincture of Christianity. Machiavelli's *Principe* was a frank guide to the secret wheels of this state mechanism, without any veil or palliation. One sees in this book, circulated after 1515, how, in a world where religion is provided by a visible church, civil government can behave much more barbarously than in any pagan or Mohammedan nation. In Athens the deity of Athens, Athene herself, gave religious dignity to the enterprises of her city. An Arabian caliph was a religious leader, and people obeyed him for the sake of their souls.

In the great deliverance wrought by the papacy for all Christian people, teaching them that rulers, kings, and princes were mere mortals and poor sinners and no better than their subjects, the secular state lost all colour of belief or salvation. It was just a machinery set up against murder and war: the keeper of earthly justice. This degradation of the secular princes is well stated by Machiavelli. He observes that a world of perfect political freedom is dawning for the mighty, because they need not even pretend to be more than secular despots. That the thirst for power justifies itself is the old teaching renewed by Machiavelli.

It was a tremendous hour in the history of human civilization when this masque of death, greed, and arbitrary power loomed on the horizon of the Western World. The year 1515, when the *Principe* of Machiavelli was finished, marks the danger of a world which has lost all faith in the Church, and because of that complete loss of seriousness cynically says "yes" to the orgies of any conqueror, dictator or despot. The mood was very similar to the temper of the nations today.

In this decisive hour Luther's sermon on the freedom of the Christian broke in like the trumpets of the Last Judgment. Why are you empty, why do you yield to the rude and shallow ambition of tyrants? Because you cling to artificial safety in a visible Church. This Church has mutilated, crippled and paralyzed your moral courage. You cannot believe that the state of affairs at court and in the government might be touched by Christian faith, baptized by Christian promise, redeemed by Christian love, because you keep Church and State in two watertight compartments. You go on Sundays and Holy Days into a stone house which you call a church, and you tax yourself highly to adorn this church with pictures and sculpture. On week-days you frequent the visible palace or market and deal with the things of your greed. And this ridiculous duplication—two systems of law, two visible orders of society—you call, in your superstition, "Church" and "State." The result is, of course, the complete degeneration of both bodies politic. The Church becomes a theatre with splendid decorations; the State can receive no real stream of power or influence from a Church which is only a neighbour in space instead of a precursor in time.

The arbitrary power of princes, attacked by the English in 1641 and by the French in 1789, was attacked by Luther in

1517. Reformation, Glorious Restoration, *Grande Révolution,* each rekindled for another 120 years the faith of a cynical world. The Tudors in England, with the great reign of Elizabeth, cannot be imagined without Luther; the same is, of course, true of the Huguenot Henry IV, the most popular King of France.

These princes were no mere Machiavellian *"principi,"* though they were stained with many of the vices of the type. The new invisible form of church interpolated into the life of every Christian a phase which was wholly devoted to his systematic training in catechism. A prince passed through this phase of pre-instruction, and later he would reinforce his conscience by the support of well informed counsellors. As a symbol of this change in character the prince might renounce his power. Charles V on the Catholic side, and Christine of Sweden on the Lutheran, stand like pillars of the century of Reform. Both abdicated from the throne, one at the beginning, the other at the end of the struggle (1556 and 1654). These are the two great acts of the new class of princes. And in so far as Erasmus of Rotterdam was the reformer who recommended this last decision to the young Charles V in his institution of a Christian prince,[7] he certainly belongs to the Reformation, as its Kerenski. The abdication made the prince into a human being, since it distinguished his dutiful struggle for power from his individual lust for power.

The Lutheran new learning kept the world alive and human for another century.

The Lutheran form of Christian State is as important, for the doctrines of political science and for the living memory of Europe, as English parliamentarianism or French democracy. This can be brought to the test by comparing Luther and

[7] See on this point Pierre Mesnard, *L'Essor de la Philosophie Politique au XVI Siècle,* p. 96, Paris, 1936. Erasmus says, page 27 of the edition of 1518: *"depone potius ac cede tempori."* The modern translators misunderstand the *"ac"* as though it meant "and"; this deprives Erasmus' advice of all dignity; he would say: escape. In fact, *"potius ac"* in Latin signifies a comparative; Erasmus says: "before you agree to become an opportunist, you had better put down your crown."

Bodin, the French theoretician, who became so famous because he spared his readers the necessity of knowing anything about theology or religion or church.

Jean Bodin is a good example of the laziness of man. The lawyers can read him and feel themselves experts; they can enjoy being left alone in their field, apart from this bothersome clergy and these quarrelsome theologians. Bodin's writings *De Republica* fascinate us by their complete break with the dualism of State and Church in the Lutheran sense. Bodin's king has all the qualities of the Protestant prince: he is Luther's High Magistrate. And Bodin owes all the basic elements of his concept of "Sovereignty," "Superanitas," to the structure of the Lutheran government, where the Christian servant, in his struggle to reform the church, had to make his sovereign a High Magistrate. But Bodin isolates the highness of the Prince into an independent function. He ignores the religious balance of power between the systematic fight of the learned Christian *against* the abuses of the church and his fight *for* the Christian state. Bodin bisects the problem. He is a philosopher. He is not interested in the Reform of the Church. He keeps the visible half, the sovereign prince, who is here to rule his territory without the old bondage of canon or imperial law; but in doing so Bodin cut his own country off from the tree of Christianity. That was outrageous and could not work: the King of France had to remain Catholic for another two hundred years. And in 1789, when the Catholicism of the King was finally given up, France made the sacrifice, not for the sake of her own miserable sovereignty, in Bodin's sense of the word, but for the sake of a new community of Europe and of all civilized nations. Bodin is the devil of territorial and moral sovereignty stealing into the garden of the Christian Commonwealth. He was never able to win a full victory for his ideas; or when he did, as in the World War, it meant disaster. No State is morally sovereign. That is the difference between a Christian and a pagan government. Religion is free and sovereign, and governs the individual State, because no government can *make* the religion of its subjects. And as the government itself is run by subjects, by people who are either Christians and believers or unbelievers, no government is sovereign in matters of religion; each is subject to the religion and the inspiration which pervades its territory. This is the concept of the Christian World of States in which each government carries out exactly the same duties in its casual district, as does any other government elsewhere. The doctrine is common to all German doctrines of government, and—except for the Prussian heathens and followers of Bodin—the *"Christlich-Germanische Staatenwelt"* stressed the *solidarity of government* against the frictions or rivalries between different governments. I may quote here some sentences of the famous Prince Metternich which Martin Luther might have written and which are advocated today by French and English statesmen as the quintessence of political wisdom. "Politics is the science of the vital interests of states. Since, however, an isolated state no longer exists, and is found only in the annals of the heathen world, or in the abstractions of so-called philosophers, we must always view the society of nations as the essential condition of the present world. Thus, then, each state, besides its separate interests, has also those which are common to it with other states. The great axioms of political science proceed from the knowledge of the true political interests of *all* states. In these general interests lies the guarantee of their existence, while individual interests possess only a relative and secondary value. That which characterizes the ·modern world is the tendency to enter into a social league, which rests on the same basis with the great human society developed in the bosom of Christianity." [8]

Bodin is not aware of this fact. To him, the philosopher, in the Horatian sense of a man with a little leisure, a library, and a taste for reflection à la Montaigne, embodies the only liberty there is in his prince's territory. The philosopher, so Bodin thinks, cannot be coerced by the prince's sovereign power. He, Bodin or Montaigne, is a free individual even in the sovereign State because he can think *ad libitum*.

Here we are at the very source of most of the misunderstandings between the Germans and the Western nations. Bodin is

[8] Clemens Metternich, *Memoirs*, I, 36, New York, 1880.

interested in thought alone. To him the mind is an appurtenance of the individual thinker. The mechanism of a sovereign State and the tiny, tiny cell of the philosopher are all he can conceive.

For Luther, teaching and learning have nothing to do with the individual mind or soul. Love has created a stream of language, a Word, an inspiration, and sent it into the valley of tears, where men live blinded by their sins and in despair. First set this stream of instruction flowing, let love and spirit have their way; then all the chains of the oppressed, all the tears of the blind, will cease to be. For the preceding and preforming voice of the Redeemer restores Creation to its old glory and true meaning. "And the Truth shall set you free" is the song of triumph of the Reformation. The stream of teaching and learning flows through the unworthy vessel of teachers and students; but since God *had pity* and *has pity,* all our misunderstanding cannot resist the pure, unmixed and genuine *"Evangelium." "Das lautre Evangelium," "Die reine Lehre,"* take the place in Germany of the mere philosophical, after-dinner reflection of a Bodin or a Montaigne.

The purity of the teaching is the essence of his gospel because on it can be established a Church of teachers and preachers to purify all learning, after the utter darkness of the Middle Ages.

Luther and his pupils created the term Middle Ages. Middle Ages meant the times which were not interested in the purification of the Gospel. The Middle Ages meant the times when Aristotle had silenced St. Paul, when the joy of additions, of affiliations and branches, had complicated the Gospel instead of simplifying it. The *Nachtigall* of Wittenberg proposed to sing only the old, pure Gospel; he tore down the elaborate cathedrals and regulations and began with the white communion-table and the one Bible on the pulpit as the only essential sources of this stream of spiritual life whose drops touch us and turn us from brute animals into men.

The term "Middle Ages" has been denaturalized by English and French historians. But though they have filed off some of its sharp edges, and changed its dates, they have not been able to do away with it altogether. This term makes no sense when it is connected with geographical discovery or other humanistic achievements. As we have seen, neither Machiavelli, the natural scientist of the State, nor Bodin, the modest philosopher under a sovereign King, founded an epoch.

UNIVERSITY LEADERSHIP.

Luther separated the Middle Ages and the modern era because he believed in the fruits of *time:* The Gospel preceded the political reality; the pulpit of the university trained boys of twenty so that, as men of fifty, they might run the government. In other words: Luther changed the Church from a neighbour in space to a prophet in time. The Church was to be not a hundred steps from the palace or the town-hall, but a hundred hours or days or months ahead of what was transacted in either of those houses.

As a symbol of this relation, the Lutheran closed his church during the week. It was open only on Sunday because then the *"Donnerwort* of Eternity" could break in upon the temporal and secular world. The pulpit being a prophetic voice, sowing the future by its preaching of the pure Gospel, the *"Katheder"* of a German university was surrounded with all the halo of a sacrament.

But we can go further. Surveying the Lutheran State during the last four hundred years, we can say that the promise has come true and that the State has been inspired again and again by prophecies from the chair. The various faculties have succeeded each other in this function. The theologians, of course, dominated the whole of the first century. After the terrible blow of the Thirty Years' War the parsons had lost much of their influence. The lawyers—and not just any lawyers, but the professors at law—took up the leading rôle. Thomasius and Pufendorf, Schlözer and Moser, reorganized the German civil service. Schlözer, in Göttingen, was called "the European Conscience." We can add the name of the philosopher Christian Wolff, because he, too, drew up a code based on the nature of things. This century of lawgiving ended in the great Codes of the end of the eighteenth century.

While France and America were establishing the Rights of Man in their Constitutions, Germany was systematically developing the public and private rights of the citizen in stupendous codifications. The general law of the land for the many territories of Prussia was drawn up in the years after 1747 and finished in 1786-88. The same thing was done in Bavaria and Austria. The great systematic view of the monarchical state is symbolized by these great codifications. They have nothing to do with the codifications of Roman Law or Canon Law during the Middle Ages. Those codes had been collections of individual decisions. In a German Code all traces of precedent are carefully obliterated: it begins with the individual and leads on step by step to the family, the partnership, the village, the county, the free associations, etc., the old Lutheran investigation of the "liberty of a Christian man" always looming in the background. As late as 1900 a general code was formulated for the Bismarckian Reich, though it never became as vigorous as were its predecessors in the individual German State. The new unity of the modern "Reich," with its lack of competition, lowered the standard of the *"Bürgerliches Gesetzbuch"* and made it unpopular and boring reading. However, it was a late reverberation of the great century of German professors of law.

In the nineteenth century, inaugurated by Immanuel Kant in Königsberg and subsequently dominated by Fichte, Schelling and Hegel, the political leadership of the university shifted its centre once more. It migrated from law to philosophy. In this transformation of theology into philosophy German learning once more became well-known all over the world. But this thought and poetry can only be understood as a translation of the Lutheran learning. The preforming quality of the arts and sciences as a kind of first instruction, through which each soul must pass, had been well understood in the sixteenth century. Erasmus of Rotterdam, the forerunner of Luther in the reform of the classics, had pointed out that they should be the preliminary to Christian instruction. As in biogenesis, Erasmus wished to see men pass through the stage of paganism before they entered the Holy of Holies. As a preparation for Chris-

tianity, the classics gained a new prestige in the eyes of the
Reformers. Since the central idea was that of running a courageous race in this dark world, rather than of building a comfortable house, the addition of one more antechamber could
not shake the foundations of the Lutheran dualism between
the sovereign pulpit and the High Magistrate. Philosophy became the external and more general application of Christian
principles to the universe. That is the key to all the obscurities
of German philosophers. They meant by *"Weltanschauung"*
the re-phrasing of theology in the language of the layman.
They expanded the Lutheran war-cry of "Every Christian a
priest" into the philosophical principle of "Every man a bearer
of the torch." These philosophers—Lessing, Herder, Fichte,
Schelling, Hegel, Feuerbach, Nietzsche—and their lesser colleagues, Fries, Krause, Natorp, etc., were descendants of parsons, or former theologians themselves, and clung to the universality of the theology they inherited. Not one of them could
be an empiricist, an adventurer on the ocean of scattered data,
as an English thinker could. The Protestant philosopher in
Germany had to defend a certain system of values. He stood
for the universe, for pure learning about the totality of things.
He had to publish his system, even if he had got only the first
principles of a first chapter of the prolegomena to a system.
The famous, nay, notorious systems of German philosophy during the nineteenth century have nothing to do with French
or English philosophy. They were an act of self-defence of German civilization against English empiricism and French Cartesianism. They were intended to save the traditions of the
Reformation in a period of foreign constellations and influences. German idealism was a romantic counter-revolution to
the French Revolution, which made as many surface concessions as necessary, in order to save the essence. It would lead
us too far to investigate in detail how Fichte, the Utopian—
before the defeat of Napoleon—built up a system of Christian
eschatology in his ethics; how Hegel, the historian, bound the
Prussian *"Geheimräte"* and *"Räte"* who sat in his classroom in
Berlin between 1817 and 1830, to the service of the *"Weltgeist,"* that is, the march of inspiration from Adam through

Christ to himself; how Schelling, the mythologist, identified our psychic life with the evolution of Mother Earth and made men a part of a grandiose myth of nature. It is enough to say that they all sacrificed the letter of theology to save the spirit of the Reformation for an enlightened world. Through their efforts the Lutheran gospel of the living spirit became the *"deutscher Geist."* This much-abused phrase is not a nationalistic conception at all. It is the translation of the Holy Ghost into philosophical terms, adapted to the corrupted world which followed the French Revolution—or as Schleiermacher, the theological exponent of the group, called it, an exhortation addressed to the *"Gebildete"* among those who disdained religion.

Being rooted in the Lutheran order of things, German philosophy could not be refuted from outside. Its dependence on theology, though on a critical and evolutionary theology, remained constant throughout the nineteenth century.

The German professor of the nineteenth century remained the preacher and confessor of a power which he felt to be responsible for the *"rechte Geist,"* the right inspiration of the *"Weltgeist"* everywhere. And the government, too, realized its obligations. In the eighties a young Baltic scholar, professor in Giessen, had published a revolutionary book on the Christian faith of the first three centuries. Laying bare the long struggle to formulate the Christian dogmas, the book seemed to shake the apostolic creed still used in every church. The Berlin faculty asked the Prussian minister of instruction to call this man to Berlin.

The Empress in her narrow piety favoured a protest from the High Consistory against the wicked innovator. The minister of instruction laid the matter before the cabinet. Under the chairmanship of Bismarck himself the protest of Empress and fundamentalists was rejected, and in 1889 Adolf Harnack was called to teach in Berlin. The bishop-like authority of the universities and government as the upper half of the church, far above the level of the individual congregation, was confirmed by this action. Harnack became the leader of liberal theology all over Europe and America. He became the president of all the Institutes of Research established in Berlin-Dahlem about 1900. For the last time a theologian had played a central rôle in the interplay of government, universities, public opinion, and progress in Germany.

In this connection a word or two about the specific meaning of the word "culture," "*Kultur*," in German may be helpful to the English reader.

While the French Revolution was proclaiming the gospel of a European civilization of free and equal brothers, Germans felt constrained to look for some way of saving the treasures of German inspiration from the invasion of this crude enlightenment. Against the geometrical over-simplification of French armies, soldiers, *organisateurs*, *intendants*, they defended the older Protestant civilization of the many hundreds of educated governments in Germany. They called this long process of the spirit cultivating a nation, "*Kultur*," and demanded that its inner core be kept intact in spite of the sudden inbreak of French civilization.

Like "*deutscher Geist*," *Kultur* makes sense only as a German answer to the French ideas of 1789. It was an act of self-defence. And for that reason it was still used against the French in 1914.

In the heat of a battle, both parties have the habit of not seeing the beam in their own eye. All kinds of reproach were heaped upon *civilisation* or *Kultur*, as the case might be, by the two nations that faced each other across the Vosges.

It would be absurd to take these Homeric discussions too seriously. But the creation of the word "*Kultur*" in contrast to "*civilisation*" is a serious and instructive matter. We see here how one group-mind reacts to the creative eruption of a neighbouring group. An older re-birth of man, the Lutheran Reformation, keeps its old place under changed circumstances by calling its ways of reform "*Kultur*," thus quenching the white-hot enthusiasm of the German henchmen of Robespierre and Marat. As the inundation or imitation of foreign ideas is always dangerous, the success of the wall built up by *Kultur* is an example of patriotism based on penetrating discrimination.

MUSIC AND GOVERNMENT.

The German university can be called a church-like institution. Like the English Parliament or the society of Paris, it had a sovereign moral personality and influence, without which no German government can be conceived.

In taking over the function of the bishops and archbishops, councils and the saints, the universities became the Church in progress, in continuous process of reform. They are the "Reformation in Permanence."

Now the liturgy of such a revolutionized Christendom had to be reformed as well. The purified Church replaced pictures by music, bodily pilgrimages by singing. "Luther sang many millions out of the Catholic Church" is an old saying. The German chorale is unequalled in beauty and variety. The German nation, robbed of its visible ornaments, takes refuge in the world of sound. In German an influential man does not "set the fashion," he "gives the tone" (i.e., the pitch). Music became a *politicum,* a religious institution in Germany. As in the field of learning, where three centuries were dominated successively by theology, law, and philosophy, so German music has three periods, from Luther to Bach, from Bach to Mozart, and from Beethoven to Wagner and Strauss. "Music and government are like church and state," wrote Luther himself. *"Potestas ecclesiastica non impedit politicam potestatem sicut ars canendi non impedit politicam administrationem."* Ecclesiastical power does not hinder political power any more than the art of music hinders the political administration.

The art of chanting is the symbol of the invisible Church. Four hundred years of German music have used Luther's suggestion as a working hypothesis. The invisible home of the Christian people in the States of Germany is music. When you visit Leipzig you find the Thomas Church, the home of a venerable tradition. Since the days of Johann Sebastian Bach, every Friday evening and every Saturday at noon, a concert has been given by the choir of St. Thomas' church. The boys of the Thomas School sing pieces of classical religious music, and, especially, they sing pieces composed by Bach. University and town attend these concerts; it is bad form to miss one of them. Bach is the patron of all German music which has not already broken loose from its Reformation basis. His own life at the courts and in the towns of Central Germany is a wonderful illustration of our argument that music became an institution in Germany. Talented and congenial composers may rise in any country; but only the Germans established music in the way in which Luther speaks of it, as a corollary to political administration. Thus, German composers are no casual by-products. Bach, for example, is clearly not an individual, but a universal, personality. He profited by the musical development of three or four generations. When we pursue the history of his family, which occupies so unique a position in the artistic life of Germany, we have the feeling that everything that happens there must end in something consummate. We feel it to be a matter of course that some day a Bach shall come, in whom all those other Bachs shall find a posthumous existence, one in whom the fragment of German music that has been embodied in this family, shall find its completion. The members of his family had a very great attachment to one another. Since it was impossible for them all to live together in one place, they made a point of seeing each other at least once a year. The rendezvous was generally one of the Thuringian towns, Eisenach, Erfurt, etc. The manner in which they passed the time during the meeting was wholly musical. As the company consisted of cantors, organists and town musicians, all connected in some way with the church, the first thing they did when they met together was to sing a chorale. From this devout beginning they passed to jests. They improvised folk-songs together in such a way that the various impromptu parts made a kind of harmony, though the words were different in each voice. It was a kind of extempore counterpoint.

Thus Johann Sebastian Bach is a historical postulate. The grandest creations of the chorale from the twelfth to the eighteenth century adorn his cantatas and passions. Bach makes the chorale the foundation of his work. To give his true biography is to exhibit the nature and the unfolding of German art. This genius was not an individual but a collective soul. If a soul is life able to express itself, we cannot but attribute to it a complete tonal language. In long connected stretches of sound—as in larger, smaller, or even the smallest fragments—his music became the vowels, syllables, words and phrases of a language in which something hitherto unheard, unspeakable, could find voice. Every letter of this language was of infinite intensity, and in the joining of these elements there was unlimited freedom of judgment. "In music," Richard Wagner said, "you can be at home as in a veritable mother-tongue; when I had anything to say, I no longer had to trouble about the formal side of expression." "Music is the universal language of Mankind." (Longfellow.) A political system based on music as a national institution cannot but be a universal contribution to humanity.

A good instance of this German contribution to the rest of the world is the German hymnody. Of it an English writer says: "German hymnody surpasses all others in wealth. The Church hymn was born with the German Reformation, and has ever since been most extensively cultivated by the evangelical church in Germany. The number of German hymns cannot fall short of one hundred thousand. We may safely say that nearly one thousand of these hymns are classical and immortal. This is a larger number than can be found in any other language. To this treasury of German song several hundred men and women of all ranks and conditions—theologians and parsons, princes and princesses, generals and statesmen, physicians and jurists, merchants and travellers, labourers and private persons—have made contribution.

Thus these hymns constitute a most graphic book of confession for German evangelical Christianity, a clear mirror showing its deepest experiences.

Now Paulus Gerhardt, the greatest of these hymnwriters, next to Luther, begins sixteen of his hymns with "I." It is not so much the individual soul that lays bare its sometimes mor-

bid moods *as it is the representative, speaking out* the thoughts
and feelings he shares with his fellow members of the Church,
i.e., with every Christian man.

It gives me comfort to transcribe this judgment of an English
expert, John Julian, the author of *The Dictionary of Hymnol-
ogy,* because any German is biassed by the power German
music possesses over his mind and soul. To make the difference
even more striking, one may remember that the non-Lutheran
Protestants did not approve of the use of original hymns in
public worship. The Puritans were long satisfied with metrical translations of the Psalms. A famous German, Albert
Schweitzer, in his biography of Bach, says: "At the first glance
it may seem incomprehensible that Calvin, by making the
Psalter the hymnbook of the people, should from the very
beginning condemn his church to infertility." [9] Schweitzer, as
a German, cannot help identifying the chorale with church
music itself. We have already seen how inevitably the English
turned to the Psalter. But, for the Reformation, music was the
way in which every Christian man could reach the goal which
the priest had already attained in the wonderful rhythms of his
Latin prayers. The layman after Luther, in his fight for equality with the priest, had to rival, not the prose of a sermon but
the tunes of the mass, which lie between speech and song. The
German in his singing is attacking a privilege and making men
equal before God. Secular music was sovereign music still!

From Beethoven to Strauss, philosophical music led the way.
It is true, Schubert, Schumann, Brahms were faithful to the
unphilosophical tradition. Felix Mendelssohn, the Christian
descendant of a Jewish philosopher, revived with fervent faith
the evangelical Bach, and himself composed the wonderful
songs of "Paulus" or "Elias." But in spite of all these other
trends, the political and religious force of German music was
transferred during the century of liberalism to the heroic, the
Promethean music of Beethoven. In the era of individualism,
Ludwig van Beethoven could become the very genius of music
to every liberal, every individual, every self-made man. Any

[9] See also P. A. Scholes, *Music and Puritanism,* Lausanne, 1934.

American or Frenchman who is dried up by the formula of his own nationality takes comfort when he listens to the quartettes of Beethoven. Here the Christian soul of man has expressed in undenominational form the universal secret of the child of the nineteenth century, beyond the limits of class or ideology or economics or nationality.

Beethoven, and the worship of Beethoven by people like Romain Rolland—whose many-volumed story of a musician, Jean Christophe, is but a translation of Beethoven into French —teach a great lesson in revolutionary interplay. The nineteenth century being "French," "liberal," "democratic," Germany had to adapt herself to the new situation. But her adaptations in the way of democracy, capitalism, or other imitative forms of political machinery, were much less important than the great contribution she made through her own genuine national institutions.

In the field of music, Beethoven bridged the gulf between Lutheranism and modernity; and he, therefore, could become the best interpreter to foreign democracies of the eternity which lay behind Germany.

There is a sharp contrast between Beethoven and Wagner in this respect. Beethoven emancipated German music. Wagner introduced into the German instrument of psychic expression, by a tour de force, all the varied spices of the nineteenth century.

Beethoven clarifies, Wagner mixes. Schopenhauer's philosophy, Parisian perfumery, proletarian anti-capitalism, anti-Semitism—all the passions, prejudices and heresies of the nineteenth century were pressed into German music till it bellied like a sail in the full wind of contemporaneity. Wagner was so engrossed in being the super-individual, the artist and genius of the nineteenth century, that he had no time to be a gentleman of the eighteenth. His music, in its perfumed sultriness, but also in its grandeur and pomposity, replaced the pure, simple worship of the Lutheran Church by a baroque opera-worship.

Beethoven was a secularized Bach, manly, courageous. Wagner's music is not courageous. It is mystifying and obscuring.

But it had the great merit of giving to the isolated, weakened and nervous soul of a German *"Gebildeter,"* who no longer went to church, a substitute for his lost religion. At Bayreuth the atmosphere of melting polyphony was consciously used to play on the nerves of the middle-class man, who was impotent as soon as he was left alone, whose emotions had to be kneaded as if in a Turkish bath. Bayreuth, as Nietzsche exclaimed, was already a relapse from the Lutheran courage-to-stand-alone. It was a secular Rome again: "Rome's songs without its words, but with its incense."

For 350 years German music had accompanied the German soul in its voluntary exile from the visible church, until the day when it became too weak to bear the pressure of this loneliness and went back to bathe in the comfort of the senses.

But Wagner was no longer a Protestant musician, and it would be very unfair to measure him by Protestant standards. Wagner dreamed of a reconciliation of the religious parties. It was no accident that he was aided by the great Catholic family of Franz von Liszt. This family has made a wonderful contribution to Bayreuth. From 1840 to 1869, while Wagner was in exile, the Magyar, Franz von Liszt, the composer of the *Saint Elizabeth*, promoted, financed, consoled and protected him. His daughter, Cosima Liszt, did the same. She betrayed, left, wounded her first husband, she sacrificed everything to "Hans Sachs," the old master, who married her when he was fifty-seven. She gave him all her tears, all her self-denial. When he died she cut her long hair (then the only possible hair-dress for a woman) and laid it in his coffin. She watched the traditions of Bayreuth like an Argus. After Cosima and Franz, Siegfried sacrificed himself, serving his father with the devotion of a Liszt and abandoning his own originality as a Wagner, until he died in 1932.

Three generations of a Catholic family from Austria-Hungary faithfully carried on and realized the Wagnerian dream of an absolute music.

German music, in order to become universal, absolute, a *"Gesamtkunstwerk,"* had to find a way of representing not one half of the German nation but its totality.

Germany: we have spoken of it as though it were merely Lutheran. But its great national revolution had created parties of reform; and the Catholic party was even more numerous than the Protestant. Wagner's background is not Lutheran Germany, but all Germany; hence his music goes beyond the split between Protestants and Catholics.

In the chapter on Austria the antagonism between these two religious parties, each with equal rights, will appear more clearly. The history of German music must be treated as beginning in its purest forms in the Protestant half of the country and nourishing generations of teachers, parsons, cantors, composers, on its faith in the invisible.

Music was the audible symbol of a church struggling against too much clearness and visibility. But the State, too, in its temporal rule, had to find a symbolic language for its own ideals and purposes. In what form could it best be made clear that this State was not a papal State, that it was ruled by a secular prince, not a priest—and yet by a prince who was a deeply believing Christian?

THE GREEN MOUNTAIN GLADE.

On the Continent, the ship of State did not move on a sea of troubles such as faced the Englishman when he sailed the five oceans of the world. The object of the recurrent and never-ceasing care for a territorial ruler in Central Europe was the forest. After a thousand years of chopping and cutting, 27 per cent of the area of Germany is still covered by forests. More than one quarter of a country where every square inch has been "cultivated," furrowed, turned, is covered by trees even today. Forestry was a national concern for the German rulers. The notorious word *"Kultur"* carries, to begin with, the notion of *Landeskultur,* cultivation of the soil. A German thinks of planting trees whenever he hears the word *"Kultur."* Trees take a long time to grow. It is *this long period* of cultivation that constitutes the outstanding privileges of a government's economic policy as against that of the individual. The far-sightedness of a paternal government has protected the German woods. "Paternal" means being unmoved by immediate profits; "paternal" stands for patience and indifference to the incentives of the day. Sports, movies, radio, newspapers, take advantage of our childishness. The German individual State was rigid and austere, its people unswayed by the demagogue; it was paternal because it took thought for a long future. It restored the chief wealth of the soil: its trees. For a poor, sandy, rainy and foggy land, it is the greatest of all services to foresee and discount the results of any waste far in advance. In a rich country waste is less disastrous. In a poor district, where tomorrow is as poor as today, any encroachment of today upon tomorrow leads to destruction.

The woods of Germany are its most popular institution. Innumerable songs have been sung in their honour. The German passion for walking is connected with them. Carl Schurz, the great American German, wrote in his brilliant *Reminiscences* about his inner relation to the German woods:

"In these lonely walks, when roe, fox, rabbit and now and then a wild boar rustled past me, I learned to love the woods and to feel the fascination of the forest solitude, with its mysterious silence under the great leaf-roof and the whisper of the wind in the tree-tops. Soon I cared less for the bird-trapping than for the enjoyment of that woodland dream. This love for the woods has never left me, and often in later life, at the aspect of a beautiful spreading landscape or of the open sea, I have asked myself whether what I had seen and felt in the forest, did not surpass all else."

The likeness of man in all his dignity to a tree in the forest is an everlasting German concept.

When German boys in their wanderings sing:

> "Who has built thee, shining wood?
> I wish to praise thy builder,"

they are not under the spell of a jungle, a virgin forest of primary growth; nor is it a wilderness of second growth which has got out of hand. It is an inter-play of mastership and free, vigorous growth, telling not of the man who made it, but of the lawful order to which he has reformed it.

The German student songs about Prague and Innsbruck,

Heidelberg and Jena, are songs of forests and hills, of wanderings through green woods and fields.

If the German composers have built the invisible church
of music, German poets have glorified the natural scenery of
the State: its woodlands. In his greatest political poem, *Ilmenau,*
Goethe, the most universal poet of Germany, translated Luther's hopes into secular speech.

Like any German counsellor, Goethe had obeyed the call
of a young prince, younger than himself. The son of a proud
republican, a titulary counsellor of the Empire, he became the
privy counsellor of a petty prince in Thuringia. These native
princes had divided the territories of their houses like any
inheritance, and had only one common enterprise left: the
University of Jena was maintained by the Saxon princes of
Gotha, Weimar, Meiningen, Hildburghausen and Altenburg
in peaceful partnership. By virtue of the university Thuringia
was still a unit, still recognizable as the old fatherland of
Luther.

But everything else seemed changed when Goethe arrived
in Weimar in 1775. French language, philosophy and poetry,
as well as English aristocratic principles, ruled at the court.
Goethe, because he was not a noble, had to eat at the Lord
Steward's table instead of the Duke's! Only in 1782, when the
Emperor ennobled him by letters patent, was he allowed to
sit where princes—as we should think—or Lutheran tradition
might have placed him from the very beginning.

Goethe devoted himself to the friendship of the young duke.
Both revelled in mountains and woods, like prophets of nature,
and not rhetorically like Rousseau, but everywhere asking after
the poor man's needs, working at a fire-patrol, spending the
night outdoors. And when the poet and the duke, after five
years of life together, wished to erect a monument to their
friendship, it became a poem in honour of the forest. *Ilmenau*
seems to be one of the six or seven important poems of Goethe
which have never been translated into English. This in itself
points in the direction of our thesis, that the political scope
of forestry is a specifically German thing. The forest is more
than the scene of the poem. Goethe begins:

"Delightful vale and you, green mountain glade,
Once more I bring you greetings from the heart.
Spread your deep-laden branches wide apart,
And welcome me into your friendly shade!
How often in the midst of fortune's changes,
Exalted peak, have I returned to thee!
Oh grant me now, today, that I may see
A young, new Eden on thy pleasant ranges!
You owe it to me, for with care unseen,
I watch and wait while you are growing green."

It is not a dialogue with Nature, but one with a cultivated soil which receives constant care, but always escapes the absolute domination, of man. The forest is an *eternal task,* never a garden, never a desert. It bears fruit, but never for the man who plants it. Always it asks for patience and thrift, and prays to be spared from greed, haste, or carelessness. Goethe, at the end of his *Ilmenau,* makes the forest the pattern of government.

"So may this corner of thy land, O Prince,
Suggest the pattern of thy days!"

In no other language could one taste the sweetness of this verse which makes the forest a model of our own "days," our march through time.

Forests give and receive; we penetrate Nature by serving her and yet leaving her free. The small Continental state is bounded on all sides, and gets its constitution from this fact of being a frontier. The Prince de Ligne, known Austrian general, said wittily of the English constitution: "Well, its most important provision is the ocean that surrounds England." The most significant item in every German constitution was, as a matter of course, this fact of the territorial frontier. Like the Czechoslovak Republic of today, the single German State had political boundaries everywhere. The efficiency of the central government was everywhere confronted by its visible limit in space. It could be creative only by virtue of its intensity. It could not move indefinitely but had to reshape, reform, cultivate limited resources. No growing empire to the westward, but wooded mountains surrounding a little area; and this little area is ruled with the parsimony of a father. To be paternal means to permit no waste.

Paternalism became the common token of every prince, every civil servant down to the last policeman. When Goethe introduced a parliament into his little "State," he welcomed the deputies with these remarkably German verses:

> "The man of good husbandry is chosen counsellor,
> Everybody must be a father at home:
> Then the prince can be father of the fatherland."

Goethe wrote these verses in 1817.

The "Deputy," the French parliamentarian, was introduced into German in the form of the counsellor, already familiar to us. Husbandry, paternalism, was what Goethe wished to see at work in every part of the State. Then the parliamentary groups would produce, by their collaboration and co-ordination, a prince who can act as a kindly father rather than as a stern judge. Without the homogeneity of the parts, the throne would be unnatural. But when paternalism is at work on all levels, one explains the other.

Earth is not deaf to the courageous. The mysterious dialogue between man and creation was represented to the Germans by the Christmas tree. In Germany the Christmas tree is not a children's toy. In the woodland, among a mining population, as in Luther's fatherland, Christmas is the central event of the year. Children and parents count the years from Christmas to Christmas. The whole promise of the forest comes into the modest *"Stube"* of the German peasant or craftsman with the lighted tree. Its candles, shining in the darkest night of the year, are a sign to him of how the world, in response to his labour, has been reformed, brought back under the hand of his Father in heaven.

TRUNK AND BRANCHES.

Quite generally the forest emphasizes the limitations of human influence. It therefore takes in the German imagination, the place of the ocean in English literature. It is a limit; and it explains the essence of the German State and government as a limited concept. The State is not omnipotent. The prince himself, in Goethe's poem, is addressed by his friend as "the scion of an old princely stock." The limits of good government are found in the territorial limits which define the claims of an hereditary prince. The prince governs a section of the German nation. This faith in the *"angestammten Fürsten"* is inconceivable to the Anglo-Saxon who has never had a native dynasty. *"Angestammt"* is not simply "native" or "inborn" or "ancestral," as it is translated in dictionaries; for in this case, as in all cases where a national language reveals itself as a political creed instead of a mere local mechanism, the lexicographers find themselves at a loss. Languages are not mechanical means to an end, as they appear to be in the commercial world. The business man must use language as he finds it. He can perhaps make words artificially; and thus most people think of language as though it were made by man. But the true man speaks a language as he speaks the truth, not making speeches but speaking out what crosses his mind, as a filament glows in the electric bulb. The bulb does not make its own light. Our speech, the Logos of the gospel, leads all of us who are of good will. Anybody who thinks that men invented language as they have invented the making of buttons or coins or stamps, is certainly incapable of understanding one word of the history of mankind. Words are not our tools; since Adam first called things good and evil men have cried, spoken, shrieked, screamed, sung, called and commanded because they *must,* not because they would. True language is an expression of necessity, not a tool in a man's hand.

If a word like Revolution or Reformation, Commonwealth or police, *"angestammt"* or "birthright" cannot be translated from English into German, or vice versa, without misgivings, it is precisely because these words are of overpowering weight, dominating us like matters of life and death, not like mere products of someone's fancy. For every honest fellow language is prayer. And if it is not, he becomes an empty shell, perhaps with some remnants of parliamentary speech still dribbling out of him.

This is the way in which I must try to explain the full meaning of the "scion of an old princely stock" in Goethe's *Ilmenau*. For thanks to this attitude the "stemmed" prince, the monarch, is anchored deep in his people. He belongs to them like the trunk to the branches.

In a system of civil service it is a difficult question how to co-ordinate so many individual experts. The English Civil Service lacks one of the essential points of the German tradition: the head of a department does not always take the responsibility for his inferiors. It often happens that the subordinate is made the scapegoat. It is of the essence of the idea of a civil service or an efficient bureaucracy that the superior has to answer for the sins of his men. And that is something he can do only if he is in moral contact with them and can answer for them not through legal forms but through his personal relations. But then he must be looked upon as the trunk and his staff as branches.

In the individual Lutheran State the formation of a model servant would have been impossible if the ruler had had to pay the slightest heed to suggestions from the bosses. The constituent element of a good civil service is that it does not depend on favours from outside. Bureaucracy has to serve the poorest of the poor and do right, not because the petitioner has a letter of introduction but because he is in the right. The detachment of the civil servant, which makes him no respecter of persons, is impossible wherever his appointment is the result of a bargain between the head of his department and some outside power or boss.

The monarchic faith of the Lutheran throws a cross light on his courage for reform. How can you reform the abuses of popery, clergy, darkness, if you are in danger of losing your very footing in the territory where you work? Only the "stemmed" prince, the native dynasty, can give stamina to the arbitrary scrap of land called a State.

The German, in fighting the papal hierarchy, clung to the rooted trunk of an established central power. The disease of

an incapable monarch was not unknown to the Reformers. But
they looked upon a wicked prince as we today look on the
depression, or as the Chinese and Russians regard famine.
These things are inconvenient, but it is no use to start a riot
or a little revolution against the depression. Misrule is terrible,
but it is better than violent change. In a famous poem Chamisso
relates in four stanzas the answer given by an old woman to the
demands of four successive generations of lords of the manor
to which she belongs. At first she angrily resists the new tax
imposed upon her. She succeeds; the old lord abdicates. But
the next is worse, and the third worse still. At the end of the
poem she prays, "Let this lord be saved, though he is wicked."
Bad government is no specific attribute of monarchy; it is the
curse of government itself.

The Germans established a constant pole around which all
the particles of the new body of reformers could be grouped.
Where a presidential election must be held every four years
there can be no efficient bureaucracy. Under the threat of frequent change the honest public servant must entrench himself
behind the letter of his instructions or regulations; the moment he leaves this shelter he is exposed to any and all pressure
from outside. The dishonest official yields to personal motives.
Now I do not believe that the majority of the people in any
department is ever dishonest. But they are forced to lose all
initiative. They live in fear. Red tape is a symbol of the
despondency of a civil servant under outside pressure. He becomes a pedant.

Germans may be pedants in scholarship, but they are not
pedants as officials. The competition between so many small
individual states, the exchange between many staffs, the reliability of the central "stock" effectively supervising all its
branches because it itself depends on nobody's vote or favour,
made the German civil servant both sovereign and responsible.
He knew the letter of his regulations, but he did not lose himself in them. He was completely detached from the surrounding populace, from rich and poor alike. The German monarch,
with his democracy of scholars, was a prince of the poor against
the rich, a *prince des gueux,* a king of beggars. As late as 1900,

the King of Prussia could be acclaimed by Schmoller, in all seriousness and with all emphasis, as the *Roi des Gueux*. The gratitude of a Lutheran country towards its scion of old princely stock was formulated three hundred years ago in classical terms: "No nation on earth has been blessed with greater benefits than this nation now enjoyeth, having the true and free profession of the Gospel under our most gracious sovereign Lord King, the most great learned and religious king that has ever reigned therein, *enriched with a most hopeful and plentiful progeny, proceeding out of his royal loins,* promising continuance of this happiness and profession to all posterity." This truly "Lutheran" language and "Reformed" doctrine of government was used by the English Parliament, after the Gunpowder Plot, on November 5, 1605.

The religious belief of Germans in this balance of power at once explains the last repercussion in 1918, when all Central Europe was despoiled of its "stocks" of princes. Complete chaos and confusion reigned. The "cadres," the whole structure of society, broke down. The trunks were uprooted and the branches fell with them. After 1918 the old dynastic religion lingered in the background, haunting the national conscience. Hitlerism and racial superstition are the direct result of Woodrow Wilson's discrimination between the nations of Central Europe and their bad governors. Once the stocks of kings were uprooted, King Demos, King Mob, set up a new dynastic dogma. The mass, of itself, is now descended from Valhalla, Teuton in blood, Germanic in breeding, sprung from the old pagan stock of Wotan and Thor. Though this be madness, yet there is method in it; and he who does not lose his head under certain circumstances, has probably no head to lose.

Hitler's "Racism" is a reasonable, nay, rationalistic transformation of the dynastic dogma. A nation accustomed to look to several scores of dynasties as the immutable trunks and pillars of law and order for the many millions of its members, has transferred this tradition to the people themselves, since the dynasties disappeared. The people have to replace the tradition of dynasty by the myth of race—since the former High Magistrates had been dynastic rulers.

GOETHE'S FAUST.

The German artisan and his relationship to his raw material, is, in every branch of German craftsmanship, very much akin to the attitude of the forester or the father.

In both cases, that of forestation and that of the fatherland, things are produced which outgrow their progenitors. When Goethe in his first years at Weimar was almost in despair over his attempt to educate the Prince, he formulated the great prayer of his life thus: "O high fortune, let me achieve the day's work of my hands. No, these are not empty dreams; these trees, now lifeless sticks, will one day give fruit and shade." He might not see the results, but the future would bring with it a recurrent life. In this there was no vanity or ambition on his part. Goethe is not thinking of immortality, like a romantic hero. His trees neither will nor shall bear the name Goethe. But in their life he will be represented. Goethe also said: "He who has not begotten a child or planted a tree is no man."

To plunge into an objective world which follows its own rules but allows you to serve it, is the aim of the true civil servant. He is a layman, but he has a *field* (*Fach*). This objective world of "fields" is no mechanism: it embraces peasants, trees, animals, craftsmen, arts, sciences. It is growing and organic. It is God's world. You cannot mould it arbitrarily to your shape or in your image. The things of creation shall be carried to their destined goal by the help of man. His best inspiration, his knowledge, his training, have to give up their personal character, their *namedness* or fame, before they can penetrate into matter and make the son greater than the father.

This is not a townsman's vision. In the town a man earns his living by his visible labour, sees what he visibly does, and hears his reputation proclaimed most audibly every day. The civil servant in the remote corner of a wooded mountain belongs to an *invisible order*. Without this moral power, no brain trust can build up a civil service free from graft and the spoils system.

The good government of German *Kultur* was interested

in the frontier, the remotest parts of the country. Here, above all, the system had to work. The systematic training of the university graduate made him a collaborator "par distance." His methodical training overcame the limits of personal contact. The new hierarchy of the civil service devoted itself to long-term enterprises carried on far from the court centres, without éclat.

The anti-*town* character of the German civil service is what makes it so important today in a world of outspoken reaction against big-city civilization. The limiting concept of the German frontier is reflected again and again in the greatest of German poems, Goethe's *Faust*. Faust rushes through the world. But the world of Faust is not Africa nor America, it is the present life of a small German town, with meadows and mountains around it, projected into the Greek classical past and into an ultimate vision of the future. Faust "rushes through the world," seizes every "moment by the forelock"; but his is a small world.

Wherever a group of men gives its time and labour to a field of nature, and thereby helps nature to its fulfilment, there you have the whole world, and the whole church, too.

Faust is in the invisible church. He is put by Goethe into the sixteenth century, the century of the Reformation. Faust, like any Lutheran, must answer these questions: Has he mistaken anything for the invisible church? Has he bowed down to the idols of this life? And his answer is: "No, I have not. I only rushed through life." Life itself was his pilgrimage, but not in the sense of a Bunyan.

Faust was never blinded by care nor possessed by worldliness like most men. No moment, however beautiful, ever absorbed him. He went on and on. Even in his last enterprise he does not ask to share in the fruits of his own plan:

"The swamp, abutting on the mountains, breeds a pestilential
    vapour—mars my loftiest deeds.
That spot, well trenched and aptly underdrained,
    Would give salubrity to what I've gained.
Then would the space which I've embanked become

A paradise!—a prosperous people's home.
Those only merit competence and freedom
Who daily watch and vigilantly heed them.
Such busy fellowship—with pleasure I could see—
Standing on ransomed ground—encircled by the free!"

Thus Earth—by the current that passes through a man's soul
—is brought back to its own destiny. Man's destination is invisible to himself. To the last, Goethe remains a Lutheran
in poetry. Faust cannot see his free land and his free people,
but he can hear them like celestial music in his ear. The click-
ing of spades sounds to him like the chorale of a singing congregation; he knows this is the sacrament of atonement for
earth, fallen from its divine destination:

"The crowds are delving, banking, piling,
Earth with itself *re—reconciling.*"

The poets, even the religious poets, must express themselves
in a worldly style. Goethe's *Faust* is a secular chant: it is the
translation of Luther into the vernacular. Goethe concentrated
in his work the wealth of the German language. And he knew
it. He was, as he explains in *Poetry and Truth*, by nature a
speaker, talker, narrator; in another nation, he would have
become a great orator. In the German nation, the man whose
genius lay in speech and words was forced into literature,
poetry and thought. Yet Goethe took over all the finest coinage of Lutheran speech from pulpit and chair. Literature was,
so to speak, his doctor's gown, as Luther had replaced his
monk's hood by the preaching of God's word.

A good instance of this transformation can be found in the
use of the word *Hoch* (high). The German predilection for
Hoch dates from the discovery of the highness in State and
University, as against the visible church of Rome. Goethe,
according to a new investigation by Wilhelm Ruoff, though
not at all interested in the quarrel of religious parties, sublimated the word and made it the keystone of his metaphysics.
"*Hoch* is Goethe's most important word. It plays a similar
rôle to that of 'eternal' among his concepts of time. In fact

it is still more important, because it can be extended still further and because it has a still greater wealth of meanings. Goethe pours everything into this word. It is his real metaphysical idea. This appears most clearly in the comparative 'Höher,' 'das Höhere,' which Goethe loves because it really does nothing but hint at an upward movement. The word is in a peculiar state of suspension. From below it is understandable; but when we look upward it is open, and it remains unexplained what the 'Höhere' really consists in. Thus it keeps somewhere about it a touch of the indefinite. *And to imply everything by this word, and yet leave a mystery around it—* that is the important thing to Goethe."

Goethe sang in the golden days of the German nation, 1763-1806, when the Reformation was harvesting its ripest fruits. The humiliation of the Thirty Years' War had been finally outgrown; the Napoleonic wars were still ahead. Three hundred and fifty princely households were competing for the best talents in music, in the arts and sciences, and in the cultivation of the soil. Klopstock, Herder, Schiller, Wieland, were writing and creating. The German Parnassus was in full splendour. Lessing, a secular Luther, had assailed the obscurantists and the narrowly orthodox in his famous exclamation, recalling Huss, recalling Hutten, recalling Luther himself: *"O sancta simplicitas!*—But I am not yet at the point, my dear pastor, where the noble man [Huss] was who uttered these words and could utter *nothing more* than this. Only he shall hear us and judge us who can and will hear and judge! O that he might hear it, he who I most fondly wish were my judge—Luther! Great, misunderstood man! And by no one more misunderstood than by the short-sighted blockheads who saunter along the road you pioneered, with your slippers in their hands, shouting, but indifferent at heart. . . . And so my knightly challenge in a few words. Write, my dear pastor, and have your associates write, to your hearts' content; I will write, too. If I yield to anything you say in the slightest matter that concerns me or my nameless friend, when you are wrong, then I will never touch my pen again."

Lessing was preparing the way for *Faust* when he cried in his *Nathan the Wise:* "Religion is a party also." Lessing, by expressing the great principle that we are all on the road to truth, each of us representing a party of religion, but only a party, enabled Goethe to make ideally accessible to everybody what had been limited, in reality, to the Lutheran faith. Before Goethe the Lutherans were impenetrable to the outside world. There was no osmosis by which the Catholics could share the experience of the Reformation. The times of Lessing and Goethe were golden times because they made transparent to the outside world what had been confined to those who had paid the full price of life.

The Lutheran faith, which lived in its hundreds of thousands of singing and serving members, was translated into the worldly poem of *Faust* so that its gospel, of the invisible church and of salvation through faith alone, might become intelligible to the members of all denominations. In the classical language of our nation's golden epoch, the heritage of the Reformation could be spread abroad. The German Catholics could not be converted before the time of Goethe because they had to resist Luther. The essence of the Reformation was only revealed in a second stage, that of high art, to those who were excluded from it in life. This is the political function of great art; for as Abbot Thayer said: "Art rescues man from his state of being limited to a point and to a moment. Contrive as you will, your camera cannot exclude the peculiarity of the moment and the place. This is the torture of the intellect, that it is condemned to still-photography. But it longs to see from all points, from all moments, as God does. The bliss of contemplation of a work of Art is this sense of emancipation, of seeing as God sees, and as we may sometimes see. What if it were prophetic?"

A man like Goethe is, in fact, a political and a religious phenomenon. We have already mentioned Dostoevski and Tolstoi, Balzac and Zola. Milton's *Paradise Lost* and *Paradise Regained* turned men's eyes from preformation (Luther's creed) to predestination. In Dante we shall have to face once more the political function of temporal poetry. The re-integration of the poet into the body politic today should be made easier by a new insight into his political function in the past.

PROTESTING POLICY.

To belong to a party in matters of religion meant, of course, a complete break with hierarchy in the Church; it destroyed the complicated hierarchy of the clergy, which had a different religion in every cloister. The "religious lappets and fringes" of a hundred monastic orders had to give way to a single *"religio christiana,"* the common religion of all Christian laymen. The six Sees whose interdicts (eleven in all) had troubled the peace of Saxony during the reign of Frederick the Wise now lost all territorial power.

In a curious anticipation of the storm, the last mediæval monarch of Germany, the so-called "Last Knight," Emperor Maximilian (1493-1518), had planned in 1512 to become pope himself. The scheme was not so fantastic as it looks: It would have been the Anglican solution of Henry VIII, by which the king became a pope. The Holy Roman Emperor had no way of heading a Germanic church; he had to attack the church at its very centre in Rome, because his Holy Empire, too, centred in Rome. His accession to the papacy would have concentrated the military and the civil rule in one hand. He would have become the strong monarch apostrophized by James I. When we remember that the taxes of the Holy Empire for the wars against the Turks were collected on Good Friday at the doors of the churches in every parish, from every participant in the Communion, we see the tremendous interpenetration of Church and State, and ask ourselves why this step of Maximilian's toward reforming Rome herself might not have been successful.

Instead of allowing the Emperor, the advocate of Rome, to swallow up the papacy, the princes of Germany swallowed up the whole hierarchy: councils, popes, bishops, abbots, prelates, and priests. One unified *"religio christiana"* sufficed for the outer garment of the Christian faith in each territory. The various sixteenth-century books with the title *Religio Christiana* have a penchant toward equality, liberty, fraternity, in matters of religion. *Religio Christiana* is not a pious tract like the book of the same title written by Augustine one thousand years before. It is a revolutionary treatise, because it subverts the whole varied and elaborate hierarchy; it unites a hundred "religions" under a single generalization. Henceforth the only possible variety in religious customs is a local variety; no other differences exist between Christians. The Holy Ghost showers its gifts upon any place, any nation, as Luther said, like a sudden downpour of rain. No body of "lords spiritual," no clergy, has a genuine right to call its own office more "inspired" than that of any other man in the community. The local magistrate alone is responsible for the unification and fitting observance of divine worship among his people. These are matters of ethics, of taste, of convenience, of education. They are not sacraments, they are merely sound policy. The phrase "good police" is the first expression of what the Germans later called *"Kultur."* Police is derived from the Greek *"polis,"* exactly as "civilization" is derived from the Latin *"civitas."* The reform of the Church is not a matter for one pope, one emperor, one visible head; it is a matter of good police in every jurisdiction in the world. By coining the word police and by glorifying it, the Germans established a united front against the hierarchy; because, by its Greek origin and by its intention, "police" did not belong to the magic circle of Roman Church and Roman Empire. It was a free, pluralistic word, accessible to every magistrate of good will and proper education.

The democratic character of Protestantism, the generality of its Christian form of life, was the battering-ram, "police" was the instrument which moved the ram, and the preaching of the word was the trumpet which made the walls of Jericho—the hierarchical church—fall without a serious fight.

The Lutheran "party of religion" is therefore a democratic party in the Church and a monarchical party in matters of government. It is exactly the opposite of the situation in England, where, as we have seen, the Commons fettered the King in Parliament but had to leave him, the "Defender of the Faith," as head of the Anglican Church.

The Lutheran "party of religion" not only had the pope to deal with, it had to do away with an overcomplicated structure of different clerical functions and offices. The German princes had to inherit and transform the functions of councils and synods, of Paris and Bologna, of cardinals and bishops. And some of these functions were quite indispensable. With all its abuses, the Mediæval Church had set up a number of absolutely necessary institutions.

The "police" of the High Magistrates had to build schools, hospitals, colleges for young men. Like Wolsey at Oxford, the German princes founded training schools for their staff. For example, in 1559 the Duke of Württemberg founded his *Collegium Illustre*. This was the princes' monastic inheritance. The maintenance of a good "police" obliged the father of his people to listen to the united voice of the universities and the unanimous creed of his party of religion. This was his heritage from the great democratic institutions of the Church in the fifteenth century. The religious party of the Reformation was the true successor of the princely opposition against the pope at the great councils of Pisa, Constance, and Basel.

The reforming princes had been the organized and permanent opposition in these councils, claiming the right to reform the church in "head and members," root and branch.

As the opposition at the mediæval councils, the Magistrates had emphasized that they as an organized body were part of the universal Catholic Church; though in an Opposition, they had remained Catholic Christians. Now they dropped the word "Roman" and avoided all disastrous substitutes like "Anglican." They were Christians pure and simple, not Anglicans or Roman Catholics. There is a famous story of how Bismarck, being asked with an ironical smile by a Cardinal of the Roman Church, "I dare say Your Excellency thinks we Catholics cannot go to heaven at all?" replied with the same smile: "A Catholic layman might, of course. About a priest I am not so sure." Made as it was 350 years after Luther's time, the remark illustrates very well the Protestant's opposition to all hierarchies.

The Catholic hierarchy had committed itself so deeply that the corruption could only be healed by the secular arm. At the councils, the party of Reform had found itself opposing a degenerate clergy. When Luther encouraged the princes to do without the pope, neither he nor they had rejected the summons to a universal council. But they made certain conditions in order to test the efficacy of their opposition. When the pope finally fulfilled one of these conditions by summoning the universal council to meet at a German place, namely in the southernmost city of Germany, Trent, the Protestants doubted his good faith; but until this day the Lutheran churches have never rejected the possibility of such a council. By this theoretical possibility the Protestants are still connected, even today, with the Roman Catholic Church. For in theory the sovereign of the local territory was nothing but an emergency-executive, not the normal bishop or head of the church.

But this local sovereign *was* allied with his colleagues in a political body of permanent character which had survived from the councils of the Church, and which for that very reason did not seriously desire any council. All that they needed they could accomplish just as well through their party organization. The Holy Spirit, the inspiration in matters of the Faith, was assured by the new learning. The new vicars of Peter, the territorial emergency-executives called forth by Luther, were willing to be guided by the vicars of Paul, the leader of the Gentiles, in all questions of universal doctrines.

The violence of German criticism, the habit of cross-lighting a question from all possible angles, and the harshness of the German police are still all relics of this truculent opposition to the established hierarchy and its abuses. In this sense Protestants are always "anti"; they are always dependent upon the existing darkness which they attack. The German, with all his critical capacities, is not ready to take over the government he has attacked. German parliamentary government has always failed because the opposition never dreamed of moderating its criticism and relating it to the practical issue at stake. The first rule of the parliamentary game is: as soon as one has failed, the other has his turn. German parliaments or Diets always criticized without limit, but were never ready to act themselves. Radical prophesying seemed enough. Three short examples from the last century may illustrate the German ways: One is taken from the notorious "Era of Metternich," the reactionary period after the Napoleonic wars; the next from '48, the year which gave so many good citizens to America; and the last from the Weimar Republic after the World War.

In 1819, the conflict between the free conscience of a great nation and the despotism of the many States, based on their police forces, came to a head in the following scene: A German professor, who had spontaneously led the German students into the war against Napoleon and so enjoyed a certain authority, went to Berlin to discuss with the Prussian government the political dissatisfaction among the students. In good keeping with the old dreams of 1524, ay, of 1460, he advised the chancellor to hold a convention or convocation of professors which would represent the nation's public spirit. He hoped to bridge the gulf between the interests of the many separate States and the united national spirit, by such a representation of German learning. But the old confidence of the governments was already gone. The chancellor replied: "Public opinion? Public opinion is in no need of a special representation. Public opinion is sufficiently represented by my police force."

An opposite mistake was made by the professors in 1848. They thought they could be victorious without real force.

In 1848 the German professors gathered in Frankfurt-am-Main in a real national Council of Doctors à la Luther. It was in perfect harmony with their Pauline tradition that their meeting place was the Church of St. Paul. They tried to do what the German doctors had been expected to do at the National Council in 1524, and before in 1460. The "Professors' Parliament" of 1848 was a secular version of the part played by the "new learning" at Wittenberg and all the other universities. Beseler, Dahlmann, Waitz, Gervinus, Uhland, Sybel, Grimm—the best scholars and civil servants of Germany—were assembled in Frankfurt from the spring of 1848 to the spring of 1849.

But they kept the Christian order of things: prophecies preceded action. And their theories were not "deduced from facts established by themselves," as they were in the English Parliament. The party of religion, not being inflexible, astronomical, i.e., moving opposition as in England, but fixed in permanent protest, made a spasmodic effort at Frankfurt, not to govern itself, but to protect itself from being governed by others. But not being at a distance of three thousand miles from their rulers, like the American colonies, the professors in Frankfurt lost the advantage of time. The kings and princes sent their police against the professors and dissolved their parliament.

The walls of Jericho can only fall if there is time to blow the trumpet. 1848 was not the time to preach, but to create a democratic police and army instantly; the professors only preached, and so they failed. The State of the Reformation proved Revolution-proof. Once more the police were able to paralyze freedom of speech outside the universities. The ban of too much police fell upon Germany again.

After the World War, the Social Democrats had no real authority because their unlimited criticism destroyed authority itself. Such a Socialist official, on Constitution Day of the Weimar Republic, would hoist the Red Flag of Marxism from his private house; at the same time, over his office, the republican tricolour was flying; and in his official capacity, he would insist that all the old monarchists should use and respect this tricolour which they hated. Thus, the man protested against the order of things (by his red flag) which he represented himself, and which he enforced upon his political enemies, officially. This, really, was the caricature of Protestantism. And so Protestantism was doomed.

HITLER.

The system of religious parties has been overruled in Germany today. Hitler is a pre-Reformation type, by race, education and character. He is immune to the last four centuries of German history. He is neither a Protestant nor an academic person nor a civil servant nor an army officer. With true instinct, he has declined any honorary degree in a university and any emblem of special rank in the army. He is the unknown soldier of the rank and file and for that reason he is able to begin all over again like an unreformed man. To him, as a stranger to Reformation Germany, the spiritual victory of Paul over Peter does not mean anything. He himself has become pope, bishop, monk and council in one person. What he has restored is the immediate divine inspiration of the political "leader." The distribution between the two powers, the inner prophetical, and the outer political, one, is dismissed. What the Reformation had abolished, a visible hierarchy in matters of faith and conviction, is restored today by a yearning nation that has missed too long the splendour of a visible spiritual authority.

The German nation, in its smaller diameter of formerly imperial territories—that is to say, with the exception of Alsace, Luxemburg, Switzerland, Bohemia, the Netherlands—makes Hitler as much a pope, a doctor of souls, a saint, a sovereign over conscience, as any Saint Peter with the keys. When a parson of the German faith was interviewed about political murder, he simply pointed with his finger to the picture of "The Leader" on the wall; no further justification was given.

The reaction against the Protestant tradition is most violent in the north. In the territories of Habsburg-Austria, the Hitler type is well-known of old. For that reason he is less contagious there. Even in Hohenzollern-Germany, no eminent Catholic or Jew would envision anyone as the Messiah. But Protestants in the north simply give way to the temptation of being admitted again to the worship of a visible power.

I am sorry to say that, in my own room in Berlin, the adviser of the then new Reichsbishop told me that "Of course, Hitler *is* Christ." A certain Dr. Frank preferred, in all earnest, to compare Hitler to God the Father. In a theological summer school on the Hainstein, near Luther's Wartburg, the future ministers were taught to see Christ in every Storm Trooper. Everything is popish, is Catholic, in the new system, except the names; the word "pope" or "church" or "heresy" or Saint or martyr cannot officially be used. Still, when one wishes to understand the function of Hitler and Goebbels as compared to the army, the only equivalent can be found in the ecclesiastical vocabulary of the Middle Ages.

After four hundred years of reform the *raison d'être* of German Protestantism is gone. The weekly sermon against popery has lost its meaning when all Christians line up together. The tension which bound together, in one person, the two attitudes, that of a responsible pastor and that of a free, protesting Christian, has been broken. The rock of a racial religion is needed today in Germany because its High Magistrates, the sponsors of the free profession of the Faith, are gone. The downfall of the twenty dynasties in Germany necessarily brought on the most terrible outbreak of fear and hysteria: without the dynastic States, the German intellectual attitude of constant Protest has become a nuisance.

A great nation like the German could live without a visible church just as long as the thoughtful criticism of "every" Christian was balanced by the prerogative of "every" prince. Then, the unending criticism might produce the sublimation of politics into reform. The World War destroyed this balance by destroying the power centres, and what was left of the Christian's liberty appeared as the sulky grumbling of mud rakers. Without a powerful state, a dreaded sovereign, a victorious army, a possible expansion, the individual German could not sit and sulk or philosophize or protest. He only could crave for a moral or religious unity of sacred character which would alleviate the offences from the outside and the anxieties within the flock. The system of the German Reformation has been destroyed in Germany today.

The three essentials of the Reformation: civil service, universities, music, are of no importance any longer. They have been sacrified, after the princes fell, by a young generation full of fear, full of superstitions, full of the need for a simple universal faith, and its personification in Hitler. A Storm Trooper like the Potemba murderers who trampled to death a political enemy in the presence of his mother, and who were acclaimed by Goebbels and acquitted by Hitler for doing so, is far away from the civil servant and wise counsellor of his prince; the *Parteischulen* and *Ordensburgen* in which *Mein*

Kampf or "The Myth of the Twentieth Century" are studied, are strange contrasts to the Universities of Jena or Heidelberg where the "Word" of the Bible set in motion the stream of systematic criticism; the *Horst-Wessel-Lied* is no music.

The only thing continuing the experiences of the past is the army. And if we wish to make a real biological diagnosis of the German situation, we may ask ourselves if there has not been a similar situation, for another great European form of life, in former days. That will help to explain the stripping naked of Germany, the philosophy of the hammer of destruction swung by Hitler.

When the French Revolution started, the downfall of the Roman Church seemed inexorable. And the bodyguard of the pope, the Jesuit order, was sacrificed. Between 1772 and 1815 the order was formally dissolved. In 1815, however, the Jesuit order was restored. And a restoration befell the footstool of the papacy, the garden of the world, Italy, which seemed to take the life out of this great nation. In Piedmont, one member, at least, of every noble family was executed between 1815 and 1830. The Jesuit restoration marked the whole Catholic Church during the nineteenth century. The climax of Jesuit influence was seen in 1870, when the dogma of infallibility was proclaimed. The Roman Church of today, we may say without exaggeration, is the result of this comeback of the Jesuits. They saved the whole Church and imbued it with their spirit when they seemed to have disappeared forever.

What does accrue, from this example, to the understanding of our own day? When the papacy, Italy, the Jesuits, were restored to their mediæval function by force, in 1815, they were separated (from their own great achievement in Trecento and Quattrocento) by three other revolutions, German, English, French. Their own spirit was more than weak. The Jesuits, belonging to the sixteenth century, had still more vitality left, and the bodyguard of the papacy lent to the body of Christ the tendencies of the company de Jesu so completely that, during the nineteenth century, Church and Jesuits seemed to be one and the same thing to any outsider. This explains the rôle of the German army today. Between the German Reformation and our present day, three revolutions occurred: the Glorious, the Great, and the World Revolution. The body-guard around the German dynasties, the Prussian army, was in eclipse for the time from 1918 to 1933. And German militarism was said to have been crushed forever. And at the end of the period 1918-1933, the very elements graciously permitted the Germans by the Allies, as universities, music, and civil service, naturally disappeared, and the only institution that was destroyed under compulsion, the army, was restored. No human group of honour can behave otherwise. The popes had grave misgivings about the Jesuits. They could not help restoring them, after the persecution from the outside. Good Germans had their doubts about Ludendorff, and the Nazis themselves are no militarists. But what else could they do, after Germany's demilitarization under duress?

Now, this army is the "Counter-Bolshevik," as the Jesuits became the Anti-Jacobins during the nineteenth century. The interesting fact about both, however, is that they came into being much later than the civilization they defended; German particularism had produced Bach and Goethe, before Frederick the Great fought the Prussian War of Seven Years, with its "Diplomatic Revolution" in Europe.

The Jesuits were restored and have restored the Church. But have they? The Prussian army was restored and has restored Germany. But has it?

Such, however, is the consistency of political biology that any violence perpetrated against a really created political creation—and out of revolution, real creation takes place—leads to a regenerative effort. Hitler is one of the deepest lessons in political reproduction of created political forms; the consistency of political biology is enhanced by, not destroyed under, duress.

And the comparison between Italian and German reaction will enable the reader to draw his own conclusions as to the timing of English and French developments.

NON-RESISTANCE.

"The doctrine of passive obedience and of non-resistance, which a sort of men did of late, when they thought the world would never change, cry up as a divine truth, is, by means of the happy revolution in these nations, exploded, and the assertors of it become ridiculous." Thus wrote the man who had to justify the Revolution of 1689 in New England. Non-resistance, ridiculous in 1689, was the essence of the Lutheran Reformation. In 1525 the peasants had taken up arms. Luther had summoned the princes to exterminate the rabble. His exhortation is pitiless, but pithy. He conjures the princes to kill and hang, to crush and burn the rebellious populace. Nobody shall bear arms but the High Magistrate and his armed police. Anarchy is the only possible outcome of several private armies within one territory.

The Peasants' War marks an epoch because it destroyed for good and all the co-existence of different armed forces in one territory. Since then, it has been forbidden to carry arms except in the service of the government. Vendetta and private warfare still flourished in the days of Luther. Both peasants and knights subscribed to the customs of private warfare. The man in New England, writing in 1690, was already so sure of Luther's success that he could ridicule the opposite of it; but he had no intention of reviving the feuds or the anarchical state of affairs in Europe before the Reformation.

I know that the formula of passive obedience is what makes Luther unpopular with Anglo-Saxons; but since the two revolutions came one after the other not much can be done to reconcile their two different ways of thinking. They were made in dialectical opposition. The plea of the English Revolution is based, however, on the achievement of the German. The right of resistance, in England, was a right of *common* resistance, not one for the individual lord or knight. This common resistance, established in England, was impossible before a territory had been consolidated into one commonwealth by monarchy.

For that consolidation the princes had to be encouraged.

How could Luther preach resistance against the princes when he had to teach them themselves to resist? His life and his work depended on *princes who resisted*. Woe to him if they did not resist! He was lost if the princes did not defy the pope's bulls and beadles. Non-resistance is bad wherever a government can do what it pleases. But in Luther's day no government could! In a thousand and one cases the Church ruled and passed judgment on the actions of the local ruler. The magistrate was constantly exposed to the censorship of a visible church. Luther summoned the laity to abolish this censorship. Should he ask, in the same breath, for a check upon his deliverers? Only a fool or a *"Schwärmer"* would abolish all government. Luther had to turn *against the "Schwärmer"* with all the violence of his temperament, like Cromwell against the Levellers. Ranting and carrying arms were ruthlessly stamped out in Germany by the Reformation. Hitlerism is the first recrudescence of pre-Reformation feeling in Germany. The Peasants' War is very much in the mind of modern German youth. But anarchy and bloodshed are inevitable when people wear coloured shirts. Against both dangers, monarchy was built up.

Luther's non-resistance was not cowardice. If either murderers and brigands or princes and magistrates search out the secrets of a Christian man's conscience, Luther advises him to say openly: "I will not do what you command; take my body and estates, and thereby injure Him by whom you will be called to strict account. We must smite the devil in the face with the Cross." (April 11, 1533.) It was the principle for which Thomas More suffered martyrdom in England.

THE BIRTHDAY OF THE MODERN CONSTITUTION.

Luther reformed the Church and made it the free source of inspiration for each Christian soul. This exalted the kings and princes into highness and sovereignty, but it also emancipated house and court, stable and barn. Luther's Catechism never forgets the ox and the ass, the maid-servant and the man-servant, the housewife at her washing and her husband ploughing the fields. This emancipation of all labour is well described in Luther's own words: "The world does not know the hidden treasures of God. It cannot be persuaded that the maid working obediently and the servant faithfully performing his duty, or the woman rearing her children, are as good as the praying monk who beats his breast and wrestles with his spirit," and in the words of the earliest Lutheran song-books, written by Klara Zellin in 1534: "the journeyman sang these new songs at his work, the maid while she washed her pots and pans, the husbandman or vintager in the field, and the mother to the crying child in the cradle."

"Laity sanctified" is the true title of the Reformation. The only day which is unanimously added to the Catholic holidays in the calendar of all the reformed churches is the birthday of Martin Luther. The saints have their places in the calendar on the days when they were born in heaven. They are celebrated on the anniversary of their last day on earth; the Christian calendar is a collection of Good Fridays, of martyrdoms and farewells to earth. Jesus and John the Baptist are the only men whose birthdays are kept in the reformed Christian churches. But the tenth of November is kept also. It is the birthday of the one man who did not revolutionize nature, who restored no birthrights. Luther knows nothing about a sinless nature or an innate right. But he stands for the laity, for the immediate relation of the soul to God. He reformed the Church into a lay-church, he reformed it even to the point of profanation—bringing the faith outside the fanum (pro-fane: before the temple). He does not belong to the visible church, which he broke down. He certainly belongs to the Church.

In England the King's birthday is a vestige of the Lutheran Reformation. Each territory got its own day for the layman. The prince's birthday was what Labour Day is meant to be in our times: the day when every man is sanctified in his calling. The birthday of independence, the Fourth of July, is a still further translation of Luther's birthday into the day of American promise. America afterwards supplanted the stock of a dynasty by the strong trunk of a constitution. The scions of a race wither and die; the Constitution is immortal.

By virtue of this sanctification of Luther's birthday, all forms of government which have arisen since the Reformation have something in common: laity, dynasties (Germany), Commons, custom (England), natural genius (France), and pre-Adamitic forces (Russia) have come forward to restore the truth confided to the universal priest: man.

TRANSITION

CHAPTER EIGHT

Polybius, or, The Reproduction of Government

Rotation of Government—"Love Thine Enemy" in Politics—Marching in Echelon—"Open" versus "Public"—A Nation's Religion—European Dictionary—Bionomics of Western Man

ROTATION OF GOVERNMENT.

BETWEEN 1517 AND 1918 FOUR GREAT FORMS OF GOVERNMENT arose which entrusted the regeneration of society to the laymen, to a secular power. All these revolutions stand for a sovereignty of the temporal. The secular mind is made the sovereign, possessing in its own right the knowledge of good and evil. The layman, the commoner, the individual, the cog in the machine—everybody may now understand government. The secrets of the State are laid open to the public, step by step. The four great forms of government all have one and the same passion: to be free from the visible Catholic Church. But they also have many other things in common. By comparing them we shall get the best available material for a real political science of mankind. We can then present to the political scientist certain statements which are more than mere abstract definitions of our own.

First of all, these forms of government are the well-known, ancient forms described by Aristotle: monarchy, aristocracy, democracy, and dictatorship. Monarchy, as the hereditary form of government; aristocracy, as the system of co-optation; and democracy, as that of election, are represented by Germany, England and France respectively. And Russia ended the series by returning to the most comprehensive form, dictatorship.

Secondly, these forms of government follow each other in

order, but not within the same country. Once they have appeared, each in its own country and in its proper order, they co-exist. Kings, parliaments, capitalists and proletariats rule simultaneously.

Thirdly, the European countries form a unity in spite of their plurality. By acting as independent revolutionary bodies, they have achieved something in common, and each has achieved something for all. The European concert is a fact, not a dream. It goes deeper than a mere concert of ministers or presidents. It is a common campaign for the best form of government.

Fourthly, the ancients knew the rotation of constitutions. Polybius described it in detail, telling how every form of government degenerated and thereby failed, not because of its wrong measures but because it fell into the hands of the wrong men. Polybius and Aristotle were considered classics on this topic of the wheel of political fortune.[1] But nobody ever asked, during the Christian Era, whether the classical statement could be tested by the experience of Christian nations. There was a good reason for this neglect of so natural a question. Christians, knowing all the failures of paganism, hated to think of such an unreasonable rotation: the world was redeemed from the curse of blind repetition.

Today, Christians are much more modest; they make no distinction between antiquity and the Christian era. Few people can answer the very moderate question: "Is there any difference between the Christian era and antiquity?" Many would say, off-hand, in a pessimistic tone: "None whatever." After all, Christians even kept slavery among their legal and constitutional forms until 1865. How, then, is there any difference? Christianity is a beautiful ritual which we observe on Sundays; but a Christian era does not exist.

We do not share this conviction. The Christian era has established something which is completely outside the Sunday ritual and yet is universal, something quite simple, and yet miraculous. Aristotle and Polybius were right in their day;

[1] Polybius, VI, 3 _ff._; Aristotle, _Politics,_ VIII, 5, 12.

their pessimistic outlook for a permanent rotation of governments and constitutions was justified; the forms of government were mortal and transient. But the Christian era has achieved something very different from the pagans, with their undeniable law of mortality. It has not been content with the rotation of monarchy, aristocracy, democracy and dictatorship; it has made them coexist. The coexistence of these four political forms in one world is not a bare coexistence; it means the inter-penetration of each one with all the rest. The abuses of one form of government, at the circumference of its sphere of influence, led to reaction. Since Germany's party of religion does not exist in England, the King of England must step down and become the first gentleman of his kingdom. Since the English type of Commonwealth does not exist in France, the aristocrats must step down and become the *élite* in a republic. Since the French variety of capital does not exist in Russia, capital must step down and become one social force among many.

Thus, regeneration occurs not at the centre but at the outer fringe. Through this happy kind of safety-valve, the centre of each form of government remains for centuries without change. The coexistence of different countries obviates the crude rotation of antiquity. The peoples co-operate and co-exist, not merely geographically or mechanically, but morally, as one collective system of interplay and mutual dependence.

This mutual dependence, by its very nature, is opposed to the domination or subjection of one country by another. It is revealed best in times where the motherland of one form is most deeply humiliated in its power abroad. Never was France more successful in urging national unity and indissolubility upon her neighbours, Italy and Germany, than in the period of Napoleon III, when she was at the lowest ebb of internal debasement and oppression. It was as though the Italians and Germans—and the English, too—could only be completely bewitched by the Gospel of 1789 when it no longer carried any notion of French superiority, as it had in the days of the first Napoleon (see p. 135).

English parliamentarism made its way to the Continent at

the time of the loss of its first empire. In the days of England's greatest distress the rules of the House of Commons, hitherto kept secret, were revealed to the Colonies in America and to the Continent of Europe. The House of Commons became the Mother of Parliaments in the dark hour when habeas corpus and free speech were suspended at home. Then it was that all the English parliamentary expressions became the public property of the civilized world. The efficient civil service of the Lutheran monarchy was not copied by France until the Thirty Years' War, under Richelieu and Mazarin, i.e., at the low ebb of the German Reformation.

All these forms of government were first brought forward by a tremendous and formidable explosion. Protestantism, Common Law, Constitutionalism, Sovietism, first tried the way of loud, noisy and belligerent expansion. The Huguenots, the Fronde, Napoleon, the, Catalonians, the Bolsheviks, all are types of violent expansion; each belongs to the first chapter of a World Revolution. But they all reached their limit very soon. None of these forms of government was allowed to carry the day completely. Each revolution had to settle down in a particular European area; it had to occupy one certain part of the earth's surface. And this part of the world was given its very shape by the fact of its undergoing the immediate influence of one of the World Revolutions. Neither the German nor the English nor the French nor the Russian nation existed in its modern form before the specific revolution which centred within its borders.

England had no unity with Ireland and Scotland; France had not assimilated Alsace or Provence; Russia had contained the Western Catholic and Protestant territories; and Germany had embraced Switzerland and the Netherlands, before the split of Religious Parties determined the new boundary of the German nation. No Great Power in Europe has ever successfully incorporated a territory into its frontiers unless that territory has shared the uniting, spiritual experience of its revolution. The German part of Austria can be annexed today by Germany only because, from 1914 to 1918, as well as from 1517 to 1866, Austria and Germany had lived together.

Alsace is in the peculiar position of having lived through the Reformation with the German, through the French Revolution with the French. It went through the German Reformation from beginning to end (1517-1555 and 1618-1654), and by this experience it was incorporated into the German nation. It cannot be compared with Switzerland, which left the Empire before the Reformation in 1499. Later, in its French days, the expulsion of the Huguenots was not extended to the Alsatian Protestants. On the other hand, it was in Alsace, which had been governed by the French King since 1680, that the *Marseillaise* was composed by Rouget de Lisle. Alsatian soldiers were in the forefront of the Napoleonic wars, and Marshal Ney hailed from Saarlouis.

The Alsatians have lived through two different World Revolutions. Under German rulers they maintained their French ideas of citizenship born of 1789, and now, under French government, they are again standing for the old German liberties of the Reformation. They are, necessarily, the famous *Hans im Schnakeloch*, of whom the Alsatian popular song runs:

> "Johnny in the midge's hole
>   Has everything his heart could wish—
> And what he has he does not want,
>   And what he wants he does not have.
> Johnny in the midge's hole
>   Has everything his heart could wish. . . ."

The World Revolutions all start without reference to space, with an absolute programme for the whole of mankind, and a vision of a new earth. They all believe themselves to be the vessel of eternal, revealed, definite truth. Only reluctantly do they come back to the old earth. Every revolution makes the painful discovery that it is geographically conditioned. Nothing seems more insulting to its great leaders and great minds than to be reminded of the earthly premises on which their conclusions rest. The history of the first revolutionary period is nothing but this process of reluctant habitation, taking root in a particular soil.

In Russia we have the spectacle of an international revolution turning national before our very eyes. But France was limited in the same way by the restoration of her frontiers of 1792 in 1815. The European scope of the British Commonwealth had to be made clear to the English Parliament by William III. In return for their liberties on the seven seas, they had to pay the full price, guaranteeing their European neighbour, the Netherlands, and participating in the wars against Louis XIV on the Continent as allies of the Catholic Emperor. The British Parliament even endured the Hanoverians, although they remained absolute monarchs on the Continent. In other words, 1688 ended the possibility of splendid isolation for the English gentry. This was the *conditio sine qua non* of William's accession. The end of a revolution comes when it ceases to believe in its own universality—when its natural hope of expansion is given up. This is what happened in 1555, when the opposition to the pope had to recognize that no universal reformation of the Church was possible. It was in the Peace of Religion of 1555 that the individual territory was made the battlefield of reform.

What the fanatical first period, with all its noise and tumult can never do, is accomplished during the period of humiliation. Only then do the forms of the revolution become articles of export which find willing buyers in other nations; for only then can a neighbour-state take the same free attitude which was the mainspring of the revolution in its motherland.

All great revolutions presuppose a colossal effort of human liberty and free will. They all arrive at their limits because they underestimate the freedom of their neighbours. The Great Revolutions never take into account the fact that mankind cannot act all at once. They overestimate the capacity of humanity for simultaneous change. They are bound to do so, because they appeal to only one class of mankind.

Every class has, no doubt about that, a common interest all over the world. High Magistrates, gentlemen, bourgeois, and proletarians are all international classes. Marx's mistake was that he believed in only two classes, capitalists and proletarians. In actual fact, land-owners and rulers have opposing interests; and Fascism has been successful in opposing Marxism because it has rediscovered the existence of two types of men who are neither capitalists nor proletarians. The type of Magistrate, judge, politician, officer, and the type of sailor or farmer had fought their battles against popes and kings long before Labour arrayed itself against Capital.

"LOVE THINE ENEMY" IN POLITICS.

Our first observation in this chapter was that the Polybian rotation of the forms of government was changed in the Christian era into a coexistence of all these forms in one civilization. This fact throws a crosslight on Marxism, which completely neglected the Christian element of contemporaneity between antagonists. In politics "love thy enemy" means that we must learn to bear the existence of a conflicting form of government. All these forms of government survive thanks to the faith and belief of their supporters. And the rationalist, who believes in a certain best form of government, cannot help feeling that this threatens his most sacred principles. The more realistic political scientists have gone to the opposite extreme and made government the empirical product of soil, earth, history, climate, environment.

We can adhere neither to the idealists, the best-government dogmatists, nor to the geographical, nationalistic school. Both theories would split humanity into meaningless atoms. He who is interested only in the "best" form of government cuts all ties between the different phases through which political institutions have passed; he destroys all respect and reverence for continuity. And, on the other hand, the admirer of England's or Andorra's romantic peculiarities cuts across our loyalties to a world-wide order. Man can neither bear to be cut off from his roots in the past, nor to have all his highest beliefs confined within the bounds of one nation or continent. The results of our survey go against both; against the destroyer of continuity and the destroyer of our unity in space. For all these revolutions attempted the same great thing, at different times and with different means, but for exactly the same purpose!

All of them faced a disintegration of the type of man who was produced by society. All of them were haunted by a worthless, slavish, dwarfish order of things. All thought of man as the image of God. The Bolsheviks would not take so much trouble to be godless if they did not feel godlike themselves. Each of these revolutions could have cried with Nietzsche: "If God exists, how can I bear not to be God?"

Each revolution, originating at the circumference of a preceding revolution, faced the eternal dilemma of a divine and a bestial nature in man. Each entrusted the solution of this dilemma to a different class, that is, to:

> Nobility
> Gentry
> Bourgeoisie
> Proletariat

In each of these classes, despair over the past and hope for the future kindled the spark of passionate love for a world reborn. The bearers of the gospel of man as the Son of God, and of nations as the nurseries of the sons of God, scorned the caricatures of humanity whom they met in real life. These men found in the monasteries of Saxony, at the Court of St. James, at Versailles or St. Petersburg, were too clearly sons of man, ay, of cattle. They had forfeited their share of divinity and inspiration.

This caricature of the former man or type was called "capitalist" by Marx, "aristocrat" by Robespierre, "tyrant" or "despot" by Pym, and the "Antichrist" or the "Whore of Babylon" by Luther. And the Nazis call the proletarian "underman," "*tchandala,*" in order to demolish him. Thus we get a list of aggressive names, contrasting vividly with our own sober and prosaic sequence:

> Whore of Babylon
> Antichrist

Nobility	Tyrant
Gentry	Aristocrat
Bourgeoisie	Capitalist
Proletariat	Underman

The torchbearers of a new revolution push out the degraded type and set about creating a new, unheard-of race. For that purpose cold, descriptive names would have been useless. The new sovereign of France had to be a self-made man and was proclaimed a citizen. The new sovereigns of Great Britain became Commoners and Christian gentlemen. The Prince, still a monster in 1515, in Machiavelli's *Principe,* was elevated by Luther in the years after 1517 to the respectable position of a High Magistrate. And today the workers, rough and ready, have been turned into proletarians, the distinguished first members of a classless society.

PROPAGANDA TITLE	DESCRIPTIVE NAME	SWEAR-WORD
. . . .	Pope	Anti-Christ
High Magistrate	Prince	Tyrant
Christian Gentleman	Noble	Aristocrat
		Tory
Citizen	Bourgeois	Capitalist
Proletarian	Worker	(Underman)

It reads, left and right, like obverse and reverse of a medal, the medal itself in reality embracing both sides.

But the list is not complete. The propaganda title of the pope is lacking. The slanderous name for the proletarian is doubtful too, because it is not used by a subsequent post-proletarian revolution, but by the defenders of the pre-Marxian order of things; in other words, by the counter-revolutionaries.

Thus the two corners of the picture, beginning and end, cannot be defined on the basis of the investigations put before the reader in this first part. Fascism and papacy—the present-day reaction against Communism in the form of black, blue, silver and brown shirts, and the existence of a Catholic Church in Europe and America—are left unexplained. Yet they are sovereign powers for the modern masses; and they turn people into friends or enemies with all possible thoroughness.

Al Smith could not become President of the United States because he was a Catholic. Fascism could not succeed in Italy until it made peace with the papacy. It works both ways, but it works. And the reproduction of mankind in the Christian world depends on the relative power or weakness of these elements. Italy, Rome, Florence, Venice, Vienna, have not been mentioned in the preceding chapters. Fascism and papacy are both at home in Italy. Our excavations in the revolutionary lava have unlocked the geological secrets of English and German religious language and of the capitalistic and proletarian vernacular; but we must turn to Italy if we wish to understand the liberties of the Roman Church and the aspirations and prospects of Fascism.

But the results reached in this second part will also give a new and better interpretation of the modern revolutions. Their very essence was, as we found, to be universal and totalitarian without being unique. One coexisted with all the rest, and that was the chief feature of modern civilization which gave it the right to bear the name European.

The coexistence of imperialism and clericalism, with the four modern forms of temporal power, changes the picture once more. The laws for the future of mankind, resulting from its past, can only be discovered after we have deepened our perspective.

MARCHING IN ECHELON.

Still, the results of the preceding chapters already offer some hints for further research. First of all, the rotation of the forms of government from monarchy through aristocracy and from democacy to dictatorship is an advance from small territories to large.

The average State of the Reformation was a small fraction of the area covered by Cromwell's first Commonwealth. Again, the Continental mass of France is much greater than that of the British Isles. And Russia is obviously a territorial problem in itself, with forty times as great an area and six times as many people as France had in 1789.

1517 Individual *State,* Saxony for instance. Average size that of Rhode Island to that of Yorkshire, with half a million people.
1649 British Commonwealth and British Sea. Eight million people.
1789 Natural frontiers of the French *Nation,* including all parts of Cæsar's Gaul (Belgium, Rhineland); it would exceed

modern France, and in its area in 1789 there probably lived
32,000,000 people.
1917 Eurasia U.S.S.R. 150,000,000 people in an area forty times
as big as modern France.

Confusion had reigned in Germany at the beginning of the
Reformation. Every knight, every valley, every township and
municipality had undertaken its reforms separately. The wars
against Hutten and Sickingen (in 1523) and the Peasants' War
(in 1525) were the cruel answer to this foreshortening of the
picture. It was the whole of each German territory with its
forests, and not merely one village or city, that had to be
organized by the Lutheran High Magistrate.

The British aristocracy of 1649 attacked a bigger territorial
problem than the German duke or prince who had escaped
Machiavellian monism and had reformed his territory by the
two sovereign powers of an invisible church and an efficient
public service. The Presbyterians did not do justice to the size
of this problem, and were doomed and replaced by Cromwell.
The French democrats, aside from all their dreams of nature,
were faced by the grim necessity of being a great power. They
turned against their federalists quite brutally, because the latter were not equal to the magnitude of the task. The social
revolutionaries in Russia made the same mistake, and were
easily overthrown by the Bolsheviks, who immediately grasped
the immense problem of organizing a continent instead of a
nation.

This progressive ascent from little to big seems to form a
natural climax. It is fascinating to see how each form of the
rotation of government has been wrought out on an ascending scale. And this view frees the principle of rotation from
its mechanical aspect of being merely a logical process. Though
the four forms of government follow each other, they do not
by any means repeat each other. Each revolution, standing on
the shoulders of the foregoing, dares to go a step farther and
attack a bigger problem in organization.

According to the pagan doctrine of mechanical change, one
and the same community went from one temporal constitution

POLYBIUS

to the next. In the Christian Era, coexistence brought with it the possibility of growth. The moral presence of the older revolution spurred on the younger sister each time. During the last four centuries, a consciousness of the forms already achieved has kept the young revolution from relapsing into chaos, and has sharpened her own duty to achieve more.

The rotation is not mechanical and not meaningless, because the starting point of the first revolution is preserved in the consciousness of all that follow. The four European divisions—Protestant prince, Puritan gentleman, Jacobin citizen, and Bolshevik proletarian—advance in a formation which in the army is called marching in echelon, each with its front clear of that ahead.

If the Marxian revolutionary theory were correct, the revolutions would arise successively in the same territory and in the same nation. Then the march in echelon would be impossible. The French gentry would have overthrown the French monarchy, French bourgeois the gentry, and French workers the bourgeoisie. The Lutheran princes all over Germany would have been beheaded by the "Junkers," the Junkers by the German middle classes, and the middle classes by the German Socialists. But that is completely chimerical. Luther's princes revolted for the whole German nation against the Italian pope. The English nation rebelled against the introduction of Continental monarchy into England, where it meant tyranny. The French nation expelled the megalomania which had been nourished by the *"gentilhomme"* ever since the British Glorious Revolution; and the Russians expelled European capitalism.

In this way each country could aim at the target of progress in its whole breadth and height. It did not move by simple reaction, what the Marxists call the dialectical process of thesis and antithesis. The pagan and mechanical philosophy of the Socialists made most of them overlook the simple facts and rules of coexistence. The English gentry, in overthrowing Lutheran monarchy, did not fall back into Catholicism. The Russians, in doing away with democracy, have not neglected the obligations imposed upon everybody by the French Revolution. The Russians must cling to national autonomy within their system, the British to Reformation, and the French to Parliament, though for a certain time the Presbyterians or Napoleon or Stalin miss the importance of this inevitable coherence and succession.

The whole question of progress depends on the possibility of coexistence of all the rungs of the ladder. In the woods, if you completely forget your starting point, you are likely to walk in a circle. To be driven in a vicious circle is the bogey and, in most cases, the real fate of pagan or primitive man. Their whole civilization is an endless repetition, without any opening or broadening out. Mr. Spengler, with his astounding primitivism, basks in this recurrence of spring, summer, autumn, and winter in each period of civilization. Primitive social groups, because they do not manage to coexist with their enemies, except by eating them, are bound to rotate in a vicious circle. The meaninglessness of so many South American revolutions, even as seen by the most sympathetic observers, such as Joseph Conrad in his *Nostromo,* is based on the fact that they follow each other in hopeless repetition. These revolutions are revolting to our human sensibilities because humanity yearns for growth and fulfilment. The great revolutions we have treated must be carefully distinguished from this mechanism of the vicious circle. They are great because they are sown in one common field of man's experience and hope. They all try to embrace all mankind; one after the other and one beside the other; like separate branches they are all grafted on the common tree of humanity.

This sequence in time and togetherness in space only became possible through a process of branching. The totalitarian faith of each revolution carries one country away from the centre, and to make up for this displacement the other countries, who either bear in themselves the seeds of an older revolution or hold back in expectation of their own day to come, rally all the more faithfully round the common centre.

Though the revolutions take their very name from the idea of rotation, of revolving, the wheel of a world revolution does more than turn in its old orbit. It moves forward along a new track and creates a new form of recurrent, repetitive life. Revolution in this sense does not shock us like the hundred revolutions in Mexico before Porfirio Diaz. Instead, it reproduces the institutions which breed and educate man. The Reformation or the Glorious Revolution produce their first results two hundred years after their outbreak, because it takes four or five generations to beget the perfect fruit of such a rebirth. Types like Pitt or Gladstone or Lincoln or Bach or Goethe had to be ripened by a long succession of unbroken faith, by the coherent labour of centuries.

Our revolutions must be raised to the square of their power before they can be understood in their deeper significance. They are not accidents of the kind which interest the reporter or the police, they are not sensational interruptions of an evolution which went on before and is resumed afterward. They change the face of the earth. Evolution is based on Revolution. It is sheer nonsense to put before us the choice between Evolution and Revolution. Revolution and Evolution are reciprocal ideas. Perhaps we do not like to believe this. But it is my disagreeable business, though myself a non-revolutionary, to deal with revolutions; it is not for the sake of originality that I attribute so much importance to revolution. No, creation goes on as God's creation has always done. A thunderstorm of destruction clears the air; then follows the low rustle of growth and reconstruction. We may assign the noise to the devil, and the still, small voice to God. But only wishful thinking can exclude either of these sounds.

The evolutionary theory of the nineteenth century has led us astray and taught us to use the words "evolution" and "revolution" as if they were mutually exclusive. Let the scientists re-examine their own concepts in the light of the real Darwin, who—as Mr. Brewster has made clear in his book on *Creation* —did not think of evolution in terms of an imperceptible gradation, but used it in the sense of creation. I prefer the word "creation" itself.

In history creation is going on all the time, and eternal

recurrence of the created kinds is also going on all the time. The creative act that sets free new potentialities of mankind is properly called revolution. Not that creation is limited to revolutions; but in the course of history, the branches of the tree of mankind are truly regenerated—ay, by grafting they are really reproduced and changed, and this can only be done by a reconstruction of the great nurseries of men which we call nations.

Revolutions do not create man; they build nurseries, as we have said before, for his reproduction in a certain way and according to a certain type. There is no Christian country and no national character which can boast that it is founded on evolutionary institutions alone. "There is scarce a commonwealth in the world whose beginnings can in conscience be justified." (Hobbes.) Pope Pius II said that kingdoms were not taken by legality or righteousness but by conquest. The fact has been emphasized so often that these quotations could easily be multiplied—which only shows that the volcanic, illegal or pre-legal origin of all government has often been in the minds of thoughtful men.

We shall see later on why the rise of a new sovereign is really the creation of a new kind of man, in a biological sense: how a monarchical Reformation remoulded the father of every family, how an aristocratic restoration reshaped every man, how a national Revolution revolutionized every mind, and how a proletarian Revolution calls upon every body. Every father, every man, every mind, every body, are the respective consignees of the revolutionary freight. The revolutions address and extol different sides of man's being; but all the revolutions call upon him, conjure him up, usher him into the world with the same desperate faith in his responsibility. Every revolution we have investigated had something to say to every human being, not merely to a few. Monarchy, aristocracy, democracy and distatorship cannot be distinguished by the more or less dependence they put in *every* member of the group. Every one of them uses the same passionate language to all. The Russian broadcasts in 1917 "to all" men are no more universal than the Lutheran pamphlets written for all Christians or the English Great Remonstrance addressed to the public.

"OPEN" VERSUS "PUBLIC."

The Revolutions occur as much in the open as any outbreak of war or fire or earthquake. Now "open" means more than "public." Open is as far above public as public stands above private. The lawyer knows private and public law; the politician or the newspaper man cannot afford to mistake private for public affairs. Private life and public life are separate worlds. But what of the open air, the immediate presence of earth and heaven, beyond the reach of social organization?

The openness of a revolution is the positive expression of its reality. Nothing is real which does not happen under God's open sky and under the evident pressure of our mother earth. The lawless character of Revolution may frighten us; its destruction of privacy and its contempt for public law make us tremble. But we ought not to deal with these greatest experiences of humanity in negative language. They are neither public nor private. We must find a positive word to explain their character. Whenever a name is found for a thing, whenever a thing is seized and held by a word, the world grows larger; when it is only described, men stay in their accustomed grooves.

All great revolutions re-create public law, public order, public spirit and public opinion; they all reform private customs, private manners and private feelings. They themselves must therefore live in a third dimension, beyond the reach of public law and private conviction. They live in the unprotected, unexplored and unorganized space which is hated by every civilization like hellfire itself—and which probably lies near hellfire. But it lies near heaven, too. Heaven and hell are the only words left to us for this character of openness and immediacy. We nowadays have learned that hell and heaven are in our hearts. As the nineteenth century was private and individualistic, the heart, too, became a private business, and so the teaching of the gospel that heaven and hell are in our hearts reads to us like an inscription from a private album: it seems meant for private use alone.

But man's heart is the centre of creation. His is a world-heart. The son of man lives in the centre of the universe, he *is* the centre of the universe, and when his heart governs him he governs the world. Let us use an illustration for this way of life. Lovers have made a great fuss over the contrast between marriage in church and marriage by mutual private consent, yet there is little difference between them in actual fact. It is true, husband and wife can marry in public, with all the ceremonies and publicity of Church and State, or they can marry in private. But, whatever the forms, heaven and earth must participate in the wedding. The whole body must be rapt to its new calling, and the whole mind must be caught up into its new state of marriage. Then it it safe to say that something real has happened; when body and soul are completely dissolved and completely remade, you can be sure that this couple will become the founders of a new race, a new people, a new nation. After all, every marriage is the nucleus of a new race. It is nothing but statistical idolatry to judge a nation by its fifty or hundred millions of population. Those are mere abstractions. The people who marry change the nation unceasingly, if and when they meet in the presence of heaven and earth. Private relations or public ceremonies are *both* conventional disguises for the real story of marriage. The question is whether this young man and this young woman are going to be married under celestial ordination or by an "arbitrary power." Many a marriage, it is true, represents nothing but chance or a personal whim. The few that are something more regenerate their kind.

It is the same in politics. Some people rule, and more people vote, on arbitrary impulse. Those who do not, regenerate the standards of society. Revolutions try to regenerate the order of society by an inbreak of celestial powers. In both cases, hell is very near heaven. Whenever we venture to live in the open, we are exposed to all the risks of outdoor—i.e., of direct and immediate—life. Revolutions break into the framework of society from outside. They bear testimony to the very existence of free space around us. While we are under the law we are always anxious to forget its presence, like a good mother who thinks she can contract a marriage for her son. And because we are anxious to forget it, we are frightened by its sudden appearance. No power can derive its sovereignty from laws. Sovereignty comes first; everything else grows out of it. Luther first had to publish his Theses openly; the Roundheads first had to raise an army, and the Bastille first had to be destroyed before the new sovereign could become visible and begin to negotiate with the old powers.

This autocephalous origin of sovereignty is so certain that what we call the period of a revolution is nothing but the time it takes to make the new sovereign visible to the oldest veteran of the former world order. As soon as this oldest veteran has perceived its existence and its scope, peace can be restored and civil war can die down. But in this world of inertia it takes years, thirty or forty, before a new sovereign is recognized.

When Louis XVIII said on his return in 1815 that nothing had happened, only one more Frenchman was in France; the oldest veteran of monarchy had subscribed to the dogma of equality. When Charles V conceded the right of reformation to the territorial powers, and when the King of England acquiesced in a parliamentary church, the final word of a revolutionary period had been spoken. The same word which was high treason on the first day had at last become law, with the blessing of the very power against which it was first directed.

Every serious revolution begins, it seems, with a *"grande peur"* on the part of the population. *"Grande peur,"* great fear, was the name given to the inexplicable anxiety of the French nation in the summer of 1789. The same anxiety appeared in Germany in 1930. Three years before Hitler came into power the crisis could be felt and was felt by the imperilled educated classes in countless cases of nervous breakdown or temporary paralysis. For the Reformation, we know that the whole German nation must have felt the meteorological signs. Two years before the bloodshed of the Peasants'

War, Luther, the successful, beloved, and admired Reformer, wrote: "The signs of nature point certainly to a political revolution, and in especial by wars. Therefore I doubt not that Germany faces either a terrible war or the Last Judgment."

This *"grande peur"* may be observed in the Middle Ages, too, and I think for the sake of completeness, I may quote Frederick II's exclamation in 1227:

"On us, then, the end of time has come, for not only in the branches but in the roots as well the power of love is frozen. Not only do peoples rise against peoples, and empires threaten empires, not only do pestilence and hunger stir the hearts of the living with terror, but the power of love itself, by which heaven and earth are governed, seems now to be troubled, not in its later flowing, but at the very *source.*"

This great outcry leads us back to the connection between the "Great Fear" and the drying-up of the power which governs heaven and earth. The great Revolutions break out whenever the power which has governed heaven and earth dries up at the fountain-head. The great Revolutions seem to destroy an existing order; but that is not true. They do not break out until the old state of affairs is already ended, until the old order of things has died and is no longer believed in by its own beneficiaries. Ranke said of the Reformation: "When the powers of the empire had grown suspicious of each other and of themselves, the elementary forces on which the empire rested began to stir. Lightnings flashed from the earth; the currents of public life deserted their usual course; the storm which had been heard rumbling so long in the depths rose toward the upper regions; everything seemed ready for a complete overturn."

The ordinary laws of life, the fruit of millennia of struggle, go to the devil when the spirit that animated them departs. No positive law can hold a position which every good spirit has deserted. When that happens, Goethe's words in *The Natural Daughter* [2] are in order:

2 Act 5, Scene 8.

"This realm is threatened
With utter ruin. For the elements
That met to form its greatness will no longer
Embrace each other with the force of love
In unity unceasingly renewed.
Now each evades the other, and withdraws
Coldly into itself. Where is the might
Of our forefathers' spirit, that once joined them,
The warring elements, unto one end—
The spirit which to this great people came
As leader, as its own father and its king?
Vanished forever! All that now remains
Is a poor ghost that, striving against hope,
Still dreams of winning back its lost possessions. . . ."

The state of Russia before the World War was described by
Joseph de Maistre as that of a frozen corpse which would stink
horribly in our nostrils when it thawed.

The power of love which governs heaven and earth is per-
ishable indeed. Its stream sometimes runs dry. No "evolution"
can guarantee mankind against this drying-up. We are no more
protected against drought in politics than we are against
drought in nature. But the "illimitable heart" by its illimitable
Revolution restores the free working of the power which governs heaven and earth. When Dante wished to give the finish-
ing touch to his pictures of the sins and virtues of mankind, he
apostrophized the power which moves the sun and the other
stars. He pointed to the equation between heaven and earth
which we have rediscovered for modern times, the equation
between human love and the rotations of the sky.

Heaven and earth are one. Christ has implanted love as
the primary moving force in man. The times of Frederick II
and Dante had the audacity to find one and the same principle at work in heaven and earth, in human and astral bodies.
And today the physicists are finding one system of passionate
energies at work in the atom and in the universe. Niels Bohr
describes the planetary system within the atom as one of suc-

cessive catastrophes and readjustments, as in a Liliputian solar system.

Revolutions do nothing but readjust the equation between heart-power and social order. They come from the open and happen under the open sky. They bring about the Kingdom of God by force, and reach into the infinite in order to reform the finite.

Thus we have found out, for history and society, the important fact that open, public, and private are three different aggregate states for mankind. Unless it is *open,* no human law or personality is proof against the demons of life. No constitution can stand fast which has not sprung from war or revolution, which has not come from beyond public law or private pleasure. Political order is not meant for happiness or the full life or the greatest happiness of the greatest number. That is the cant of public-minded privateers who know nothing of the outdoor life of the pioneer, beyond good and evil, driven by the angels and demons of love and fear.

Revolutions come as a positive effort when the fear of a complete breakdown of order preys so terribly on the bowels of men that only a great courage and a great love can open the way to a new equilibrium of powers.

A NATION'S RELIGION.

The difference between politics and religion, confused as they are today, can be re-stated simply by the distinction of public and open. At no time can any group exist without religion and without public law. To reduce these two elements into one has often been tried, and never will succeed. Public Law asks the citizen for obedience, religion for worship. Any group obeys politically its legal ruler; but it worships religiously the opening of a new path out of chaos.

The gentry of England, the princes and professors of Germany, the *écrivains* of France and the Bolsheviks in Russia are, or were, revered by their respective nations as demigods. The worship bestowed on them as heroes corresponded to the peculiar religion these demigods stood for.

The witness of these supermen bridged the gulf between the natural man and the infinite by permitting him to take on a definite character. Much has been said and written about a nation's character. In most cases, I am sorry to say, the writers take the character like a stone, a piece of nature. This nationalistic creed in fixed characters is charmingly defended by Mr. Madariaga, the long-time member of the League of Nations Council. In his *Englishmen, Frenchmen, Spaniards,* the underlying principle is the eternity of a national character. The inevitable answer to this national fatalism is the "Revolt of the Masses," so ably described by Mr. Madariaga's fellow-countryman, Ortega y Gasset. How could it be otherwise? A man who believes in fixed types should not groan when living men do not respond. I know that the average psychologist thinks he is delving very, very deep when he says that Frenchmen are democratic, Germans obedient, and that the English have a natural liking for aristocrats. But is this not poor psychology? Is it not intolerable for any human being to feel himself condemned once for all, by the mere accident of birth, to a fixed character? In the field of political or moral values we are all competitors, all of divine nature, all changeable and transformable. But we are "nationals" because we are men, capable of feeling gratitude and of responding to this feeling. Thinking and thanking belong together. As long as we have reason to be grateful we shall always respect and repeat the reasoning of our elders. A nation never forgets its interval in the open, between fear and faith, hate and love; for in it this certain section of humanity came into contact with God. If anyone paves a road into a new love, a new faith, a new governing power, he becomes the legislator of the revolution. He vanquishes the fear of hell and disintegration: "They have knocked at all the doors that led nowhere, and the only one by which they can enter, and for which they searched centuries long, opens suddenly." (Proust.) Since he seals this new covenant between the Creator and his frightened and fearing creatures, he establishes a new faith and a new order of things. Since this order is not based on reason but on deliverance from fear, it very often takes a long time to make the new way practicable for every-day work. However, the abolition of fear precedes all practical action. For the creator of a new heaven and a new earth transforms the people. And in return his own kind becomes a severed caste and governing class; his social function becomes a church-like institution for his country.

The prince, the gentleman, the scholar, the minister—they have taught the Germans and the English when they were despondent how to pray so that they might be heard. The formula of this prayer becomes the secret law of the land, the very core of the nation's language, and makes the use of any foreign political vocabulary impossible. It produces a kind of immunity.

The German language in 1649 or 1688 was so full of "Reformation," of chorales and the Lutheran Bible, that when a historian tried to find the reaction of German public opinion to Cromwell and William III he was overcome by disappointment. To no revolution did Germany react so little as to the English. Even today, in the vocabulary of German political language the political concepts of England stand like foreign bodies, unconnected with the native tradition, whereas "cavalier" and "feudal" are high praise in a German mouth. This is because the British Revolution came too early to find a door open. The love of the Reformation had not yet died down. The Fronde in France was much more dangerous in its imitation of the Puritans.

Today, the same French nation cannot swallow the Russian Revolution: they are simply too near their own great revolutionary past. Nobody can think of Poincaré and Stalin, Clemenceau and Lenin, as contemporaries. They live on different planets, as far apart as Venus and Neptune. And this is certainly no quibble, but a serious attempt to explain the depth and stability of our political religion or our religious politics.

No man is a European who has not been educated by certain church-like institutions in his own country, institutions created once and forever by a revolution which teaches him faith, hope, and love, but mainly love. The languages of Europe are not materialistic facts, but creative expressions of a certain side of the Christian faith, used by a certain political class in a certain section of the continent.

The successful creation of a new political language by a new class, in a new section of the continent, is called a Revolution; and the territory within which it succeeds and the people whom it transforms are the components of a nation. Nations are the products of Revolutions.

Each nation depends upon a leading class, which from its inspired stand in the open danger and open warfare of revolution becomes the governing class in public law and the model of private life. The Bolshevik party in Russia, the religious party in Germany, the parliamentary party in England, the civic party in France, are not fractions of an existing nation, but the *raison d'être* of the whole.

EUROPEAN DICTIONARY.

In accordance with this rule, no country's political grammar can be literally translated into that of any other. A group of institutes from America and various European countries recently compiled a dictionary of political science. The method it followed was simply to ask each national group to contribute an article on each subject: Italians, French, Germans, and English were to work out a series on State, Government, Nation, Parliament, etc. Each group worked and kneaded those poor words in its own fashion, according to the predilection or the indifference of its own nation toward each one.

But these political words are more than scholars' terms; they lie at the heart of a nation's becoming and making. There is no reciprocity between "nation" in English and "nation" in French, nor between "civilization" in Italian and in German. A system of European political language can never be based on the meretricious superstition that these words can go through an international clearing-house. They are the minted gold of a nation's treasure. Let us give some examples:

GERMAN	ENGLISH	FRENCH	RUSSIAN
Cultivated	Countrified	Civilized	Electrified
Staat	Commonwealth	Nation	Soviets
Every Christian	Every man	Every individual	Every body
Magistrates	Commons	Intellectuals	Communists
Katheder	Pulpit	Tribune (platform)	
Prince	Gentleman	Citizen	Proletarian
High	Old	New	Functioning
Hochgesinnt	Public-spirited	Grand	
General principle	Public spirit	Esprit	
Hochwohlgeboren		Élite	Quality
		Intellectuelle	
Der gemeine Mann	The poor	Les Illettrés	Quantity
Protestant	Whig	Liberal	
Magister, Dr.	Minister, member	Écrivain	
Billigkeit	Common sense	Bon sens	
(= Equity)			
Pflicht (= Duty)	Right	Idée	Function
Geheimrat	M.P.	Académicien	
Sehr geehrter	Dear Sir	Cher ami	Tovarich
Herr	William		(comrade)
Gewissenhaft	Righteous	Bon	Efficient
(conscientious)			
Beamter ("Rat")	J.P.	Légion d'Honneur	
Geist	World	Nature	Society

The vocabulary of High in German and of Low in English has created a network of derivations. *Hoheit, Hochwohlgeboren, leutselig, herablassend, Hochachtungsvoll, Hochgemut, Hochgeehrt,* should be set off against Low, Low Church, Lower House, common sense, minister, ministry. Or the German group around *Mut (Übermut, Grossmut, Demut, Armut,* etc.) against the English "quiet," "calm," "discreet," "demure," "reserved," etc., etc.

The positive sense of *"Hochschule"* in German contrasts with the negative sense of high-brow, high church in England. A German boy is recommended as "highly" gifted; in England he does better if he has "common sense." And the French language has still a third creed. The French, being above all individuals, translate "common" by "good." All the English compounds of "well" or "good" are of French origin. In 1789 there was published in Paris the little *Code of Human Reason,* by Barbeu du Bourg, which says, "Man needs at least three things for his happiness: Health, common sense, and a clear conscience, and man needs nothing but three things: Health, common sense, and a clear conscience." But in French it runs "le *bon*heur requires *bonne* santé, *bon* sens, *bonne* conscience." The Frenchman has *bon sens* and a *bonne conscience.* But good sense and common sense are very different. Luther would never have permitted himself to call anything in his own sinful self good. Luther's conscience was *pure,* genuine; a gentleman's motives had to be based on the common weal.

Some words have invaded the European world without keeping their national stamp because whenever an institution was derived from one particular country the rest of Europe took over the terms and names for its functioning in a mechanical and superficial way. "Republic," "revolutionary" and "national" are French; "supremacy," "sovereignty," and "Ph.D." are German; "parliament," "country" and "local government" are English.

The dictionary will tell you that most of these words are Latin. "Sovereign" was invented by a French thinker. "Supremacy" occurs in Henry VIII's "Act of Supremacy." Why, then, are they German? And are not "Country" (*comitatus*) and "republic" simply international? Parliament is a French word translated from the good old German "sprakka," i.e., *colloquium;* but the Germans despised parliaments, the English believed in them.

Any number of such misunderstandings could be cited. Our list on the word "nation" is a most confusing example. This word, which our statesmen are fond of pulling like an organ-stop, sounds a different note in every country. Diplomats should be required to say, when they use it, whether they are speaking French or Russian or English or German.

Each of these European languages can be heard anywhere in Europe: they are exchanged freely among the different countries. There are Catholics in Germany, Tories in England, royalists in France, and the *"spez"* in Russia, to speak the pre-revolutionary language. To give one good example, the Royalists in France went so far as to preserve for a century the old Versailles pronunciation of the word King, calling him not "Roa," like the Parisians, but Roy, like the English "royal," as in the days when the language of Versailles was the standard. The later revolutionary languages also invade the precincts of the older European stocks. Thought jumps lightly over all frontiers. Communists are everywhere, Fascist "shirts" are everywhere. The same was of course true of the Jacobins in 1800, who could be found everywhere, and of the Conservatives after 1815, who reacted as the Fascists are doing today. For the sake of decency the Jacobins turned "Liberal," and as Liberals they conquered a world which had been closed to them as long as they were called Jacobins. The pietistic affiliates which the Whigs, the gentry, and their ministers had on the Continent were no stronger than the friends the Lutherans had in England in the seventeenth century. At that time Lutheranism was so much of a uniting force that even Henry VIII thought of joining its League. "It is not improbable that the fate of Henry VIII's second wife, Anne Boleyn, was sealed by Henry's failure to gain for his second marriage the endorsement of the Wittenberg faculty."

Is it not strange that within a year or two, any national upheaval born of truly revolutionary ambition can find supporters in every country?

It is a fact, though an incredible one to the superficial democrat, that Mr. Everyman is by no means necessarily on the side of democracy in these processes of political infection. Dictators or monarchs have supporters quite as ready and quite as devout, when the time is ripe. "Democracy" has no surer approach to the masses of men than the other three forms of government. Each form seems, strangely enough, to express a popular longing. The German civil law, the English Common Law, the French laws of nature, the Russian laws of Lenin, were all welcomed with fierce enthusiasm.

The forms of government are more than the superficial garb of certain office-holders. At least for the Europe of modern times, they are the flesh and blood of a particular body politic. The country which produces the new form is given to it heart and soul. It must let some adherents of the pre-revolutionary order survive, it is true (Catholics, Nobles, Aristocrats, Bourgeois); but on the whole its creative effort absorbs all the religious energies of the nation. This process reaches the population of the whole country. Everybody is conscience-stricken, for everybody shared in the *"grande peur,"* and by that shock was prepared for a break-up of his inner being. Monarchy or aristocracy or democracy are poor terms to define the power which so deeply ploughs the clods of a nation and kneads the clay of man into a new image of God.

BIONOMICS OF WESTERN MAN.

This totalitarian character of the Revolutions we have studied obliges us to insert them as stages in the natural creation of mankind. Such Revolutions carry on the process of creation. Thus political history ceases to be outside nature: man and the other forms of creation are closely akin, with the great difference that man was not created a hundred thousand years ago, but is being made before our eyes.

Men are reproduced, regenerated and physically influenced by the great Revolutions we have already observed. The European nations did not exist in 1000. Most of them were shaped in 1500. Today they are well-known to all of us, some of them already in decay, or reorganization, but certainly all of them transient. What existed before they were born? Or shall we say that the Revolutions did not really create them, but only built a kind of well-kerb around each nation's most particular qualities so that they might flow and come forth forever?

In each case, it was the revolutionary setting of the nation which enabled it to make its contribution to the world at large. Civil government, parliamentarism, democracy, planning, are developed in one country as an ultimate end, whereas all the others can use it as a thing of relative importance. When parents, for example, compare Russia and her terrible sufferings with France or America, they thank God that they need not bring up their children in Russia. The Roosevelt New Deal is less painful than the *Piatiletka.* The novelties of the French Revolution were introduced into England or Germany with less murder and warfare than France had to undergo. But we can be sure that without the French Revolution, England would not have seen the Reform Bill of 1832 nor Germany its Revolution of 1848. The New Deal and the devaluation of the dollar are unthinkable without a preceding Bolshevik Revolution. The Great Revolutions are eccentric, they exaggerate, they are brutal and cruel. But the life of the rest of the world is regenerated by their outbreak. It may seem doubtful who gains more, the revolutionized country or its partners. One thing is certain, the old forms of civilization, stagnating, their circulation clotted, are regenerated by the power of the new form. Life is regenerated in the rest of the world whenever a new form joins the older ones.

Not that the older forms become superfluous. A partisan of Fascism thinks, of course, that democracy is doomed, as the liberals bet in 1830 that the House of Lords in England would disappear within ten years. But the House of Lords exists, Kings govern, and French democracy will exist in 1940 or 1950. Perhaps the addition of a new form even relieves and eases the older forms of a part of their burden. They recover. Monarchy in Germany experienced a regeneration after the Napoleonic wars, and the regeneration of the English system after 1815 is well-known.

The biological secret of eternal life can, perhaps, be formulated thus: Lest the old kinds die or stagnate, a new kind branches off from the tree of life. By reason of this flowing forth of life into new forms the forms already existing are able to survive. The revolutionary creation of one new kind permits the evolution of the older kinds.

All our statements thus far are based on a short period of four hundred years. It is clear that we must try to test them in the light of a longer period. The possibility of reproducing man on the larger scale of a great national revolution is in itself a paradox. The rotation of government from Luther to Lenin, from monarchy to dictatorship, is no more than one observation in a limited field.

We must try to see more clearly the safeguards developed for civilization in the Christian Era. We shall test our results by the revolutions of the preceding five hundred years.

If the same rotation of the forms of government, the same Polybian law of development—one form giving birth to the next—can be stated for a second period, the observation will have outgrown the status of accident and blind chance.

In the midst of our present life, one old layer has proved itself long-lived. The Roman Catholic Church in Europe and America is quite a remarkable reality even today. We saw at the very beginning that the Russians, being of Greek Orthodox creed, are the first non-Roman nation to start a world revolution. Bolshevism and Catholicism are the only world-wide organized moral powers today. In order to estimate the chances of Bolshevism, we must assess the chances of the Catholic Church. So far we have done no more than to look at the Western World in its "Modern World" home. But there is also a mediæval world, Italy and Austria; and to understand them, we shall have to deal with Spain and Prussia as well. Only then shall we be equipped to deal with the New World.

The last chapter of the second part will consider the Revolution in the New World. Contemplating the American promise, we shall land again in the present world of Communism and dictatorship. But in coming back to the present day after a detour through the bionomics of European history, we shall perhaps have illuminated the great question of tomorrow, the reproduction of mankind.

A SECULAR CHRIST

He swings His axe after the World War. *Crux ergo hæc ipsa crucifigenda est.*

PART TWO

FROM THE ROMAN EMPIRE TO AMERICA

The Clerical Revolutions

A MEDIÆVAL CHRIST

Pity, Wisdom, Humility, swinging hammers to nail Christ on the Cross.

CHAPTER NINE

The Roman Emperor Without His Empire

Provinces or Nations?—Imperial Palace or Local Manor?—The Last Song on the Last Judgment (Dante Alighieri)—All Souls: The Christian Democracy of the Last Judgment

PROVINCES OR NATIONS?

NORMALLY, WE TAKE FOR GRANTED THE EXISTENCE OF SEPARATE nations with boundaries, customs, currencies, armies of their own. Yet during a great revolution these boundaries seem to disappear, and the right of nations to a separate existence is called in question. The world unrest of today, caused by the great revolution of the World War, should again bring home to us the truth that the nations of Europe are rather short-lived: when Austria has vanished from the map, it dawns upon us that the great powers themselves are temporary. Not one of them existed in the year 1000. It took three more centuries before Italy, the first of the modern nations, came into being; and it was not until 1500 that England, Germany, France, Russia, Spain, Poland, were moulded to a recognizable degree into "nations."

The nations of the Western World were called into being by five hundred years of clerical revolution. In those days the energies of man's political faith expressed themselves in religious language. But man is the same in all ages. How slight were the solidarity of our race if the centuries before 1500 were simply a relapse into barbarism, and made no contribution to the political progress of modern man! The clerical period of Christianity's struggle for life is as simple and lucid in its achievements as the cycle which we have discovered in

485

modern times. Conflict, despair, faith, pride, humiliation and fulfilment, the six notes of every revolutionary keyboard, are equally perceptible in the alleged darkness of the Middle Ages. The outcome of that half millennium, the creation of articulate nations, is so definite and so important that we may assume it had had inspired leadership from the beginning. The aversion of old-time Protestants toward the mediæval order does not excuse the civilized world today in overlooking our perpetual dependence on the forces that were set in motion a thousand years ago. The age that produced the great and original musical innovation of counterpoint, the basis of musical harmony as we know it and the underlying principle of all modern art, that built the castles and cathedrals by methods of transportation unknown to antiquity, that invented the drainage system of our lawns and meadows, had a latent energy at its disposal which may well make us jealous.

All the more curious, in view of this vitality, is the geography of 1000 A.D. Scotland was Caledonia; "Britannia" could still signify that part of the island lying west of a line drawn from the Isle of Wight to the Isle of Man. Naples and southern Italy were cut off from the rest of "Italia." "France" was a small part of Gaul; three quarters of Spain centred around the Moslem caliphates; and the frontiers of the Roman Empire cut right through modern Germany. The lands of the old Roman Empire suffered from disintegration. For the sake of peace and order they called forth a new spirit. The result was that Roman provincials became citizens of vast new empires and the static lands of old were transformed into the great nations of the modern world.

IMPERIAL PALACE OR LOCAL MANOR?

The external conditions of life in Western Europe in the year 1000 A.D. can perhaps best be described by two negatives. First, the Western World was no longer united, as in Cæsar's day, in an empire of thousands of cities; there was a nominal emperor, but there were no cities to build his empire upon. And second, the modern nations of Europe did not exist; Eu-

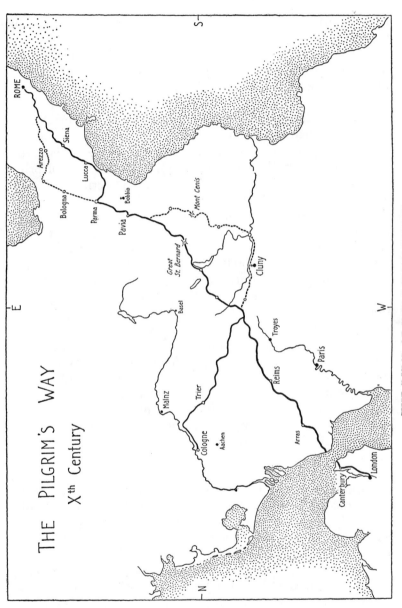

THE PILGRIM'S WAY
Xth Century

ROME

Arezzo
Siena
Lucca
Bologna
Parma
Pavia
Bobbio
Mont Cenis
Great
St. Bernard
Basel
Cluny
Troyes
Paris
Reims
Mainz
Trier
Cologne
Aachen
Arras
Canterbury
London

E
S
W
N

THE RUMP OF THE ROMAN WORLD

rope as a whole was split by tribal differences into innumerable particles.

No nation, no cities, yet an emperor, was the paradoxical situation a thousand years ago. Since an emperor already existed, the obsession of the last thousand years has been to build cities. Countless words have been derived from the Latin *"civitas"* to express this homesickness of Europe for the lost cities which had once flourished on her soil. *Citoyen*, Civilization, City (*Città del Vaticano*), Civil service, the Italian word *civilta* (culture, politeness, humanity), Civil lists, are offsprings of a permanent longing to re-endow the Western World with some kind of citizenship.

The unique experiment of the Western World consists in regenerating a former world. Not a change in quantity, but a change in quality, is the content of these thousand years of revolution. The Great or Perfect Year of Revolutions is full of attempts to recivilize a given world.

The result is, among other things, the modern nations. Nations have taken the place of the ancient city or *polis*. The word politics or policy signifies today the tendencies of national government, even though *"politikós"* is the adjective of *polis*, which means town, *urbs*. Whenever we speak of policy today, we move in the sphere which has transformed the classical city-state into a world-wide institution. The nations are the cities of today. Nations covering vast continents are the rightful heirs of Civilization, because the empire was recivilized, step by step, by a series of common and interdependent acts of city-founding.

The first attempt of recivilization was an attempt to build the whole Occident into one city, and to this city was given the name Jerusalem. The re-founder of the Roman Empire, Otto I, is represented on a liturgical vessel of the tenth century which bears the inscription *Jerusalem visio pacis*. From this we learn that an emperor, a thousand years ago, did not represent pre-eminently the power of this world. He was considered the state witness of a world beyond. In a world of scattered, continental tribes, who lived surrounded by inhospitable oceans, threatened by Vikings and pirates and Moslems, the friendly aspect of the old Roman Empire, embracing the shores of the Mediterranean, had completely changed. The Empire was a remembrance and a desire. The emperor, as an institution, could not be explained by the existing economic or social organization; he stood in open contradiction to this organization of society. The figure of the emperor stepped into this world like a stranger, and by its strangeness unleashed an unheard-of cycle of Revolutions, whose vital powers equal the processes of creation which we know in other realms of nature. By the stepping-in of a foreign principle, an absolute claim, a power belonging to past and future, the inhabitants of Europe were created into one city. We used above the equation of *polis* with the particular nation. We were wrong. It was European civilization as a whole which was called upon to represent the idea of the ancient city-state! The civilized nations are sectors of *one* city.

The concept of a universal civilization opposing a multitude of local economic units was the emperor's gift to the European tribes. Unity and Emperor were synonyms in 1000. Social changes have diluted Empire into Civilization, but Unity is still the original capital invested in European history by the person of the emperor.

The emperor was infinitely greater than reality. Stars and suns were the ornaments of his mantle; for the tent of heaven was his proper garb. Mankind, lost in the darkness of dissension and schism, received an image of the unifying sky in the person of the living emperor. He had no empire in the real sense of an established order, at least not in the sense we give to the word empire today. There were no taxation, no officials, no traffic, no money, to make it possible for him to establish a central government. His rule was unique, not central.

It is overlooked that the Church during its first millennium was never called *Una sancta,* the famous term framed by Boniface VIII in 1302. The singular would have had no meaning in a period when Rome was only *prima sedes,* i.e., the first among many sees; until the return of her King, Christ, the Church could not hope for visible unity on earth. The Church existed in endless multiplication, in every sacred spot on the globe where a martyr had shed his blood. Her Head was in Heaven. On earth the duty of maintaining visible Uniqueness and Unity belonged to the emperor. The popes of the first millennium refused steadfastly to be addressed as "universal."

Without visible centralization, Unity had to be represented by a continuous effort and movement of the emperor and his army. The Roman emperor of the year 1000 had no permanent capital. The Holy Roman Empire was without a capital to its very end in 1806; the emperor had to live on the land. His clergy moved with the imperial court, army and clergy being his only central government. The clergy, having no family nor house of their own, were as movable as the young knights and soldiers. The real life of the most Christian Apostolic emperor contradicted sharply all his universal claims. It was local. Taxation was unimportant as a source of revenue. He had certain big estates, *palatia*, which gave him such and such a number of daily services, each "service" comprising fifty pigs, twenty-five cows, ten measures of wheat, wine in Franconia, or beer in the less fortunate Saxony. The services from his palaces in Saxony would amount to 365×40 in the course of the year.

The budget of this emperor of heaven and earth was composed of the daily services of a few score of local manors! The manorial background of the imperial power was its weak point. The spiritual superlative and the material diminutive were directly related to each other.

For the rules and customs of a lord of the manor were the real organization of the imperial court. Government was set up by making an ordinary country house the organ of public administration. Happy times, when neither individuals nor community existed in the way of our modern, atomized world! Public life was tribal organization in clan and army, private life was the economic organization of husbandry. We have seen the change of husbandry and the table in the dining hall of the manor into the table of the House of Commons, on which the Lord of the Treasury places his national budget. Five hundred years before, the emperors had to manage the budget of an empire in the form of a manorial budget. The dignitaries of the empire were treated as servants of an imperial household. The pope and the bishops were the spiritual chaplains, the teachers and professors, the columnists and librarians of a universal "House." The whole imperial family was an organ of government. Ministers, princes and princesses, marshals, chamberlains, and chancellors formed an indissoluble unity, one indivisible instrument of government. Every part of Europe was covered by manors with the same comprehensive domestic organization. The problem of production was solved by incorporating as many members as the division of labour required, into a household. As in other ways, the pre-War Hungary preserved best the style of the church-castle-manor-factory Unit of older times. The view of a Transylvanian church-castle recalls the complicatedness of a feudal domestic organization. The history of fine art and of architecture has narrowed our outlook on the past, by preserving the word "house," especially for the rooms devoted to everything except work. The mediæval husbandry embraced a large *yard*. Even the *court* of the emperor was but one part of his big palace; a church would belong to it, but also stables, barns, workshops, barracks; and the assembly of his staff which lived around the yard took place in a great hall like the Homeric "Megaron." Here in the hall of the palace the order at table gave an exact picture of the social hierarchy. The Last Supper of Jesus and the Apostles impresses us as something special and peculiar in the classical time of big cities, with their disintegrated society.

In 1000 A.D., the Last Supper was not a contrast, but the crowning symbol of every day's experience. For in the palace, the society at table was a living body for work, courtship, social life and government. The emperor's throne was not a foolish old piece of furniture, used three or four times a year; it was the lord's high seat at table. His wife and the princes would sit on footstools next to him.

The complete identity of the emperor's instruments of governmental administration with every nobleman's household weakened the emperor's position. He was, after all, only the peer of thousands of house-lords. The economic system had to be administered on the spot. Consequently the emperor could not interfere with local administration. Every father and

mother ruled over the members of their household as absolutely as the emperor. Fatherhood and motherhood were *economic offices;* "son" and "daughter" were titles signifying a
definite function in society. In so far as children or servants
worked in the household, whether it was a duke's palace or
a peasant's farm, no emperor could interfere.

The uniqueness of the emperor was, then, hard to express
in a world of local government. Judge, administrator, manager
of business—every house-father was that. Patriarchalism was
nothing peculiar to the emperor. The local character of economy spurred the emperor to special efforts. Otherwise, in a
world of thousands of patriarchs, the Unity of a City of God
could not become visible.

The emperor's house had to include a set of persons lacking
in other households. Kings and dukes served at his table and
they were not allowed to sit while the emperor took his meals.
With kings as his servants, the emperor was exalted. And in
other ways his house was exalted beyond the houses of other
lords. He shared his meals with the highest priests of the Catholic Church. His companion was an archbishop or the pope
himself, and he could talk to him at table. Sharing his meals,
the clergy removed the emperor into the atmosphere of clerical
and divine remoteness. A shroud of mystery surrounded the
emperor; wherever he went, he was a member of the clergy.
He was a prebendary of the cathedrals of his empire. In
Cologne the emperor and the pope, with their following, each
occupied one side of the choir.

The first interest of the emperor was the Church and the
reform of the Church. He was responsible for the prayers re-
cited and the masses sung in his empire. For more than two
centuries (800-1056) the emperors imposed on the Roman
church the forms of mass, the ceremonials, the ritual, the creed,
and the prayers of their imperial palace and court. When
Rome was an Augean stable, the German emperors saved the
purity and growth of religious worship in Roman Christendom. But in spite of the hopeless corruption of Rome itself,
the word Roman was the only symbol of unity for a divided

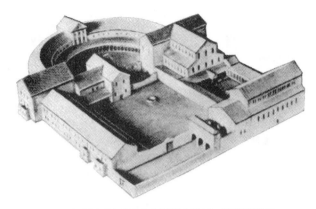

THE PALACE OF A MEDIÆVAL EMPEROR:
Ingelheim (reconstruction).

THE EMPEROR AS PROTECTOR OF THE HOLY GHOST, IN
THE FORM OF A DOVE. ABOUT 980

continent. The emperor, though a German, had to move and act as a Roman.

The millennium of creation and revolution had to revive all the dead words of the Latin language, one after the other, to resurrect the corpse of the Occident, as it had been in 900. For this continent, hopelessly divided, as it was, into small cantons and valleys, was held together by one language. The Latin tongue comforted the souls of these natives of little places in the Alps, or the northern plains, by reminding them of the great past. But the sea, the ancient road of commerce, being in the hands of Moslems, Normans, Byzantines, Danes, and the continent itself overrun by the frequent raids of Huns and Magyars, the Latin speech was more like a reminiscence of unity and universality than an everyday fact.

A comparison will help, perhaps, to explain. When in 1869 the American transcontinental railroad was finished, the workers who met at the junction were Chinese coolies and Irish immigrants. This was a peaceful meeting. To understand the longing of the Europeans for Rome, you have only to imagine that Chinese and Irish had come with the support of their respective motherlands, and that parts of several Middle Western States and of the Western provinces of Canada were the only regions free from invasion.

Let us assume that these fragments had resolved to preserve the sacred name of the United States, that they were happy to bring Greenland, thickly populated by means of her technical devices, into their league, and that after a long campaign, Washington, D. C., had been saved by these far distant Greenlanders from being absorbed either by a de Valera or by the troops of a Sun Yat Sen II.

These few States, out of so many, would base all their politics on the old claims of Washington to be the capital of the United States. Perhaps in some of them, facing the dismemberment of their territory, the restoration of the union would dominate all political thought for centuries.

A thousand years ago, the situation on the Continent of Europe recalled somewhat the one we have outlined here. The Europeans of that day struggled for Rome as the only imaginable centre. For them, the last ruler of the Roman Empire in the West had not been the little Romulus Augustulus whose downfall in 476 figures in our textbooks as the beginning of the Middle Ages. Happily enough, they enjoyed life without even knowing the term Middle Ages. It had not been invented by the Lutherans then!

Roman was the whole past millennium, and Charlemagne was looked upon as but the last in the long series of emperors of Rome. Charles' Frankish army, having conquered most of the Western provinces of ancient Rome, was regarded as the pillar of the Roman order of things.

"Roman" was the spell of unity that enabled the provinces of Europe to go along as children born of one cradle, eternal Rome, *Roma æterna*. "Public" is a Latin word, because only Latin could make Europe the field of one public law, one public spirit and public opinion. This spell of "Roman" is fast vanishing. We shall live, probably, to see its extinction or its natural death. It is after all, not more than a background before which the characters of the great national civilizations have unfolded themselves. But they unfolded themselves by translating something general, something that had been Roman, into English, French, Italian, etc. The nations of Europe gave a particular answer to a general appeal. But nations cannot build up a centennial memory without institutions. The appeal could only become real and permanent through an institution. The permanent appeal for regeneration was conveyed and enshrined in the Catholic Church, with its life of adoration and prayer. The prayers and adorations of this church were the quintessence of antiquity.

The total revolutions of our era were all answers given by the will and the unlimited faith of the laymen to a gospel preached by Latin tradition. We have regarded the answers. We shall understand them better when the appeal is revoiced directly. We have in fact listened to the dialogue between the parents—Roman Empire and Roman Church—and their children through all the centuries. We could not begin with the exhortations of the parents because our ears are deafened by the noise of recent centuries. But now the noise once being phoneticized we turn to the original language about our world, our general and universal destiny. All universal meaning and intrinsic requirements of life, a thousand years ago, were felt and expressed in the name Roman. Our own remembrance of the world of free trade of our pre-War days, now relapsing into a welter of tariffs, passport regulations, immigration quotas and all kinds of barriers, sub-divisions and sectionalism, can easily find its own likeness in the situation of a Roman empire which had lost its hold over the earth, but still conveyed to everybody who thought and fought politically, the two motives of unity and universality.

A history of the world can only be based on these two elements of unity and universality. No nation can plan or restore peace and prosperity without facing the question of what must remain united in spite of antagonism or seclusion, and what has to be universal in the future, in spite of territorial or continental particularities.

A friend of mine once tried to discover the *unum* and *universum* of the future. What is going to be the world-wide unity for our children? It seems as if it must be something in the nature of an economic unity. My friend found his suggestion corroborated by the fact that Christians today dream of the *"Una sancta"* alone, dropping the word *ecclesia* (church), to which *"una sancta"* originally belonged. That omission, he argued, forecasts a future when society, not church, will be the Universal City, the *"Una sancta,"* the "city without a temple" of Revelation, Chapter 21, 22. Many sects, many creeds, many races, many ways of education and self-expression, but one unshakable bondage or freedom of economic organization may remain for us in the future. The various creeds and denominations and national beliefs will be small parishes in a world-wide economic society.

In the beginning of European history, the opposite proportions between Church and economy prevailed. Economy was husbandry,—something local, parochial, narrow,—split into myriads of atoms. Christianity claimed universality and unity. One great ocean of creed and an archipelago of economic islands—that was the situation in the year 1000.

This unity of creed was the necessary condition of any general experience, because work and labour and capital were special, fixed to the soil. When men were summoned to join in a common purpose, a general effort, they could understand only a Roman effort, a Roman purpose, because they knew that unity and universality had existed once before in the form of Rome.

Church and economy have changed their places during the last thousand years.

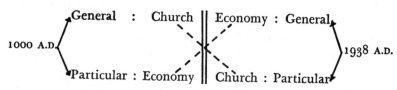

But this scheme conveys a wrong idea unless we take account of the steady march of the nations from the old situation into the new. We have to add to our scheme two arrows hinting at the movement, the revolutions which obliged the nations to move on two levels. The universal church becomes more and more particular in her operations; economy becomes more and more universally organized. We still pray for One Catholic Church. The real trouble of the future will be, whether we can pray for it sincerely or not. It is true that for ten centuries the nations carried both visions, the vision of local rights and private property, and the vision of a universal realm of peace. Private property is being attacked today on the same ground as the unity of faith. Both ideals are imperilled. Bolshevism is radical enough to make the church a private affair for the individual, and property the public affair of the community. But the question is not dependent on any subjective theory about Marxism. It is an issue for any government which subsidizes industry, taxes private educational institutions, propagates political ideas, or repopulates its deserted villages with self-subsisting homesteads.

The same question is put to us constantly: how to balance local interests and the universal welfare of humanity? Our ancestors threw in their lot for local rights and universal peace, as we try to do now. The march of the nations is always moving towards a two-fold goal. Every stage of this campaign was marked by a new compromise, a new covenant of the children of Japhet with God. Every time, the covenant was declared sacred and inviolable. Every time, a part of Christianity found the last covenant most unsatisfactory and stated a new one, producing a new order of society, a new type of man, a new form of life.

Man is but a brute when he does not struggle for both ends simultaneously. The dualism of liberty and particularity, on one side, and unity and universality, on the other side, is what makes man a man. Pitt renovating the English finances and nevertheless plunging his country into appalling debts for the Napoleonic Wars, is a good example of this double-edged character of man's struggle for life.

The American Civil War did not pay, certainly not. Yet it was inevitable because the equality of men was a universal goal which men could not forget or suppress. The other side of the medal was industrial revolution and it, too, was urgent. We gain our ends by a strange dualism. If a man thinks of money or private interests only, he will fail in the long run. His bank will go bankrupt, his children will become lazy; for once money is the highest good, why think of anything else? But the public-spirited man who lacks a healthy shrewdness for his own interests will fail as well. We walk very slowly on this earth, in a mutual interdependence of unitarian and universal duties and rights and particular and individual rights and duties.

Many people think of their interests primarily as rights, and only reluctantly as duties. They do the same in public affairs. They enjoy the rights of a voter more than the duties of a tax-payer. They think they can do as they please; it seems not to matter. But after a time, duties and rights are revalued. A bankruptcy, a war, a riot, an earthquake in the social world, upsets the scales and they cry for united support in their private affairs, and go in with their life and property for public business.

Religion can become less universal and economy can be

made less particular. Are we in earnest when we pray for a universal church? Or are we on the road to a united economy?

When Luther abolished the hundred monastic "religions" in Saxony, restoring one united religion and one common fund for the church and the schools in each territory, he made economy very much more general and universal than it ever had been before. But his church became less universal. It became at its best a national church, somewhat bigger, as we have seen, than one particular State, and extending over the whole body of a nation that comprised six kingdoms, 100 princes and innumerable High Magistrates; but the gains in economic unity and the loss of ecclesiastical universality are both unmistakable.

In England, the Anglican Church struggled hard to maintain a broader area than that of the Commonwealth. But it did not succeed. Non-conformity spread. The Commonwealth became larger than the Anglican Church. In the nineteenth century, the concept Nation was accepted as the spiritual unit; the economic reality embraced all civilized nations on equal footing; another half of the globe was treated as zones of interest, colonies, spheres of expansion. In the economic confederacy of liberalism, the colonial territories were the underdog. In the Soviet-system, there is an attempt to make the despised colonial ground the cornerstone of the social order.

The literary and political language of every nation is the result of a special balance between spirit and economy at a certain period. Each expresses a decision on the proportions between capital and faith. Each swept Europe in its own time as the best expression for the right balance between individuality (rights) and universality (obligations). And finally, because they all expressed a sincere disclosure of the human soul, each took permanent roots in one of the provinces of Europe and shaped this part by a great institution. Therefore, different as the European languages are, they are branches on the same tree since the dualism of faith and wealth is the problem of all of them. Without this dualism man is a mere brute and denies his history. We can only feel at home, and within our own family, in places where one certain form of this dualism is respected and revered and lived. The deeper meaning of civilization can be defined by referring to the ambiguity of the word citizen. City of God and City of Durham: Citizen of a place and citizen of a greater kingdom you must be if you are a human being. Two allegiances are the secret of civilization. Since the Russians are in their Restoration-period now and have joined the League of Nations, their faith will quickly take its seat among the previous creeds. It coexists with older systems.

For every modern man or political group a certain expression of this dualism in the past or abroad can be a real power of life. He can visit, as a friend, the home in which this expression of something eternal was born, and come back from his visit enlarged and better equipped for his own two-edged struggle for life.

THE LAST SONG ON THE LAST JUDGMENT (DANTE ALIGHIERI).

European history is the sequence of these equations between universal and particular, between local rights and federal government; it is a sequence as complete as a paradigm of word-forms in grammar. The oldest form of this equation is, on one side, the Emperor of Holy Rome marching on his laborious way through the Continent as the sole and universal judge, and on the other, the Lords of the Manor asking absolute loyalty, including the vendetta, from their knaves, chaplains and children.

No wonder that before anything else the final judgment caught the imagination of the Imperial period. A universal judgment—that was a political programme of truly world-wide character. It would release men from local bondage and arbitrary power. The more rarely the actual presence of the emperor secured a fair trial, the more passionately the picture of universal and efficient judgment was drawn by all the souls who longed for a definite redistribution of justice. Now, the hope of such a final and accomplished judgment was easily sublimated into a great system of thought and this system has not vanished from the earth and never will. The hope of a

Last Judgment will always reappear, and whenever it is resuscitated it will make man the brother of the Holy Emperor.

> For who would bear the whips and scorns of time,
> The oppressor's wrong, the proud man's contumely,
> The pangs of dispriz'd love, the law's delay,
> The insolence of office, and the spurns
> That patient merit of the unworthy takes. . . .
> But that the dread of something after death,
>   puzzles the will.

This old system is fully accessible, is so to speak still palpable,
in a great work of art. The quintessence of the Holy Roman
Emperor's mission in a weary world was condensed into a
majestic vision by the last great Ghibelline, the last believer
in the emperors from the North.

The Divine Comedy of the Last Judgment was sung by
Dante Alighieri of Florence. He visits the eight circles of Hell,
the mountain of Purgatory, then Paradise and the blinding
brightness of Heaven; and he dares to conceive for the first
time the great idea of Revolution. At the end of his poem he
says that one and the same power moves the life of mankind
and the life of Stars and Suns. Our actions and movements,
therefore, when prompted by love, are near to the constellations and revolutions of the celestial bodies. With this bold
equation, Dante transferred and projected our deepest and
most human experience upon the sky of the external world.
He prepared the reapplication of the world revolution to
Society. For Dante made these revolutions of the stars the symbols of life, and their motivation identical with the passions
of our own life. No wonder that his century, the fourteenth, is
the century in which the main concept of this work, Revolution, was first used by Italian chroniclers to draw a parallel
between heaven and earth, between the meteoric changes in
the sky and those in the political life of the Italian City-States.
But the most important feature of Dante's poem is that it bears
witness to the old time when the Sacred Emperor, marching
through this world, still paved the road for God's Last Judgment.

THE APOSTOLIC EMPEROR AND EMPRESS

They are ushered in by the Apostles Peter and Paul and crowned by Christ. About 1008-og.

The imperial form of the dualism pervading humanity is present and accessible to us in Dante's great poem, *The Divine Comedy*. This poem, begun in 1300, testifies to a much older dualism. The dualism for which the song of Hell, Purgatory, and Heaven was conceived as a high dirge was the dualism of the Roman Empire during the tenth and eleventh centuries. The emperors of the North, from Henry I (1002-24) to Henry VI (1307-13) were the heroes of Dante. Much trouble has been taken to show Dante's training in the Scholastic literature of the thirteenth century. It is obvious that he lived physically in the time of Giotto and Albertus Magnus; but what matter? An English country squire can live in flesh and blood in the same world with Mr. Stalin; but are they contemporaries in the real sense of the word? For any important issue, they are not. This is precisely the situation of Dante in his day. Facing a changed world, he had to sing the Last Judgment so that the great period when the emperors had acted as judges of Christianity might be eternalized in a work of art. As a simple outline of Dante's vision of the Last Judgment, we can say that he draws a line from everybody's specific and particular existence to his place in the universe which lies beyond the visible organization of earth. His Last Judgment applies the categories of unity and universality to the Beyond, because earthly life is local, parochial, particular, fragmentary. He is obliged to trace everybody's destiny to its last judgment; it is the only way to unite men who are separated on earth. The realm of faith is the only universal and unifying home for the scattered villages of the tenth century.

Manorialism prevailed in the economic world. Dante himself, it is true, already lived in the Free City of Florence, which, as we shall see, passed successfully from the manorial unit into a larger economic concept. But he was exiled when the old families of clannish tradition were driven from the town. He was perhaps the last great victim of this first step beyond the clans and tribes of imperial days! Dante was driven out by the Italian revolution into the life of a refugee. He was made, less by his theory than by his fate, into a Ghibelline, a partisan of the age of the emperors from the North. He was, like an

American Loyalist in 1790, a stranger to his time. He owed his immortality to the immortal achievements of a Roman Empire that lay between local feuds, local monasteries, local economy, and the Last Judgment of the Universe. It is the first immortal period of our past; in it we can experience the principle of Church and economy in a form far removed from our own situation and yet perfectly close to our own doubts and experiences.

Dante looked on the emperor as the only legal vicar of the terrors of the Last Judgment. On his campaigns in Italy, in Poland, in France, in Burgundy, in Hungary, the emperor protected the widows and orphans, the poor and the weak, against the local politician. The Majesty of his Sword stood in judgment over the wickedness of local despots. The lord of the manor had to tremble, because before the court of the emperor the poorest serf could bring his complaint. The emperor wore a mantle decorated with the galaxy and the sun and the moon as symbols of his universality. With his mantle covering heaven, the emperor's sword held together the local fragments of an unarticulated Continent.

The old Romans had never liked the Continent. They had organized the coasts of the Mediterranean. The ports of this well-articulated sea had formed the highways of antiquity. Antiquity had not known the rudder for steering a boat. But it knew even less about mass transportation on land by mechanical aid. It was completely ignorant of how to harness a horse or a bull for haulage over a long distance.

The indefatigable march of the Emperor and his army was therefore the only moving force for unity and universality. To understand Dante's concentration on the cruelties and blessings of the Last Judgment, we must think of the loneliness of the clans and individuals who were threatened by the merciless persecution of feud and vendetta, wandering from one country to the next to find refuge. The sudden apparition of the emperor could suppress the vendetta, restore peace, establish security. Like lightning in the dark the emperor appeared to the tribes in their local system.

The emperors found little or no support in Rome. The

bishops of Rome had degenerated. Nobody doubted the fact of the papal succession to St. Peter. But it would be fatal to think that this was a great comfort; for the Church of Rome was rotten and known to be rotten. Pornocràcy, "pig-rule," historians have called this squalid period of the papacy. The vicars of St. Peter were despised by clergy and laity alike. No wonder that the emperors who succeeded in raising a Christian army for a march to Rome appeared as the true heads and reformers of the Christian Church.

The desires and longings of the time are expressed remarkably well on the golden bowl from the tenth century, which we reproduced on p. 492, the significance of which has never been pointed out because the finding and interpretation of it are of rather recent date. The legend on the basin reads: "Jerusalem visio pacis." In the centre is the Emperor Otto, holding up a bottle for the oil of baptism and a dove, the symbol of the Holy Ghost. Otto appears on a sacramental vessel because only he can restore the Jerusalem of Eternal Peace. To him is entrusted the Dove of Inspiration. Public Spirit, to us a general force of democratic inspiration, centres in the emperor. What is certainly a blasphemy to us, is no blasphemy in a time of piggishness among the clergy, when the marching army of the empire was the only force for restoring peace. The placing of the Holy Ghost in the hand of the emperor is a colossal deviation from orthodoxy, but a deviation in self-defence. It is a real outcry for a force which can at least unite and universalize life. This force has always been idolized by mankind, and always will be. "When Otto III sat in judgment, Heaven groaned, earth boomed," sang a poet.

No wonder that this emperor sought for the model of his action not in Roman history, but in the past of the Roman Church. The pagan Cæsars did not attract him, the devoted Christian. Was he not rather the successor of St. Paul the Apostle? Was he not inculcating the Gospel in a clergy that for its worldliness was called "mundus," world, and in Christians of so little faith that a man had to become a monk before he could be called "convert" and "religious." "Conversus" and "religiosus" had become names for monks alone.

Otto III ordered a statuette of St. Paul, perhaps the most individual piece of art we have from his time. In an imperial monastery, Echternach, a master carved it and added, on a roll in the hand of Paul: *"Dei gratia sum id quod sum"*—the proud word of the apostle: "By the grace of God I am what I am." Now, this "by the grace of God" was exactly the title on which the emperors so strongly based their sovereignty. Otto went so far as to adopt St. Paul's formula from his letters, and to call himself *"servus Jesu Christi."*

It is true that when Otto III (984-1002) reformed the Holy See and installed northern-born popes, first his cousin Gregory V and later his teacher, Sylvester II, the reform itself, by exalting the bishops of Rome, was bound to weaken his own apostolic claims. Therefore he now called himself *"servus apostolorum,"* seneschal, majordomo of the apostles. On the maps of the time the earth was shown divided into twelve sections, one for each apostle. The emperor, as the majordomo of our Lord's twelve apostles, had to administer the apostolic inheritance (see illustration facing page 501).

It was with deep feeling that the renovation of the Christian Church was introduced. Sylvester was the first pope who called himself "the Second," after Pope Sylvester, who had, according to the legend, baptized Constantine, the emperor of the Council of Nicæa.

A renaissance begins where names forgotten for 700 years are brought back into man's ken. And the existence of a Pope Sylvester II suggested an Emperor Constantine II. Only, after all, Pope Sylvester I had converted the pagan emperor Constantine to Christianity, while the pious emperor Otto III in his zeal for the Church had himself installed Pope Sylvester II. No wonder that he felt himself superior to the pope. St. Paul appeared to Otto in a vision and strengthened him in certain plans for reforms in Rome, against the objections of Pope Sylvester. As Paul had preached, founded, reformed in Asia Minor and Spain, in Rome and Illyria, as a "free-lancer" of inspiration, as the faithful legate of the Holy Ghost, so Otto would hurry from Posen to Aachen, from Aachen to the south of Italy. Thus, the dove of the Holy Spirit seemed to fly over the lightless earth as the dove had flown in Noah's day, after the great flood of sin. A poet summoned the emperor "as a second St. Paul" to clean the Augean stable in Rome!

The appeal to the authority of Paul was more easily conceivable because the eastern emperors and patriarchs of Constantinople were given to playing up Paul against Peter. I shall mention only one great example of this practice of the Oriental Christians. To the second universal Council of Nicæa, in 787, the pope wrote a long letter in which his authority was duly based on St. Peter. When his legates arrived in Nicæa, they conceived how little interest Peter's authority would arouse among clergy who came from the oldest churches of Christendom. They changed or forged, in the Greek translation, the mention of Peter into a mention of Peter and Paul. The Greeks in answering did not mention Peter at all, but based their respect for Rome on the fact that St. Paul himself had praised the orthodoxy of the Romans! Whereas Peter gave Rome a monopoly, Paul was both Roman and universal, sweeping, like the Holy Ghost itself, freely over the whole earth. *"Sanctus Paulus Romanus et non Romanus est,"* "Paul is a Roman and not a Roman," was the remark of one of the popes, Victor III himself. Thus the emperor's universal task was emphasized by his acting under the special auspices of St. Paul.

The emperor was even called the vicar of God by his enthusiastic chroniclers. Today, the theory of such a government is preserved in the rights of the only respected (though not existing) Apostolic Majesty, the "kiraly" of Hungary. This kiraly-king got his name from "Karolus"—Charlemagne. And the Hungarian Crown of St. Stephen enjoys today all the ecclesiastical privileges of the Roman emperor in 1000, on Hungarian territory. Roman Catholic bishops and abbots, for example, may be appointed by the Crown, an incredible anachronism today, but an undoubted maintainer of unity in 1000; under the Regent of a country that easily never will see a king again, the "Crown of St. Stephen" still is the objective embodiment of apostolic ruling. And all through the last thousand years, the Roman See has had severe headaches from time to time, when they saw, preserved in Hungary, that which pointed to a pre-Gregorian Church of imperial reform.

ALL SOULS: THE CHRISTIAN DEMOCRACY OF THE LAST JUDGMENT.

This universal power standing above local tyranny had to be more than a naked sword and a merciless crushing force of conquest. Dante's Last Judgment reveals its moral majesty by showing all the tears and fears of a human heart under the weight of true judgment.

The emperor's Pauline dignity, when it had to restore the papacy and govern the Christian Church, could rely on an army of monks who centred around the monastery of Cluny. It was they who, for the first time, wrote the idea of super-local unity into the constitution of a monastic order, and, by inserting a new day in the calendar, wrote the notion of universality into the hearts of the Christian peoples.

They united monasticism by imitating imperial centralism. As the emperor had distributed public duties among the many imperial monasteries, so did now the abbot of Cluny for spiritual purposes. Cluny incorporated all the "Roman" monasteries which were reformed by it. The abbot of Cluny was the only abbot, the other monasteries being ruled by friars, vicars president. Cluny became a super-abbey.

For the first time in history space was conquered by the legal personality of a corporation, scattered though it was all over the empire.

The constitution of Cluny is the first trust, the trans-local corporation. It was even attacked on that ground. In a venomous satirical poem, the bishops ridiculed the "kingdom of Cluny." But in the loose fabric of the tenth-century world it was a great step forward.

One abbot of Cluny refused to become pope in Rome. The monasteries carried the reform in spite of Rome's decay. And the monasteries gave comfort to the layman, too. They invented the *treuga dei,* the truce of the land. The liturgy of the church was used to restore peace. The week of Easter, from Palm Sunday to Easter Sunday, with Maundy Thursday and Good Friday in it, was taken as a model for daily life. Monday,

Tuesday, Wednesday, a man was allowed to fight his kind. But from Thursday to Sunday, Cluny imposed abstinence from all violence. Holy Week was epoch-making in that it divided life again into peace and war, making peace and war definite, abolishing their complete confusion; and ennobling the task of the common knight as a defence of God's peace. The ritual of a king's coronation was extended to the knighting of every soldier of God.

But Cluny's greatest act was giving to mankind the day of All Souls. All Souls is a Holy Day celebrated by Catholics on the second of November, the day after All Saints.

"All Saints" represents the last feast common to Greeks and Romans, Orthodox and Catholics. Its celebration dates back to the ninth century, two centuries before our period.[1] It is a day of triumph for the redeemed and victorious part of humanity. It is the day of all those since St. Stephen, the first martyr, who by their deaths have opened the dark mystery of heaven to us. Glee and jubilation fill the day of All Saints.

All Souls is a day of purgatory. The Church in 1000 is no church of saints. It is a church of sinners, who by their blood-ties are all involved in bloodsheds: pious bishops fighting in the imperial army, innocent children being biassed by vendetta.

All Souls established the solidarity of all souls from the beginning of the world to the end of time. We learn, from the biographer of St. Odilo of Cluny, how Odilo conceived the idea of begging on the hill of Purgatory for all souls ever born or to be born. The liturgy of the mass for the day is full of deep shadows. He who has ever heard a Catholic mass at a funeral should know that it is taken from the formula invented by Odilo of Cluny, probably in 998, certainly before 1031, to celebrate All Souls.

The Empire, with all the apostolic majesty of one sacred emperor at the top of the hierarchy, was a Christian democracy. By a late ritual in Austria the corpse of the emperor was ordered to be carried to the door of an abbey. The chamber-

[1] H. Quentin, *Les Martyrologes historiques du Moyen Âge*, pp. 366 ff., Paris, 1908.

lain who leads the cortège knocks at the door. A friar opens the window and asks: "Who knocks?"—"The Emperor."—"I know no man of that name." The chamberlain knocks again. "Who is there?"—"The Emperor Francis Joseph."—"We do not know him." Third knock, and the same question. After reflection, the chamberlain now answers: "Brother Francis." Then the door opens to receive a comrade in the army of death, on equal terms with all souls.

The first universal democracy in the world was a democracy of sinners, united by their common confession of sins in expectation of the Last Judgment. That is why the members of this democracy wore the uniforms of death. It was an army in winding-sheets. The forms of this confederacy were first developed, not for a personal day of death, but for that general day. From it, the ceremony was carried over to individual burial.

Oswald Spengler says in one of his deepest remarks that every civilization sets out with a new experience of death. In so far, Europe started with a new experience when All Souls was added to All Saints. For it gave comfort to innumerable people in the loneliness of their hearts to celebrate the truth that death was universal and that all men would be rallied at the Last Judgment. And they would actually spend two thirds of their fortune to arm themselves against this last day.

I hope I have succeeded in overcoming our common notion of the Last Judgment as a mere religious concept without practical consequences. In fact, it was a political agency of the first importance; it attracted the wealth of the people like a magnet, building up an immense property in the hands of a disinterested trustee, the Church.

And this confederacy was also democratic. In Dante's poem, there are popes in hell and emperors in purgatory. From the complicated structure of Society in his time, he drew his wires to a common focus in the Beyond. All people had to be deeply impressed by the fact that they were equal in the sight of God. It is the poet's and the artist's privilege to use his art like God, to see, not with the eyes of the transient hour, but with the vision of eternity. Dante's *Divine Comedy* is divine because it reveals how men can be equal in the eyes of the Creator.

But poetry and fiction and art are always a sequel to religion. Goethe's *Faust* translated the experience of Luther and of his singing congregation to the unbelieving public of the nineteenth century. Dante, writing as a lost, an exiled, soul, at the end of the imperial period, enables us, who are not contemporaries of the eleventh century, to share the feeling stirred by the introduction of All Souls in 998.

In All Souls, every Christian anticipated through the common purgation of death, what we would call the final judgment of world history. He was changed into dust, a mere part of this passing world. World was not "without end" in 1000. "World" was an utterly unstable fog of blindness, vanity, insecurity, crisis. Yet Odilo of Cluny discovered world history as a universal order and fact, when he ordered the whole religious fraternity to pray for the liberty of *"omnes omnimodo fideles."* Up to that time, monks had prayed only for their abbey, their relatives, their friends, their connections. Odilo conjured up instead [2] the universe which lies *between heaven and hell, between saints and sinners,* waiting for our prayers, and which consists of all those who have been, from the beginning of the world to its end.

The liturgical readings for All Souls emphasize the utter naught which is man. Man is like Job, like grass, like a shadow. Yet God thinks highly enough of him to fix His eyes upon him and to call him to judgment.

In these prayers the idea of Judgment was called a privilege. "Last Judgment" conveyed more than terror; it revealed man's dignity, his claim not to be thrown into the fire like a weed, but to be judged. And is that not true? Is not a fair hearing the first human claim? Can we ask for more in this vale of tears? It is true, man trembles at the idea of being judged.

"All Souls" continues: "Spare me, because my days are nought." But the army of Christian soldiers marches with irresistible faith before the Saviour who was their comrade, and is now their judge. The triumphant outcry, in the mass

2 Migne, *Patrologia*, Vol. 142, 1038.

for the dead on All Souls, runs: "I know that my Redeemer liveth, and I shall rise on the Last Day."

Liberty was promised to all souls, liberty, the great promise of Revolution, is first heard in the Occident at All Souls. This cry for liberty divides East and West, the Eastern church being the quiet church of holiness and adoration, Western Christianity fighting for salvation and deliverance: "Free Thou," the Mass for All Souls beseeches Heaven, "Free Thou the souls of all believers from the punishment of hell, from the deep abyss, free them from the lion's maw. May thy standard-bearer, Michael, bring them into the Holy Light which thou didst promise to Abraham and his seed." *"Visio pacis Jerusalem,"* was the motto of the Empire. The vision of peace promised to Abraham, the ancestor of Jerusalem, now appeared to the Army of the Dead.

The crowning hymn of All Souls is the *"Dies iræ, dies illa,"* a song which has been translated into English more than one hundred and fifty times. It cannot be translated; the words created, the language shaped, in a real revolution of the human heart, are untranslatable. The mass being sung in Latin, the song of Thomas of Celano (1226) on the Last Judgment was in Latin, also. But Latin, which was then sung and prayed all over the Continent in the form of plain chant, was a more natural language for mankind than English or French today. On All Souls, the priest used the real first and last language of our soul, which is *before the division of song and speech.* The plain song of the mass also keeps alive the oldest of all truths, that language is living and life-giving speech. This language is not to be found in the dead, soundless prose of our daily talk and chatter. We whisper; our language is a dead branch of the living tree of speech. Souls dive into language as into their true element and where they dare commit themselves to the flood of sincere speech, there is no division of language, no Babylonian confusion of tongues. Where mind and heart are fully represented, mankind knows only one language. English psalms, French ideas, German chorales, Russian statistics and diagrams—what else have they tried to do but to restore the unity of language throughout mankind? The unifying power of all the great revolutions is what makes them life-giving, creative, restoring. The imperial democracy of All Souls and the Last Judgment attempted the same thing. The plain-song of the mass represents man in his deepest emotions. Man knows nothing of division. "The division of man" is the fall of man. It was not William Blake alone who preached this gospel. Division has been man's ruin again and again. The *"Dies Iræ, Dies Illa,"* restored unity in a divided world, restored man's union by singing and playing in child-like plasticity before the Creator.

Though the *"Dies Iræ"* was written two centuries after the inauguration of All Souls, it faithfully repeats words, ideas and associations which we find expressed in the verses of Odilo's biography. In our human world, when one faith pervades it, time works as an evolutionary force. It takes a number of generations to carry to perfection what the soul began to express in a new outbreak of inspiration. Our pragmatic history-writing exaggerates the external evidence of contemporaneity. The finest flower of a civilization springs up after centuries of growth. Dante was no contemporary of the people who asked him to apologize to them before returning to Florence. It is not only admissible, but necessary, to declare that the seed was planted when the first revolutionary set out with a new faith in the meaning of life and death. Since the year 1000 all souls have prayed the *dies iræ:*

> *Dies iræ, dies illa*
> *Solvet sæclum in favilla*
> *Teste David cum Sybilla.*
>
> *Quantus tremor est futurus*
> *Quando iudex est venturus*
> *Cuncta stricte discussurus.*
>
> *Tuba mire spargens sonum*
> *Per sepulchra regionum*
> *Coget omnes ante thronum.*
>
> *Mors stupebit et natura*
> *Cum resurget creatura,*
> *judicanti responsura.*

Liber scriptus proferetur
in quo totum continetur
Unde mundus *judicetur.*

Judex ergo cum sedebit,
Quidquid latet, apparebit,
Nil inultum remanebit.

Iuste iudex ultionis,
Donum fac remissionis
Ante diem rationis.

Lacrimosa dies illa
Qua resurget ex favilla
judicandus homo reus,
huic ergo parce, deus.

Day of wrath, that (very) day
shall dissolve the age into ashes
our witnesses being David and the Sybil.

What a tremour is to be
when the judge is to come
everything strictly examining.

The trumpet spreading marvellous the sound
through the graves of (all) regions
shall force all before the throne.

Death shall be stunned and Nature
when shall rerise the creature
to him who judges giving answer.

Book written will be brought forth,
in which the whole is contained
whence the world is to be judged.

The Judge, then, when he will take his seat
whatsoever is hidden, will appear
nothing unvindicated will remain.

O righteous judge of vengeance
the gift make of forgiveness
before the day of accounts.

Full of tears will be that day
when man shall rise again from his ashes,
to be judged, in thy court.
Spare him (for whom we here pray), O Lord.

Human prayers anticipate the inevitable, and by anticipating they create a field of force for liberty. Liberty is nothing but the taking of death into our lives. By anticipating death, we are delivered from evil. Love, prayer, solidarity, sacrifices can shorten the process of purification. So-called world history became a reality from the moment when All Souls began to work on every man.

In war there is no time. In war people have lost control over time. Then it is that the wheel of nature grinds us in its turning. Peace restores to us the room for free action. But unless we carry into this action an idea of the future, of final values, of direction, our liberty will not be of any use. In anticipating the lessons of death, Europe learned democracy, she learned Unity, she learned Universality. All Souls is the cornerstone of all our modern civilization.

The day of All Souls, proclaiming purgatory to be the stage for all contemporaries, has separated us forever from the jubilant glee of the ancient church. In a minute correction, this change was expressed most strikingly by the Cluniacs: At Easter time, everybody was happy in the experience of resurrection, and evil itself was redeemed since God can make use of evil as well as of good; in recognizing the restoration of the world, the old church sang: "O happy fault that produced this redeemer!" [3] Cluny resented this slighting of our human

[3] Adam lay ibounden
  Bounden in a bond;
Four thousand winter
  Thought he not too long;
And all was for an apple,
  An apple that he took,
As clerkes finden
  Written in their book.
Nor had the apple taken been,
  The apple taken been,
Nor had never our Lady
  A-been [of] Heaven Queen.

guilt: the prayer *"O felix culpa"* was suppressed.[4] Losses and gains in the life of the spirit are interdependent, so it seems. Man grew up to a greater knowledge of his own nature when he started the anticipation of the Last Judgment in his Great Year of Revolution.

All Souls became a popular Holy Day. It made its way from Cluny in spite of the conservative attitude of the popes. Some inhibitions against it exist even today in the Roman practice which tries to protect the day of All Saints and its claim to be a feast of two days, including the Second of November. Long before Papal Rome was able to regularize All Souls—a last regulation was tried by the Pope during the World War— the monks of Cluny flooded the Occident with an ocean of masses on this day. The monks, in an alliance with the apostolic majordomos of the Church, the great German Emperors, educated the tribes of Europe in a faith of repentance and prayer. This was done without the support of bishops and popes. Ghibelline and Dantesque Christianity is a special stratum of Catholic faith; this stratum is older than Roman Catholicism in the modern sense. Protestants and Dante's Christians easily meet. They are not in a deadly opposition. The very existence of the imperial period of Christianity prevented —in Luther's days—the Reformation from destroying the unit of our faith totally and forever. For Roman Catholicism contained many more layers than popery against which Luther raged, and especially a strong imperial and monastic admixture.

And in all later centuries, liturgical revivals like Anglo-Catholicism and similar movements have freely used the treasures of All Souls and of the Christian democracy of the Last Judgment.

Blessed be the time
That apple taken was.
Therefore we moun singen
"Deo Gratias."

Quoted with spelling modernized, from Sloane Ms. 2595 (according to Bradly Stratmann early fourteenth century) as printed in *Early English Lyrics*, E. N. Chambers and F. Sedgwick, p. 102, London, 1907.

[4] Cardinale Schuster, O.S.B., *Liber Sacramentorum*, Vol. IV (1930), p. 49, and p. 18, Note 1.

At every moment our field of free action is imperilled. The World War has destroyed it again. Where there is no choice, there is no soul. When Dollfuss, the Chancellor of Austria, was deliberately deprived of the comfort of the last anointment, when confession and the solace of a priest were denied to the victims of the German Purge in 1934, the World War revealed its destructive force as the end of a civilization. All Souls died in 1934, because the Christian democracy of the dead and the dying was no longer real. Modern man believes, perhaps, in equality of birth. But he fancies that everybody dies alone and individually.

The complete breakdown of a civilization that does not anticipate death is certain. Common sufferings create. Common tears restore. That is why the spiritual regeneration of Cluny was called *"dona lacrimarum,"* the gifts of tears. A stream of tears cleansed the soil, long smirched by bloodshed, and the lands of the former empire were inundated by a peace unknown in ancient Rome.

CHAPTER TEN

Rome: The Revolution of the Holy See

Papal Court Against Imperial Palace—The Triumph of Old Age—The Economic Revolution—Paul Helps Peter: The Technique of the Papal Revolution—The Addressees of the First Revolutionary Document—Crusade and Scholasticism—A Church Made Visible and Raphael's Greatest Painting—Anti-Christ

PAPAL COURT AGAINST IMPERIAL PALACE.

THE PALACE OF THE EMPEROR MOVED WITH HIS ARMY. WHERE the army was not, the emperor's judgment could not become a reality. This lack of permanent organization was the sore spot of the whole system. It became intolerable when the army showed itself unable to cover the whole area that longed for peace and order.

The emperor's palace was not real for a great part of Western civilization. The kingdom of Western France and of the Anglo-Saxons in England did not obey his orders. But here the local kings acted as vice-emperors; in other words, they claimed a sacred and ecclesiastical function like the apostolic majesty at the centre. *Regna,* kingdoms, were sub-divisions of an ideal empire. These anointed kings did not deny the potential uniqueness of the Empire. They were all in favour of a form of government which gave to the head of the army the advowson of the Church. The weakness of the imperial programme became conspicuous when old Mediterranean provinces of the Roman Empire showed themselves ready to renew their connections with the Holy See. Spain and Sicily changed masters in the eleventh century. They turned the scales of the Holy Roman Empire, because they laid bare its inadequacy to reform the Church in the islands and peninsulas of the former Roman world. In Spain, Cid Campeador taking Toledo from the Moslems, and Robert Guiscard ruling over Southern Italy, prepared the way for an attempt to restore a Mediterranean civilization, to organize its shores instead of the continental mass. Without a navy, without a permanent residence on these coasts, the emperor could not think of bringing his peace and his church regulations to bear on these countries. Sicily and Spain, by re-entering the orbit of Western life, opened the door to a new era. This era ejected the emperors and kings and vice-emperors from the Church, and assigned them one State among many as their jurisdiction. In 1060, when the Normans of Sicily paid their homage to the pope, they created the "State." By that act they changed the Holy See in Rome from a part of the imperial palace into an independent papal court. To have a Curia (a court) became the cry of the papacy against the palatine principle under which emperor and pope had shared one and the same chancellor.

Irresistibly, the emancipation of this first section of the imperial palace called forth the emancipation of all the rest. The Papal Court was followed in the process of emancipation by the Princes' Chamber and by the Cabinet of Ministers. The sequence of European revolutions can be illustrated by a diagram of the imperial palace and its slow dissolution. Constitutional history runs from palace to cabinet, and ends in the tent of the dictator, put up again by an army, but this time without the productive force of a household at his disposal. Mussolini or Hitler are reduced, in their governmental stock of clothes, to the shirt of a "leader." Compared to the wardrobe of the imperial palace or the Papal Court, the "shirts" of modern government—black, brown or blue—are but poor raiment. People in the eleventh century might well have considered them "nudists."

The Papal See was newly established in a section of the imperial "church fortress"; archway and cloisters around the yard were cut off and used as the field for a new organization. The Mediterranean parts of the old Roman Empire, like Sicily, Apulia and Calabria, which had never been Frankish, but remained Byzantine provinces, were conquered by Nor-

man princes for the Western Church; but they were no longer
incorporated in the Western Empire. Instead, Robert Guiscard,
the great Norman chief, paid homage to St. Peter in Rome.
Two decades later, a princess in her own right gave Tuscany to
the papacy. Though this bequest was never acknowledged by
the emperor, it marked an epoch nevertheless. Without imperial dispensation a prince within the empire had turned over
to the Papal Court what had been under imperial control for
centuries. The Papal Court was no longer overshadowed by
the walls of the imperial palace. It lay for the first time under
the open sky, an immediate, sovereign court. The hieratic
exaltation of the emperor ceased to dominate. With great conciseness, the popes now called their canon laws by a new term,
Ius Poli, the law of the firmament. Moon and stars on the emperor's mantle no longer frightened the pope. His rising sun
spread a bright daylight over the new civilization, centring
around his Court in Rome.

Central government was invented by the papacy when it
granted the free right of appeal to every Christian soul. Before
the Papal Revolution, no son of a church anywhere had been
allowed to denounce the crimes of his bishop or to carry his
grievances outside his own diocese.

The new spiritual party claimed the right to open the road
to Rome for all parts of the world. Every bishop had to be
prepared to see complaints of his own diocesans brought up
in Rome. Even today, any Catholic may refer questions of
marriage to the Roman Courts. The bishops were summoned
to visit the pope at regular intervals, *"ad limina apostolorum."*
The Papal Court broke through the forms of personal allegiance which existed in the feudal system of the empire, and
established a new system of immediate allegiance between
every bishop, every abbot, every Christian and the pope.

The emperor's chancery was accustomed to call Rome the
Mother of all Churches. The Papal Revolution, by requiring
regular visits in Rome of every bishop, and by granting free
appeal to everybody, created the situation so familiar to us,
whereby the Roman Church has become the mother of every

Catholic individual. This modern vision was not generally conceived before 1100. It was the content of a revolution.

THE TRIUMPH OF OLD AGE.

The ascetic monk on the papal throne spoke still from the beyond. At his "conversion" a monk was buried in symbolical forms; he handed over his life, his property, his family, to his patron. He died in every sense. He lived and anticipated a spiritual world.

"Civil death" or monastic death is a legal term which describes the consequences of the monastic profession. Gregory VII manifested the monk's spiritual world of after-death as a cradle of government. Ancestral wisdom from beyond the grave was introduced into a world threatened by child mortality, juvenile leadership, and the rare survival of people past middle age. Today man's life spiral so often reaches the third circle, from sixty to ninety years, that this age is not especially emphasized as a basis for a certain attitude toward government. At that time the tremendous lack of older men made it advisable to specialize in the features of old age, of the nonagenarian with his natural resignation and renouncement. The monk's existence is an artificial substitute for the man who has waived all his claims because of age. "Senescence by establishment," the papal rule could be called, if the English language had preserved the flavour of the Latin "Senectus," old age. Unfortunately, the word "senile" enjoys no distinction in English; the worship of virility has atrophied the English interest in old age as a peculiar form of life. The indifference of the English to the "third age" as deserving political representation may be compared to the failure of German paternalism to represent youth politically. In German, old age kept a good meaning in the special word "Greis" (senex), while "youth" was more and more neglected. At the end, the German word meaning "a youth" became comical: "Jüngling" ceased to have any full dignity or value. In reaction against this suppression and against paternalism, the famous Youth Movement sprang up in Germany, restoring the phases of adolescent youth as a special form of life in the community. The monks of the eleventh century could appeal to a corresponding situation regarding old age. By the distribution of ages among the population, there was a lack of proportion between young and old. The "third age" was undermanned. The special phase of German paternalism will best be understood when we come to the phase of "motherhood by establishment" which prevailed in Italian civilization. But we are here considering primarily the first phase of the papal renovation of the Church, and we can describe it as a constitution by which the ancestral cult of the "third age," the grandfather, the man who stands beyond the passions of the soul and the changes of the body, is established. "Spiritual" came to be the motto of the revolutionary party. The pope, the priestly father of all believers, was himself the clearest symbol of the new force which was to be established. Celibacy became the issue of this struggle against an imperial church.

At the outbreak of the revolution the pope called upon all laymen to expel their married priests. The married cleric shared too much in the passions and material interests of his contemporaries. In the Eastern Church, bishops and priests always married before being ordained. There the phase of priesthood came in the natural course of events as a late stage in life, after a man had experienced the preceding phases. In the Western Church, the phase of natural life for the cleric was shortened to its minimum, and the period of renunciation was lengthened. Thereby, the importance of this particular phase in the life-cycle was suddenly enhanced. By this temporal variation, old age got a most powerful representation in a century of too early mortality. The shibboleth for recognizing the true servant of the spirit became—and naturally, I think—celibacy. Any responsible cleric who felt it his duty to spare the married priests under his jurisdiction was leaning by so much toward the imperial side.

The new party among the clergy was a minority in the beginning; it took fifty years to secure the establishment of the new class of a spiritualized clergy. And in honour of its reorganization, the name *"Spirituals"* was coined under Gregory for the "new clergy"; it implied a refounding of the Church.

"Clergy" itself meant "chosen people" in Greek; but the new "spirituals" of the Papal Revolution were not the whole clergy. One part of this clergy was imperial; that is, in the eyes of the reformers it was rotten, corrupt, deserving of extirpation and annihilation. It had not passed through a true conversion despite baptism and ordination. The old clergy ceased to bear the mark of holiness. It was "*mundus,*" world, secular clergy, a contradiction in terms. It had to show by a new effort that it had turned from the world to the new life. The new effort consisted mainly in a decision to fight with the pope against the local governor and, eventually, the emperor. Whereas the imperial and royal bishops insisted that no priest could engage in warfare, the Gregorians defended crusading as a holy enterprise.

The change from secular clergy to Lords Spiritual could be expressed by no better symbol than by a new obedience and allegiance to the court in Rome. The success of the popes in their establishment of central government could not be explained without the symbolical value of this subjection of the whole clergy in the Western world. He who went to Rome reformed himself! The pope's own office was brought nearer to every congregation, because his name had to be mentioned in the public prayers of every service.

And the pope's individual name was made a weapon in the struggle for reform. From 1047 to 1146 the popes choose to be "seconds," to imitate the times of the fathers of the Church, by singling out venerable names from the first centuries. Never was there a more deliberate "Renaissance" than in this century of renaming the popes. If any period deserves the attribute of historical Renovation it is the time of the Crusades.

Gregory VII, it is true, was not a "second." But he combined two purposes in the choice of his name. One was a protest against the imperial action which had forced Gregory VI, Hildebrand's patron, out of office in 1046. By calling himself VII, Gregory confirmed the legitimacy of Gregory VI. Then, Gregory I (590-604) was the pope who more than any other was quoted and appealed to by his great revolutionary successor. Gregory VII does not contradict our list of "seconds";

THE "RENAISSANCE" OF THE ELEVENTH CENTURY

List of "Seconds" Among the Popes

1046-1047	Clemens II takes the name of Clemens I, 91-100, author of the Clementines.		1
1048	Damascus II	(I. 366-384)	2
1055-1057	Victor II	(I. 190-202)	3
1059-1061	Nicolaus II	(I. 858-867)	4
1061-1073	Alexander II	(I. 109-119)	5
1088-1099	Urbanus II	(I. 222-230)	6
1099-1118	Paschalis II	(I. 817-824)	7
1118-1119	Gelasius II	(I. 492-496)	8
1119-1124	Calixtus II	(I. 218-222)	9
1124-1130	Honorius II	(I. 625-638)	10
1130-1143	Innocentius II	(I. 402-417)	11
1143-1144	Cœlestinus II	(I. 422-432)	12
1144-1145	Lucius II	(I. 253-254)	13

(out of 18 popes between 1046 and 1145)

Interval of 313 years. No pope is a "second." As an aftermath, the list is reopened—with a joke—by Pius II.

1458-1464	Pius II	(I. 142-154) ("Pius Æneas" from Virgil)
1464-1471	Paul II	(I. 757-767)
1503-1513	Julius II	(I. 337-352)
1555, April	Marcellus II	(I. 307-309)

There are other papal names of the first thousand years still waiting for application.* Until the end of the tenth century, the Christian name, as received in baptism, held good even for a pope. Thus any intentional repetition of a name was impossible in the first millennium. Only when a second name-giving was asked could Gerbert of Reims, the friend of the Emperor Otto III, choose to be called a second Sylvester (999-1003), the first Sylvester (314-335) having been the friend of the great Constantine.

* This fact is important because from it we have evidence that neither in 1145 nor in 1555 was the stopping of the custom caused by a lack of names. Not the names, but the interest in the Renaissance-process, had passed.

he himself thought of the times of Gregory I as being now restored. It was the deliberate restoration of a past five hundred years before.

We have a precious document which makes it clear how radical the revolutionary ideology was. This document is a letter from one of the great papal abolitionists, Anselm of Lucca. Like any revolutionary group, the class which destroyed the liturgical and apostolic aspect of imperial dignity was called upon to justify its rebellion against a form of government which had lasted more than five hundred years. Every order exists by prescriptive right, and five hundred years are not a poor title to authority.

To those objections Anselm replied, and his words are as bold as those of any political radical today:

"You say that this execrable form of government over the church has lasted an immeasurable length of time, through all which time the rulers of this earth had the power of appointing bishops. That is no argument. A perversion introduced by the princes of this world can be no prejudice to the right form of government, through whatever length of time it may have prevailed. Otherwise, our Lord God himself would be guilty, since he left mankind in bondage to the devil, to the deformation of true government, and only redeemed it by his own death after the lapse of *five thousand years!*" [1] Five thousand years of rule cannot legalize the devil's government. This is really *the* boldest revolutionary argument. It turned "time" topsy-turvy by stripping the most ancient custom and tradition of its weight and significance. The wisdom of the ages suddenly became questionable and objectionable. There was now an older wisdom, a previous conception, a more genuine attempt to fall in with the original ideas and intentions of God's creation.

Five thousand years do not prove anything in the devil's favour. Empires, then, cannot be based on the prescriptive right of a mere five hundred. Any historical form can be dissolved when prehistory and future conclude an alliance in

[1] Migne, *Patrologia Latina*, 149, 466.

the hearts of men! This alliance is something extraordinary. The inertia of men gives an advantage to custom and tradition. In any settled organization of society, future is easily kept from its rights by an historical order which seems full of authority. The future is handicapped by our lack of faith. This explains the fate of ordinary revolts or rebellions, even where there is notorious misrule. Mere rebellions are nothing but "future." Bare future, without images and patterns of a visible order, frightens the mass of men. They will never have the patience to live for an invisible future. They would feel dizzy. Man needs images, rules, traditions, hand-rails by which to find his way in the throng of problems and doubts.

"Revolution" has changed the face of the earth over and over again, by its excavation of prehistory. The ghost of the first day of history is put up against all later depravity. Rousseau's Adam, Hitler's Teutonic tribes, Coke's Old England of Magna Charta, Luther's "original Christianity," are not more visionary than the papal vision of God's tolerance of the devil for five thousand years. The divine right of God knows no prescriptive right through the mere passing of time. All the revolutions of Europe share this same heroic rallying of past and future against a rotten present. What establishes the precedence of certain revolutions over the host of seditions and rebellions is the assumption of full responsibility for the whole past of mankind. The revolutions of this type deserve to be rendered prominent and conspicuous. Their generosity compensates for the necessary atrocities which make them hideous. They are devoted to more than a stupid thirst for power or an unwillingness to cope with traditional duties. The ferment of decomposition is overcome by the total revolutions through a vision of responsibility for the future *and* the past. The immediate past is shunned as a casual and accidental tyranny of man's inertia and blindness. The true past points into a new future. Revolutions project their political programmes into a distant past.

The superficial critic may think that this is but a trick, and that its discovery deprives it of all moral value. Was it not merely as a blind for ambition that Napoleon took the ancient

TWO HORSES IN THE NEW HARNESS

They pull twelve people, six times as many as before.

titles of Alexander and Cæsar, or Cromwell addressed the English as the chosen people of Israel?

No, the historical responsibility of revolutions for the universal past is not a trick. The sceptic who thinks he has freed himself from a necessary property of the human mind whenever he discovers and understands the special function of this property, overlooks the contribution made by the past to the future. The sceptic who loves to strip man of his historical garb is mistaken. To answer this disrobing scepticism, we must analyze the situation better. Revolution runs the risk of chaos. Revolution feels that an old order has died. When the spirit has left the body of an institution, the revolution breaks out. In this hour no language exists, or can exist, to lead people on. All the words and concepts that might be used are overloaded with associations rooted in the past state of affairs. All the words are dead, too! This complete destruction of the values connected with traditional words characterizes total revolution in contradistinction to the petty revolts, the *Putsch,* or the *coup d'état.*

The fighters against chaos are a relatively small group, which has to strengthen its grip on the future slowly. This group is a minority in its own country; and beyond that the country itself is only a section of a wider area. Inspiration, the *driving force* for a growing unit, seeks a universal way of expression, without which it cannot expand. In this fatal dilemma, between the trite but well-organized language of a dying past and the inspired faith of a group without visible or audible means of self-expression, universal history furnishes the needed generalities to the leaders of the future!

It equips the revolution with a language everybody is able to understand. It clothes the empty space of "Future" with an unsullied tapestry of pictures and stories.

But it does this on one great condition: the tapestry must be woven out of *universal* history, stories of all mankind, of world-wide value, global significance. The ambitious rebel or dictator would be satisfied to see his own picture on the walls of every house. Total revolutions, in search of a new language, must let in a kind of speech and of image which can be un-

derstood by an unlimited number of people all over the world
and through a long future. Western civilization, filling its
houses with Greek and Roman books, pictures, and ideas, unified Europe, because the new language of classicism was a
common, general language for Italians and Swedes, Poles and
Spaniards! The concepts supplied by universal history force
upon a hitherto local and social revolution the character of
universality, which grafts the new branch-government, the new
twig of civilization, on the universal tree of mankind.

It is not, therefore, as the sceptic thinks, any arbitrary past
which can be conjured up by a great revolution. Like a principle of mathematics, history in its full sense, in spite of all
its abuse by antiquarians, is and has always been world history, mankind's history, universal history. In history, completeness of responsibility is the only safeguard against arbitrariness
and the making of national mythologies. An influx of universal
history gives a revolution the connection with reality at its
most dangerous moment of unreality and chaos. Universal
history was the historic weapon of weak men against the strongholds of established, non-universal order. Any movement, for
example, the Russian Revolution and its counter-revolutions,
can be tested by this general criticism. If its historical perspective toward the past is special, it is a counter-revolutionary
movement. If its prehistory is universally valid, the movement
is really concerned with the future!

THE ECONOMIC REVOLUTION.

In the rebellion against the manorial system, a very tangible
social question had to be solved. A new technical invention
spread through the Western world. The increase in power
brought by this invention was as colossal as that brought in
the last century by the use of coal and electricity. No wonder
that the social unrest was similar. At that time, the harnessing
of horses was radically changed. Where before, in antiquity
and in the first millennium of our era, a carload had amounted
to four, or at most five, hundred pounds, it was now possible
to transport five thousand pounds. For the new harness exploited the full energy of the horse's shoulder-blades. Further-

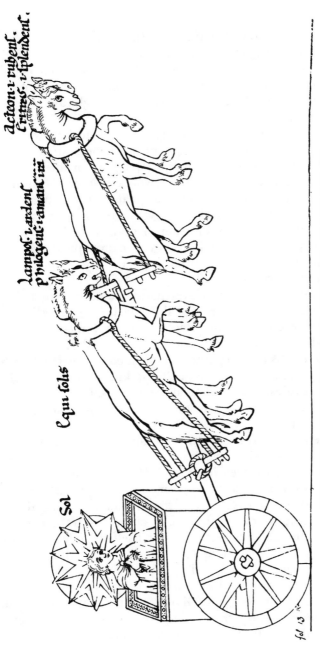

Actron · v · rubent ·
Eritreus · v · ſplendent ·

Lampoſ · v · ardent ·
Phologeuſ · amanc · 1a

equi ſolis

Sol

fol 13

THE OLDEST PICTURE OF A CAR AND FOUR. ABOUT 1200 A.D.

more, it was now, for the first time in history, possible to have a car and four or a car and six or eight, one pair of horses being harnessed behind the other. A score of people could now ride in one car. Grain, timber, stone, restricted to water transport before, now became carloads on the highways of the mainland of Europe.

The consequences of this technical revolution were numerous. It is no accident that most of the famous stone bridges of the Middle Ages were built shortly before or after 1100. The majority of churches had been wooden. Now the number of stone churches increased to the great admiration of contemporaries. Other technical improvements followed, wind-mills, for example, the transportation of grain over longer distances now being possible. The lords of the manors provided the roads with many strongholds; from 1050 to 1150, some thousands of stone castles were built.

This increase in power over nature came unexpectedly. The manorial system had been established for a society less powerful, and therefore more dependent on human labour. The dependency of the labour forces on the lord of the manor was complete. His military force was treated as a part of his household; they were knaves. Now, these knaves were sent out into distant castles; the huge manors were split into the smaller units of castellanies. The new form of life in these "branch offices" asked for a new law. Feudal law was the answer to the new technique of transportation and the far-reaching changes it made in society.

The Church placed itself at the head of the new movement. In the inevitable struggle over the issue as to whether the increased power over nature should finally belong to the old manorial lords or to the other classes as well, the Church turned the scales by establishing itself as a feudal court for the world at large. The very word for the Holy See that is most commonly used today, Curia, is not older than the eleventh century. And it means a centre of feudal law for an army which is no longer living in the home of its military commander but which is living outside on separate estates.

Feudal law, in the ears of an American an abuse of the

Dark Ages, came as a striking innovation to loosen the ties between lord and knave and to develop the latter into a Christian knight. The blessing of the Church was needed for this process in order to lend a spiritual justification to the social change. What seems to the superficial student of the Middle Ages a theological quarrel, was a struggle for applying justice to a new situation for man in nature.

Symbolically, the artists of the twelfth century placed the Church herself into the new car, to show her victorious march.

PAUL HELPS PETER: THE TECHNIQUE OF THE PAPAL REVOLUTION.

The clergy mutinied against its dependence on the palace. This mutiny is called by historians the struggle over investiture. Investiture was the appointment of a bishop or abbot by a royal order from the king's palace or chapel. During the struggle this privilege of the emperor was contested by the pope. But in so doing the pope was acting as the trustee of all Christendom against imperialism. The Papal Revolution was as complete in social depth as any modern "revolt of the masses." The popes emancipated the whole spiritual army, from primate and archbishop down to chaplain and parish priest. The papacy cut the direct and domestic relation between throne and altar in every manor or palace, and claimed the right to be guardian and spokesman for every local representative of the spirit. The vicar of St. Peter, to whom the most distinguished Cathedral in Christendom was given, now claimed to represent every pulpit or cathedral before the emperor.

Modern debates about the Gregorian revolution against the emperor are seldom fair to the viewpoint of either pope or emperor as they were in the eleventh century. One side maintains that the popes did not innovate at all but went on in the same line as before; the other speaks of despotism and arbitrary usurpation by the papacy. The one party really denies that there was a revolution, and the other is not aware of its fatal necessity. Both fail to see the precedent which was set for all Europe by the Papal Revolution, and the social-

biological phenomenon of total revolution which started at
the throne of St. Peter. One of the causes of this failure might
be found in the fact that the revolution was carried out by one
man, who acts and speaks in the solitude of a hermit. We are
so accustomed to thinking of revolution in terms of masses and
appeals to the populace that the one-man principle of the
Papal Revolution seems irreconcilable with the modern parallels. But revolutions change their technique. How else can
they effect the surprise which is the *conditio sine qua non*
of their success?

The Papal Revolution is outwardly a revolution of one man,
one dignitary, the pope alone. But simply because Lenin's
revolution is disguised as a revolution of the proletariat, it is
none the less the action of one man and a very few of his
friends. Revolutions, as we have seen, run down the scale from
palace to tent, from wardrobe to shirt. Numerically they run
through the scale from 1 to infinity. The ostensible basis
of support for the revolution has increased all the time; the
real basis was always universal. The avowed share of one particular leader has become less and less outspoken; the real
leadership was always restricted. In each revolution, a balance
exists between 1 and infinity, between the few who know and
the many who follow. The Papal Revolution was the most
general and intensive social earthquake Europe has ever seen.
It shook the *only* stable, unblemished and respected symbol
of unity: the economic, racial, religious, and moral unit of
palace and manor. It emancipated the *sons, clergy, knights,
and servants* of every manor in Europe. By a revolutionary act
the pope set up a new balance between economic particularism and spiritual universalism.

The initial impulse of the Papal Revolution was the Synod
of Sutri in the year 1046. The emperor, in his pious zeal for
reform, deposed three popes and installed another. This Synod
of Sutri was extolled by his monk-allies of Cluny as a very
miracle of heaven. But a new generation in the clergy felt it
as an insult. Walloon and French writers venomously attacked
this whole-hearted union between emperor and pope which
gave the former a power of censorship over the pope.

"Better the whole earth be changed into one jurisdiction, and the bishops of the whole earth come together and elect the pope, than leave him the serf of the emperor," exclaims the first revolutionary pamphleteer. In these words he revealed the true problem of Roman Catholicism, as it survives today. Who shall elect the pope? The group which elects the pope is master of the Church, because through it the pope rules. And the group which controls the papal election is the pre-formed model for appointments for every church in the world.

Today the pope is elected by the cardinals, i.e., nominally, by the bishops, priests, and deacons of the city of Rome. But today their Roman title is a matter of form. Instead of being Roman priests, they are customarily one half Italians and one half foreigners. The papacy is an Italian, not a Roman, dignity. But this is something quite foreign to the eleventh century, the practical result of the struggle of investiture. It is interesting to notice that the first author who treated the problem on principle foresaw a solution which still occupies the Catholic world in our time.

What the reform party did tackle immediately was the exclusion of the Roman nobility from the election of the pope. The clergy alone is entitled to elect the pope. The *populus Christianus* of Rome, the laymen, were excluded from the election. The bishop of Rome ceased formally to be the chosen of his city by the decree of 1059, which empowered the cardinals alone to elect him. The decree recognized the possibility of an imperial veto. And this veto also survived for nine hundred years. It was exercised for the last time in 1903 by the apostolic majesty of the Hapsburg emperor against the election of Cardinal Rampolla as pope. The Crown Cardinal of the Apostolic Majesty once more acted in the conclave as the spokesman of his house-lord, the emperor, as he had in the times of the Ottos.

After 1046, a break was inevitable between a Northern emperor and an independent pope, capable of shifting the balance of the Church to the classic shores of the Mediterranean. With the growth of southern Italian, Spanish, and Balkan questions, the papacy was forced to lay emphasis on its independ-

ence from any particular temporal monarch. A unique
emperor became intolerable as soon as he abused his ecclesiastical claims in order to conceal the defects of his political

THE OLDEST TYPE FOR PETER AND PAUL
Third Century.

expansion. His only possible justification would have been the
reality of his totalitarian government. If he was not the judge
of the globe, his close alliance with the Holy See in Rome was
prejudicial to every action the pope might think necessary
in a country outside the sphere of imperial influence. The
threat of a Caliphate was not fictitious in the Western civilization of the eleventh century. It was necessary that this fatal

TRANSFORMATIONS IN THE ICONOGRAPHY OF ST. PAUL:

FROM SCROLL THROUGH KEY TO SWORD

course be eschewed by the new emancipation of the clergy. The word orb (circle, world) became the obsession of papacy. Never before had Rome thought of its place in the world in other than organic terms. It had been extolled as *prima sedes, caput mundi,* the brightest star in the galaxy of churches. The revolutionaries made it, as one of their leaders wrote to Gregory in his letter of welcome, 1074: "The centre of an orb, to which radii must be drawn from the circumference." The *Urbs* (City) of Rome was to be the centre of the Orbis, the circle of the earth. When the revolution had completed its victory, a universal council was convened in the Lateran, of which it was said that the *"orbis"* seemed to be contained in the *"urbs."* The Pope pronounced his blessing and gave his commands *urbi et orbi.* This notion of a central power made an archbishop say: "The pope is changing the bishops into his tenants and stewards." At the œcumenical council of 1139 it could be proclaimed that all the dignities of the Universal Church were derived from the pope like the fiefs of vassals.

By summoning the Christians to Jerusalem, the papacy resuscitated the maritime character of the old Roman Empire. The Crusaders, going from France to Sicily and Palestine, built up a route of traffic and exchange which crippled the old continental axis of the Empire, from the North Sea to Rome. The symbolic figure of St. Peter, long depressed by the corruption of his vicars, was supported in his new undertaking by St. Paul, whose office had helped to interpret the emperor's office. St. Paul, the apostle of the Gentiles, was the natural apostle of the *orbis.* The popes of the struggle for investiture multiplied the instances in which they acted as vicars of Peter *and* Paul.

The emperor was denied apostolic character. He became one king among many. Gregory VII gives the lie to the emperor's claim by aligning him with all the other kings, in the plural. The only singular and universal power was the papacy; the "true emperor," the only unique name and dignity, had to be the Pope.

The Pope, by the struggle for investiture, by preaching the Crusades, undermined the kingdoms of this earth. The emperor, fierce against the ungrateful prelate whom he had confirmed, deposed him; and all the princes of the empire shouted: "Descende, descende: go down, Hildebrand." In that revolutionary hour of history, the pope turned his face from earth to heaven. He was not answering any human being. He banished the princes, shouters and slanderers as he thought them; but he did not speak to them. He did not face the emperor, who to him was but one king among many. Where did he turn?

The first revolution of the Christian era began in the loneliness of a monk's cell and a monk's heart. The incredible technique of this first world revolution, unchaining fifty years of bloodshed, disorder and despair, was the resolution of Gregory to make himself "monk-emperor." Gregory fused the functions of Cluny and of the Apostolic Majesty, the "religiosus" (monk) and the judge of this world.

Hildebrand had been a monk; and so his adversaries reproached him with the many embassies and journeys of his younger days. They were thinking of the old Benedictine rule by which a monk was the inmate of one monastery, at one consecrated spot. But Gregory inherited the Cluny idea of amalgamation in space. He had been prior of San Paolo at Rome before he was made bishop of St. Peter. And the very friend who had called him the "Holy Satan" had sung the praise of the trans-local power of St. Paul. Gregory had listened to this psalm, by Petrus Damiani, of the precedence of St. Paul over Peter: "Paul resembles Christ. Christ was crucified in Jerusalem, but he did not make the place of his death the capital of the world. Christ is present in every church. Likewise, Paul has no predilection for one church. He has no special cathedral. He is the right arm of God, held out *over the whole breadth of the earth,* presiding over all churches." "A world heart like Christ himself, and supplementing the sufferings of Christ by his own," Paul had been worshipped at his grave. Now the Praise of Paul as the Right Arm of God [2] raised him from the grave up into the bright sky of a new dawn. The saints of a

---

[2] *"Qui divinæ dexteræ non ambigitur exercere virtutem"*—"Who undoubtedly exerts the power of the right arm of God."—Petrus Damiani, *De picturis principum apostolorum c.2* Migne, Patrologia Latina, Vol. 145, 591.

church outside this world now became real, immediate guiding stars to political organization. Paul, so long worshipped at his grave, now rises to establish the *Ius Poli*, the law of the firmament, as the ecclesiastical legislation began to be called about 1100.

Paul furnished another power symbol, that of the two swords. Paul corresponded to Benjamin in the Old Testament allegorically. And of Benjamin it was said (Judges 3, 15) that one might use both hands, the temporal and the spiritual, simultaneously.[3] It is scarcely an accident that Paul is represented later with two swords, whereas before 1100 the Apostle never carried a worldly weapon.

Papacy profited from the new symbolism.

The sword of faith, which Paul himself had spoken of, was now given into the pope's hand for the first time. It was emphasized, as against older traditions, that Paul had died on the same day as Peter, not a year later. The papal statute-book, the canons, inserted new paragraphs on Paul who had never been mentioned before. Coins were sold to the Pilgrims to Rome, showing Paul and Peter each carrying the famous key which gave the power of binding and loosing.[4] Gregory VII was the first to put Paul together with Peter on his coins and later popes put them on their seals. In the official concordat of 1122, the Church Universal was distinguished from St. Peter's in Rome. It labelled the new centralized power of the pope to transact any business with the temporal power in the name of all other bishops, the church of Peter and Paul, whereas the Holy See in Rome itself was simply called St. Peter.[5]

Paul was glorified with new fervour. The wandering apostle was transformed into a stabilized, central, yet universal symbol

[3] Carl Erdmann, *Die Entstehung des Kreuzzugsgedankens*, p. 147 f., Berlin, 1935.

[4] This irregularity, which fits so badly into the static picture most of us entertain about the Roman traditions, also is found in a document contemporary to Gregory VII; here, too, both apostles, Peter and Paul, will "close the gates of paradise to a trespasser." *Cartes de Cluny*, IV, 752, no. 3594. And another contemporary can speak of pope Gregory "cum predecessore suo beato Paulo" Monumenta Germaniæ historica, Libelli de Lite I, 308.

[5] This feature of the document was discussed in detail in my paper read before the Mediæval Academy of America in 1934.

of the new Church. The pope, who for a thousand years had anxiously avoided calling himself universal or œcumenical, because he feared that the expression would be derogatory to the other churches, was now settled, as Paul's vicar, on the universal apostolic throne of the whole earth and dropped his resistance to the title "universal." The symbol of St. Paul, now reclaimed from the emperor, ceased to lead the unorganized movements in the Church against the established order. This prophetic function was forgotten for four hundred years, until it was re-invoked by Luther. For four hundred years people identified, practically, the functions of Peter and Paul and if anyone looked beyond this state of affairs, he foresaw only a Johannine age. The mediæval critics of papacy looked for a new era under the sign of St. John the Evangelist. Paul was not mentioned in this great vision of the future. He had become identified with papacy; the Pope had taken over his function.

Paul, the strongest prop of imperial theocracy in 1000 A.D., was regained for the papacy. This needed a special effort. Though buried in Rome under Peter's jurisdiction, though a co-founder of its apostolic church, he had not more belonged to Rome than to Christianity at large. The friend of Gregory VII could exclaim that Peter presided over Rome, Paul, like Christ himself, over all the churches of Christendom. But now the Pope—acting as the legal spokesman and plenipotentiary of the universal clergy for any settlement between kings and bishops—took to himself this Pauline presidency over all the churches.

Rome and the New Jerusalem, *urbs* and *orbis,* the City of Rome and the circumference of the globe, were united by permeating all places with one supernatural vision. Spengler has called Greek antiquity Euclidian, local, atomistic, without the Faustian character of perspective and background, fusion and shadows. Gregory is the man who discovered the fusion of omnipresence and centralization, the anti-classical and anti-pagan concept of the Middle Ages.

What we call Middle Age begins with the ubiquity of the abbot of Cluny, in all the many abbeys of the Western world, and the transference of this ubiquity to the monk on the papal throne.

Was it only seventy-five years before that an emperor was worshipped as a second Paul, cleansing the *Urbs?* Well, he, Gregory, was the vicar of Peter and of Paul, cleansing the *orbis.* Monk and Emperor blended into one; Gregory restored the episcopal, i.e., mundane, See of Rome to its religious leadership. In the famous document that answered the emperor, he looked up to Peter and Paul as to the lords of everything in *urbs* and *orbis.*

THE ADDRESSEES OF THE FIRST REVOLUTIONARY DOCUMENT.

The greatest proclamation of his revolution was given him by the spirit and he dictated it for his private recollection. The *"dictatus papæ"* explains to us the technique of the first universal revolution in our history. Corrupted by the fiction of a crowd of millions on whom the modern dictators train their loud-speakers and their broadcasting systems, we easily miss the criterion which constitutes the real revolution. Lenin, and not one hundred and fifty millions of Rusians, formulated the whole content of the Russian Revolution. Though all the contents of the Papal Revolution were utterly opposed to Lenin's formula, we must understand that in the orbit of revolutions, the last one is so extreme in its mass-ideology only because it is the last; the number of allegedly conscious revolutionaries seems to grow from one revolution to the next. But this increase in numbers is one of the unavoidable technical devices in the mechanism of revolutions. Nothing in history can be repeated. If two events are to have the same effect on men at different times, the forms of the two events must differ. In the course of nine centuries, man had to pass through the orbit of possible arrangements. Gregory the Seventh's *"Dictatus Papæ"* for his private use and the Bolshevik broadcasts "To all and everybody" are two ends of a series. We shall find that in 1200 the Pope started the Guelphic Revolution by addressing himself to the College of Cardinals assembled in a consistory. With this later development in mind, we can draw one clear line from the technique of Gregory to that of modern times.

FORM AND ADDRESS OF THE FIRST REVOLUTIONARY DECLARATIONS

1075	*Dictatus Papæ*	The Holy Spirit speaks to the Pope and he puts it on record.
1200	*Deliberatio de statu imperii*	Pope reads an allocution to the Cardinals in his consistory.
1517	Luther's 95 theses	Nailed on the doors of the prince's church in his university, inviting opponents.
1641	The Great Remonstrance	Printed copies of the document, which the Commons are sending to the King, are sold to the public.
1789	The *États Généraux* in Versailles	Changed into the "National Assembly," which summons the Nation. The deputies speak to the galleries.
1917	The Bolsheviks	*Address all and everybody* in radio broadcasts.

The pope's decision appears even more sublime if we consider the pressure under which he acted. The *"Dictatus Papæ"* formulated a programme, in the sense that the writing down of these paragraphs was a way of justifying them. For such is the property and the honour of true human speech that the user stands sponsor for its validity and asks to be taken at his word. Some of the items of the *"Dictatus Papæ"* deserve to be repeated here:

1. The Roman Church is founded by God alone.

2. Nobody except the High Priest of Rome can be named œcumenical (universal).

3. The pope alone can, according to circumstances, make new laws, found new congregations, change foundations into monasteries, divide a rich bishopric and consolidate a poor one.

8. He is the only one who shall wear imperial insignia.

9. The pope's feet all princes shall kiss.

10. His name is the only one which must be recollected in the

prayers in all churches. (The emperor's name had been inserted in former days, never the pope's.)

12. He can depose emperors.

18. His judgments can be changed by nobody. He alone can oppose the judgments of everybody else.

19. No paragraph and no code are canonical without his authority.

20. Nobody can judge him.

21. Every pope is—by the merits of St. Peter—sanctified.

25. The pope can judge bishops without a synod (i.e., as the Holy Ghost dictates the decision, the pope is master of the Holy Ghost without the inspiration of a council).

This document itself is the revolution. For how could the infallible have mere thoughts about his office? When he thinks, he thinks right, since the Spirit is with him. Therefore his inspiration is in itself an action. The *"Dictatus Papæ,"* in appearance a mere private memorandum, was nevertheless a revolution and decision of a competent authority. The first revolution of the Occident broke out in the breast of one man. In the loneliness of his heart, he dictated to his own soul the programme of the Papal Revolution. This first political programme of the Christian world should be studied carefully by students of political theory. They will find that no such programme can be understood without interpreting it in a dialectical way. In fact it is a dialogue. Gregory says, for example, *"unicum nomen est papæ."* Why this haughtiness? Because we have seen the emperor alone had been thought unique until then. The pope has the Holy Spirit "without any council." Why this wilfulness? It means that his Italian council in Rome, the local clergy of Rome, cannot help the pope sufficiently in the questions of the whole Church—that he must act in those matters as the permanent secretary, so to speak, of the Universal Church in Council. Thus he becomes the spiritual seismograph, not of Rome, not of Italy, but of the world.

Since then, the Pope's breast, *il petto del papa,* has been the seat of the political secrets of the Holy See. We are so accustomed to think of the largest possible audience in politics that to speak to your own heart, and to govern *"in petto"* seems rather odd. After all, this fashion of the popes is mentioned in the newspapers even today. But it has established once and forever a second power of political inspiration, an immediate connection of the spiritual leader with the inspiration of the day. The Spirit, if he is to become the Spirit of Creation, must work without delay. Councils, emperors, space, mean delay. The human heart moves immediately. The political togetherness and contemporaneity of our present world has its origin in the isolation of a human heart. A monk breaks down the humble walls of the Cluny monastery, grows and grows until his heart begins to move heaven and earth, and his voice to frighten like the Trumpet of Doom. That is the true emperor, who needs no physical marching through space, whose very word at the world's end is as terrible as a sword, though he himself remains at Rome. Gregory was so full of this vision that he even anticipated the modern telephone. He told Odilo of Cluny, when they passed a broad river and Gregory was far in advance, that he saw a thread leading from Odilo's mouth to his own ear and transporting to his understanding every word Odilo thought. (Migne, 148, 45.) And the earth answers to the sonority of the new voice of the "true emperor" (verus imperator). Not only do the knaves of the manor become Christian knights, emancipated by the Crusades, but one law of the firmament begins so to govern all marriage and all clergy in Christendom that the soldiers of the new spiritual army leave wives and children and devote themselves to celibacy, like true pilgrims and strangers to all localized and established family life.

A contemporary hymn, partly imitating the ancient John Chrysostomus, describes the new church government in these verses:

"Tuba domini, Paule, maxima
De celestibus dans tonitrua
Hostes dissipans cives aggrega."

"Oh, Paul, greatest trumpet of the Lord;
Who sendest the thunderbolts down from Heaven,
Disperse thy enemies and gather those who belong to Thy city."

Paul's spiritual sword governs the world-wide city of God. The popes tested their spiritual power by demanding to be obeyed.

Gregory died in exile, in Salerno, after eleven years of struggle against the inertia of a baffled world. The bishops did not like to be treated as his stewards, and the emperor did not understand how he was expected to govern without two thirds of his budget. The pope himself, on his deathbed, was despondent at his exile from Rome, and complained: "I have loved justice and hated iniquity. That is why I die in exile." But to that a bishop gave a fitting answer: "You cannot call yourself exiled, my father, because the earth is given to you as your possession, and the nations of it are your heredity." Indeed, invocation of the guiding stars of a new firmament had made the pope at home on the whole earth illuminated by this firmament. The bishop's answer made the pope the prince of a new city, the *civitas Romanæ ecclesiæ*. Henceforth the whole earth was conceived as an edifice in shining marble, one city, one Church. The unity passionately believed in the catacombs now appeared in the full light of day. Against the picture of the Holy Emperor crowned by Christ, the new vision, with a bold inversion, shows St. Peter crowning the Church.

Gregory died with this solace in his ears. Forty years later, the peace between Church and emperor was restored by a "concordat." As the first believers had become one heart and one soul, so emperor and pope, it was thought, should become one heart and soul again. Till today the name originated in 1122 has been used for any treaty between Church and State; but in our modern world we are so blind that we overlook the fact that a concordat cannot be either a treaty between governments or a contract between individuals.

A concordat makes a presupposition otherwise known only in marriage; namely, that each partner can be expected to think of the salvation of the other's soul, under certain circumstances, even more than of his own. Without this interplay shared by both parties, we cannot help misunderstanding the sound relationship between Church and State: they are then merely parties to a contract. Since the radical faith of

Christians may carry them away into non-governmental channels, any government may be imperilled by the religion of the people. It need not be the Roman Catholic denomination. But any ruler reaches the limits of his power whenever his people begin to believe that something else is worth dying for other than that which they believed in before. No money, no power, no soldiers, can hold a fortress or a nation if the spirit is gone which bound all the inner loyalties of his society into one faith and one infinite willingness to die for it. Anything a man is ready to die for is stronger than anything people merely live on.

The concordat expresses the experience of the Christian world that government relies on the faith in the infinite, endless, unconditioned absolute for which men are ready to die, and that any institution entitled to influence this faith is a sovereign of the first importance. Because people had suffered persecutions and exile and boycott for half a century, pope and emperor recognized each other's sovereign power. Acquainted with the lessons in sovereignty presented by the revolutions a government will understand the meaning of the concordat. It will not act as a sceptic philosopher, like Bodin, nor will it try to make itself the object of religious worship, like a caliph. Every such heresy of a worldly power has called forth a violent rebellion. Luther, Cromwell, Napoleon, Lenin, all introduced a new sovereignty either because the old one seemed anæmic or because it claimed for itself a religious worship. The concordat of Worms in 1122 grew out of the experience of a caliphate and therefore limited the absolute power of the emperors. The emperor's son even deserted his own father, saying that he had a father in Heaven, represented by the pope, whom he must obey before his earthly father. This may seem too simple for a modern reader who has forgotten that, and why, and how far, we are to obey our earthly father indeed. In the days of vendetta, it was a great discovery for the crown prince of the empire to be faced by the fact of a double allegiance. Now this is the secret of political liberty. Liberty becomes vital when man is faced by a dilemma. No man is free to do what he likes. He can never do more than choose between two things: for example between peace and war, past and future, security and adventure, his mother and his bride, his employer and his trade union, the nation and his party, and so on. But every choice proposes one loyalty which you prefer and one which you neglect.

The Papal Revolution of the eleventh century introduced the principle of dualism into the political world. Jesus had spoken of God and of Cæsar, it is true; but God is not a visible institution. The dualism of institutions enables men to seek Him. In Western civilization, at least since Gregory VII, two sovereign powers have always balanced each other. This, and this alone, has created European freedom.

Theoretically, all philosophers praise liberty. Practically, it can exist only when every human soul has two loyalties. Every monism leads to slavery. The modern democracies are leading to slavery, because they have no guarantee against the monocratic tendencies of popular government.

The Papal Revolution, by asking the Roman monarch to give back his right of investiture to the universal church of Peter and Paul, expressed the idea of a new sovereign, co-existing with every king and emperor in every parish. The dreams of Cluny and of Gregory had come true. The idea of a trans-local organization, a corporation, was realized. The Catholic Church is not at all international. It would be bad taste to call her so. And in the mouths of her detractors of the Fascist or Teutonic or Freemason type it is an intentional slander. The Church never was international; she was trans-local and universal. She was present in the same way and with the same intensity in the home of the coal-miner and in the court of the prince. The lord of the house had to allow his servants the right of pilgrimage and crusade. And this active pilgrimage emancipated them.

The sovereignty of Peter and Paul in 1122 restored the dualism necessary for our moral freedom, which had been invaded when the emperor was welcomed as a second St. Paul.

The idea of the new sovereignty was expressed, too, when the Crusaders who took Jerusalem in 1099 elected Geoffrey of Bouillon king. For this noble lord, well aware, like Crom-

well the Protector, that the papal struggle for liberty of the
Church had been fought by the kings of this earth, took the
name, not of a king, but of a defender of the Holy Sepulchre.

Space itself is seized upon by the movement toward Jerusalem. It is common knowledge that Christian churches are
oriented, and that orientation means to look toward the East.
This is not enough for the Age of the Crusades. The church
stood hidden among houses, or outside the town on a hill,
with its crypts deeply rooted in the earth. The new desire of
the heart transcends the Alps and the seas. It blasts open the
walls and the roofs of the earthly house. The walls of Cluny
are the first to show symptoms of upheaval. The diagonal ribs
of the vault heave; they were called ogives (*augivi*) because
they augmented its power, added to its capacity for becoming
a vault. Ogive was a new word then; and so, too, was "vault."
It branched off from the word "*volvo*," the root which is present in revolution and evolution. Thus "vault" is in itself
an exorbitant word, leaving the orbit of general tradition,
according to which a roof and a shelter must obey the laws
of gravity.

There can be no revolution where the law of gravity rules
the hearts of men. Man has to be inspired to overcome his
inertia. When he does that, he re-creates creation. The Papal
Revolution goes against the laws of gravity. The vaults of a
Gothic cathedral are an inverted ship. *Nave* equals *navis*, ship;
the house of stone in the Gothic style is not a local house, fixed
in space, but a symbol of pilgrimage, suspended in time. The
regions from which the first Crusaders came were the first
to develop the new style. The Germans and the English followed enthusiastically. But it is very important to remember
that the Gothic style never gained ground in Italy. The Papal
Revolution in its first stage is not an Italian business. It is a
dialogue inside the orbit of Christendom. Every spiritual power
on the periphery is magnetized by the new central power of
the Sepulchre. The new dualism which delivers the local resi-
dent from his local gods, ancestors, vendetta, is based on the
contrast between *home* and *pilgrimage* or *crusade*. The Papal
Revolution is successful, in so far as it gives to everybody's life

some tinge of a spiritual mission as a pilgrim. The seven sacraments, from baptism to the extreme unction, were established in the twelfth century, creating a psychic biography, adding to every "body's" physical experience the "soul's" psychic pilgrimage. The cathedrals help us to see that the dualism between the two swords, the temporal power and the spiritual power, does not mean a geographical division. It means the liberty of all souls to leave their country and their friendships. The Christian democracy, under the spiritual leadership of the popes, delivered the cathedrals from their spatial fixity.

The Gothic minster is a ship in a fleet that sails the sea of the spirit. All souls seek the Holy Sepulchre and therefore embark in this navy. In the fleet of the Gothic cathedrals the Papal Revolution of the Church majestically moves on.

CRUSADE AND SCHOLASTICISM.

The Crusades and the struggle for investiture changed the map of Europe, the Western world. The concept of a potential Roman Empire gave way, at least at the periphery and in the South, to an orb, to be governed by the mother of all churches, the Roman Church. The Holy Sepulchre in the East helped to build a new axis, leading from Northwest to Southeast (which was eccentric to the former North-South axis), Aachen, Cluny, Alps, Roncaglia (near Milan), Rome. It led from Canterbury and Rouen to Genoa or to Marseilles where Gregory VII even tried to erect a rival of Cluny, and by Sicily to Palestine, or by Barcelona into crusading Spain.

The mother of all churches became the Mother Church. The orb was held together as one *civitas*. For Augustine the City of God and the city terrestrial had not met. In the twelfth century a new city was planned, with the pope as its true emperor.

The old emperors had represented the light of the stars in the darkness of time. The "true" emperor was hailed as a rising sun, bringing daylight to the world. The broad noonday of civilization was present wherever the new concept of *ecclesia Romana* was formulated or used. How often had Christ been compared to the sun! Now the popes were declared to be vicars

of Christ for Heaven and Earth, the eternal and the temporal.
The pope, therefore, was the sun; the emperor was at best his
steward, the moon. "Thereby," a canonist writer, Hostiensis,
declared, "it is evident that the priest's dignity is 7,644½ times
higher than the royal. For thus the proportion between sun
and moon is stated in the fifth book of the Almagest of
Ptolemæus." [6] No wonder then, if the dignity of tens of thousands of priests was condensed into the united power of the
pope, that he seemed to be a sun. His Roman Church now
appeared as a bright city in which every Christian could taste
the joy of citizenship. The times of Christ himself were at
hand. Christ's words were in the mouths of the popes as though
he were alive again. With Christ's words at the Last Supper—
"Desiderio desideravi hoc pascha manducare vobiscum": "With
desire I have desired to eat this passover with you" (Luke 22,
15)—Innocent III welcomed his council in 1215. In the daylight of an effective organization of life, the paths of men were
visible at a glance. This led to a transformation of the concept
of a sacrament. Before the Crusades, in the night of the world,
every act of the Church had seemed an act of atonement to
God, a lightning worthy to be called sacrament. The deeds of
saints, the prayers of monks, the victories of the emperor, were
glimpses of light piercing the fog connecting heaven and earth,
replacing the unreal shadows of man's will by the decrees of
Providence. Now the arch of reality made a vault over the
earth. A thousand years of sacrament could be summed up.

The twelfth century felt itself the *Summa Summarum* of the
treasures and sacraments of the Church. The list of "second"
popes recapitulated the whole past of the Roman Church. A
rich literature parallelled the undertaking of the Roman
Church, reconciling the discordant traditions of the fathers.
Abailard's famous *"Sic et Non"* was described in our French
chapter; Magister Gratianus of Bologna wrote *Concordia discordantium canonum,* a parallel to the idea of concordat in the
political field. Once more the old patristic ways of thinking

---

[6] This statement still recurs, 350 years later, in Jean Bodin's famous *Six Livres
de la République,* 182, 1577.

were re-embodied in the "Last Father of the Church," Bernard of Clairvaux. On the whole, the world had definitely changed. A new science was started. Its name itself, "theology," so trite today, was new and bold. The Fathers of the Church carefully avoided this pagan term, that hinted at a rational knowledge about the gods. Now, the new "theologians," to the despair of Bernard, declared the Bible to be down below, in the crypt of the Church, as its foundation; their new science, however, had to erect up from the ground the eight storeys of theological thinking. The walls of the new cathedral of theology were to reflect the mysteries of the sacraments. In this programme, Hugo de St. Victor in Paris pictured the future architecture of the Gothic cathedral. (Migne, 176, 803.)

The much-admired style of the Gothic arch, then, reflects a new mental vision, conceived, not by masons only, but by the theological scholars first.

The teachings of eleven successive centuries, thirty-three generations, were brought together and made present simultaneously by the lectures and glosses of a new scholarship. Scholasticism was the grandiose Renaissance of Christian learning, precisely in the same way as Humanism resurrected classical learning, during modern times. Paul's apostleship to the Gentiles was replaced by a new apostolate among the Christians. A "doctor of the Gentiles" seemed less needed than doctors for the Christian kingdoms.

The corporations of professors and students, the universities, armed for their doctorate in the form of a mission. They claimed the privileges of knights. It was a crusade of mind and spirit. Yet it was a crusade, not a mission. Missions require virgin countries; crusades reconquer districts formerly orthodox, but since lost. Similarly, scholasticism developed a Christian doctorate, an inner doctorate for a world outwardly orthodox, but completely pagan under the surface. The populace of a thousand years ago had no unified Christian culture; that is a romantic prejudice of certain nineteenth-century souls like Novalis or Henry Adams. As a doctor for re-paganized Christians, Hugo de St. Victor "overroofed" the crypt of the Bible by his idea of the eight Orders of the Sacraments of Divinity which correspond exactly to the ideologies of Revolutions:

Hugo de St. Victor	Revolutions	Chapter
1. Creator		
2. Creation of Matter	1917	IV
3. Freedom of Will and Fall of Man (Adam)	1789	V
4. Natural Law (Noah)	1776	XV
5. Old Testament (Israel)	1649	VI
6. New Testament	1517	VII
7. Church	1075	X
8. Last Judgment (Resurrection)	998	IX

He goes on: "This is the whole Divinity, this is the whole spiritual building, and as many sacraments as it contains, by so many storeys does it rise into the sky."

Scholasticism tried to unify and to Christianize the people of its time because they were slipping back into paganism. The doctorate of the new scholars was something completely unknown in antiquity. It was an effort for human solidarity. They were fighting the hell of paganism from the inside, because since the Empire and All Souls everybody had learned to care for everybody else. These people of the twelfth century, under the leadership of the pope, knew that perfectly well. They could not give up the solidarity of mankind, embodied in the concept of a world-purgatory and a world history. They knew of no science for science's sake. They thought like the Crusaders, one for all. The subject of their crusade of restoration was Christendom, all and every man united. Scholasticism outdistances Platonism and any classical philosophy by virtue of this clear service in a crusade. In both periods, it is true, thought is cultivated in schools. But in the Christian Era universities are organs of one solid body politic which sends out doctors and knights to recover its lost provinces both inwardly and outwardly.

The thought of the last thousand years is Christian by establishment. Pagan thought reflects on the world from outside the *polis,* because it was pushed out of the particular *polis* into the universal cosmos. Christian thought was reborn of

ST. THOMAS AQUINAS IN HIS SCHOOL, BY FRA ANGELICO

The Scholastic Dream: The heart made visible

a conflict between two forces in one society, Pope and Emperor. This conflict created a scientific method unknown to Greeks and Romans: it forced upon European thought its dialectical sagacity and its comprehensive power of thinking in paradoxes and in contradictions. All possible varieties of thought were still embraced by a universal society, because two ways of explanation were presented by the two protectors of thought, Emperor and Pope. Western civilization was built on a "citizenship in the universe" from the start. The "Cosmopolitanism" of modern free-thinkers is but a tardy translation of the mediæval citizenship in the Church. For the same reason, neither scholasticism nor modern free thought reflects the doubts or whims of private individuals or schools. They represent a process of meditation and regeneration going on in the *new city of the Holy Ghost, the city of revolutionized Christendom.*

A CHURCH MADE VISIBLE AND RAPHAEL'S GREATEST PAINTING.

Now we are equipped to understand the transformation of the sacraments. Where the old Church had known only countless acts of grace which built up its mysterious body, the scholastic period of the Crusades surveyed the whole process at one glance. All the sparks of divine light ever emitted at any time were now collected into one centre: the papacy and the visible Church. The famous fight of Luther against the "visible" church is often misunderstood by both Catholics and Protestants, because neither see that Luther stopped, not the process of embodiment and realization in the old church, but the conscious tendency to *"make* visible" in the scholastic Church. In the period of the old church the hidden treasures and mysteries of man's soul were experienced and revealed. The period of the "Scholastic Church" made these treasures and mysteries visible to the mind and eye of a "mundane" Christendom. The favourite literature of the visible church was *"specula,"* mirrors. Thousands of books used the name as a title. Why? Because they tried to *make visible.* The "visible church" attacked by Luther was the result of a reconquest, the aim of which was to *make visible* its treasures. From Gregory VII to 1500 the Church was more than the audible and visible Body of Christ. It was, besides, a stormy party of reform within the Corpus Christi, waging war against the mundane decay of clergy and laity by means of Crusades and Doctorates, making its internal treasures visible. Mysteries were unfolded, secrets explained; the ways of life were made clear. The multitude of Sacraments was simplified. Seven sacraments dealt with every Christian's life-cycle from cradle to bier. Baptism, Confirmation, Marriage, Ordainment, Repentance, and Extreme Unction were the recurrent stations of every soul's pilgrimage. All Souls, the night-watch of the monks in memory of the Last Judgment, was supplemented in the daily life of the crusading church by this curriculum for every soul.

The seventh sacrament—actually the first—was, of course, Holy Communion itself. The reconquest of theology especially centred around the Last Supper. The real presence of Christ in the consecrated wafer became the obsession of all thoughts and disputes. By granting it to mankind, the Lord seemed to have revealed the unique secret of the whole structure. In order to make this secret visible, no effort was spared. The sacrament of the host appeared in the annual calendar on Maundy Thursday, as a station in the life and passion of our Lord. It was a part of the entire history of Christ's Passion. The new campaign to reveal even the most mysterious elements of the creed, detached Holy Communion from its historical place in Passion Week. It was also observed separately; the tie between the omnipresence of the sacrament, and its historical genesis in the course of events, was loosened. Not only at the beginning of spring, at Easter, but at the full height of summer, after the Holy Ghost had built up Holy Church, the Eucharist had to be celebrated on a special day.

At the climax of the Church's crusade to recover its lost possessions in time and space, Thomas Aquinas composed the order of the Service for Corpus Christi. Raphael reached the zenith of his art when he told the day's origin in his "Mass of Bolsena" in the Vatican. Instituted in 1264, the feast was made compulsory for the whole Roman world in 1310, and fixed on the Thursday after Trinity. Unknown in the Orient, a scandal to any Protestant, the Feast of Corpus Christi commemorates the *opus operatum*, the real reality of the Church's work of reconcentration. The crusading Church believed in

RESULT OF THE PAPAL REVOLUTION
St. Peter crowning the Church.

its capacity to concentrate the light of all priesthood in one pope, the thoughts of all saints in one *summa*, the problems of all fathers in one concord. It believed, therefore, in its right to celebrate this process of *reconcentration* by one feast, which concentrated the revealing power of a whole millennium of sacraments into the triumphant procession of one bright summer day. Corpus Christi leaves the crypt and choir, the altar and nave of the church building. The crusading Church celebrates in procession. Led by the Lords Spiritual, on Corpus

Christi Day the Church recalls its fight for liberty. The result
of the Papal Revolution is well expressed in the text of the
service. The faithful pray for protection against the persecutors of the Church; they pray for the pope, "whom Thou
has destined to *preside over Thy church.*" (This singular—
"Thy church"—would have been impossible three centuries
before.) They pray for the new barriers established against the
emperor's "simony" with the words: "Let Thy church serve
thee, resistance and heresies being utterly destroyed, in protected liberty."

The liberty of the Church was and remained the great war-
cry for four centuries. Even in the four centuries after the Reformation the liberties of man were only translations of this
liberty of the church. The Rights of Man were a translation
of the Rights of the Christian people, the Rights of the Christian people were a translation of the Rights of the Universal
Priesthood and the Rights of Priesthood were deduced from
the Rights of the Trustee of Priesthood, the Pope, against
the threats of the Anti-Christ.

ANTI-CHRIST

For such was the revolutionary change in the underlying
principles of civilization that the Anti-Christ now became
the favourite theme of curialist literature. The fear of Anti-
Christ is something different from the fear of the Ghibelline
age before the Last Judgment. The vision of the Last Judgment concentrates all our attention on our fate after death.
The vision of the Anti-Christ cannot be based on this interest
in immortality, because the Anti-Christ is expected on earth,
long before the Last Judgment. Man's asking whether this
world is threatened by the advent of the Anti-Christ proves
that he has become interested in the world itself. How could
it be otherwise? The reform of the popes had built an edifice
as like as possible to the celestial order. Space was organized,
a visible centre established, temporal forces checked and limited, the past regenerated, the earth civilized. Nobody but the
Anti-Christ could trample under foot the seeds of this new

sowing. An oath of allegiance, phrased by the great Innocent III himself for a king of Aragon, gives us a glimpse of
contemporary thought. This oath gives the lie to the naïve
presumption of modern man that the name Christ meant, after
all, nothing very different from Jesus of Nazareth. The mediæval oath carefully distinguished the pope's "succession" from
his "vicarate." "Succession" was used to point back to Peter;
here the unbroken historical chain gave proof of legality. But
the new authority of the popes, won in the twelfth century,
was not based on the historical aspect of his office. Europe,
though scholastic, was not historistic. The life-cycle of mankind did not seem to point from a preponderance of Christianity in the past to a preponderance of secularism in the
future. Christianity lay before mediæval men as a growing
future, a process of salvation. They were marching *towards*
Christ. The pope, therefore, balanced his descent from Peter
with his service to the future emperor. Not the humiliated
and defeated Jesus, but the triumphant Christ, was the pope's
authority. The pope was in authority till Christ came again.
He judged the world before the Anti-Christ should tempt
Christ's church; he was the superior of kings as Christ's vicar.
Here is the oath:

"With my heart I will believe and with my mouth I confess that
the Roman Pope, successor to St. Peter, is vicar of Him by whom
the kings reign, who is the master of the world's kingdoms and
gives kingship to whom he will."

In this oath the papacy is the sole representative of Christ's
world government. Thus the Roman Emperor is detached from
any claim to finality. The Roman Emperor descended from the
pagan Cæsars, the contemporaries of Peter and Paul; but any
emperor who claimed connection with the final goal, the Day
of Atonement, was clearly the Anti-Christ. Indeed, once the
vicarate of Christ was conjured up by the popes of the twelfth
century, the rôle of the Anti-Christ, the devilish power tempt-
ing the nations by secular pride, got a new actuality.

The new Vicar of the Last Judge, the Pope, unchained an
historical process, a real torrent of actions because he wanted to

be the "Concorder" of Christendom. The old apostolic Emperors had fitted into quite a different frame, that of a timeless, eternal Church of the Saints. In an unaltering Body of Christ, a mystical growth had gone on, but time was not split in past present and future; anything touched by the Church was lifted out of time and became eternal.

This frame was destroyed. The actual emperor is removed from his place as a reformer or as the High Commissioner in the history of Salvation. He is a mere bailiff, needed by the pope for special support in the secular branch. *"Imperator potest dici officialis ecclesiæ Romanæ,"* says Canon Law. Whenever the imperial throne is vacant, the pope fills the vacancy. He is the only pilot to the proper end of time. Compared to the disordered plurality of kingdoms, the pope is not a prince of this world. That is the basis for his claim to authority. "To be in authority" is a phrase preserved in English tradition from Catholic times. These two words authority (*auctoritas*) and power (*potestas*) were strangely transformed by Scholasticism.

In ancient Rome Augustus Cæsar had claimed both power and authority. In so doing he was assuming a dignity comparable to that of George Washington; for like Washington he held more than the highest office in the country—he was first in the hearts of his countrymen. This Augustus expressed by juxtaposing the legal *potestas* and the moral and imponderable *auctoritas* enjoyed by the best and wisest men in the community. A millennium later, "authority" came to express the wisdom revealed by Christ's death and the resurrection from the grave against the powers of the natural world. "Authority" is, so to speak, the most papal word still in use today. It covers more than the legal claim of a man who has grown up from natural birth and inherited the apostolic succession; his authority is derived from and reflects a last judgment over men and things. It co-ordinates the world in the direction of its final goal. As a matter of course, and as with Augustus or Washington, the pope's authority outweighs his power. By it he is able to see through the temporal divisions here on earth. The papacy looks with the eye of immortality, with God's eye, upon the passing scene of human troubles.

The practical gain from the pope's vicarate was stupendous. A new time span was wrested from death and decay. Mankind no longer had to fear an immediate inbreak of the Last Judgment. The formula of the "rapidly approaching end of time," so common in the documents between 800 and 1100, now disappears.

The new threat is the coming of the Anti-Christ. And the Roman Church keeps a vigilant watch; it protects Christendom against this eventuality. And the coming of the Anti-Christ has not quite the paralyzing quality of the Last Judgment. Even though the Anti-Christ was an eschatological figure, it was a great release for the mediæval mind, to be removed from the immediate contemplation of the Last Day, to the lighter problems of his coming. For, it was a problem, not of the Beyond, but of this lower world.

The doctrines of authority on one side and of Anti-Christ on the other brought men back to a definite interest in the history of the world. We have begun "the *witness* of the ultimate faith," says the historian of the First Crusade. This seems, perhaps, still pretty near the abyss of the Last Day; but to contemporaries the change amounted to a rediscovery of the world. This world of creation had come into real being; a precarious being, to be sure; yet from the bottomless depths of smoke and cloud there had emerged a new vision, that of a garden protected by the authority of the Holy See.

Before we deal with the garden of the empire, *"il giardino dell' impero,"* as created by the Papal Revolution, I wish to combine our statement in this chapter with our previous findings about modern eschatology. Actually the Papal Authority was committed to a postponement of salvation. The more efficiently it delayed the coming of the Anti-Christ, the more powerful it became, and the less real seemed the end of time. The Anti-Christ was the vision which circumscribed the historical vision of the papal party bewteen 1200 and 1500. Whenever an emperor or a prince was proclaimed the Anti-Christ, like Frederick II of Sicily in 1245, the end of history seemed near. By so much it becomes clear that Oswald Spengler or Georges Clemenceau were not the first to fear the end. Every form of civilization has its own vision of the end of things. The dictatorship of the proletariat, the so-called revolution in permanence, is limited, even threatened, by the possibility of a state-less and class-less society. The English Revolution is circumscribed by the inbreak of the "pride of man," by Lucifer and the downfall of the angels. Luther's gospel ends with the kingdom of God which is never here, always unattainable, always ahead of us.

Each new form of civilization can therefore be discovered, or divorced from its predecessor, the moment it loses interest in the horizon of the former historical vision. As a matter of fact, Luther, Cromwell, Robespierre, and Lenin were all well aware that they lived in a different world from their predecessors. To Lenin, the downfall of civilization was not a threat, as it was to Clemenceau: it was a fact upon which to build. For Robespierre, the fall of the angels had already happened; Lucifer reigned and should reign; Shelley and Byron were innocent romanticists compared to the brazen and conscious genius of the French self-made man. Cromwell accepted the kingdom of God as being either here or nowhere. He hated men who passively faced the unattainable, in the Lutheran way. Up to the present day, Anglo-Saxon Christians sigh at the rigid inactivity of the Lutherans and their disbelief that we can realize the kingdom of heaven on earth. All German philosophy is but an attempt to remove the kingdom of heaven to a transcendental space and time which is inaccessible for mortals but which nevertheless stimulates us constantly to make a new (though hopeless) effort in the direction of the ideal. The list is completed by Luther. Luther broke out of the narrow circle of the Roman ideas when he conceived of the pope as the Anti-Christ. He brought the vision so terribly feared by the Guelphs, the papal party, down to earth: the Anti-Christ had come. One had only to single him out: he was papacy itself! Meanwhile, between Anti-Christ and the kingdom of God, the Protestant Christian had to find his way in the dark.

We find the same principle at work in the Papal Revolution itself. To us it seems that the Last Judgment cannot have been anticipated. And yet it was: literally. The curialists clearly had the idea that pope and Holy Church could pass judgment on all and every thing, as *vicars of Christ*. They actually no longer waited for the Last Judgment.

The vicarate of Christ, claimed by the popes since the middle of the twelfth century, has found a poor interpretation in modern times. Historians have not considered the problem of eschatology. Reading of the pope as vicar of Christ, they thought of him, as vicar of the *historical Jesus Christ* of the year 30 A.D., the revealed God on the Cross; whereas the people of the twelfth century thought of Christ primarily as the Last Judge of this world. A vicar of Christ was therefore a vicar of the Last Judgment. In the eleven-forties, when the new doctrine was formulated that the pope was the vicar of Christ, it was combined with his claim to wield the spiritual and the temporal sword. Now the temporal was that part of our world which proved vain and worthless in the eyes of the Last Judge. To the pope the temporal sword was given in this sense, that he alone could descry the relative values of the temporal, because he alone could judge it from the final vantage-point of heaven and hell. The vicar of Christ, therefore, according to scholastic ideas, did not look forward into the future; he looked backward from the end of things into this world of sham and fiction.

Looking backward from the final goal of all mankind, the pope perceived the truth about this world. He anticipated the Last Judgment. And it was this anticipation of Christ's Last Judgment which aroused Luther's fury.

In Lutheranism the lost horizon was replaced by the limiting concept of the kingdom of God. Yet soon, the new party of the Puritans felt that the Lutherans did nothing to bring about this kingdom of heaven. So they marched into it boldly, as the chosen people. Where was an end to their kingdom? For the Elect, the ultimate danger was pride, Lucifer's sin. This would mean the renewed loss of paradise regained.

Into this abyss of Lucifer's pride, into the earthly paradise of man's genius and self-made arts and sciences, mankind plunged intentionally after 1789. Lucifer lost his diabolical character. He was hailed as Prometheus. To this Promethean civilization of the nineteenth century the old curses no longer sounded terrible. The only future that seemed dreadful was physical decay and disintegration. The downfall of all higher values, the desertion from the beautiful, the good and the true to the primitive standards of violence, vitality and regularity was forecast and deplored by all the prophets of the liberal century. The Soviets by abolishing truth, the Nazis by abolishing justice, openly broke away from the liberal tradition of the French Revolution.

And again, the new Russian masses of the perpetual revolution get their corresponding historical horizon. They, too, must be located and sheltered in a certain phase. They are told that they are in the midst of an everlasting turmoil. The spasms of class-war will last till the Classless Society shall make its entrance on earth. That will not happen for a long time to come. In the meantime, the governing party is safe in its claim for dictatorial power.

With the speed appropriate to our era of aeronautical time— as Mr. Lindbergh so happily baptized it in his Berlin speech— the modern counter-revolutions against Bolshevism are trying to anticipate "Classless Society." If successful, they would annihilate the historical horizon of Marxism. But they are merely counter-revolutionary; for they are not overawed by the end of time.

Gain and Loss of Historical Horizons:

> Last Judgment anticipated 1080;
> Anti-Christ anticipated 1517;
> Kingdom of Heaven anticipated 1649;
> Earthly Paradise (Adam) anticipated 1789;
> Decadence, Disintegration, anticipated 1917;
> Downfall of Liberty, New Barbarian Classless
> Society anticipated 1933.

To the sceptic observer and enlightened historian, these desperate acts of transforming "the ends of time" may seem sheer madness. And they will not even admit that there is a method in it. They are unwilling to admit the facts because for the modern historian the only facts that exist are facts of the past. Yet the facts of the past, for the living, would be of no importance whatever except for the facts of the future!

So we find all the written history of today at a loss to deal with the change in perspective without deep pity for the folly of man. Of Gregory VII, the distinguished scholar Mr. Hauck said caustically: "It is in vain to ask where there is any gain made by Rome during Gregory's reign." [7] He is right in the world of *his* facts. Bloodshed, exile, humiliation, rebellion, disorder, reached a climax in the year in which Gregory died. But men like Gregory or Cromwell or Robespierre do not come to construct a new house but to allot a new area on which to build! Since we are ascribing to the total revolutions of our era an intention that is not admitted by the average sceptic, two examples may show the preoccupation of the real beginner of a new era. The first is taken from Gregory VII, the second from the English conquerors of the kingdom of heaven.

In his Bulls in which he humbled the Roman Emperor into a Teutonic king, Gregory asserted: "We are taking victory from his arms, we are binding him not in the spirit only, but in the physical world and in the thriving of his life as well." "He will have neither power in any battle nor victory for the rest of his life." These assertions show clearly that the pope meddled with the decrees of Providence quite literally: he anticipated the Last Judgment.

Of a contemporary of the English Revolution, R. M. Jones writes: [8] "He did not propose to postpone the practice of the principles of the kingdom until it had finally come in its final triumph. *If that course were pursued there would never be a kingdom. The way to bring it is to start courageously to be the kingdom so far as the person can reveal it.* Instead of postponing it to a heavenly sphere or to a millennial dawn he boldly undertook to begin living the way of the kingdom." This describes accurately what "anticipation" means in each Total

---

[7] Hauck, *Kirchengeschichte Deutschlands*, III, 832, Leipzig, 1896.
[8] *Hibbert Journal*, 23, 39.

Revolution. As soon as we grasp for what these people were fighting it becomes clear that they were highly successful. These anticipations have little to do with an immediate result "in cash," be it territorial or financial. The Cromwellians sanctified the waves of the Western world; Gregory VII emancipated the nations of Europe from the fetters of the Roman Empire and changed knaves of the manor into crusading knights. The same victory over the encircling gloom was carried by Robespierre, when he attacked the kingdom of the Elect, the privileged classes; by Luther, when his Christian faith survived the fact that the Anti-Christ had already risen to might and yet Christianity survived. All these acts have nothing to do with politics in the trite sense of the word. Yet, what generations of men have feared as the final death-blow to civilization is suddenly recognized as the chiming of a new hour of history. What was labelled end or death is now called start or birth. The leaders of a revolution re-name the era. That is all they do. Only when we are acquainted with man's encirclement by an evolutionary horizon can we do justice to the heroes who destroy and create these horizons. Why should they be successful in any other sense than that which they intended? When Oliver Cromwell, on his death-bed, assured his stunned physicians that, by direct revelation he was certain not to die, he was mad as a mortal and right in his vision of a permanent place for himself in the evolution of man.

For the evolution of man, the so-called successful people who are praised by the opportunists are utterly unimportant. Evolution of Man is but another term for perpetual victory over death, over the encircling gloom. The so-called successful people don't touch this problem. They move contentedly within the conventional gloom of their epoch.

Christian civilization has always faced more than the death of the individual; it anticipates the death of its most sacred ideals and institutions. In contradiction to nature, civilization is not interested in the survival of the fittest. It is interested in something more modest and more important, something too simple to be mentioned by philosophers. It is interested in survival after death. Individuals die anyway. Man is mortal.

Yet man lives to build a shell of civilization around him which will be quasi-immortal, like a turtle's shell. The Church, however, has taught us the mortality of any such shell which is void of the spirit of life. Man must have the power to build these shelters and must keep the power of destroying any one shelter.

After the renovation by emperors and monks, the Church itself had to learn to bury its old shell. Kings, aristocrats, bourgeois, and labourers learned to distrust the immortality of their respective civilization in a process of eternal vigilance. In anticipating the Anti-Christ the mediæval Church watched for the slightest symptom of decay. By anticipating the final threat, any form of society can attain immortality. By anticipation of the hour of death, the life cycle can be governed consciously. The life of civilization is eternally recurrent, it is immortal, whenever the fear of its last hour is kept present by frank criticism.

The famous critical power of the Western world is one of its most important Christian qualities. This inner criticism of institutions from the point of view of their death has made them eternal. Papacy exists today, in spite of all odds and in spite of all its enemies. England and France exist in spite of the proletarian revolution. The anticipation of a Last Judgment looming over our own civilization is the best remedy against its inevitable downfall. This is the paradoxical wisdom of European revolutions.

CHAPTER ELEVEN

Italy: The Garden of the Italian Renaissance (The Second Clerical Revolution)

National Millennium Versus "Middle Ages"—Key Soldiers—Diplomatic Whisper—Italian Geography—"Hourly Rule": The Secret of Secular Government—Landscape in Politics—The Poverty of St. Francis

NATIONAL MILLENNIUM VERSUS "MIDDLE AGES."

FROM 1200 TO 1517 THE POWERS OF THE ROMAN POPE CHECKED every temporal power in Europe. Modern nationalists deplore this degradation of national "sovereignty." They repeatedly accuse the Church of degrading national pride and the nature of man by making both depend upon a priesthood. But these same secularists and Fascists, Freemasons or Die-hards, take every chance to visit Italy and to fall in love with the Italian cities and the beautiful landscape of Tuscany or Umbria. Their admiration for Florence, Siena, Assisi, Perugia, Urbino, these pearls of the Italian Middle Ages, give the lie to their national fanaticism against popery. Before the World War, a Swedish Protestant wrote a book [1] on Western Democracy, in which, after 250 pages on modern popular government, the reader is surprisingly transported from modern London to mediæval Siena. In a rapture of enthusiasm Mr. Steffen tells him that here, in the Italian Free-Cities of the Middle Ages, all the liberties of modern Europe and America were hatched. Now, if the Italian City-State was really the cradle of the Rights of Man, it was a cradle which was possible only under the authority of the Roman Catholic Church. Italy would not have seen

[1] Gustav F. Steffen, *Die Demokratie in England*, Epilogue, Jena, 1910.

any of the glories of the Renaissance without the Papal Revolution and its continuous work. Furthermore, the downfall of Italian civilization clearly came about with Luther's attack on popery. In the Catholic world, revolutionized by his sermons, the notorious *sacco d'Roma* (1527) was like a conflagration marking the end of Italian liberty. The conquest of Rome by the pillaging hordes of the imperial army, Germans, Spaniards, and all the rest, was the symbol of Luther's victory over the Anti-Christ of Rome. But it also put an end to the three hundred years of Italian liberty!

Every form of civilization is a wise equilibrium between firm substructure and soaring liberty. Childlike people praise the liberty and ignore the substructure which creates this liberty. They wish to have Sunday without week-days, sugar without salt, civil peace without police. They do not ask the price of one's privileges. Pacifists, liberals, Protestants, Socialists, in their genuine passion for improvement, forget the delicate equilibrium that underlies a civilization. Mankind always stands on the edge of barbarism and universal warfare; a matter of inches separates it from ruin. The breeding-place of man which we call civilization is no impregnable fortress. It is easily destroyed. Civilization, as a living body politic, is mortal. It is bound to die by its own accomplishments. Death is the goal of life. Dead things, like porcelain, cannot die. It is the honour of living bodies that they can die. Living forms have a history, from birth to death, because it is of the essence of life to be directed by an experience of death.

Italian *civilita*—the Italian form of city—was in dynamic equilibrium between Roman authority and local *potesta*. Therefore, with the defeat of Roman authority the tradition of Italian city-power ended. Modern papacy alone keeps alive the old glories of Italy as a vital force in European civilization, by calling its possessions in Rome "La Città del Vaticano." In the name *Città del Vaticano,* coined by the Concordat with Italy in 1929, the great character of the Italian nation and the great Italian contribution to humanity are well combined. The paradoxical basis of Italian liberty was exactly what modern nationalism deprecates. Italy lived by excluding all universal rule from the peninsula except the papacy.

Italy did not exist in 1200. When the Church harvested its first great victory, in its Concordat of 1122, the concept of Italy did not fit into the geographical conception. From the empire one piece is detached: the Teuton kingdom. Italy is not mentioned, it is no political term. This is the more important to state as our text-books maintain the opposite: they report on the struggle between emperors and popes as if the popes had kept "Italy" in 1122. The negligence of our text-books is, perhaps, more significant than the terms used in 1122 themselves. From this negligence springs the laziness with which people will repeat again and again the time-worn word "Middle Ages." This word is useless for all the purposes of modern men who wish to understand their own antecedents. All our antecedents are twofold: Roman and Christian on one side, national on the other. The first millennium created our Roman and Christian past, the second, by *restoring* Roman Church and Christendom, created the Christian nations. Without dropping the term Middle Ages, this clear distribution of two different millennia cannot be taught to our children. If our children cannot learn some simple facts about the last two millennia, they will give up and follow the line of least resistance. Sacrificing all chronology, they will place prehistory, ten thousand years b.c. before their own past. The skulls and bones of primitive man will act as an historical charm and nobody will penetrate into the thicket of facts about our real past. In restoring the Church, the papacy had to create Italy: this is the great transformation from a universal revolution of the Roman Church (1075-1198) to a national revolution of Rome and its allies in Italy, the so-called Guelphs. The first nation to be established in Europe had a universal, a Christian, a spiritual head: the Pope. All nations of today cling to this claim that saves us from barbarism. The conscious alliance between the papacy and Italy did not begin until the times of Innocent III and Francis of Assisi. The memory of the second half of the Papal Revolution was embodied in the life of

Francis, and in the actions of the popes after Innocent III's election to the papal throne in 1198.

KEY SOLDIERS.

The Crusade, the recovery of the Holy Sepulchre, lost its hold on the leading men of the new time. The papacy, the heart and soul of the undertaking, no longer hoped for the Crusades as a magic charm, a way of counter-balancing the world axis from Aachen to Rome by a permanent highway from the British Channel to Marseilles, to Palermo, Rhodes, and Palestine. For the Roman emperors had managed to acquire Sicily and Southern Italy. True enough, they did not govern it as emperors. They gave up the universal claim of "Roman Empire" by promising the pope that the Sicilian kingdom should be kept outside the empire. They did not bring the moral pressure of a united, universal empire to bear on the Church. Yet the geographical fact of an emperor who ruled seven eighths of Italy and the surrounding sea was, if anything, worse than a legal theory of universalism. In 1198, practically all Italy obeyed the emperor. The pope's only salvation lay in ordering him off on a crusade; but this was more or less an artifice. The crusade in the hands of the emperor was a contradiction in terms. Its very concept had been anti-imperialistic. No wonder that the popes lost interest in the political symbols of the Crusades.

New emblems were needed to combat the emperor's sphere of influence. And they sprang up. With the beginning of the thirteenth century, the independent use of the keys of St. Peter as emblems or badges of the papacy makes its appearance. The new symbol of warfare for the specific ends of papal policy was a flag bearing the keys of St. Peter, which is first mentioned under Innocent III.[2] His successors recruited troops against the emperor under the name of key soldiers—a name

[2] Examples of the independent use of the keys as emblems or badges of the papacy are unknown before the beginning of the thirteenth century. Donald Lindsay Galbreath, *A Treatise on Ecclesiastical Heraldry*, Vol. I, p. 6, Cambridge (England), 1930.

which survives today for the Swiss bodyguard in the Città del Vaticano.

The new flag betokened a changed world. The popes now began the attempt to recover the papal territories in Italy, and to loosen the grip of the emperor on Rome. The technical term was "Recuperation"; and we may call the second half of the Papal Revolution by this term "Recuperation." For geographical integrity was the endeavour which guided every step of the papacy between 1198 and 1268. The House of Swabia, with its claim to the empire and the Kingdom of Sicily, became an obsession with the popes. They did not cease from their fight against the "poisonous tree" of this family until papal key soldiers, after 1250, marched into its hereditary Kingdom of Sicily and until its last descendant, Conradin, was beheaded.

Conradin of Swabia was fourth in the line of "persecutors of the Church" from this house. When he came to Italy and was defeated near Tagliacozzo by Charles of Anjou, and later captured, the allegation brought against him was that he had offended against the Church, his nurse. Charles of Anjou, himself a knight and a prince, based the prosecution on a crime against the Church! He acted as the steward of the pope, called into Italy against the Ghibellines. The relation between the sword of the Angevin Prince and the spiritual sword of papacy is well illustrated by the legend that during the battle of Tagliacozzo, Clement IV, though far away in his palace, experienced the whole battle internally, so to speak, as an intense vision. The popes direct, equip, instruct the secular arm: they are not able to act themselves, but they find arms and legs to carry out their intense will. The stirring story of this papal vision marks the climax of the papal rebellion against geographical encirclement. After the death of Conradin no emperor ever re-established a political domination over the Italian peninsula. The papal "Recuperation" was accomplished.

But the exhaustion after those seventy years was terrible. Clement IV died soon after the final victory, and the papal throne stood vacant for three years, nine months and twenty-one days. "The simple-minded found this long vacancy of the papal throne most astounding," wrote a chronicler. It showed how tremendous the effort had been on both sides, and how small the advantage had been which had brought the final victory—an experience that recurs in every serious world struggle.

DIPLOMATIC WHISPER.

We began intentionally with the end of the revolution, because it sharpens our insight into the revolutionary character of the beginning. The struggle was ended by a vacancy in the Papal See; it was begun by a vacancy on the imperial throne, in 1198.

The newly elected Emperor Frederick was an orphan whose Norman mother lived in Sicily and for whom, therefore, according to the Frankish law, no regency could be established. The orphan's next-of-kin, his uncle, could take his nephew into his own house, but he could not be made a regent in the orphan's house and conduct the business of the empire in the child's name. The old concept of the House as a real economic unit prevented Philip of Swabia from becoming regent for his nephew Frederick. He resolved, therefore, to go "under crown," that is, to act as emperor, but to omit the sacrament of anointment. By this device he could act as temporary king until Frederick became of age.

This gave the papacy a chance to intervene. A counter-candidate, a Guelph, was anointed as quickly as possible. By this act the pope drove Philip into a defensive position; Philip took belated refuge in anointment, in spite of his loyalty to his nephew. But the anointment, being a sacrament, made Philip irrevocably king and destroyed his plan for a temporary arrangement.

In this chain of events, the pope found the pretext for an attack on the honest and over-scrupulous Philip. He banned him for having repudiated his loyalty to his nephew! He accused Philip of a *violated conscience*. The term is important; it was destined to become epoch-making. The *wounded* conscience of Philip was an artificial construction by the pope, so that he might condemn him. Nobody was ever more honest and correct than Philip. His tender conscience had even made him avoid being anointed immediately, for fear of damaging his nephew.

Martin Luther's restoration of the personal conscience reads like a reply, after the lapse of three hundred years, to the Pope's Machiavellian accusation of Philip. Perhaps in no other case is the grandeur of historical continuity clearer than in this dialogue between the papal attack on the German prince's conscience and Luther's restitution of the princely conscience. The dialectical process between the revolutions takes the form of a dialogue carried on across a valley of centuries. And the full weight of a revolution can be tested by asking whether it has such a contradictory answer to give to another.

The document which formulated the papal right to ruin Philip stands, as might be expected, half way between the *Dictatus Papæ* of 1075 and the 95 theses of Luther in 1517. It was a *deliberatio de statu imperii,* read to the cardinals in consistory in 1200. No longer does the pope begin the revolution *"in petto,"* by a monologue. Yet we are still far from the public disputation of theses in a university. The pope does not address an uncertain number of people. He makes no public speech or protest or thesis. He deliberates with his cardinals within the walls of the papal court. The document fittingly opens a period of aristocratic government in the Church. During the long vacancies of the Holy See, the duty of governing the Church fell, practically, on the cardinals. The second half of the Papal Revolution is carried out, less by a monarchical than by an aristocratic, form of Roman Church. Aristocratic chapters became the form of government in every bishopric.

The "deliberation" of 1200 is a statement of interest. It asks: "What is necessary, what is fitting, what is convenient (*quid oportet, quid decet, quid expedit*)?" And the reader is left in no doubt that the *"expedit,"* the interest, carries the decision. The document is a masterpiece of diplomacy. In the *Dictatus Papæ* of 1075, a man holds a soliloquy before his God. The sin of Simony is fought. In the *deliberatio* of 1200 we hear the halftones of a diplomatic whisper. A political danger is flaired.

Papacy now has at its command both the superhuman strength of the last trumpet—and the halftone of diplomatic language. The *deliberatio*, in its bodiless whisper, reminds us of the bodiless presence of the pope's mind at the Battle of Tagliacozzo. It was not any full-blooded virility, but the cultivated wink of the diplomat, which made the papal curialists famous all over the world. Papal diplomacy became one of the great artistic achievements of civilization. All European diplomacy learned its trade from the papacy. The methods of diplomacy differ from the ringing sound of "papal bulls" and exhortations as the grooves on a modern gramophone disc differ from a monumental style.

ITALIAN GEOGRAPHY.

The *deliberatio* of 1200 advanced the cause of the Guelphic candidate. After innumerable detours, the papacy always came back to this deliberate effort to destroy the union between the Northern empire and Sicily.

In this annihilation of the Hohenstaufen, the popes undoubtedly were involving themselves in a purely secular struggle. But emperor and pope could not be room-mates in Italy. We owe to this struggle the first concept of a secular kingdom or "state." In 1221, Frederick II had to promise the pope that he would never use the same seal for his empire and for his Sicilian kingdom. As a result the emperor's insignia disappeared from the Seal of Sicily. Instead there appeared a clumsy map, probably the first secular map in European history. Its trees and bridges and the straits of Messina, symbolize the dawn of secular government under the pressure of papal authority. The word "pressure" should be taken as literally as possible. This map was not the result of the free play of an artist's imagination; it was literally extorted from Frederick II. It marked the end of the emperor's sacred character on Italian soil, and ushered in the period of the city-state with its purely worldly character.

From the beginning of his reign, Innocent III worked to "recuperate" the possessions of the Church. In re-assembling what had been gathered piece by piece for a thousand years, he was led to organize the papal possessions once more, and this time in the form of a single political unit. In writing to all

Sacred or Secular Government

I. FREDERICK II AS ROMAN EMPEROR

(Eternal Rome and her eagle are on his seals.)

II. FREDERICK II AS *SECULAR KING*

The oldest secular map, gives the Straits of Messina, castles, fruit trees, cities of Sicily, Calabria, and Apulia.

his cities and towns, in summoning all his subjects to conferences, the pope created the Papal State. This state borrowed its light and existence from his universal authority, but was itself merely a geographical area, a state without a racial, national, or historical unity, a bishop's state. The case of Sicily and its new geographical seal had its counterpart in the organization of Central Italy.

But the pope could not stop at this point. For his opposition to the legitimate house of the Ghibellines, he had to find allies. This time not Norman princes from the South, but the cities of Northern Italy offered their support. However, they annexed certain conditions. The pope could not longer act, as Gregory VII had acted, as an impartial, super-local authority beyond space and time. He was forced into a coalition as an Italian prince.

As early as 1180 the cities of Verona, Venice, Vicenza, Bergamo, Treviso, Ferrara, Brescia, Cremona, Milan, Lodi, Piacenza, Parma, Modena and Bologna had written to the pope: "We were first to bear the emperor's attack, so that he might not destroy *Italy* and suppress the *liberty of the Church.* We refused, for the *honour and liberty of Italy* and for the dignity of the Church, to receive or to listen to the emperor." Innocent III, in one of his first letters, written on April 16, 1198, recommended "the interest of Italy" to the cities of Tuscany. The same papacy which as recently as in 1150 had depended upon the emperor to overthrow the revolutionary Arnold of Brescia in Rome, now committed itself irrevocably to the "common cause against a common enemy"! (Potthast no. 8425.) The biography of Innocent III explains that the year 1200 was the turning-point, after which the pope was unable to act from a purely ecclesiastical point of view but had to become definitely Italian: "Our Lord the Pope thought the conditions of peace [with the emperor] reasonable. Yet many were scandalized, as though he were going to favour the Teutons in Italy, who through cruel tyrants had subjected them to a most grievous servitude. He, therefore, deflected his course in favour of Italian liberty and did not accept the terms."

A deflection in favour of Italian liberty was the new course urged upon the papacy. The Italian view of the struggle was clearly expressed in the terms of the alliance which the cities of Northern Italy concluded in 1226: "No emperor shall march from Germany to Rome with more than 1,200 soldiers!" Between 950 and 1250 the Northern emperors had personally come to Italy eighty-five times. The territories between the Alps and Rome felt themselves abused, degraded into a mere highroad for constant expeditions to Rome. They were but a means to an end. And they suffered the more as the Northern tribes rose one by one to an equal footing with the old Frankish stock, the backbone of the realm, through their tribal dukes becoming emperors. With the Swabian dynasty the last of the tribes had given the empire a ruling house. Hence the contrast of an emancipated Germany and a subdued Italy was now at its zenith.

On the other hand, Italy had no big ecclesiastical territories like the North. Also, after 1122, the Italian bishops were under the control of the popes. In 1161 the emperors had destroyed the rich city of Milan. For the Italian revolt against the North, this cruel act was that "last straw," that final event which we have found at the bottom of every great revolution. After 1161, Italy was in ferment. The revolution went "underground." But "Italy" still meant the highway of the emperors from the Alps to Rome. It was still a special mediæval concept, by which the name Italy was reserved for the northern two thirds of the peninsula.

In the South, no league of cities made itself respected by the popes. In Sicily, Campania, Apulia, Calabria, 153 bishoprics formed the stronghold of papal policy. When we read that in 1215 the "orb" met in Rome for the Lateran Council, an analysis of the figures illustrates the special character of this orb. Of 412 prelates, more than a hundred came from the Kingdom of the Two Sicilies. There, in the South, the classical tradition survived which gave a bishop to every town. In Sicily the *"polis"* of antiquity had remained through the centuries. In Southern Italy the Roman popes inherited a province of Greek institutions. Therefore the Roman bishop, in his councils, had three hundred Italian bishops to set off against the thirty-five of Germany or the eighty of France! Secular Italy, in the modern sense of the word, showed no political homogeneity in 1200. But, for the papacy, the smallness of each episcopal jurisdiction and the multitude of bishoprics in Italy, were big with consequences. The pope became the born leader of the whole Italian body of Lords spiritual [3] despite all the differences of government in the peninsula. The *"Natio Italica"* in the councils of the fifteenth century was naturally led by the pope himself, as the foremost Italian prince, while Spain, Germany, England and France had difficulty in finding a true national representative.

"HOURLY RULE": THE SECRET OF SECULAR GOVERNMENT.

All "authority" being reserved for the pope, Italian "liberty" unfolded itself in the direction of *"potestas."* It seems incredible that the modern word "power" is the same word as *"potestas,"* so great is the change in meaning. *"Potestas,"* in Italian political thought, meant the reverse of modern power. *"Potestas"* was a transient public function in a temporal order of things. *"Potestas"* entered the plan of the creator best when it was as transient and short-lived as possible. The Italian experiment in *potestas* is a grandiose experiment in the fleeting character of time. *"Potestas,"* the power of office, given, according to St. Paul, by God to magistrates, became the name for the head of an Italian city. This *Podesta* was appointed for one year; and to emphasize the fleeting character of this "power" he was fetched from outside, and left the city after his term of office. The Lord Mayor of London and the rectors of the universities in Germany are appointed for one year only. "A year and a day" was a set term in European courts for the right of possession; any officer who stayed on for more than a year was presumed to be in lawful possession forever. The one-year rotation of office made it plain that in a republic nobody had

[3] A vivid picture of this leadership occurs as late as 1807 in Napoleon's talk with the Papal Nuncio, described in Clemens Metternich, *Memoirs,* I, 292, New York, Scribner, 1880.

power as his own property. It opposed *potestas* to property, and its "modern usage," as they called it, to the feudal life tenure of hereditary succession. Around the *podesta* a new kind of literature sprang up.[4] His power came from God, because it carefully avoided all sacramental authority. Feudal society was scorned as having misused power by treating it like property. The thrill of a new discovery in the application of short set terms, originally used only in court, can still be felt if we analyze the hundreds of Italian "statutes" established in the thirteenth century. We find: "Rights of Men," "Bills of Rights," *ordinamenta della Giustizia*, all animated by the greatest political optimism. In spite of their variety, these statutes are all devoted to one serious effort. Power must be established between and beyond individuals. Nobody can be, or represent, the body politic. Man as a temporal being shall organize his society in forms of temporal, i.e., provisional order. Often one year seems too long a period, and the appointed time was shortened to six months, four months, two months. During each term, instead of one individual, six or four or twelve, might be in power together. These men formed an intimate comradeship during their term of office. The Russians would call their group a "collective." They slept together and took their meals together. They were not allowed to go home or to speak to their families during the term. They were construed as one indivisible body. As the emblems of power had to be entrusted to this group, the constitution divested them of all attributes of power after their term expired. Lots were drawn to select the group. Nobody should aspire to office. Not per-

---

[4] Dr. Fritz Herftter, *Die Podestaliteratur Italiens im 12. u. 13. Jahrhundert,* Leipzig, 1910. Chapter 129, "Johannes v. Viterbo": Appendix, *De duabus potestatibus.*

Cognoscant igitur et manifeste sciant ex predictis potestates et civitatum et aliorum locorum rectores, se a deo esse, et nulla inde excitatio de cetero moveatur in cordibus eorum, et cognoscant gladium habere ab ipso domino deo. Nec sine causa datus est eis gladius temporalis; quia ad vindictam malefactorum, ad laudem vero bonorum. Ergo precipue deum et equitatem habeant ante oculos suos,* ut supra dictum est. Scituri pro certo quod non magis alios iudicant quam ipsi iudicabuntur. † Qua enim mensura mensi fuerint eadem remetietur eis. ‡

* Dig. XIII, 4, 4.   † Cod. Just. III, 1, 14.   ‡ Mark. IV, 24.

sonal aspiration, but the impersonal inspiration of office, was wanted. The Italian city-state freed the State once and for all from its identification with individual rights or the physical life of one of its citizens.

It is true, in modern times, that society is organized by the division of powers into a variety of simultaneous functions. The Lutheran State made civil service and military service parallel. English parliamentarianism distinguished king in parliament from king in council, judiciary from executive. America and France divided government into three branches, one checking the other: the judicial, the legislative, and the executive. Division of power has been a departmental arrangement of different activities during the last four hundred years.

In Italy, for the three hundred years preceding, power was also divided, but by a successive arrangement of men in the same activity. If the men in power alternated three times a year, then the annual power was divided into three different sections, an arrangement in series, which people then thought as efficient as we now think our departmental divisions. The Presidency in the United States is a modern example of mediæval principles; great power must be vested in one man, but for a very short time.

The "temporal" organization treated society as temporary. That is the clue to all the grandeurs and ineptitudes of mediæval politics. Italian thought and Italian political experimentation in the cities led the way. This was the revolutionary Guelphic idea of the years between 1200 and 1500.

In our days, in the midget Republic of Andorra, the "temporal" is still sanctified in a mediæval way. Six valleys in the Pyrenees form the Republic. The result is that the six valleys try to form a temporal power. Six men are sent out from the valleys on a certain day, their mandate being valid only for this day. They get a "diet" for their going, staying and returning; the very word "diet," "*dies*," being the mediæval word for a "temporal" assembly instead of "parliament." The six men gather in the "Iron Cabinet" which contains the chest with the governmental archives. Here the charters and privileges of the

"State" are kept. They must be laid upon the table before the men at every meeting, to endow the group afresh with the power of government. Six locks secure the chest. Each of the six parish representatives brings one key with him. Six men turn their keys in the lock—the chest is opened—government can begin. When they depart, no authority is left behind them. The day's power has been exercised, it expires at sunset.

Here we have the metaphysics of the secular state: the order must remain a day's order; it may not exceed the orbit of the year. Under the empire, Passion Week had stood for peace. Now the ecclesiastical calendar of the year, successfully rivalling the emperor, begins to subdue the temporal power and compress it into the short span of the twelve months. Everything beyond a year was dangerous because it created abuse. Thus the transience of human things was made the essential principle of political institutions. The political body and will were built up out of the days of various and varying men, and not out of the life-times of particular men. The Guelphic city subordinated man's calendar to the church calendar. It forbade the body politic to go beyond the year of the religious soul. This "Guelphic" concept was so general that it spread over all Europe. The kings and princes took it up for the government of their realms, by giving a temporal share to the estates of the country. I say, a temporal share; for it was the "diet," the representative of the country in "going, staying, and returning" that gave the estates their power. What we have mentioned in little Andorra, can be found just as well in Great Britain. The famous dictum of Henry VIII, on the splendour of parliament, must be read with a careful eye to this conception of temporal or transient order:

"We be informed by our judges, that we *at no time* stand so highly in our state royal as *in the time of parliament,* wherein we as head and you as members are conjoined and knit together in one body politic, so as whatever offence or injury *during that time* is offered to the meanest member of the House is to be judged as done against our person and the whole court of Parliament." (Pollard, p. 231.)

Henry VIII transformed this temporal State into a modern State, by making the king head of the Church. Thereby the State inherited the eternal timelessness of the Church. The notorious divine right of kings was a discovery or invention of the sixteenth century. The period between 1200 and 1517 knew of no such divine right, because the secular order proceeded by diets and year-books; any time-span exceeding the space of a year was under the authority of the Church. Men dealt with "a year and a day," and they were happy because, frankly accepting the fugitive character of time, they felt that they were not imperilled by the slavery or idolatry of any secular power.

LANDSCAPE IN POLITICS.

The vision of the territory to be governed by this temporal power underwent a definite change also. By the concentration of power into the time-span of a "diet," it seemed possible to feel the whole territory as present on that one day. The diet made the political power so real that it ceased to belong to individuals: the countries and valleys and boroughs were represented, embodied, on the spot.

This new vision of space was clearly developed in the Guelphic states. As early as 1192 all the peasants in the county of Genoa were made citizens of Genoa. In 1235 the Florentines enrolled all the farmers of their Tuscan possessions as citizens. The equal status of every man, despite the distance of his home from the political centre, is so natural to our political thought that we forget how utterly difficult it was to arrive at this concept and to carry it through. Dante, the man of Ghibelline traditions, always protested against the Guelphic mixing of peasants and citizens. (Ercole II (1928), 26.) Yet this was one of the most important changes of his century. His protest against it made Dante once more a stranger to his time.

Dante's antipathy to the artificial citizenship of the husband-man was shared by all the Northern princes. In Germany, for example, this Italian principle was considered an outright soviet system. Time after time in the next two centuries the empire forbade by law the existence of "pseudocitizens" ("*Balo-*

burger," *"Pfahlburgertum"*). Neither peasants nor knights could become citizens in the Northern cities. Meanwhile the progress of Italy depended on this Guelphic generosity towards the country-side. The peasants had civil rights, and joined the minor guilds and crafts of the city. The great artists of Florence came from her villages. Settignano gave her Michelangelo, Vinci the great Leonardo, Vespignano produced the first painter of the *"stilo nuovo,"* Giotto. In exchange, the city gave something to the country which no peasant or knight could have given. The alliance between city and country created what modern man enjoys as landscape. No "landscape" whatever was in existence before 1200. It has long been noticed how great a detachment and distance is needed to perceive a landscape. A peasant is a part of his environment; he cannot see it, or treat it as his object. Scientists have investigated the way in which a native of the Alps contemplates high mountains. An authority reports his findings: "The peasant or farmer often seems to overlook mighty ridges or summits or extensive valleys. Instead, he names a multitude of trifles. As a genuine child of nature, he is not detached enough from it to visualize the main forms of the landscape. Like all the impressions of primitive men, 'landscape' is split into a mass of details." This quotation from the Alpinist Finsterwalder may be rounded off by a few words from Carl Schurz's *Reminiscences:* "The perception of natural beauty is not primitive, but the result of education, of culture. Naïve people seldom possess it, or at least do not express it. The aspects of nature, mountain, valley, forest, desert, river, sea, sunshine, storm, etc., etc., are to them either beneficent, helpful, or disagreeable, troublesome, terrible. It is a significant fact that in Homer, with all the vividness of his pictures, there is no description of a landscape or of a natural phenomenon from the point of view of the beautiful. We remark the same in the primitive literature of other countries."

Guelphic Italy discovered the landscape as the background of its cities, because the landscape was no longer owned by separate and greedy proprietors. It was changed into the field of political potestas, of *"civilitas."* Landscape became a politi-

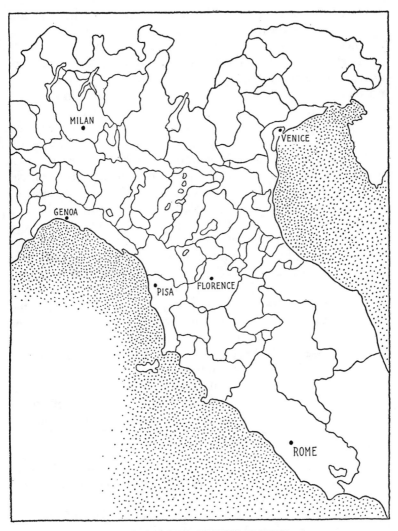

THE GARDEN OF THE EMPIRE

City States and small principalities in Italy—circa 1300. All the lines are
political boundaries.

cal and an artistic reality. In looking at the Guelphs and Ghibellines of Italy we are reminded of the difference between the Social Revolutionaries and the Bolsheviks in Russia. Here it was the Social Revolutionaries who were in love with the individual peasant or village. They distributed the land among individual settlements. The Bolsheviks conceived the unifying vision of one Russian economy. The Italian city-state is so small that modern national historians always wonder why the Italians did not unify the whole peninsula in the Ducento. This absurd projection of present-day proportions into the past hinders us from learning by the past where it is really identical with our own situation. The Guelphic effort was as real as modern economic planning, because the economy of the city was something new, something bigger than manorial husbandry had been. The division of labour between the craftsmen was something startling and confusing in a time when 183 crafts contributed to one knight's equipment. The knight being, so to speak, the heavy artillery of the Guelphic period, the organization of the crafts around his panoply meant what the armament industry means to us: the most complicated and most efficient branch of technical production. A vision which bound the vinedresser and wheat-farmer together with the artisans of this industry, did not lack boldness and grandeur. It overcame the idea of local autarchy; it changed locality into territory. Three thousand square miles may seem a contemptible piece of land today. Yet, as it embraced a most complicated mechanism of production, its social problem was not less difficult than ours.

We find a steady increase in size from revolution to revolution. 3,000 square miles in Italy, 25,000 in Germany, 140,000 square miles in Great Britain, 360,000 square miles in France: such were the units to be organized. Soviet Russia measures forty times the size of France; its problem is the problem of organizing a continent.

> Manor,
> City-State,
> Princedom,

United Kingdom,
Nation,
Continent,

form one after the other the substratum of a social revolution. The majority, during such a revolution, misses the point of concentration, the bigger issue. The new rulers are those who are bold enough to organize a new area by means of a new vision. They are always a minority when they begin. But they solve problems inaccessible to the old ways of thought, because they think in a new order of magnitude.

The break between two worlds is a shift in the size of the area to which political thought is applied. The jump from local to "territorial" economy was as dangerous as the jump from "national" to continental economy. In mediæval Italy as in modern Russia this jump was made abruptly, by violent revolutions; whereas the other countries temporized more or less between the two radical solutions. The boldness of the leap into a new comprehension of the world frightened man, as it always does. A new horizon dawned before the eyes of men in the thirteenth century, leaving the dark walls of palace and church, opening out into the dim colours of the last cloud and the last hill in the distance, where earth and heaven seemed to meet.

The co-operation of papal authority and secular *"potestas"* gave rise to a new political symbolism. The art of the Renaissance was the expression of a unique political constellation. The new governments of the Italian cities lacked the dignity inherent in an anointed king or a sacred emperor. They were, by principle, republics of this world. The Italian city-state left worship, theology, religion, to the Roman Catholic Church; and the citizen of Italy was easily led to exalt her, the One Church, into the common nurse and mother. Where Rome had been the Mother of all Churches, it now became "Our Mother Church." The symbol of this spiritual motherhood was the adoration of the Virgin Mary. The ebullition of Italian liberty was intimately connected with a new effort to increase her worship. The Rosary, by which the Ave Maria and the Lord's

Prayer were combined into a chain of prayers, was invented in the thirties of the Ducento, i.e., in the thirteenth century. The dignity of Holy Mary's position on Earth and in Heaven became the subject of increasing debate between the two groups of friars, Franciscans and Dominicans. Mary's intercession was construed as the intervention of the mother for her family and servants in a manor or palace of the time. An empress or a queen or a farmer's wife, being in charge of the whole economy of her household, was not only entitled, nay, in duty bound, to raise her voice and interpose her authority in any transaction concerning one of her labour-forces. Among the privileges of the Empress or the Queen, this intervention is regularly mentioned. The comprehensive protection of a "house" being the chief feudal conception of society, the Virgin Mary's intervention with her son was much more natural than in modern days, where the mother is no longer the undisputed queen.

Now all the discussions about Mary reacted directly on the Church. The Church stood sponsor, not theologically but practically, for the real presence of Mary, as Holy Communion bestowed the real presence of the Saviour. The stone edifice of a cathedral, embracing the altar with the sacred host, was like the womb of the Virgin embracing her blessed child. Yet better than stone or glass would "Mother Church" give to every Christian the warm feeling of protection and guidance. The Roman Church seemed omnipresent in the life of the Christian, the World ceased to be unfeeling and cold, the Madonna appeared anywhere and everywhere. Her mantle reached from Heaven down through clouds and snow to the earth, and warmed the children of men in the field, in the forest, at sea, and in their workshops. The Sienese, before the battle of Montaperti, dedicated their city to the Holy Virgin. They gave to Siena the title of *"Civitas Virginis,"* and the bishop collaborated with the *Sindaco* in the cathedral to offer the city solemnly to the Mother of Christ. No wonder that the Sienese, on the battlefield, saw the mantle of the Madonna floating over their troops. All over Europe Our Lady's churches became the churches for the new commons.

The Madonna was so near that her representation behind the altar now became a rule. Beginning in 1200, the Catholic priest elevated the sacred wafer; moreover in doing so, he turned away from his congregation toward the East. The space into which he looked had to be filled. It could not be filled more naturally than by the picture of the Madonna; and so it was. The three hundred years of Madonna-painting are celebrated today by countless books on mediæval art. The triumphant vision of the new political movement in Italy became the "Madonna in the Landscape."

What distinguishes painting after 1300 from all previous art? Perspective. What distinguishes Occidental art from Chinese, to which it owes perhaps the knowledge of landscape painting? Perspective. The gilded background of Byzantine art is exchanged in Italy for a new perspective. The Madonna, the fixed visual centre of the divine service in the church, is framed by the political vision of the new city-state: the Landscape. The *stilo nuovo* in painting was what books on planning are today, or what written literature was to the national revolution in France: the expression of a *common effort* and a *common faith*. The Mother Church, and the citizen protected by her, were felt to be the centre from which light shone into the darkness of the world. A landscape is the country viewed from within the city. When Petrarch wrote his famous verse, *"Fior, frondi, erbe, ombre, antri, onde, aure soavi,"* the painters had blended cathedral and country. A whole territory lay before the charmed eye, delivered from local tyrants, centralized under the lawful power of purely temporal government. The deeply felt opposition between the new temporal and the old local order may help us to sympathize with the enthusiasm of the people whenever a Madonna was painted in the *stilo nuovo*. Nicolo Pisani is, I think, the first artist to receive special homage from the community for his famous *relievos*, in 1260. About 1300, Duccio of Siena, an eye witness of the battle during which the Virgin had spread out her mantle of protection, painted a Madonna which was received by bishop and clergy, governors and people, and was conveyed to the cathedral amid

the ringing of all the bells. In his verse-subscription to this
painting, the artist treats himself as an equal of the city:

> Mater Sancta Dei Sis Senis causa requiei,
> Sis Duccio vita te quia pinxit ita.

> Holy Mother of God,
> Be thou the cause of peace to the Sienese;
> Be thou life to Duccio because he painted thee thus.

The relationship between the pope and Raphael or Michelangelo exceeds by far the customary relation between princes
and artists in other countries. Even in Venice, the proud pa-
trician city, we read in the Cathedral of St. Mark: "First contemplate carefully and acknowledge the art and labour of
brothers Francesco and Valerio Zuccati, of Venice, then judge."
The painter, being an artisan (artista) himself, and being honoured for painting the symbol of the city's liberty, could represent all the crafts and guilds of his community. He was no
isolated, impressionable genius like the artist of the nineteenth
century. He was the best man in his craft.

THE POVERTY OF ST. FRANCIS.

The independence of the city-state was such a great enterprise that one really wonders how the papacy itself survived
the violent impetus of secular feeling. We have called the
period from 1200 to 1269 the second half of the Papal Revolution. Looking into the heresies in the Italian cities, their religious indifference, their anti-clerical legislation, we wonder
in what sense this Guelphic movement was really religious at
all. Our astonishment increases when we turn to the general
situation of the papacy in this period, and to its greatest defeat,
the failure of the Crusades.

The more Italian the interests were which the pope was
forced to consider, the less real became the idea of the Crusades. It is true, the Crusades still loomed like a spectre on the
horizon of the eighteenth century. The Roman calendar ordained Crusaders' holidays for victory over the unbelievers as
late as 1700. On the eve of the Reformation in 1495, the Ger-

man peasants of the *"Bundschuh"* dreamt of a crusade to end all their miseries. Luther had to explain seriously that "God cares no more for the empty spot called the 'Holy Sepulchre' than for all the cows in Switzerland." Æneas Sylvius, the humanist pope who called himself "Pius" in memory of Virgil's pagan hero, the "Pius Æneas," nevertheless planned a crusade against the Turks as late as 1460. Knowing all this, I still maintain that the Crusades ceased to be the leading idea of the papacy after 1200. In 1204 the so-called Latin Empire was set up in Constantinople by the Fourth Crusade. The violation of the Greek churches in Byzantium shocked everybody who took the word "crusade" to heart. The Children's Crusade, in 1212, ended in a hecatomb of innocent victims. In 1226 the atrocities of a crusade against the Waldenses and Albigenses put public opinion to the test again. The climax was reached when the Emperor Frederick II, though solemnly banned by the pope's excommunication, stood in the Church of the Saviour in Jerusalem and crowned himself by taking the crown from the altar. The Crusades had definitely turned out to be a two-edged weapon. Had it not fallen into the hands of a rebel against the Church, and of people who compromised the pope by unspeakable mistreatment of other Christians? The terrible abuses of the Crusade compelled the papacy to bow before a new and pure vision.

After 1226, when the pope banned the emperor, and when this emperor carried out his Crusade in spite of the papal ban, the pope found moral comfort and spiritual solace by visiting the man whose merit it was to knot together papal and national revolution, the Saint of whom his bishop could say in the words of the 142nd Psalm: "God gives not such a man to every nation." In 1228 the pope visited Assisi and knelt at the deathbed of him whom we may call the last Crusader and the first friar of the Occident.

Francis of Assisi is the coping stone in the vault which was raised by the Guelphic revolution over "the garden of the Empire." He was a rich young man of knight-like education, who dreamt of a crusade. He went to Apulia from where he meant to embark for the Orient. Instead, he returned. The idea of a crusade proved, by his heart's own experience, to be unreal or obsolete. This return from Apulia is the greatest event in his life. It closed, for this deep soul, the door to a past form of expression which still sufficed for many of his contemporaries. His turning about in Apulia was a demand for a new form of Christian life to replace the Crusades. We do not know whether, on his way South, he came in contact with friends of a certain Abbot in Calabria, Joachim di Fiore, but we are sure that he and Joachim di Fiore came to be connected in a providential way. The great historical prophet Joachim di Fiore was the John the Baptist of the *"poverello."* The prophecy of Joachim was a new monastic religion; and its fulfilment was the life of Francis. Joachim turned against the *scholastici* of the twelfth century who, in a period that would last only sixty years before the Johannine "third age" began, were still preoccupied with their school-doctrines. Joachim forecast the end of the existing form of the Church; the Holy Ghost moved on. In his terms, the Virgin Mary had to conceive a new son by the spirit. This son was a new people, with all the power (*potestas*) under heaven that was promised by Daniel. Here the people's sovereignty is proclaimed to be a seed of the spirit. The year 1201 begins a new era in the history of the world's salvation, which was to be awaited with the greatest anxiety. The prophet dated the great change from the ancient form of the Church to a new form, to the epoch between 1201 and 1260.[5] In his philosophy of history, Odilo of Cluny's great conception of All Souls is kept alive, but with the additional idea of revolutionary change. After the era of the Church will come an era of the Holy Spirit. We find here the temptation of a change in era so characteristic of every total revolution. Joachim calls the future "Johannine"; Paul being tied up with Peter in the visible church of Rome, John, the Apostle of charity, is made the patron of the new age of pure

[5] The greatest general of the Franciscan order, Bonaventura, fearing to keep his spirituals from getting out of hand, around the dangerous date 1260, scolded Joachim di Fiore for "irreverence." This slip of the greatest Franciscan thinker marked the end of the inspired period in this revolution.

spirit. Joachim's writings had so great an influence that other books were forged in his name. An *Evangelium æternum* was published, around which a strong party of so-called Spirituals, especially monks, gathered. The pope's spiritual sword was no longer acknowledged by the Spirituals as the climax of spiritual life. Preceding Wycliff, Huss and Luther, they, the Spirituals, taught that the clerical functions of the Church bore the name of spiritual improperly, and at best figuratively; that the gift of the Holy Ghost came long before all clerical ministrations; and that next to the famous seven gifts of the Spirit, the free utterances of inspiration would still precede the hierarchy in spiritual rank. It was a complete revolution of values, taught by the left wing, the Joachimites, and it prepared the way for Luther. A victorious papacy had destroyed Simony, but it had appropriated the silver and gold of the faithful to its own uses. The Church had become wealthy. The Vicar of Christ, wishing to wield both swords, was clearly fighting for earthly riches when he armed his soldiers of the keys for the "Recuperation" of Italy. The second clerical revolution had to cure the disgust created by this spectacle. The Recuperations might have extinguished the flame of allegiance to the visible church if there had not been the new ideal of poverty. Poverty is the great gospel of the mendicant Orders as celibacy had been the price paid by the Gregorians. Poverty meant conjuring up the early life of Christianity in its darkness, abjection and starvation, to balance this late period of sun-like radiancy. The prayer for poverty is the greatest expression of the new program. It contradicts the abuses at the Holy See. Like the *Dies Iræ,* or like Dante, this prayer connects us forever with the clerical era of man's revolutions on earth. Again and again poets have entered into the beauty of this prayer, most recently the German poet, Rainer Maria Rilke. But it is not beauty alone, it is political power, it is a new life which surrounds us in these terse and stringent lines: "Poverty was in thy crib, and like a faithful squire she kept herself armed in the great combat that thou didst wage for our redemption. During thy passion she alone did not forsake thee. Mary thy mother stopped at the foot of the cross, but *poverty mounted it* and clasped thee in her embrace unto the end; and when thou wast dying of thirst, like a watchful spouse she prepared for thee the gall. Thou didst expire in the ardour of her embraces, nor did she leave thee when dead, O Lord Jesus, for she allowed not thy body to rest elsewhere than in a borrowed grave, O poorest Jesus, the grace I beg of thee is to bestow on me the treasure of the highest poverty. Grant that the distinctive mark of our Order may be never to possess anything as its own under the sun, for the glory of thy name, and to have no other patrimony than begging."

Yet, this poverty could have remained a negative attitude, in opposition to papacy and clergy. In St. Francis the political vision of Joachim found one who realized and embodied the new era, and yet did not condemn the past.

St. Francis dared to sanctify the temporal. The days of his life were called *"Fioretti,"* a wonderful illustration of the special emphasis laid by his contemporaries upon the temporal; for every one of his days was considered as modest, as beautiful, and as unstable as a flower. His poverty and his principle of mendicancy enabled his followers to lead a new form of life, far away from the manor, in the cities, with the townspeople. Francis did not retire from the world into a monastery and devote himself to agriculture and cattle-breeding. The Franciscans lived in the city. The new world of stone cities, built by free men, and the new horsepower, now was sanctified.

Yet Francis kept his filial devotion to the Church, which alone could make his experience of Christ's life on earth a valid experience for all Christianity. Toward the end of his life he received the five stigmata of the Crucified Himself. Hands and feet showed the traces of the wounds caused by the nails of the Cross. The age of the Spirit was clearly at hand. By spiritual identification, the *poverello* relived the experiences of the Saviour Himself. The impression which the friars made was tremendous. In 1300 there seem to have been 200,000 friars, organized in two orders, Dominicans and Franciscans, their existence no longer debatable. *Nobody* doubted that he should join one of the two, the only possible question being, Which? These friars covered Italy with a network of arbitration and peacemaking. The cities, no longer recognizing any superior, were faced by permanent feuds with neighbouring towns. Friars would travel from city to city, invoke Our Lady, and command peace. In 1233, for example, the pope sent one of the friars, John of Vicenza, to Tuscany for the reconciliation of Siena and Florence. John thought it more important to work in the Marchionate of Treviso. All the cities of Lombardy, Venetia, and Romagne were represented on the day of his "Great Devotion" in Verona.

Simultaneously, the people in Parma started the "great Alleluia." Ave Maria was sung with a three-fold Alleluia. The whole population marched in procession. The sparks of this general fraternizing in Parma reached Bologna and Modena. In 1260, the year forecast by Joachim as the beginning of the Great Johannine form of life, had arrived. No wonder that this year saw the outbreak of the greatest movement of the Franciscan type. "The people," wrote a chronicler, "seemed to fear a 'Visitation of God,' " because all Italy was visited by misery, feuds and crimes. Suddenly in Perugia, a hermit raised his voice. The inhabitants marched, headed by bishop and clergy, in a long train as far as the next city. In spite of winter's cold, all were naked to the belt and scourged themselves till the blood came. From church to church they marched. Peace, charity, *misericordia,* were the words they uttered with signs.

At first they are ridiculed. But soon the whole neighbouring city was infected. All threw off their coats and scourged themselves. All confessed their sins and made peace. From Perugia to Rome, in Tuscany and in Liguria, in all of Lombardy, one city visited the other, and for the period of a month or two all Italy was at peace. The exiled could go home. The prisons were opened. The political problem was always the same: peace in an archipelago of independent cities. And the begging monks, living not on the country, but with the citizens, were the organs of this peace.

Modern Europeans know of flagellantism only vaguely from its mechanical revival in the fourteenth century. During the Babylonian captivity of the Church, when the popes were far from Rome, Italy and the papacy had an experience similar to the French sufferings under Napoleon III. In every respect, the Second Empire in France was the reverse of the first, and yet it lived by imitating the slogans of the first. In the same way, the formulas of Francis and the Spirituals were repeated between 1305 and 1377. The Black Death in 1348, in Boccaccio's day, led to a new outbreak of flagellantism.

Perhaps the Flagellants of the Ducento expressed the moral need which was felt after the violent destruction of feudalism in Italy. Half a million people or more had shaken off the manorial servitude of local seigniors and had begun to breathe the free air of the cities. It is not easy for a class to keep its balance after the sudden breakdown of immemorial allegiances. Flagellantism replaced, perhaps, the rigid discipline in the manors by a voluntary self-chastisement.

We turn once more to the great healer of the evils of the Ducento, Francis of Assisi. To the average historian, Francis is simply a Saint of the Church. The Guelphic centuries seem to continue the line of their predecessors. Then "modern" times would begin with Petrarch. Let me cite the example of a leading scholar, Mr. Vossler. In his book on Mediæval Culture, he deals exactly with the Guelphic period, the time of Francis of Assisi and Dante, and he says that the famous Sun Hymn of St. Francis is, in general, a repetition of the 148th Psalm. Now I am the last to disparage the Psalm. And at the first reading, it may seem that the Psalm, like the Hymn of St. Francis, seeks the glory of God in Nature.

"Praise ye the Lord, from the Heavens, praise Him in the heights.
Praise ye Him, sun and moon, praise Him all ye stars of light.
Praise Him, ye heavens of heavens, and ye waters that be above the heavens. Let them praise the name of the Lord: for He commanded and they were created.
Praise the Lord from the earth, ye dragons, and all deeps;
Fire and hail; snow and vapours, stormy wind fulfilling His word;
Mountains and all hills; fruitful trees and all cedars."

I pause: could we wish more than to go on in endless repetition of this praise?

But the terrible price paid by the chosen people for this exaltation of the Lord was the prohibition of any graven image or any likeness of anything that is in heaven above or that is in the earth beneath. The Jews, having no home on this earth, teach the other nations not to adore created things, not to bow before any secular order.

If Francis of Assisi in the thirteenth century transforms the 148th Psalm, it is to redeem the secular order. What the Jews have anticipated, the Christians are allowed to carry out, to put into action, nay, to transform into temporal and secular forms. To understand St. Francis' hymn, one must see the 148th Psalm against the background of the secular state. Cluny still detested the temporal: *"Solvet sæculum in favilla,"* the secular will be brought to ashes. We have seen that between 1200 and 1500 the secular is pardoned, rediscovered, restored; and the last aim of this chapter is to show the difference between the original text of the 148th Psalm and its projection into the "Secular," which our modern civilization so takes for granted today.

Man is a flower, the world the Garden in which he is planted; this was St. Francis' great experience. He discovered a new world, within the old world of monasteries, emperors and manors. All these powers avoided the external world, feared nature, were frightened night and day by demons and wicked spirits. In his vision of Christ, Francis himself feels that Jesus' heart was with all creation, that He came not to redeem mankind only, but the whole cosmos. The heart of man moves toward creation. For the first time the walls of a house were felt to be hostile to the reconciliation of man and nature. Francis made creation his family. He praised the glory of the Lord in His creation. But he did not, like the Psalmist, look up to the Lord after having looked down at His creatures. He kept his eyes on the soil. In this his attitude differed from that of the Hebrew psalter.

Mr. Vossler says: "There is not much difference between the 148th Psalm and the Hymn of St. Francis." We cannot ignore our discoveries about the landscape, which in the German *"Landschaft"* is not simply an esthetic term, but also means a

political representation of the country. This has left more than
a trace in the hymn of the *poverello*. Does it not make a great
difference to say Thou and Thee to God's creatures, to live
intimately with the land, to be a member, one flesh and blood,
with the land?

St. Francis' hymn describes his discovery of physical creation. When one reads, one understands why it makes an epoch,
why Raphael and all the painters of the Renaissance are the
fulfilment of thirteenth-century Spiritualism. One understands
that there is one stream of life running through the whole
period. Henry Thode was right when he said that the Italian
Renaissance began with St. Francis. The political and religious
life between 1200 and 1500 is a unit, preceded by the Crusades
and followed by the Reformation. Here is the Hymn of
St. Francis:

"Most High, Omnipotent, good Lord, thine is the praise, the glory
    and every benediction;
To thee alone, Most High, these do belong, and no man is worthy
    to name thee.
Praised be thou, my Lord, with all thy creatures, especially my
    Lord Brother,
Sun, that dawns and lightens us; and he, beautiful and radiant
    with great splendour, signifies thee, Most High.
Be praised, my Lord, for Sister Moon and the Stars, that thou hast
    made bright and precious and beautiful.
Be praised, my Lord, for Brother Wind and for the air and the
    cloud, and the clear sky, and for all weathers through which
    thou givest sustenance to thy creatures.
Be praised, my Lord, for Sister Water, that is very useful and
    humble and precious and chaste.
Be praised, my Lord, for Brother Fire, through whom thou dost
    illumine the night, and comely is he and glad and bold and
    strong.
Be praised, my Lord, for Sister, our Mother Earth, that doth cher-
    ish and keep us and produces various fruits with coloured
    flowers and the grass.
Sister Our Mother Earth who cherishes us,
    Our Brother Fire, who is glad and bold
    Our Sister Water who is chaste. . . ."

This is final. For "Sister, our Mother Earth" is the sublime paradox of this faith. It preserves the full pagan value of "Mother Earth" within the Christian "Sisterhood." The term "Middle Ages" is a negative political challenge thrown out by the German Reformers; Guelphic Franciscan Italy is the positive creation of a human heart, which made men brothers and sisters of the creatures around them, which re-clothed itself in a sweet, new style under the protection of the Lord and his Church. In the dialectic of the clerical revolutions, man turned from the judge to the judge's mother and extorted from her the solution that the judge seemed to withhold.[6]

[6] This is no figure of speech. *Extorting* Mary's grace is a contemporary expression, stated by the Jesuit Verley, Vol. 125 of the *Études par les pères de la Compagnie de Jésus,* pp. 161 *ff.* (1910). And Abailard sang:

> "To the Judge's mother fly,
> Who from the Judge's wrath do fly.
> To pray for them she is compelled,
> Man's mother becoming when in bail he is held."

CHAPTER TWELVE

Polybius Once More: Our Economic Future

EUROPEAN THOUGHT IN 1900 WAS ACCUSTOMED TO DATE THE modern era from the days of Cola di Rienzi in 1347 and the *Decamerone* of Boccaccio. Mr. Friedell's history of modern civilization [1] begins with this period. Modern liberals start at this epoch with as good reason as if someone began the history of the French Revolution with Napoleon III! Certain modern terms that came into use in the fourteenth century attracted the attention of people who had already decided that the Middle Ages were uninteresting or "dark."

However, by the use of this date things which are related to each other like original and caricature are separated by force. The curve of the Guelphic revolution is distorted. Alleluia and flagellation were great realities in the Ducento; they were shallow memories of the past in the days of Boccaccio.

Let us fix the periods of the Papal Revolution so clearly that superficial enlightenment can no longer divorce what belongs together.

The dialogue between the revolutions is as real in the clerical revolutions as in those investigated by Marxians. It need not be said that this fact proves nothing for the economic causation of any of these revolutions. It proves that revolutions are undertaken, in our era, in the face of mankind, in an open dialogue, and are carried on on a wave-length of several centuries. The exaggeration of the particular idea of the Last Judgment inevitably led to the reaction in which another side

[1] Egon Friedell, *Cultural History of Modern Civilization*, New York, Knopf, 1930-32.

of the ecclesiastical tradition was put in the centre of the map.

The Gregorian and the Guelphic revolution were like a spiritual and an earthly expression of the same effort. Gregory and Innocent III, the dictating monk and the deliberating diplomatist, set out, one crying loudly, the other whispering, toward one and the same goal. The deliverance of the Holy Sepulchre opened the door to liberty for the Gregorians, whereas the two Innocents (III and IV) cared only for the deliverance of Italy. Yet they seem to be two halves of one and the same majestic process. The clergy of Christendom changed all the ways of life in the Occident. If the national revolutions of modern times led to a regeneration of the peoples, the clerical revolutions in the time of the Crusades regenerate the face of "Our Sister, our Mother Earth" with no less thoroughness. And as they aroused all the great passions of humanity, it is only natural that we should find, in the course of the clerical revolutions, the same swings of the pendulum which we observed in the French or English volcanic eruptions.

Both the Gregorian and the Guelphic revolution pass through a period of frivolous arrogance and presumption:

1122 to 1147
1269 to 1302

The *"Enrichissez-vous"* of Louis Philippe is a mild expression compared to the presumption of the curialists in these two periods. In the first the emperor was treated as the pope's vassal. An impertinent picture in Rome kept alive the humiliation of this serfdom. But scandals in Rome brought the papacy near to the abyss; and finally, the enraged Romans drove out the pope, who fled to foreign countries. The same carelessness prevailed after the Guelphs' victory over the Ghibellines a hundred and fifty years later. After the death of Urban IV, the cardinals delayed the Conclave for two and a half years. We mentioned before how bewildered the people were at this outcome, after seventy years of suffering for the sake of the papacy. Some years later, when the pope had to pass through a city which was under his interdict, the gossip went that he lifted the ban on entering the town, and renewed it when leaving! The crowning expression of this era of presumption was the famous bull, *"Unam Sanctam,"* of Boniface VIII, promulgated in 1302. In a time when every prince and layman was nauseated by the insolence of the clergy, this pope re-emphasized his apocalyptic claim to the control of all secular power. He had the two-headed eagle of the empire stitched on his robes.

One cannot avoid the impression that the defeat of the Holy See was conjured up by this pope's arrogant decree. He was made a prisoner by French knights, and the king of France debased the papacy's moral dignity by the trial of the Templars. Papacy was stripped of its crusading organization; the Order of the Knights Templar, founded to protect the Holy Sepulchre and Christian pilgrims, was persecuted, disavowed and annihilated by the French kings. These auxiliaries of the first Papal Revolution against the apostolic dignity of the emperor, had nowhere been stronger than in those regions in which the popes of the struggle for investiture, had taken refuge from the empire. It was in France, therefore, that the institution of Crusading Knighthood had become most burdensome and troublesome. Now, the *auto da fé* of the Templars in 1314 showed how far the basis of papal liberty had shifted from the emancipated warriors of the Crusades to the territorial devices of the Guelphs in Italy. But the sway of counter-attacks even forced the popes out of their Italian domain and exiled them for seventy years to Southern France, to Avignon.

For three quarters of a century, Italy, the garden of the empire, lived without the presence of the pope to whom she owed the sovereignty of the cities. The Babylonian exile at Avignon (1309-1377), with its seventy years, is of equal length with the time of exaltation (1200-1269). The exile is that period of humiliation well-known to us from other revolutions. The time-span of seventy years is longer than in any other case. Even the first clerical revolution, the Gregorian, had only about fifty years of exaltation and fifty of humiliation.

THE CLERICAL REVOLUTIONS CORRESPOND TO
EACH OTHER IN THE FOLLOWING WAY:

	GREGORIAN	GUELPHIC
Point of departure	1046	1161
Exaltation	1075-1122	1200-1269
Humiliation	1147-1198	1309-1377

But the period of humiliation is not the last word in the course of a revolution. For the Italian cities and the Roman Church there is a golden period beginning in the middle of the fifteenth century. The so-called "Renaissance" is like a golden age of fulfilment.

The German nation has something similar long after its humiliation in the Thirty Years' War—in the peaceful times between 1763-1805. The classical period of German music and literature, with Goethe, Mozart, Beethoven, Schiller, Klopstock, Lessing, Herder, Kant, can easily be compared with the classical period of Italian art, when Leonardo, Raphael, Lorenzo de' Medici, Michelangelo, were alive, when the Vatican Library and the Singing Schools of the Sistina were founded, and when the pope acted as *arbiter mundi* in the quarrels over the newly discovered American world.

For English civilization, the Victorian Age offers a similar aspect of achievement and satisfaction between the Corn Laws and the Boer War (1846-1900).

The golden age of German princely particularism ended suddenly with the Napoleonic invasion. The door of Italy's paradisaic age was banged by the French invasion in 1498.

	ITALY	GERMANY	ENGLAND
Exaltation ...	1075-1122	1200-1269	1517-1555	1641-1688
Humiliation..	1147-1198	1309-1377	1618-1648 (54)	1776-1815
Golden Age..		1450-1498	1763-1805	1846-1900

The famous Italian "Renaissance" has little to do with the conquest of Constantinople in 1453. The Renaissance is the legitimate outcome of a five-centuries-long effort.[2] Its painters

[2] For the anti-Protestant bias in the modern use of the term see part III, chap. 16.

and architects and poets translate the great inspirations of Gregory and Francis of Assisi into secular garb and classical forms. But the landscapes of Raphael's Madonnas, and the background of the Cæsaric Judge in Michelangelo's "Last Judgment," are translations into humanistic terms of the whole-hearted effort of more religious centuries. The fashion, ay, the idolatry, of the Renaissance in our day should not blind us to the fact that the Renaissance was a sunset. The cynical humanists of the Quattrocento spoke the last word, not the first. They dissolved, they could not construct. They did for Scholasticism what Goethe did for the Reformation: they secularized its mysteries. By Renaissance art, the Guelphic revolution was made accessible to the agnostic and the snob, and to the educated man of modern Europe.

Italy's contribution to mankind is immense. Her glories were compressed into the masterpieces of fifty years; these kept Europeans and Americans under her charm for another four hundred. Italy very early became the Holy Sepulchre for the European traveller.

But the periods of the clergy's revolutions should be considered under another aspect, also. For the rest of Europe, the Renaissance was no golden age. Italy's advantage was the world's misfortune. The fifteenth century is a terrible, unhappy, dark, and cruel period. The orgies of the Italian princes (Borgia!), and the sufferings of all the European nations, throw a lasting shadow over all its amenities in art and literature. The fifteenth century was a time of dissolution, of disappointment, of wildest reactionism. The fifteenth century offers, in some respects, the key to our own present situation: it was a premature time, with many pressing problems, and nothing prepared to solve them.

For the purposes of a comparison, we must go into the constitutional evolution of the Church; for, after all, this evolution had a world-wide bearing, and made every member of Christendom suffer.

The Schism of 1378 which ended the exile in Avignon aroused all the critics of aristocratic government in the Church. Not only had the cardinals become omnipotent, as they often ruled for years without electing any pope, but throughout the Church the chapters dominated and overruled the bishops and abbots. The aristocratic principle was now bitterly criticized by the friars who detested the snobbish life of the upper 10,000. The insecure, the poor, and the intellectual groups in the Church united for the attack. After 1377, the left wing of the Franciscan Movement united with the responsible teachers of theology when two and more popes were struggling simultaneously for recognition. The Professors of Paris and all the Doctors of Christendom, the Intelligentsia of the Church, easily found support among their secular princes and lords. Between 1377 and 1460 the Church would not have survived the disgust, hate and envy of the laity, without a definite attempt by the theologians to broaden its foundations and to base its constitution on a clerical democracy. Democracy of the clergy was no luxury to the great Gerson of Paris or to Nicolaus Cusanus. It was the only way to save any authority for the clergy of Europe. St. Peter had been rehabilitated in 1075 by borrowing from St. Paul the principle of universality in space. This centralization had enabled the popes to dethrone the emperor. After 1200 the Johannine church of the Spirituals, forecast by Joachim di Fiore and embodied in Francis of Assisi, had again supported St. Peter's authority. Now, after another one hundred and fifty years, the nations organized themselves with the purpose of regenerating the Church. The years 1378 to 1449 might well be labelled: The nations support St. Peter. The nations were organized at the great democratic councils of Pisa (1409), Constance (1414-18), and Basel (1431-49). The University of Paris led the French nation, while the greatest nation, the German, embraced six different kingdoms. Spain and England were represented also. Scheduled parliaments of the whole Church, in the form of councils, were demanded for thirty years in advance, and when they finally met, expectation ran high. The national Doctors were full of the pride which every young class shows in its first political action. They were much more eager than the popes or cardinals not to expose themselves to any charge of heresy, or even indifference in matters of orthodoxy; and this led to their defeat. They plunged the world into the disastrous wars against the Hussites.

The mistakes in the trial of Huss at Constance in 1415 can be explained by the jealous desire of the young parliamentary democracy to equal the Roman curialists. The councils, by their inexperienced eagerness, unchained the violent rebellion of the Hussites: for, like all democracies, the councils were weak in their foreign policy. What they really wished was to fight their "King": they turned against the pope. Frequent universal councils, at least one every five years, had to be granted by the popes; for a continent of such size, and without modern transportation, a very Utopia of parliamentary power. The greatest victory was the formal subjection of the popes to the council's authority in 1432: here the nations, the five clerical bodies of the universal Church, declared themselves to be sovereign. Thus princes and doctors tried to carry out the Reformation within the Church one hundred years before they left its walls.

But the clerical democracy of the councils was not able to stop the Hussites, who rejected all organized clergy. The Hussites were the Nihilists of the time. Like those Marxists who cannot bear to see a defective "state" at work, and wish to abolish all government, the Hussites not only disapproved of the Church, but concluded that it was better to have no visible church whatever.

Between papacy and Hussites, the nations showed no united front. It was easy for the popes to divide the national bodies and to satisfy each nation by special concessions. In 1449 the last council was dissolved. The popes after 1450 began to live in Rome permanently, and to rebuild their residence with great care and foresight.

The world outside Italy was deeply disappointed. Everything seemed to have been in vain. The outraged laity scorned the whole clergy. Democracy was despised as it is today. The canonists seemed nothing but politicians of the worst type. Cynicism prevailed, the popes were taunted with their forged Donation of Constantine, monks and priests with their dissipation, canonists and doctors with their graft and their vexatious practices.

The new secular needs brought forward new kinds of men, who tried to satisfy them by a queer mixture of holiness and political leadership. Lack of civilized state government is the proper explanation of characters like Joan of Arc, Savonarola, the Swiss prophet Nicolaus von der Flue. Half saints, half politicians, they tried to bridge the gulf between the old priestly organization and the political one of modern times. The fifteenth century is a time of endless travail.

Hitler is very much a political "saint," in the peculiar sense of the fifteenth century. He especially resembles Giovanni Capistrano, the Crusader against the Turks, later canonized as "*apostolus Europæ*," an anti-Semitic leader who had a tremendous following between 1445 and 1455. Capistrano fought the Hussites, as Hitler fights Communism; he introduced a new symbol, namely, the rays of the sun surrounding the name I H S, appalling to good Christians then. He and his like delayed the Reformation for another fifty years by defending the dictatorship of a ruthless papacy. The European masses, disillusioned by the democratic rule of the universal councils, and frightened by the Bolshevik experiments in Bohemia, listened to his Italian speeches with complete idolatry. In these mass meetings after four or five hours of unswerving attention to a speaker of whose words they could not understand a syllable, when the interpreter began to translate it into the native idiom, the crowd would disperse immediately. Capistrano scorned the doctors of democratic councils, burned the Jews, attacked the Turks, the Hussites, intimidated the Humanists, the princes. He preached the restoration of the papacy in the intolerable form which this institution took on between 1450 and 1517.

A venerable old institution it was, but its own members and defenders no longer believed in it. The Pontificate of Æneas Sylvio Piccolomini as Pius II (1458-1464), with its mingling of pagan and Christian symbols, is an example of the sterile compromise concluded by such a humanist. Old Virgil had spoken of his Trojan hero as "Pius Æneas." The Sienese

Æneas chose Pius as his new name on account of this Virgilian phrase. Any institution in its senility goes back to a kind of primitive restoration; all the detail and the refinement of subtle forms are given up. The papal government of 1460 was much more brutal and primitive than that of Gregory, Innocent, or Boniface had been. It was an undisguised dictatorship that met with disgust, suspicion, rebellion and contempt inside and outside.

The so-called Renaissance was, for the world at large, a desperate period of delay. From 1460 to 1517 the world was through with its mediæval constitution; yet the Bolshevik attempt of the Hussites, abolishing the visible church without any substitute, clearly offered nothing acceptable to the countries which suffered. The negative impression made by the radical destroyers of the visible church threw the nations once more into the arms of an obsolete form of government. The Middle Ages culminated through the efforts of the then Fascists, like Capistrano, in dictatorship. In 1460 the pope promulgated the notorious bull *"Execrabilis,"* which forbade appeals to any synod of the Church. Its violent language seems to be taken from modern anti-democrats. From the *Dictatus papæ* in 1075, through the cardinals' Consistory of Innocent III in 1200 and the democratic claims of the councils between 1377 and 1449; to this bull *"Execrabilis"* of Pius II, the rotation of government is unmistakable.

Monarchy in the visible church 1075-1200
Aristocracy 1200-1377
Democracy 1377-1460
Dictatorship . . . . 1460-1517 [3]

It is true, these changes did not shake the older groundwork of the Christian Church. The papacy of 1075 was a limited enterprise. It did not build up a new Christianity. It only made the pope the trustee of every monk and clergyman in Europe, abolished the unique office of the emperor inside the Church, and exalted the pope, the successor of St. Peter, into the Vicar of the world's Last Judge. These three acts of external defence

[3] For the present-day papacy, compare pp. 244, 604, 608.

were necessary to the internal revival of the Church. They enabled a world of tribes and clans to advance from superficial baptism *en bloc* to the virtual conversion of all and everybody. However, the papacy had to use political means to make this process of regeneration visible.

The deliberate campaign to make conspicuous the mysteries of the old Church was based on secular, centralized methods of government. From 1075 to 1517 human and natural law came to make up the bulk of Canon Law. The *Ius Divinum*, the divine forms of life of the first thousand years, remained the foundation; but the superstructure was completely political and rational.

This visible, unmystic part of the Church could no longer lead a timeless existence in worship and adoration and holiness. It became a body politic, entering the life of the world and following the course of the world. No wonder that this part of Christianity behaved like any great political form. It underwent the Polybian rotation of government. In spite of its unchanged name, the rulership of the Church was monarchical in 1100, aristocratic in 1300, democratic in 1430 and virtually a dictatorship after 1460.

The interesting question is how the equilibrium between change and continuity was preserved. A special study will have to be made of this equilibrium by students of political science who feel that the rotation of government must now be seriously investigated. For our purpose, it suffices that rotation of government occurs twice in the history of Europe, once for the government of the Church, between 1075 and 1517, and again for the national governments between 1517 and our day. Both times it is by no means a mere stumbling from change to change. The Church of the Crusades and the nations of modern times both escaped the hopelessness of the circle which had opened before the eyes of ancient thinkers. In the Christian world no form, so to speak, was completely forgotten or lost. Yet political forms are mortal forms. Monarchy, aristocracy, democracy, dictatorship, are parts of our existence which belong to the passing world. They wear out in their very application. They cannot survive for an unlimited time. One must be replaced by the next, and the order of succession between the four forms seems unalterable. The following table gives evidence of an interplay between eternity and temporality, between timeless and passing order in the last millennium.

CHRISTIAN CIVILIZATION

	PAPAL ORGANIZATION OF THE CHRISTIAN CLERGY	NATIONAL ORGANIZATION OF THE CHRISTIAN PEOPLES
Main emphasis on the monarchical side	1075-1200	1517-1648
Main emphasis on the aristocratic side	1200-1377	1640-1789
Main emphasis on the democratic side	1377-1460	1789-1917
Dictatorship, Fascism, etc. ..	1460-1517	1917 ....

Church and State in Christendom have delved deeply into reality and the nature of things. I do not think that it diminishes their new dignity to see them in their struggle for existence. In 1929, when the pope abandoned his full claim to a papal state and was satisfied by a reminiscence of the Guelphic revolution in the form of his *Città del Vaticano,* he showed how the fruits of the past are gathered in at the beginning of a new period. For I see no reason why the clerical and national organization of the world should be the only two periods of our civilization.

An economic organization of the world will probably be the problem of the future, and it will demand ample time for its fulfilment. The comparison between the two periods of rotation of government suggests why, for the moment, the world is unable to shift immediately from its national to an economic organization. When the Church had gone through the trials of Hussitism and conciliarism, the new national forms of life, in Germany, France, Spain, England, etc., found their warmest advocates in the enlightened clergy of the Church. In the fifteenth century the wisest reformers were clerics. But in spite of their wisdom, clerics could not build up the secular government of modern times. Their clerical bondage stood in

EXCESSES OF PILGRIMAGE, SIXTEENTH CENTURY
(Inserts: Centenary Medal in memory of Huss.)

their way. Being honest bishops or theologians or monks, they could not face the destruction of their own political and social existence. Their programme remained sterile because it could not propose as its first paragraph the exclusion of priesthood from matters of State.

Our statesmen since the World War are to a large extent aware of their shortcomings. National policy prevents economic recovery, and they know it. National interests have closed the world market. However, a statesman is paid by his own nation. The more disinterested and the more honest a patriot he is, the less effective will all his wisdom be. MacDonald, Briand, Wilson, had to remain national statesmen in spite of their deeper insight. Mussolini, Hitler, De Valera, draw the conclusion that nothing but national statesmanship is needed. They are wrong. State sovereignty is doomed. Yet it cannot be sacrificed until some other road is open.

In 1460, no staff of civilians existed to inherit the political responsibilities of the clergy. In 1938, no economic staff exists to inherit the social responsibilities of the politicians. Bankers, Bolsheviks and trade unions alike seem utterly unqualified for such a task. For the gigantic task of an economic organization of the world, the effort to produce a technical staff must be carried on for at least another fifty years. Statesmen will balk at many of the steps which might lead to training this staff. Dictators will crush all such anti-national attempts. But, I am afraid, the democratic Isolationists will persecute them with no less conviction. Neither the purity of heart nor the sincerity of mind needed for such a work can be found in a sceptical and cynical post-War world of crisis and disintegration.

Only those who prove immune against the germs of this disintegration, against Fascism, Communism, Humanism, Racism, etc., will be fit to undertake the final task. But a glance into the past may encourage them. There is really no hurry.

The modern economic stand-still has a striking parallel in the fifteenth century. After 1400 no city increased in size; and the economy of the city-state of those times corresponds to the national economy of today. The whole Occident was tortured by disappointment and cynicism. Racism celebrated its orgies then as today. Yet the life of humanity was not suffocated. In a completely new way, man was enabled to renew the natural rotation of political life for another four or five hundred years. The cynical humanists of the Renaissance did not open the new way. They extirpated their own faith and hated any belief. More courageous souls discovered the new approach to life by a new positive faith. If this statement encourages one young reader to smile at the facile talk of busy intellectuals, and to think in time-spans worthy of man's nature, I will gladly suffer the hatred of the new sceptic.

CHAPTER THIRTEEN

The Survival of Austria-Hungary

THE MEMORABLE FEATURES OF EUROPEAN CIVILIZATION IN ITS
ecclesiastical period were all based on permanent elements in
human nature: on the weariness and resignation represented
by the monks of Cluny, on the seniority of a spiritual overlord, the pope, and on the maternal care of "Mother Church"
and her wandering friars. One after the other, these elements
prevailed because they offered light and warmth in the struggle
against disintegration. These three remedies served their purpose well, and seemed therefore to be precious European traditions. The revolutionary leaders in each phase were men of
a monastic type: Odilo of Cluny, Hildebrand, St. Francis of
Assisi. With the Reformation, a secular type replaced the
monkish. Luther, the prophet of the secular state, left his
monastery and married a nun. His remedy was paternalism—
paternalism in the state and in the family. Luther was succeeded by a line of military leaders. The revolutions of more
modern times were led by men like Cromwell, George Washington, Napoleon, and Lenin—all of them descendants of country proprietors. Monks and country gentlemen represent the
two halves of the European millennium of revolutions. Different as the two types are, they nevertheless ought to be
regarded as carriers of the same mission. Furthermore, the secular leaders were not able to destroy the achievements of their
spiritual predecessors; they could do no more than exploit
another part of human nature, hitherto neglected. That explains why the monkish type was not simply wiped out by the
Reformation. And so we need not wonder that Catholicism,

papacy, monasticism, are still among us, even though their principles were attacked by the four modern revolutions.

The papacy, in its stronghold of self-chosen absolutism, donned the armour of a merely secular policy when Julius II, as head of the papal state, took it upon himself to act the part of a second Cæsar. The Counter-Reformation surrounded the purified Church with an army of defenders, the Jesuits. For four centuries the Church developed its absolutism and centralism. It is true that the French Revolution seemed to usher in its final decline. The army of the papacy, the order of the Jesuits, was disbanded, and the pope himself made a prisoner of Napoleon.

But the nineteenth century saw another revival of Catholicism. Never before had the Catholic Church paid so much obedience to the Apostolic See. The movement of Solesmes united all the churches of the Catholic world by introducing the Roman mass and liturgy into every diocese. Centralization in cult and worship reached a climax. Today bishops and priests have become what they seemed to be slated for under Gregory VII, when Archbishop Liemar groaned, "The bishops are becoming the pope's stewards and bailiffs." The process of centralization is pervading the whole structure of the Roman Church, throttling the initiative of its branches, desiccating the soil wherever an unconscious growth might seem possible. Through the incessant attacks of secularism, the spiritual Church of Scholasticism was forced into a straitjacket of vigilant self-defence. In an age of reason and naturalism, the Church surrounded itself with a rational and highly sceptical system of thought—the Jesuit literature—and with the most natural weapon of government: power. Today the Catholic Church appears in the rôle of a centralized organization, a natural power of the highest efficiency, because it lives in a world which believes in nothing but reason, nature, organization and power.

The different steps by which the Roman Church adapted itself to a changing environment are all quite logical. Yet they have only a secondary interest for the bionomics of European civilization, because they are self-evident reactions of an organism struggling for survival. They do not surprise us by striking out along new paths, as in the era of complete regeneration of the Church. Thus they add little to our knowledge of human nature; whereas Odilo of Cluny, Gregory VII, and St. Francis of Assisi conquered realms in our own life which would not exist but for their having championed them. From pioneering, the energies of the Church have turned to apologetics. At no period in its history was the clergy simpler, more ethical, more orthodox, more correct, more disciplined than now. This means that the purposes of the past have been accomplished. That accomplishment means a great deal: it brings the world nearer to its end. But it cannot be creative, because it has to be loyal to foregone conclusions. The Church is no longer politically creative in the way it was during its Renovation, when it acted as a driving and revolutionizing force. It now carefully follows the movements of the world.

To give one important example: When the maternalism of the Guelphic centuries was challenged by Luther's rugged paternalism, that is, when the Reformation began, the Church met the attack on St. Mary and the Mother Church by concentrating on the cult of St. Joseph, the foster-father of Jesus. At the beginning of the sixteenth century St. Joseph's day, the nineteenth of March, was emphasized, fraternities in his honour grew numerous, and the limiting concept of Joseph's sublimated fatherhood was the well-chosen weapon of the Church against the world's secular paternalism. In 1500, the new emphasis on the cult of Joseph was an intelligent reaction, but it was inevitably more a symbol than a real force.

In her progress through two thousand years the Church generally moves by infinitely small steps. The shift from St. Mary to St. Joseph was accomplished with a minimum of discontinuity; yet it is attested by Catholic historians themselves. The coincidence of this gradual shift with the rising paternalism of the Reformation is a precious argument for the deep wisdom by which the different stages of European civilization are interconnected. The forces which bring on each constellation in the political sky logically exclude each other like two opposite principles—in our example, maternalism and paternalism. Logically they are like water and fire, purely hostile elements. Yet the sequence represented by the different revolutions turns out to be necessary and complete. The exhaustion of one phase or form is proved not only by the outbreak of a violent revolution, but by the concessions which the leading power of the older phase itself instinctively makes to the next period—as in our case of St. Joseph.

During the last four centuries the Roman Church has been put on the defensive against a universal secularism. Yet the hundreds of millions who lived under its crosier are still a reality. It should not surprise us to find that this survival of a Catholic laity long ago acquired a political form of its own to symbolize its existence and *raison d'être*. The Catholic laity kept its representation in modern Europe. Up to the World War, one great European power survived which united the heritage of imperial and papal and Guelphic centuries in one comprehensive structure. Here the old empire of St. Henry and the Apostolic realm of Otto the Great and St. Stephen of Hungary survived.

Austria-Hungary was an astonishing combination of the entire list of elements that made up European civilization. This *"Völkermonarchie,"* this "international nation," was a riddle by the very fact of its existence. Yet it existed, against all logic and reason.

Friedrich Schlegel (1772-1829), the inspiring genius of nineteenth-century Romanticism, tried to express the collective character of Austrian civilization by founding a magazine in Vienna under the title *Concordia:* the name hinted at the time of unbroken harmony between spiritual and temporal power. The conversion of the Hanoverian Schlegel into an Austrian loyalist may help us to explain Austria's achievement for humanity. Friedrich Schlegel stood all his life for totality. He knew that thought laid claim to completeness, that in thinking a man should try to act as a representative of his species, not of his individual, subjective interests. True reason, therefore, by its own nature, must be universal. To think along party lines may be good politics, or piety, or loyalty, or chivalry; it cannot be thought in its purest form, which means that he who thinks feels himself responsible for the very existence of truth among the other powers of this world, who concern themselves with adapting thought to thoughtless ends.

By this responsible attitude, Schlegel, in a period of factional and national tendencies, preserved the universality of scholarship. He was the founder of the European school which deserves most of the credit for the scientific successes of the nineteenth century. He drew a clear line between the natural and the social sciences. He foresaw our own attempt to deal with the continuous process of creation in mankind itself. He distinguished clearly between a description of the permanent properties of man and a science that would interpret man's *qualitative variations*, as species and as specimen, through the course of history. Thereby he defined the human soul and character as the irreplaceable object of scientific history. Schlegel knew that the acquisition of new qualities could alter man himself, that saltations and mutations occurred. As a *thinker* he could not but be comprehensive; although a political fighter must think partially, Schlegel, without denying the relative claims of the French Revolution, was concerned with the representation of all the features of civilized man.

By birth he was a Protestant from Northern Germany; under the influence of the revolutionary emancipation of the Jews, he married a divorced Jewess in Berlin. When Napoleon gave the Holy Roman Empire its knockout blow, Schlegel, in a magazine published in Paris, tried to build up a new solidarity and called his review *Europa*. He settled in Vienna; he became a devout Catholic. He made himself famous by his lectures on world literature, and in Vienna he published his *Concordia*. This magazine was meant to be something like the mediæval *Concordantia discordantium*, to restore peace between denominations, parties, and nations. And Schlegel experienced the mutual interpenetration of different forms and stages of civilization in the phases of his own life. He himself was a European by virtue of a long and painful course of training. His settling in Vienna was the free choice of the conscientious, responsible universalist, who could find no other asylum in divided Europe for his comprehensive aspirations.

And Austria *was* more than an agglomeration of fourteen different nationalities. As such, it was treated by short-sighted European nationalists as a *"contresens dans l'Europe moderne."* [1] But Palacky, the founder of Czech national self-consciousness, had shown deeper insight when he wrote: "If Austria did not exist, it would have to be invented." In space, the Austrian empire was a sum-total of fourteen nationalities.[2] Yet this was only one side of its constitution. It was likewise a comprehensive sequence in time. The title of the Austrian emperor bore witness to every layer of Western civilization. He was an apostolic monarch who appointed bishops and abbots, vetoing the pope's election like the apostolic emperors of Saxon-Roman times. As a good ally of St. Gregory VII, he was a faithful supporter of the pope's claims to temporal power and canonical jurisdiction. He was a staunch supporter of the friars. This same emperor was *podesta* of the Free City of Trieste, using the title made famous by the glorious city-states of Italy and governing the city under a special constitution. In his hereditary lands he ruled as a father of his people, with an unparalleled staff of civil servants, the *"Hofrat"* being the outstanding type in this system of civil service. In Hungary, where the Crown of St. Stephen was the symbol of a victorious gentry, he was, for all secular purposes, an English "king in parliament." By granting universal manhood suffrage to his subjects, he paved the road for nineteenth-century democracy in his empire. And finally, to complete the circle, in some of his territories he acted with dictatorial powers, under the martial law of conquest and occupation.

Like a Frankish king, he was loved and worshipped by his army; whatever form of government the individual soldier might be subject to in the different sections of the empire, he was proud to join the army. With deep understanding, Grillparzer, the greatest Austrian poet, hailed the army camp as

[1] Before the World War, this expression was used in official French textbooks of geography.

[2] H. A. L. Fisher (*A History of Europe*, Vol. II, p. 734, London, 1935) "sees in [the Austrian Empire] an attempt to realize upon a small scale the ideal of a Christian society, embracing all races and tongues."

the true home of Austria; and this was no love of despotism, because at the same time he violently denounced the inorganic autocracy of Russia and promised that Austria herself would carry out the duty of destroying Czarist Russia in the name of liberty.

I hope that our short list of the different forms of government in the Austrian empire has made it clear, not only that the results of all the volcanic eruptions of a thousand years had been precipitated in the Austrian area, but that the precipitates were preserved in completeness and integrity. I do not mean to overlook the fact that in every country in Europe history had blended different phases of civilization into an irrational unity. Yet the distinction between this part of the Continent and the other civilized nations of Europe was very definite: throughout the rest of Europe the attempt was always to establish a single principle by violent means. One principle was exaggerated, others were attacked and suppressed. The area of states and nations was fixed by conscious efforts based on theoretical claims: the *dominium maris* (dominion of the seas), the "natural frontiers," the divine right of kings. Austria-Hungary was Christendom itself, was Western civilization in its totality. Faced with the Turkish danger on its eastern frontier, Austria-Hungary had kept up the traditions of the defenders of the faith, the emperors of the Holy Roman Empire. Its institutions, in their completeness, differed from the particularistic traditions of the rest of Europe. Austria's completeness was a "completeness by establishment." To preserve the results of all the phases of historical evolution in one whole was the essence of her existence. It was that fact which made Schlegel an Austrian.

The political principle of this constitution was real, though it cannot be interpreted from the narrow viewpoint of German, Hungarian, or Czech policy. For the provinces of old Austria-Hungary were too narrow to explain her *raison d'être*. Austria's frontiers were accidental; they were imposed on her from outside. She represented something bigger than she could be herself. She stood for the heritage of Christianity. Patiently, in a passive way, very often suffering, she bore the burden of a unity which was threatened by one member of the family of nations after the other. The errors of the European nations which mistook themselves for independent individuals rebounded from the flexible constitution of this part of the Christian world, complete as it was by definition. New forms were added; but there still remained the old palace of the emperor, the *"Kaiserliche Hoflager"*—the last special head of which was Count Montenuovo—with its special Hungarian representative, the *"Minister am kaiserlichen Hoflager,"* and its strict Spanish ceremonial, in which the "monk-emperor" type of Cluny was consciously revived.

Austria's entire mission depended on a relative sacrifice of particularism and individualism by the groups that composed the empire. This bulwark of Christianity was based on a paradox. No attempt was made to force the component nations and countries into a colourless unity. Their particularities were frankly recognized; but march they must with a discipline like that of the Crusaders—who had also hailed from different nations. The self-denying sacrifice of the Slavic races in Austria was the price that had to be paid for the existence of the last remnant of togetherness and completeness in Europe.

The World War emancipated the Slavic elements in Austria and gave them a short Indian summer of State particularism. Jugoslavia, Czechoslovakia, Lithuania, and Hungary are stragglers in the march of European nations. Their post-War independence should not be overrated. Six hundred years and more of common traditions cannot be eradicated by fifteen years of nationalism. The new States in Europe are particular States very much as Saxony or Bavaria were a hundred years ago: they presuppose a unity. Not one of these States can think seriously of going to war. Their shape forbids it, their minorities forbid it, their permanent state of martial law forbids it. For in these countries war means the arming of everybody; peace means the arming of the ruling half only. Accordingly, they prefer peace.

At the dawn of modern times, Central Europe, the field of the Reformation, was divided into "Reich" and "Nation," i.e., Empire and particular States. In the beginning, the empire held the countries and regions from Ostend, Antwerp, and Brussels to Liége, Strassburg, the Lake of Constance, Arlberg, the Tyrol, Styria, Carinthia, Slavonia, and north again as far as Schwiebus, a place two hours by railway from Berlin (see map on p. 154). The central area which was thus surrounded by the emperor's *"Erblande"* (hereditary possessions) was split into innumerable territories governed by high magistrates, so well described by Carlyle in *Sartor Resartus* or Gobineau in *Les Pléiades* or Romain Rolland in *Jean-Christophe.* The high magistrates were civilians; the ring of imperial dominions was a military frontier.

This was four hundred years ago. When we study the map of Europe in 1938, we find exactly the reverse of the environment in which Luther lived. The inner group of particular States has been amalgamated into one "Reich," under the military command of a "Realm leader." There is no Bavaria or Saxony, no Free Cities or principalities in this block. On the other hand, the small countries around this block amount to a score: Finland, Latvia, Esthonia, Lithuania, Poland, Czechoslovakia, Hungary, Rumania, Jugoslavia, Liechtenstein, Switzerland, Disannexed France, Luxemburg, Netherlands, Belgium, Denmark.

The new situation is as complex as the old. Obviously, in this new political arrangement, nothing is settled; but a new process has been initiated. The States of the Danube basin and of Western Europe, between France, England, and Germany, are situated in a special field of force. They are not in a cosmopolitan world, with its centre of gravity in Paris. They are in a very definite world, of less universal character. The rôle played by the France of Henry IV and Richelieu in relation to the small princes of the inner Reich is performed in our day by Italy toward the succession-States. Before 1938, Mussolini guaranteed the existence of Austria; he counterbalanced Hungary's sympathies for Germany; he checked Jugoslavia.

But diplomatic manœuvres of this kind do not go deep enough to destroy the ties which bound the old Austria-

Hungary together. The secret of Austria's "international nation" was intermarriage. Our current phraseology of "nation" and "internationalism" is rather anæmic. When we think of international relations, we think of trade, of treaties and conferences. But the most important relation between two separate groups is that of matrimony. Every marriage eventually works for the making of a new nation. A wedding is an act which may found a new people. The wisdom of Abraham was right, and is always right. There was a famous dictum which distinguished Austria's princes from Machiavelli's *principe:* "Let others wage war; thou, happy Austria, shalt marry." Not only was this true of the emperor's house, it was also the secret of the nations under his sceptre. Officers, landowners, business men, civil engineers, masters and foremen, diplomats, civil servants, and pedlars intermarried. The nations in Austria-Hungary are nothing but nationalities of Austria, that is to say, they are subdivisions and subspecies of a dominant type. Agram, Ljubljana, Budapest, Cracow and Prague are Austrian cities, in spite of the passionate efforts of the Hungarians to make us think of Budapest in more heroic terms.

The dominant type of man in Austrian civilization was developed by a system of marriage rules which, from the point of view of the particular nationality, may be called outbreeding, but which was inbreeding as it concerned the one great area of Austria-Hungary. Thus a type with specific qualities of character was produced, which necessarily differed from the dominant type in other European countries. Its speech was bilingual; its heritage was translation, transformation, metamorphosis. The husband's official "nation" could not remain unchanged by the inheritances that came from the wife's side.

The daughter who leaves the house of her parents behind her brings into her husband's house a treasure of instincts, rules and ways of living, habits and customs, values and traditions, which are really subject to an "evolution." Here the much abused word "evolution," or development, means what it says: thirty or forty years of married life bring a disentangling and unfolding, provided there is a real heritage which comes down through the "daughter" from her father's house to her children's cradle. From this point of view the modern increase in divorce is easily explained. Where father and daughter are no longer seriously connected, where the life of two generations is no longer a twofold expression of one soul, a man's interest in a girl cannot endure more than a few years. What she learns in college is not very interesting to her husband.

A man does not become a husband in the full sense of the word on his wedding-day or during the honeymoon; and the reason is that he marries something more than an individual. A wife brings to her marriage the full past of her kin. If we were all men, the clans and races of men would never amalgamate. The rugged male, armed with his rigid convictions and his fighting spirit, is inaccessible to the influences of another race. But in the form of a wife's devotion, her inheritance from her ancestors gains a foothold in her husband's soul. It takes a whole life to make such influences bear fruit in the man's ways of living and thinking. These are a woman's deepest secrets and treasures, unknown even to herself. A woman's secrets are more important than her smile; her smile is only the curtain that covers them. Modern feminism gives us a mere face value, like the famous grin of the Cheshire cat or like a Sphinx without a riddle. In the recurrent monotony of a mechanical society, the full meaning of daughterhood seems to be disappearing rapidly. In an age where men do not dare to become real fathers or elders or patriarchs, girlhood, bridehood, womanhood and motherhood are less seriously threatened than daughterhood.

Of the Austrians their poet, Anton Wildgans, said, "We have often been compared to the Phæacians. Our nature might better be symbolized by Nausicaa, the king's daughter on the island of the Phæacians. To the stranger who hails from a foreign land and is driven to her shore by adverse winds, the princess is sent by her divine instinct." Nausicaa and Odysseus furnish the true parable of *"tu, felix Austria, nube"*—Thou, happy Austria, shalt marry.

The symbolical character in Austrian history was Maria Theresa, the *"Erbtochter,"* "the daughter of succession," who took over the immense legacy bequeathed by her father. By her forty-year reign she transformed the territories that protected the Holy Roman Empire into a secular Austrian Empire. As a woman, she herself could not become emperor; nevertheless she kept up the Hapsburg monarchy and the union between its different countries. Austria underwent a real revolution when Europe tried to divide the spoils of an apparently easy victory over Maria Theresa. She left Vienna and placed herself in the hands of the Hungarian gentry; and for two hundred years the liberties of the Crown of St. Stephen dominated Austria because Maria Theresa, in her fight against the Estates of the Empire, guaranteed the liberties of the Magyars.

With her successors, the golden crown of the emperor emblematized more and more the mere dominance of the Hungarians over the rest of the empire. At the end, seven million Magyars were sole rulers of Hungary—twenty million people— and held two thirds of the population in complete subjection; and Hungary, in turn, governed the whole empire, forty-six million people, though she paid only 30 per cent of the taxes. In 1914, the real constitution of Austria-Hungary was not expressed by its name. In fact, it was a Hungary-Austria, where, by a most complicated system, the Hungarian gentry swayed a great empire. The exemptions and privileges of Hungary were the price paid by Maria Theresa and all her successors for the transformation of the Austrian parts of the Holy Empire into an Austrian Empire. Attempts at treating Hungary like the rest of the provinces always failed. The irregularity that was undoubtedly involved in this favoured position can be compared to a revolution; for an illogical and objectionable constitution was forced upon the heiress in her own right, by insidious and reckless adversaries. Moreover, this revolution followed the rules which we have stated for other revolutions. It went through its period of humiliation, between 1805 and 1813. In those years the Austrian constitution was shown to have been too mechanical, too naturalistic. It was not enough for Austria to have ceased to be a Holy Roman Empire and to become an hereditary monarchy. The great powers of Europe are either representations of something absolute, seed-beds for the growth of man, or they are lost. Austria seemed lost at the end of the eighteenth century because it was nothing but a natural agglomeration secularized through the accident of feminine succession, not a living body politic with a definite rôle in the European concert.

We have seen how and why Friedrich Schlegel and his friends threw in their lot with Austria and imbued her, in spite of her dependence on Hungary, with the proud consciousness of representing completeness and totality. Thus Austria was able to sublimate the rôle of Maria Theresa and of the daughter of man. The patient sufferings of Austria in this rôle of the daughter, the famous Viennese charm—all the virtues of a great soul that learned to speak universally in the midst of a Babel of tongues—produced an Austrian language which we all know: music. Haydn, Mozart, Beethoven, Bruckner, Franz von Liszt, Johann Strauss, Mahler—a stream of music that watered the gardens of Austrian civilization. Of Vienna Eduard Hanslick wrote in 1886: "By her supremacy in the art of sound, Vienna is more than the musical capital of Austria; she is a powerful empire in herself. The sovereignty of this empire extends far beyond the borders of the political monarchy. Slight overtones of Slavic, Magyar, the Italian melody, blend with the eminently German character of this music; and like any successful mixture of races, they revivify and embellish it."

Austria's Catholicism and her "daughterhood" stood in opposition to the Protestant paternalism developed by the Reformation. The passive attitude of the receiving, enduring, forbearing, abiding part of Christendom found a way of spiritual sublimation; and thanks to this sublimation Austria survived. "The survival of the fittest" leaves us asking: Who, after all, is fit? In the case of Austria we can answer this question. When a living being delves into the very depths of its potentialities, it will prove to be fit. Considered from the outside, Austria was illogical, impossible, a hopeless case of contradictory political principles. But a city is protected by men, not by walls. Austria strengthened her weak political foundations by creating a new type of man. Here again, as in all other revolutions, man regenerated himself by going back to an eternal trait in human character.

We have explained why even the Little Austria of today cannot be called a linguistic province of Germany. Language is a more complicated matter than nationalists suspect. It is not a cellophane wrapper thrown around several millions of people. Language is language in the full sense only so long as it expresses the deepest impulses of human life. National tongues which refuse to serve the great biological purpose of our species cease to speak. Since nationalism severs the purpose of speech from the deepest desire of man and woman (which goes far deeper than the noisy national slogans), the languages degenerate into propaganda. They decay before our eyes, though they may survive as fossils for another thousand years. Their future will be very interesting, because people who speak the same language will understand each other less and less, while classes, professions and groups of different nationality will find themselves closer to each other, all over the globe. The arrogant destruction of the Hapsburg monarchy was based on a gross heresy concerning language. The Austrian character was a great character because it was conceived as a unity in spite of variety, through the faith of generations of devoted men and women who based their actions on magnanimous patience, daughterly candour, and unaffected hospitality.

Lest the reader be confused by what he is reading in the daily papers, it might be well to say that the annexation of "Austria" by Hitler in 1938 was not the annexation of Austria. His reunion was nothing more than what happened to Jugoslavs, or Czechs, or Rumanians, or Poles, in 1918. Hitler only fished the driftwood of the German Austrians out of the flooded area of a world catastrophe. The German Austrians are only one sixth of that Austria with whom we were concerned in this chapter.

The daughter in Europe, Nausicaa-Austria, destroyed by the World War, will find her resurrection in the world.

CHAPTER FOURTEEN

The Mills That Grind

The Rehabilitation of the Repressed—Emancipation from the Old Gods—
Europe's Second Peace

THE REHABILITATION OF THE REPRESSED.

THE DISINTEGRATION OF EUROPE AFTER THE GREAT WAR REVEALS another set of mechanisms at work in revolutions. Here we can study the technique of readjustment. In ancient times, a defeated group like Troy or Carthage ceased to exist. Modern nations do not die. Ireland, Poland, Lithuania, for example, seem immortal. To make this possible, the mechanism of readjustment must function unceasingly. But how is readjustment possible for a nation which has received its national institutions as a religion and a worshipped creed? If nations were loose groups of some millions of individuals, existing for certain general purposes like food and shelter, readjustment would be easy. Nations are something much more complicated, a permanent apparatus of special selection. The members of such a group must be ready to die for the values selected by their national experience and their national traditions; and they are. The readiness of men to die for a cause makes readjustment a highly difficult task. If people prefer death to seeing the inherited order shaken, the attempt at change may simply cost the life of the radical leaders, without any practical result. Blear-eyed patriotism imperils the evolution of any group.

For such is the nobility of man that he can overcome his love for existence, and die for a lost cause. He can exclude his own body from the life-interest he wishes to embody. Without the courage to die for his class, country, child, ideal, a man could never represent any form of historical life. Parents who are not courageous enough to fight a kidnapper, mariners who will not save the passengers of their burning ship at the risk of their own lives, have ceased to fulfil the minimum requirements for mankind. Fortunately, in the majority of cases, the readiness of people to suffer for the survival of the group transcends the cowardice of the tenderfeet. Thus readiness for duty guarantees the perpetuation of any body politic.

Revolution can never succeed where people are ready to die for the existing order of things. Revolutions fail where the troops fire, where the police disperses the mob, where a handful of volunteers takes up arms for the legitimate government. It is only when the mass of the people prefer their own struggle for life to the sacrifice of their lives that revolutions prosper. Such a state of affairs proves that the old order no longer contains a valued element of truth. For without exaggeration it can be said that the value of any order of things is tested by martyrdom, by the willingness of people to die for it.

The French constitution survived the wave of violent feeling in 1934 because the mass of the French nation is still imbued with the stream of ideas that inspired the founders of the republic in 1789. They still believe in the pricelessness of their contribution to the true self-expression of mankind. Therefore even Russian Communism has made no impression on them. The French are the youngest group in the civilized world in respect of their revolutionary experience. The revolution of the oldest nation in Europe, Italy, is six times further removed from the Bolshevik experiment than is the French. Italy, therefore, reacted most violently of all the European nations to the world revolution of the World War. That is why Mussolini was the first symbolic figure on the post-War stage of events. Hohenzollern and Hapsburg Germany, divided in the Reformation, reacted ten years later than Italy (1933 and 1938). England, America and France resist better on account of their more recent creation. Yet England will react more fundamentally than France; and it is easier for the

French to resist than for the Italians. A nation's faith in its own revelation lasts only a relative length of time.

The vital reactions of the older forms of civilization to the World War and the revolution brought about by the War deserve special attention. For if they prove to be merely mechanical means of defence and counter-revolution, the simplest way of explaining them would be inertia. Shabbiness, stupidity, and hunger for life would suffice to bring about such counter-movements.

Now a short survey of Europe since the War shows that the following courses have been taken. Italy solved the papal question: it finally overcame the division into Guelphs and Ghibellines, that is, the protest of the Vatican against the unification of Italy. Today Italy is imperialistic. True enough, the name of Emperor, outlawed in Italy since 1200, remains excluded from Italy herself. Yet Mussolini is a Roman emperor in every respect except the name. Italy's obsession during the last four centuries had been that foreigners did not take Italian politics seriously. Italy gave the world musicians, painters, actors, cardinals and diplomatists; but for the rest she was the Holy Sepulchre of a past civilization. Beggars, late trains, dirt and hilarious disorder—this conception of their country enraged the Italians. Mussolini tries to change all this. From a country of art and religion, he has made Italy into the hegemonic power among the succession-States. As Louis XIV dominated Europe after the Thirty Years' War, Mussolini dominated Central Europe. For the first time in fifteen hundred years Italian influence reached out beyond the Alps. As Louis XIV was imitated by the German princes, so Mussolini's Fascism was imitated in all the impoverished and vanquished nations of the former imperial area. The nations have changed rôles. Mussolini overshadows the former Italian contribution to our world —the papacy—by the political game he is playing in the North and East and West. He plays empire whilst, strangely enough, the old imperial country, Germany, has before her a religious task, that of tribal, *"völkischer,"* regeneration. Nazism is the outbreak of popular energies against the overweight of the German "State." Hitler is the true expression of the repressed desires of peasants and lower middle-class, who were under the yoke of the *"Gebildeten"* and can now avenge themselves upon that class. The foreign observer who mistakes Nazism for Fascism can test this point by the following facts: Not one name or memory from the Guelphic times between 1200 and 1517—the very times so forgotten and ignored in Italy today —has been overlooked in the national revival of Germany since the War. Whereas the last four hundred years offered little or nothing for the purposes of this revival, every successful trend has pointed to the times of Joan of Arc, the Teutonic Order, the *"Vehme,"* the Peasants' War, Matthias Grünewald, *Ordensburgen,* and *Marken des Reichs.*

In Germany the division of the nation into two separate bodies, Catholics and Protestants, has been overcome by a Messiah. The result of the Reformation, the system of scholarly trained civil servants, is being revised; the rigid organization of the States is superseded by a sort of nationalistic papacy. The Germans long for something like the mediæval papacy, though in a secular form. Hitler is as much a national pope as Mussolini is an Italian emperor. In Germany there was no need to produce a strong State; in fact, the spontaneity of the German people had been throttled by too much government.

The *"Völkische Revolution"* does not solve the problem of Capitalism or of Communism. It looks beyond both and anticipates the classless society of complete racial identity. The word "revolution," deliberately used by the anti-Marxian movement in Italy and in Germany in order to captivate the revolutionary youth of the nations, does not have the same meaning in both countries. In Italy it is used for an imperialistic effort. In the field of foreign affairs, the German Nazi revolution is really going back to the forests of *Germania antiqua.* It needs world peace more than anyone else. The repressed instincts of pre-State existence turn up again and are deliberately fostered. The Germans are anticipating the tribal organization of an economically united world.

The English are also returning to a pre-revolutionary development. Through the law passed in November, 1934, an

Englishman's house has ceased to be his castle. The Crown is being made the centre of a restoration of centralized government, police and civil service, and of serious and methodical training. Music returns to the English-speaking nations. The Puritan inhibitions against systematic thinking give way to an influx of intellectual and philosophical energies. Ramsay MacDonald presided over a "national" government. Every move made by the English during the last few years is a step back toward the Tudor State. The Judges of the Common Law, especially the Lord Chief Justice, Lord Hewart, write books against "the New Despotism." And Edward VIII seems vituperable to the same church that came into being by the divorces of Henry VIII.

The French, little as they are able to change, are going in for regionalism and self-government of provinces and professions. For the first time political unrest is stronger in the provinces than in Paris. Bretons, Alsatians, Basques and, perhaps, Catalonians rekindle the flame of federalism stamped out as it had been by the unitarian ideals of 1789.

In every great nation in Europe we observe a resurgence of the repressed. Those features of the human life-cycle are being regenerated which the great national revolutions had suppressed or shortened. The one-sidedness of the national character is supplemented by features which were silenced for centuries. This process gives the lie to the superstition that national character is eternal. Man is too proud a creature to bear the stigma of partial development; he cannot help longing for completeness. And the consequence is that the established division of functions between the European nations is being revised. Though the achievements of the great revolutions cannot be cancelled, the lost phases of the human soul —spent as the price of the revolutions—are being rediscovered and reannexed. The Europeans are going home to a more complete concept of humanity. Yet there is one law which governs them: No European nation can have a real second revolution. The slogan of "revolution," the word "revolution," so freely used for these post-War processes, cannot hide the relative smallness of the events they cover. The post-War change within national areas cannot be compared to the colossal creative acts of earlier centuries. Europe has been "revolutionized" by the World War and the subsequent World Revolution; but its single "revolutions" are all partial processes of adaptation in one general world-readjustment. A score of national revolutions today are no more than enough to equal one genuine, complete revolution.

Everywhere it is the underdog of the last revolution who is being released from the pressure of the great national system. This underdog is not an individual; he is neither the poor man nor the proletarian. We, in our modern individualism, fancy that oppression and injustice can be done only to human individuals. In actual fact, any social system is unfair to certain ways of life. In Germany the mediæval peasantry was crushed in the Peasants' War; in Italy, the Imperial Roman tradition was trodden under foot by the popes; England, in 1688, abolished royal conscience and centralized government; and the living voices of the *"pays de France"* were silenced in 1789. The achievements of civilization are sublime. Only psychoanalysis discovers the price of any sublimation. We become aware, today, of the price of civilizations. By a revolution, whole systems of behaviour are put under a taboo and fall into desuetude. At such a moment the famous "inhibitions" begin to work. A gentleman cannot scratch himself in good society, under the threat of being automatically outlawed. He foresees his social death and prefers to suffer. And that is not all. The negative fear-explanations of psychology fall short of explaining the mechanism of national character fully. It is true that a member of, let us say, French society can foresee that he will be outlawed if he does not know the *bon ton*. The threat of social capital punishment prevents most of the outbreaks of unco-ordinated instinct. But the positive love for the established ideal of national character does more than fear could do. A gentleman does not behave like a gentleman because he is afraid of being an outcast. He does it because he feels that he *must* be a gentleman! It is a positive desire to strengthen the code of national character which pervades the average member of a group. He grafts and trims his own nature like a gardener—a gardener in the service of the god or goddess who created the group. It is the secret of any ruling class that it wars against its native instincts in the service of its god. It is a priesthood which believes that the national character, represented by certain habits and beliefs, is ultimate. A continuous procession of pilgrims join in worshipping at the various temples, of good breeding, genius, statecraft, motherhood, asceticism.

In all the great national forms of life the World War brought a crisis. The colossal bloodshed among the governing classes weakened the priesthood of the national tradition. The ruling group lost a much bigger proportion of its young men than did the rest of the population. This misproportion between the loss of officers and that of private soldiers forced a readjustment upon the nations. There were no longer enough educated and voluntary representatives of the divine tradition to represent it in the feeble hearts and souls of natural men, caught in the cogs of the industrial machine.

At this point the great nations show the wisdom of their post-War reaction. The divine element being so weakly represented, after the heavy death-toll among the educated classes, the proletarian might sway the whole civilization if the basis of civilization itself could not be enlarged and broadened. The personality of the gentry, of civil service, of inspired individualism, is not accessible to the mass-men or to post-War youth. Bolshevism would be inevitable for them. At the same time, the heroic achievements of the national efforts made in the World War largely support and justify the various national traditions. Even Germany, though financially defeated by the Americans, would never have succumbed to her European enemies alone. The war between the Europeans was a stalemate. The great nations of Europe have all proved indestructible.

In this twilight of the national gods, the masses would have been lost without some indirect inducement to follow the national tradition. They would feel incapable of bearing the terrible burden of priesthood; the divine ego of the national will would crush these mechanized beings. Therefore they have been allowed to worship gods belonging to a pre-natal stage of national character. The European nations cannot civilize the modern proletariat directly. Such a straightforward attempt would be asking too much responsibility and self-denial of the mass-man.

The process of amalgamation into the traditional civilization works indirectly. All we can hope from these labour-forces is that they may still have some moral vitality. The masses are no longer expected to conform to the standards of the national élite; they are permitted and encouraged to be primeval. That is, they are trained to embody the specific pre-revolutionary shapeless type, the underdog that was repressed by the national revolutions. Meanwhile the real national responsibility rests on the shoulders of an inner group. These leaders of the post-War readjustment necessarily have two faces. Outwardly they resemble the underdog set free in post-War days: Mussolini looks like a proletarian Cæsar and Hitler like a peasant pope. Inwardly they are heirs to the pre-War national policy.

Under these circumstances, public education no longer has the function of training the crown-princes and candidates for government office, as naïve national education always did. Since the Great War, the mere vitality of the masses has become, for the first time in history, an independent item in national education. Even if these masses will not produce leaders for the nation, they must be organized. So they are put through a training stage which serves as *preliminary* in the real national history. The mythology which modern democracies are beginning to teach their masses is no longer simply a glorification of the national institutions. It runs riot among the lost opportunities, the suppressed instincts, the reminiscences of the nations' pre-civilized days.

This is a new mechanism of adaptation. The Nazi of today is related to the true German Lutheran type created after 1517 by the fact that he is encouraged to live through the previous stage, that of the German of 1500—which once again leads to the type of the Lutheran public official. After the French Revolution, the technique of adaptation differed: the best qualities of the English "gentleman" could be parallelled in the middle classes by the type of the "good sport." The sportsman is not, by himself, a gentleman; yet he resembles him in every respect. And the ritualism that governed the daily life of the gentry who hunted the fox was made accessible, by a second codification, to everybody who owned a bath-tub. The adaptation in the Reformation countries consisted in replacing theology by philosophy. In Germany and in all countries which adopted its type of scholarship, the philosophical leaders of 1800, Hegel, Fichte, Schelling, Schleiermacher, persuaded the shopkeeper that he was no longer getting theology but real natural philosophy as his moral nourishment.

But the anti-Bolshevik reaction of today is not based on a philosophical translation of the older values: the modern masses would not care for philosophy. It is effected by a psychological technique which satisfied their pre-natal instincts.

This reaction deprives the national institutions, as we know them, of their splendour and prestige. The chief organ of a complicated organism abandons its claim to form the visible model for the rest. For this process, however, there is a historical parallel. In the horrible times of the Borgias, when the papacy became a dictatorial organization, it ceased to be understood. It handed the masses over to leaders and movements of which it itself did not approve. The education of candidates for the inner circle, and the education of common men, were deliberately separated. Yet this senile organization saved the unity of the Church for another hundred years. It was at this time that Erasmus of Rotterdam canonized the separation of clerical and secular education by doing the same thing we do today. He, and the secular governments of his days, did with humanism what we are beginning to do with primitivism: namely, prefix it as antecedent in education to the existing curriculum. Erasmus said: Of course, Christianity is the crown, but why not start with the classics of Greece and Rome? In the same way our colleges are beginning to teach primitive sociology and barbarism and anthropology more and more, as one other precinct to the sanctuary of our "real values," whatever this may mean. The modern masses will soon be led through a maze of precincts: pre-history, Pre-natal Man, Stone Age, Egypt, perhaps some hours will remain for the Greeks, and the humanities; Christianity will be post-poned till St. Tib's eve. Once more mankind is patching on some chapters to the education of man which probably will become the chapters most violently taken in. The step from humanism into anthropology today is as final as the step from Christianity to Humanism. Again, political need asks for a simplification. The European nations have been forced since the World War into the segregation of two types. On the one side they established a dictatorial group, and on the other they emancipated the repressed instincts of the underdog. By the use of this mechanism the particular State may prolong its national sovereignty for another period of years, in spite of the fact that the natural conditions for it are gone.

The return of the repressed means that the nations are mark-ing time and preparing for the economic organization of the whole world. By admitting the irresponsibility of their masses for the traditional national priesthood and creed, the nations unconsciously acknowledge the inadequacy of these national traditions themselves. They have absolved the masses of an allegiance which would eternalize nationalism and which would make it impossible for the peoples to start afresh with a new human image of God.

EMANCIPATION FROM THE OLD GODS.

This is an era of psychoanalysis. Whatever its merits, no analyst certainly can be compared to the Great War. Emanci-pation from the old gods was perpetrated by an analytical process on a colossal scale. The national concepts and ideas of the belligerent parties concerning their own situation in the world were challenged and used up during the World War. While at war, the nations clung to those reminiscences of the past which seemed most fitted to stimulate every com-batant, at the front and at home, to the utmost energy. Through the constant application of these familiar associa-tions during the War itself, their force was spent. This process of exhaustion has never been taken into account. And yet the using up of familiar national sentiments occurred everywhere.

Even America's sentiment, which one might think relatively free from historical traditions, was overstrained by war propaganda. When General Pershing landed in France, he was reported to have uttered his message to French civilization in these words: "Lafayette, we are here." [1] The crusade of the Star-Spangled Banner led to the defeat of the Central Powers of Europe. Once before, the United States had been involved in European quarrels in spite of its determination to keep aloof. In 1812 America threw its weight in the scale with revolutionary France against conservative England. It was a fight for new principles, for the rights of man, against Georgian Great Britain. There was a portion of gratitude for Lafayette in the War of 1812. Every textbook admits that the old alliance with France played its part in the events between 1812 and 1815: the war was a last act in the revolutionary campaign begun in 1776.

A crusade is not a revolutionary war. And though it is not our business to decide how much of a crusade America's partnership in the World War was, it cannot be doubted that the situation in 1917 here was very different from that at the dawn of liberty, in 1812 or 1776. The very name "Crusade" is a term, not for progress, but for the regaining of old, lost territory or preventing its loss.[2] The difference between a pioneer discovering a new world and a crusader fighting for Europe and democracy is exactly the same as that between a missionary on one side, and the Crusaders of nine hundred years ago on the other. Missions and campaigns for missions are concerned with converting pagan countries which are now to hear the Gospel for the first time. A crusade is conservative. Its purpose is to stabilize the very background and premises of progress: the salvation of the oldest provinces of the faith. During her courageous advance towards the West, America was called back by cries for help from the cradle of modern civilization. This

---

[1] For the whole story, see Gen. John J. Pershing, *My Experiences in the World War*, p. 93, New York, Stokes, 1931.

[2] See p. 547.

was a parallel to the alarming news which once came to the Western world of the conquest of the cradle of Bethlehem and the Holy Sepulchre in Jerusalem by the Mohammedans.

Thus we see that in 1917 "crusade" was a very special term, which had a meaning only for America. The European countries themselves, deeply interwoven in one old world, were like Bethlehem, Jerusalem, Nazareth and Transjordania, fighting against each other and themselves destroying the land of promise. But, for the New World, the "crusade" persuaded a westward-facing continent to look back toward the east and the dawn of its own civilization.

"Crusade" was only a name. But such a name lifts a new event out of the grey limbo of every-day existence. It frees it from any possibility of being confused with egoistic or imperialistic enterprises. It dedicates, separates and distinguishes. Protecting this war against pettiness and coarseness, it shows that gratitude reaches across hundreds and thousands of years.

Thus the value of some such exalting name was felt in every belligerent country. The memory of an older heroic or brilliant struggle for life was present in the minds of all the European nations. As we have seen, the word "crusade" was not available to them; but there were other reminiscences to strengthen their morale. We give a list of these associations.

WORLD WAR PARALLELS

The following list contains two classes of comparisons which were made during the years 1914-18, with the intention of interpreting the catastrophe.

One was used by responsible patriots, statesmen, and teachers to ascertain the ideals of their own nation. The other was found in the more detached writings of scholars. The scholarly parallels all showed the weakness of intellectual abstraction, because they picked out events entirely outside the experience of any contemporaneous belligerent. The political parallels were all invoked because they suggested very real scars and experiences of a particular body politic.

A. POLITICAL COMPARISONS

1912	*for:*	Bulgaria: The War of the Balkans.
1870		France: The War with Prussia.
1800-1815		England: The Napoleonic Wars.
(1772) 1793, 1795		Poland: Her Partitions between Russia, Prussia, Austria.
1776-1783		America's First Comparison: The Collaboration with France.
1756-1763		Prussia: Frederick the Great and the Seven Years' War.
1742-1748		Austria: The War of Succession under Maria Theresa.
1568-1579		Belgium: The Struggle of the Low Countries against Spain.
1453		Russia: The Loss of the Cross of the Hagia Sophia in Byzantium.
1415-1434		Bohemia: The Martyrdom of John Huss and the War of the Hussites.
1099-1274		America's Second Comparison: The Crusades.
951-1268		Italy: The Invasions and the Rule of the Nordic Emperors.

B. ACADEMIC COMPARISONS

French:
410 A.D. Alaric and the Goths in Rome (defeatistic mood).
452 A.D. Attila and St. Genevieve (victorious mood).

German:
202 B.C. Rome (Prussia) against Carthage (victorious mood).
168 B.C. Macedonia's War against Rome (defeatistic mood).

Russian, Marxist:
End of History. Last capitalistic catastrophe, no parallel, properly speaking.

These recollections are as different as the wave-lengths of different radio stations. France was taking its *"revanche"* for 1870, and Bulgaria for the Balkan Wars of 1881 and 1912. These two countries had the shortest memories, or, to put it more carefully, used the most recent past as a parallel to the present war. Other countries looked further back. England saw herself fighting the new Napoleon: Lloyd George, with his "Hang the Kaiser," was repeating the English slogans of 1810. Prussia and Austria had a precedent in the Seven Years' War, 1756-1763, and the War for the Austrian Succession, 1742-1748. The very foundations of both countries had been laid in these two great struggles; and since their existence was at stake in the World War, many authors have stressed the analogy. Thomas Mann wrote a famous and very serious essay which drew a comparison between Saxony's alleged neutrality in 1756 and Belgium's neutrality in 1914. The destruction of Prussia and Austria as a reslt of the War has fully justified the comparison. Both powers had really lost their basis of existence, laid down one hundred and seventy years before. They invoked the ghosts of this past with good reason. It was a last effort, as a drowning man surveys his whole past; swift as lightning, all the chief remembrances of his life turn up in his imagination, probably because the mind hopes to recall a former situation which might offer an experience, a remedy, a way out of its mortal danger. Our list goes on and shows the interesting parallels for the Czechs and the Poles. The "oldest" country, in the sense of the remoteness of its historical parallel, is Italy. Italy was the only great European power that fought under the spell of the clerical period of the Occident. She was fighting for the last time, in the person of the Austrian emperor, the emperors from the North who had possessed and maintained the Roman Empire of the Middle Ages. Thus her reminiscence peered back almost as far as the American vision of a crusade. Every nation read into the World War a great chapter from its own past. And all these images were wasted. Not one of the parallels proved satisfactory. The World War transcended the boldest expectations, as well as the usual concepts, of historiography. A German historian was so ingenuous as to confess during the War that it offered little interest to the historian. So little did it fit into his framework of historical periods and motives!

When a post-War generation had to be introduced into national life, the exhaustive use of historical traditions and real memories during the War made necessary a return to still older layers of remembrance. That is why the European countries turned to the language extirpated by their own formation. These new languages have already been explained. Today, in every country in Europe, the traveller will find sympathy if he pulls the stop which opens the memories of the repressed.

But how shall we speak in America? Crusading America differed from the Old World. When the United States of America went through its revolution in 1776, it had neither 130 millions of people nor even 24 millions, as France had in 1789. In the course of 150 years America bred at home, and attracted from the Old World, a hundred million people and taught them the American Revolution. The problem of its political education after the War was less intense, therefore, than in Europe, where whole nations had to face right about at once. In America the experiment made by two and a half million people in 1776 had already been repeated and memorized by scores of millions of immigrants. Thus, it was spared the rehabilitation of the repressed which is going on all over Europe.

EUROPE'S SECOND PEACE.

From 1914 to 1917, six great nations went to war, five of which had made their contribution to the life of mankind in former centuries, whereas one, Russia, was only entering its period of self-revelation. In 1917 Europe reached a stalemate. The European War gave way to World War and World Revolution. Something bigger than Europe now proved to be the field of force of this catastrophe.

From 1917 to 1920, America extinguished the fire of open warfare, and peace was re-established on the surface. However, the technical war had run off faster than the evolution of the minds and souls involved in the struggle. In the Napoleonic wars, the Thirty Years' War, the Hundred Years' War, the cumbersome technique of warfare made hostilities last so long that a new generation grew up during the war itself. The technical achievements of our age condensed military events and destructions into five short years. For that reason our wartime generation grew up in the twilight of a so-called post-War period.

For all practical purposes this allegedly post-War period was nothing but a hangover of the pre-War ideologies. It was the Indian summer of national sovereignties. By 1930 these national ideologies had worn off definitely. And when President Hoover sent his message on a war debts moratorium to Europe, the French, the leading nation in the century of national sovereignty, immediately realized the decay of their pride. They exclaimed, *"On nous a traités comme Nicaragua."*

Finally new problems that emerged from the War itself, each a world problem instead of a European, battered at the doors of the diplomatic chanceries, and asked for recognition. A mental war ensued, fought under different names in different countries, putting up dictators in Portugal and Poland, in the Baltic States and the Balkans, producing Hitlerism in Germany, the Italian conquest of Abyssinia, Roosevelt's visit to Buenos Aires, and the first socialist government in the bourgeois republic of France.

This mental warfare found a restricted outlet for its passions in Spanish territory. Spain lent itself as the ideological battlefield of Europe, like the Balkan battlefield before the World War. The goal of all these movements is a second peace, superseding the so-called peace of Versailles and of St. Germain.

Therefore nothing new is being enacted now; only a new generation is introduced and integrated into a situation created by the World War. Thus the Spanish civil war itself is corroborating the new dilemma of a technical era; here again the technical destruction has been so efficient that the problems raised by the war itself overshadow the issues existing on the eighteenth of July, 1936. Neither the childish simplicity of the generals nor the stubborn doctrinairism of anarchists, Communists and syndicalists has survived. Their queer idea was to eliminate the other party. This term "elimination"—by shooting or bombing—is the interesting contribution of this new civil war to revolutionary terminology. Unfortunately, elimination is not going to work. Ten thousand children, women, workers, protestants, priests, nuns, may be "eliminated"; but no problem of society will be solved. The cost of the destruction will have to be paid off by whole generations. Airplanes may race at top speed in hours; man lives up to his real experience pretty slowly.

A new political science, then, is bound to differentiate between technical and political time. Statesmen of the future will become aware of the dualism between the inevitable lag for political action (till the masses may be introduced into reality) and the inevitable settling of accounts which comes as certainly as the rotation of the planets.

To this bilateral law we owe the second, mental, warfare that has been raging since 1931. A thoughtless and largely aimless world war is being repeated today in theory and reflection. When we analyze the attitude of the nations in this aftermath, we may observe how lawfully the march of the nations proceeds. For what are these nations actually trying to do? They are all trying to reclaim the valuable features of the epoch of the World War; they are all trying to avoid the mistakes and blunders of that period. They do this by instinct more than by any clear understanding of the new law of technical precocity and mental make-up. Of course, the leaders who tried to calm the masses during the depression ignored the fact that our modern military technique works faster than national thinking can follow. Nevertheless, they all acted on this assumption.

President Roosevelt scarcely remembered Wilson's mistake in going to Versailles, into the den of the lion. Fortunately, Roosevelt went to Buenos Aires instead of to Europe. His social policy, after much wavering and experimenting, liquidated the war problems. Baruch and Nye, in compliance with Roosevelt's wishes, moved for legislation that would take the profits out of war. He had to accept the veterans' bonus, and realized that the twelve millions of unemployed could not be left in the lurch like individual losers in life's gambling. Loss of their opportunities was no individual bad luck in their case. Labour lost its capital in the World War, because the growth of foreign markets came to an end then. Americans are unemployed as the result of the War. It is true that after the War the American loans to Europe postponed this result. In 1929, however, the simple issue had already become: Who should pay for the

World War—capital, labour, or the farmer? To a certain extent Roosevelt simply acknowledged the problems of the Wilson administration.

This "handwriting on the wall" was clearly exposed by the scientist, Arthur D. Little, as early as 1928, when he wrote, in the midst of prosperity: "The War developed amongst us a new Bushido, another Samurai class pledged to service. Its membership included those who toiled for the common good in a supreme emergency; devoted women; our youth who on land and sea and in the air dared the impossible, and achieved it. Shall we permit this unity of purpose, this capacity for co-operative effort to become dissipated in the perpetuation of past mistakes, or shall we direct these new and potent forces to the development of our estate? It is well to be wise in a great moment." [3]

England and France have tried to be wise during this mental war. These two arrogant victors of 1919 have been volunteering as the vanquished from 1932 to 1937. France did not go to war for any of the many violations of the Versailles treaty, not even for the remilitarization of the Rhineland, which made national sovereignty impossible in Europe. She allowed Germany to play the victor in this mental war because Versailles had falsified France's real achievement.

After all, Germany did not lose the World War in the East. The Germans saved the world from Czarism. The winning-away of all the Baltic States from Russia was due to the German victories only. Neither England nor France would have emancipated these countries, and so the simple truth that Central and Eastern Europe formed one administrative unit at the end of the World War is coming forth again in the frantic overrunning of Austria, the alliance between Poland and Germany, the ousting of the Francophiles in the Balkan countries, etc. However, though Germany did not lose the World War in the East, neither did she win it. The arrogance of Lloyd George and Clemenceau is replaced by Hitler's pride today. Whenever mankind does not reach its destiny by humility and

[3] Arthur D. Little, *The Handwriting on the Wall*, p. 25, Boston, 1928.

justice, it will reach it by a sequence of two self-conceits and two injustices. Likenesses of Lloyd George and Hitler should be carved on one side of a war memorial, and the mourning daughter of man, Europa, on the other. Then the soldiers of Europe, the 800,000 killed in action around Verdun alone, might come to rest in their graves.

The second peace, of course, means that the sovereignty of national states in Europe has gone for good. I know that the sceptic will point to the noisy chauvinism of all countries. Let it be understood that the mental war, though conducted on lines of the most violent nationalism, is eating out the very heart of patriotism. For the national gods are degraded today. As we have seen before, the World War resulted in degrading national gods into idols and inefficient dreams. The second war is degrading the idols into cash. They are advertised by travel bureaus like merchandise, and broadcast daily by loudspeakers. This accelerates the selling out of nationalism.

On the other hand, rulers in Poland, Hungary, Italy, Germany, Spain, are forced to enter a new international combination. The Communistic International, and the Warriors' International, are racing for hegemony today. The result of the World War, then, is the emerging of a nationalist-international party in Europe. Unconsciously and inadvertently, this party of the warriors is doing away with any possible sovereignty of the single European state. Modern dictators exclaim, like Marx and Engels in 1847, "Soldiers of Europe, you have nothing to lose, unite." The direction of this process is easily overlooked because their philosophy is the soldier's philosophy; its prophet, Friedrich Nietzsche, baptized it "the philosophy of the hammer." This is difficult for educated people to grasp, since their ingrained ways of thinking date back to the "Revolution of Ideas" of 1789. The Philosophy of the Hammer is the reverse of the Philosophy of Ideas. Veteran idealists still expect that the actors in the political drama should make speeches announcing their actions and conforming to their actions. Unfortunately, the World War means a material revolution; it is anti-ideological, anti-bourgeois, and anti-liberal.

Its champions, therefore, are no revolutionary idealists, they are materially revolutionized masses. It is significant that the very word "revolutionary" is out of date today. It is too conscious, too active. To modern masses the philosophical consciousness of a liberal mind no longer applies. Robespierre was revolutionary; modern mass-man is revolutionized passively. Has anyone noticed that the catchword of 1789, "Revolutionary," is dropped today? We contemporaries of the World War have accepted man's cosmical and social passiveness by adding to the term "revolution" of 1688, and to the adjective "revolutionary" coined in 1789, the new term "revolutionized."

So we need not be surprised if the Fascist International should execute the death warrant of the sovereign state against their own wish. By making nationalism cheap and unpalatable all over the small promontory of Asia called Europe, they produce the nausea that will end nationalism. On the other hand, the Warriors' International ends where European nationalism ends. Russia dropped her national flag as early as 1917 and, by aiming at the whole world, united one sixth of the globe; to her, then, the unity of the nations of Europe is nothing very big. She dreamt of a world-wide union and does everything in her power to outdo any particular unity of the old European countries by her international radicalism. And, west of the Atlantic, America, too, is far too vast a continent to feel or act like one European nation. America is a whole world, opened up by all the nations of Europe.

Russia and America, then, are too big to share the problems of atomized Europe. Europe, from Gibraltar to Danzig, and from Dublin to Stamboul, is the battlefield of the specific campaign of this world war to end the sovereignty of the individual European nation. For any one of them, it has become impossible to go to war simply. In this area, therefore, some order is required by which Europe be organized economically as America and Russia are organized already. In the light of geographical exclusivity, we ought to read the speeches of Hitler against "Communism." I think we all have to admit, that the Western World never will nor can "go Russian." The old Roman and Protestant countries are impervious to the Soviet experiment that fitted an area in which no living faith had changed society for a thousand years. If this is so, non-Russian Europe is compelled to search for a new social union of her own. And this search is accelerated by the Warriors' International. They may never find it. The geography of Europe is most unfavourable to any such tendency. Eccentric interests are too strong.

The solution for Europe that would serve the purpose, probably, would be the common administration of Africa. In handling Africa, Europe would acquire the unity of purpose that made the thirteen American colonies into a union. In America the vast continent beyond the Alleghenies was a federal enterprise. Common enterprises are the only ties that bind groups together. Unfortunately, in Europe they all talk, still, of dividing Africa instead of organizing it, as Europe's last chance. However, the mental war puts this question squarely before Europe for the first time.

The prospects for any real merger of Europe are dim; the British Empire is not European, and France is responsible for the achievement of the last 150 years, and therefore is as slow on the trans-national road as Wellington's England was slow in 1815. When the British are willing to admit the European Continent as junior partner into their empire, and the French are ready for the conception of a true confederacy, the taming of the shrew may happen. A second peace then may be concluded. Unfortunately neither France nor England may go so far, for they represent previous steps in the adventure of the human race which still are significant.

The second peace, therefore, that is bound to come at the end of the mental war of the last years, will be no more than an armistice. Japan, India, China, South America, Africa, Australia are only materially connected with the organic whole that we mean when speaking of Europe. They all will have to be integrated sooner or later into the working whole of the human race. Meantime it is better to speak frankly of an armistice. On an armistice pacifists and militarists may agree, and a reasonable armistice often outlasts an arbitrary peace.

We are in a twilight zone between peace and war, and the diplomats who still think of pre-War rules for a world in which there was either war or peace, are helpless in this new situation. The "accidents" that worry them and for which they use up their fountain pens, as in the case of the *Panay* accident, cannot be classified with the sign: peace or war? The Warriors' International laughs at this obsolete classification. Every step today is half belligerent, half peaceful. Diplomatic notes do not fit the new situation: swift but only partial action is expected. No moral complaints, no eternal sanctions, but energetic moves on a chessboard: retaliations, limited and yet real acts, flash through the twilight zone between peace and war. There no longer exists the clear cut "either-or" of "French" clarity, just as French ceases to be the language of diplomacy. The new world of energies wants to be aware of day and night, peace and war, sun and shadow, at the same time. The nations begin to talk the truth to each other, they shout indecently, they bite, scratch, in short, they drop diplomacy. This only means that they are integrated into a whole. Within one organism, no diplomatic shyness any longer survives.

CHAPTER FIFTEEN

The Americans

Independence—Equality—Forerunner and Failure—A "Half-Revolution"—The Rhythm of America—The New World—"Promise" and Natural Law in America—Due Process of Law

INDEPENDENCE.

AN AMERICAN HISTORIAN ONCE TOLD ME THIS ANECDOTE OF HIS student days. A professor of history had asked his class for the cause of the American Revolution, and had announced that of all the many possible answers he wanted only one. His students were at a loss; they knew too many answers. His answer ran; "Because the Colonies were three thousand miles away." Only experts have the right to ask such questions, and only experts can give such answers. I am no expert in American history, I am an expert in revolutions; and so when I look at the professor's question, and listen to his answer, I can only say; "This may be the right explanation; but if it is true, then there was no revolution." Birth is not rebirth. A far distant colony does not make a revolution merely by becoming independent. Cutting the umbilical cord of the new-born child is no revolution!

Hence our question: Was the American Revolution a true revolution, with revolutionary effects, effects that were permanent and that forecast a particular form of life? Fortunately, the question has often been asked by American historians themselves. We shall listen to what they and the contemporaries of the Revolution have to say. There is much more evidence in the sources than I can quote or cite, but at least the question will become answerable; and the answer will show why it is possible for me to say something new about the significance of the American Revolution as a revolution.

"The very term American Revolution is not without difficulties, and its use has led to misconception and confusion. In letter after letter John Adams tried to teach a headstrong generation some degree of accuracy in the use of an expression of which they had knowledge only by hearsay. 'A history of the first war of the United States is a very different thing from a history of the American Revolution,' he wrote in 1815. . . . 'The Revolution was effected before the war commenced. The Revolution was in the minds and hearts of the people.'" [1]

Now the same John Adams wrote in 1821:

"That there existed a general desire of Independence of the Crown in any part of America before the Revolution, is as far from the truth as the Zenith is from the Nadir . . . for my own part, there was not a moment during the Revolution, when I would not have given every thing I possessed for a restoration to the state of things before the contest began, provided we could have had any sufficient security for its continuance. I always dreaded the Revolution as fraught with ruin, to me and my family, and indeed it has been but little better."

Now, which statement is true? In history, diverse and even contradictory aspects of the same fact may each be true. Both statements must be taken as sincere.

All we can be sure of is that there were two different concepts of revolution in the world between 1750 and 1775. The one was French, the other English. [2] The British tradition of 1688 made glorious revolution a return to old historical principles. Let me give some examples of this side of the question. In the letters forged by John Randolph, uncle of Edward Randolph, and purporting to be written by George Washington, Randolph, who had been a friend of the Washington family, makes the general write:

[1] Arthur Meier Schlesinger, *New Viewpoints in American History*, p. 161, New York, Macmillan, 1922.

[2] See my study on *Revolution als Politischer Begriff in der Neuzeit*, Breslau, 1931.

"Having been brought up in revolution [sic] principles, I thought I trod surely when I traced the footsteps of those venerable men. Wonderful! These too are the principles of our opponents; so that all our misfortune and fault is the having put in practise the very tenets which they profess to embrace."

Barrett Wendell, in his delightful *Stelligeri*, develops these conservative ideas of the leading class at length when he writes:

"For looked at in the light of the centuries, our own constitution and all that has grown up beneath it are but outgrowth, strong with the strength that comes from natural, undistorted growth, of that firmest known system of human rights—the common law of England.

"It was the purpose of our native conquest to impose no system on anybody or on any territory; but only to maintain, in the face of all the military force of England, those rights which by the common law of England not even the English Crown had the right to touch. This is the trait that distinguishes our revolution from all the others that have since troubled the Old World and the New. Ours, and ours only, strove not to innovate but to preserve; not to manufacture a ready-made system of law and government, but to guard and protect in its normal growth a system of government which had been proved sound and wholesome by centuries of ancestral experience.

". . . The Americans were in the right, and in the right because what they fought for was no abstract principle, but rather the maintenance of their vested rights.

"In so doing, however, they were forced to be for a moment rebels. As rebels it was their inevitable misfortune to find opposed to them that great part of the best and worthiest people in the land who in any crisis feel bound to throw themselves on the side of the established authority. And the old grey house of the Pepperells typifies what few of us allow ourselves to remember—the tremendous sacrifice of good men and true that was the inevitable price of our national independence."

On this same subject of the close connection between 1688 in England and 1776 in the colonies, the American edition of William Blackstone's *Commentaries on the Laws of England* remarks in a footnote to the paragraph on the Convention of 1689: "The student who has read with care the Declaration of

Independence will see that the framers of it had this declaration [i.e., of 1689] in mind and *intended to keep strictly within the precedent.*"

This simple view, which laid nine tenths of the weight on the maintenance of vested rights and one tenth on the necessary inconvenience of rebellion, was re-emphasized in a dark hour of American history, namely, in 1862:

> "We will glance now at our fourth and last historical example, the American Revolution of 1776. . . . The American Revolution was not a revolution in the sense in which the Southern rebellion is necessarily a revolution, if it attain to that dignity at all. It was no organic disruption of society, no radical disintegration of the framework of government. It was a mere separation of certain governmental dependencies from a distant sovereignty, with which, though largely affiliated in origin and language, they had scarcely anything in common in respect to governmental policy and tendencies. The colonies were not incorporated, functional members of the British government, and their severance left that government whole and sound in all its parts." [3]

But a more abstract concept of the word "revolution" was involved in the course of events from the very beginning. The French spies in America and the French ministers at home shared the interest of all the French in *"les révolutions des empires,"* the revolution of empires. And in 1776 the young American statesman who perhaps more than most of his colleagues was brought up in French philosophical ideas, Gouverneur Morris, wrote to his mother:

> "What may be the event of the present war, it is not in men to determine. Great revolutions of empire are seldom achieved without much human calamity, but the worst that can happen is to fall on the last bleak mountain of America, and he who dies there, in defense of the injured rights of mankind, is happier than his conqueror. . . ."

But we know now from the books of Doniol and Van Tyne that as early as the 1760's Choiseul, Durand and others were

[3] Rev. Joseph Clark, *The History and Theory of Revolutions*, Philadelphia, 1862.

expecting a revolution in America. Not only was "The Independence of America" a common toast in the French West Indian Islands (*New England Chronicle,* May 2, 1776), but Raynal, in 1770, wrote on the "English Revolutions," in the plural. Durand reported to Choiseul:

> "*Il n'y a personne en Angleterre qui n'avoue que, faute de prévoyance, les colonies qu'elle possède en Amérique formeront un jour un état séparé; c'est la forme de cette révolution que je désirerais de prévoir."*

"If there were a man in New York with the genius of a Cromwell, he could set up a republic there more easily than did the great Oliver." "It is for France and Spain," [Durand] urged, "to make that man appear."

There is good evidence that the great leaders were counting as early as 1769 on help from France. And: "Pontleroy believed that Revolution would be the end of all England's efforts to better the lot of her colonists."

In all these French statements the English-American connotation of "*the*" Glorious Revolution is dropped. The new revolution is but one of many; and French curiosity is indifferent to its content. An early French visitor soberly links the two notions of independence and of new forms of government:

> "There is a gentleman here of French extraction, whose name is Du Simitière, a painter by profession. . . . This M. du Simitière is a very curious man. He has begun a collection of materials for a history of this revolution. He begins with the first advices of the tea ships. He cuts out of the newspapers every scrap of intelligence, and every piece of speculation. . . . He has *a list* of every speculation concerning independence, and *another* of those concerning forms of government." [4]

The two lists are excellent, because they show two very different trends, one emphasizing the English principle of "no taxation without representation," and, derived therefrom, independence, and the other facing the problem of a *new* form

[4] John Adams, in *Letters of Members of the Continental Congress,* II, No. 77, p. 49 *ff.*, August 14, 1776.

of government. Independence, as a return to Whig principles and methods of action, is certainly only one side of the American Revolution.

EQUALITY.

The colonies desired equality with the motherland. The French word *égalité*, the rallying-cry of 1789, meant equality within one country. Equal the citizen should be, regardless of vocation or profession. The American word equality, in 1776, was much less individualistic. The whole body politic of the colonies was jealous of the pretensions of the body politic at home. The colony of Massachusetts called itself the Commonwealth of Massachusetts; the name United States recalled the United Kingdom. George Washington could be compared with the noblest and best type of English gentleman. The American state papers were written in a peerless style of parliamentary English. The content of the American Revolution was no novelty, no new discovery of the nature of man; it was, first of all, an assertion of the *equal* right of the pioneers to have their English way in the new world.

The inferiority complex of many educated Americans has its counterpart in the epoch of independence; the unquestioned leadership of Europe is to give way to an equality of the new States with the old Monarchies, or, as the Preamble of the Declaration says, "an equal station among the Powers of the Earth." This Equality of 1776 still belongs to the Anglo-Saxon world of values; whereas the *Égalité* of 1789 was a radical outcry of men's individual nature. That explains, among other things, the compromise which was made on slavery. In 1776 nobody thought of forcing the gentlemen of Georgia and South Carolina to abolish slavery. It existed in other English colonies. It was not the objective of the Natural Rights of Man. But of course slavery was the reverse of the medal.

The first version of Equality had been: We, the colonies, are the peers of the motherland. The second version, eleven years later, took cognizance of the tremendous universality of every word that is uttered by human faith. In revolutions, we believe in a new word without divining its full scope, without knowing what hopes or fears our own word raises in the hearts of our fellowmen. The sudden or slow reaction of our neighbours, our enemies, our servants or employers, to our word of faith shows us how much we have been in the dark, and how much the word itself was like a seed buried in the darkness of a new soil. To our faith and to the words of our faith the answer comes from the outside world. In the non-Whiggist world of French friends of America, of free-thinkers, of negroes, the word "equality" found an echo which resulted in changing the word itself. It became a word of hope for new peoples, slaves, immigrants, Indians, who had not been so much as thought of in 1776.

The Jeffersonian Ordinance of 1784 was the first solution and compromise between faith and hope in the word Equality. This ordinance, the only practical constitutional advance made between 1780 and 1787, is remarkable indeed, for it balances admirably the two notions of equality. On the one hand it gave to the United States the power to own territories in common; this common ownership and sovereignty was necessary before the United States could take the place of the United Kingdom of Great Britain and Ireland or the United Empire of the Loyalists in Canada. It established full equality between the colonies and the British Commonwealth. The United States inherited the colonial adventure of the English. The frontier, the winning of a continent abandoned by the French in 1763, now became the united enterprise of the thirteen colonies, and added to their provincial and parochial local governments an imperial task commensurate with the First English Empire. The Revolution appeared clearly as the result of the Anglo-French war and the expulsion of the French from the continent. It crowned the equality of the colonies and the motherland with the only crown worthy of the name: the crown of free and full growth into the future. It placed the responsibility for the continent on the thirteen colonies united.

The ordinance ruled that the new territory, ceded and to be ceded, should be divided into prospective States, to which names were given; each of them to receive in due time a temporary or territorial government, and ultimately to be admitted into the Confederation of States upon the express assent of two thirds of the preceding States. The West was made an equal of the East. The colonies recognized the equality of each territory and its admission "on an equal footing with the original States."

Now one of the five fundamental conditions to the establishment of both their temporary and their permanent governments foreshadowed the reverse of the medal, announced the change of Equality from a word of faith to a word of hope. Jefferson, as author of the Ordinance, had inserted the following paragraph: "That after the year 1800 of the Christian Era, there shall be neither slavery nor involuntary servitude in any of the said States." This paragraph was the first word of love spoken in mediation between faith in equality and hope of equality as elements in American constitutional life. But the fifth provision was lost through the absence of a member from New Jersey, rendering the vote of that State null and void for want of a quorum. Sixteen members had voted for Jefferson's prohibition of slavery, seven against; six States for, three against. But an affirmative vote of a majority of all the thirteen States was required. Thus by a vote of 6½ to 6½ the prohibition of slavery failed in 1784. This indicates clearly how little progress Equality had made from faith toward hope.

Three years later—and, by that token, three years nearer the French Revolution—Jefferson's Ordinance was reframed for the territories northwest of the Ohio, excluding, by its silence, the territories south of that river. Here the Jeffersonian principle was incorporated by Nathan Dane of Massachusetts: "There shall be neither slavery nor involuntary servitude in the said Territory." Instead of a vote of 6½ to 6½ it was a division of the continent into two halves. Equality in the body politic was granted to every colony. Equality of the individual was granted in the northern half only.

When the grandsons of the sons of the Revolution reopened the proceedings in 1860, the word equality was read from the other side. Colonial equality weighed, so to speak, one fourth or one eighth in the scale; the equality of the individual overbalanced it. And this experience was not peculiar to America. The absolutist Czar of Russia likewise had to emancipate the bondmen and serfs of his landlords. Cheap, free, mobile labour had appeared on the market. The word of hope for the serf or the slave had been made intelligible to the governing class in America by the factory system. In 1860 the word of hope met, in the capitalist class, not so much faith in a new world as clear knowledge of the conditions of the new world. A religious faith had enabled the fathers of the Revolution to go forward. In 1860 it was a secular knowledge, a sober insight into the machinery of the industrial system, which accepted the religious hopes of the coloured people as an ally. The brunt of the old religious faith in the equality of the colonies was borne by the Southerners. The song *Maryland, My Maryland* is a queer example of this frenzy of the religious belief in the States' rights established by the Revolution.

The American Revolution, by this ambiguity of the use of the word "equality," offers a lesson in political language in general. Equality began in the dark, as a word of faith. It meant equality of the colonies with the motherland. Its other side, the word of hope—equality for the slaves—first appeared in 1784 and 1787.[5] It had already achieved then, one half of the new order. But the hour for its universal application in both ways, in the way of faith and in the way of hope, did not strike until the War of Secession. And as this was a war and not a committee-vote as in 1787, the religious faith of 1776 in equality was on the side of the South. The Northern industrialists were led to hear equality as a word of hope, and with a new energy and vigour, because all over the world liberalism was advancing triumphantly. The waves expanding from the centre of Europe reached Russia and America simultaneously, and in both countries they carried reluctant and unsentimental rulers in the direction of "hope for equality."

Here we look deep into the machinery of human speech and spirit. Every revolution starts from faith; hope alone can never cause or excuse the terrible evils of a revolution. *Despair* must reign before faith in the Creator and in the dignity of human-

[5] According to older Declarations (Delaware, 1776, etc.), "Every man is created free and equal"; but slaves were not touched by these statements.

ity can enter the scene in such a brutal form as it does in times of revolution. Faith is a belief in things unseen; it goes against hope, it defies all odds, all probability, all chances. Faith in your mission enables you to break down the protecting walls of law and continuity. Faith drove Abraham from his country. And faith, in times of real necessity, is always accounted righteousness. It is a *passive* attitude, a strike in an impasse, a walkout.

It is only in a later stage of the revolution that Hope replaces Faith. When those who have uttered, stammered, cried out the new word in the dark of despair and revolution, when they have passed away, their grandchildren who have listened to it in the open day of revolution, try to write the next chapter. Hope is *active*. And action is, in spite of the great heresy of the nineteenth century, completely sterile without a foregoing promise, without the Word. Without the promise of faith, and its desperate decision to *bear the worst,* the later activities of hope would be of no practical result.

Faith, hope and love, the religious forces of mankind, are not limited to denominational purposes. Faith, hope and love are universal. They are the only real motive forces of history and of political life and language, for the simple reason that they alone connect the words men speak and use as means of communication with a real power working in time and space.

In the Civil War we can study the decay of this religious language. The profiteers from the North who abused the South after the War, the carpet-baggers, disorganized and dismantled the American political credo so passionately defended by Lincoln. After 1868 the words of religious promise and the acts of their fulfilment were debased to rational and deliberate uses. Interests, rationalism, scepticism, racketeers, littérateurs and traders reduce our creative words to the level of mechanized speech. They use them as advertisement, as talk, and as a means of hiding their thoughts.

So this is a lesson we should draw from our study of this one side of the American Revolution. Faith, Hope and Love are not individual qualities of the so-called individual soul. Neither are we, as humble members of a church or synagogue or lodge, expected to bother about these allegorical ladies. They are beyond our individual "intentionality." Whole generations are given over to them. Periods of faith, periods of hope, and periods of trading in words seem to follow each other with inescapable logic. The only liberty left to the individual is whether his actions during these different periods shall be dictated by love or fear. Self-forgetfulness or self-conceit makes all the difference in our individual appearances on the scene of history. Abraham Lincoln is the everlasting hero of self-forgetful devotion, who bridged the gulf between faith and hope, fear and salesmanship, with the one timeless quality of man.

FORERUNNER AND FAILURE.

Equality was one important promise of the Declaration of Independence. But that it was the only one is emphatically denied by so careful and conservative an American as Henry Cabot Lodge. There was a universal aspect of the American Revolution which had nothing to do with the struggle between colonies and motherland. When we turn to this aspect we feel delocalized. We are no longer listening to local gods, jealous of their territorial rights. We can hardly understand why this thing happened, of all places, in America. It becomes human, universal, inevitable, a psychic adventure of the whole species of man. Lodge says:

"From the American point of view, then, there was nothing inevitable about the American Revolution. It was created by a series of ministerial mistakes, each one of which could have been easily avoided. From another point of view, however, it was absolutely inevitable, the inexorable result of the great social and political forces which had long been gathering and now were beginning to move forward.

"When the great democratic movement started, at the close of the eighteenth century, it began in England, where there was no despotic personal monarchy, where personal liberty was most assured, and where freedom existed in the largest measure. The abuses of aristocracy and monarchy in England were as nothing to what they were on the Continent. The subjects of George III were not ground down by taxes, were not sold into military service, were not trampled on by an aristocracy and crushed by their king, they were the freest, best-governed people on earth, faulty as their government no doubt was in many respects. Yet it was among the English-speaking people that we detect the first signs of the democratic movement, for, as they were the least oppressed, so they were the most sensitive to any abuse or to any infringement upon the liberties they both prized and understood. The entire English people, both at home and abroad, were thus affected. The Middlesex elections, the career of Wilkes, the letters of Junius, the resolution of Burke against the increasing power of the Crown, the rising demand for Parliamentary reform, the growing hostility to the corrupt system of bargain and intrigue, by which the great families parcelled out offices and seats and controlled Parliament, all pointed in the same direction, all were signs of an approaching storm.

"If the revolution had not come in the American colonies it would have come in England itself. . . . The colonies were the least-governed, the best-governed, and the freest part of the dominion of Great Britain. . . . America rebelled, not because the colonies were oppressed, but because their inhabitants were the freest people then in the world and did not mean to suffer oppression." [6]

Here we are within the British Empire. We are facing a question, not primarily of independence, but of ideas versus other ideas. Jonathan Boucher said in 1797, "Now the American Revolution was clearly a struggle for pre-eminence between Whigs and Tories." But when Du Simitière began his lists on forms of government, in August, 1776, the Whigs in England and the revolutionaries in America had already separated.

The Declaration of Rights, written by George Mason, recommends, it is true, a frequent return to fundamental principles. This is good English style. But Article Five introduced that minimum of new principles, over and beyond Whiggism, which constituted the real break. As the expression is particularly sober and modest, it seems to me the more striking. Mason recommends, on the authority of Cicero, *De Legibus*, III, 2, a

[6] Henry Cabot Lodge, *The Story of the Revolution*, I, pp. 14-16, New York, Scribner, 1898.

uniform equable rotation of obedience and command: and the Virginia Declaration of Rights reads in his draft;

"(5) That the legislative and executive powers of the state should be separate and distinct from the judicial; and that the members of the two first may be restrained from oppression by feeling and participating the burthens of the people, they should, at fixed periods, be reduced to a private station and return unto that body from which they were originally taken."

This rotation is indeed the pregnant expression of democratic principles. The "reduction to a private station" and "return to that body from which he was originally taken" was in operation when Washington refused the third term; it made President Grant, in his old age, write books so that he might pay his debts. The return to a low station is utterly objectionable in an aristocracy. In England, "once a member of society [that is, of good society], always a member." In America, a man can be as often out as he is in, and there is no self-pity about it.

Nature is the political principle and the spiritual force of the Revolution. Thomas Paine dwelt at length on nature; but he was not alone in doing so. Even Gouverneur Morris, after he had turned poor Paine out of Congress, wrote in the same vein in his *Observations on the American Revolution*. These were published by a committee of Congress, in accordance with a resolution of that body, in 1779. Now this enemy of anarchy and democracy could not help declaring on the title page:

"The great principle is and ever will remain in force that *men are by nature free.* As accountable to Him that made them, they must be so; and so long as we have any idea of divine justice, we must associate with it that of human freedom. The right to be free can never be alienated. Still less is it practicable for one generation to mortgage the privileges of another. . . ."

Here the conservative who in 1814 uttered the remarkable words, "Rejoice, America, the Bourbons are restored," opened the door to the mighty goddess of Nature, who if she is invited in will bring with her the emancipation of all creeds, all races, all nations. Lord Charnwood said of Lincoln:

"His affection for his own country and its institutions is curiously dependent upon a wider cause of human good, and is not a whit the less intense for that."

And Lincoln himself, in 1860, said with deep feeling:

"I have pondered over the evils that were endured by the officers and soldiers of the army who achieved that independence. . . . It was not the mere matter of separation of the colonies from the motherland, it was the sentiment in the Declaration of Independence which gave liberty, not alone to the people of this country, but I hope to the world, for all future time. It was that which gave promise that in due time the weight would be lifted from the shoulders of all men."

The nature of man, of the individual man, is exorcised. The Whigs in America are obliged to adopt a vocabulary unknown to their English ancestors. What the Levellers, the left wing, the lunatic fringe of Cromwell's revolution, had first arrived at, in 1648—the idea of a law paramount—was now put into practice in the form of a written Constitution. And the colonists cannot dispense with Thomas Paine, this typical Leveller, this English radical. He crosses the threshold of the English sanctuary, Canaan, he relinquishes the language of Israel, and dares to set foot outside, in free space. Paine exclaims: *"We have it in our power to begin the world over again.* A situation, similar to the present, hath not happened since *the days of Noah* until now." We are outside Revelation, in the free world of Nature.

The ideas of the French Revolution seem, and are, similar. "Nature" had arisen to power all over Europe between 1688 and 1770. But how different is the situation! This time Nature is rediscovered, not in Paris, the intellectual centre of mediæval Christianity, but in Boston and Philadelphia. Nature is not reimplanted in a refined country by revolutionary forces; on the contrary, a capital is artificially projected into the wilds of a new continent. The revolution mobilizes the inhabitants of thirteen British colonies against the wild Nature of a half-unknown area.

There are three significant features in this attempt to support independence by exorcising nature. Two of them are not peculiar to the American Revolution; they can be found in other forms of government which sprang from other revolutionized areas. The third feature is unique and belongs to America alone.

Of the two regular features which the American Revolution has in common with all other periods of revolutionary preparation, the first is its connection with the upheaval which follows it; the French Revolution. We find that the main revolutions, for example, the Russian, the English, the Italian, each had a precursor. And the precursor is always a failure. From this viewpoint shall we call the American Revolution a failure too? We must look deeper into the question of precursors.

Normally, it is the radicals, the left wing within the sphere of the last great revolution, who take the next step. The idea of Henry Cabot Lodge is perfectly justified, that the freest country is always full of the forces which are preparing the next revolution.

Nowhere have there been more Communists than in France under Napoleon III. It is in Paris that they start the Commune in 1871. It breaks down. The Communists are destroyed for a long time. Fifty thousand are condemned to deportation. Paris is not Russia. It is totally unfit for the proletarian dictatorship. It remains the meeting place of inspired individuals.

Germany lived through the Reformation in her little principalities. The Calvinists, the left wing, felt strongly that they should bring the reformed church into the hands of the lower estates, and they began a real Puritan revolution in Bohemia. The Elector Palatine was made king in Prague for one winter. This Bohemian simile to the later William III of England suffered a total breakdown, at the famous battle of the White Mountain in May of the next year, 1620. The Puritan Revolution had to migrate from continental Bohemia to insular Great Britain. The King of England, father-in-law of the king-for-one-winter, became the target of the Puritans; his brother-in-law, Charles I, was brought to the scaffold. Bohemia had all the qualities of a continental country, with the need for a strong central power. Only in Shakespeare does Bohemia lie on the sea-coast. The ideas of local self-government, and of democracy in the congregation, would not work there. They were transplanted to the island which calls for self-government, in its capacity as domestic centre for a new commonwealth across the seas.

By now, the reader will not be surprised to find the same form of precursor revolution in the cycle of clerical revolutions. Arnold of Brescia, and Savonarola are well-known cases in point. Both tried to overcome the abuses of the preceding civilization by an attack at its very centre. Savonarola attacked the Guelphic city-state in Florence in 1495. Arnold of Brescia anticipated the new Franciscan vow of poverty by his struggles in Rome in 1146, but since emperor and pope turned against him unitedly, he failed. Four times, the seed seemed to be ripe. Four times, in 1146, 1495, 1620, 1871, the seed, though ripe, could not bear fruit, because it remained within the old environment. The stormy petrels of a revolution must go from the centre of the previous revolution to its fringe, as the seeds of plants are carried over to another specimen.

With the lesson of these four distinct cases of precursor revolutions in mind, we turn to the American Revolution again. It is a minor point, but of a certain interest, to compare the politics of the Stuarts and the Bourbons just before their fall. Louis XIV and James I both supported the precursor revolution abroad and by supporting them, became the unconscious instruments of the real and total revolution which went against themselves. The ways of Providence are inscrutable! More general is the statement that, as in the four other cases, the radical opposition against the abuses of the last total revolution was strong within the whole British Commonwealth, and the outburst in America was only its symptom. And the colonies, in accepting all these radical forces, rid the motherland—to a certain extent—of their infection.

But when we look at the thirteen colonies as a part of the British Commonwealth, we realize immediately how utterly unprepared they were to expand their ideas so as to include the world. The struggle for existence was much too hard. In France, nature is a relief from an aristocratic civilization; in the colonies, nature is attacked day after day by a body of pioneering individuals, who must stick to facts and have no time for abstract ideas. In a virgin country, Nature is not lazy. She threatens you with annihilation if you do not move faster than she does. Nature marches against you if you do not out-march her in time. A thinly populated country faces a constant relapse into a second wilderness, a repeated loss of regions already conquered for plough and pasture.

The sound of the axe is the natural philosophy of America. Nietzsche's desire to philosophize with a hammer in his hand is artificial in comparison with the natural philosophy of the woodchopper in the West. Facts, facts, facts, are the reality in a new world. Men, men, men, are the need of a pioneering group. It is not the salon, not a feminine culture, but bosses who run America. Not inspired writers, but shrewd politicians, not genius, but self-made men, are what is wanted.

Now all this does not vary greatly from the English type. The pioneer is necessarily harsher, coarser, more ruthless than the fighting gentleman; but he is by no means his antitype, as the Frenchman is. Thus no really new type was created by the American Revolution. In this respect, America is like her sister-areas. All the "precursors" remain geographically, spiritually, and morally too much within the orbit of the previous great revolution to be original. A certain variation is attempted, but no really new variety of man is produced, based on a new aspect of the human soul.

After 1780, the American advance reached its limit. Thomas Paine's sharpest anti-British protest lost its influence. Paine's success in 1776 was not a beginning but an end.

That the forward leap had not gone far enough for a "total" revolution becomes clear not only when one compares the fate of the other harbingers of revolution, but when one recurs to purely American observations. What says John Adams' mar-vellous letter to H. Niles in 1818 (*Works*, X, 282)?

"The Revolution was in the minds and hearts of the people; a change in their religious sentiments of their duties and obligations. While the king and all in authority under him were believed to govern in justice and mercy, according to laws and constitutions derived from the God of Nature and transmitted to them by their ancestors, they thought themselves bound to pray for the king and queen and all the royal family, and all in authority under them, as ministers ordained of God for their good; but when they saw those powers renouncing all the principles of authority, and bent upon the destruction of all the securities of their lives, liberties and properties, they thought it their duty to pray for the Continental Congress and all the thirteen State Congresses. . . ."

How excellent! Modern rationalists easily forget that in every American household and in every parish in the thirteen colonies a day came when the words in the prayers had to be changed and were changed; that in the year 1776 any such change was still felt as a religious conversion, a deep break in the life of the people. The daily form of expression for the visible body politic was transferred from the whole to a part, from the British Commonwealth to the Commonwealth of Massachusetts. Even today, the judge in any State still prays for the common weal of his State!

True enough, it was the beginning of a new era in America when King George was no longer mentioned from the pulpit on Sunday; but the warmth of the old prayers of the pioneers for their European homes could not simply be transferred to the Continental Congress. The prayer for Continental Congress was a substitute, not an equivalent. We hear that a dead silence prevailed when the word "nation" was first adopted by Congress. The British nation could as little be replaced by an American "nation" as the king could be replaced by Congress. "Nation" is one of those artificial words of European coinage that swim on the surface of America's political talk. But above and beyond the particular colonies, beyond the Commonwealth of Massachusetts and beyond Rhode Island and Providence Plantations, America is neither a state nor a nation nor an empire. All these names reduce America's stature to the petty level of political institutions. There is, to be sure, a Federal government serving as a lever by which Americans can move the world. But the space they live in is neither State nor Empire nor any other human and social substitute for nature; it is nature itself. To pray for Congress was a poor thing; it meant, in effect, that one no longer prayed at all.

"The colonies had grown up under constitutions of government— so different, there was so great a variety of religions, they were composed of so many different nations, their customs, manners and habits had so little resemblance, and their intercourse had been so rare, and their knowledge of each other so imperfect, that to unite them in the same principles in theory and the same system of action, was certainly a very difficult enterprise." (John Adams, X, 283.)

Let us keep in mind this hollow, incomplete religious situation and the sudden shrinking, the crippling of the idea of "Commonwealth." It will help us later to understand what the real faith of America has been since her breaking away from England.

The American Revolution was a precursor, and as a precursor it was as unable to create a new language as the Romans, the Bohemians, or the forerunners of revolution in Paris and Florence had been incapable of tearing down the traditions of their environment. In that respect America, as she appears in the *American Letter* of MacLeish, must be interpreted as an unfulfilled promise, snuffed out between the two great forms of life and education which were created by England and France respectively. Something has happened to America; she has lost one political language without finding another. She has suffered a psychic loss. In France the walls of the Bastille, because they were of stone, allowed of a real total revolution. Dynamite will not accomplish much in a desert. The same is true of a revolution three thousand miles away from its base. Our professor's answer on the cause of the American Revolution really ought to be changed into its opposite; the American Revolution could not go deep enough to be a true revolution, for the very reason that it happened three thousand miles from England!

A "HALF-REVOLUTION."

The tremendous remoteness of America brings us to the question of geographical chance. Poland's sandy provinces resisted the aristocratic domination of a gentry. The gentry, which in England was the nation's chief pride and glory, brought only division and disintegration to Poland; for, to paraphrase the witty remark of the Prince de Ligne, she had no British sea in her Constitution. The Polish Revolution of the gentry failed, after a great beginning. As I mentioned before, the American Revolution might be placed in the same class. This class is more difficult to explain. It is earmarked by the fact that it stands halfway between the solitary catastrophes and the long, long march of the great revolutions. We have seen that in any revolutionized territory periods of pride and humiliation alternate for centuries like strophe and antistrophe. And we find that these periods correspond in length for the various revolutions.

There exists a series of what may be called "half-revolutions": a concomitant phenomenon to the great revolution. Half-revolutions cannot create an original key or melody of political language, being placed for one reason or another too near the focus of some other realm of influence. But they represent a real and externally successful revolution; only the achievement is undone by a period of demolition. Spain, Sweden and the Netherlands are the great examples of such a process.

A list of half-revolutions would show that Spain became a real great power as the result of a rather brief effort. Between 1566 and 1581 Spain crushed the Netherlands, Portugal and the Grand Turk; and the Spanish order of the Jesuits conquered the field of education at Rome. The might established in so brilliant a campaign spread over all Europe. In 1658 Oliver Cromwell was buried according to Spanish ceremonial; the Puritan leader was carried to the grave with all the ceremonies used at the burial of Philip II of Spain. What a lesson in the hegemony of Spain over Europe during the seventeenth century! And at the beginning of the eighteenth, Frederick

William of Prussia copied the code of honour of the Spanish orders of knighthood for his new staff of officers. Spanish etiquette, with its strict separation of king and queen, survived all changes in Austria down to 1917, when it was discarded by the young Charles I. In their common bed-chamber, the Empress Zita was allowed to interfere in matters of state: she even held conversations with cabinet ministers over the telephone. The austere majesty of the Catholic king was turned into the privacy of a middle-class couple. It meant the certain collapse of the Hapsburg throne; but it also meant the vanishing of the last Spanish glory. This glory had already been dimmed as early as 1700, in the War of the Spanish Succession. For twelve or thirteen years Spain had proved to be merely a pawn in the game of the rest of Europe. With the treaties which ended this war, Spain ceased to be a great power.

The same sudden extinction befell Sweden. Its periods are 1630-1651 (from the entrance of Sweden into the Thirty Years' War to the abdication of Gustavus Adolphus' daughter Christina), that is, the period of its revolutionary influence on Europe; and 1700-1721 (the reign of Charles XII), that is, the era of extinction. Nobody can read Voltaire's famous *Charles XII* without a shudder, without the feeling of Nemesis at work. All the merits of Gustavus Adolphus and Oxenstierna, the wise chancellor of the king and of Christina, are undone. A prestige earned by twenty years of hegemony over Europe is wasted in a fool's adventure that lasts another twenty years.

Both Spain and Sweden are less concerned with making a revolution in their own national character than with imposing it ready-made on the rest of Europe. And so they fail. The terrible attempt of Philip II to turn the wheel of history backward is expiated by the complete obliteration of Spain in its War of Succession. The same is true of the Netherlands, whose brilliant fight against Spain, together with their aristocratic system and their Cromwell-like Lord Protector, successfully anticipate the Bohemian adventure in 1620.

The reason why these half-revolutions are so different from their greater brothers is that they meet no full martyrdom at home. The test of the Great Revolutions is that they were most fertile during the period when their countries were most deeply humiliated. By that token they have an immortal soul. The half-revolutions expire; and in the hour of their expiration nobody is concerned for their former achievement. All that is gone. It was only on the surface. But I should add that there are many questions here open to discussion; the inquiry ought to be carried on from the point at which we have arrived. A special volume should be devoted to the comparative study of half-revolutions. It would reveal the brutal character of political life, which never delivers anything without its full price of psychic depth, of faith, hope and love.

It may not be clear how the American War of Secession really fits into the list of half-revolutions. But that it belongs in a series of correlations, strophe corresponding to antistrophe, I am convinced. Over long periods of time each revolution calls for its sequel. Time is a field of interplay as well as space; and we are only beginning to divine the rules of this interplay. These correlating conditions are certainly remarkable. What they prove is neither a rough and ready individualism of purely atomic events, nor a crude, astrological, meaningless fluctuation of abstract principles.

These correlations are asymmetrical. Mankind lives in a system which is forever *opening* and *changing.* The thirty years of the German Reformation, and its downfall in the Thirty Years' War, mean the same for the substance of the process, as the twenty-six years of the French Revolution or the twenty years of the English Civil War. They form an equation with the sixty-eight years of the Italian revolution and the exile of the popes in Avignon. Thus the door is opened wide to the individual shape of each event. But though they are full of variation, nevertheless the periods are rhythmical.

I say all this because I promised to make a contribution toward reintegrating the scattered atoms of history. But we also need it for the very practical purpose of grasping the relation between the American Revolution and the Civil War. Everybody feels that there is such a relation. The nature of man revolted in 1861 against the fictions of a Constitution based on the nature of man. And the principle of independence was put to the test as well. The South had to realize that this independence had not meant a permanent separate existence for any and every region, but a single Declaration of Independence at a unique historical moment. As against the States' Rights the liberal ideas of the French Revolution had invaded the American world. The slaves were emancipated.

But do the years of the War of Independence correspond to the years of the War of Secession? And do they correspond to the periods of upheaval (1640-1688) and humiliation (1776-1815) in England as well? Let the new science of Revolution answer these questions.

THE RHYTHM OF AMERICA.

The States of the continent of America, united in 1776, offer a peculiar and, so far as I know, unparallelled lesson in Revolutions. A close relationship between war and revolution has often been mentioned in these pages. Revolution begins with wars (Russian), or ends with wars (French), or is focussed by wars (German, England), etc. But in all these cases the relationship is obvious; no one doubts, for example, that the Thirty Years' War was a chastisement of the religious party in Germany. In the peculiar case of America we find a Freudian repression which forbids all mention of the interplay between war and revolution. American history began by suppressing it, and continued to repress it. This suppression was not invented or devised by politicians or users of rhetoric; it merely happened.

The three, ay, the four, turning-points of American policy were each preceded, at a distance of half a generation, by a war. The experience of war sank deep into the womb of the time, and fertilized, in a population with little time or leisure for reflection, the common thinking and common understanding of a change to come. When this new phase of life appeared, the fact that it had been begotten in the preceding war was overlooked. War and revolution, though secretly interdependent, were not *visibly* connected.

Every American war had the same effect on the country; a political outbreak after a generation, or in about fifteen years.

The fact is not apparent so long as you begin American history with the Boston Tea Party or the Declaration of Independence, because then the greatest interplay of war and revolution is automatically excluded. Let us admit the working hypothesis that there might be an interdependence between external wars and internal revolutions. Then set up the following list:

1756-1763	French and Indian War
1776-1783	Revolution
1812-1815	War of 1812
1829-1837	Jacksonian democracy; spoils system
1845-1846	Mexican War
1860-1868	Civil War
1917-1918	World War
1933-	New Deal

The difference between the Revolutionary War against the British Crown and the War of 1812 is made especially clear by this comparison: the Revolution is an answer, given in the form of a civil war, to the expulsion of the French rivals. The personality of George Washington links the War of 1756 and the Revolution of 1776; Washington owed his fame at the beginning of the Revolution to his pre-eminence in the foregoing war. The War of 1812 was a real external war. True, it was also an aftermath. People still remembered 1776. Otherwise Napoleon might equally well have been the foe. But the War of 1812 was a war pure and simple; it had no idea, no constitutional purpose, no reforming intention whatever. It was an aftermath of the era of humiliation for the English, the era between 1775 and 1815. Here American was under the spell of European meteorology, as it had been in 1756.

However, the War of 1812 brought forward a new leader: Jackson. Old Hickory did not become President until 1829; but when he did, the nation he led into the spoils system was a new nation. The English-American War of 1812 had shaken the remnants of English Whiggism in America. The moral atmosphere of the English-American War, with the open recalcitrance of New England, had been thoroughly rotten. Now, since it had been a war of resentment and prejudice against England, the populace could put up for the first time an absolutely un-English type of man, the man of the people and of the frontier. But it took them fifteen years to do so.

The war against Mexico brought a third empire, the Spanish, into the hands of the United Colonies. The way to Texas and to California was no longer to be paved by individualistic settlers or sailors: California and the Spanish third of the United States had to be unified by the concentrated effort of railroad-building. The Union Pacific was the organizing force of the new period, which had to deal for the first time with East, Middle West, and West as three essential parts of the United States. Railroads meant big business, vast agglomerations of capital, cheap labour, proletarian immigration.

The War of Secession was the constitutional and political solution of the economic problems raised by the Mexican War. Whiggism, which was significant only for the thirteen original colonies, and Federalism, which had no meaning in the new West, were replaced by Republicanism. Republicanism meant the Industrial Revolution. This has often been said; in repeating it we wish to stress two facts: first, that the new West was conquered by that vanguard of fortune-hunters which is concomitant with early capitalism; and second, that the word "industrial" means the united and centralized effort of big capital and hundreds of thousands of employed hands.

This third of the United States was not won piece-meal, acre by acre, farm after farm; it was taken as one big field for industrial organization. For that very reason the people who were employed in the task were distinguished very sharply from the people who had settled the Middle West. The Irish or Polish or Italian or Chinese workers who built the railroads across America and made the steel and iron and copper to run them, were not individuals like the farmers and squatters of old. The personalities of the Industrial Revolution were the big corporations which hired those thousands of men.

The Civil War ended with the amendment protecting every person in life and property. It was the hopeful ideology of

Sumner and the Abolitionists which was reflected in this word
"person." The Fourteenth Amendment, in 1868, inherited
from the Northwest Ordinance the formula: "No person shall
be deprived of life, liberty, or property without due process
of law." Lincoln had wished to use the old text of 1787, for
obvious reasons of conciliation.

At first the Supreme Court limited the word "person" to
human beings; but later they extended it to include corporations. A statute which had been the Magna Charta of individual liberty north of the Ohio from 1787 to 1868 became the
Magna Charta of corporations, with the ultimate result of the
Delaware Corporation. The corporations were victorious in
1868 because the task laid upon the nation in 1846 could only
be solved by their organizing capacity.

The World War swept over the United States at the end of
their Industrial Revolution, as the War of 1812 had swept over
them at the end of the first period of revolution. Both times
they thought themselves "too proud to fight"; and both times
they were drawn into the European maelstrom.

1763	reads not unlike	1846	
1776	Washington reads like	1860	Lincoln
1812-1815	is comparable to	1917-1919	
In 1829	a new era began as in	1933	

Take the times of good feeling between 1815 and 1828, for
example, and compare them with the prosperity after the
World War. Coolidge and Hoover were conservatives of the
John Quincy Adams stamp. Mr. Harding proclaiming the
withdrawal from all European activities, from the League of
Nations, etc., and Monroe formulating the principle of hands
off America, have something in common. The situations in
which they found themselves were not at all the same; but the
same spirit guided them both, and the same attitude made
them both popular—and unreal.

The unreality is especially evident in both post-war situations. In 1815, as in 1919, a completely exhausted Europe and
a prosperous America conclude the peace. But prosperous

America was governed for another half generation by a group of men who had lost contact with the new structure of the national life. The frontier rose up suddenly in 1828, to the inexpressible shock of the older generation. The explosion in 1933 came just as unexpectedly. Trade Unions, Socialism, Brain Trust, subsidies . . . a torrent of new blessings and new questions, and no brains or hearts prepared to meet them.

The World War turned the scales against the big "corporations" protected by the Fourteenth Amendment. Collective capital had been organizing America for fifty years. Now collective labour, collective groups of immigrants, class-groups, various sections of the country, are restless in America because the World War destroyed European civilization upon which they had relied as a background. Up to the War, the social and cultural groups of American life drew on Europe for nourishment. In spite of "Equality," engineers, historians, physicians, trade unions, parsons and social workers, foresters and farmers found corresponding groups in Europe, based—as it seemed— on inexhaustible funds of reproduction and regeneration in the field of thought and taste, remedies and ideas, beauty and imagination. As a result of the Great War the respective groups in America have lost these props of their moral existence. The standards of beauty, piety, scholarship, parliamentarism, craftsmanship, are no longer delivered on post-card order from Europe. Bolsheviks, Fascists, depression and dissolution beset Europe. Meanwhile, at the back of all American institutions, a gap begins to be felt. The sudden enthusiasm for Scandinavia is an attempt to fill this gap. It is a makeshift.

The American crusade did not save Europe. Of the unforeseen results of the American crusade in 1917-18, the fate of Austria is, I think, an undisputed example. The "Balkanization," the atomization of Europe has lowered all the standards of her culture. In consequence, many elements of American life are being forced into a readjustment of their backgrounds.

The word "immigrant" is not welcome in American public discussion; but it is less the individual immigrant than his racial or cultural background which now claims reception into a new whole. America's immigrant groups could once live by tracing back independent and individual ties with a particular European influence or institution, but that will not work any longer. At this time, immigration of individuals is negligible. The emphasis can be shifted now. The formative energies which were reflected in the new-comers of the last hundred years must now be transfused into the American system. Unassimilated, these energies will produce, as they have at times already produced, embolism and paralysis.

It is not our business to prophesy. But we can see that recovery is no important part of the New Deal. The New Deal has little to do with the business cycle; it is not a question of one particular failure of the economic system. It must accept, willy-nilly, the results of the World War: Europe destroyed, markets closed, and America's cultural groups left to desiccate by the drying up of their fountainheads. The New World is only now returning to its first great vision, that of being really a New World. After all, the four wars, 1756, 1812, 1845, 1917, and their four applications, 1776, 1829, 1860 and 1933, have only developed and circumscribed the one theme proposed by the first war of 1756. The contemporaries of the Revolution knew, to an astonishing degree, how far the true American principle lay beyond any particular political principle. They knew that all forms of government, all schemes and proclamations, were dwarfed by the Star-Spangled Banner and its galaxy of States. The *completeness of America* was the American premise from the very beginning.

But before illustrating this faith of the fathers of the Constitution, I wish to point out the astonishing fact that the political turns of American life were always rather unforeseen, rather unprepared. There was a period of incubation during which the seed planted by a previous war was ripened. Then, suddenly, a new group of men came to the fore and tried out the new forms of government befitting the changed situation which that war had brought about. It is fatal for any great truth to be thought of as a textbook truism. Nobody will make any use of it. "War is the father of all things" is such a worn out phrase; it has never been applied in political science as a working hypothesis. The peculiar trait of American history seems to me only the long period between cause and effect, between external war and civil change.

Perhaps in older countries a greater sophistication of the ruling classes, and a greater differentiation and variety of ideas, permits a subtler interweaving of events with the consciousness of those events. Only in the Great War, it seems, did Europe show something comparable to the innocent and ingenuous American habit of digesting the results of a war half a generation later. Hitlerism, at least, offers many features which hint at the fact that Germany entered the War without any thought, any goal, or any insight into the future. It took a new generation of youth to bring the "movement of the unknown soldier" into political power, fifteen years later.

External war is the father of domestic law. The community of war times is always the new community.* Peace writes down the constitution which was tested in time of war. Rights, liberties, privileges, the wheels and checks of a system, depend not on arbitrary notions of individual leaders, but on the scars of experience left on the body politic by the period of its most radical testing. It is a comfort, I think, to find that our human affairs do not depend so much on volition or brains or chance as on the real fact of trial and sacrifice. That wars should bring about, after a rather long time of secret influence, a form of government tested by these very wars, seems a convincing example of the super-individual forces at work in society. Roosevelt may never quote Wilson or refer to the World War situation; yet the emergency measure of 1933 had to take up the problem of economic organization at the exact point where it had been left in 1918. The war-machinery of the country in 1918 is being rebuilt today for peace-time purposes; but it is being rebuilt, no doubt about that.

The march of nations is slow, but at least it is not arbitrary; it is march from war toward peace. War means sacrifices, peace means profits. Government is the Colossus that bestrides war and peace. Wherever scarcity and self-denial are virtues, there

---

* Eugen Rosenstock-Huessy, *Kriegsheer und Rechtsgemeinschaft*, Akademische Festrede, Breslau, 1932.

is war being waged. Wherever plenty and happiness are extolled, there is peace.

Social forms reflect the experiences of war, and reconcile war-time mobilization with peace-time reconstruction. Any suppression of this interplay between war and New Deal will only prolong the crisis. Politicians, frightened by the supposed cowardice of the masses, are easily led to gloss over such serious truths. The forgetfulness of the man in the crowd deters even those who have some memory of the past from applying it. But unless the United States recognizes this interconnection of war and peace, the country will stumble into one international puzzle after the other. Its withdrawal from Europe since the war is an expression of the American dismay at learning that war is never the end, but always the beginning of a new social order.

THE NEW WORLD.

The contemporaries of the Revolution often conjured up the great promise of a new world, united by the abandonment of the French colonies in North America and by the spontaneous effort of the English colonies during the war of 1756.

The States founded in the Revolution are called the United States. The name reminds one of the United Kingdom of Great Britain. The new unity was no kingdom, and a unity nevertheless. At the end of the eighteenth century such a unity was unheard of. Now the newness of this unity was not a mere legal or formal fact. The Federalists were mistaken in considering it simply a constitutional issue. Jefferson was more far-sighted; and this insight was what brought him his triumph in 1800. For the new unity was a unity not in being, but in becoming. It was not a togetherness of possessions but the potentiality of an unfolding, ever widening system. As Thomas Paine shouted: "We have it in our power to *begin* the world over again. The birthday of a new world is at hand, and a race of men, perhaps as numerous as all Europe contains, are to receive their freedom." He was much less interested in the constitution of 1776 or 1787 than in the concept of a world in space and time, destined "to begin all over again."

This jubilation may be scorned by the Philistines. But a

Machiavellian statesman like Vergennes stated the same fact, when he wrote in 1775:

"But it may be said that the independence of the English Colonies will produce a revolution in the New World . . . that they will scarcely be quiet again and assured of their liberty before they will be seized with desire for conquest." [7]

Let us consider the words of Vergennes; for they give us the key to America's calling. He takes the independence of the thirteen colonies for granted; he is indifferent to forms of government. He makes a new point. He foresees a *revolution* in the New World, *after* independence and the new government are established. "Even supposing," he goes on, "that the Americans should overrun the Spanish possessions, it is by no means certain that such a revolution would be prejudicial to France." The revolution is to be carried on indefinitely by the fiery nucleus which pioneers the new world. The American Revolution is a permanent revolution by a little nucleus of two and a half million people *within the new world,* with the mission of unifying it. "By adding an unmeasured world, we rush like a comet into infinite space." [8]

A growing unity is not a natural thing, it is revolutionary. Not a federal government, but only the glories of this growing unit with all the future before it, could counterbalance the old desire expressed in the prayers for the British Commonwealth. The wealth of space beyond the Commonwealth of Virginia and the Continental Congress was filled by the endless desire for a new world. The God of Nature is deaf and dumb. The God of eight hundred years of English history had to be—and may I add, has been—superseded by the God of a creative future. "God of Nature," for the Americans, covered the naïve faith in a *Nature waiting for them.*

This was very well formulated by T. Pownall as early as 1780:

[7] Charlemagne Tower, *Marquis de La Fayette in the American Revolution,* I, 93, Philadelphia, Lippincott, 1926.

[8] Fisher Ames to Gore, October 3, 1803; *Works,* I, 324, Boston, 1854.

JOINT ENTERPRISE OF THE AMERICANS

199 million acres for wagon roads, canals and railroads granted by the Federal Government and Texas, 1823-1870.

"North America is become a very primary planet in the system of the world which, while it takes its own course in its own orbit, must have effect on the orbit of every other planet and shift the common centre of gravity of the whole system of the European world." [9]

Pownall goes on—and this, too, was written in the year 1780:

"Being thus planted in a New System in a New World . . . if they take up this character and hold out its operation and effect to the Old World, they will become a Nation *to whom all nations will come,* a People to whom the Remnants of all ruined people will fly, whom all the oppressed and injured of every nation will seek for refuge. The riches of the sea will pour in upon them; the wealth of Nations must flow in upon them. . . ."

Thomas Paine said, "A situation similar to the present, has not happened since the days of Noah until now."

And President Stiles of Yale, in his election sermon in 1783, shows a perfect harmony with Thomas Paine's point of view. He too is enthusiastic over the age of Noah now returned. But he makes it clear that the Revolution is a revolution toward a new world:

"Heaven has provided this country, not indeed derelict, but only partially settled, and consequently open for the reception of a new enlargement of Japhet. Europe was settled by Japhet; America is now settling from Europe. *And perhaps this second enlargement* bids fair to surpass the first. . . . In two or three hundred years this second enlargement may cover America with [a population of three hundred millions]. . . . The United States may be two hundred million souls, whites. . . . Can we contemplate their present, and anticipate their future increase, and not be struck with astonishment to find ourselves in the midst of the fulfillment of the prophecy of Noah that his sons, Shem, Ham and Japheth should replenish the earth?" [10] (Genesis IX, 11-19.)

Now this is not simply the Monroe Doctrine or the imperialism of Theodore Roosevelt; it is much more. Regarded

[9] T. Pownall, *A Memorial . . . to the Sovereigns of Europe on the Present State of Affairs between the Old and New World,* p. 4, London, 1780.

[10] J. N. Thornton, *Pulpit of the Revolution,* pp. 405 *ff.,* Boston, 1860.

from the inner side, it seems that the task of America is not limited by any static Constitution. From the very beginning it is a new, complete unit, which shall be created, but with a clear aim; to be complete, to lead into the new continent not one branch, not one offshoot, but the full life of the human race. The *complete* representation of all forms of life, of all the types of men, of all human achievements in government and education, can be an expression of mere curiosity, but it can also become a duty. The Americans of the Revolution, in appealing to the world, did much more than defend their cause: they made an offer. I am not thinking of the offer to individuals; they made an offer to the world to be complete, to establish in the New World a complete image of Europe. Europe had the visible unity of the Roman Empire as its origin. America, from the beginning, took a continent for its visible unity in the future. The revolutionary idea of the New World was to become politically united and humanly complete. The revolutionary element in the term "the American Revolution" is not to be found in the word "Revolution" which is simply the exercise of the British Right of Resistance. It is hidden in the word "American."

Congress was called the Continental Congress. And a human being became an American by two steps: integration into one of the colonies, and pioneering (or at least speculating) somewhere on the continent.

Without that polarity between unity and completeness the United States cannot breathe. For the movement toward completeness must balance the movement toward unity. The balance beween the two principles was kept, by the moving frontier on the one side, and the European immigration on the other. The thirteen colonies started the Revolution in the New World by moving the frontier and by drawing in new people. Then they had to develop unity of government and the complete range of human characters. One without the other would be meaningless. The aspiration for totality is, as we know, a feature of the Revolution. The totality of the American Revolution consists in making America an epitome of the race.

In this present hour, America, in her tradition of tolerance and hospitality, has allowed European influences to make her a kind of pandemonium. All the races, all the voices, all the creeds, all the teachings of divided and hostile Europe, meet here. Pandemonium is not a goal, it is the inevitable new start. A polyphonic organization of life might make that pandemonium a panchronion, uniting all the voices of the human race. By "pandemonium" I mean the babble of voices caused by the flood of irrelevant, accidental European problems and solutions, by "panchronion," their appropriate sequence and recurrence.

America, as we have seen, hardly keeps abreast of her own achievement. She is seldom consciously up to the stage which, practically, she has already reached. We have observed that in the restlessness and unreflectiveness of the American advance, it took wars to force new issues upon the nation. And even after these wars, as in 1815 or 1847, it took another half generation before the issue was grasped not only practically but consciously. Formulation has always come late in American history. James Russell Lowell, like MacLeish, calls America by a name which alludes to her half-consciousness:

"O strange New World that never yet was young,
Whose youth from thee by griping need was wrung . . .
Thou, skilled by freedom and by great events
To pitch new states as Old World men pitch tents . . ."

But this continent also knows something about men. America stands for more than pure geographical expansion.

"Thou, taught by fate to know Jehovah's plan
That man's devices can't unmake a man,
And whose free latch-string never was drawn in
Against the poorest child of Adam's kin."

In an eloquent prose parallel to Lowell's verses Herman Melville exclaims, in the thirtieth year of his life, in the fulness of manhood:

"For who was our father and our mother? Or can we point to any Romulus and Remus for our founders? Our ancestry is lost in the universal paternity; and Cæsar and Alfred, St. Paul and Luther, and Homer and Shakespeare are as much ours as Washington, who is as much the world's as our own.

"We are the heirs of all time, and with all nations we divide our inheritance. On this Western Hemisphere all tribes and peoples are forming into one federated whole; and there is a future which shall see the estranged children of Adam restored as to the old hearthstone in Eden!"

The whole depth and height of European institutions is summoned to emigrate to America today! The collapse of Europe makes America the heir of all time in a less primitive, but even more comprehensive, sense than that in which Melville spoke. The creations of the last two thousand years, down to the least and poorest, are asking shelter and protection in America. And the Americanization of the foreign-born is no longer a problem of education for the individual immigrant. America, with its wealth of European "goods" and institutions, still has to integrate these individual legacies to make them her living property. Museums of art and science are all very well; but the task at hand lies outside and beyond the museums. "And there is a future which shall see the estranged children of Adam restored as to the old hearthstone in Eden!"

America, by the very fact of being the New World, is bound up with the whole world! She has never tried to make a world revolution; but her very existence has changed, and is changing, the World War into a World Revolution.

"PROMISE" AND NATURAL LAW IN AMERICA.

"As there is a law in England called the common law which takes precedence of all other, as there is a law in America, called the natural law which takes the same precedence, so there is in the world the fundamental law, which is above Statutes or constitution, which the religious mind calls the law of God, the philosophical mind calls the law of nature, and the judicial mind calls the law of human society. It is not a law; it is the law, supreme over all other law, and defending the individual against all human society. . . . The nation which overrides them [the rights which every human being possesses] is the enemy not of one nation but of all nations." [11]

Americans, fighting against Europe for independence and equality, were not interested in a maximum revolution, in which high was to be turned into low, old into new, natural into social as in the total revolutions. They wished to divorce the mother country as little as possible. In this minimum revolution, then, the political vocabulary was not turned topsy-turvy. The British concepts were kept, Common Law retained. The necessary revaluation came by a shift of emphasis *within* the words.

Still, this shift was important enough to give America a particular place in the language of mankind. In the history of mankind's thought on religion and politics, America occupies a place of universal interest, not for any vocabulary of its own but for the *"Umlaut,"* the transformation of meaning she has produced within the given English vocabulary.

"Promise," "natural law," and "due process of law" harbinger a highly original change in emphasis, a change of which it may be said that like Voltaire's God, *"s'il n'existait pas, il faudrait l'inventer."* We should have to invent the rôle played by America because this rôle was forecast and foreshadowed from the beginning of European political life as one essential part of the whole drama. In this respect, I feel it to be my privilege to enlarge the findings of American scholarship, so ably put together in the books of Charles Grove Haines, *The American Doctrine of Judicial Supremacy* (1932), R. L. Mott on *Due Process of Law* (1926), and B. F. Wright on *American Interpretations of Natural Law* (1931). I wish to trace the process of specification by which these elements, after having been parts of a more comprehensive system for six hundred years, took over the full content of the whole system. Natural Law in America is not different from Natural Law in the Christian tradition in general, as long, at least, as we compare

[11] In Robert McElroy's *The Social and Political Ideas of the Revolutionary Era*, London, 1931. "Theorists of the American Revolution," p. 22 *f*.

each tradition with the other as a thing by itself. It is only when we investigate the place of natural law within the whole fabric of thought that we become aware of the American drama. Without changing the content or the vocabulary, the Americans changed every bit of it, by placing it elsewhere.

To Cromwell and Blake and the Anglo-Israelites and to numerous British, England was the promised land. The laws of the chosen people, their judges, their sabbath and their faith had been resuscitated ever since the streets of London heard the cry: "To thy tents, Israel!" as the summons to arms of the Puritans. The spirit of the God of Israel was the Spirit of the British Commonwealth. And the promises given to Moses came true when the Egyptian darkness of Stuart despotism was destroyed.

For America, too, "promise" was a biblical word. It was good English Rule that the people of Massachusetts or Connecticut established in their alleged theocracies of the seventeenth century. The same gap which the Puritans in New England filled by referring the courts to the Bible [12] puzzled the English after 1640. For on both sides of the Atlantic sore need was felt for an equivalent to the former ecclesiastical and royal courts in moral matters. The promises of God were for the righteous only, and therefore it was resolved, in 1641, that a court might pass judgment "in the case of the defect of a law in any particular case by the word of God." [13] As an emergency measure, the word of God, the promises of the Bible, crept into the court records on both sides of the Atlantic. But in the second half of the eighteenth century the vision of the promises of God migrated from Israel to a broader area of meaning. We described this re-migration from Israel to nature, from the circle of revelation to the universe, in our section on precursor revolutions. And in our section on the New World, Pownall, Thomas Paine and Ezra Stiles bore witness to the fact that the times of Noah were back again, when

[12] William MacDonald, *Select Charters and other Documents*, p. 53, New York, 1899.

[13] F. N. Thorpe, *The Federal and State Constitutions*, I, 529, Washington, 1909.

man first took possession of the whole earth. Noah's promise was more complex and more adaptable to the new world than the promises to Abraham. The *natural* covenant between God and Noah and his sons took the place of the *Holy* covenant between God and Moses at Sinai. This is the original meaning behind "the promise of America," "God's country," and similar terms.

Now, Noah was intimately connected with natural law according to the unbroken chain of Christian tradition. God had not failed man, from the beginnings of the world. And one of the phases of the evolutionary history of his dealings with man, was labelled the stage or period of Natural Law in the textbooks of the Middle Ages.[14] Natural Law bore the proud name of a Sacrament and held the fourth place among the eight sacramental orders. Because the word sacrament has gone out of business today, we may translate Natural Law as the eight evolutionary phases of creation. Natural Law had its specific historical time in which it was *sovereign* according to God's plan. And like any other phase of God's creation, this period could be restored and resuscitated from the dead. Modern thought has erected a wall against the appreciation of natural law by treating it as an idea outside time and space. Then, of course, it is debased into a whim. Its authority and bearing become inexplicable. Lest we underrate its immortality we should pay more attention to the chain in which it was meant as one link. This special link rivalled all the other links in unbreakable proof that "from the start until the end of time God is taking care of his world." (Migne, 176, 802 A.) The system of natural law in the Christian era never was an abstract system of rules. It had its place in the biogenetic ladder of mankind's climb upward. It was a peculiar and permanent independent stratum in the geology of human salvation.[15] And since it had its clear period in the chronology of the race, it kept its distinct rank as a permanent stratification in the order of every society. The eight sacramental orders,

14 See above p. 547 *f.* our report on Hugo de St. Victor.

15 "In each epoch we find all these different kinds of man simultaneously; but each time a different type is leading." Migne, 176, 688. (Hugo de St. Victor.)

after having dominated a period completely at one time in the past, were now all perpetual potentialities of political behaviour. The eight orders distinguished by Hugo de St. Victor as early as 1150 were both historical orders and perpetual qualities of social life. Without the interplay between its lawful place in history and its being available daily, natural law loses its power.

Christian doctrine held that, between the fall of Adam and the covenant with Abraham, the unspoiled elements of man's will were at work for the restoration of society. Individuals co-operate spontaneously to build up a reasonable and peaceful order. The mortar is consent. They can never achieve the building completely because man is not an author and legislator only, he is a product too; therefore he never quite recaptures the forces of his being through his own reason; too much of other people's reason permeates him. In this natural order of society something is achieved; ay, everything that can be produced by agreement between individuals. The lesson of what can be achieved is unforgettable, for it is now in incessant operation as one element in the historical process. In the restoration of the last millennium, the day of doom, the last of the evolutionary phases in scholasticism, displayed regenerative power first. Later, the seventh, the sixth and the fifth grade were resurrected from the dead. Precisely as scholasticism taught, first Church, then New, then Old Testament were used as separate orders upon which a new life could be modelled. Accordingly, we find the complete sequence from the Last Judgment to Church, New Testament, Old Testament, re-lived in Cluniacs, Gregorians and Guelphs, in Luther and the Protestants, and finally in Cromwell and his Commonwealth. In this series of restorations, Natural Law obviously got its chance when the Jewish analogies of the British Revolution had run their course. The Anglican Restoration of the promises given to the chosen people, was exhausted. Like its predecessors—Last Judgment, Church of the Fathers, New Testament—it had been overworked and abused. Hence Noah's promise and the Natural Law of consent, with its place between Moses and Adam (reading backward), found the gates open. They spelled the Mosaic promise and the revealed law of the Jews in the rôle of a persuasive set of values for peace among men.

Natural Law, then, in the texts of the eighteenth century, is no arbitrary choice. It did not come as a break with the theological tradition. It did not lead away from theology to physics. All this our dim eyes read into the story. Only the next paragraph of the creed common to all Western man, was now read aloud. Because "revelation" in its specific British meaning proved an abomination, Natural Law was put on the map. When the Judges in the High Court of England-Israel killed the spirit behind the letter of "revelation" America gave Noah and Natural Law their legitimate chance. "Reason," in this American context, gets its proper colour, too. The American does not think of reason in the European way, of *raisonner, raesonnieren,* i.e., private reasoning. "Boost—and don't knock!" Since consent is the life of natural law, American reasoning is not arbitrary or passionate individualistic reasoning; instead it is co-operative reasoning of the men of good will. "Co-operate" is the most striking phase of the American vocabulary. For concrete co-operation, not for abstract philosophy, reason was given to men. This was the principle underlying Hugo de St. Victor's doctrine, and it became the principle of American life. Reason in America is co-operative and practical.

America differs from all other countries in that it was settled by the free choice of its citizens whether they came with the Pilgrims or in the last immigrant ship. By this free choice of millions and millions (the principle of natural law), free consent became a living reality time and again. And this reality, that spontaneous agreement may solve the problems of society, transcended by far the narrow concept of natural law as a source in the courts and for the bar. As with scholasticism, to which the phases of the Old Testament and of Natural Law or of Creation were real patterns of life, "Natural Law" in America meant neither a system of government nor a code, but a design for living. And its identifying mark is that nothing in it is fixed. The mind of America is not set and does not want to be set. "Her inhabitants know no lasting city, no ancestral acres, no unbreakable habits. They are as fluid as drops of water in a society as fluid as themselves. The American moves so fast that he takes in his unthinking stride the transformations that have the effect of violent revolutions in other countries." [16]

DUE PROCESS OF LAW.

Since 1776, French ideas and Russian economics have had their day, and they have instilled their gospel into some Americans. America as a whole, however, lives under stars of her own. And she can see more clearly than the trembling masses in Europe that the spirit behind all the seven evolutionary phases of sacramental orders of society is one and the same spirit, revived whenever one phase becomes a dead letter. All these forms are elements only. Despite their temporary decay or triumph, they are, every one of them, everlasting elements of creation. This is man's Magna Charta of Freedom. For at any given moment in our history or biography, we may take up any one of these elements as the adequate expression of our faith. And this liberty is not badly protected under the law of nature that underlies the American Constitution.

Hence, one thing before all others asked for protection when "the European Frontier in America" was independently organized: mobility, flexibility, free movement all over the new world. Strangely enough, the right to this free movement has not even a specific name in American law, whereas the Germans, to whom it was new, invented the term *"Freizuegigkeit"* (right of roaming wherever you like). The Constitution of the United States, however, guaranteed to every citizen the opportunity of "rushing like a meteor into infinite space." [17] And this opportunity cannot be taken away from him without due process of law.

The peculiar emphasis given to this concept by American practice reveals the power of natural law in America. Due process of law was a "protection of the general rules which

[16] Fourth-of-July editorial, 1936, New York *Times.*
[17] See p. 673, note 8.

govern society." [18] "Old" in the British language, "new" in the French, may well be translated by "natural" as much as by "big" in a Dictionary of Correlative Values. Correspondingly, the British would evaluate "parliamentary procedure," the French "passionate discussions or conversations" as highly as Americans appreciate "due process of law." The appeal to a natural law, promising a chance and an opportunity to everybody, is the great hymn of praise throughout the years of the American people. And due process of law is the wall around this sanctuary.

And walls need watchmen; for men, not walls, protect a city. This Constitution had to be protected by special guardians. And here, American Law was confronted with an impasse at first. How could a "design for living," the new American pattern, be protected by political institution or legislature? Any political agency will crave power; here, power was to be withheld from the political agencies. Government by common consent means a government weaker than the wills of those who consent. In 1935, it was still considered possible to hold a Constitutional Convention in Rhode Island; in other words, the people still felt it to be in their power to recast their government completely. In the English Common Law, no safeguard existed against Parliament. And the American Bar was so thoroughly filled with the British tradition that as late as 1817 the Chief Justice of New Hampshire declared that due process of law could "not limit the powers of parliament; to rule otherwise would make the whole statute book a dead letter." [19] The chosen people of England-Israel relied on the public spirit embodied in the High Court of Parliament. This court of courts was considered inspired, as a "congregation of congregations" listening to the king of kings. In America, the whole foundation for a special moral rank of Parliament was lacking, all the more so since this very institution failed the Americans in their struggle. The historical and the social functions of the English Parliament were trans-

---

[18] Daniel Webster in the Dartmouth College case.
[19] *Reports of Cases in New Hampshire,* I (1819), 129 and 131.

ferred to Congress, the House of Representatives reflecting the social changes, the Senate the historical continuity. The quasi-religious function of Parliament was untransferable to a political agency. The moral conscience that is neither social nor historical is represented in America by the nine interpreters of the written Constitution. The co-operative sons of Noah reply on the wisdom of the fathers of the Constitution, as Shem, Japhet and Ham, and their latest progeny, had to trace back their claims to their father's covenant with the God of Nature, in case of a dispute. The spirit enabling the individuals of good will to co-operate is not embodied in an inspired assembly as in England. It is an "antefact," antedating all visible institutions, only to be found in the settlement that precedes all divisions.

For these reasons, Parliament in England is sovereign to interpret the meaning of due process of law. Congress in America is not. Otherwise the glorious march of forty-eight new States, built up out of thirteen colonies of the British Commonwealth, would have been impossible. Shem, Japhet and Ham populated the earth, thanks to the promise given to Noah. All the races of the world populated America under the protection of due process of law granted by the Fathers of the Constitution, and upheld by the Spirit vested in their representatives.

This part of the American Constitution was the latest to become self-conscious. Long after the Executive and the Legislative took up their operations, the Judiciary found its place. That delay may seem an accidental development. In fact, it was the keystone of the building, and probably could not be disclosed before the Fathers of the Constitution saw their dreams of personal power, or party-power, pass away. When the Federalists died as a party, their own rôle as a moral sovereign power rose as a phœnix from their ashes. John Marshall saved their authority by capturing for the Supreme Court the power of interpreting the American "design for living." The Supreme Court *is* the Fathers of the Constitution made present. They make the promise of America a reality by guaranteeing everybody his natural rights through the protection of due process of law.

EPILOGUE
THE METANOMICS OF SOCIETY

CHAPTER SIXTEEN

Articulating Periods and Co-ordinating Memories

Government by Textbooks—A Nation's Memory—Unifying Memories: The Task of the Historian—A Nineteenth-Century Myth: The Renaissance—Microscoping or Telescoping?

GOVERNMENT BY TEXTBOOKS.

NEW EXPERIENCES CREATE THE CONSCIOUSNESS OF NEW HISTORical periods. When we begin to talk quite naturally of a time called "after the depression" or "after the World War," we mark an epoch. This is as much a new creation of history as "after the Revolution" (of 1776 or 1688). Thus we should not be surprised that the nineteenth century, inspired by Rousseau and Voltaire, with its great wave of scientific discoveries, and its pride in the arts and sciences, revolutionized the history of mankind in thousands of textbooks for colleges and schools.

But it is astounding how little attention was paid to this new dogmatism. For the first time in the history of the world, the values cherished by a child's parents became less noticeable in its education than the traditions created by its schoolmaster's textbooks. The individual, having too short a life in himself, must always be transformed into a living conductor of the historical current, by a special device. In former days, a child's ancestors were made present to his mind in two ways: by the holidays and customs and furniture of the house, and by the tales of older people: grandfather, grandmother, uncle and aunt helped the parents to tell the stories of the past in such a vivid way that the listener could fill in the gaps. The child felt he had been actually present at Lexington or Gettysburg.

Modern man no longer trusts in aunts and grandmothers; they, like old furniture, became the outfit of museums. He does trust in textbooks.

This makes a textbook a thing of political significance and of catechizing power. Hence all dictators now excel in the swift recruiting of textbooks. In Turkey, all professors were dismissed or curtailed in salary who did not teach that Turkish was the main language from which all others—English, Russian, etc.—had sprung. And Turkey only stands for all the other new or regenerated nations with dictatorial textbook-administration. It is true, in more democratic countries, the periods of history vary from year to year, according to the newest historical discoveries. I myself learned two different beginnings for modern times, and three different dates for the end of antiquity; and the number of periods or epoch-making events collected from books, documents and textbooks during my later studies is not to be counted. Whenever I can pick out a new "chronology" or era, I feel like a collector who has discovered a new butterfly.

The more the periods differ in the different countries and schools, the greater the confusion. Thus the advance of scholarship in history seems to replace certainty by ambiguity, lucidity by a dark fog of dates, only to be pierced by the acumen of college examiners.

In this situation, the simple statement seems permissible that most authors of textbooks do not know what historical periods are. An inquiry made among Amercian history teachers, splendid high school staffs, showed me how naïve they were about the political bearing of "modern times" or "A.D." They overrated "facts" and underrated "periods." But a thousand facts, whatever they are, cannot weight the scale against the authority of a system of periods, for a system of periods embodies the hierarchy of values of a generation. As long as the Middle Ages are called the Middle Ages they must remain dark and romantic.

Today every system of periods is a scholarly system and reflects the domineering influences of scholarship. Any scholar is privileged to introduce a new system of periods, basing it on new documents found in the archives of Erewhon. The public thinks of periods as interchangeable, quite arbitrary divisions for purposes of chapter headings. Yet "antiquity," the Christian Era, the future, modern times, are landmarks of reality.

They tell a story of two professors who held chairs of mediæval and modern history in the German University of Halle. When a thesis was submitted to them on the years between 1490 and 1510, they both declined to criticize it, because one man's duty ended with 1500 A.D., and the other's began there. These gentlemen went a little far with their faith in the absolute righteousness of the principles ruling the guild and craft of the historians.

Still, the periods of history are not historian-made. Every mathematician relies on the fact that A is not B. In the same way the historian does homage to the eternal truth that the Middle Ages were intrinsically different from his own more modern times. A simple restatement of the relations that should prevail between historical periods and their narrators cannot be skipped in a work which centres around the making of epochs by revolution. To us, the pluralism of eras is not a curse but a blessing, because it delivers the historian from his greatest danger—that of mistaking himself for an explorer of mute nature instead of a servant of society.

If this seems a bit obscure at first, we may simply ask what the object matter is on which the historian works. What are his facts? Most answers would run: the historian's facts should be as simple, as well-tested, as objective, as the facts of natural science. Man describing man's actions should be as precise as any biologist describing the Drosophyllum or oxalate crystals. This first blunder degrades the writing of history into a natural science. Not one of the achievements in the field of natural sciences can be equalled by the scientific historian. He seems to know much more, but his readers feel they understand much less. The function of history is not to march in the rear-guard of natural science: the historian's subject matter is not life or nature. As soon as this becomes clear, his aspiration to be treated as a natural scientist can be dropped. For if the endeavours are completely different, they will no longer be mixed up together in one faculty or technique, of the natural explorer, and of the historical narrator. Then the historian's system of chronology will also cease to be the result of his whims or subjective theories. Whenever he fixes new periods, he will do so not in his quality of scholar but as leader and prophet of his nation.

In the nineteenth century historians were, in fact, the political leaders of the community. They were trusted as knowing the past of mankind and of their own country. Knowledge of the past and leadership for present and future did not seem to be in conflict. Historians represented both the memories and the good conscience of the community. Guizot and Thiers, Dahlman and Gervinus, Mommsen and Sybel, Macaulay and Bancroft, are well-known cases in point.

These golden days are gone. The historian is no longer the born political leader, and he is no longer completely trusted. The predicament of modern history arises from its no longer being in harmony with the memories and traditions of any clearly defined group. The neglect of the double rôle played by the historians during the nineteenth century easily explains the chief difficulties of history in the post-War world. The historian is no longer the standard bearer of a nation's or a church's best traditions. He has become merely a scholar.

A NATION'S MEMORY.

What, then, do I call memory or tradition, as opposed to the writing of history? Edmund Burke has unanswerably described the memory of a nation, though he seems only to be defining the nation itself:

"A nation is not an idea only of local extent, and individual momentary aggregation, but it is an idea of continuity, which extends in time as well as in numbers and in space. And this is a choice not of one day, or of one set of people, not a tumultuary and giddy choice; it is a deliberate *election* of the ages and of generations; it is a constitution made by what is ten thousand times better than choice; it is made by the peculiar circumstances, occasions, tempers, dispositions, and moral, civil and social habitudes of the people which disclose themselves only in a long space of time. It is a vestment which accommodates itself to the body. The individual is foolish, the multitude, for the moment, is foolish; but the species is wise, and when time is given to it, as a species, always acts right." (Ed. of 1856, VI, 146.)

Let us apply this statement of Burke to the situation of history-writing today. The scientific historian does not enter virgin territory when he begins to write. He enters, not a world of animal nature, but a world which mankind has previously conquered by action, discovery, sacrifice, emotion. The historian's facts are not facts in the common sense of this abused word. His facts are man's experiences.

Consciously experienced life, *erlebtes Leben,* as we say in German, is more than life. It shows its higher complications in a simple event like the battle of Waterloo which ended the French Revolution. The soldiers on the battlefield are involved in a manœuvre which they do not understand. Men swear, children cry, horses run, women try to save little things, and the soldiers are marching, marching, marching, Heaven knows why or where. Stendhal or Tolstoi, describing the complete blindness of the individual sharer in a great event, are perfectly right. Yet the deeper the embarrassment, the more dangerous the confusion, the more violent is the effort of all those involved in it to establish a common experience and a common intelligence. Probably because the confusion which reigned during the battle was so tremendous, the battle of Waterloo became a name, an impression, and a reality long before the historians sat down to write of it. Some features, some actions, some human traits, tower above the mire of incomprehensible sufferings and hardships as the individual tradition of this particular victory and defeat. Fears and hopes, envy and generosity, collaborated to coin the names "Belle-Alliance" or "Waterloo." Man is a name-giving animal. Conscious experience is the presupposition for a new name.

History is incapable of producing names. It proceeds by concepts, definitions, and corrections of names. Research is unable to create names. The process of commemoration is under way long before the critic argues about the importance or unim-

portance of an event. Gettysburg, Saratoga, Yorktown, Mara-
thon, are not facts, but creations of a nation's memory. This
creative process precedes historiography by as great an interval
as that by which it follows the confusion of the thousands of
soldiers or civilians who, among countless facts, did not know
what it all meant. The Peloponnesian War was in the hearts
and bowels of the Greeks long before Thucydides clarified its
memory in the first scientific book on history.

The memories of an individual or a group are not built
up by science. They are a process of selection by the group
which goes through a decisive experience of victory or defeat.
Memory differs in its working from literature or science. Memory uses other means, because it is not an effort of the intellect.
The whole being of the nation is at stake in a great event. The
new name is only the minimum requirement for the assimilation of an overwhelming experience. And assimilated it must
be, lest it become an obsession. Monuments are built, ceremonies are devised, to keep the memory awake.

The periods of history are products of this creative process.
The Crusades, the Reformation, the Middle Ages, Antiquity,
the Glorious Revolution of '88, are—like all important divisions of era—expressions of a group-morale, and not in the least
the outcome of scientific research. We see the same thing happening today when people begin to date things in relation to
the World War. The scholar is not the master of the periods
he uses. He only corrects those which exist.

The climax is reached when an event is incorporated into
the calendar as a recurrent date. Memory is fixed by the calendar of a group or a nation. Seven hundred and sixty years ago,
Thomas à Becket was put into the calendar of the Christian
Church as a martyr to its liberty. He—the victim of an English
king—replaced in the calendar the ideal of true righteousness;
he took the day of King David himself, directly after St.
Stephen, the first of all martyrs. The introduction of such a
day into the English kingdom, two years after the murder,
under the authority of the Pope in Rome, tells us more about
the mediæval relations between Gregorian Rome and a local
kingdom than do many discussions of the Anglicans during

the nineteenth century. The pilgrimage to Canterbury once
more underlines the fact that the day of St. Thomas was
the "Fourteenth of July" of the Papal Revolution, and the
Magna Charta of the common man from 1174 to 1535. The
ceremony of re-reading Washington's Farewell Address in the
Senate is another example of the formation of memory. In
this case, reading is a means to the chief end of tradition—it
gives time for reflection. "Those who remember the past are
not condemned to repeat it." (Santayana.) Burke observed that
the species is wise when time is given to it. Since only a few
events can make an epoch or become holidays, names or monuments, traditions are based on a selective process. Memory
is tyrannical. It represses and excludes; it exalts and prefers.
Thus it may be unfair; but it is real. Group memory is a barrier between the alleged facts and the historiographer's task.

UNIFYING MEMORIES: THE TASK OF THE HISTORIAN.

Let us analyze now the historian's duty; let us turn to the
Greek, Thucydides. To our mind he is the first great scientific historian because he is conscious of his duty of detachment. He has "distance." He opposes the "agalma," the monument which a group dedicates to its gods after a conscious
experience. He corrects Athenian tradition by giving the intentions and purposes of the other side. He writes the history
of the war between Greeks in a way acceptable to both sides.
His speeches are no mere ornament. They are Thucydides'
great discovery. All our modern scientific apparatus is nothing
more than the evolution of his speeches. In using the forms
of legal pleading, Thucydides transforms the "national monument" into a "possession for ever," partial tradition into universal history. History, after Thucydides, can be defined as
the bilateral restoration of two unilateral memories. History
is corrected and purified tradition, enlarged and unified
memory.

Why must the history of the Great War be tried and tried
again? Its history must be written because it has left memory
paralyzed by prejudice. Disgust prevents many people and
whole nations from thinking of it. *John Brown's Body* deals

with all the scars of partial memory left by the Civil War. An eminent pragmatic historian, Samuel Eliot Morison, called Stephen Vincent Benét's poem the best history of the Civil War. Benét not only resuscitated the memories of the few leading men, and the traditions of North and South; he went further and balanced the experience of the soldiers with the emotions of the folk at home. Thus his poem ends the *"infandum dolorem,"* as Virgil called the unspeakable pains of war and defeat.

The historian is the physician of memory. It is his honour to heal wounds, genuine wounds. As a physician must act, regardless of medical theories, because his patient is ill, so the historian must act under a moral pressure to restore a nation's memory or that of mankind. Buried instincts, repressed fears, painful scars, come for treatment to the historian. The historian regenerates the great moments of history and disentangles them from the mist of particularity.

Scientific interpretations of history, like the Marxian or the Hegelian scheme or Henry Adams' law of acceleration, are little more than his gadgets and tools for building another scaffold around the old house of mankind's memories for his work of repair. The historians of the last century particularly sinned: they took their scaffold for an end in itself. Hegel and Marx, Carlyle and Spengler, over-cultivated the historian's pride. The machinery of their individual scaffolds appealed to them too much. They remind one of the famous Viennese medical school which took less interest in the patient than in the theory of the disease. However, all the great historians instinctively preserved their loyalty to great events. But today they are less read by the masses than are the "constructors" of laws and generalities.

One thing seems to be especially responsible for the emancipation of history from its service to real memory. Traditions were entering into dissolution and anarchy during the nineteenth century. History and written literature became substitutes for all other forms of tradition. This monopoly in matters of the past was an emergency measure. With an industrial revolution, a weakening of the Church, a lapsing of immemorial home and trade traditions, the historian seemed the only available protector of tradition. The Romantic historian acted in an emergency. And since all great historiography of our days owes its very existence to the historical faith and passion of the Romantic school, it is only fair to say that history partially rescued memory in a period of forgetfulness and destruction of tradition.

But history-writing cannot replace the memories of the layman. It is the birthright of man to build up a memory and to have faith in the future. Memory and faith are properties of a man as a layman, a member of the people. It is the privilege of the historian to unify dualistic memory; and for this healing capacity he must be made independent in his research. Both the layman's birthright and the historian's privileges have been sacrificed by modern philosophy. It ascribed to the historian both the non-scientific faith of the natural man and the unlimited access to unrecorded facts enjoyed by the natural scientist. This has become something of a disgrace now, when natural scientists themselves no longer claim such an immediate access to their facts. Physics and mathematics have no inexplicable advantage over the rest of man's reasonable attempts to cope with the riddle of creation. Thus the apologetic philosopher, following always at the heels of science, was perpetually duped, and history-writing itself lost its honourable place as a helper of memory. The historian became a champion of one of the traditional abstract scientific theories.

The divorce of national memory from history-writing is being answered today by an outbreak of national, social and racial mythologies. "Myth," as modern literati use the word, is a substitute for lost memory. Scientific history, in self-defence against mythology, must base itself frankly on previous group-traditions; otherwise history cannot demonstrate that its conceptions are rooted in empirical reality. If history were the only human activity for representing the past, it would remain arbitrary and would have no means of distinguishing itself from mythology. As long as other ways of forming memory coexisted, the historian's book could play its proper synthetic rôle. Nowadays, any violent and partial book on history will find millions of readers who have not learned to digest a real historical experience. In these cases the best-intended history plays the rôle of a dangerous soporific. It once more weakens the creative power of the reader to experience history for himself.

Oswald Spengler is the clearest type of a writer of "history without memory." In his *Decline of the West* he gives a world history without mentioning one word or expression used by the contemporaries of his events. No *"Dieu le veult,"* no "rights of Man," no "To thy Tents, Israel," no "These are the times to try men's souls." He looks at the world of man as if man had no memory. He writes for those who despair of ever acquiring a memory and a tradition, to the children who wish never to become adults.

Why, then, has he become so popular? His readers are people weary of their own memories—people shaken by the earthquake of the World War and quite willing to surrender their own traditions and memories! At the end of a period, traditions are so shaky that the stylus of Clio gives way to the brush and the obliterating sponge. Spengler's book outdistanced all European and occidental traditions by subordinating them to a scheme that was suitable for the struggles of the second or third millennium B.C. It dumped the burden of our own forefathers' history into an abyss where it lay together with the rubbish of five or six other "civilizations." Spengler enabled post-War society, especially in Germany, to bury its own traditions, since it now had as little contact with the names and dates of its own past as with the external facts of any Saharan civilization.

Thus the historian is as often the grave-digger of our memories as their restorer. His work tests the duration of living memory, strengthens the rising, and buries the withered. Liberal society was vigorous enough in 1815 to build up a new historical faith; Spengler obliterated the same society's tradition after 1918.

The blight which the World War laid upon national traditions is perhaps best made clear by contrast with the powerful myth set up by scholars a hundred years ago. They created a new "periodization" of mankind's history in order to make it fit into the Jacobin scheme of progress and self-made manhood. They did it so well that the workings of the new machinery have only recently been laid bare.

A NINETEENTH-CENTURY MYTH: THE RENAISSANCE.

Today all our schoolboys and schoolgirls are taught a "French" myth. Not by a contemptible trick, but through the naïve faith of three or four generations, what we may rightly call the "French" periodization of history was created—unknown and inconceivable before, but now believed, worshipped and learned by heart in every civilized nation. All the former total revolutions had done the same. Odilo of Cluny re-erected the great framework for one united history of all mankind, believers and infidels. Joachim di Fiore distinguished successfully, first, an ecclesiastical history of the Christian centuries before him, and, second, a post-ecclesiastical, i.e., political, spiritual and cultural history for our millennium, beginning in his own time. And Luther's disciples separated what they labelled the Middle Ages from modern times. All these three divisions are of permanent value. They are all unforgettable. The same is true of the French contribution to mankind's recasting its memory time after time. The French invented the period of the "Renaissance," beginning about 1450 and ending in 1498 or 1500 or 1517. Today every college president knows of this Renaissance period as a golden age.

Actually, the time between 1450 and 1517 is one of the ugliest and darkest hours of the past. The growth of the cities ceased all over Europe, and the men of the guilds and crafts, for lack of employment, streamed into the gangster life of Armagnacs and Landsknechte. Petty tyrants destroyed the foundations of local rights. The Church nearly collapsed under the disillusionments of the universal councils and the wars against the Hussites. Christianity ran wild. One might almost say that the gargoyles of the Gothic cathedrals tried to become political leaders and alleged saints. One of these had his followers daily take notes of his achievements, lest they be missed or his canonization delayed. And canonized he was. Louis XI

of France was only one among the refined torturers of those
days. Popes killed their cardinals, and princes their brothers
and fathers. The Roman emperor's son was imprisoned by
a petty town. The Spanish Inquisition was set up, and the
notorious *Hammer of Witches* published. Constantinople
was conquered by the Turks. By that mysterious cyclical process, the monarchical, aristocratic and democratic institutions
of the clerical period of Europe entered the decadent phase
of dictatorship.

This period of atrocities was turned into the Golden Age of
the Renaissance after 1815. The French Revolution of 1789,
bringing a new day for natural humanity, could no longer
admit that a supernaturalist's Reformation had decried and
ended the Egyptian darkness of the Middle Ages, and began
"modern times." The *"Neuzeit"* of German Protestantism,
beginning about 1517 or 1518 or 1526 and extending indefinitely into the future, would have embraced the Great Revolution of '89, and by this enclosure would have reduced the
importance of the latter. Thus, genuine modernity had to begin with 1789. Everything before was ancient, *"ancien régime."*
On the other hand, it could not be denied that France was
already surrounded by a preceding civilization whose own
warcries were "newness," *videlicet* Protestantism. In order to
reconcile the two elements, the accent was shifted from the
Reformation, as the great beginning, to a more splendid age
destroyed by the Reformation. The times of dissolution for
the clerical authority which preceded Luther's outburst, were
now severed from the rest of the Middle Ages as a period of
alleged secular emancipation. The religious laxity which had
enlarged the field of scholastic interest to include the Greek
and Roman classics, was proclaimed the greatest asset of the
later fifteenth century. It is true that in the Quattrocento many
of the clergy saw no great harm in dressing as Romans or
Greeks. Pope Julius II (1503-1512) certainly did not object
to being likened to Julius Cæsar and a beautiful Parmesan
abbess of his times can be seen on the wall of her own monastery, portrayed during her lifetime, as a Greek goddess. This

revival of pagan beauty, of Hellas and Rome, which in the nineteenth century refounded Greece and the Olympic games, was seized upon as the glory of a Renaissance "Humanism." It would be a mistake to ascribe the new period to one man's sudden idea. Long before it was formulated, the Protestant pattern showed signs of decay. The old admiration for the Reformation was gone; the atrocities of the fifteenth century and the human monsters it produced—like Pietro Aretino who showed his impudence as a blackmailer by calling himself *"per la grazia di Dio uomo libero"* (a free man by the grace of God) and implied libertinism instead of liberty—were sufficiently far away to become interesting for the age of Beaumarchais and Figaro. People began to forget exactly why the cut was made in the reign of Charles V (1519-56). This state of transition before the "Renaissance" was established, with the previous epoch of Luther fading away, is reflected lucidly in an essay written by a German in Paris in 1796: Wilhelm von Humboldt, in dealing with the mysterious three periods "antiquity," Middle Ages," "Modern Times," betrays the impasse out of which "Renaissance" was to become a way out. Humboldt's first period is no longer the era of the Old Testament, but the "antiquity of Greece and Rome" only. Jerusalem is eliminated from his horizon. Consequently, the Middle Ages no longer are connected with the New Jerusalem, i.e., the Church. He literally says of the Middle Ages: "They are the era from the decline of taste and scientific culture until their steady and full regeneration." He seems fully to apply the yardstick of Humanism. However, the spell of the Protestant tradition lingers in his memory too. For he clings to its starting point for modernity in the sixteenth century, instead of in 1450, which latter year is the high water mark for Humanism. Humboldt solves this perplexity in a telling way: "The era of the Middle Ages," he goes on to say, "extends from the middle of the fourth to the middle of the sixteenth century; for at that time [1550] only the *results* of the restoration of sciences *which happened more than a century before*[!] began to become really conspicuous." ("*Da erst um diese Zeit die Folgen der mehr als hundert Jahre frueher geschehenen Wiederherstellung der Wissenschafter recht sichtbar zu werden anfingen.*") [1] Humboldt, then, anticipated fully the evaluation of the later admirers of the Renaissance. And since the leading class of writers like Humboldt did not even mention the destinies of the Church any longer, the cut needed no longer to be simultaneous with Luther. It was transposed to 1450. History-writing Humanism was now purified from any respect for religion. Instead of the confession of the monk Luther, the interest of the professions in 1789 and 1800 determined the formula of the historians. A knowledge of Renaissance art became a kind of religious liturgy for every educated free-thinker of the nineteenth century. The new chronology, fixed about 1825, and rapidly spreading from France to England and Switzerland, and from both countries to Germany and Italy, got a worldwide significance through the personal relations of scholars and artists. A Viennese scholar and patron of the arts, Geymüller, wholly French in culture and outlook, though a deeply Christian soul, in his correspondence regularly addressed the famous Swiss author of the *Culture of the Renaissance,* Jacob Burckhardt, "We citizens of the Renaissance!" In this complicated way, English Tories and Prussian Junkers, Swiss Conservatives and Austrian Catholics, all of whom openly detested any communion with the ideas of 1789, nevertheless became imbued with them in the forms of their most important reflection on man's way through time. They began to recast history, as though it had foreshadowed in 1450 the humanism of 1789. From Jacob Burckhardt and Friedrich Nietzsche to Berenson and R. Roeder, the new glorification of the intellectual emancipation four hundred years ago outshone all the deep shadows of that dying age.

It is only today that the historians of art begin to criticize their own creation of a thing called "Renaissance Art" and "Humanism" as a definite period. The newest book on the subject published during the Great Depression (Richard Hamann's *History of Art*) drops the whole concept of a specific

[1] *Werke*, II, 24.

style to be labelled Renaissance.[2] His new volume, as if dating from an age ignorant of a "Renaissance," was intentionally written without mentioning either the word or the period "Renaissance" that thrilled us in our youth.

Thus we see that today the French Revolution, having exhausted its dynamic elements, is repelled from one of its most aggressive outposts. An allegedly separate "Renaissance" as a specific period dividing the Middle Ages from Modern Times, begins to vanish even in its central field of origin, the history of art itself. Popular writers on the period, like R. Roeder, begin and end their writing with the amazing statement that they could not find what they had expected—a real Renaissance —but much decay and despair. In fact, as early as 1885, Henry Thode, the son-in-law of Richard Wagner, reacted against the idol of Liberalism by publishing a book in which he traced the Renaissance back to St. Francis of Assisi in 1200! We ourselves, after listening to the voices of contemporaries, drew the line for the origins of a new civilization at 1200; and so we might happily accept Mr. Thode's thesis. But what use would it be to call the Saint who received the five stigmata of the crucified in his body, the beginner of Europe's repaganization? If the humanistic Renaissance began about 1200, there was no such thing as a Renaissance.

Now if the reader will look up our chapters on the cycles of Polybius and on the latest phase of the Guelphic revolution, he will find that between 1450 (end of the Councils; rebuilding of the Vatican began) and 1517 (Luther) there is a clearly marked period which ends the one great cycle reaching from 995 to 1517. In pointing this out we are not trying to break up real periods in history-writing; we are merely opposing an unanalyzed, self-confident naïveté of certain experts. They honestly believe in the prejudices of their own time! Yet they think themselves unbiassed by any faith or creed! By this assertion they constantly violate the rules of the game that brought them to the top, and forfeit the immunity which their function enjoys in modern society.

[2] *Geschichte der Kunst von der Altchristlichen Zeit bis zur Gegenwart,* 2nd edition, Berlin, 1935.

With the laity it was a different story. They showed a magnificent spirit in their worship of the "Renaissance." They spent millions and millions of dollars on its cult; and founded numberless museums and university chairs for its study. It will take centuries to erase from our textbooks all the blind and dogmatic panegyrics on its achievements. Probably they never will be erased. For the work was not futile. By detracting from the German Reformation, it helped to overcome the anti-Catholic complex of the Protestant countries. It delivered one phase of pre-Protestant "darkness," 1450 to 1517, from the curse of belonging to the deplorable Middle Ages, and it revealed the trick of the Lutheran Revolution which was to create a unity, "the Middle Ages," out of Roman, Frankish, Cluniac, Papal and Guelphic periods. Rightfully it purified our denominational memory. However, it is revealing that, after all, the new scientific treatment never became as simple as memory. For the time limits given for the Renaissance epoch in textbooks differ widely, whereas periods really experienced by mankind have an unmistakable birthday and an irrevocable end. John Addington Symonds has a memorable article on the "indefinite space of time" for the Renaissance in the *Encyclopædia Britannica*. According to him, not only any time from Dante to Milton can claim a share of it, but without the achievements of the nineteenth century, the "Renaissance" would have no meaning! This unconscious confession by one of the faithful bears out our thesis.

The wholly secondary character of the division is best compared to the British device in substituting an "Industrial Revolution" for the real French Revolution in their textbooks. In both cases the instinct of the evolutionist was at work, putting his evolutionary scheme above the revolutionary. This would be all right if the new scheme were not explicitly bound up with the old. "Industrial Evolution," "Renaissance of the arts and sciences," would be unobjectionable; whereas "Industrial Revolution" carries with it the conscious suppression of the other (French) Revolution and its un-English principles of government. "Renaissance of the arts and sciences" would be all right, but putting the period just before Luther, conjuring up as starting points purely negative events like the loss of Constantinople in 1453, or a purely technical change like the invention of printing, and closing the period of Humanism in 1499 or 1498, before the world becomes inhuman (read Protestant) once more, tends to belittle the Protestant and to minimize the definite break made by the Reformation. Periods like that of Humanism or of the Industrial Revolution are afterthoughts, not born of original, contemporary experience but of secondary tendencies. It would be unfair to call them artificial; but secondary they are. They lack the candour and elemental greatness of the historical calendars built up immediately in the wake of revolutions. They should not be allowed to dominate the Great Year of mankind as it is pictured in the creations of real holidays and traditions by monks, papacy, free cities, princes, parliaments, citizens and workers. Separated by the World War from the naïve faith in Renaissance and Humanism, we may even go a step further and indicate that the period between 1870 and 1914 brought a kind of golden fulfilment to the ideals of Modern Times, and for that reason it is possible to look back to the care-free days of pre-War Europe as to a golden age. My guess is that later historians will do so and compare the mediæval epilogue of the "Renaissance" to the epilogue of pre-War peace and security. Let them not exaggerate the happiness of the two sunsets of a long day. Of the spirit of pre-War Europe, 1870-1914, Friedrich Nietzsche could say: "God was dead." And for the fifteenth century, Martin Luther used a strikingly similar epithet: "God threw the cards on the table and refused to play the game any longer."

MICROSCOPING OR TELESCOPING?

Naturally our own attempt to bring back a respect for the creative moments in history is the positive supplement to the negative criticism we have had to make in this chapter. Our attacks on the tacit bias of the "scientific" history should be read in the light of our own scruples against deviating one inch in our narrative from mankind's self-revelation. We know that men like Ranke never overrated the intellectual afterthoughts of historians or scholars. Historians in all times have made the people themselves speak again. And in this respect the good historian of a limited period could and can escape Spenglerianism much more easily than I who have had to deal with the Great Series of Revolutions.

That is why my historical technique differs from that of most of my colleagues who can fill many chapters with the events of a day, a month and a year. I am trying, by my technique, to do what they do, only for long periods. Modern man is interested more and more, not in days, but in centuries and millenniums. Many writers have a flair for what the modern reader is demanding. He will not read the diary of Alfred's third counsellor or every letter written by Daniel Webster to his political friends in Massachusetts and New Hampshire. He wishes to revive a bigger unit of man's history. For that purpose, there are other documents than diaries or letters or records, these favourite sources of the national historian. The calendar and its holidays, the monuments and fashions of a country, the words and names of its speech, are equally important sources in this book. By emphasizing their bearing on the moulding of a nation's or a class's memory and—by that—its character, the teacher of history can steer between the two extremes of our present history-writing—the confusion of endless detail and the charlatanism of cheap and irresponsible constructions.

The scholar, in his desperate fight for truth, usually prefers finiteness of detail; the public, in its longing for thrill, seeks lightheartedly the "broad view" of the march of civilization. The detail known and handed down to us about the last thousand years is overwhelming and practically unlimited. For the earlier millennia, the main outline is easily drawn. Hence primitive and distant times are analyzed in the geologist's manner, into large strata of diluvium or stone-age. Modern times are microscopically searched for minute data. Thus, one and the same history of man is treated with telescopes or microscopes according to distance. Today, this most undesirable divergence of methods bars the way to a common historical perspective.

In attacking our own immediate present and past—those last inevitable thousand years still represented and continued by our every thought and action—we have had to overcome this divergence between telescopical and microscopical history. Our macroscopical method looks into the birth throes of birthdays and holidays, into the creation of words, into actions that called forth permanent reactions, into those revolutionary processes which have fixed certain permanent processes of national education. In doing so, we may have to brave the ire of responsible scholars, and take the wind out of the sails of irresponsible writers, and thereby irritate both, though we wish to bring them together again. Still, even our failure would not relieve the scholar and the writer from their common duty; to avoid the Scylla of disordered detail and the Charybdis of meaningless generalities.

Let us go back to the unity of man's history and yet listen to the inimitable variety of his original tongues. For when God said, "Let us make man, historical man, the varieties of man," he let all these varieties speak for themselves. Each type and kind, each tribe and nation, sprang into life as a particular tongue. When they were called into existence, they themselves called their existence with new names. The other creatures were produced without any such spontaneous contribution of voicing the issues themselves; whenever new men were created, they were carried away by the living word so that they labelled the new phase in the life of mankind by a "before" and "after" the event.

CHAPTER SEVENTEEN

The Future of Revolution

Viva Voce Biography—Viva Voce Concerto—The Suspension of the Cosmic Laws—The Passing of the Inspiration—Post-War Economics—Face to Face with Mankind

VIVA VOCE BIOGRAPHY.

ALL THIS BOOK LONG, ONE VISION THAT SLOWLY ASCENDED BEFORE my inner eye on the winter morning at Verdun, more than twenty years ago, and that has been tried, tested, rejected, forgotten, reproduced, corrected and transformed and yet has remained real ever since, had to be placed before my readers. Here, finally, I can pause. I am no longer under its spell, since it has crossed the bridge to you. I have said it. And I am free to consider, for you and for myself, some conclusions and practical results. We all spring from this pedigree of revolutions. As cousins, then, we may elicit from the autobiography of our race some guiding principles for our own conscience. What conclusions have we to draw from this long epic of passions and beliefs? In fact we cannot trust our narrative of revolution until we can test its human validity by applying it to our own nature. Until we have the revolutionary vein within ourselves as something quite independent from politics, this narrative can be belittled as mere theory. But our book can be personally tested: *De te fabula narratur;* it is your own story that is told in this volume. That is to say: Any real man behaves in the volcanic hours of his own life as people behaved during revolutions. Those hours are extreme and terrible, yet they tell us more about the unity of human nature than soft days of peace from which behaviourists are apt to derive their political concepts.

Physicists must speak about *things;* for things cannot speak themselves. Mathematics helps us to describe the mysteries of the matter which we observe and investigate from the outside. Figures and equations attack the mysteries of the world.

Man is not like the world outside man. Man—that is what we are ourselves. Man does not allow any other fellow to express his own secret of existence. Man can only be understood by listening to his own word. That is the great object-lesson of revolution for our own personal situation. In the white heat of revolution, a society reaches the height of its sincerity, penetration and clairvoyance into its own self. In the same way there exist in the life of every living soul one or two solemn moments when he speaks the full truth about himself.

This climax of insight must not be mistaken for anything like the conscious self-complacency of a salesman or a soldier. It is not the boastful John Falstaff, but St. John lying on the ground like one dead, to whom we must compare a nation in the birth-throes of conversion to its eternal rôle. In every-day life the most similar event was perhaps the act of the bride who passed from her parents' house into that of her suitor by the one word "Yes." If she meant it, the full content of her life, her choice and her destination, was implied in this moment. That is why the word spoken at such an hour has little to do with the gabbling which is also called language, but which is only the rubbish and off-scourings of creative speech. The bride's single word of reply has a power as divine as the "Let there be light" of the world's first day. Like the cry in an hour of revolution, her "yes" carries a weight as heavy as the most heroic action. It is a revelation of the woman's whole future, a decision over her whole past. It is irrevocable, and it is true.

Such words and such moments are rare in the life of the individual, and in the life of mankind as well. Daily life prefers half measures and half lights. The pressure and danger must become tremendous, it must be a question of life and death, before our cold reason, our conventional language, and our fear of committing ourselves, will give way to the unmistakable and unique sounds of truth.

This is astounding enough; the outcry of a group, suddenly placed outside the world's century-long conventions, this monologue in the darkness of the first minute. Men and nations speak out their own secret; to be a historical being means to have one's hour of perfect sincerity.

If human life can express itself in the unshielded, unguarded moments of despair and ecstasy, it is not the philosopher's business to go behind or beyond that expression. Woe to him who would abstract, deduce, comment and interpret these clearest expressions of the one and united soul of mankind for the sake of his logical concepts. Society mocks the philosophers or sociologists who try to get *behind* the scenes. All we can learn is to listen better and better. And listening is difficult enough. The daily life of the nations recoils from the open sincerity of great hours. The fictions and pleasures of every day divert our attention from the deeper symbols. A deadening clatter of cheap gossip and excitement deafens our ears to the true creations of life. Yet in the hours of danger the simplest emotions return and throw blind millions back into the ruts in which the car of destiny is driven.

So this is the answer to your question: We must cease to look around or behind the great facts of our past or future. The great events are the great events. We, born after the event and living on the surface, need a special training before we can even hear a voice from the depths. Most men judge depth by surface-standards, with the ugly self-complacency of the globe-trotter. Please judge the surface by the standards of viva voce biography. Stephen Vincent Benét warned us, in *John Brown's Body:*

> "This is the monster and the sleeping queen
> And both have roots stuck deep in your own mind.
>
>   •   •   •
>
> "So when the crowd gives tongue
> And prophets old and young
> Bawl out their strange despair
> Or fall in worship there
>
>   •   •   •

"Before the flame hoping it will give ear,
If you at last must have a word to say,
Say neither, in their way,
'It is a deadly magic and accursed,'
Nor 'It is blest,' but only 'It is here.' "

Then the true sounds will come to our ears in the nights of growth and the nights of sorrow, and we shall know whether these sounds of past realizations still bind us with fear and hope, or whether, released from our old loyalties, we must bury our dead and emigrate into the new country of the soul given to the faithful by the Lord over Life and Death.

VIVA VOCE CONCERTO.

If we had discovered only the fact of viva voce biography we should have reconciled the laws of life for the individual with those for his kind.

But we have found a deeper secret—the monologues of the different revolutionaries form a dialogue among themselves. England praises its "lower" House because Germany had become obsessed by the idea of "highness." The French speak of *"bon sens,"* because "common sense" had been pre-empted by its glorification in the British Commonwealth. The Germans praise paternal methods as applied to the world, because the centuries of Italian hegemony had praised the maternal ways of the Church beyond the world. Noah was praised by the Americans because they came after the English revival of the chosen people of Abram's seed. The Soviets are organizing the pre-Adamitic forces of society so that the bourgeois prejudices for *L'homme libre,* Adam, may not remain the last word in the history of creation.

One revolutionary self-confession, then, depends logically upon those which precede. This logical dependency does not diminish its sincerity or spontaneity. For the logical contradiction to the previous set of values occurs before it clothes itself with political power. The self-confessions of Gregory's *Dictatus Papæ* might seem to be the most secret and wordless kind of speech. Yet they were the seed which bore fruit in the majestic public manifestations of eight centuries. Rousseau's private

Confessions had to precede Robespierre, as Colonel Hutchinson's austere prayers preceded Cromwell's passionate outbursts. If the interdependence of all the utterances and the spontaneous character of each are both true, we cannot explain this relationship by the cheap motives of jealousy, imitation, intellectual dependence or other circumstances of human frailty. On the other hand, the interplay cannot be treated as an atomistic fact, outside our other system of ideas; it is no accident. The fact of a meaningful dialogue between the nations in their most sincere and self-centred utterances is surprising. I do not wish to hide my own surprise. But at least one consequence is clear; this interplay proves that one spirit makes its way through the letters of this alphabet.

The great and totalitarian Revolutions are the test of the unity of mankind. They refute all the theories which followed in the wake of Darwinism proclaiming the "autocephalic" origin of every race, kind and nation. The tremendous impetus which carries every revolution out to all the world refutes the idea that men are separated by territorial limits. The differences themselves between the nations spring from unity. They can be compared to processes of mutual polarization. Revolutionary ideas call mankind to order. They put the great questions which are going to divide and rally the next century.

Not one of these national revolutions is local in purpose or result. The grain of seed is hidden in one part of the earth. Like any earthly form, it must secure a local seed bed and a field in which it can root itself. But the tree planted in such a national area bears fruits for all mankind. The fruits of the revolution tree are articles of export for the various countries. German theology, English government, Italian painting, French literature, are known to everybody as the most significant contributions of each country to all the rest.

THE SUSPENSION OF THE COSMIC LAWS.

The life-cycle of man leads him through different physical stages. Child, adolescent, youth, man and old man; each is different from all the others. Girl, bride, mother, housewife, and grandmother are even more sharply divided. The human race has exploited the potentialities of this life-cycle. It has based its different forms of organization on the properties of different ages in the two sexes. Whereas 1000 A.D. saw an emperor governing an unamalgamated, unspecialized agglomeration of tribes, nine hundred years later we find a civilization which has exploited all the advantages of the different stages in the life of our kind.

Old age, motherhood, fatherhood, manhood, bridehood, sonhood and daughterhood have been utilized to establish the papacy, the free cities of Italy, the German system of civil service, English parliamentarism, French national democracy, the international empire of Austria, and the Russian soviets. The old phrase, "Europe a family of nations," seems to have an almost too literal sense when we think of a real family and consider the completeness of our list. Here the qualities of man's biographical stages or of a family's members are transformed and exalted into national characters. The properties of age and sex belong to all men. It is therefore not ridiculous to call the civilizations of Italy, France and Austria by names taken from "womanhood." In everybody's soul both sexes [1] are present. It throws no shadow of humiliation on the Italian or the Frenchman to say that he has helped to personify qualities which through the lameness of our language seem to be limited to one sex. The artist's genius, for example, has the gifts of conception and begetting developed to an enormous degree. Now, the artist is an eternal potentiality as man. Yet the artist is nearer to the feminine side of life, the receptive, magic, creature-like forces of our existence, and his dwelling in the depths of "Sister, our Mother Earth" is what makes him a genius. Thus the most virile artist, the inspired writer or speaker, can represent bridehood or motherhood with better right than can a spoiled flapper. The same can be said of the priest or the thinker. On the other hand, the statesman, the explorer, the soldier, are akin to masculine elements. A German

[1] In an epoch of sex obsession it may be useful to recall the utterly dry meaning of *sexus* in Latin: part of the race. From this meaning it is obvious that mankind cannot exclude any "part of the race" from its ambition.

woman can represent the paternalism of her country without losing an inch of her dignity as a woman.

The properties enumerated above are primary forces in the character of men and nations. Beyond their physical meaning, they embrace moral, intellectual and social processes necessary to any human existence. They are the great forms through which man can root himself in the cosmos and govern it.

The pedigree of revolutions shows that each tried to realize one neglected or imperilled potentiality of the life-cycle, and stressed its importance by establishing one great national institution to take care of the reproduction of these special processes and types. Each Revolution started permanent cultural processes to mould a specific character out of plastic humanity.

This evolution began by using the end of the life-cycle, by the conscious re-establishment of "old age" at a time when old age was especially misrepresented.[2] Then it continued dialectically, following the series of ages or phases backward to Mother, Father, Man, Woman, Daughter, Son. The stage of the Russian proletarian is the stage of the delocalized emigrant, the boy of twenty, the born revolutionary, the prodigal son. But no stage was left out. Arbitrary revolutions might happen. But they failed. Only those revolutions were successful and memorable which obeyed the deepest need of the life-cycle. This need may be called its desire for complete representation. Each embodiment gave birth to the next form, for otherwise the completeness of the cycle would be interrupted. The list of man's revolutionary personifications, going backwards, shows that the cycle of *conscious* revolutions is complete. For, back of the adolescent, man lives unconsciously.

The name for the revolutionary inspiration will change in the future as it has changed over and over again. All the different names were derived from the inspiration revealed to many by the Holy Ghost, that unruly power that bloweth where it listeth. The list of nouns runs:

[2] Chapter Ten.

Spiritual (both: Lords Spiritual and "The Spirituals" in the Franciscan sense)
"Geist" of the New Learning
Public Spirit
Esprit
Class Consciousness

But the verb "to inspire" is the same for all, it even cannot be spared for the latest phase of revolutionary inspiration, where people act under the spell of "instinct," the racial or Fascist antagonist of class-consciousness.

It is true the change of names will be connected with a change of procedure. Future revolutionary phases are unavoidable since life is not going to die out immediately on our earth. What will be their form? We have already foreshadowed the answer. With a conscious economic organization of the whole earth, subconscious tribal organizations are needed to protect man's mind from commercialization and disintegration. The more our shrinking globe demands technical and economic co-operation, the more necessary it will prove to restore the balance by admitting the primitive archetypes of man's nature also.

Dr. Jung asked for a restoration of the archetypes of Indian or Chinese or Malayan traditions because he found his patients from America and Europe were "in search of a soul." The problem is more crucial. For Christian civilization was built on the worship of a child in its cradle. It went out into the world to regenerate and reimplant all processes and types of man's life. Since Jesus himself, however, passed away at thirty-three, he had lived only from childhood to early manhood. Therefore Christianity, when restoring the dignity of old age, motherhood and fatherhood by creating sublime institutions, was not exposed to comparisons with the life of the perfect man. Papacy (1075), mother church (1200), paternal state (1517), proved immune against jealousy. This lack of rivalry is most conspicuous in the case of St. Francis with his patience and faith in his mother church. The inspiration of the first total revolutions of the Holy See, of Guelphic Italy and Lu-

theran Germany and the Christian Gentry, were therefore unswervingly Christian; in fact, they were wholly aware of their
indebtedness to Chrsitianity for their own new life by the ways
of the spirit. They depended, for their own self-realization,
on the good conscience granted to them by Christianity.

The aspect changed when the stages near to the biographical
tradition of Jesus' own life were about to be re-established.
The French and the Russian revolutions are particularly jealous of Jesus. Before them was the task of representing a single
stage in our life-cycle which can also be found in the life of
Jesus. The life of Jesus knows of no exclusivity for one phase.
For on it was founded the whole concept of re-birth in the
Christian era. His life therefore, as far as we know of it, by
being more universal, overshadows any absolute pretensions
on the part of a young proletarian or a liberal genius. The professions of artist and writer are secular by principle and are
rooted in matter and earth. The French creative mind and
nervous receptiveness, as detached from Jesus' manhood, was
illustrated by types like Prometheus, Herakles, Alkibiades, and
any self-made man. Later, the Russians in worshipping Judas
Iscariot found a most paradoxical way of eliminating Jesus.
Judas is sterile, without real faith, a traitor, but he is the
realist, to dream of an immediate dictatorship. Such a notion
is congenital in a group of revolutionaries who must organize
a proletariat on principles suitable to the unreliable age between fifteen and twenty-one.

This does not alter the fact that the French and Russian
revolutions are results of the Christian era. They depend upon
it, they complete it. Christianity is not a mutual admiration
society. It may allot to a certain form of life the necessary
area in which to establish its own realm. The chief duty of
any member of the Corpus Christi is to strengthen the other
forces of humanity and thereby to assure the later co-ordination
of the Russian antitheistic form with the rest of the Christian
community. The economic unity of the world will probably
offer an opportunity for co-operation between forces of life
which are consciously Christian and others which suppress
their Christian inheritance for the sake of restoring one single

vital phase. Still the un-Christian forces play their part in the process of reimplantation of every branch of mankind into the one tree which is the perpetual effort of our era. During the last millennium the scattered nations of the whole earth were remoulded into parts of a whole.

In the future, many buried instincts will have to be revived in the white man if he is really to survive in this age of "childhood regained" into which a senile world is plunging. Here, senility is no metaphor. In this world of one-child families, old age pensions, birth control and the abolition of illness, youth is in a minority, with its proper contribution neglected, as was old age a thousand years ago. Gregorian Papacy was then the cure for too much clannishness and tribalism. Today clannishness and primitivism may be recalled to life, to restore the balance of a senile world in which there are three adults to one child. The longing to dance, behave, forget, dream like a child is felt increasingly. The stages of the first twenty years of man's life, which in former days were treated as steps preparatory for old age, are changing before our eyes into ends in themselves. Though this cult of childishness is spreading everywhere, Germany, removing its harness of paternalism in a kind of orgy, is anticipating the tribalism of the next three hundred years. They especially long to return to the "archetypes" of childhood and primordial dawn, to rites of initiation and pagan sacrifice because Germans crave a fountain of youth. But until the economic unity of the world is estblished, the return to dream states would prove fatal. These dream states are admissible only as an antidote, in the education of the masses in the national sectors of the globe.

Before any tribe or group can sacrifice reason to the unreal myth and magic of pre-history, its food and shelter must be guaranteed by the peaceful world-wide organization of production. Nazism is premature; it cannot coexist with the potentiality of war. Frightened by the proletarian Revolution, the Nazis are attempting "a classless nation," a solution which lies even beyond the Russian society. They are developing the characteristics of the primitive tribes before they can commit themselves to such an adventure. And the professed pacifism

of Hitler hinges upon the fact that the Nazis plan to return
into the forests like the Germanic tribes. The Jews, who represent the universal history of mankind, stand in their way. Yet
it is perhaps only through the Jews that the world may become
a playground for tribal primitivism! Possibly the Jews will
contribute more than others to that universal organization of
production which makes wars impossible and leads in a world-
wide economy. This is the necessary presupposition for the
revival of primitive archetypes in different sectors of the globe.
Since this revival is interested in buried instincts, it can be
neither Christian nor philosophical, in the sense in which the
English, American or French Revolutions were philosophical
or the Roman, Italian, and German were Christian.

The early stages of human development will be the goal of
efforts which will no longer pretend to be deliberate or logical
revolutions. They will be "Relapses" into instinctive phases
of primitive life and "Reproductions" of archetypes. That is
why our future evolution will lead to a variety of special reproductions. A relapse toward the dawn of civilization is opposed
to any world-wide generalization. It will become the pride of
such a relapse to be anti-universal and limited to a single local
or social group. Economy will be universal, mythology regional.
Every step in the direction of organizing the world's economy
will have to be bought off by a great number of tribal reactions. The clans of the future cannot follow the same technique which we described through the two cycles of clerical
and secular revolutions. Even so, it remains probable that the
tribes of the future will pass through the forms of monarchy,
aristocracy and democracy like Church and State in the past.

If this future cycle of political forms occurs—breaking up
the dictatorships of our present stage of transition—it will have
nothing to do with the course of the season through the year,
as Spengler thought. Civilization is not a counterpart of the
seasons, spring, summer, autumn and winter in perpetual recurrence. For man answers the threats of nature by heroic
efforts which counterbalance her eccentricities. In the "spring"
of civilization man was not at all springlike, but cultivated old
age instead: whereas modern civilization, with its character of

an end and a terminus, is reviving youth and boyhood by desperate efforts. The power of going up-stream is the revolutionary force in man. It is never comparable to the seasons of nature, because man goes against the inertia of his own habits.

Man has the specific gift of closing a rift in the cosmos. By realizing the peril of death or decay in time, nations or individuals stem the tide of events. Man is the creature who lifts himself and climbs up-hill; he overcomes the inertia inherent in nature. The waters join the sea; men, in a revolution, flow to the mountain tops and descend on the other side in a new course. Man's symbolical place in nature would be a great divide from which the waters run down in varying directions. Man dares to climb upwards, in an unnatural direction, stopping the natural descent of the life-cycle by forcing life to pause. He forces his own nature to dwell at one level of his natural, physiological life-history longer and more consciously, and transforms a phase which seemed unimportant into a dwelling-place for generations to come.

THE PASSING OF THE INSPIRATION.

The Great Revolutions succeeded because they achieved something that was necessary. The dialogue between them is the more majestic for this intrinsic necessity. True statesmanship and true direction of one's own life are guided by instinct for the necessary, the *unum necessarium*. Arbitrariness is the death of men and of nations. He who forces superfluous actions on his fellow men is a political charlatan or a despot. Each great revolution accomplished something necessary. By this fact they are exalted above the Satanic caprices of tyranny or anarchy.

The category of necessity is beyond abstract good and evil. Inevitable necessity—like manifest destiny—is a category of the true future. That is to say: present hardships can be transfigured by the gleam of the future, whenever men are ready to volunteer for a sacred goal. Our social grammar should be divided into one futuristic and one past. This hits the moralists hard. For their usual epithets of "good" and "evil," as applied to history and politics, spring from a timeless, static mind which ignores the differences between past and future. The moralist and the creator live in different tenses. This is usually overlooked; yet if we mix the ethical with the political aspect of life we shall never be able to do justice to our own best actions.

Every soul that faces reality is perfectly aware of this distinction and acts accordingly with the best of consciences. Only if a man tries to take his stand outside the world, as the philosopher of ethics does, he deliberately and constantly neglects the triplicity of past, present and future. It is a great secret, unknown to children or adolescents, but one which is revealed and becomes familiar to everyone who grows up to full manhood, that our ideas about good and evil are one thing, and the right time to introduce a change for the better is another. The idealist who thinks anything can be good outside of time and space only makes a fool of himself. Timeliness is everything. Reality is "good" when it proceeds timely; it is bad when too late or too early. "Good" and "evil" themselves in their deepest sense mean ripeness and immaturity. Any man who looks around him finds a great many desirable points which might make for the improvement of his environment. It is a wise man who realizes that it will take all his energy to carry one per cent of these good and desirable points into reality. The rest of the "good" is excluded. Reality is closed to the empty pretensions of the "always" idealist. Reality seems to hate the abstract good with the intense hatred the first Christians felt toward their idealistic rivals, the Gnostics. Real life can certainly never hate "the" good, but it does hate the abstract idea of the good. It has always spat out the abstract, and always will.

Real life's only approach to a fuller, better form of existence is through necessity and timeliness. Bring a thing into fashion, create a fresh interest, make it timely, and, as a climax, let it be clear that it is inevitable and necessary—and it will be incorporated into the lists of reality.

Fashion expresses a tendency, timeliness launches us on the current of irresistibility, whose driving force leads into the future with the power of "manifest destiny." And if we call

the whole mechanism for attaining the future by one comprehensive word, "necessity," then all the minor items mentioned
here, such as modes and fashions, are included as subspecies
or "feelers" into the "fulness of time."

True action is not responsible to so-called ethics. A vital
issue rises above the known good and evil because it leads into
the unknown. Is it good or evil to marry? Ridiculous question.
Yet such a decision is always answerable to the question: "Is it
arbitrary or is it necessary?" It is strange that, though every
human being acts on these principles, they are rarely mentioned. If a kidnapper invades my house and I fire at him, this
shot cannot be measured by abstract standards of good and evil.
While I am shooting my only responsibility is for perceiving
the true inevitability of this action. I must not shoot from
blind fear. The danger must be real, and any other means
must be impossible for me. The fellow who uses his gun whenever he gets a chance is as despicable as the other who is unable
to throw the intruder out of his house. The delicate line of
distinction between the virile man, the milksop, the saint, is
drawn by nothing but "necessity." A man's behaviour in an
emergency is the test of his relation to the future, to the things
held in store for mankind by time.

The results of all our crucial actions are hidden from us. We
attempt to foresee the success of our actions repeatedly by our
intellect; but it never works. Pre-calculated action fails when
it meets the full reality of life. I know, of course, that many
pre-calculated actions do succeed. But they all happen in a
field from which the full inbreak of free and divine future has
been excluded by careful organization. Car-driving under rigid
regulations, teaching under the inflexible time-schedule of the
classroom, social gatherings with their certainty of being over
at half-past ten, all avoid an exposure to the real future. In all
these fields, time is limited to re-presentation, repetition, of
pre-calculated acts. Here life is immured in the categories of
past and present. In the recurrent parts of our social organization life has become cyclical. A complete cycle means the exclusion of novelty and real future.

To propose to a girl, to settle in a new place, to read a great book—these are dangerous things. To have a date, to drive up to an inn for tea, to read the *Saturday Evening Post,* are less dangerous because so little real future is at stake. Of course we must not allow names to mislead us. One and the same name may cover both "futuristic" and purely "cyclical" happenings. To a man of seventy, meeting a new person generally means little. His capital of future time is nearly exhausted. A boy, as long as he is not blasé, finds in every "date" the excitement of a final commitment. If this youngster is willing to expose himself to the full impact of the occasion, the date suddenly loses its character of a mere date, and can signify everything or nothing. Then the shallow ethics which has framed the rules for our behaviour on a "date" is soon forgotten. The boy's whole being enters the game, past and future included. The only justification for Romeo's infringing the traditional morality on his "date" with Juliet is the tragic necessity of their love. Fortunately, in Romeo and Juliet, the completeness of their surrender to the future asserts its own right. Even the spinster has learned that. In a tragedy the hero belongs to the future and is defeated by the chains of the past and the standard of the present. Whereas in a farce the people we laugh at are obsolete, petrified and unchangeable types. They are not surprising; the plot is. Human tragedies and comedies may be divided according to the relation between the past or future character of hero and plot. And any great play will mix tragical and comical elements as life does.

Unfortunately the political spinster is less educated than the poetical spinster. And most political spinsters are men. They will not admit that the case of true lovers is rather like the "cases" of other departments of social life. Yet love and hatred remain the powers which govern the sun and all the other stars, nations and individuals, in so far as their desire for a full and true future is capable of lifting them out of their rutted tracks and orbits. In any field of action, necessary changes are justified whether they be legal or not. The whims of crowd emotion or mob brutality are not excusable. They remain in the sphere of arbitrariness, though irresponsible politicians may help to legalize and constitutionalize them. There is an illegitimacy about mere legal forms which is a greater offence to life's exigencies than an open breach of the law. A very frequent procedure in modern society is to pass arbitrary measures in a legitimate or at least legal form. But the mechanical prolongation of existing life by legal tricks and the genuine creation of future life in dangerous action are at opposite poles of political development.

A man acting responsibly tries to answer a real demand. His conscience is visited by a question. In the old days the hero who asked us a question of life and death, and wrested a vital answer from us, was called a god. The human being within ourselves that was willing to listen to such a question, to obey its impact on heart and conscience, and answer it, was called man. The slave, who could not listen, had neither name nor gender, nor speech like the men who could. He was a thing. What then was a "thing"? Any thing involved in the dialogue, any content of question or answer, was a thing, *id est;* whatever was treated as a *theme* was an object, a part of the objectivated world. In this sense God himself, when treated as the helpless and analyzed subject matter of discussion, as the Divine, becomes a "thing"; but any part of the world, sun, earthquake, crisis, revolution, can become a god when we feel that it is a power urging questions upon us.

God—man—world are the three eternal components of spiritual life. Any process of thought, speech or inspiration must restore the tripartite order between divine question, human answer and subject matter. The triplicity is inevitable since any serious question is beyond the individual that is struggling to answer it; any theme, on the contrary, is beneath the man who is analyzing it. Names, of course, are ambiguous. The name God may degenerate into a mere word, the "world" may be proclaimed God; but the mechanism of the three levels is present in every breath of life. No attempt at replacing them by calling everything divine, or everything worldly, or every power social or human, stands the logical test. Where there is no question, no standard, no command, no conscience, God and man both disappear and only brute nature remains. When we put all the divine power into man by worshipping society or humanity, man's truly human side evaporates into dust, and God and world remain the only realities.

That is what happened to the age of science. Man asked wonderful, divine questions at random. He imitated God's divine power of raising the issue, without limiting himself to necessary issues, and forgot that man is responsible only as an answerer of powerful and overwhelming questions or demands. He got drunk on arbitrary, unnecessary "problems." On the other hand, science reduced his human side into a natural organism, a part of the world's mechanism. Liberalism treated man's mind as divine and man's body as matter. The human soul, which is the only specifically human element in man, was throttled by the pressure from both sides. Practically all the books of the nineteenth century use mind (mind and body, etc.), where the twentieth century is learning to discriminate between mind and soul. We no longer believe in man's God-like and world-like behaviour as his only *human* features. But if man has abused the name and power of God so terribly that he can no longer call upon Him by the name "Creator," we can still grasp the triunity of question, answer and object, in this dialogue which goes on in mankind and in every soul.

Let us forget all our foolish notions about God and the world; let us analyze the curious fact that we are all the time answering this appeal. That which "asks" within us may be our own genius; or it may be some very different power. Art, or truth, may ask our allegiance. Scholarship may take its toll from man by demanding his time, his sleep and his good health. Manifold are the powers which raise their voices in man. Anything may become his "god," anything his "world." Atheists, for example, may bring the "concept of God" before their tribunal in the name of their own God, matter. In other words, their God is matter, and their doubts and questions are aimed at a dead thing, the definitions of theology. But this heckling of theological concepts has little to do with the name of the *living* God. A God is present in the materialist's question as in any other. God is not a concept. He is always a person, and he bears a name, that name in which we are asked to ask others.

For instance, when I ask a sportsman: "How may a good

sport do such and such a thing?" I invoke the power of sport. The sportsman in question shall not justify himself for my personal satisfaction. He is summoned to satisfy "Sportsmanship" and Her Imperative. I am evading the disagreeable situation of somebody setting himself up as in authority, by putting Sport on the higher level and myself remaining on the same human level with the other fellow. Yet there can be no doubt that I am relying on the existence of two levels, one of human democracy, the other of ruling powers. This becomes utterly clear when the alleged sportsman shrugs his shoulders and replies: " 'Sportsmanship' can go to H——; I don't care." In that case, my whole argument was in vain, because he simply refuses to acknowledge Sportsmanship's authority. Perhaps I am myself on the college team and believe unswervingly in Sportsmanship; then I am deeply shocked by my friend's blasphemy.

The power who puts questions into our mouth and makes us answer them, is our God. The power which makes the atheist fight for atheism is *his* God. Of course God is not a school examiner. Man never gives his real answer in words; he gives *himself*. When a man asks if a girl loves him he hopes that she will give not an empty phrase, but herself. The more completely she gives herself the greater her response, the more divine has she made the question. The gods whom we answer by devoting our lives to their worship and service ask for obedience, not for a lip-confession. Art, science, sex, greed, socialism, speed—these gods of our age devour the lives of their worshippers completely. They trace every line in the faces of their servants. Yet servant and master are never the same. The asker and the answerer remain different units. I summon you to "love me," "obey me." You answer this with an "I will" or "I will not." But the I which urges you to react, and the you which reacts, more or less reluctantly, are not in command of the same powers. The "you" that answers has not the same weapons at its disposal as the "I" that presses you for an answer. God's questions come to us through the meek yet irresistible forces of heart and soul; our answers may rely on the thousand devices of our intellectual and social equipment. The

I that asks me to seek the vital truth of an issue is in command of all the good angels of truth.

The old meaning of the word "to ask" included the ideas of command, demand, search, and question. When the modern mind began its scientific adventure, it limited the verb "ask" to the sense of a purely intellectual process. By this lowering, it became possible to ignore the difference between the divine "I" that asks and the human "you" that endeavours to answer. Descartes fell into an heroic fallacy when he identified the majestic "I" of the God in his soul, who asked a response from him, with the responsive "you" from which the answer is wrested. He labelled the two interlocutors with a single ambiguous term, "ego." This self-conversing personality is an invention of modern times. Neither Plato nor Aristotle knew anything of such a chimeric "Ego," who was neither God nor man; but Godlike and yet anthropomorphical. On the one hand, all the real distinctions between men—sex, age, colour, race—were neglected; the "Ego," so we were told, transcended them all. On the other hand, the really superhuman powers, those veritable "I's," were denied. As a scientist, man was given a superindividual, transcending capacity which nevertheless still claimed that it was not divine. This unreal I, the Ego, once manufactured, God, Man and World all three collapsed.

No man ever lived or ever will live in whom God and man are the same. He who knew the secret of our two-fold nature to perfection cried out with the sincerity which exalted him to the first-born son of man: *"Eli, Eli, lama sabachthani."* This one phrase from the Gospel gives the lie to any heroic philosophy of the Ego. It remains for ever the touchstone of man's position between God and World: "My God, my God, why hast thou forsaken me?" By that cry the limits between divinity and humanity in man were established for ever.

When we rediscover the inexchangeability of God, man, and world, their axiomatic coexistence in every act of the spirit, when the triunity of the three levels (questioning power, answering man, and discussed subject matter) is re-established, we shall enter the last era of history. Under the new trichotomy we shall no longer be frightened by the multiple shape of God.

There are many questions and many answers. But none of the multiplex deities who demand our thanks, thought, and service can enslave all the elements of our being. There may be a time when we must worship them. Yet when we analyze our whole life between birth and death, we cannot assign the whole life of any human being to a single one of these many deities and powers. No one of them is supreme. Some enter the scene rather late. Science is too severe a god for children. Venus abdicates her authority over old age. Socialism annoys the man of sixty, and greed is hardly conceivable to a young person. The gods pass. When the individual realizes their passing, their unceasing change, he is converted to God—the living God who invites us to obey the *"unum necessarium,"* the one thing necessary and timely at every moment. This man discovers his complete liberty, the unbelievable freedom of the children of God, who are independent of all specific codes and traditional creeds, because the God of our future and our beginning is superior to the gods he has put around us in the short periods of our conscious efforts.

In the Bible there are two names for God: one is grammatically a plural, Elohim; the other is the singular Jahve. The Elohim are the divine powers in creation; Jahve is he who will be what he will be. When man sees through the works of Elohim and discovers Jahve at work, he himself begins to separate past from future. And only he who distinguishes between past and future is a grown person; if most people are not persons, it is because they serve one of the many Elohim. This is a second-rate performance; it deprives man of his birthright as one of the immediate sons of God.

In the Sistine Chapel of the Vatican, Michelangelo shows God creating Adam, and keeping in the folds of his immense robe a score of angels or spirits. Thus at the beginning of the world all the divine powers were on God's side; man was stark naked. We might conceive of a pendant to this picture; the end of creation, in which all the spirits that had accompanied the Creator should have left him and descended to man, helping, strengthening, enlarging his being into the divine. In this picture God would be alone, while Adam would have all the Elohim around him as his companions.

POST-WAR ECONOMICS.

What we have tried to state for the individual is also true for the nations of Europe. Today they face a dilemma: either destruction through loyalty to their national deity or conversion to a living faith. A scholar who sacrifices marriage, health, and active citizenship to his learning is deaf to the temptations and commands of any power except scholarship. A nation, naturally, never could devote itself to such narrow aims. A nation is bound to contain farmers, scholars, lawyers, business men. Its national type embraces a wealth of callings and interests. The danger for a nation lies not so much in its one-sided greed for money, land, knowledge or material things, but in the impoverishment of its types of man.

Each of the nations of Europe has aimed to represent one definite member of the human family. And the particular goal of each nation was legitimate so long as it was meant as a safe-guard against exaggerating another. By studying the origin of each national type, we were able to make transparent the mutual dependence of the great national characters. They balanced each other. Each one furiously and absolutely driving ahead in its own direction, they together achieved a process of permanent regeneration. Each sang its theme in that symphony. Each spoke with a thousand idiomatic tongues its part in the common drama. The ultimate ends of these revolutionary processes were far beyond the goals of individual professions; out of the tremendous and universal effort a true form of mankind was reproduced.

Why can this no longer go on as it did before? The innocence of effort has vanished. Today we know too much about the merits of other members of civilization. When man feels the divine touch on his shoulder, he must follow. Nothing of real divine truth can remain excluded from man's desires. Such is his divine nature that he can never bear to be deprived of one of God's powers for all time. When a German sees and experiences the virility of England, when an English-

GOD WITH HIS ELOHIM CREATING ADAM, BY MICHELANGELO

woman sees the lovely qualities of an Austrian girl, a process of borrowing, of longing, of mutual permeation is begun; and this is inevitable, because man can never be confined to the worship of any single god. He cries out for the one God of all mankind.

The stalemate of the World War has spread the application of this truth which was always valid for individuals, to the nations themselves. Even the English nation trembles in its shoes because it knows—as a nation—that its type is no longer sufficient, not even in the Anglican Church. The great nations are being forced to make allowances for the inadequacy of their own types. They are shocked by this. They meet the shock by violent revulsions and all kinds of escapes and arrangements by which the shock may be neutralized. By their convulsions and self-encirclements they clearly admit that this mutual permeation is at work.

Man will no longer be satisfied to remain shut up within the limits of one nation's institutions and ways of life. Lenin, Stalin, Mussolini, Hitler, and even second-rate leaders in Germany like Hess, Goering, Darre, Rosenberg, have drawn their inspiration from outside, from living in foreign countries, from hailing from other countries, or from marrying from abroad. That is to say: even these leaders of ultra-nationalism stand in a dualistic situation, in which at least two different environments and national experiences are fused together.

The relativity of each nation's particular type and standard means the end of the modern era and its secular revolutions. The World War, with its sequel, the Russian Revolution, was the last total revolution tending to cast all men in one mould. Henceforth more than one type has to be made accessible to the souls of men. The absolute power of each separate god is gone.

The future task is to lead man's life through a sequence of different phases and well-timed allegiances. No single allegiance can claim domination any longer over our whole life. The place of the old Christian conversion will be taken by a solemn and deliberate change of allegiance in mid-life. Man is called to fulfil himself. How can he, if parts of human life remain inaccessible to him? Youth and adults, men and women, children and old men, will live and worship in different ways. This change during the course of life is becoming more and more the great issue for a mechanized world.

By this time, perhaps the reader is convinced of the sterility of the so-called revolutionaries or reactionaries in this, our present age. The time of "one-type" revolutions is over. When Marx discovered the class-war, he thought of the proletarian as the ultimate type for all mankind. No proletarian himself, he gave a special type the character of totality. Looking beyond Marx we take the proletarian as typical of one stage only in the life of the individual, and one phase only in the life of mankind. The juvenile type of the proletarian, with its dynamic and nomadic tendencies, immediately calls up all the other phases of a man's complete life-cycle. In this respect the modern class-warrior is handicapped in comparison with the bourgeois. The *"citoyen"* really felt that aristocrats were superfluous. But no proletarian can conceive of a social machinery without entrepreneurs. The proletarian class is not the only one to survive; they should recognize the variety of character and calling among the phases of life.

The Marxian demands a monotonous, one-type organization of Communistic youth; the post-Marxian will crave a polyphonic economy. Because man is man he cannot live, and never has lived, in one form of economy. I know, of course, that modern thought circles around the two systems of capitalism and Communism. They may be attacked or defended, but they are always praised as modern in comparison with an alleged third system—feudalism. Capitalism and Socialism may be systems which the modern man does not like; but the third system seems so contemptible that we simply need not know anything about it. Feudalism, they say, is just the economy which immediately preceded capitalism.

Nothing is less true. Capitalism was preceded by at least four different economic systems; all of which have survived to a certain extent; and modern economy is based on an interplay between them all. Setting out from the immediate local "Services" of a manorial organization, the economic system has now reached the stage of continent-wide economy. In this progress Manorialism was replaced by Curialism, Curialism by Cameralism, and Cameralism by Colonialism. The complete list, as evolved in our various chapters, should be:

1. Manorialism
2. Curialism   especially in Rome and the centralized orders of the Church
3. Cameralism   especially in the German states
4. Colonialism   especially in the British Commonwealth
5. Capitalism   especially in the industrialized areas
6. Communism   especially in Eurasia

Never was any one of these systems more than the prevailing tendency of an age. Its respective adherents were but "more manifest in their conversation and in a more shining station," as Hugo de St. Victor put it nicely. All government mixes monarchic, democratic, dictatorial and aristocratic elements. Well, economics mixes the elements of all the "isms" catalogued here. When we wish to study economics, we must not restrict our tools of understanding to the concepts of one single "ism." It was the political and intellectual blindness of the liberal economist to mistake his tools for ideals. It is clear that these systems are ideal types. In a way they are timeless. In reality some of them have always coexisted; not one of them can stand alone. A modern college student may pass through all of them in the course of his life. As a farmer's son, he may have lived for fifteen years in a household which, so far as his own horizon goes, is still a seignorial manor. He then passes through college with a scholarship from a quasi-ecclesiastical foundation. He may serve in the army as the servant of a cameralistic state. He may work in a factory as a proletarian. He may open a shop as a capitalist, on his own responsibility, and hold shares in foreign enterprises in Shanghai or Straits Settlements which are managed by a British firm on a colonial basis.

The economic interpretation of history is perfectly right in seeing and stressing one side of the revolutionary process by which the way was paved from manor to continent, and through which the economic unit has grown beyond Church and State into a new geographical order of magnitude. The economic interpretation explains, for example, many of the colonial problems of American history, where capitalism was delayed by the possibilities of colonial exploitation. All the total revolutions of mankind have resulted in changes of a social and economic order. Yet none of them would have happened if each people had talked only of economics. *The secret of the due process of revolution is a progressive change in vocabulary.* The Russian Revolution took the guise of an economic revolution because the previous revolutions had stressed other sides of the social order. Society is based on an economy of forces, of which economy, in the usual sense, is only one force. Soul, body, mind, hands, breeding; any one can be made the centre of a revolution. The material side is always present in history. But our study includes man's other allegiances in Society. Man can live as man only because he can choose various ways of approach to the organization of mankind. He cannot be limited to one social or economic system. Systems are man-made. In consequence of this truism, man can never be enslaved by his own tools. The whole talk of a one-principle economy seems inhuman. The dynamic transition from one form of economy to another is the central problem for the individual members of society. Any working economy always has been and always will have to be a polyphonic economy, made up of different forms of work and development for the different phases of our life. A child needs a patriarchal economy; an adolescent is perfectly happy in a communistically organized camp; a man or woman at forty is concerned about savings and private property; and an old man is perhaps most interested in defending his hermit-like solitude. At one point in our lives we must expand consumption; in another we voluntarily cut down all our needs. Man is too complex a being to be imprisoned in one phase of his biographical evolution. Socialism is wrong, for no other reason than for its monotony. The Socialists have believed too easily that capitalism was the curse of all previous civilizations. Man has the undeniable right to outgrow any form of social organization, because he is the creator of his society as much as its creature. It is easier to preach and propagate economic uniformity than to acknowledge man's natural multifariousness. The only stable unity which we can know is beyond our reach. We are not God.

The age of total revolutions has passed away. A unified society with a multiplicity of tribal characters and national types will be the *"leit-motif"* of the centuries before us. Meanwhile, Communism and dictatorship are the daily political fare of a humanity which was thrown into the post-war world unprepared. Since the Marxists belong to the last generation of the nineteenth century, their fallacies have come to light a bit later than their nationalistic predecessors. The World War refuted both. Our common experience now forces upon us a new concept of the world's revolutions.

FACE TO FACE WITH MANKIND.

A great revolution is the meaningful creation of a new variety among the existing varieties of mankind. Not one of the leading national characters of Europe is older than a millennium. Not one of them was created without regard to the types of character that already existed. Each nation was called upon to play its part in the great symphony in which man has listened to the revelation of his own character and destiny. The European "nation" is one variety, conscious of its relations to the other varieties of man. At the bottom of revolutionary variations, we can draw the distinctive line between chance variation in nature and man's varieties in society. Man's distinction, as compared with animals and plants, depends upon his action in the face of the other varieties of his kind.

In other respects man shares the fate of nature's children. Especially is he subject to the tremendous thirst for "divergence of character" which pervades all creation and which contributed so much to Charles Darwin's reflections on the origin of species. Every genus in nature splits into hundreds and thousands of classes; every human language splits into some scores of dialects and variants. Life is not to be thought of without constant variation. "To live" means to search and to experience change and differentiation. This is a biological axiom, equally valid for plants, animals and men.

Still there is a deep gap between natural reproduction and the revolutions of our era. As we said before, civilized man in Europe and America is not the offspring of unconscious evolution. He is the product of a revolution. The melting-pots of revolution are full of images, revivals and reminiscences. Man —not the individual, but man as the family of nations—was created by a series of volcanic explosions to which people gave themselves up heart and soul; and the result was a type hitherto unknown, yet connected by a secret harmony with the previous revolution-born types of Europe. From these unmistakable results of our survey of the last thousand years, it becomes clear that most of the dogmas of the nineteenth century about man are untenable.

Men being products of revolution, we cannot continue to speak of "man" in the singular without grave misunderstandings. This "singular of man"—that is, the unity of mankind present in each individual—is not so easily attained as our ancestors thought. Of course it exists, since every man is potentially a "great divide" and a "transformer." Every man is "revolutionizable" from one status of aggregate into another. In this quality of changeability we are all peers. Both the sociological statement that man is capable of any change and the theological doctrine that we are sinners to be converted, are true. He can be transformed into the most extreme type on the scale of types by the creative act of a total and world-wide revolution. This is the one general truth about every man which makes brothers of us all. We either are or can become sons and descendants of certain creative acts called revolutions. Yet all being products of revolution, we are differentiated by the different stages represented by these very revolutions. Each European became what he is because his brothers were what they were.

Every national character arose because other types of men existed which called urgently for a supplement or an antagonist. The nations and classes of Europe are interdependent. Through their respective great historical hours they came to occupy the different stages of man's biographical progress; that is, they exploited the great ages in the life of man. They did not vary unconsciously. They enriched and re-created life consciously. Nothing is gained when we try to explain the rebirth of life through man by the operation of the glands or by thermodynamics. The application of chemical or physical concepts to society loses all meaning in the face of man's power for the "re"-making of life. By the modest "Re" as in Revolution, Restoration, Renaissance, Renovation, Recuperation, Reversion, Reproduction, man is separated from the rest of his fellow creatures.

Man wishes to reproduce his kind. His kind being by principle a changing species, *homo sapiens mutabilis,* man is concerned with the actual course of "re"-generation. He selects one or the other course; his "re"-building is a responsible act in the face of the rest of mankind. Neither the mere reproduction of tall brutes full of vitamins nor the idealistic celibacy of the philosopher is the theme of human history. Human history tells the tale of a free man's reproduction. The everlasting man is always free and always a son, always an heir and always an innovator. That is expressed by the syllable "re" in revolution. Even in the moment of history when man seems wholly concerned with change and obviously despondent about any tradition, he still paints his experience as a re-volution, bringing back something pre-existing or prefixed in the order of things. Out of millions of possibilities, one certain action is taken with the support of the "re." The syllable "re" signifies that his action implies selection. The riddles of our human existence lie in the fact that we are reproducing a changeable kind. That is why we are neither angels nor bees, and why the childless angels of heaven and the swarming beehives of nature do not suffice to explain human behaviour. The angelic light of inspiration and the busy persistence of the bees have to be re-conciled afresh in every century. Every century demands a new selective principle reconciling the two.

It is up to us to find, to prepare for, and to establish pending forms of reconciliation in creating new varieties. In nature, the endless species of fishes, insects, of plants, spread downward into innumerable subspecies and individuals, without involving any discussion between these varieties; man is the only species aware of its own varieties. From the very beginning of primitive societies, from the totems of bear and fox and wolf for the sections of a tribe, man has been moved by his urge to justify his variations explicitly. The totems, by including more than one species of animal, recognized man's plea for conscious completeness. "Wolf" and "fox" in human society knew of each other and existed for each other. Yelling and shouting perhaps, they still named each other. In their language the primitive tribes always embraced more than their own variety. Classes, Nations, Types, are not at all like the mute varieties of natural species, because they feel proud or humiliated by being varieties. This draws a clear line between Sociology and Biology. The Marshal Niel rose is not yellow because the La France rose is deep red. But a king was a king because a knight was a knight and a slave a slave. Mothers and daughters, fathers and sons, artists and scholars, monks and generals, French and Germans, English and Americans, are obviously related to each other. Among men one variety presupposes all the others, and justifies its right to exist among the others.

Marx's vision of the individual being moulded into a kind of type by the specific organization of his society is true. But, strangely enough, his vision excluded just the creative results of revolution. In our era the social relationship between the classes in one city or country—rich and poor, gentry and knaves, princes and subjects has been dominated by a more sublime process. Social relations in one territory are subordinate to the meaningful embodiment of human types in national bodies. Thus, when Marx re-discovered the polarizing processes between Capital and Labour, the civilized world was concerned with the more complex problem of reproducing all genuine forms of man in a family of nations. Marx cared for the Reproduction of Capital and Labour. But in the sober reality of our era, Christians and Europeans are concerned with more than a bread-and-butter policy. They have sacrificed their very blood to provide one great power as a centre of reproduction for every truly human type. Western man's types are not atomistic units, to be numbered and labelled as French, Russian, English, Nicaraguan, Arabian, and so on and so forth. There may be sixty-six equal members of the League of Nations in Geneva; but they are only single and special characters on the tree of life of mankind. Only as implanted in a functioning universe for a unique task are they real nations.

One very simple form of interplay between the different specimens of man prevents us from forgetting our interrelation. All men can speak to each other. Speech is the universal attribute by virtue of which man is the one animal conscious of his variety. Divergent animals of the same family cannot speak to each other except in human fairy tales. But it is no fairy tale that men can speak to each other.

I hear the atomistic linguist of the nineteenth century objecting: there are some three hundred different languages in the world, and he thinks of them as housed in watertight compartments, with only a little osmosis between them. Latin, French, English and German seem languages—irrevocably plural.

I do not doubt the plurality of speaking groups and linguistic units. But I challenge the common interpretation of their plurality as merely a meaningless sum. This is the greatest fallacy of the nineteenth century. Were not the Italian of Dante, the English of Milton, the German of Luther and Goethe, and the Russian of the Bolsheviks created by the revolutionary desire of one part of Christendom to express itself to the others? Have we not found every important word in a nation's vocabulary deeply rooted in the human dialogue to which it committed itself in its hour of revolution? "Country," *"Obrigkeit,"* State, Civilization, Revolution itself, visible church and Soviet Union—these were not particles of a local or material stock of words, called French or English; they were outcries coming from mankind in the throes of rebirth.

Each new stratum of revolution-born Europe spoke a new language. Scholastic Latin was one of these regenerated idioms, spoken by all Europe till her other members added their new keys to the concert. Even in the nineteenth century, with its faith in nationalism and its philological creed of three hundred distinct, permanent, objective languages, the faith that mankind has a universal speech was kept alive. The age of Beethoven, Verdi, Wagner and Bizet answered the philological heresy: that man does not speak to every man. "Music," it said, "is the universal language of mankind." For speech is more comprehensive than is suspected in grammar schools.

Mankind does not try to speak one language. It does not monotonously speak the same words. But this is only because in every dialogue the two partners assume different parts, represent different points of view, use different arguments. Variety is of the essence of real speech between men. In the old days when priest and layman, chief and henchman, spoke together, they used two idioms as a matter of course. In language the principle of idiom and dialect is inherent from the beginning. By the multitude of dialects we are reminded of the innumerable quarrels, dialogues, disputes between the men of the past. But interplay and mutual relation are at the bottom of the tower of Babel which linguists study today by the queer method of approaching each language separately. Each human variety has its particular coagulated speech. Every speech is dissoluble; it is retranslatable into the universal language behind one separate tongue. Through translation, each variety of man remains in contact with all the other varieties.

An efficient philology cannot believe in the material impenetrability of languages. It is not by chance that mankind restored its unity after the Babylonian confusion of tongues, by translating a single book into almost every tongue. The translation of the Bible into three hundred languages made up for man's loss of unity in speech. Furthermore, this restoration by common terms of thought was the pride and rallying cry of every total revolution in Europe and America. So definitely is the revolutionary process of the last thousand years bound up with the unification of thought by the common possession of the Bible that every revolution passionately claimed a special section of Biblical history as the classical text for its own drama.

The popes of the Gregorian Revolution, from Victor II to Eugene III, clearly recalled the last chapter of Biblical history: the early centuries of the Church, during which the very canon of the sacred books had been fixed and developed. The

Guelphic leaders, Saint Francis and his followers, as well as Innocent III, lived the passion and cross of Christ and His disciples. Luther, by enthroning the *"Predigtamt"* of the German *"Geist"* (Spirit) as the controlling power of secular government, restored the prophetic office of the times of Elias, John and Jesus. Cromwell's and William's England reinstated the Judges' function and the divine voice of public spirit which had ruled Israel before the Kingdom of David. France went in for the period before the age of revelations—natural man, the God of nature and the rights of Adam before the Fall. And Russia and we contemporaries of Bolshevism delve deep into the pre-adamitic and pre-historic forces of labour, sex, youth, primitive tribes and clans, hormones and vitamines.

This exact sequence, an inverted Biblical chronicle from 300 A.D. back to the first days of life on earth, was traced by revolutionaries who thought themselves completely free, independent and original, and who violently opposed the terms and slogans of every other revolution, preceding or following. Yet they were all under the invincible spell of "One Universal Language for all Mankind." The vigour of this epic unity, binding the national revolutions together, was tested to the utmost by our investigation of the American vocabulary. Halfway between the English and the French, America might not have shared in this strange Biblical retrogression. But this was not so at all. We found in the pamphlets and sermons of the War of Independence the figures of Noah and his sons symbolizing the new cradle of nations in these United States! Noah, Shem, Ham and Japhet, taking their places exactly between the Puritan Judges of Israel and the Rousseauist "Adam," bear witness to the unity of "language" throughout the Christian era, in spite of all national languages. Regeneration of Language would be no faulty name for the due process of Revolution. This process was the means of survival during the sixth day of creation.

CHAPTER EIGHTEEN

Farewell to Descartes

THE YEAR OF HARVARD'S TERCENTENARY, 1936-1937, WAS ALSO the tercentenary of a great intellectual event. Three hundred years ago the rational foundations of modern science were established. It was then that the *"Weltanschauung"* which lies at the root of our modern universities was first put into a book. Its author had intended to write some comprehensive volumes under the proud title, *Le Monde.* But that philosopher, René Descartes, was dissuaded by religious dangers from publishing them in full, and limited his task to the famous *Discours de la Méthode.* In it the great idealistic postulate of the *"Cogito ergo sum"* was formulated, and therewith the programme of man's scientific conquest of nature. Descartes' *"Cogito ergo sum"* opened the way to three hundred years of incredible scientific progress.

When Descartes came forward with his "wondrous strange" Discourse, the scholastic type of university had long since been in decay. He replaced the principles by which mediæval thought had been guided ever since Anselm's *"Credo ut intelligam,"* with his *"Cogito ergo sum."* Among the possible starting points for our powers of reason, scholasticism had singled out man's faith in the revealing power of God: Descartes seconded it with his no less paradoxical faith in the rational character of existence and nature.

The *"Cogito ergo sum,"* for its rivalry with theology, was one-sided. We post-War thinkers are less concerned with the revealed character of the true God or the true character of nature than with the survival of a truly human society. In asking for a truly human society we put the question of truth once more; but our specific endeavour is the living realization of truth in mankind. Truth is divine and has been divinely revealed—*credo ut intelligam*. Truth is pure and can be scientifically stated—*cogito ergo sum*. Truth is vital and must be socially represented—*Respondeo etsi mutabor*.

Our attack on Cartesianism is inevitable since "pure" thought encroaches everywhere on the field of social studies. Historians and economists and psychologists cannot stand the idea of not being "pure" thinkers, real scientists. What a frustration!

I am an impure thinker. I am hurt, swayed, shaken, elated, disillusioned, shocked, comforted, and I have to transmit my mental experiences lest I die. And although I may die. To write this book was no luxury. It was a means of survival. By writing a book, a man frees his mind from an overwhelming impression. The test for a book is its lack of arbitrariness, is the fact that it had to be done in order to clear the road for further life and work. I have done all in my power to forget the plan of this book again and again. Here it is, once more.

Through Man's own revolutionary experience, we know more about life than through any outward observation. Our ecodynamic moving through society is the basis for all our sciences of nature. Distant nature is less known to us than man's revival, through constant selection of the fittest, and through conscious variation. Man's memories of his own experiences form the background of all our knowledge of society and of creation.

Science, and history in its positivist stage, underrated the biological element in both nature and society. They took physics and metaphysics, measurable and weighable matter and logical and metaphysical ideas as the elementary and basic foundations on which to build our knowledge. By beginning with abstract figures in physics, or general ideas in metaphysics, they never did justice to the central point in our existence. For neither physics nor metaphysics can offer us any practical base from which to enter the fields of biology or sociology. Neither from the laws of gravity nor from the ideas of logic or ethics is there any bridge to lead into the realms of life, be it the life of plants and animals or of human society. Dead things are forever divided from the living; figures and ideas belong to the limbo of unreality.

We can drop the methods of the past. The schemes of that era, whatever they might be, were based on either physics or metaphysics. Some were subjective and some were objective; some were idealistic and some were materialistic, and many were a mixture of both. But they were unanimous in assuming that scientific thought should proceed from the simple facts of physics or general ideas. They were unanimous in assuming that either the laws of gravity or the laws of logic were primary and central truths on which the system of knowledge must be built. They all believed in a hierarchy with physics and metaphysics at the bottom, as primary sciences, and a ladder reaching upwards to the second and third stories of the house of knowledge. Once we see the cardinal fallacy of this assumption, Marx becomes as much the son of a bygone era as Descartes or Hume or Hobbes. They all look astoundingly akin. They all set out with abstract generalities on man's mind and on the nature of matter.

We renounce their approach to knowledge. "Thought" and "being," mind and body, are not the right points of departure for the masteries of life and society. Physics, interested in the mere being of abstract matter, and metaphysics, speculating about man's ideas, are at best marginal methods for dealing with reality. They do not touch the core, since they begin by investigating dead things or abstract notions. They are not concerned with the real life, either of natural creatures or of society. It is quite true that the universe is full of dead things and the libraries of men full of abstract concepts. This may *explain* the former presumption that, in studying a vast quantity of stones, gravel and dust, or an endless series of doctrines and ideas, one was attacking the substances which preponderate in the world. Yet this presumption remains a vicious circle. In a whole valley of stones and lava, one blade of grass is enough to refute a system which pretends to explore the grass by weighing and measuring all the gravel in the valley. In the same way, the presence of one living soul among the three million volumes of a great library offers sufficient proof against the notion that the secret of this soul is to be found by reading those three million books. Coal can be explained as the embalmed corpse of ancient forests; no tree can be explained by investigating anthracite only. Physics deals with corpses, and metaphysics with formulas from which the life has passed away. Both sciences are concerned with secondary forms of existence, remnants of life. The scientific treatment of these remnants may be very useful; yet remains a secondary form of knowledge. Life precedes death; and any knowledge of life in its two forms of social and cosmic life can rightly claim precedence over both physics and metaphysics. The two modern sciences of life, biology and sociology, must cease to take orders from the sciences of death, physics and metaphysics.

In a recent series of publications on biology, called "Bios" and inaugurated by the leading American, German, and English biologists, the first volume, written by A. Meyer and published in 1934, is devoted to this Copernican revolution. Meyer shows that physics has to do solely with an extreme case in nature, its most remote appearance. Therefore physics can more fittingly be described as the last chapter of biology than as the first chapter of natural science. The same holds good for the social sciences in their relation to metaphysics. And the details which interest the sciences of death and abstraction, are useless for the task which lies before the explorers of the life that goes on between heaven and earth, in the fields of economics and bionomics.

By the way, since the sciences under the spell of the old hierarchy of physics and metaphysics are usually characterized by the ending -ology (viz., sociology, philology, theology, zoology, etc.), a different suffix for the emancipated sciences of life would be convenient. When we speak of physiology, psychology, etc., we generally mean the sciences in their old form still biassed by the physicist's and the metaphysician's errors. While speaking of Theonomy—as now commonly used by German thinkers—Bionomics—as the English usage goes—and Economics, we have in mind the mature and independent sciences of life which have become conscious of their independence from the sciences of death. Since we are facing the emancipation of these bio-sciences from "amalgamate false natures," a change in name is highly desirable to discriminate between their enslaved and their emancipated status.

The reality that confronts the bionomist and economist cannot be divided into subject and object; this customary dichotomy fails to convey any meaning to us. In fact, Mr. Uexkuell and the modern school in bionomics insist on the subjective character of every living object that comes under the microscope. They have rediscovered in every alleged "object" of their research the quality of being an "Ego." But if we are forced to agree that every It is also an Ego, and every Ego contains the It, the whole nomenclature of subject and object is revealed as ambiguous and useless for any practical purpose.

Sociologists like MacIver have taken the same point of view in the social sciences. The division of reality into subject and object is becoming worthless, ay, even misleading. It should be clear that in the fields of bionomy and economy it is an outrage to common sense to divide reality into subject and object, mind and body, idea and matter. Whoever acted as a mere subject or a mere body? The Ego and the It are limiting concepts, luckily seldom to be found in vital reality. The word "it," which may not give offence when applied to a stone or a corpse, is an impossible metaphor for a dog or a horse, let alone a human being. Applied to men it would reduce them to "cheap labour," "hands," cogs in the machine. Thus a wrong philosophy must necessarily lead us into a wrong society.

The four hundred years' dominance of physics inevitably leads up to the social revolution of the "It's," the "quantity" into which the workers are degraded by a mechanistic society. The politics and education of the last centuries proved a disaster whenever they tried to establish the abnormal and most inhuman extremes of Ego and It as norms. An imagination which could divide the world into subject and object, mind and matter, will not only accept the cog in the machine with perfect equanimity, but will shrink even less from the cold scepticism of the intellectual. His disinterested yet self-centred attitude, typical of the *déraciné,* will be thought of as normal.

Moreover, when humankind approaches a development by which one of its members, a class or a nation or a race, is to be enslaved and made into an "it," a mere stock of raw material for labour, or freed to become, as a group or class, the mere tyrannic Ego—a revolution will arise and destroy these extremes. Idealistic subject, the Ego, and materialistic object, the "It," are both *dead leaves* on the tree of mankind. Our survey of revolution shows that they are both insupportable extremes. The positions of Ego and It are deadening caricatures of man's true location in society. The great European family of nations was not concerned with the production or fostering of ideals or material things, but with the reproduction of types of the everlasting man, such as daughter, son, father, sister, mother and, of course, their combinations.

The abstractions and generalities that prevailed in philosophy from Descartes to Spencer, and in politics from Machiavelli to Lenin, made caricatures of living men. The notions of object and subject, idea and matter, do not aim at the heart of our human existence. They describe the tragic possibilities of human arrogance or pettiness, the potentialities of despot and slave, genius or proletarian. They miss the target at which they pretend to shoot: human nature. Though man tends to *become* an Ego and is *pressed* by his environment to behave like an It, he never *is* what these tendencies try to make of him. A man so pressed into behaviourism by awkward circumstances that he reacts like matter, is dead. A man so completely self-centred that he is constantly behaving as the sovereign Ego, runs insane. Real man enjoys the privilege of occasionally sacrificing personality to passion. Between action as an Ego and reaction as a thing, man's soul can only be found in his capacity to turn either to active initiative or to passive reaction. To veer between Ego and It is the secret of man's soul. And as long as a man can return to this happy balance he is sound. Our knowledge of society should no longer be built on non-existent abstractions like Godlike Egos or stone-like It's, but based on you and me, faulty and real "middle voices" as we are in our mutual interdependence, talking to each other, saying "you" and "me." A new social grammar lies behind all the successful twentieth century attempts in the social sciences.

King Ptolemæus' grammarians in Alexandria first invented the table which all of us had to learn in school: "I love, he loves, we love, you love, they love." Probably that table of tenses set the keystone into the arch of the wrong psychology. For in this scheme all persons and forms of action seem to be interchangeable. This scheme, used as the logic of philosophy from Descartes to Spencer and as the principle of politics from Machiavelli to Marx, is a grammar of human caricatures.

How far, in fact, does the "I" apply to man? For an answer to this question let us look into the Imperative. A man is commanded from outside for a longer time in his life than he can dispose of the "I." Before we can speak or think, the Imperative is aiming at us all the time, by mother, nurse, sisters and neighbours: "Eat, come, drink, be quiet!" The first form and the permanent form under which a man can recognize himself and the unity of his existence is the Imperative. We are called a Man and we are summoned by our name long before we are aware of ourselves as an Ego. And in all weak and childlike situations later we find ourselves in need of somebody to talk to us, call us by our name and tell us what to do. We talk to ourselves in hours of despair, and ask ourselves: How could you? Where are you? What will you do next? There we have the real man, waiting and hoping for his name and his Imperative. There we have the man on whom we build society. A nation of philosophizing Egos runs into war, a nation of pure "cogs in the machine" runs into anarchy. A man who can listen to his Imperative is governable, educationable, answerable. And when we leave the age of childhood behind us we receive our personality once more by love: "It is my soul that calls upon my name," says Romeo. It cannot be our intention at this moment to follow up the implications of this truth in all detail. The hour for such a discussion will quite naturally arise after the facts expounded in this volume have received better consideration by the general public.

However, one central result cannot be repressed even at this early stage of the "re-alignment of the social sciences" through the study of human revolution; and that is, that this study offers more realistic notions for man than the study of his mind or body. For the famous concepts derived from mind or body were, as we have said, "subject" and "object"; and they are not to be found in healthy men in a healthy society. Man as a subject or as an object is a pathological case rather. The everlasting man as a member of society can only be described by reviewing the faculties which he has shown to us in the due process of revolution. He proved to be a beginner and a continuator, a creator and a creature, a product of environment, and its producer, a grand-son or an ancestor, a revolutionary or an evolutionist. This dualism that permeates every perfect member of the civilized world may be summed up by two words that fittingly should supersede the misleading "objectivity" and "subjectivity" so dear to the natural scientists. The new terms are "traject," i.e., he who is forwarded on ways known from the past, and "preject," i.e., he who is thrown out of this rut into an unknown future. We all are both, trajects and prejects. As long and in so far as our civilization follows a clear direction we all are sitting in its boat of peaceful evolution, and are safely trajected to the shores of tomorrow according to the rules of the game. Whereas whenever society shows no sign of direction, when the old boat of its institutions seems no longer afloat, we are challenged by the pressure of an emergency to take to an unknown vessel that we have to build ourselves and in the building of which more than one generation may be devoured. To build a new boat without precedent in an emergency, is the imperative of the revolutionary. Our trajectedness and our prejectedness, then, are our social imperatives. Their interplay is the problem of the social sciences. Traject is the evolutionary; preject is the revolutionary predicate for man.

We are aware of the bearing of this attack on Cartesian science, bound up as it is with Descartes' formula, *"Cogito ergo sum."* We take the full risk of leaving his platform forever. Thought does not prove reality. Modern man—and one need not turn to exaggerations like *Ulysses* by Joyce—is made into a bundle of nerves by thought. The modern man is pervaded by so many "foreign-born" ideas that he risks disintegration by thinking. The mind is not the centre of personality.

Before bidding farewell to the *"Cogito ergo sum"* we should once more realize its power and majesty. This formula invited us all to join the army of research in its fight against irrational nature. Whenever a man was trained for the abstract Ego of the observer, our mastery over nature was at stake. On this unifying war-cry of "I think therefore I am" man founded his glorious technical conquest of the "objective" forces and raw materials of the world. The George Washington Bridge across the Hudson is, perhaps, one of the finest results of this religious co-operation between rational Egos. Nobody can remain unmoved by its crystal-clear form. The alliance between all the thousands and millions whose co-operation was needed before man was capable of such a technical miracle is certainly inspiring. Or as President Coolidge said when he welcomed Charles A. Lindbergh home from his flight to Paris: "Particularly has it been delightful to have him refer to his airplane as somehow possessing a personality and being equally entitled to credit with himself, for we are proud that in every particular this silent partner represented American genius and industry. I am told that more than one hundred separate companies furnished materials, parts or service in its construction." And Lindbergh himself added: "In addition to this, consideration should be *given the scientific researches that have been in progress for countless centuries.*" This army of men enlisted against nature under the password of *"Cogito ergo sum"* deserves our lasting support.

But among men, in society, the vigorous identity asked of us by the *"Cogito ergo sum"* tends to destroy the guiding Imperatives of the good life. We do not exist because we think. Man is the son of God and not brought into being by thinking. We are called into society by a mighty entreaty, "Who art thou, man, that I should care for thee?" And long before our intelligence can help us, the new-born individual survives this tremendous question by his naïve faith in the love of his elders. We grow into society on faith, listening to all kinds of human imperatives. Later we stammer and stutter, nations and individuals alike, in the effort to justify our existence by respond-ing to the call. We try to distinguish between the many tempt-ing offers made to our senses and appetites by the world. We wish to follow the deepest question, the central call which goes straight to the heart, and promises our soul the lasting certainty of being inscribed in the book of life.

Modern man no longer believes in any certainty of existence on the strength of abstract reasoning. Yet he is dedicated, heart and soul, to man's great fight against the decay of creation. He knows that his whole life will have to be an answer to the call. And here, near the end of this book, a short formula may be of some use, to condense our whole endeavour into a sort of quintessence. The formula we propose, as the basic principle of the social sciences, for the understanding of man's group life is as short as Descartes' *"Cogito ergo sum."* Descartes assumed, in his formula, that the same subject that asks a question and raises a doubt solves the problem. This may seem true in mathematics or physics, though today with Einstein even this limited hypothesis has become undemonstrable. In any vital issue, he who asks and we who answer are widely separated. The problem is put to us by a power which far transcends our free will and by situations beyond our choice. Crisis, injustice, death, depression, are problems put to us by the power that shaped our miseries. We can only try to give a momentary answer, our answer, to the everlasting protean question. Our knowledge and science are no leisure-hour luxury. They are our instruments for survival, for answering, at any given hour of life, the universal problem. The answers given by science and wisdom are like a chain of which every link fits one special cog on the wheel of time. The greatest and most universal answers that man has tried to give, like the Reformation or the Great Revolution, even these, as we have seen, *were temporary answers,* and had to be supplemented after a century had passed.

The "I think" has to be divided into the divine: "How wilt thou escape this abyss of nothingness?" and the man's or na-tion's answer, given through the devotion of his whole life and work: "Let this be my answer!" "Man" is the second person in the grammar of society.

Having discovered, in every serious problem, the dialogue between the superhuman power that puts it and those among us to whom it appeals, we transfer the questioning I to regions more powerful than the individual. Environment, fate, God, is the I that always precedes our existence and the existence of our fellow creatures. It addresses us: and though we may perhaps voice the question, we are no egos in serving as its mouthpiece. Persons we become as addressees, as "you." We are children of time and the emergency of the day is upon us before we can rise to solve it.

Whenever a governing class forget their quality of addressees, a suppressed part of mankind will raise its voice instead for an answer. Society shifted from an unsupportable dualism of haughty Ego and suppressed It into its proper place as God's addressee at the point of outbreak of every great revolution. A new psychic type took over the part of answering the question of the day whenever a province of Christianity was denied its own proper voice. When Italy was a mere tool of the Holy Empire, as in 1200, when Russia was an exploited colony of western Capitalism—as in 1917—a new sigh was wrung from the apparent corpse: and no Ego, but a new appealable group was born. No governing class ever survives as a mere self-asserting Ego. It will always survive by responding to its original claim as God's "you."

Nations are grateful. As long as a shred of the original problem is before the nation and as long as the members of the governing group show the faintest response to it, nations tolerate the most atrocious eccentricities in a perfect patience. This patience and gratitude may truly be called the religion of a nation. When a man—or a nation or mankind—wishes to be re-born, whether from too much solitude or out of the crowd, he must leave both the study of the Platonic thinker and the machinery of modern society behind him, and become an addressee again, free from egocentric questions and from the material chains of the It. In our natural situation, that of being an addressee, we are neither active like the over-energetic

Ego nor passive like the suffering under-dog. We are swimmers in a buoyant and everlasting medium. The dawn of creation is upon us, and we await our question, our specific mandate, in the silence of the beginnings of time. When we have learned to listen to the question and serve towards its solution, we have advanced to a new day. That is the way in which mankind has struggled forward, century after century, during the last two thousand years, building up the calendar of its re-birthdays as a true testament of its faith.

The responsibility of inventing questions does not rest on the living soul. Only the devil is interested in bringing up superfluous and futile problems. Rightly, Tristram Shandy begins with an outburst against the "If's." The real riddles are put before us not by our own curiosity. They fall upon us out of the blue sky. But we are "respondents." That is man's pride, that is what makes him take his stand between God and nature as a human being.

Thus our formula has been given in three simple words: *Respondeo etsi mutabor,* I answer though I have to change. That is, I will make answer to the question because Thou madest me responsible for life's reproduction on earth. *Respondeo etsi mutabor:* By self-forgetting response, mankind stays "mutative" in all its answerable members. The *"Cogito ergo sum"* becomes one version of our formula, that version of it which was most useful when man's path opened up into the co-operative discovery of nature. In the person of Descartes, mankind, sure of the divine blessing, decided on a common and general effort, valid for all men, that would transform the dark chaos of nature into objects of our intellectual domination. For the success of this effort, it was necessary to cast the spell of the *Cogito ergo sum* over men to overcome their natural weaknesses and to remove them far enough from the world that had to be objectified. *"Cogito ergo sum"* gave man *distance* from nature.

Now this distance is useful for a special phase within the process of catching the questions and pondering over the answers and finally making the answer known. For the phase during which we *doubt,* we are sure of nothing but our thought; for that phase, then, the Cartesian formula was fortunate indeed. And since, in natural science, this phase is the most essential, natural scientists thought mankind could live on this philosophy at large. But we know already that the *expressing* of truth is a social problem by itself. In so far as the human race has to decide today on a common effort how to express or represent truth socially, the Cartesian formula has nothing to say. And the same is true about the *impression* of truth on our plastic conscience. Neither the centuries that prepared and finally produced Descartes nor we post-War people can found our common international and interdenominational efforts on a formula that says nothing about the dignity of impressions and expressions, of learning and teaching, or listening and speaking to our fellowman.

The centuries of the clerical revolutions were concerned with giving us the good conscience and the certainty of the illumination on which Cartesius was able to found his appeal to the general reason in every one of us. They had to study the problem of *impression,* i.e., how man can learn what to ask from life. For that purpose, they had to establish another kind of distance within the thinking process. And the establishing of this kind of distance had to precede that secondary distance between subject and objects as established by Descartes. If Scholasticism had not done away with all the local myths about the universe, Descartes could not have asked the reasonable questions about it. In order that man might become able to think objectively at all, he had to know first that all wishful thinking of our race was outwitted by a superior process that originated and determined the part played by ourselves in the universe.

The real process of life that permeates us and gets hold of us, that imperils us and uses us, transcends our off-hand aims and ends. By revering it, we can detach ourselves from our fear of death, and can begin to listen.

As a principle of efficient reasoning, this detachment was transferred into philosophy by the greatest English philosopher, Anselm of Canterbury, in a sentence rivalling with the Cartesian in conciseness: *"Credo ut intelligam"* is the principle distancing men from God in their intellectual practice. We might translate the Latin (which literally means: I have faith in order that I may come to understand) in our terms: I must have learned to listen before I can distinguish valid truth from man-made truth. This, again, turns out to be but another version of our proposed formula in its triangular relation. In Anselm's statement the emphasis is on the hearing, as the organ for inspiration by truth. In Cartesius', it is on the doubting as the organ for transformation of this divine truth into human knowledge. In our phrasing, the emphasis shifts once more, and now to the process of making known, of speaking out at the right time, in the right place, as the proper social representation. We no longer believe in the timeless innocence of philosophers, theologians, scientists; we see them write books and try to gain power. And this whole process of teaching again needs the same century-long self-criticism applied by Anselmists and Cartesians to the processes of detaching us from God and from nature. In society, we must detach ourselves from our listeners before we can teach them.

Both the *Credo ut intelligam* and the *Cogito ergo sum* worked very well for a time. However, finally the *Credo ut intelligam* led to the Inquisition and the *Cogito ergo sum* into an ammunition factory. The progressive science of our days of aircraft-bombing has progressed just a bit too far into the humanities, precisely as theology had dogmatized just a bit too much when it built up its inquisition. When Joan of Arc was questioned under torture, her theological judges had ceased to believe. When Nobel Prize winners produced poison-gas, their thinking was no longer identified with existence.

Our formula *"Respondeo etsi mutabor"* reminds us that human society has outgrown the stage of mere existence which prevails in nature. In Society we must respond, and by our mode of response we bear witness that we know what no other being knows: the secret of death and life. We feel ourselves answerable for life's "Renaissance." Revolution, love, any glorious work, bears the stamp of eternity if it was called into existence by this sign in which Creator and creature are at one. *"Respondeo etsi mutabor,"* a vital word alters life's course and life outruns the already present death.

CHAPTER NINETEEN

The Survival Value of Humour

LET US TURN A LAST TIME TO THE VENERABLE DESCARTES, OUR adversary, the great seducer of the modern world. In his booklet on method, he seriously, without any trace of humour, complained that man had impressions before his mind developed to the full power of logic. For twenty years, so his complaint runs, I was impressed confusedly by objects which I was unable to understand. Instead of having my brain a clean slate at twenty, I found innumerable false ideas engraved upon it. What a pity that man is unable to think clearly from the day of his birth, or that he should have memories which antedate his maturity.

Have these naïve confessions of the demigod of modern science, the inventor of the mind-body dualism, met with the only success that they deserve: unending laughter? This brings up the serious question of what the omission of laughter, or its application, mean in the evolution of science. Scientists seem to be unable to grasp the folly of Descartes' remark. Common sense, however, acts on the principle that a man who fails to apply laughing and weeping in the discovery of vital truth simply is immature. Descartes is a gigantically expanded adolescent, full of curiosity, loathing his mental childhood, and frustrating his mental manhood.

Descartes wished to have man's plastic age erased. He wished to transform man from a plastic preject thrown into life and society so that it might be impressed and educated, into an empty subject to be filled with objectivity. This amounts to saying that the human mind should decipher only the impressions made on those parts of the world that are outside himself. Consequently the scientists today, for they all represent the practice of Cartesianism, think that they must not be impressed themselves, that it is their duty to keep cool, disinterested, neutral and dispassionate. And they try hard to develop this lack of humour. Their inhibitions and repressions are such that they give vent to their passions for trifles, and most unconsciously, only because they do not dare to admit them as the greatest capital of human investigation.

The more a man represses the impressions made upon himself, the more he must depend, in his orientation and conclusions, on vestiges and impressions made by life on others. He is suppressing some of the evidence of the world he is studying when he claims to work with pure mind. Let us compare very briefly the physicist or geologist, the biologist or physician, and our own economics and metanomics of society. Then, it will become clear that they all form a logical sequence.

Geology depends on impressions made by floods, earthquakes, volcanoes. The mountains tell the story of their oppressions and rebellions. The outstanding data of this science of Mother Earth are those furnished by the most violent impressions that mark an epoch in evolution.

Turning to medicine, we easily observe that a physician will not recommend a new drug before some living beings have tried it out. The serum or antidote becomes of interest when it leaves a real impression on or in a living organism.

All true sciences are based on impressions made on parts of the world, on stones, metals, plants, animals, human bodies, from atom to guinea-pig.

Very well, if the impressions made on stones have brought forth a special science, that of stones, and if the impressions engraved in bodies have built up modern medicine and biology, then the impressions that are powerful enough to shake our minds must be of greatest scientific fruitfulness. Aping, however, the natural sciences, the brahmins of the knowledge of man boast of their own neutrality and impassive indifference to the issue. No science being possible without impressions, they turn to an artificial laboratory where they produce effects on guinea pigs, and substitute the experiences of the guinea pigs for their own.

The truth is that the great Cartesius, when he obliterated the impressions of the child René, maimed himself for any social perception, outside natural science. This is the price paid by any natural scientific method. As far as it is applied, and neutralizes the geologist or physicist or biochemist, it obliterates their personal social and political experiences. Hence, the sciences develop a habit which is disastrous for the social thinker.

No scientific fact may be verified before it has made an indelible impression. The terror of revolutions, war, anarchy, decadence, must have made an indelible impression before we can study them. "Indelible" is a quality that differs widely from "clear." In fact, the more confused and complex and violent the impression, the longer it will stick, the more results will it produce. A revolution, then, is the most important fact for understanding, because it throws our minds out of gear. By definition, a revolution changes the mental processes of man. The scientists who sit in objective judgment before they are overwhelmed simply disable themselves for their real task, which is to digest the event. They do not expose their minds to the shock. In other fields of life, this is called cowardice.

The cowardice of the social thinker who denies that he is impressed and shell-shocked personally by a revolution or a war-scar, makes him turn to statistics describing the buttons on the uniforms of the soldiers, or makes him list the botanic names of the trees on the parkways where the insurgents fell. The impressions that matter, as they are given, for instance, in Tolstoi's *War and Peace* (his own fears, hopes, etc.), he is at a loss to admit: and so he looks for second-rate impressions that are too funny for words. And again, nobody dares to laugh.

Hence, scientific progress in the social field depends on the regulating power of humour. Humour precludes wrong methods, by simply ridiculing them. *Le ridicule tue.* And as much as chemists need laughing gas, we need, to exclude the pretensions of impassionate thinking, a strong dose of humour.

If we could place mirth on the throne of society, the war-scar that produced this volume would finally have vanished.

My generation has survived pre-War decadence, the killing in the War, post-War anarchy, and revolutions, i.e., civil war. Today, before anybody awakens to conscious life in this narrowed world, unemployment, or airbomb-strafing, or class-revolutions, or lack of vitality, or lack of integration may have cast the die of his fate, and stamped him forever. We daily emerge out of social death by a miracle. Hence, we no longer care for Cartesian metaphysics which lead man's mind beyond his physical death in nature. We are groping for a social wisdom that leads beyond the brutal "nomical" facts of economics and the monstrosities of the social volcano.

As a survivor, man smiles when realizing how narrowly he has escaped. This smile, unknown to the dogmatic idealist or the scientific materialist, twists the face because a human being has survived danger and therefore knows what matters. Humour illuminates the inessential. Our modern sciences, on the other hand, die from the carloads of inessentials that are dumped daily on the student's brain. In modern society the idea prevails that science is on the increase in bulk. They are adding, adding, adding to the mountain of knowledge. The man who survives is starting, starting, starting. For he is recovering his mental powers after a social catastrophe. And he looks into the blossom of a flower with greater surprise and delight at seventy than when he was a child. The survivor in us, though he may lose in curiosity, gains in astonishment. The metanomics of human society, as put forward in this book, are tokens of the surprise that man survives. Beyond, that is to say "meta," the nomical, the all-too-mechanical brutalities of social chaos, metanomics arise. They constitute the gay knowledge that Nietzsche was the first man to acclaim as "gayza Scienza," mirthful science. The results of metanomics form the frame to the joyous exultations of life; they allow life to be resuscitated and revitalized whenever it has spent itself. The results of a "gay science" do not neutralize life, they protect its exuberance. They bind together, in a common mirth, the survivors and the new-born. Thus, metanomics has its definite place in the autobiography of the race. Whenever the survivors have experienced death they are able to instil their dearly bought humour into the vigorous joy of youth. Never did mankind acquire a common knowledge by storing it away in libraries. Tell me, however, that you are willing to experience your life as a sentence in humankind's autobiography, tell me how far you share responsibility with the blunderers of the past, and when you have shown me to what extent you are capable of identification with the rest of mankind, I shall know whether your knowledge is survival knowledge, metanomics of society as a whole, or merely your private metaphysics.

My generation has survived social death in all its variations, and I have survived decades of study and teaching in scholastic and academic sciences.[1] Every one of their venerable scholars mistook me for the intellectual type which he most despised. The atheist wanted me to disappear into Divinity, the theologians into sociology, the sociologists into history, the historians into journalism, the journalists into metaphysics, the philosophers into law, and—need I say it?—the lawyers into hell, which as a member of our present world, I never had left. For nobody leaves hell all by himself without going mad. Society is a hell as long as man or woman is alone. And the human soul dies from consumption in the hell of social catastrophe, unless it makes common cause with others. In the community that common sense rebuilds, after the earthquake, upon the ashes on the slope of Vesuvius, the red wine of life tastes better than anywhere else. And a man writes a book, even as he stretches out his hand, so that he may find that he is not alone in the survival of humankind.

[1] See the author's essay, *"Die Krise der Universität,"* in *Die Hochzeit des Kriegs und der Revolution,* pp. 204 ff., Patmos Verlag, Würzburg, 1920.

Explanatory List of Maps and Illustrations

Front Endpaper Map, The World Adjudicated to the Twelve Apostles.

The heads of the twelve Apostles are distributed according to their missionary districts. St. Paul has no particular section; on this point see our text on pages 534 and 536.

The map is "oriented"; that is, East is shown at the top, where Paradise is placed. The "Antipodes," in the South, are marked by a man lifting his foot. The more than humble position of Western Europe is significant; all the more so since the map originated in the extreme West of Europe, in Northwest Spain, where it was drawn by the monk Beatus, in 776, for a commentary to St. John's Revelation. (The text, without pictures, was reprinted in 1935 by the American Academy in Rome.) The map was reconstructed by Konrad Miller (*Mappæ Mundi,* I, p. 35, Stuttgart, 1895). See also Edna Kenton, *The Book of Earths,* New York, William Morrow and Company, 1928.

For four hundred years, this type of world-map dominated the monastic manuscripts. A revision took place only with the Crusades: Jerusalem now was put in the centre. This geographical exaltation of the Earthly Jerusalem was quite abhorrent to the ancient Church, which cared only for the spaceless celestial Jerusalem (see our picture on page 491). The revision depended on the rationalization which we describe on pages 531-536. The revised edition is contained in the map from the *Chronicle* of St. Denis on page 293 of this book.

Page 28, The New Freedom in Choosing a Profession (*Die Berufs-wahl*). Woodcut by Hans Burgkmair (1473-1532).

The original caption, in old German verse, says: "Many estates are signified here; hence my reason commands me to choose wisely among them lest I be tormented by horrible repentance." G. Hirth, *Kulturgeschichtliches Bilderbuch,* I, p. 224, No. 360, Leipzig, *sine anno.*

Page 36, Map of Pre-Siberian Russia.

Russiæ, Moscoviæ, et Tartariæ Descriptio auctore Antonio Jenkensono Anglo, Londini, anno 1562, here taken from *Theatrum Orbis Terrarum* by Francis Hogenberg, Antwerp, 1570.

Page 44, Two Iconostases.

An iconostasis is the pictured wall separating the laity from the clergy in the Orthodox (Greek, Russian, Bulgarian, etc.) Church. The first, schematized, drawing is taken from Michael Rajewsky, *Euchologion* (in German), plate XI, Vienna, 1861.

The second, an actual Iconostasis from E. Golubinski, *Istoria Russkoi Tserkoi,* Atlas, plate LI, No. 1, Moscow, 1906.

Compare also N. P. Konakov, *The Russian Icon,* Oxford, 1927.

Page 52, Map of U.S.S.R. (Soviet Russia).

See the periodical *USSR in Reconstruction,* 1931, No. 6.

Page 156, Bird's-Eye View of Paris about 1610.

From Antoine Fontanon, *Les Édits et Ordonnances des Rois de France,* IV, Paris, 1611.

Page 154, The Hapsburg Danger to France. Original map drawn by T. H. Thomas.

The French territory is shaded; the Hapsburg possessions in Spain, Italy, Germany, are in lines; the shifting allies or neighbors of both are left white.

Pages 293 and 296, England's Place in the Middle Ages and in Modern Times: two maps.

1. This map, from the *Chronicle* of St. Denis, 1364-1372, is briefly discussed in our remarks on the front endpaper map. Jerusalem is in the centre; England is on the left part of the lower rim. Shakespeare must have this map in mind when he speaks of England as "the utmost corner of the globe" in *King John*.

2. Best's map of the world, 1578. The map was printed when the English Court and the City of London speculated on the discovery of the Northwestern Passages to Cathay. Now England is in the middle, between the familiar and a new world. Mark the "Frobishers Straightes."

Further material in Miller Christi, *The Silver Map of the World*, London, 1900, and A. E. Nordenskjoeld, *Periplus*, maps XXXIX, X, XII, XLIII; text pp. 19, 56a, 103, Stockholm, 1897.

Page 300, The British Vision: Two Seals.

1. Reverse of the Great Seal of 1651. This Seal, drawn by Simon, shows on the obverse the House of Commons with the Table of the House (pp. 306 ff.), and the legend: "In the third yeare of freedome by gods blessing restored" (pp. 277 ff.). The Great Seal of "the First Yeare of Freedome Restored" dates from 1648 and is called "Seal for the Count of Common Bench at Westminster." It already has the "marinorama" (p. 294), as given in our picture, even more sharply accentuated. It is, however, far less developed in detail. See A. and B. Wyon, *The Great Seals*, p. 36, London, 1887.

2. Seal used by the Admiralty Office, 1662 (right after the taking of Tangier and the Portuguese alliance). Charles II on the waves. It is, however, noticeable that the inscription (our text, p. 302) does not speak of the king but of the Britons as the kings of the orb; the restoration of 1660 stressed the fact that by no means the king only, but much more the whole nation, was restored (pp. 304 f). See G. Vertue, *Medals, Coins and Great Seals*, plate 23, London, 1753.

Any reader who wishes to study the contrast to the pre-Restoration period may look up the Armada medal of Elizabeth and the Seals of Charles I in 1640 and of his son used in the fifties, *i.e.*, before the royal "Restoration." In their picture of the king anointed, these Seals still belong to the type shown on page 570 (King of Sicily) of Guelphic days.

For the Britannia-Rule-the-Waves concept, see also Ben Jonson, *The Fortunate Isles and their Union,* a Masque, 1626.

Pages 376 and 377, The Case for Wittenberg: two maps. Original drawings by Thomas H. Thomas.

The conflict between Church and State that compelled the States to reform is shown by contrasting two maps covering exactly the same territory, one under the title, "One prince yet many territories," the other, "Many bishoprics yet one university."

1. Secular Saxony in 1520. The wondrous meandering of the lands of Luther's prince, the Prince Elector Friedrich der Weise. Down to 1918, the curious shape and small size of the Thuringian and Saxon principalities, with Weimar, Gotha, Erfurt, Jena, Meiningen, Eisenach, etc., has been an inexhaustible gold mine for romanticism and political humour.

2. Clerical Saxony in 1520. Pre-Reformation boundaries of ecclesiastical administration. The residences of the majority of the bishops concerned were located outside Saxony. In addition to this "absentee" régime by "extramural" bishops, part of the circa 100 Saxon monasteries depended on superiors who resided outside the principality. (Consult text p. 437.)

This map, though it is hard to believe that the real political background of the Reformation should have been so little studied, had to be drawn from poor resources. See Hans Beschorner in *Amt und Volk,* V, pp. 12 ff., 1931, and in *Catalogus Mapparum Geographicarum ad Historiam pertinentium,* p. 169, Warsaw, 1933. For the neighbouring principality of Hessen, with the University of Marburg, the material is available in the book of Wilhelm Classen, *Kirchliche Organisation Althessens im Mittelalter samt einem Umriss der neuzeitlichen Entwicklung, mit 21 Kartentafeln, Schriften des Instituts für geschichtliche Landeskunde von Hessen und Nassau Nr. 8,* Marburg (Lahn), 1929.

Page 396, Right and Wrong in the Reformation: two medals.

1. Medal struck for the Bicentenary of Wittenberg University,

1702. On one side, the Crown Prince of Saxony in his capacity as Rector of the University (see page 401); on the other, God (His name in Hebrew) illuminating the town of Wittenberg, with university and church. Two sovereignties: one of the prince, one of the university. An engraving of 1540 enlarges on this topic well and may be used as a running commentary to our medal: its inscription reads (in Latin):

> Wittenberg, Glorious City of God,
> See and Castle of the True Catholic Doctrine,
> Of the Academies of Europe the Most Famous,
> And in the Last Millennium by Far the Holiest Place.

(Walter Koehler in Pflugk-Harttung, *Im Morgenrot der Reformation*, p. 379, Halle, 1917.)

2. The Anglican distortion which made the Puritan Restoration necessary: Medal struck in honour of the Supremacy of Henry VIII of England, 1535. The king is proclaimed Head of the Church in the three sacred tongues: Hebrew, Greek, and Latin. At the same time, England is only one of the territories which he governs (origin of the Irish problem).

Page 482, Christ swinging the axe, after the World War, and destroying His Cross. Mural by J. C. Orozco, Baker Library, Dartmouth College, Hanover, N. H. See *Baker Library Bulletin,* March, 1938.

We have added a sentence from Augustine which, strangely enough, empowers us to express this idea: *Crux ergo hæc ipsa crucifigenda est—*The Cross Itself has to be crucified. (*Epistulæ* 241 in the Viennese edition—38 of the former editions.)

Page 484, A Mediæval Christ. The Christian Virtues, Pity, Humility, and Wisdom, eagerly crucifying Christ.

From a Dominican Legendary of German origin, end of the thirteenth century, now in Keble College, Oxford, folio 7. See J. Sieghart, *Mitteilungen der Zentralkommission,* pl. LXXXIII, Vienna, 1865; Hanns Swarzenski, *Die Deutschen Buchmalereien des XIII. Jahrhunderts,* No. 343, pl. 61, and text pp. 19, 38, 96 n. 1, Berlin, 1936. Swarzenski gives five more samples of the same theme; he traces it to a sermon of Bernard de Clairvaux (Migne, *Patrologia*, 183, 275).

Page 487, The Pilgrim's Way in the Tenth Century. Original drawing by Thomas H. Thomas.

The documentary evidence for this road as in regular use dates from the year 993 (Konrad Miller, *Mappæ Mundi*, III, 156-158, Stuttgart, 1895). This map deserves the title "Rump of the Roman World."

Not only does this road touch nearly all land that is "Roman" in the tenth century, but it also uses, and that for the last time, Roman roads and bridges. Later, the bridges collapsed, and other roads, as for example after 1215, the St. Gotthard Pass, became popular.

It is the rump of a Roman "World," because the Empire as well as the Church of Rome, in their ramifications, are comprehended. The reader will observe that the map is "oriented" like the front endpaper map of Beatus, because the contemporaries would look this way (East at the top). Not one of the modern nations is fully contained in it. The borderlines cut through Spain, France, England, Germany, Italy, in the modern sense of these names. Most of the seashore was in the hands of infidels, Normans, Moslems, or Greeks. Huns made their inroads to west of Basel (see page 502). The central location of Cluny is obvious, too (see pages 506 ff.).

Page 492, 1. Palace of a Mediæval Emperor. Reconstruction of Ingelheim on the Rhine, built by Charlemagne. See Adolf Zeller, *Rheinhessische Bauten,* Berlin, Walter de Gruyter, *Heft,* 2 (1936), page 8, pict. 26

The palace, of course, contained a church, one of those *"chapelles élevées dans les châteaux, comme un tour de plus de l'enceinte fortifiée"* (J. Puig I Cadafalch, *Géographie du Premier Art Romain,* p. 258, Paris, 1935).

2. The Emperor as Protector of the Holy Ghost, about 980.

A bronze vessel. The Emperor Otto (either Otto I, 936-973, or, more probably, Otto II, 973-983) carries a dove for the chrism and

a tank of oil for the catechumens. Legend: *Hierusalem Visio Pacis.*
Witte, *Zeitschrift für Christliche Kunst* 32 (1919), p. 58, n. 7.

Page 501, The Apostolic Emperor and Empress.

Christ crowns the Emperor Henry II, the Saint, and the Empress
Kunigund; the Apostles Peter and Paul are officiating by ushering
them in. This miniature is from the manuscript clm 57 = no. 4452
in Munich. It was painted between 1008 and 1014. Even Gregory
VII did not dare to withhold the title of Saint from this emperor,
who forced on the Romans the form of mass which was observed
by the Franks in Aachen. In Bamberg, the bishopric founded by
Henry, and to which he gave this manuscript, in the hymn *ad sex-
tam,* Henry was called "Apostolus." See also *Monumenta Germaniæ Historica, Scriptores,* XI, 235; Percy Schramm, *Kaiser, Rom
und Renovatio,* pp. 156-60 and 34, Leipzig, 1929.

Page 524, The Greatest Invention of the Middle Ages I.

Harnessed with a collar, two horses are shown pulling twelve
people, that is, six times as many as before 1100. From *Bible Mo-
ralisée Illustrée,* edited by Count de Laborde, V, folio 48, p. 328,
Paris, 1911. We are adding this picture to the collection in the book
of Lefèbvre. In the *Hortus Deliciarum,* Herrad, on planche 47/48,
draws the new collar; and two donkeys are able to pull fourteen
men and Dame Luxury. Two groups of facts in the sources of the
twelfth century get their explanation now, one having been overlooked, and the other misinterpreted by the historians of art.

1. The Church herself, during the twelfth century, and apparently neither before nor after, is shown as a car with the twelve
Apostles packed in it, and the four Evangelists pulling. See ms.
Bodleiana, 270B, folio 32, col. 1, no. 2; Louisa Twining, *Symbols
of Early and Medieval Christian Art,* pl. 61, text p. 124, London,
1852.

2. The much discussed *Culte des Carts* is not a merely hysterical
outbreak. Noblemen and women of the time would vie with their
peasants in pulling by hand the cars loaded with stones for the
church. We see, from our own reactions to the Labour Camp Move-

ment today, how a new machinery provokes a moral reaction for labour. Mortet et Deschamp, *Rescuil des Textes* II (Paris 1929), 66 f.

For the contrast with the days before the invention, see two wagons on plate 65 (from a tenth-century manuscript) of Adolf Merton's *Buchmalerei von St. Gallen*, Leipzig, 1923.

Page 527, The Greatest Invention of the Middle Ages II.

The oldest picture of a car and four, about 1200. From *Hortus Deliciarum* by Herrad von Landsberg, pl. V bis., Strassburg, 1879-99. Also given in the systematic treatment of the invention by Count Lefèbvre de Noettes, *L'Attelage, le Cheval de Selle à Trayers les Âges. Contributions à l'Histoire de l'Esclavage*, 2nd ed., figure 151, Paris, 1931.

Pages 532 and 533, Transformation in the Iconography of the Apostle St. Paul: From Scroll through Key to Sword: seven pictures.

1. Peter and Paul seated, Latin inscription, third century (page 533).

2. St. Paul. Ivory (about 1000), from the Imperial Abbey of Echternach, now in the Musée Cluny, Paris. Text: *Dei gratia sum id quod sum*. See our text, page 504, and A. Goldschmidt, *Elfenbeinskulpturen*, II, no. 25, Berlin, 1918.

3 and 4. Pilgrim Tokens, showing Peter and Paul, each with a key. These keys were sold to pilgrims in Rome before the end of the twelfth century (Anton de Waal, *Römische Quartalsschrift für Christliche Altertumskunde und Kirchengeschichte*, XIV (1900), p. 64, pl. I, 1-4).

5. Peter and Paul, with key and sword, flanking the door of San Pietro di Ferentillo in Umbria. We give this specimen of the new, Gregorian symbolism, first because it shows the final attribute of Paul, and second because it so often has been misdated as being of the eighth century (Herzig, *Die Langobardischen Fragmente in der Abtei San Pietro di Ferentillo, Römische Quartalsschrift*, XX (1908), p. 77, fig. 7; P. Toesca, *Storia dell' Arte Italiana*, I (1927), 151, no. 2; correct: A. Bertini-Calosso, *Enciclopedia Italiana*, XV, 20a, Rome, 1932). A similar misdating for a Greek picture of Paul with Sword is to be found in Jameson, *Sacred and Legendary Art*,

pl. 69, pp. 177, 191, London, 1857. Another pre-Gregorian Paul with Sword was eliminated, incidentally, by Adolf Goldschmidt in *Die Elfenbeinskulpturen aus der Zeit der Karolingischen und Sächsischen Kaiser*, pl. 155e, Berlin, 1914: an ivory fan, of undoubtedly Carolingian origin, in the Carrand Collection at Florence, contains a Paul with Sword. Goldschmidt showed that his figure has taken the place of an original, Carolingian, St. Agnes. A thorough house-cleaning of the material is highly needed, with the motto of the old Muenter, *Sinnbilder und Kunstvorstellungen der Alten Christen*, II (1825), p. 35: "There are no monuments with the swords, prior to the end of the eleventh century, which can be absolutely trusted." A. K. Porter, *Crosses of Ireland* (1931), pp. 42, 59.

6. Peter carrying the key, Peter the sword. Pilgrim tokens sold in Rome after 1190 (O. Wulff, *Altchristliche Bildwerke*, II (1911), p. 72, pl. VI, no. 1898).

7. The earliest known sculpture of St. Paul with Sword, 1120-25, in Maguelonne-Hérault. The dating is from A. Kingsley Porter, *Romanesque Sculpture on the Pilgrimage Roads*, fig. 1288, text I, pp. 268 ff. He analyzes the parts of the church architecture and sculpture. Since the cathedral was rebuilt in 1172, this date was incorrectly given to the St. Paul also by P. Dobschütz in his *Der Apostel Paulus*, II: *Seine Stellung in der Kunst*, Halle, 1928.

For the symbolic significance of the sword still valuable, Auber, *Histoire et Théorie du Symbolism Religieux*, II, p. 151, Paris, 1871. The sources are Ephesians 6, 17: the sword of the spirit, and Hebrews 4, 12: the word of God is powerful and sharper than a two-edged sword. The frequent assumption, that Paul's sword is nothing but the application of the later general rule that any martyr is painted with the instruments of his martyrdom, is refuted by the fact that in the days when this rule prevailed Paul was shown with *two* swords.

Few historians have paid sufficient attention to the revolutionary newness of the doctrine of the two swords. Most were satisfied to quote a Carolingian source in which the *emperor* claimed two swords! The best collection of the material is in the index to volume III of the *Libelli de Lite, Monumenta Germaniæ Historica*.

In general, three mistakes may be mentioned because they explain why the great significance of this change is ignored by the experts: 1) our numbers 3 and 4 went unheeded; 2) several monuments were misdated or undated and blocked the road; 3) the degradation of Peter, by the decay of Rome, and the special value of Paul for the new universality of the "orb" were as little evaluated as the specific Gregorian emphasis on the two swords. (A. J. Carlyle, in his *Medieval Political Theory*, II, p. 206, New York, 1928, writes: "There was here nothing new or revolutionary," with which compare our quotation from Hauck on page 559.)

For contrast, see coin of Pope Victor II (1055-1057). Although already a reformer, Victor put only Peter with his key on the coin (Charles et Rohault de Fleury, *Les Saints de la Messe*, VI, pl. XXIX).

Further literature: R. C. Gillie, *The Pauline Period*, in W. S. Sparrow, *The New Testament in Art*, pp. 64 ff., London, Hodder & Stoughton, *sine anno;* Stefan Beissel, *Bilder aus der Geschichte der Kunst in Italien*, pp. 134 and 226, Freiburg, 1899; Anton de Waal and Kirsch, *Roma Sacra*, p. 47, 1925.

Page 548, St. Thomas Teaching. The Scholastic Dream: everything, even the heart, made visible.

Painting by Fra Angelico da Fiesole (1387-1455).

Page 551, The Result of the Papal Revolution: St. Peter Crowning the Church.

From Louisa Twining, *Symbols and Emblems,* pl. 60, no. 4, London, 1852. See our text on page 541.

Page 570, Sacred or Secular Government: Two Sets of Symbols.

1. Frederick II as Roman Emperor. Eternal Rome and her eagle are on his seals and coins. The models are ancient coins. From Huillard-Bréholles, *Historia Frederici Secundi Diplomatica*, I, page following title page, Paris, 1852.

2. Frederick II as Secular King of Sicily. The oldest "secular" map gives the Straits of Messina, castles, fruit trees, cities of Sicily, Calabria, Apulia (Huillard-Bréholles, *op. cit.,* VI, pp. viii, 800, and page following title page, Paris, 1860).

Page 579, The Garden of the Empire. Original drawing by Thomas H. Thomas.

The City-States and principalities which claimed to have no superior *("superiorem non recognoscentes"),* north of Rome and south of the Alps about 1300. All the black lines on the map represent political boundaries.

Page 604, Excesses of Pilgrimage and the Commemorative Medal of Jan Huss.

Pilgrimage to the miracle-working Virgin at Regensburg, Bavaria, with tumultuous scenes, by Michael Ostendorfer (1490-1559). Left and right of the church steeple are the obverse and reverse of a medal in memory of Huss. It belongs to a series of coins struck in 1515 and after for the centenary of the burning of Huss at Constance in 1415. The coins were struck in Northern Bohemia by Count Stephen Schlick (1487-1536). The legend runs: *"Centum revolutis annis deo respondebitis et mihi"*—When a hundred years have turned you will have to answer God and myself. Hence, the date on the medal is 1415. Zeitschrift für Numismatik, 14 (1887), p. 225; Eduard Fiala, *Beschreibung der Sammlung Böhmischer Münzen und Medaillen des Max Donebauer,* pl. LXIII, no. 3738, pl. LI, no. 3451, Prague, 1889.

Page 674, Joint Enterprise of the Americans. Original drawing by Henry Copley Greene.

The 199,000,000 acres of land for wagon roads, canals and railroads granted by the Federal Government and the State of Texas between 1823 and 1870. The grants given by Texas amounted to some 33,800,000 acres, one sixth of the area of the state (which equals the percentage granted by the Federal Government). They are included in our map because the United States had no public domain in Texas, so that this state itself exercised the right which the Federal Government held in the rest of the new states. See Department of Commerce and Labor, Bureau of Corporations, *The Lumber Industry,* I, pp. 220, 231, Washington, 1913.

All the publications on this matter are based on a map published in 1878, and they all omit the Texas grants. Compare *Atlas of the*

Historical Geography of the United States by Charles O. Paullin, Edited by John K. Wright, map 56D, Carnegie Institution of Washing, 1932; J. W. Powell, *Report on the Arid Lands of the United States*, Washington, 1879; *The Public Domain*, Washington, 1883. Our map purposely omits all detail.

On the map, a blank space is noticeable east of the northerly angle of Texas; this blank space is Indian territory in which land grants, quite properly, were not made, although a railroad crossed the area.

Page 728, Michelangelo Buonarotti (1475-1564): God with His Elohim Creating Adam.

From the Sistine Chapel, Vatican City, Rome.

Back Endpaper Map, The World Adjudicated to Nobody: No Nation or Continent Is in the Centre. The map is given twice.

A bipolar, transverse, elliptical, equal-area map. Like a Mercator projection, this map distorts forms; unlike a Mercator map, it represents areas exactly, and shows all the connections possible across the poles. The first map of this type was drawn, perhaps in an unimpressive technique, by Sir C. F. Close in *Great Britain's Ordnance Survey, Professional Papers, New Series*, volume II, 1927. This seems to be omitted in the otherwise exhaustive study by C. H. Deetz and Oscar S. Adams, *Elements of Map Projection*, U. S. Department of Commerce, Coast and Geodetic Survey, Special Publication No. 68 (Fourth edition revised April 2, 1934). See also C. H. Deetz, *Cartography* (Special Publication No. 205), pp. 50 ff., Washington, 1936, and this book, pp. 465, 604 f., 630, 715, 717, 729.

INDEX

INDEX

The sign — in the text repeats the catchword: war; World — = World War. "See" means that the quotations are put under the other catchword. Additional references to related topics are given in parenthesis; "Atlas (geography)," means that relevant material may be found under the catchword "geography," too. When names of persons are mentioned in the text the index supplies the dates of their lives in parenthesis. St. Denis seek under Denis. For the word "revolution" the changes in terminology and concept are listed completely; for the different revolutions the various chapters should be consulted.

773

784

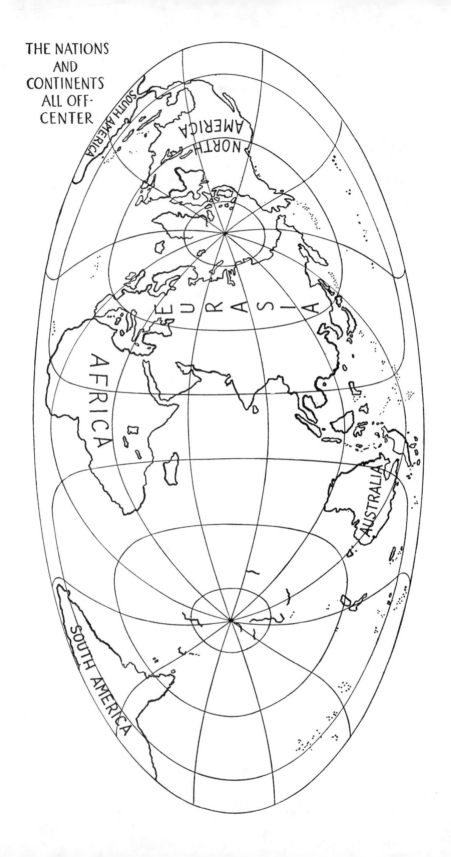

THE NATIONS
AND
CONTINENTS
ALL OFF-
CENTER

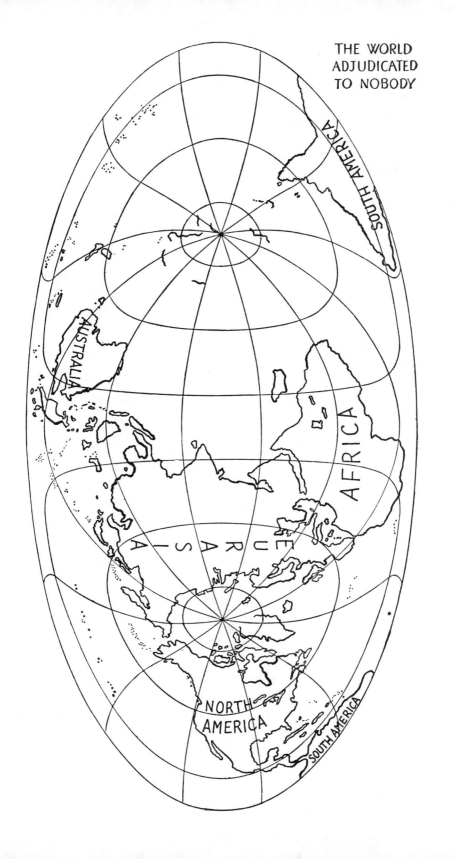

THE WORLD
ADJUDICATED
TO NOBODY